Contents

KT-362-042

About the Author

Zoe Thomas is a journalist and education writer. She has worked on *The Times and Sunday Times Good University Guide* since 2005 and is a former staff journalist for the Sunday newspaper. For the past 12 years, she has written extensively for the *Guide*, both its UK and Irish editions, and its sister publication *The Sunday Times Schools Guide*, *Parent Power*, the annual review of Britain's leading primary and secondary schools. She has a degree in media studies from the University of Sussex.

Acknowledgements

We would like to thank the many individuals who have helped with this edition of *The Times and Sunday Times Good University Guide*, particularly Alastair McCall, Editor of *The Sunday Times Good University Guide*, and John O'Leary, journalist, education consultant and the former author of this *Guide*. Thanks also go to Catherine North, the lead consultant with Andrew Farquhar, for UoE Consulting Limited, which has compiled the main university league table and the individual subject tables for this *Guide* on behalf of *The Times*, *The Sunday Times* and HarperCollins Publishers.

To the members of *The Times and Sunday Times Good University Guide* Advisory Group for their time and expertise: Patrick Kennedy, Consultant, Collective Intelligence Limited; Christine Couper, Head of Planning and Statistics, University of Greenwich; James Galbraith, Senior Strategic Planner, University of Edinburgh; Daniel Monnery, Head of Corporate Strategy, Northumbria University; Jackie Njoroge, Head of Strategic Planning, University of Salford; Steve Walsh, Head of Planning, Aberystwyth University; David Totten, Head of Planning, Queen's University, Belfast; Jenny Walker, Planning Officer, Loughborough University; to Denise Jones, Emily Raven and Jonathan Waller of HESA for their technical advice; also to Richard Puttock, Director of Data, Foresight and Analysis, Office for Students. To Nick Rodrigues, Sue Leonard, Charlie Burt, Georgie Campbell, Catherine Lally and Katie Meynell for their contributions to the book.

We also wish to thank all the university staff who assisted in providing information for this edition.

THE TIMES
THE SUNDAY TIMES

Good University Guide

2022

Zoe Thomas

Published in 2021 by Times Books

An imprint of HarperCollins Publishers
Westerhill Road
Bishopbriggs
Glasgow G64 2QT
www.harpercollins.co.uk
times.books@harpercollins.co.uk

HarperCollins Publishers,
1st Floor, Watermarque Building,
Ringsend Road,
Dublin 4, Ireland

First published in 1993. Twenty-seventh edition 2021

London Borough of Hackney		
91300001139569		
Askews & Holts		
	£19.99	
	6444698	

© Times Newspapers Ltd 2021

The Times is a registered trademark of Times Newspapers Ltd

ISBN 978-0-00-841946-2

Catherine North was the lead consultant with Andrew Farquhar for UoE Consulting Limited, which has compiled the main university league table and the individual subject tables for this *Guide* on behalf of *The Times*, *The Sunday Times* and HarperCollins Publishers.

Please see chapters 1 and 13 for a full explanation of the sources of data used in the ranking tables. The data providers do not necessarily agree with the data aggregations or manipulations appearing in this book and are also not responsible for any inference or conclusions thereby derived.

Project editor: Alan Copps
Design and layout: Davidson Publishing Solutions

A catalogue record for this book is available from the British Library.

Printed and bound by CPI Group (UK) Ltd, Croydon, CR0 4YY.

MIX
Paper from
responsible sources
FSC™ C007454

This book is produced from independently certified FSC™ paper to ensure responsible forest management.

For more information visit: www.harpercollins.co.uk/green

Timeline to a University Place

This book will help you find a university place in September 2022. That date may seem somewhere in the dim and distant future right now, but the application process is a bit long-winded and some of its various deadlines crop up sooner than you think. Those who want to study medicine, for instance, starting in September 2022, must complete their application by 15 October 2021 – almost a year before their studies start (all going according to plan), by which time they need also to have had some practical experience of helping to care for people and to have taken an aptitude test. Getting your ducks in a row well ahead of application and decision deadlines will give you time to breathe, as well as more flexibility and choice. Leave it to the last minute and your choices will become more limited. What you study and where you study it, will be game changers in your life to come; these are big decisions, and they merit proper consideration.

So where to start? Use the dates below to find the key stages to a university place.

Key dates
February to July 2021
This is the time to develop your thinking on the subject you would like to study and where you would like to be at university. See overleaf for where to find advice in this book on choosing a subject and a university.

March 2021 onwards
Go to university Open Days, coronavirus restrictions permitting. Open Days give you a personal impression of what a university feels like, its location, and what studying in a particular department or faculty would be like. In pre-Covid times candidates would only have the time and resources go to a small number of Open Days, and our advice was to plan carefully and make them count. At the time of going to press though, almost all Open Days were virtual events – making it easier to 'attend' more of them. But with the possibility of restrictions being lifted at least some of these may become physical events, which is why we advise consulting each university's website for Open Days in Chapter 15. Check these out to ensure you get the best experience.

July 2021
Registration starts for UCAS Apply, the online application system through which you will apply to universities. You will have a maximum of five choices when you complete your form.

September 2021
UCAS will begin to accept completed applications.

15 October 2021
Deadline for applications to Oxford or Cambridge (you can only apply to one of them), and for applications to any university to study medicine, dentistry or veterinary science. Be aware that some courses require you to have completed a pre-application assessment test by this date.

15 January 2022

Deadline for applications for all other universities and subjects (excluding a few art and design courses with a March 2022 deadline). This is the last date you can apply by, but it is better to get your application in beforehand; aim for the end of November 2021.

End of March 2022

Universities should have given you decisions on your applications by now if you submitted them by 15 January 2022.

April onwards

Apply for student loans to cover tuition fees and living costs.

Early May 2022

By this time, you should have responded to all university decisions. You have to select a first choice, and if your first offer is conditional, a second choice, and reject all other offers. Once you have accepted an offer, apply for university accommodation if you are going to need it.

First week of August 2022

Scottish examination results. If your results meet the offer from your first choice (or, failing that, your second choice), your place at university will be confirmed. If not, you can enter Clearing for Scottish universities in order to find a place on another course.

Second week of August 2022

A-level results announced. If your results meet the offer from your first choice (or, failing that, your second choice), your place at university will be confirmed. If not, you can enter Clearing to find a place on another course offered by any university.

Mid to late September 2022

Arrive at university for Freshers' Week.

NB: It is vital to consult UCAS Apply and the website of your chosen universities for developments. At the time of going to press, the possibility of basing offers on actual results, rather than predicted grades, was being widely discussed. No decision had been taken but candidates are advised to keep checking for changes.

How This Book Can Help You

Making a successful application to university has many stages. Fundamental to the whole process are your decisions on which subject to pick and where to study it.

How do I choose a course?

Most degrees last three or sometimes four years, some even longer, so you will need enthusiasm for, and some aptitude in, the subject. Also consider whether studying full-time or part-time will be best for you.

» The first half of chapter 2 provides advice on choosing a subject area and selecting relevant courses within that subject.

» Chapter 13 provides details for 67 different subject areas (as listed on page 36). For each subject there is specific advice and a league table that provides our assessment of the quality of universities offering courses.

How will my choice of subject affect my employment prospects?

The course you choose will influence your job prospects after you graduate, so your initial subject decision will have an impact on your life long after you have finished your degree.

» The employment prospects and average starting salaries for the main subject groups are given in chapter 3.

» The subject tables in chapter 13 give the employment prospects for each university offering a course.

» Universities are now doing more to increase the employability of their graduates. Examples are given in chapter 3 and in the profiles in chapter 15.

How do I choose a university?

While choosing your subject comes first, the place where you study also plays a major role. You will need to decide what type of university you wish to go to: campus, city or smaller town? How well does the university perform? How far is the university from home? Is it large or small? Is it specialist or general? Do you want to study abroad?

» Central to our Guide is the main *Times* and *Sunday Times* league table in chapter 1. This ranks the universities by assessing their performance not just according to teaching quality and the student experience but also through seven other factors, including research quality, the spending on services and facilities, and graduate employment prospects.

» The second half of chapter 2 provides advice on the factors to consider when choosing a university.

» Chapter 15, the largest chapter in the book, contains two pages on each university, giving a general overview of the institution as well as data on student numbers, contact details, accommodation provision, and the fees for 2021–22. Note that fees and student support for 2022–23 will not be confirmed until August 2021, and you must check these before applying.

» For those considering Oxford or Cambridge, details of admission processes and of all the undergraduate colleges can be found in chapter 14.

» Chapters 9 and 10 give advice about the latest changes to university life, including aspects of behaviour, mental health and coronavirus precautions.

» If you are considering studying abroad, chapter 11 provides guidance and practical information.

» Specific advice for international students coming to study in the UK is given in chapter 12.

How do I apply?

» Chapter 5 outlines the application procedure for university entry. It starts by advising you on how to complete the UCAS application, and then takes you through the process that we hope will lead to your university place for autumn 2022.

Can I afford it?

Note that most figures in chapters 4 and 7 refer to 2021 and there will be changes for 2022, which you will need to check.

» Chapter 4 describes how the system of tuition fees works and what you are likely to be charged, depending upon where in the UK you plan to study.

» Chapter 7 provides advice on the tuition fee loans and maintenance loans that are available, depending upon where you live in the UK, other forms of financial support (including university scholarships and bursaries), and how to plan your budget.

» Chapter 8 provides advice on where to live while you are at university. Sample accommodation charges for each university are given in chapter 15.

How do I find out more?

The Times and Sunday Times Good University Guide website at **https://www.thetimes.co.uk/gooduniversityguide** will keep you up to date with developments throughout the year and contains further information and online tables (subscription required).

You can also find much practical advice on the UCAS website (**www.ucas.com**), and on individual university websites. There is a wealth of official statistical information on the Discover Uni website (which has replaced Unistats) **https://discoveruni.gov.uk**

Introduction

When our previous *Guide* was published, the uncertain outcomes of Brexit were the major issues looming for UK universities. Little did anyone know what else was on the horizon. Among the many things recent history has taught us is just how enduring UK universities are. They braced to deal with the Covid-19 aftershock and plummeting applications, only for more candidates to apply in the 2020 cycle than had done so in the year before. Overall, more than 289,500 UK 18-year-olds applied in 2020, and almost 258,000 were accepted – close to 7% more than in 2019. Universities weathered the storm of the A-levels grading fiasco, and then braced again for an onslaught of deferrals by students wanting to avoid a socially-distanced first year, but no such rush materialised. People got on with the business of going to university in 2020, albeit with some major interruptions and in a far more online or face-covered way, not to mention with sparklingly clean hands.

There is clarity, finally, regarding Brexit's effect on universities. The move for new students from the EU, EEA and Switzerland from home fee status to paying the much higher international rates is not a popular one in the sector. There are fears that, inevitably, fewer European students will study here and the prized diversity of UK campuses will suffer, while the steeper price of a UK university education will slow down social mobility. Universities are rallying to ride the expected dip in applications from the Continent, however, and at this stage there is no sign of the demand from other international students weakening. Students from outside the EU accounted for more than 89,130 applications in the 2020 admissions cycle, compared with 49,650 from EU countries. EU students who were already on UK courses before the clock struck midnight on 31 December still qualify for home fees, but they will have to register with the EU Settlement Scheme by 30 June 2021.

This edition of our *Guide* has been written on the basis that university life will continue as (the new) normal. There is no reason to expect any different for applicants looking to start courses in 2022. In fact, they should enjoy something of a buyers' market. The rise in the 18-year-old population is not expected to be back to its 2010 peak until 2024 and with offer rates continuing to rise in most subjects, opportunities should be plentiful. If applications from the EU do take a plunge, this will broaden the pool further for those from the UK and Ireland (whose home fee status in Britain is unchanged), and for those from abroad who are undeterred by international fees.

School-leavers whose gap year plans were disrupted by Covid-19 contributed to an uplift in the numbers finding university places via Clearing in 2020. Clare Marchant, chief executive of the admissions service UCAS, predicted 80,000 enrolments, versus 73,325 in Clearing 2019. The shift to a blend of online and face-to-face learning has been widely accepted without protest. The digital native student population was not put off by virtual lectures and adapted naturally to the new delivery methods. Some academics are treating 2020 as year zero and working around a probable framework that the following two years will continue to be extraordinary in some way.

Certainly, universities have been forced to critically review what they do and how they do it. Even before the pandemic, lectures were being recorded for playback and online teaching was being developed to different extents. Covid-19 has pressed the fast forward button, signalling a new approach to teaching that is bolstered by readily available and user-friendly technology. Just as the majority of people quickly became comfortable working from home, Covid-19 has accelerated changes in higher education.

Zoom could not save university sport from its pandemic-induced hit, however. The British Universities and Colleges Sport (BUCS) intramural league competitions were forced into an off-season. But a special exemption to the 'rule of six' meant teams returned to play last autumn, and newcomers in 2022 should be able to look forward to getting stuck into university sport, whether for fun, fitness or at elite level competition. Our *Guide* traditionally features a chapter on enjoying sport at university, but as with the BUCS league we paused it this year, making space instead for an in-depth look at the impact of Covid-19 on higher education.

The progress being made across higher education towards a more socially equitable distribution of places risked considerable disruption by the health pandemic. As it happened, though, far from Covid-19 adversely affecting the drive to diversify university intakes, it provided an unexpected boost. Such was the demonstrable unfairness of the Ofqual algorithm, initially used to calculate A-level results, that universities took drastic action to ensure that those from disadvantaged backgrounds did not miss out disproportionately on places. Colleges at Oxford decided to admit all those to whom offers had been made, effectively by-passing A-levels. Once the dust settled, it emerged that Oxford had admitted more students educated in the state sector than ever before – 68%, up from 60.6% in the 2019 admissions cycle and 55% five years ago. As our chapter on where students come from explains, the university has committed to recruiting 25% of its undergraduates from previously under-represented backgrounds by 2023.

Chapter ten of our *Guide* offers a fresh spin on how to help and support the student in your family. Looking at trends in drinking, drug-taking and personal safety on campuses, the chapter aims to set a realistic tone. Letting go of the reins is no easy task for today's hands-on parents, but as the chapter explores, it is possible to give your child autonomy whilst also checking in with them around the matters of drink, drugs and staying safe.

Issues concerning mental health among students remain an area of concern that the effects of the pandemic seem likely to exacerbate. Jenny Smith, policy manager at Student Minds, is particularly worried for new students. "The start of a new academic year is a key pressure point for many, even before you take difficulties related to the pandemic into consideration. Students may be worried about their academic capability, establishing new friendships, or making ends meet financially," she explains in chapter ten. Universities are struggling to meet demand for mental health services and long waiting times are par for the course. Find out what the support is like at the universities you consider applying to, as access to care can vary. UCL invested an extra £140,000 in student mental health services in recent years, after a protest by students. The University of Bristol offers a ten-week Science of Happiness course to all students, which teaches exercises to improve mental wellbeing, and Manchester's four universities and the Royal Northern College of Music are in the second year of £1.6 million pilot mental health service linking psychiatrists, psychologists and mental health nurses with students.

Even with the potentially lasting impact of coronavirus, university remains an undeniably exciting and worthwhile investment, as evidenced by the increased numbers enrolling each year, although they have to pay £9,250-a-year for teaching. The price of tuition fees has not gone up for students from the UK and Ireland for now, but it has not gone down either – as had been proposed by the Augar review in 2019. But in February 2020 research by the Institute for Fiscal Studies (IF) reconfirmed the salary premium, finding that a degree from a UK university increases a person's net earnings by at least £100,000 over their lifetime, after student loan repayments and taxes are factored in.

Some degrees do not offer good value for money though, and applicants need to find a sensible balance between following their dreams and getting into debt unwisely when choosing what and where to study. Investigate the findings of the new Graduate Outcomes survey, which shows what graduates of the 67 subject areas featured in chapter 13 are doing 15 months after finishing their degrees. Ideally, in the subjects you want to apply to you will see high proportions in high-skilled jobs and/or postgraduate study, and far fewer in jobs deemed low-skilled, or even unemployed. The remodelled survey's census point is an improvement on its previous incarnation, which canvassed graduates only six months after university. The longer timeframe offers a more realistic reflection of modern work patterns and should be a useful tool for new applicants.

Most graduates do not regret going to university and carry fond memories of their undergraduate years with them through life – along with career advantages and intellectual enrichment. Britain's universities are a magnet for students worldwide, and for those who have them on their doorstep they offer a valuable resource. The right university cannot be pinpointed simply by a league table, but this *Guide* should provide all the information needed to draw up a shortlist for further investigation, which will help you make the right choice in the end.

Evolving higher education

In the 27 years that this book has been published, higher education has experienced numerous changes. Recommendations made by the Augar review into post-18 education and funding have been slow to bear fruit however. Its headline proposal was to reduce tuition fees to £7,500, however in light of the pandemic Philip Augar himself, who led the panel, said such a move would be too destabilising. The government promised more detailed feedback on the review's suggestions in the latest spending review, but then went quiet on the issues and we are back where we started.

Britain's withdrawal from the European Union has brought significant change for students coming to the UK. As part of the Brexit divorce deal, students from EU countries, Iceland, Liechtenstein, Norway (EEA) and Switzerland will no longer be eligible for 'home' tuition fees of up to £9,250 in Britain. Nor can they continue to access tuition fee loans here. Instead, from the 2021–22 academic year EU, EEA and Swiss students will qualify for the same, higher rate of 'international' tuition rates payable by those from the rest of the world. These vary by course and by university but were mainly between £12,000 and £20,000 in 2019–20, although some cost £39,475, while medicine reached £61,435.

The pattern of applications and enrolments has changed since the introduction of higher fees in 2012. Students are opting in larger numbers for subjects that they think will lead to well-paid jobs. While there has been a recovery in some arts and social science subjects, the trend towards the sciences and some vocational degrees is unmistakeable. Languages have suffered particularly, and so have courses associated with parts of the economy that were hardest hit by recession. Building is one example, where numbers are only now beginning to recover, even though the subject is in the top ten for employment prospects.

Most students take a degree at least partly to improve their career prospects, so some second-guessing of the employment market is inevitable. But most graduate jobs are not subject-specific and even the keenest future forecasters are hard-pressed to predict employment hotspots four or five years ahead – which is when today's applicants will be looking for jobs. Demand for computer science, for instance, plummeted when the "dotcom bubble" burst, and courses closed. Now the tech industry is booming and there is a skills shortage.

Just as it may be unwise to second-guess employment prospects, the same goes for the competition for places in different subjects. Universities may close or reduce the intake to courses that have low numbers of applicants, while some of the more selective institutions may make more places available, especially to candidates who achieve good grades at A-level. Bristol, Birmingham, Exeter and University College London have all taken hundreds more students than usual since the recruitment restrictions were relaxed for high-grade candidates. Others plan to follow suit – as long as they can attract enough students.

Using this Guide

The merger of *The Times* and *Sunday Times* university guides seven years ago began a new chapter in the ranking of higher education institutions in the UK. The two guides had 35 editions between them and, in their new form, provide the most comprehensive and authoritative assessments of undergraduate education at UK universities. There are no new names in the main table this year. But, although Hartpury makes a first appearance in our profiles. ministers are keen for new institutions to shake up the higher education system. Even those with university titles – the first criterion for inclusion in our table – take time to build up the body of data required to make meaningful comparisons.

Some famous names in UK higher education have never been ranked because they do not fit the parameters of a system that is intended mainly to guide full-time undergraduates. The Open University, for example, operates entirely through distance learning, while the London and Manchester Business Schools have no undergraduates. Birkbeck, University of London, which operates a broadly part-time course model, has dropped out of the table this year.

There are now 67 subject tables, and others will be added in due course because there is growing demand for information at this level. Successive surveys have found that international students are more influenced by subject rankings than those for whole institutions, and there is no reason to believe that domestic applicants think differently.

Since the separation of National Student Survey (NSS) scores, outlined below, there has been no change in the basic methodology behind the tables, however. The nine elements of the main table are the same, with the approach to scores in the 2014 Research Excellence Framework mirroring as closely as possible those for previous assessments. In order to reflect the likelihood of undergraduates coming into contact with outstanding researchers, the proportion of eligible academics entered for assessment is part of the calculation, as well as the average grades achieved.

The graduate prospects measure, derived from the new Graduate Outcomes survey, has made allowance for 15 months' worth of feet-finding among graduates before taking a census of their job status, which makes it a better reflection of their prospects than the six-months-on survey that went before it.

The methodology for the new edition remains stable. The *Guide* has always put a premium on consistency in the way that it uses the statistics published by universities and presents the results. The overriding aim is to inform potential students and their parents and advisors, not to make judgments on the performance of universities. As such, it differs from the Government's Teaching Excellence Framework (TEF), which uses some of the same statistics but makes allowance for the prior qualifications of students and uses an expert panel to place the results in context. Our tables use the raw data produced by universities to reflect the undergraduate experience, whatever advantages or disadvantages those institutions might face. We also rank all 131 universities, while the TEF uses only three bands, leaving almost half of the institutions in our table on the same middle tier.

The TEF represents the first official intervention in this area since the Quality Assurance Agency's assessments of teaching quality were abolished more than a decade ago. Scores in those reports correlated closely with research grades, and the first discussions on the framework in the Coalition Government envisaged one comparison taking account of both teaching and research. This remains our approach, to look at a broad range of factors (including the presence of excellent researchers on the academic staff) that will impact on undergraduates.

Guide Award Winners

University of the Year	**Oxford**
Runner-up	**Queen Mary, London**
Shortlisted	**Bath**
	Coventry
	Strathclyde
Scottish University of the Year	**Robert Gordon**
Welsh University of the Year	**Cardiff Metropolitan**
Modern University of the Year	**Lincoln**
Sports University of the Year	**Nottingham**
University of the Year for	
Teaching Quality	**Abertay**
Student Experience	**West London**
Graduate Employment	**Imperial College London**
Student Retention	**Manchester Metropolitan**
Social Inclusion	**Sunderland**

This year's tables

Cambridge and Oxford remain unshakable at the top of the academic table. The gap has narrowed this year between second-ranked Oxford and its ancient rival Cambridge in first place. Oxford takes our University of the Year award 2021–22, in recognition of its work to develop a vaccine for Covid-19, along with its response to the A-level grade mishandling in the summer of 2020. Scientists at the university's Jenner Institute and the Oxford Vaccine Group were early leaders in the race to inoculate against the novel coronavirus.

Cambridge is top in almost half (32) of the 67 subject tables, an extraordinary achievement. Oxford leads in five, followed by Glasgow (four) and Loughborough (also four). St Andrew's, in third place overall, remains Scotland's top university by a clear margin, and Queen's Belfast occupies the same position in Northern Ireland, while in Wales, Cardiff has regained the top spot from Swansea. Its neighbouring university, Cardiff Met, has climbed 33 places to 79th, and wins our Welsh University of the Year award, while Robert Gordon, up 17 places, takes Scottish University of the Year. Other impressive rises include Bishop Grosseteste, in Lincoln, which has gained nearly 40 places to 64th, Edinburgh Napier, up 38 places to 63rd, and St George's, London in 49th place – an 18-place rise.

Going in the opposite direction, London South Bank has fallen 37 places to 123rd and De Montfort has declined by an even bigger margin of 45 places, to 119th. The upper reaches of our table are fairly stable, other than some minor reshuffles. Bath has re-entered the top 10 for the first time since 2014, while the London School of Economics has overtaken fifth-ranked Imperial College and occupies fourth place. Warwick, in tenth, has maintained its record of never dropping outside our top 10.

Runner up for our University of the Year award, Queen Mary, University of London, continues to prove that academic success and social inclusion are not mutually exclusive. It has risen eight places to rank 41st in our academic ranking and is five places up at 46th for social inclusion. Lincoln, our Modern University of the Year, is one of five universities that have opened new medical schools in the past two years.

A number of modern universities continue to feature above some older foundations. The first edition of *The Times Good University Guide* predicted the development of a new pecking order in an era of growing competition between universities, many of which had newly gained that title. Harper Adams reached the top 20 last year, though it has fallen to 28th this year and Chichester and Coventry are also in top 50 positions.

Making the right choices

This *Guide* is intended as a starting point to finding the right course, a tool to help navigate the statistical minefield that applicants face, as universities present their performance in the best possible light. There is advice on fees and financial questions, as well as all-important employment issues, along with the usual ranking of universities and 67 subject tables.

While some of the leading universities have expanded considerably in recent years, most will remain selective, particularly in popular subjects. Although the offer rate is promising, that does not mean that all students secured the university or course of their dreams. The demand for places is far from uniform, and even within the same university the level of competition will vary between subjects. The entry scores quoted in the subject tables in Chapter 13 offer a reliable guide to the relative levels of selectivity, but the figures are for entrants' actual qualifications. The standard offers made by departments will invariably be lower, and the grades those departments were prepared to accept were often lower still.

Making the right choice requires a mixture of realism and ambition. Most sixth-formers and college students have a fair idea of the grades they are capable of attaining, within a certain margin for error. Even with five course choices, there is no point in applying for a degree where the standard offer is so far from your predicted grades that rejection is virtually certain. If your results do turn out to be much better than predicted, there will be an opportunity through the Adjustment system, or simply through Clearing, to trade up to an alternative university.

Since the relaxation of recruitment restrictions, universities that once took pride in their absence from Clearing have continued to recruit after A-level results day. As a result, the use of insurance choices – the inclusion of at least one university with lower entrance standards than your main targets – has been declining. It is still a dangerous strategy, but there is now more chance of picking up a place at a leading university if you aimed too high with all your first-round choices. Some may even come to you if you sign up to the UCAS system that allows universities to approach unplaced candidates on Results Day if their grades are similar to those of other entrants.

The long view

School-leavers who enter higher education in 2022 were not born when our first league table was published and most will never have heard of polytechnics, even if they attend a university that once carried that title. But it was the award of university status to the 34 polytechnics, over a quarter of a century ago, that was the inspiration for the first edition of *The Times Good University Guide*. The original poly, the Polytechnic of Central London, had become the University of Westminster, Bristol Polytechnic was now the University of the West of England and Leicester Polytechnic had morphed into De Montfort University. The new *Guide* charted the lineage of the new universities and offered the first-ever comparison of institutional performance in UK higher education.

The university establishment did not welcome the initiative. The vice-chancellors described the table as "wrong in principle, flawed in execution and constructed upon data which are not uniform, are ill-defined and in places demonstrably false." The league table has changed considerably since then, and its results are taken rather more seriously. While consistency has been a priority for the *Guide* throughout its 27 years, only six of the original 14 measures have survived. Some of the current components – notably the National Student Survey – did not exist in 1992, while others have been modified or dropped at the behest of the expert group of planning officers from different types of universities that meets annually to review the methodology and make recommendations for the future.

While ranking is hardly popular with academics, the relationship with universities has changed radically, and this *Guide* is quoted on numerous university websites. As Sir David Eastwood, now vice-chancellor of the University of Birmingham, said in launching an official report on university league tables that he commissioned as Chief Executive of the Higher Education Funding Council for England: "We deplore league tables one day and deploy them the next."

Most universities have had their ups and downs over the years, with the notable exceptions of Oxford and Cambridge. Both benefit from top research grades – a measure that carries an extra weighting in our table. They also have famously high entry standards, much the largest proportions of first and upper-second class degrees and consistently good scores on every other measure. Imperial College and University College London have seldom been out of the top five, with St Andrews joining them in recent years, while the London School of Economics, Durham and Warwick have all been fixtures in the top ten.

There have been spectacular rises, however. West London was bottom of our rankings in 2001, as Thames Valley University, but ranks equal 61st this year and wins our award for Student Experience. Lincoln is another former incumbent of the bottom spot, in 1999 when it was the University of Lincolnshire and Humberside, and sits in 45th this year.

Since this book was first published, the number of universities has increased by a third and the full-time student population has rocketed. Individual institutions are almost unrecognisable from their 1992 forms. Nottingham, for example, had fewer than 10,000 students then, compared with more than 30,000 now. Manchester Metropolitan, the largest of the former polys, has experienced similar growth. Yet there are universities now which would have been too small and too specialist to qualify for the title in 1992. The diversity of UK higher education is celebrated as one of its greatest strengths, and the modern universities are neither encouraged nor anxious to compete with the older foundations on some of the measures in our table.

The coming years may bring more transformation in the higher education landscape, not just from increased blended online learning, but from private sector institutions competing strongly with established universities in some fields. Even before Covid-19, distance learning was becoming more popular, and investment in Massive Open Online Courses (MOOCs) was increasing. The rising 18-year-old population will boost the demand for higher education places over the next few years, but it remains to be seen whether the finances of universities and the regulatory restrictions they might face will enable them to satisfy that demand. There may, indeed, be university closures and mergers, although they have been predicted before and seldom come about. As mentioned at the start of this introduction, universities are among the most enduring of the UK's institutions, and will take some shifting.

1 The University League Table

What Makes a Top University?

The introduction of tuition fees across UK universities more than two decades ago sharpened everyone's focus on the importance of picking the perfect degree at the best university. Forking out hefty sums of cash tends to have that effect. Higher education was a relative snip back then though, at £1,000 a year, but the mental leap was arguably more significant; a degree was no longer an entirely government-funded rite of passage that could be taken for granted. Fees first crossed the £9,000-a-year threshold in 2012 and are now a bit higher still.

Universities know that budding students and the Bank of Mum and Dad have every right to feel well-informed and confident that they are making a worthwhile investment, not only financially but academically, socially and in terms of future career prospects. They have responded by issuing reams of statistics about themselves, and the government has taken a similarly transparent approach – so much so that for those embarking on applying for a university place, navigating the plethora of information is a complicated and at times confusing process.

The Times and Sunday Times Good University Guide weighs up university performance measures and combines them in a straightforward way that has armed generations of students with the knowledge and insights to make informed choices. The table in this chapter focuses on the fundamentals of undergraduate education and makes meaningful comparisons. Every element of the table has been chosen for the light it shines on the experience undergraduates encounter during their degrees, and their future prospects.

Over 27 years of publication our *Guide* has maintained consistency in its evaluations, confident that the measures used are the best currently available for the task. Some changes have been forced upon us though, naturally enough during the course of nearly three decades. When universities stopped assessing teaching quality by subject our table lost its most heavily-weighted measure. However, we now have the benefit of the National Student Survey (NSS), which allows us to reflect the student experience. More than two-thirds of final year undergraduates give their views on the quality of their courses, a remarkable response rate that makes the results impossible to dismiss.

The student satisfaction measure is split in two. The "teaching quality" indicator reflects the average scores of the survey's sections on teaching, assessment and feedback, learning opportunities and academic support. The "student experience" indicator is drawn from the average of the sections on organisation and management, learning resources, the student voice and the learning community, as well as the final question on overall satisfaction. Teaching quality is favoured over student experience in our table and accounts for 67% of the overall student satisfaction score, with student experience making up the remaining 33%.

The basic information that applicants need in order to judge universities and their courses does not change, however. A university's entry standards, staffing levels, completion rates, degree classifications and graduate employment rates are all vital pieces of intelligence for anyone deciding where to study.

Research grades, while not directly involving undergraduates, bring with them considerable funds and enable a university to attract top academics.

Critics may have reasons to discount any of these measures, but the package has struck a chord with readers. Our ranking has built a reputation as the most authoritative arbiter of changing fortunes in higher education.

The measures used are kept under review by a group of university administrators and statisticians, which meets annually. The raw data that go into the table in this chapter and the 67 subject tables in chapter 13 are all in the public domain and are sent to universities for checking before any scores are calculated.

The various official bodies concerned with higher education do not publish league tables, and the Higher Education Statistics Agency (HESA), which supplies most of the figures used in our tables, does not endorse the way in which they are aggregated. But there are now numerous exercises, from the Teaching Excellence Framework to the annual "performance indicators" published by HESA on everything from completion rates to research output at each university, that invite comparisons.

Any scrutiny of league table positions is best carried out in conjunction with an examination of the relevant subject table – it is the course, after all, that will dominate your undergraduate years and influence your subsequent career.

How *The Times and Sunday Times* league table works

The table is presented in a format that displays the raw data, wherever possible. In building the table, scores for student satisfaction (combining the teaching quality, student experience scores) and research quality were weighted by 1.5; all other measures were weighted by 1.

For entry standards, student/staff ratio, good honours and graduate prospects, the score was adjusted for subject mix. For example, it is accepted that engineering, law and medicine graduates will tend to have better graduate prospects than their peers from English, psychology and sociology courses. Comparing results in the main subject groupings helps to iron out differences attributable simply to the range of degrees on offer. This subject-mix adjustment means that it is not possible to replicate the scores in the table from the published indicators because the calculation requires access to the entire dataset.

The indicators were combined using a common statistical technique known as z-scores, to ensure that no indicator has a disproportionate effect on the overall total for each university, and the totals were transformed to a scale with 1,000 for the top score. The z-score technique makes it impossible to compare universities' total scores from one year to the next, although their relative positions in the table are comparable. Individual scores are dependent on the top performer: a university might drop from 60% of the top score to 58% but still have improved, depending on the relative performance of other universities.

Only where data are not available from HESA, are figures sourced directly from universities. Where this is not possible, scores are generated according to a university's average performance on other indicators, apart from the measures for research quality, student/staff ratio and services and facilities spend, where no score is created.

The organisations providing the raw data for the tables are not involved in the process of aggregation, so are not responsible for any inferences or conclusions we have made. Every care has been taken to ensure the accuracy of the tables and accompanying information, but no responsibility can be taken for errors or omissions.

The Times and The Sunday Times league table uses nine important indicators of university activity, based on the most recent data available at the time of compilation:

» Teaching quality
» Student experience
» Research quality
» Entry standards
» Student/staff ratio

» Services and facilities spend
» Completion
» Good honours
» Graduate prospects

Teaching quality and student experience

The student satisfaction measure has been divided into two components which give final-year undergraduates' views of the quality of their courses. The National Student Survey (NSS) published in 2020 was the source of the data.

Where no data were available in the 2020 survey, the score from the 2019 survey was used. Where no data from the 2019 survey were available, the 2018 score was used.

» The National Student Survey covers eight aspects of a course, with an additional question gauging overall satisfaction. Students answer on a scale from 1 (bottom) to 5 (top) and the score in the table is the percentage of positive responses (4 and 5) in each section.
» The teaching quality indicator reflects the average scores of the first four sections, which contain 14 questions.
» The student experience indicator is drawn from the average scores of the remaining four sections, containing 12 questions, and the additional question on overall satisfaction.
» Teaching quality accounts for 67% of the overall score covering student satisfaction, with student experience making up the remaining 33%.
» The survey is based on the opinion of final-year undergraduates rather than directly assessing teaching quality. Most undergraduates have no experience of other universities, or different courses, to inform their judgements. Although all the questions relate to courses, rather than other aspects of the student experience, some types of university – notably medium-sized campus universities – tend to do better than others, while those in London in particular tend to do worse.

Research quality

This is a measure of the quality of the research undertaken in each university. The information was sourced from the 2014 Research Excellence Framework (REF), a peer-review exercise used to evaluate the quality of research in UK higher education institutions undertaken by the UK Higher Education funding bodies. Additionally, academic staffing data for 2013–14 from the Higher Education Statistics Agency have been used.

» A research quality profile was given to every university department that took part. This profile used the following categories: 4* world-leading; 3* internationally excellent; 2* internationally recognised; 1* nationally recognised; and unclassified. The Funding Bodies have directed more funds to the very best research by applying weightings, and for the 2015 Guide we used the weightings adopted by HEFCE (the funding council for England) for funding in 2013–14: 4* was weighted by a factor of 3 and 3* was weighted by a factor of 1. Outputs of 2* and 1* carried zero weight. This meant a maximum score of 3. In the interests of consistency, the above weightings continue to be applied this year.

» The scores in the table are presented as a percentage of the maximum score. To achieve the maximum score all staff would need to be at 4* world-leading level.

» Universities could choose which staff to include in the REF, so, to factor in the depth of the research quality, each quality profile score has been multiplied by the number of staff returned in the REF as a proportion of all eligible staff.

Entry standards

This is the average score, using the UCAS tariff (see page 32), of new students under the age of 21 who took A and AS-Levels, Scottish Highers and Advanced Highers and other equivalent qualifications (eg, International Baccalaureate). It measures what new students achieved rather than the entry requirements suggested by the universities. The data comes from HESA for 2018–19. The original sources of data for this measure are data returns made by the universities to HESA.

» Using the UCAS tariff, each student's examination results were converted to a numerical score. HESA then calculated an average for all students at the university. The results have then been adjusted to take account of the subject mix at the university.

» A score of 144 represents three As at A-level. Although all but five of the top 40 universities in the table have average entry standards of at least 144, it does not mean that everyone achieved such results – let alone that this was the standard offer. Courses will not demand more than three subjects at A-level and offers are pitched accordingly. You will need to reach the entry requirements set by the university, rather than these scores.

Graduate prospects

This measure is the percentage of full-time, UK-resident graduates undertaking further study or in a high-skilled job 15 months after graduation. The high-skilled employment data came from the new Graduate Outcomes survey published by HESA in June 2020. It is based on 2018 graduates interviewed up to September 2019. The results have been adjusted for subject mix.

Good honours

This measure is the percentage of graduates achieving a first or upper-second class degree. The results have been adjusted to take account of the subject mix at the university. The data comes from HESA for 2018–19. The original sources of data for this measure are data returns made by the universities themselves to HESA.

» Four-year first degrees, such as an MChem, are treated as equivalent to a first or upper-second.
» Scottish Ordinary degrees (awarded after three years of study) are excluded.

» Universities control degree classification, with some oversight from external examiners. There have been suggestions that, since universities have increased the numbers of good honours degrees they award, this measure may not be as objective as it should be. However, it remains the key measure of a student's success and employability.

Completion

This measure gives the percentage of students expected to complete their studies (or transfer to another institution) for each university. The data comes from the HESA performance indicators published in March 2020 and based on students entering in 2017–18.

» This measure is a projection, liable to statistical fluctuations.

Student/staff ratio

This is a measure of the average number of full-time equivalent students to each member of the academic staff, apart from those purely engaged in research. In this measure a low value is better than a high value. The data comes from HESA for 2018–19. The original sources of data for this measure are data returns made by the universities themselves to HESA.

» The figures, as calculated by HESA, allow for variation in employment patterns at different universities. A low value means that there are a small number of students for each academic member of staff, but this does not, of course, ensure good teaching quality or contact time with academics.

» Student/staff ratios vary by subject; for example, the ratio is usually low for medicine. In building the table, the score is adjusted for the subject mix taught by each university.

» Adjustments are also made for students who are on industrial placements, either for a full year or for part of a year.

Services and facilities spend

The expenditure per student on staff and student facilities, including library and computing facilities. The data comes from HESA for 2017–18 and 2018–19. The original data sources for this measure are data returns made by the universities to HESA.

» This is a measure calculated by taking the expenditure on student facilities (including sports, grants to student societies, careers services, health services, counselling, etc.) and library and computing facilities (books, journals, staff, central computers and computer networks, but not buildings) and dividing this by the number of full-time-equivalent students. Expenditure is averaged over two years to even out large projects that may distort figures (for example, a computer upgrade undertaken in a single year).

Rank	Last year's rank		Teaching quality (%)	Student experience (%)	Research quality (%)	Entry standards (UCAS points)	Graduate prospects (%)	Good honours (%)	Completion rate (%)	Student-staff ratio	Services & facilities spend per student (£)	Total	Page
1	1	Cambridge	n/a	n/a	57.3	212	91.4	92.9	98.7	11.2	3,828	1,000	362
2	2	Oxford	n/a	n/a	53.1	203	90.6	94.0	98.1	10.3	3,436	982	492
3	3	St Andrews	86.7	86.3	40.4	211	81.9	90.6	95.0	11.2	3,725	967	520
4	6	London School of Economics	77.3	74.3	52.8	170	92.5	92.2	97.2	11.9	2,941	898	464
5	4	Imperial College London	75.5	78.5	56.2	189	95.4	91.5	96.8	11.1	3,914	859	432
6	7	Durham	79.0	76.2	39.0	188	87.0	91.7	95.6	14.7	3,498	841	390
7	5	Loughborough	82.4	84.8	36.3	153	83.6	84.4	93.3	13.4	3,410	810	468
8	9	University College London	75.4	75.7	51.0	175	86.1	88.9	94.6	10.4	2,823	798	562
9	11	Bath	79.1	80.9	37.3	174	89.4	89.0	96.2	14.9	2,736	790	332
=10	10	Warwick	78.6	77.9	44.6	171	85.2	86.7	94.9	13.8	2,580	769	564
=10	8	Lancaster	79.4	77.8	39.1	150	81.9	79.6	93.0	12.5	3,588	769	442
12	12	Exeter	78.4	79.3	38.0	163	83.3	86.7	94.6	15.2	2,805	741	404
13	15	Bristol	76.4	75.0	47.3	169	83.6	90.1	95.0	13.3	2,548	730	354
14	16	Glasgow	78.4	79.4	39.9	204	81.3	82.6	88.0	13.4	2,747	729	408
=15	13	Leeds	77.7	77.2	36.8	163	82.0	87.2	93.5	13.7	3,096	727	444
=15	20	Southampton	79.0	78.8	44.9	153	81.6	85.8	92.0	13.3	2,700	727	538
17	25	Edinburgh	72.8	72.9	43.8	187	81.2	89.5	93.8	11.9	2,379	724	398
18	18	Manchester	76.7	75.5	39.8	165	83.0	82.9	93.5	13.1	3,349	718	470
19	14	Birmingham	76.4	74.9	37.1	159	84.7	86.2	94.6	14.1	3,331	712	340
20	22	York	80.7	78.7	38.3	151	81.7	82.4	94.3	14.4	1,982	700	582
21	23	East Anglia	80.7	79.1	35.8	138	79.6	84.7	87.8	13.5	2,924	696	392
22	19	Royal Holloway, London	79.7	79.2	36.3	134	75.0	81.5	91.2	14.7	2,913	689	518
=23	24	Dundee	80.9	80.7	31.2	176	84.4	76.5	87.7	14.3	2,779	676	388
=23	36	Strathclyde	78.5	79.5	37.7	200	83.4	84.9	87.8	19.5	2,090	676	544
=23	26	Sheffield	79.7	80.6	37.6	152	81.8	82.7	93.2	14.7	2,327	676	528

Rank	Last year's rank		Teaching quality (%)	Student experience (%)	Research quality (%)	Entry standards (UCAS points)	Graduate prospects (%)	Good honours (%)	Completion rate (%)	Student-staff ratio	Services & facilities spend per student (£)	Total	Page
26	21	Nottingham	77.0	75.6	37.8	150	84.9	84.4	92.1	14.5	2,888	672	486
27	27	Aberdeen	78.4	80.3	29.9	183	79.8	86.2	88.9	16.2	2,517	666	316
28	17	Harper Adams	84.6	82.7	5.7	124	71.2	73.0	87.6	14.8	4,029	665	418
29	29	Liverpool	80.0	80.2	31.5	143	80.6	78.8	92.7	14.4	2,899	660	456
30	30	King's College London	72.5	70.8	44.0	164	86.3	85.5	91.4	11.9	2,810	654	438
=31	35	Queen's Belfast	76.1	76.3	39.7	152	84.7	85.0	91.6	14.6	2,423	652	506
=31	28	Newcastle	76.4	77.1	37.7	150	81.4	82.0	95.1	14.2	2,483	652	476
=31	=38	Reading	78.1	77.2	36.5	127	78.9	81.9	91.3	15.8	2,880	652	510
34	34	Cardiff	76.9	75.8	35.0	154	83.1	81.7	91.8	14.3	2,581	645	366
35	33	Heriot-Watt	77.1	78.0	36.7	168	80.8	79.3	84.4	17.8	3,268	644	422
36	31	Swansea	80.6	80.7	33.7	129	82.6	79.1	89.2	15	2,293	643	554
37	41	Leicester	77.0	77.3	31.8	132	76.9	78.9	94.0	13.7	2,830	630	452
38	47	Stirling	82.2	78.6	30.5	165	77.4	76.3	81.3	16.2	2,011	625	542
39	32	Surrey	75.0	76.9	29.7	146	85.5	79.9	88.9	15.8	2,800	616	550
40	37	Essex	78.8	78.0	37.2	107	73.6	75.4	84.3	16.7	3,691	610	402
41	49	Queen Mary, London	72.8	73.9	37.9	152	80.3	86.0	90.7	13	2,208	602	504
42	45	Aberystwyth	87.3	86.4	28.1	123	66.9	70.7	82.8	16.8	2,493	598	320
43	48	Aston	77.8	77.9	25.8	128	81.3	81.9	89.9	16.1	2,126	594	328
44	=38	Sussex	76.1	73.6	31.8	142	76.2	75.3	89.9	17.4	2,563	579	552
45	51	Lincoln	82.4	81.3	10.3	120	72.9	75.9	88.7	15.3	2,295	578	454
=46	50	Coventry	82.4	80.5	3.8	122	78.6	74.6	81.8	13.9	2,625	572	378
=46	71	Chichester	83.8	81.1	6.4	122	69.5	75.6	90.5	14.4	1,926	572	374
48	54	Kent	77.9	76.8	35.2	131	72.9	78.0	88.8	17	1,952	569	436
49	67	St George's, London	71.7	73.1	22.2	156	90.3	78.1	94.4	13.3	5,211	564	522
50	44	Soas, London	75.0	71.3	27.9	158	68.5	82.5	82.0	11.6	1,469	562	532

Rank	Last year's rank		Teaching quality (%)	Student experience (%)	Research quality (%)	Entry standards (UCAS points)	Graduate prospects (%)	Good honours (%)	Completion rate (%)	Student-staff ratio	Services & facilities spend per student (£)	Total	Page
=51	46	Keele	80.5	79.0	22.1	123	78.2	76.0	86.9	14.3	2,266	560	434
=51	=58	Ulster	79.6	78.9	31.8	128	76.6	78.6	80.3	18.1	2,574	560	560
53	40	Nottingham Trent	82.3	81.3	6.5	125	71.7	69.7	86.7	14.8	2,495	558	486
54	43	Arts Bournemouth	86.5	83.2	2.4	147	57.3	68.3	91.4	14.5	1,745	556	324
55	=56	Leeds Arts	83.5	79.6	n/a	152	62.4	76.7	93.6	14.1	1,334	554	446
56	64	Oxford Brookes	76.3	76.3	11.4	122	78.5	78.8	89.4	14.7	2,408	549	494
57	=65	Northumbria	79.4	77.0	9.0	143	75.2	78.7	83.8	15.5	2,332	544	482
58	=58	West of England	83.9	83.0	8.8	121	76.8	74.5	82.5	15.4	1,897	541	568
59	76	Plymouth	82.7	80.0	15.9	128	76.5	73.7	83.5	16.2	2,342	538	496
=60	77	Hull	80.3	78.6	16.7	125	75.0	73.7	82.9	15.1	2,594	537	430
=60	52	West London	86.3	85.2	1.6	123	68.0	75.4	77.8	15.2	2,483	537	566
62	70	Bangor	81.1	79.6	27.2	125	73.2	72.0	83.8	15.7	1,932	536	330
63	101	Edinburgh Napier	81.6	80.2	4.6	152	74.3	78.8	81.1	18.2	2,524	535	400
64	=102	Bishop Grosseteste	84.7	81.2	2.1	109	71.0	70.7	89.0	18.4	2,445	532	344
65	=62	Manchester Metropolitan	80.2	78.1	7.5	131	66.5	72.8	85.1	15	2,831	530	472
66	83	Robert Gordon	84.3	82.2	4.0	156	78.5	72.0	84.5	18.7	1,706	528	512
67	=65	Sheffield Hallam	80.6	77.4	5.4	116	77.1	75.7	85.5	16.8	2,702	525	530
68	94	Bournemouth	78.3	76.2	9.0	115	79.0	78.8	84.3	17.6	2,455	524	348
69	=79	Chester	82.4	80.1	4.1	116	67.8	71.5	79.7	15.1	2,879	511	372
70	55	Edge Hill	78.0	76.7	4.9	130	72.0	71.3	84.2	14	2,587	510	396
71	42	Creative Arts	81.9	74.5	3.4	136	54.2	73.5	84.8	13.7	2,775	509	380
72	=56	Portsmouth	81.1	79.4	8.6	113	72.9	73.6	83.8	16.1	2,281	504	500
=73	61	Huddersfield	78.5	75.6	9.4	128	72.0	75.6	83.5	15.5	2,455	502	428
=73	=89	Royal Agricultural	78.4	77.3	1.1	120	70.3	67.6	94.4	19.8	3,130	502	516
75	=96	Glasgow Caledonian	80.8	79.0	7.0	159	74.6	80.3	85.0	21.4	1,881	500	410

Rank	Last year's rank		Teaching quality (%)	Student experience (%)	Research quality (%)	Entry standards (UCAS points)	Graduate prospects (%)	Good honours (%)	Completion rate (%)	Student-staff ratio	Services & facilities spend per student (£)	Total	Page
76	53	Staffordshire	83.7	79.4	16.5	120	66.7	73.4	79.7	17.5	2,289	498	540
77	=62	Norwich Arts	80.5	76.9	5.6	130	56.2	70.8	84.1	15.2	3,013	495	484
78	69	Roehampton	79.0	77.9	24.5	103	61.6	66.7	75.1	14.8	3,321	493	514
79	112	Cardiff Metropolitan	81.1	80.2	3.9	128	72.2	70.6	80.1	18.1	2,561	492	368
=80	=98	Abertay	87.0	81.2	5.1	148	67.3	75.8	74.3	21.2	1,853	490	318
=80	60	Liverpool Hope	83.1	79.4	9.2	114	62.9	71.8	77.3	15	2,147	490	458
82	73	City, London	71.7	72.1	22.6	136	76.7	75.6	87.5	17.3	2,709	488	376
=83	81	York St John	84.4	80.7	4.1	103	66.9	73.6	86.4	18	2,204	487	584
=83	=79	Arts London	76.7	69.7	8.0	135	57.9	72.2	84.2	13.7	3,178	487	326
85	78	Liverpool John Moores	79.8	79.5	8.9	145	69.8	73.7	82.1	16.8	1,829	484	460
86	85	St Mary's, Twickenham	82.0	80.1	4.0	110	70.1	75.1	82.8	18	1,922	479	524
87	75	Central Lancashire	78.4	75.7	5.6	127	72.5	72.3	76.2	13.3	2,629	476	370
88	100	Brunel London	73.9	73.9	25.4	119	75.0	75.6	87.5	17.7	1,945	471	356
89	82	Queen Margaret, Edinburgh	80.3	76.1	6.6	153	71.8	79.6	79.3	19.5	1,676	469	502
=90	=96	Birmingham City	80.3	76.7	4.3	123	71.4	74.4	84.0	16.6	2,102	468	342
=90	114	South Wales	82.0	78.0	4.0	121	68.0	70.4	81.7	15.1	1,955	468	536
92	87	Teesside	82.1	78.7	3.6	120	78.1	71.6	77.9	18.2	2,634	467	556
93	=89	Solent, Southampton	82.5	79.9	0.5	124	64.1	70.7	78.5	15.8	2,149	466	534
=94	91	Derby	83.0	80.4	2.5	118	68.7	66.9	78.3	14.6	1,957	465	386
=94	72	Falmouth	81.7	77.2	4.6	126	59.7	76.4	86.9	17.3	1,704	465	406
96	=98	Winchester	79.8	75.9	5.8	110	66.5	74.3	84.2	16.5	1,810	463	574
97	68	Goldsmiths, London	70.0	63.8	33.4	127	62.4	79.6	78.0	14.9	3,106	461	414
98	84	Greenwich	78.0	76.3	4.9	122	73.0	77.1	81.4	17.8	2,314	460	416
99	88	Hertfordshire	79.3	78.1	5.6	107	71.3	65.7	82.0	14.8	2,859	458	424
100	111	Salford	79.4	76.7	8.3	127	72.8	71.7	81.9	16.5	2,100	456	526

Rank	Last year's rank		Teaching quality (%)	Student experience (%)	Research quality (%)	Entry standards (UCAS points)	Graduate prospects (%)	Good honours (%)	Completion rate (%)	Student-staff ratio	Services & facilities spend per student (£)	Total	Page
=101	=92	Worcester	83.6	81.7	4.3	117	72.4	66.0	82.1	17.8	1,715	453	578
=101	=102	Wales Trinity St David	84.9	79.3	2.6	135	57.3	73.5	77.0	16.3	1,873	453	558
103	109	Sunderland	80.4	78.1	5.8	113	66.2	61.3	78.4	15.5	2,946	450	548
=104	106	Kingston	79.1	77.3	5.1	117	70.2	71.3	80.9	16.8	2,761	445	440
=104	110	Bath Spa	77.5	73.1	7.9	112	62.4	80.1	84.0	17.2	2,165	445	334
106	105	Bradford	76.5	76.3	9.2	125	75.6	79.9	82.5	18	2,217	444	350
107	123	Leeds Beckett	81.8	80.3	4.1	107	69.7	71.3	76.1	19.2	2,325	443	448
108	=92	Buckingham	82.5	81.0	n/a	121	74.7	63.5	83.1	15	805	442	358
109	95	Gloucestershire	81.1	76.9	3.8	116	64.5	71.8	81.4	17.7	1,979	441	412
110	117	Leeds Trinity	80.4	78.7	2.0	104	68.3	78.7	80.3	21	1,952	439	450
111	116	Northampton	80.1	74.7	3.2	102	69.0	66.9	78.8	16.2	2,889	438	480
=112	113	Bucks New	82.5	79.8	1.5	109	69.6	58.2	79.3*	16.5	2,796**	437	358
=112	115	Newman	84.4	82.2	2.8	110	63.5	66.8	78.1	17.1	1,778	437	478
114	121	Cumbria	81.0	75.4	1.2	120	75.0	63.9	82.9	15.7	1,760	429	382
115	=102	Plymouth Marjon	82.5	79.7	0.0	114	70.4	73.8	79.1	20.5	1,603	426	498
116	108	West of Scotland	81.6	78.4	4.3	130	72.0	70.9	78.5	22.6	2,389	423	570
117	120	Anglia Ruskin	80.0	78.1	5.4	113	73.8	75.6	78.1	17.7	1,525	415	322
118	125	Bolton	85.6	81.3	2.9	114	64.2	60.4	72.2	14.4	2,179	411	346
119	74	De Montfort	75.2	74.6	8.9	111*	71.0	72.5	81.4	19.8	2,407	408	384
120	122	Brighton	76.8	72.4	7.9	114	76.2	67.8	80.7	17.5	2,003	407	352
121	107	Middlesex	76.1	74.3	9.7	115	61.9	68.7	78.1	17	2,734	402	474
122	129	Suffolk	78.3	74.2	n/a	105	75.7	71.0	72.5	16.7	2,591	400	546
123	86	London South Bank	77.9	75.5	9.0	107	70.6	70.7	76.4	16.3	2,327	388	466
124	130	Wrexham Glyndŵr	83.0	78.2	2.3	110	67.1	71.0	74.2	19.4	1,784	385	580
125	126	London Metropolitan	80.8	78.4	3.5	97	60.0	60.4	64.8	17.8	4,053	381	462

Rank	Last year's rank		Teaching quality (%)	Student experience (%)	Research quality (%)	Entry standards (UCAS points)	Graduate prospects (%)	Good honours (%)	Completion rate (%)	Student-staff ratio	Services & facilities spend per student (£)	Total	Page
126	119	Westminster	76.8	76.0	9.8	119	63.9	66.2	82.4	20.9	1,764	363	**572**
127	118	Canterbury Christ Church	79.2	73.5	4.5	106	70.9	66.7	67.3	15.6	1,904	359	**364**
128	124	Wolverhampton	80.5	77.2	5.9	109	65.9	65.6	70.4	17.2	2,098	349	**576**
129	127	East London	78.6	75.5	7.2	111	59.7	70.3	73.1	19.7	1,699	324	**394**
130	131	Ravensbourne, London	71.7	65.1	n/a	112	70.7	82.9	72.4	24.2	1,466	298	**508**
131	128	Bedfordshire	76.8	72.4	7.0	103	70.1	65.6	58.5	19.7	2,043	277	**336**

last year's data

2017-18 data only

2 Choosing What and Where to Study

Going to university is a momentous stage in life, and it can shape a future like no other. Putting in some legwork now to carefully research your options should lead to a happy and successful undergraduate experience. As the pandemic reminded us, the future can be unpredictable, and you want to find a university where you can feel settled and supported as well as a course that will not sell your investment short after you graduate.

Having fun and making friends have always been big parts of an enriching university experience, along with learning. These are the years when social circles are often forged for life, and many people meet the partners they end up marrying. You may find yourself feeling so at home in your university's city, town or region that it becomes the place you put down roots after graduation. The years devoted to developing your intellectual curiosity stay with you as an adult, too.

Increasing numbers of students are choosing university as their next step and more are enrolling each year. In London, 60% of the working age population are graduates. The appeal of university is such that even in 2020, students carried through with their plans to start courses in the autumn, in spite of the A-levels fiasco and the social distancing measures that were going to seriously dampen the fresher spirit. Predictions that swathes would defer did not materialise. Quite the opposite; by UCAS's June deadline the application rate from UK 18-year-olds was the highest it had ever been. People had used the lockdown period to apply to higher education, it appeared, with a 17% year-on-year increase in new applicants during this time. The charms of university are perhaps all the more appealing when the alternatives are so limited, with opportunities to travel restricted and job prospects confusing and/or bleak.

Clearly, the debt incurred through student loans to cover £9,250 per year tuition fees, plus living expenses, has not put undergraduates off. Such investment means the financial outcomes after university should be a significant consideration. The price of tuition fees has not gone up for students from the UK and Ireland, but they have not gone down either – as had been proposed by the Augar review in 2019. Meanwhile fees for new students coming to UK universities from the EU, EEA countries and Switzerland are subject to a major hike. Brexit's conclusion has meant these students have lost their right to home fees and funding, and they will be charged the same, much higher, international tuition fee rates as those from the rest of the world from the 2021–22 academic year.

There is a pay-off, though, even if it is not immediate. In February 2020 research by the Institute of Fiscal Studies (IF) found that a degree from a UK university increases a person's net earnings by at least £100,000 over their lifetime, after student loan repayments and taxes are factored in. The report confirms most other research into the graduate salary premium, and represents 20% more in earnings on average for graduates, compared to those without a degree. The benefits of a higher education cannot all be boiled down to higher salaries, however. Those whose ambitions lie in public service, third sector careers or the arts, for instance – careers which generally require a degree and have high social value – are unlikely to end up highly paid. Pursuing a passion for a subject is one of students' main reasons for going to university – as it should be – though this should be balanced with finding out what to expect job and income-wise after graduation.

The new Graduate Outcomes survey shows what graduates of the subjects you are interested in are doing 15 months after finishing their degrees. Ideally, you will see high proportions in high-skilled jobs and/or postgraduate study, and far fewer in jobs deemed low-skilled, or unemployed. The remodelled survey's census point is an improvement on its previous incarnation, which canvassed graduates only six months after university. The longer timeframe offers a more realistic reflection of modern work patterns and should be a useful tool for new applicants.

Some subjects and some universities carry more prestige than others. Such judgements are worth bearing in mind, as your future CV will be assessed according to them. This kind of thinking may not sit easily with everyone, but employers treat universities and subjects as yardsticks, not just the results gained on courses. Certain universities, however, may not occupy our upper rankings, but they might have particularly strong departments for individual subjects. Make the most of out of this *Guide*, and cross reference the subject-by-subject information in chapter 13 with the university profiles and rankings in chapter 15.

Lots of things will influence where you go to university and what you study, from wanting to explore a subject you love in more depth and taking the first steps in your career path, to the desire for greater independence in a new location and the freedom to socialise how and when you please. Or you may want to study part-time and live at home. The options are not endless, but they are many.

Be realistic in your choices, the course you apply to should be within your capabilities, though it will also need to keep you interested for three or four years. A degree should broaden your options later in life, so be sensible about choosing one that can do that for you and keep an eye on the jobs horizon. The technological advancements of the fourth industrial revolution are continually reshaping the world of work, and you want to be abreast of developments.

Computer science degrees tailed off in popularity following the bursting of the dotcom bubble but now they are highly sought after again. Medicine is unlikely to decline, and the number of places to study it is growing. Languages meanwhile are falling in popularity at degree level, not because employers do not want them – they do – but more likely because fewer people are taking them at A-level, as they are considered harder than some other options. Maths is experiencing a similar issue. Narrowing your focus at degree stage could limit what is open to you in five to ten years' time. This *Guide* can inform you of what is possible, and what will make a wise choice.

Is higher education for you?

Being carried along with the flow is all too easy. Maybe your whole friends' group is going to university, or your parents expect it. If you apply for a course in your strongest A-level subject, things should work out OK and your career will look after itself, right? Or perhaps your driving motivation is to leave home and go a bit wild. Such considerations are natural and will not necessarily lead to a disaster. But now is the time to question whether university is the best way of fulfilling your ambitions. There are degree apprenticeships, or training schemes at big firms which could equally help you achieve what you want, minus the massive debt.

If studying for A-levels or equivalent qualifications has felt like torture, now may not be the time for you to go to university. Perhaps a job would be better, and possibly a return to education later in life would suit you more. Love of a subject is an excellent reason for taking a degree; it will help you focus your search on a course that reflects your passion. But if a degree is a means to a career end for you, look carefully at employment rates for any courses you consider.

Setting your priorities

The majority of graduate jobs are not subject-specific; employers value the transferable skills that higher education confers. Rightly or wrongly, however, most employers are influenced by which university you went to, as mentioned above, so the choice of institution remains as important as ever.

Consider adding value to your degree in the jobs market by going to a university that offers some sort of employment-related scheme. It could be work experience built into your degree, or a particularly active careers service that reaches out with activities.

Narrowing down the field

There is only a scramble for places on a relatively small proportion of courses that attract intense competition. Otherwise, there are plenty of places at good universities for candidates with sufficient qualifications, you just need to find the one that suits you best. For older applicants returning to education, relevant work experience and demonstrable interest in a subject may be enough to win a place.

Too much choice is more of an issue. There are the 130-odd universities featured in this *Guide* plus lots of specialist colleges to consider, which between them offer thousands of course combinations. Narrow down your options by choosing a subject – or subject area – first, rather than a university. This can reduce the field considerably as not all universities offer all subjects. Having made this first edit by subject, then factor in personal preferences such as location and type of university – campus or city – and by this point you may already have the beginnings of a manageable list.

Next up is course content and what life is really like for students. Today's budding undergraduates are at an advantage in this regard. As well as having access to the informative and accurate contents of university prospectuses and websites, they can connect with current students online and do some digging. Most universities have an 'Ask a Student' function, or similar, on their website, which will link you with a student ambassador for a live chat or call back. Another helpful source of information is **www.thestudentroom.com** the country's largest online student community. You may already have used it while studying for your A-levels. The peer-to-peer platform offers forums for students to discuss their options, ask for advice and build relationships. Current students on the courses and at the universities you are interested in may be happy to share their appraisals – though bear in mind that what they tell you may be biased in some direction or another, and cross reference anything you have been told with factual sources of information such as ours, or the UCAS website.

The National Student Survey is an objective source of information which is available online, with a range of additional data about the main courses at each institution, at **www.officeforstudents.org.uk/advice-and-guidance/student-information-and-data**. Visiting the university will give a truer picture yet; better still go to the department where you would be studying.

What to study?

Choosing a subject and a course before picking a university is the most common means of whittling down your options. As well as an interest that is sustainable for three-plus years in the subject you pick, you need to ensure you have the right qualifications to meet its entry requirements. Many economics degrees require maths A-level, for example, while most medical schools demand chemistry or biology. The UCAS website **www.ucas.com** is a good starting point; it contains course profiles and entrance requirements, while universities' own sites offer more detailed information. The Russell Group of 24 leading universities' Informed Choices website is another go-to source of information regarding required subjects.

Your school subjects and the UCAS tariff

The official measure by which your results will be judged is the UCAS tariff, which gives a score for each grade of most UK qualifications considered relevant for university entrance, as well as for the International Baccalaureate (IB). The tariff changed three years ago. The new points system is shown on page 32, but most applicants are not affected – two-thirds of offers are made in grades, rather than tariff points. This means universities may stipulate the grades they require in specific subjects, and determine which vocational qualifications are relevant to different degrees. In certain universities, some departments, but not others, will use the tariff to set offers. Course profiles on the UCAS website and/or universities' own sites should show whether offers are framed in terms of grades or tariff points. It is important to find out which, especially if you are relying on points from qualifications other than A-level or Scottish Highers, more of which are included in the new tariff.

Entry qualifications listed in the *Guide* relate not to the offers made by universities, but to the actual grades achieved by successful candidates who are under 21 on entry. For ease of comparison, a tariff score is included even where universities make their offers in grades.

UCAS tariff scores for main qualifications:

A-levels		AS levels	
Grade	Points	Grade	Points
A*	56	A	20
A	48	B	16
B	40	C	12
C	32	D	10
D	24	E	6
E	16		

Scottish Advanced higher		Scottish higher	
Grade	Points	Grade	Points
A	56	A	33
B	48	B	27
C	40	C	21
D	32	D	15

BTec Level 3			
National Diploma (post-2016)		Extended Certificate	
Grade	Points	Grade	Points
D*	28	D*	56
D	24	D	48
M	16	M	32
P	8	P	16

International Baccalaureate*			
Higher level		Standard level	
H7	56	S7	28
H6	48	S6	24
H5	32	S5	16
H4	24	S4	12
H3	12	S3	6

*The Extended Essay and Theory of Knowledge course are awarded A 12, B 10, C 8, D 6, E 4
For Foundation Diploma, Extended Diploma and other BTec levels see UCAS website
For other qualifications see: ucas.com/ucas/ucas-tariff-points

"Soft" subjects

These are another big factor in what and where you study. The Russell Group of 24 research-led universities scrapped its controversial list of preferred A-levels in 2019, after criticism that it contributed to a devaluation of creative and arts subjects. Previously however the group's Informed Choices website had a list of "facilitating subjects", comprising: maths and further maths, English, physics, biology, chemistry, geography, languages (classical and modern) and history, which are required by many degrees and welcomed by Russell Group universities generally. The website advised sixth formers to pick the majority of their A-levels from this list and to include at most one "soft" subject. Although these "soft subjects" were not listed specifically, a previous Informed Choices report named media studies, art and design, photography and business studies among the subjects that would normally be given this label. The new Informed Choices website offers more personalised guidance on A-level choices instead.

The facilitating subjects list may be gone, but its legacy is entrenched, and applicants to these universities should be very aware of that when selecting A-levels. It is better to keep more doors open than close any off at sixth form. For most courses at most universities, there are no such restrictions, as long as your main subjects or qualifications are relevant to the degree you hope to take. Even so, the Russell Group lists are an indication of the subjects that admissions tutors may take more or less seriously, especially if you plan to apply to at least one leading university. Although only the London School of Economics has published a list of "non-preferred" subjects (see below), others may take a less formal approach but still apply similar weightings.

General studies is a separate matter, and some universities still do not regard it as a full A-level for entry purposes, while others – including some leading institutions – do.

Vocational qualifications

The Education Department downgraded many vocational qualifications in school league tables from 2014. This has added to the confusion surrounding the value placed on diplomas and other qualifications by universities. The engineering diploma has won near-universal approval from universities (for admission to engineering courses and possibly some science degrees), but some of the other diplomas are in fields that are not on the curriculum of the most selective universities. Regardless of the points awarded under the tariff, it is essential to contact universities directly to ensure that a diploma or another vocational qualification will be an acceptable qualification for your chosen degree.

Admission tests

The growing numbers of applicants with high grades at A-level have encouraged the introduction of separate admission tests for some of the most oversubscribed courses. There are national tests in medicine and law that are used by some of the leading universities, while Oxford and Cambridge have their own tests in a growing number of subjects. The details are

---

"Traditional academic" and "non-preferred" subjects

The London School of Economics expects applicants to offer at least two of the traditional subjects listed below, while any of the non-preferred subjects listed should only be offered with two traditional subjects.

Traditional subjects

» Ancient history
» Biology
» Classical civilisation
» Chemistry
» Computing
» Economics
» Electronics
» English
» Further mathematics
» Geography
» Government and politics
» History
» Law
» Mathematics
» Modern or classical languages
» Music
» Philosophy
» Physics
» Psychology
» Religious studies
» Sociology

Non-preferred subjects

» Any Applied A-level
» Accounting
» Art and design
» Business studies
» Citizenship studies
» Communication and culture
» Creative writing
» Design and technology
» Drama/theatre studies
» Film studies
» Health and social care
» Home economics
» Information and communication technology
» Leisure studies
» Media studies
» Music technology
» Physical education/ Sports studies
» Travel and tourism

General studies, critical thinking, thinking skills, knowledge and enquiry, global perspectives and research and project work A-levels will only be considered as fourth A-level subjects and will not therefore be accepted as part of a conditional offer.
Accounting and Drama/theatre studies may be considered by certain departments.

Admissions tests

Some of the most competitive courses now have additional entrance tests. The most significant tests are listed below. Note that registration for many of the tests is before 15 October and you will need to register for them as early as possible. All the tests have their own websites. Institutions requiring specific tests vary from year to year and you must check course website details carefully for test requirements. In addition over 50 universities also administer their own tests for certain courses. Details are given at: **www.ucas.com/undergraduate/applying-university/admissions-tests**

Law

Cambridge Law Test: for entry to law at Cambridge; candidates called for interview sit the test in late November.

Law National Admissions Test (LNAT): for entry to law courses at Bristol, Durham, Glasgow, King's College London, London School of Economics, Nottingham, Oxford, SOAS, University College London. Register from August; tests held from September to July.

Mathematics

Mathematics Admissions Test (MAT): for entry to mathematics at Imperial College London and mathematics and computer science at Oxford. Advised but not compulsory for applicants to mathematics at Warwick. Test held in early November.

Sixth Term Examination Papers (STEP): for entry to mathematics at Cambridge and Warwick (also occasionally requested by other universities). Check for registration and test dates at **www.admissionstesting.org/for-test-takers/step/about-step**

Test of Mathematics for University Admission: results accepted by Bath, Cardiff, Durham, Nottingham, Lancaster, London School of Economics, Sheffield, Southampton, Warwick, registration opens early September, test held early November.

Medical subjects

BioMedical Admissions Test (BMAT): for entry to medicine at Brighton and Sussex Medical School, Cambridge (also for veterinary medicine), Imperial College London, Keele (international applicants only), Lancaster, Leeds (also for dentistry), Manchester (for some groups of international students only, check university website), Oxford (also for biomedical sciences) and University College London. Applicants take BMAT – September or BMAT – November.
Check: Check **www.admissionstesting.org/for-test-takers/bmat** for registration and test dates.

Graduate Medical School Admissions Test (GAMSAT): for graduate entry to medicine and dentistry at Cardiff, Exeter, Liverpool, Nottingham, Plymouth (and dentistry), St. George's, London, Swansea, Keele and St Andrews, Dundee, Sunderland and Ulster. Register by July 20, test held September 3–16.

Health Professions Admissions Test (HPAT-Ulster): for certain health profession courses at Ulster.Register by January 11, test held 22–23 January.

University Clinical Aptitude Test (UCAT): for entry to medical and dental schools at Aberdeen, Anglia Ruskin, Aston, Birmingham, Bristol, Cardiff, Dundee, East Anglia, Edge Hill, Edinburgh, Exeter, Glasgow, Hull York Medical School, Keele, Kent and Medway, King's College London, Leicester, Liverpool, Manchester, Newcastle, Nottingham, Plymouth, Queen Mary, University of London, Queen's University Belfast, Sheffield, Southampton, St Andrews, St George's, London, Sunderland, Warwick. Register between early May and mid-September; tests held between late July and late September.

Cambridge University

Pre-interview or at-interview assessments take place for most subjects. Full details given on the Cambridge admissions website. See also STEP and BMAT above.

Oxford University

Pre-interview tests take place in many subjects that candidates are required to register for specifically by early October. Full details given on the Oxford admissions website. Tests held in early November, usually at candidate's educational institution. See also LNAT, MAT and BMAT above.

listed on page 34. In all cases, the tests are used as an extra selection tool, not as a replacement for A-level or other general qualifications.

Making a choice

Your A-levels or Scottish Highers may have been straightforward to choose, but the range of subjects at university is vast. Even subjects you have studied at school may be quite different at degree level – some academic economists prefer their undergraduates not to have taken A-level economics because they approach the subject so differently. Other students are disappointed because they appear to be going over old ground when they continue with a subject that they enjoyed at school. Universities now publish quite detailed syllabuses, and it is a matter of going through the fine print.

The greater difficulty comes in judging your suitability for the many subjects that are not on the school or college curriculum. Philosophy and psychology sound fascinating (and are), but you may have no idea what degrees in either subject entail – for example, the level of statistics that may be required. Forensic science may look exciting on television – more glamorous than plain chemistry – but it opens fewer doors, as the type of work portrayed in Silent Witness is very hard to find.

Academic or vocational?

There is frequent and often misleading debate about the differences between academic and vocational higher education. It is usually about the relative value of taking a degree, as opposed to a directly work-related qualification. But it also extends to higher education itself, with jibes about so-called "Mickey Mouse" degrees in areas that were not part of the higher education curriculum when most of the critics were students.

Such attitudes ignore the fact that medicine and law are both vocational subjects, as are architecture, engineering and education. They are not seen as any less academic than geography or sociology, but for some reason social work or nursing, let alone media studies and sports science, are often looked down upon. The test of a degree should be whether it is challenging and a good preparation for working life. Both general academic and vocational degrees can do this.

Most popular subject areas by applications 2020

1 Nursing	186,115
2 Psychology	133,160
3 Law	123,575
4 Computer Science	100,580
5 Design studies	89,135
6 Management studies	85,770
7 Medicine	84,380
8 Combinations with Business & Admin Studies	77,455
9 Other Subjects allied to Medicine	69,495
10 Sport and Exercise Science	66,235

Source: UCAS End of Cycle report 2020

Most popular subjects by acceptances 2020

1 Nursing	37,630
2 Psychology	37,630
3 Law	23,760
4 Computer Science	20,035
5 Design studies	19,140
6 Combinations within Business & Admin Studies	18,565
7 Business studies	16,560
8 Management studies	16,205
9 Sport and Exercise Science	15,555
10 Other subjects allied to Medicine	13,745

Source: UCAS End of Cycle report 2020

Subject areas covered in this *Guide*

The list below gives each of the 67 subject areas that are covered in detail later in the book (in chapter 13). For each subject area in that chapter, there is specific advice, a summary of employment prospects and a league table of universities that offered courses in 2018–19, ranked on the basis of an overall score calculated from research quality, entry standards, teaching quality, student experience and graduate employment prospects.

Accounting and Finance
Aeronautical and Manufacturing
  Engineering
Agriculture and Forestry
American Studies
Anatomy and Physiology
Animal Science
Anthropology
Archaeology and Forensic Science
Architecture
Art and Design
Biological Sciences
Building
Business Studies
Celtic Studies
Chemical Engineering
Chemistry
Civil Engineering
Classics and Ancient History
Communication and Media Studies
Computer Science
Creative Writing
Criminology
Dentistry
Drama, Dance and Cinematics
East and South Asian Studies
Economics
Education
Electrical and Electronic Engineering
English
Food Science
French
General Engineering
Geography and Environmental Sciences

Geology
German
History
History of Art, Architecture and Design
Hospitality, Leisure, Recreation and Tourism
Iberian Languages
Italian
Land and Property Management
Law
Librarianship and Information Management
Linguistics
Materials Technology
Mathematics
Mechanical Engineering
Medicine
Middle Eastern and African Studies
Music
Nursing
Other Subjects Allied to Medicine
Pharmacology and Pharmacy
Philosophy
Physics and Astronomy
Physiotherapy
Politics
Psychology
Radiography
Russian
Social Policy
Social Work
Sociology
Sports Science
Theology and Religious Studies
Town and Country Planning and Landscape
Veterinary Medicine

Nevertheless, it is clear that the prospect of much higher graduate debt is encouraging more students into job-related subjects. This is understandable and, if you are sure of your future career path, possibly also sensible. But much depends on what that career is – and whether you are ready to make such a long-term commitment. Some of the programmes that have attracted public ridicule, such as surf science or golf course management, may narrow graduates' options to a worrying extent, but often boast strong employment records.

As you would expect, many vocational courses are tailored to particular professions. If you choose one of these, make sure that the degree is recognised by the relevant professional body (such as the Engineering Council or one of the institutes) or you may not be able to use the skills that you acquire. Most universities are only too keen to make such recognition clear in their prospectus; if no such guarantee is published, contact the university department running the course and seek assurances. In education, for example, by no means all degrees qualify you to teach.

Even where a course has professional recognition, a further qualification may be required to practise. Both law and medicine, for example, demand additional training to become a fully qualified solicitor, barrister or doctor. Neither degree is an automatic passport to a job: only about half of all law graduates go into the profession. Both law and medicine also offer a postgraduate route into the profession for those who have taken other subjects as a first degree. Law conversion courses, though not cheap, are increasingly popular, and there are a growing number of graduate-entry medical degrees.

One way to ensure that a degree is job-related is to take a "sandwich" course, which involves up to a year in business or industry. Students often end up working for the organisation which provided the placement, while others gain valuable insights into a field of employment – even if only to discount it. The drawback with such courses is that, like the year abroad that is part of most language degrees, the period away from university inevitably disrupts living arrangements and friendship groups. But most of those who take this route find that the career benefits make this a worthwhile sacrifice. Growing numbers of traditional degrees now offer shorter periods of work experience.

Employers' organisations calculate that more than half of all graduate jobs are open to applicants from any subject, and recruiters for the most competitive graduate training schemes often prefer traditional academic subjects to apparently relevant vocational degrees. Newspapers, for example, may prefer a history graduate to one with a media studies degree; computing firms are said to take a disproportionate number of classicists. A good degree classification and the right work experience are more important than the subject for most non-technical jobs. But it is hard to achieve a good result on a course that you do not enjoy, so scour prospectuses, and email or phone university departments to ensure that you know what you are letting yourself in for. Their reaction to your approach will also give you an idea of how responsive they are to their students.

Studying more than one subject

If more than one subject appeals, you could consider Joint Honours – degrees that combine two subjects – or even Combined Honours, which will cover several related subjects. Such courses obviously allow you to extend the scope of your studies, but they should be approached with caution. Even if the number of credits suggests a similar workload to Single Honours, covering more than one subject inevitably involves extra reading and often more essays or project work.

The number taking such degrees is falling, but there are advantages to them. Many students choose a "dual" to add a vocational element to make themselves more employable – business studies with languages or engineering, for example, or media studies with English. Others want to take their studies in a particular direction, perhaps by combining history with politics, or statistics with maths. Some simply want to add a completely unrelated interest to their main subject, such as environmental science and music, or archaeology and event management – both combinations that are available at UK universities.

At most universities, however, it is not necessary to take a degree in more than one subject in order to broaden your studies. The spread of modular programmes ensures that you can take courses in related subjects without changing the basic structure of your degree. You may not be able to take an event management module in a single-honours archaeology degree, but it should be possible to study some history or a language. The number and scope of the combinations offered at many of the larger universities is extraordinary. Indeed, it has been criticised by academics who believe that "mix-and-match" degrees can leave a graduate without a rounded view of a subject. But if you are looking for breadth and variety, scrutinise university prospectuses closely as part of the selection process.

What type of course?

Once you have a subject, you must decide on the level and type of course. Most readers of this *Guide* will be looking for full-time degree courses, but higher education is much broader than that. You may not be able to afford the time or the money needed for a full-time commitment of three or four years at this point in life.

Part-time courses

Tens of thousands of people each year opt for a part-time course – usually while holding down a job – to continue learning and to improve their career prospects. The numbers studying this way have dropped considerably, but loans are available for students whose courses occupy between a quarter and three-quarters of the time expected on a full-time course. Repayments are on the same conditions as those for full-time courses, except that you will begin repaying after three years of study even if the course has not been completed by then. The downside is that universities have increased their fees in the knowledge that part-time students will be able to take out student loans to cover fees, and employers are now less inclined to fund their employees on such courses. At Birkbeck, University of London, a compromise has been found with full-time courses taught in the evening. For courses classified as part-time, students pay fees in proportion to the number of credits they take.

Part-time study can be exhausting unless your employer gives you time off, but if you have the stamina for a course that will usually take twice as long as the full-time equivalent, this route should still make a degree more affordable. Part-time students tend to be highly committed to their subject, and many claim that the quality of the social life associated with their course makes up for the quantity of leisure time enjoyed by full-timers.

Distance learning

If you are confident that you can manage without regular face-to-face contact with teachers and fellow students, distance learning is an option. Courses are delivered mainly or entirely online or through correspondence, although some programmes offer a certain amount of local tuition. The process might sound daunting and impersonal, but students of the Open University (OU), all of whom are educated in this way, are frequently among the most satisfied in the country, according to the results of the annual National Student Survey. Attending lectures or oversized seminars at a conventional university can be less personal than regular contact with your tutor at a distance.

Of course, not all universities are as good at communicating with their distance-learning students as the OU, or offer such high-quality course materials, but this mode of study does give students ultimate flexibility to determine when and where they study. Distance learning is becoming increasingly popular for the delivery of professional courses, which are often needed to supplement degrees. The OU takes students of all ages, including school-leavers, not just mature students.

In addition, there is now the option of Massive Open Online Courses (MOOCs) provided by many of the leading UK and American universities, usually free of charge. As yet, most such courses are the equivalent of a module in a degree course, rather than the entire qualification. Some are assessed formally but none is likely to be seen by employers as the equal of a conventional degree, no matter how prestigious the university offering the course. That may change – some commentators see in MOOCs the beginning of the end of the traditional, residential university – but their main value for now is as a means of dipping a toe in the water of higher education. For those who are uncertain about committing to a degree, or who simply want to learn more about a subject without needing a high-status qualification, they are ideal.

A number of UK universities offer MOOCs through the Futurelearn platform, run by the Open University **www.futurelearn.com**. But the beauty of MOOCs is that they can come from all over the world. Perhaps the best-known providers are Coursera **www.coursera.org**, which originated at Stanford University, in California, and now involves a large number of American and international universities including Edinburgh, and edX **www.edx.org**, which numbers Harvard among its members. MOOCs are also being used increasingly by sixth-formers to extend their subject knowledge and demonstrate their enthusiasm and capability to admissions tutors. They are certainly worth considering for inclusion in a personal statement and/or to spark discussion at an interview.

Foundation degrees

Even if you are set on a full-time course, you might not want to commit yourself for three or more years. Two-year vocational Foundation degrees have become a popular route into higher education in recent years. Many other students take longer-established two-year courses, such as Higher National Diplomas or other diplomas tailored to the needs of industry or parts of the health service. Those who do well on such courses usually have the option of converting their qualification into a full degree with further study, although many are satisfied without immediately staying on for the further two or more years that will be required to complete a BA or BSc.

Other short courses

A number of universities are experimenting with two-year degrees, encouraged by the Government, squeezing more work into an extended academic year. The so-called "third semester" makes use of the summer vacation for extra teaching, so that mature students, in particular, can reduce the length of their career break. Several universities are offering accelerated degrees as part of a pilot project initiated under the coalition government. But only at the University of Buckingham, the UK's longest-established private university, is this the dominant pattern for degree courses. Other private institutions – notably BPP University – are following suit.

A growing number of short courses, usually lasting a year, are designed for students who do not have the necessary qualifications to start a degree in their chosen subject. Foundation courses in art and design have been common for many years and are the chosen preparation for a degree at leading departments, even for many students whose A-levels would win them a degree place elsewhere. Access courses perform the same function in a wider range of subjects for students without A-levels, or for those whose grades are either too low or in the wrong subjects to gain admission to a particular course. Entry requirements are modest, but students have to reach the same standard as regular entrants to progress to a degree.

Higher and Degree Apprenticeships

Apprenticeships have been a serious alternative to university for more than a decade. But now students can have the best of both worlds at a growing number of universities, with higher or degree apprenticeships, which combine study at degree level with extended work experience with a named industrial or business partner. The programmes are already popular but are only available in a limited range of subjects, such as accountancy, computing, healthcare sciences, management and some branches of engineering. Universities are planning to expand their offerings.

Such apprenticeships take up to five years to complete and leave the graduate with a Bachelors or even a Masters degree. Employers including Deloitte, PwC, BMW and the BBC are offering higher-level apprenticeships, although naturally not all are with household names such as these. Students are paid employees of the sponsoring company, with a contract of employment and holiday entitlement, as well as salaries averaging £17,875 a year in 2019. Some are available through UCAS, but most require a direct application to the company. The best starting point to weigh up the options is the gov.uk website, which has a 'Find an Apprenticeship' section. Once you register, you can set up email and text alerts to inform you about new apprenticeship roles. You can also find a range of vacancies at **www.ratemyapprenticeship.co.uk**, which carries thousands of reviews.

Further details of the structure of courses and the areas in which apprenticeships are available can be found at **www.gov.uk/government/publications/higher-and-degree-apprenticeships**. In addition, *Which? University* and the National Apprenticeship Service have produced a more detailed publication, *The Complete Guide to Higher and Degree Apprenticeships*, which is available online and in print.

Universities with highest and lowest offer rates

Highest			Lowest		
1	Aberystwyth	96.1%	1	Oxford	21.8%
2	Roehampton	93.9%	2	Cambridge	28.5%
3	Bishop Grosseteste	92.2%	3	LSE	35.2%
4	Portsmouth	89.9%	4	St George's London	39.0%
5	York St John	89.4%	5	Arts, London	41.9%
6	Leeds Trinity	89.0%	6	St Andrews	42.3%
7	Nottingham Trent	88.9%	7	Imperial College	43.0%
8	=Newman	88.7%	8	Edinburgh	43.8%
9	=Exeter	88.7%	9	Leeds Arts	46.7%
10	St Mary's Twickenham	88.3%	10	Dundee	48.8%

UCAS: Applications 2019

Yet more choice

No single guide can allow for personal preferences in choosing a course. You may want one of the many degrees that incorporate a year at a partner university abroad, or to try a six-month exchange on the Continent – which in future will probably be via a UK-run alternative to the European Union's Erasmus Programme. The situation post-Brexit was uncertain at the time of writing. Either might prove a valuable experience and add to your employability. Or you might prefer a January or February start to the traditional autumn start – there are plenty of opportunities for this, mainly at post-1992 universities.

In some subjects – particularly engineering and the sciences – the leading degrees may be Masters courses, taking four years rather than three (in England). In Scotland, most degree courses take four years and some at the older universities will confer a Masters qualification. Those who come with A-levels may apply to go straight into the second year. Relatively few students take this option, but it is easy to imagine more doing so in future at universities that charge students from other parts of the UK the full £9,250 for all years of the course.

Best paid graduates

(Median salary 15 months after graduating)

1	Imperial College London	£33,000
2	London School of Economics	£31,000
=3	Cambridge	£30,000
=3	Oxford	£30,000
=3	University College London	£30,000
=6	Bath	£29,000
=6	King's College London	£29,000
=6	St George's, London	£29,000
=6	Warwick	£29,000
10	Queen Mary, London	£28,000

HESA 2018 graduates

Where to study

Several factors might influence your choice of university or college. Obviously, you need to have a reasonable chance of getting in, you may want reassurance about the university's reputation, and its location will probably be important to you as well. On top of that, most applicants have views about the type of institution they are looking for – big or small, old or new, urban or rural, specialist or comprehensive. Campus universities tend to produce the highest levels of student satisfaction, but big city universities continue to attract sixth-formers in the largest numbers. You may surprise yourself by choosing somewhere that does not conform to your initial criteria but working through your preferences is another way of narrowing down your options.

Most popular universities by applications 2020

1	University of Manchester	79,925
2	University of Edinburgh	64,225
3	University of Leeds	62,250
4	UCL (University College London)	58,690
5	King's College, London	57,470
6	University of Birmingham	55,935
7	University of Nottingham	54,170
8	University of Bristol	52,385
9	Manchester Metropolitan University	48,270
10	Nottingham Trent University	46,670

Source: UCAS End of Cycle report 2020

Entry standards

Unless you are a mature student or have taken a gap year, your passport to your chosen university will probably be a conditional offer based on your predicted grades, previous exam performance, personal statement, and school or college reference. Many universities followed Birmingham's lead in making unconditional offers to candidates in selected subjects who have a strong academic record and are predicted high grades. But the practice drew criticism from ministers and was then banned during the health pandemic until September 2021. It remains to be seen whether many universities will return to such offers once the restrictions are lifted.

Supply and demand dictate whether you will receive an offer, conditional or otherwise. Beyond the national picture, your chances will be affected both by the university and the subject you choose. A few universities (but not many) at the top of the league tables are heavily oversubscribed in every subject; others will have areas in which they excel but may make relatively modest demands for entry to other courses. Even in many of the leading universities, the number of applicants for each place in languages or engineering is still not high. Conversely, three As at A-level will not guarantee a place on one of the top English or law degrees, but there are enough universities running courses to ensure that three Cs will give you a chance somewhere.

University prospectuses and the UCAS website will give you the "standard offer" for each course, but in some cases, this is pitched deliberately low in order to leave admissions staff extra flexibility. The standard A-level offer for medicine, for example, may not demand A*s, but nearly all successful applicants will have one or more. In Scotland, universities have started to publish two sets of standard offers: their normal range and another with lower grades for applicants from disadvantaged backgrounds. A similar practice elsewhere in the UK uses contextualised information about applicants to reduce entry grades for those from equivalent backgrounds.

As already noted, the average entry scores in our tables give the actual points obtained by successful applicants – many of which are far above the offer made by the university, but which give an indication of the pecking order at entry. The subject tables (in chapter 13) are, naturally, a better guide than the main table (in chapter 1), where average entry scores are influenced by the range of subjects available at each university.

Location

The most obvious starting point is the country you study in. Most degrees in Scotland take four years, rather than the UK norm of three, which makes them more expensive, especially given the loss of the year's salary you might have been earning after graduation. A later chapter will go into the details of the system but suffice to say that students from Scotland pay no fees, while those from the rest of the UK do. Nevertheless, Edinburgh and St Andrews remain particularly popular with English students, even though they charge £9,250 for each year of a four-year degree. Others in Scotland cap the fee at the equivalent of three years. The number of English students going to Scottish universities has increased almost every year since fees went up, although there would be no savings, perhaps because the institutions have tried harder to attract them. Fees – or the lack of them – are by no means the only influence on cross-border mobility: the number of Scots going to English universities rose sharply, in spite of the cost, probably because the number of places is capped in Scotland, but not any longer in England.

Close to home

Far from crossing national boundaries, however, growing numbers of students choose to study near home, whether or not they continue to live with their family. This is understandable for Scots, who will save themselves tens of thousands of pounds by studying at their own fees-free universities. But there is also a gradual increase in the number choosing to study close to home either to cut living costs or for personal reasons, such as family circumstances, a girlfriend or boyfriend, continuing employment or religion. Some simply want to stick with what they know.

The trend for full-time students who do go away to study, is to choose a university within about two hours' travelling time. The assumption is that this is far enough to discourage parents from making unannounced visits, but close enough to allow for occasional trips home to get the washing done, have a decent meal and see friends. The leading universities recruit from all over the world, but most still have a regional core.

University or college?

This *Guide* is primarily concerned with universities, the destination of choice for the vast majority of higher education students. But there are other options – and not just for those searching for lower fees. A number of specialist higher education colleges offer a similar, or sometimes superior, quality of course in their particular fields. The subject tables in chapter 13 chart the successes of various colleges in art, agriculture, music and teacher training in particular. Some colleges of higher education are not so different from the newer universities and may acquire that status themselves in future years.

Further education colleges

The second group of colleges offering degrees are further education (FE) colleges. These are often large institutions with a wide range of courses, from A-levels to vocational subjects at different levels, up to degrees in some cases. Although their numbers of higher education students have been falling in recent years, the current fee structure presents them with an opportunity because they tend not to bear all the costs of a university campus. For that reason, too, they may not offer a broad student experience of the type that universities pride themselves on, but the best colleges respond well to the local labour market and offer small teaching groups and effective personal support.

FE colleges are a local resource and tend to attract mature students who cannot or do not want to travel to university. Many of their higher education students apply nowhere else. But, as competition for university places has increased, they also have become more of an option for school-leavers to continue their studies, as they always have been in Scotland.

Their predominantly local, mature student populations do FE colleges no favours in statistical comparisons with universities. But it should be noted that the proportion of college graduates unemployed six months after graduation tends to be higher than at universities, and average graduate salaries lower. However, 14 further education colleges secured 'gold' ratings in the first year of the Government's Teaching Excellence Framework (TEF) – although more than twice as many found themselves in the lowest 'bronze' category.

Both further and higher education colleges are audited by the Quality Assurance Agency and appear in the National Student Survey, as well as the TEF. In all three, their results usually show wide variation. Some demonstrate higher levels of satisfaction among their students than most universities, for example, while others are at the bottom of the scale

Private universities and colleges

Another alternative to mainstream university has been relatively insignificant in terms of size until recently, but the current fee regime may cause numbers at private universities and colleges to grow. Courses are mainly in business and law, and also in some other specialist fields.

By far the longest established – and the only one to meet the criteria for inclusion in our main table – is the University of Buckingham, which is profiled on Page 358. The best-known "newcomer" currently is BPP University, which became a full university in 2013 and offers degrees, as well as shorter courses, in both law and business subjects. Like Buckingham, BPP offers two-year degrees with short vacations to maximise teaching time – a model that other private providers are likely to follow. Fees were £9,000 a year for UK students taking BPP's three-year degrees in 2020 and £13,500 a year for the accelerated version.

The New College of the Humanities, which graduated its first students in 2015, started out with fees of nearly £18,000 a year for all undergraduates, guaranteeing small-group teaching and some big-name visiting lecturers in economics, English, history, law and philosophy. The college is now matching the 'public sector' at £9,250 a year and has been bought by the Boston-based Northeastern University.

Two other private institutions have been awarded full university status. Regent's University, attractively positioned in London's Regent's Park, caters particularly for the international market with courses in business, arts and social science subjects priced at £18,500 – £21,500 a year for 2021–22. However, about half of the students at the not-for-profit university, which offers British and American degrees, are from the UK or other parts of Europe. The University of Law, as its name suggests, is more specialised. It has been operating as a college in London for more than 100 years and claims to be the world's leading professional law school. It offers law degrees, as well as professional courses, with fees for three-year degrees set at £9,250 in 2020–21 for UK students and £11,100 for the two-year version. The university has 14 UK campuses, in locations including London (where it has two), Nottingham, Birmingham, Bristol, Chester, Guildford, Manchester, Leeds and Sheffield, as well as at Exeter, East Anglia, Reading, and Liverpool universities.

There are also growing numbers of specialist colleges offering degrees, especially in the business sector. The ifs School of Finance, for example, also dates back more than 100 years and now has university college status (as ifs University College) for its courses in finance and banking.

Some others that rely on international students have been hit by tougher visa regulations,

Top 10 Universities for Quality of Teaching, feedback and support 2019
% satisfied with teaching quality

1 Aberystwyth	87.3%
2 Abertay	87.0%
3 St Andrews	86.7%
4 Arts Bournemouth	86.5%
5 West London	86.3%
6 Bolton	85.6%
7 Wales, Trinity St David	84.9%
8 Bishop Grosseteste	84.7%
9 Harper Adams	84.6%
10 = Newman / =York St John	84.4%

Source: National Student Survey 2020

Top 10 Universities for Overall Student Experience 2019

1 Aberystwyth	86.4%
2 St Andrews	86.3%
3 West London	85.2%
4 Loughborough	84.8%
5 Arts Bournemouth	83.2%
6 West of England	83.0%
7 Harper Adams	82.7%
8 = Newman	82.2%
8 = Robert Gordon	82.2%
10 Worcester	81.7%

Source: National Student Survey 2020

but the Government is keen to encourage the development of a private sector to compete with the established universities. Two newcomers will focus on engineering, for example. The Dyson Institute of Engineering and Technology, based at Malmesbury, in Wiltshire, welcomed its first 33 undergraduates in 2017. Funded entirely by Sir James Dyson, there are no fees, and students will work at the nearby Dyson headquarters for 47 weeks a year. The New Model in Technology and Engineering, in Hereford, has received more than £20m in Government funding and promises to "totally reimagine and redesign the higher education experience".

So far, there are few multi-faculty private institutions, but the range of specialisms is certainly growing. There are two high-profile colleges specialising in football, for example, and, from this year, an Interdisciplinary School, based in London. Inevitably, they will take time to build up a track record, but there should be a market in the areas they offer. A listing of some of the more popular private institutions begins on page 587.

City universities

The most popular universities, in terms of total applications, are nearly all in big cities with other major centres of population within the two-hour travelling window. Students are drawn by the best nightclubs, top sporting events, high-quality shopping, cultural diversity and access to leading galleries, museums and theatres. Especially for those who live in cities already, city universities are a magnet. The big universities also, by definition, offer the widest range of subjects, although that does not mean that they necessarily have the particular course that is right for you. You might not actually go clubbing a lot or hit the shops that much, in spite of the inspiring marketing material that suggests you will, either because you cannot afford to, or because student life is more focused on the university than the city, or even because you are too busy studying.

Campus universities

City universities are the right choice for many young people, but it is worth bearing in mind that the National Student Survey shows that the highest satisfaction levels tend to be at smaller universities, often those with their own self-contained campuses. It seems that students identify more closely with institutions where there is a close-knit community and the social life is based around the students' union rather than the local nightclubs – at least in the first-year when more students tend to live in campus accommodation. There may also be a better prospect of regular contact with tutors and lecturers, who may also live on or near the campus. Few UK universities are in genuinely rural locations, but some – particularly among the more recently promoted – are in relatively small towns. Several longer-established institutions in Scotland and Wales also share this type of setting, where the university dominates the town.

Importance of Open Days

By far the best way to be confident that any university is for you, is to visit. But with continuing Covid restrictions, the pattern of Open Days is likely to vary and many may remain virtual rather than physical events. Our profiles give each university's website for the latest information. Schools often restrict the number of open days that sixth-formers can attend in term-time, but some universities offer a weekend alternative. A full calendar of events is available at **www.opendays.com**. Bear in mind, if you only attend one or two, that the event has to be badly mismanaged for a university not to seem an exciting place to someone who spends his or her days at school, or even college. Try to get a flavour of several institutions before you make your choice.

How many universities to pick?

When that time comes, of course, you will not be making one choice but five; four if you are applying for medicine, dentistry or veterinary science. (Full details of the application process are given in chapter 5.) Tens of thousands of students each year eventually go to a university that did not start out as their first choice, either because they did not get the right offer or because they changed their mind along the way. UCAS rules are such that applicants do not list universities in order of preference anyway – indeed, universities are not allowed to know where else you have applied. So do not pin all your hopes on one course; take just as much care choosing the other universities on your list.

The value of an "insurance" choice

Until recently, nearly all applicants included at least one "insurance" choice on that list – a university or college where entry grades were significantly lower than at their preferred institutions. This practice has been in decline, presumably because candidates expecting high grades think they can pick up a lower offer either in Clearing or through UCAS Extra, the service that allows applicants rejected by their original choices to apply to courses that still have vacancies after the first round of offers. However, it is easy to miscalculate and leave yourself without a place that you want. You may not like the look of the options in Clearing, leaving yourself with an unwelcome and potentially expensive year off at a time when jobs are thin on the ground.

The lifting of recruitment restrictions in 2015 has increased competition between universities and seen more of the leading institutions taking part in Clearing. For those with good grades, this makes it less of a risk to apply only to highly selective universities. However, if you are at all uncertain about your grades, including an insurance choice remains a sensible course of action. Even if you are sure that you will match the standard offers of your chosen universities, there is no guarantee that they will make you an offer. Particularly for degrees demanding three As or more at A-level, there may simply be too many highly qualified applicants to offer places to all of them. The main proviso for insurance choices, as with all others, is that you must be prepared to take up that place. If not, you might as well go for broke with courses with higher standard offers and take your chances in Clearing, or even retake exams if you drop grades. Thousands of applicants each year end up rejecting their only offer when they could have had a second, insurance, choice.

Reputation

The reputation of a university is something intangible, usually built up over a long period and sometimes outlasting reality. Before universities were subject to external assessment and the publication of copious statistics, reputation was rooted in the past. League tables are partly responsible for changing that, although employers are often still influenced by what they remember as the university pecking order when they were students.

The fragmentation of the British university system into groups of institutions is another factor: the Russell Group **www.russellgroup.ac.uk** represents 24 research-intensive universities, nearly all with medical schools; the million+ group **www.millionplus.ac.uk** contains many of the former polytechnics and newer universities; the University Alliance **www.unialliance.ac.uk** provides a home for 18 universities, both old and new, that did not fit into the other categories; while GuildHE **www.guildhe.ac.uk** represents specialist colleges and the newest universities. The Cathedrals Group **www.cathedralsgroup.ac.uk** is an affiliation of 16 church-based universities and colleges, some of which are also members of other groups.

Checklist

Choosing a subject and a place to study is a major decision. Make sure you can answer these questions:

Choosing a course

» What do I want out of higher education?
» Which subjects do I enjoy studying at school?
» Which subject or subjects do I want to study?
» Do I have the right qualifications?
» What are my career plans and does the subject and course fit these?
» Do I want to study full-time or part-time?
» Do I want to study at a university or a college?

Choosing a university

» What type of university do I wish to go to: campus, city or smaller town?
» How far is the university from home?
» Is it large or small?
» Is it specialist or general?
» Does it offer the right course?
» How much will it cost?
» Have I arranged to visit the university?

Many of today's applicants will barely have heard of a polytechnic, let alone be able to identify which of today's universities had that heritage, but most will know which of two universities in the same city has the higher status. While that should matter far less than the quality of a course, it would be naïve to ignore institutional reputation entirely if that is going to carry weight with a future employer. Some big firms restrict their recruitment efforts to a small group of universities (see chapter 3), and, however short sighted that might be, it is something to bear in mind if a career in the City or a big law firm is your ambition.

Facilities

The quality of campus facilities is an important factor in choosing a university for most students. Only the course and the university's location tend to have a higher priority. Accommodation is the main selling point for those living away from home, but sports facilities, libraries (24-hour, ideally) and computing equipment also play an important part. Even upgraded campus nightclubs have become part of the facilities race that has followed the introduction of higher fees.

Many universities guarantee first-year students accommodation in halls of residence or university-owned flats. It is a good idea to know what happens after that. Are there enough places for second or third-year students who want them, and if not, what is the private market like? Rents for student houses vary quite widely across the country and there have been tensions with local residents in some cities. All universities offer specialist accommodation for disabled students – and are better at providing other facilities than most public institutions.

Special-interest clubs and recreational facilities, as well as political activity, tend to be based in the students' union – sometimes known as the guild of students. In some universities, the union is the focal point of social activity, while in others the attractions of the city seem to overshadow the union to the point where facilities are underused. Students' union websites are included with the information found in the university profiles (chapter 15).

Sources of information

With more than 130 universities to choose from, the Discover Uni and UCAS websites, as well as guides such as this one, are the obvious places to start your search for the right course. Discover Uni, the successor to Unistats, includes figures for average salaries at course level, as well as student satisfaction ratings and some information on contact hours, although this does not distinguish between lectures and seminars. The site does not make multiple comparisons easy to carry out, but it does contain a wealth of information for those who persevere. Once you have narrowed down the list of candidates, you will want to go through undergraduate prospectuses. Most are available online, where you can select the relevant sections rather than waiting for an account of every course to arrive in the post. Beware of generalised claims about the standing of the university, the quality of courses, friendly atmosphere and legendary social life. Stick to the factual information.

While the material that the universities publish about their own qualities is less than objective, much of what you will find on the internet may be completely unreliable, for different reasons. A simple search on the name of a university will turn up spurious comparisons of everything from the standard of lecturing to the attractiveness of the students. These can be seriously misleading and are usually based on anecdotal evidence, at best. Make sure that any information you consider comes from a reputable source and, if it conflicts with your impression, try to cross-check it with this *Guide* and the institution's own material.

Useful websites

The best starting point is the UCAS website **www.ucas.com**, there is extensive information on courses, universities and the whole process of applying to university. UCAS has an official presence on Facebook **www.facebook.com/ucasonline** and Twitter **@UCAS_online** and now also has a series of video guides **www.ucas.tv** on the process of applying, UCAS resources and comments from other students.

For statistical information which allows limited comparison between universities (and for full details of the National Student Survey), visit: **www.discoveruni.gov.uk**

On appropriate A-level subject choice, visit: **www.russellgroup.ac.uk/for-students/school-and-college-in-the-uk/subject-choices-at-school-and-college** or **www.informedchoices.ac.uk**

Narrowing down course choices: **www.ukcoursefinder.com**

For a full calendar of university and college open days: **www.opendays.com**

Students with disabilities:Disability Rights UK: **www.disabilityrightsuk.org/how-we-can-help**

3 Assessing Graduate Job Prospects

You do not have to go to university in order to build a career. For many students who do choose higher education, though, improving their chances of a well-paid, professionally fulfilling future may be a driving force behind taking a degree. Flying the nest, having fun and exploring a subject you have an intellectual curiosity in, used to be enough to warrant spending three-plus years as an undergraduate. Career considerations could arguably take a back seat for a bit, at least for those studying broad-based rather than vocational degrees. But since tuition fees became part of the equation, students have been prompted to weigh up whether the investment is worth it or not.

From the government's perspective, a degree should provide value for money to the taxpayer as well as to the student, partly because so many student loans will not be fully paid back. Graduate salaries are one way of evaluating whether a degree represents a good bet, but they are a blunt tool and liable to vary depending on whether a university is located in an area of high or low employment, with high or low wages. In 2019 the long-awaited Philip Augar review on post-18 funding recommended cutting tuition fees from £9,250 to £7,500. It called on the government to make up the funding difference, and to adjust support for different subjects to reflect the economic and social 'value' of degrees, and how much they cost to teach.

The proposal rang alarm bells for institutions that major in the arts and humanities, where graduates are less likely to earn high salaries early in their careers. Universities UK, the umbrella group for vice-chancellors, rallied in defence of a rounded university experience, commissioning polling by Comres in 2020 which found that only one in three students and recent graduates said their decision to go to university was to get a higher salary. Julia Buckingham, vice-chancellor of Brunel University and president of Universities UK, called on government to broaden its definition of 'value' beyond a student's expected future salary alone, saying:

"We should all be asking ourselves if we really want to live in a culture that identifies success by salary alone. It is time to listen and take notice of what students, graduates and society really value about the university experience and consider how we can ensure prospective students have access to the information they want to inform their future decisions."

The Times and the Sunday Times Good University Guide agrees, and our league table rankings have never used salary data as a performance measure. Few would attempt to argue that trainee nurses and teachers, for example, should be put off going to university because the professions they are studying towards do not promise megabucks. We do, though, list median salaries for each subject group in this chapter's second table, and with the subject guides in Chapter 13, for reference.

While no one can see into the future, applicants must attempt to evaluate the kind of career trajectory their potential degree could lead to. To spend money and time on university and then work in a job that could have been accessed without a degree adds up to a bad deal, however much fun you had, or intellectual curiosity you explored at university. The post-Covid, post-Brexit jobs market only heightens the need to make considered decisions about whether to go to university, and which degree to take. The freshers of 2021 and even 2022 are likely to be feeling anxious about how the pandemic and the end of the transition period could affect their career opportunities.

The measure we use to assess graduate prospects takes account of the rates of employment for graduates of the 67 subject areas in our *Guide* and distinguishes between types of work. After several years in development a new way of making these assessments is introduced this year. The new Graduate Outcomes (GO) survey has replaced the Destination of Leavers from Higher Education (DLHE) survey. Both measure the same thing: what graduates do next, but their crucial difference (for the purposes of this *Guide*) is the point at which they take their census. The previous system gathered information six months after graduation, whereas GO conducts its survey 15 months after graduates have finished their degrees. The longer timeframe better reflects changes in work patterns, with many graduates (in Covid-free times) doing internships, travelling or sampling the jobs market before plumping for a career path.

The new GO survey has caused our graduate prospects measure to evolve; so we now look at the proportion of graduates in high-skilled (instead of graduate-level) jobs or postgraduate study. This *Guide* uses a definition of a high-skilled job from the Higher Education Statistics

---

Median earnings by degree subject five years after graduation (2011–12 graduates)

Medicine and Dentistry	£49,300	Philosophy & religious studies	£26,600
Economics	£41,600	Biosciences	£26,300
Engineering	£35,400	Allied health subjects	£25,600
Mathematical Sciences	£34,300	English studies	£24,800
Pharmacology, toxicology & pharmacy	£33,200	Materials & technology	£24,800
Architecture, building and planning	£33,200	Sport and exercise science	£24,500
Physics & astronomy	£33,200	Health & social care	£23,700
Veterinary Science	£32,800	Education & teaching	£23,700
Medical sciences	£31,000	Media, journalism & communications	£23,700
Computing	£29,900	Sociology, social policy & anthropology	£23,400
Politics	£29,600	Combined & general studies	£23,400
Chemistry	£29,600	Psychology	£23,400
Nursing & midwifery	£28,500	General, applied & forensic sciences	£23,400
Geography, earth & environmental studies	£28,500	Celtic studies	£22,400
Languages & area studies	£28,500	Agriculture, food & related subjects	£21,900
Business & management	£27,700	Creative Arts & Design	£21,500
Law	£26,600	Performing Arts	£20,400
History & archaeology	£26,600		

Source: Department for Education, Graduate Outcomes March 2020

Agency (HESA), which conducts the GO survey. Universities that got the best graduate prospects scores in the previous measure have been largely unaffected by the new measure and continued to perform strongly, while for some universities very different results emerged, triggering unusually big swings in our overall rankings.

The latest figures from the UK Labour Force Survey, run by the Office for National Statistics showed that graduates remain at a career advantage over those without degrees. The employment rate for graduates in 2019 was 87.5%, a slight decrease on the 2018 rate (87.7%) that goes against a general trend of increases since 2011. The 72% employment rate among non-graduates in 2019 means those with degrees maintain a clear lead in the jobs market. The gap has been narrowing since 2014 however, as it did in the latest year compared with the 71.6% employment rate for non-graduates in 2018.

The UK Labour Force Survey also looks at the proportions in high-skilled work, where the gap widens to more of a gulf between graduates and non-graduates. In 2019, 65.9% of graduates were working in jobs deemed high-skilled, compared with 23.9% of non-graduates. The highest proportion (78.9%) in high-skilled work were those with postgraduate qualifications.

As a general rule graduates of UK universities enjoy a salary premium, which a report by the Institute of Fiscal Studies in 2020 put at £100,000 or more over a lifetime. Research by HESA and Warwick University the year before suggested this premium has declined in recent years, however, as the number of students has grown and the economy has deteriorated. At whichever rate is the most accurate, a degree does still bring a salary premium and if at any point, graduates' annual earnings slip below £26,575, they do not need to make repayments on any student loans (although the interest will continue to stack up).

This does not mean that every degree is a passport to a higher-paying job than life without one. Salary figures for graduates five and ten years into their careers show marked differences between universities and subjects in their graduates' earning power.

Future-proof degrees?

In the current fourth industrial revolution, automation is reshaping some jobs and the traditional nine-to-five is giving way to more independent ways of working. Economists have said young people should plan for five careers in a lifetime. Yes, lots is changing, but the oft-quoted estimate that 65% of primary school age children will end up working in jobs that don't yet exist was debunked as a statistical urban myth. A BBC investigation found such a high proportion unlikely and without factual roots, a figure of around a third was more likely, it suggested. Everyone knows that there have been changes to the world of work in the last few decades, but repeating to young people that the jobs they will do have not been invented yet can be unhelpful, dispiriting and confusing.

Advances in robotics and artificial intelligence will mean some jobs are on the way out, but roles needed to develop new technologies and new solutions are expanding. The stuff that makes us different from machines, such as emotional intelligence, analytical skills and caring, will also be vital in the future jobs market, as will creativity and resilience. A rounded university education with experience in and out of the classroom or laboratory will help to hone such 'soft' skills. As for resilience, current and incoming students who have adapted to blended online learning, dealt with exam marking fiascos and had to develop a socially distanced way of student life, are already building their bounce-back-ability.

Parents' well-meant career advice is often 20 or 30 years out of date. Careers experts recommend finding something you care about, and something you are good at, and linking the two together to find a job that will be rewarding. Some suggest looking at the United Nations' Sustainable Development

What graduates are doing 15 months after leaving university by subject studied

Subject	High-skilled job %	High-skilled job and studying %	Studying %	Lower-skilled job and studying %	Lower-skilled job %	Unemployed %	Total with positive outcome %
1 Medicine	91	6	2	0	0	0	99.7
2 Physiotherapy	94	2	0	0	1	1	97.4
3 Nursing	93	3	1	0	2	1	97.2
4 Veterinary Medicine	96	0	1	0	2	1	97.0
5 Dentistry	90	6	1	0	0	3	96.9
6 Radiography	92	2	1	0	2	2	95.6
7 Land and Property Management	83	10	2	0	2	3	94.6
8 Civil Engineering	79	3	8	0	5	5	90.2
9 Pharmacology & Pharmacy	72	5	12	0	5	6	89.8
10 Building	81	4	1	0	9	4	86.7
11 General Engineering	71	3	11	0	8	6	86.0
12 Physics & Astronomy	54	4	28	0	9	5	85.9
13 Town and Country Planning and Landscape	74	4	7	1	10	4	85.7
14 Architecture	74	4	7	0	7	8	85.1
15 Other Subjects Allied to Medicine	67	4	13	1	12	3	84.8
16 Chemistry	55	3	26	0	10	5	84.7
17 Chemical Engineering	67	3	14	1	9	6	84.6
18 Mechanical Engineering	72	3	8	0	11	5	84.0
19 Computer Science	74	3	6	0	10	7	83.2
20 Economics	67	7	8	1	13	4	83.1
21 Mathematics	62	7	13	0	12	5	82.5
22 Materials Technology	59	3	20	0	13	4	82.3
23 Electrical and Electronic Engineering	71	2	8	0	12	6	81.5
24 Anatomy & Physiology	49	4	27	1	15	3	81.3
25 Aeronautical and Manufacturing Engineering	66	3	10	0	14	6	79.6
26 Food Science	66	3	11	0	17	4	79.4
27 Geology	52	2	24	0	16	6	78.7
28 Russian	64	2	12	0	17	5	78.5
29 Librarianship & Information Management	68	4	3	1	16	9	75.2
30 Law	53	6	13	1	20	6	73.6
31 Geography & Environmental Sciences	54	3	15	1	22	5	73.2
32 French	54	4	14	1	22	5	73.1
33 Iberian Languages	57	3	11	1	21	6	73.1
34 Biological Sciences	43	3	26	1	21	6	73.0
35 Celtic Studies	50	2	16	5	24	3	72.9
36 Social Work	63	4	4	1	24	4	72.2
37 German	55	3	12	1	22	7	71.4
38 Politics	52	4	13	1	23	6	70.9
39 Education	61	2	6	1	26	4	70.2

Subject	High-skilled job %	High-skilled job and studying %	Studying %	Lower-skilled job and studying %	Lower-skilled job %	Unemployed %	Total with positive outcome %
40 Theology & Religious Studies	45	7	17	1	25	5	70.0
41 Middle Eastern and African Studies	54	7	8	0	24	6	70.0
42 Business Studies	60	4	4	1	25	6	68.7
43 Accounting & Finance	50	11	4	3	26	6	68.7
44 Philosophy	48	5	14	1	26	6	68.6
45 Music	55	4	8	1	27	5	68.1
46 Sport Science	50	5	12	1	29	4	67.6
47 Classics & Ancient History	44	5	18	1	25	8	67.2
48 East and South Asian Studies	51	4	11	1	24	9	67.0
49 Italian	51	4	12	0	27	7	66.6
50 Linguistics	49	3	14	1	29	5	66.2
51 English	48	4	13	1	28	6	65.9
52 Anthropology	47	5	13	1	26	8	65.8
53 Agriculture and Forestry	58	3	5	1	31	3	65.7
54 History	43	3	16	1	29	6	64.7
55 Archaeology and Forensic Science	45	2	15	1	29	7	63.4
56 American Studies	47	3	12	1	32	5	63.3
57 Art & Design	56	1	3	1	31	7	61.5
58 Communication and Media Studies	54	2	4	1	32	7	60.6
59 History of Art, Architecture and Design	41	3	14	1	33	8	59.4
60 Creative Writing	42	4	9	1	33	10	56.4
61 Drama, Dance and Cinematics	49	2	4	1	37	7	55.6
62 Psychology	36	4	13	2	39	6	55.5
63 Sociology	40	3	11	2	39	6	55.1
64 Hospitality, Leisure, Recreation & Tourism	48	2	3	1	40	6	54.2
65 Social Policy	41	3	8	2	40	6	53.7
66 Criminology	40	2	7	1	43	6	51.0
67 Animal Science	24	1	11	4	55	5	40.3
TOTAL	59	4	10	1	21	5	73.4

Note: This table is ranked on the proportion of graduates in high-skilled jobs and/or further study, and those combining lower-skilled jobs with further study. This total is shown in the final column in bold. Source: HESA, 2017–18

Goals (SDGs) and aligning careers to them: improving health and education, reducing inequality, spurring economic growth and conserving the environment – these are problems whose solutions are long-term, and their higher purpose chimes with the interests of the current generation of students. You could work as an expert in these fields or use other professional skills within the context of these SDGs.

By keeping your eye on the horizon to see what trends and changes are coming, you stand a chance of picking a future-proof field of work. Automation is changing professions, but not wiping

What graduates are earning 15 months after graduation by subject studied

	Subject	High skilled work (median) £	Low and medium skilled £
1	Dentistry	38,000	—
2	Medicine	34,000	—
3	Veterinary Medicine	31,000	—
=4	Chemical Engineering	30,000	22,000
=4	Pharmacy & Pharmacology	30,000	19,500
=6	Economics	29,000	20,000
=6	General Engineering	29,000	21,500
8	Electrical and Electronic Engineering	28,350	20,850
=9	Aeronautical and Manufacturing Engineering	28,000	21,500
=9	Building	28,000	20,000
=9	Materials Technology	28,000	19,500
=9	Mechanical Engineering	28,000	21,500
=9	Physics & Astronomy	28,000	19,000
=9	Social Work	28,000	17,535
15	Civil Engineering	27,500	19,300
=16	Computer Science	27,000	18,500
=16	Mathematics	27,000	19,000
18	Land and Property Management	26,500	—
=19	Librarianship & Information Management	26,000	20,500
=19	Politics	26,000	19,500
=19	Russian	26,000	—
=22	Accounting & Finance	25,000	20,000
=22	Anatomy & Physiology	25,000	17,600
=22	Anthropology	25,000	18,750
=22	Business Studies	25,000	19,500
=22	Chemistry	25,000	19,500
=22	Classics & Ancient History	25,000	18,500
=22	Criminology	25,000	18,000
=22	East and South Asian Studies	25,000	20,000
=22	French	25,000	19,500
=22	Middle Eastern and African Studies	25,000	18,000
=22	Philosophy	25,000	18,500
=22	Town and Country Planning and Landscape	25,000	21,000
=34	Agriculture and Forestry	24,000	20,000
=34	Education	24,000	17,100
=34	Food Science	24,000	18,500
=34	Geography & Environmental Sciences	24,000	19,000
=34	Geology	24,000	18,000
=34	German	24,000	19,500
=34	History	24,000	18,500
=34	Iberian Languages	24,000	19,500

Subject	High skilled work (median) £	Low and medium skilled £
=34 Italian	24,000	22,864
=34 Nursing	24,000	17,500
=34 Other Subjects Allied to Medicine	24,000	17,500
=34 Social Policy	24,000	17,750
=34 Theology & Religious Studies	24,000	17,000
=34 Physiotherapy	24,000	—
=34 Radiography	24,000	—
49 Biological Sciences	23,500	17,500
=50 American Studies	23,000	20,000
=50 Celtic Studies	23,000	—
=50 English	23,000	18,125
=50 Linguistics	23,000	18,000
=50 Psychology	23,000	18,000
=50 Sociology	23,000	18,500
=50 Sport Science	23,000	17,750
=57 Architecture	22,000	18,500
=57 History of Art, Architecture and Design	22,000	19,000
=57 Hospitality, Leisure, Recreation & Tourism	22,000	19,000
=57 Law	22,000	19,000
=57 Music	22,000	17,500
=62 Animal Science	21,000	18,500
=62 Archaeology and Forensic Science	21,000	18,000
=62 Art & Design	21,000	17,900
=62 Communication and Media Studies	21,000	18,000
=62 Creative Writing	21,000	16,500
=62 Drama, Dance and Cinematics	21,000	17,500

Note: The salaries table is ranked only by the median salary of those in highly skilled employment in each subject area.

Source: Higher Education Statistics Agency, Graduate Outcomes Survey 2017–18 (published November 2020).

them all out entirely. It is taking over the number crunching parts of accountancy, for instance, but accountants are still needed and some are moving into a more people-oriented, trusted business advisor role with their clients.

Graduate employment and underemployment

Competition for graduate jobs, with their salary premium over a working lifetime, remains stiff. There are 14 million graduates in the UK, and in London they make up 60% of the adult population. The North East is the region with Britain's lowest proportion of graduates, yet 34% of those aged 20-plus have a degree. The high proportion of graduates in the overall population means that they may now take longer than their predecessors to find the right career opening, and might experiment with internships before committing themselves.

Employers' ideas of which jobs require a degree, and of the roles for which they prefer graduates, change over time. Nurses have not always been required to take a degree, but the job now needs skills that were not part of the profession 20 years ago. The same is true of many occupations. Even in jobs where it may be possible to do the work involved without a degree, having taken one makes it easier to get hired in the first place.

Surveys have found that a sizable proportion of graduates consider themselves working in a job that does not requires a degree – an experience known as being underemployed. Scoping out a job via internships rather than going for whatever is immediately available for the highest salary, can be a wise move. Almost 60% of graduates said they would take a lower salary for a more fulfilling job when surveyed by Accenture around seven years ago, and only 55% were working in their chosen field.

The graduate labour market

The long-term effects of higher education are more encouraging. The government's Longitudinal Education Outcomes (LEO) data were published at the end of 2016, showing average salaries and employment status three, five and ten years after graduation. Some of the measures were updated in the 2016-17 tax year and published in 2019. The original reports showed that 55% of graduates a year out of college had steady employment, but that a decade after graduation, the figure had hit 69%. Graduates were shown to be on a steadily ascending salary ladder, with median earnings rising from £16,500 a year after graduation to £31,000 a decade later. The figures also show predictable differences between subjects in employment and salary rates, as well as illustrating the lasting impact of university choice. Among law graduates, for example, the top earners from Oxford and Cambridge averaged more than £75,000 (and the lowest some £35,000) after five years, compared with less than £10,000 for low earners from the University of East London.

The contents of this *Guide* – particularly in the subject tables – should help to create a more nuanced picture. A close examination of individual universities' employment rates in your subject – possibly supplemented by the salary figures on the Discover Uni website **www.disoveruni.gov.uk** – will tell you whether national trends apply to your chosen course.

At the time of writing a no-deal Brexit looked to be on the cards, and the health pandemic continued to impact businesses and the economy. Even without such circumstances, for the boom years of graduate employment to return, there will have to be stronger recruitment by small and medium-sized companies, as well as the big battalions. The number of self-employed graduates will increase, in line with universities reporting growing demand for their business start-up and incubator services. If you are considering the graduate entrepreneur route, explore what your chosen university offers, because business hub services vary considerably in scale and sophistication.

Subject choice and career opportunities

For those thinking of embarking on higher education in 2021 and 2022, the signs are still positive. But in any year, some universities and some subjects produce better returns than others. The tables on the pages that follow give a more detailed picture of the differences between subjects at a national level, while the rankings in chapters 1 and 13 include figures for each university and subject area. There are a few striking changes, but mainly among subjects with relatively small and fluctuating numbers of graduates.

In the employment table, subjects are ranked according to the proportion employed in jobs categorized by HESA as high-skilled, and include those undertaking further study, whether or not combined with a high-skilled job. The level of detail we provide about types of job is illuminating; some similar tables do not make a distinction between different sorts of work, which can mislead applicants into thinking all universities and subjects offer uniformly rosy employment prospects.

The definitions of both a high-skilled and a graduate job are controversial. But HESA relies on the Standard Occupational Classification, a complex series of definitions drawn up by the Office for National Statistics (ONS). New universities, in particular, often claim that the whole concept of a graduate job immediately after graduation fails to reflect reality for their alumni. In any case, a degree is about enhancing your whole career, your way of working and your view of the world, not just your first job out of college.

That said, the tables in this chapter will help you assess whether your course is likely to pay off in career terms, at least to start with. They show both the amount you might expect to earn with a degree in a specific subject, and the odds of being in work. They reflect the experience 15 months after graduation of those who completed their degrees in 2018, so the picture may have improved by the time you leave university. The pattern of success rates for specific subjects and institutions are unlikely to have changed radically though.

The table of employment statistics from the new Graduate Outcomes survey reveals some unexpected results. For example, only 68.7% of business studies graduates are working in high-skilled jobs or doing further study, exactly the same proportion of accounting and finance graduates who achieved similar positive outcomes. The food scientists and town and country planners fare a lot better. All six branches of engineering are in the top 15 subjects for graduate earnings, and the top 25 for successful graduate outcomes.

The employment table also shows that graduates in some subjects, especially sciences such as physics and astronomy, biological sciences, chemistry and geology, are more likely to undertake further study than in others, such as those in art and design or hospitality. A range of professions now regard a Masters degree as a basic entry-level qualification.

Those going into subjects such as art and design appreciate that it too has its own career peculiarities. Periods of freelance or casual work are common at the start of a career and may become an enduring choice. Less surprisingly, doctors and dentists are virtually guaranteed a job if they complete a degree, as are nurses. HESA found that not one medicine graduate was unemployed 15 months after finishing their degrees, and only one in 100 phsyiotherapists, nurses or vets was out of work at the same stage.

The second table, on pages 54-55, gives average earnings of those who graduated in 2018, recorded 15 months after leaving university. It contains interesting, and in some cases surprising, information about early career pay levels. Few would have placed social work in the top 10 for graduate pay. However, nursing is now one of a large group of subjects sharing 34th place, having been in the top 20 a few years ago.

It is important, of course, to consider the differences between starting salaries and the long-term prospects of different jobs. Over time, the accountants may well end up with bigger rewards, despite being only £1,000 a year better off than the nurses in our early-career snapshot.

In any case, it is important to realise that once you ignore the higher incomes available to medics and other elite professionals, early graduate incomes vary less than you might think from subject to subject. Twelve subjects ranging from accountancy and finance to criminology and chemistry tie for 22nd spot in our salary ranking. A further 15 tie for 34th. But the difference between these two groups is only £1,000 a year, with the first set on £25,000 and the second on £24,000. That's why you should consider the lifetime earnings you might derive from these subjects, and your own interests and inclinations, at least as much as this snapshot.

Enhancing your employability

Graduate employability has become the holy grail of degree education since higher fees were introduced in most of the UK. Virtually every university has an initiative to enhance their graduates' prospects. Many have incorporated specially designed employability modules into degree courses; some are certificating extra-curricular activities to improve their graduates' CVs; and many more are stepping up their efforts to provide work experience to complement degrees.

Opinion is divided on the value of such schemes. Some of the biggest employers restrict their recruitment activities to a small number of universities, believing that these institutions attract the brightest minds and that trawling more widely is not cost-effective. In 2019–20, High Fliers reported that the ten universities most targeted were Manchester, Birmingham, Warwick, Bristol, Cambridge, Nottingham, Leeds, University College London, Sheffield and Oxford. Some top law firms and others in the City of London have introduced institution-blind applications, but big employers' links with their favourite recruiting grounds are likely to continue. Widening the pool of universities from which they set out to recruit is costly, and can seem unnecessary if employers are getting the people they think they need. They will expect outstanding candidates who went to other universities to come to them, either on graduation or later in their careers. But most graduates do not work in the City and most students do not go to universities at the top of the league tables.

University schemes

If a university offers extra help towards employment, consider whether its scheme is likely to work for you. Some are too new to have shown results in the labour market yet, but they may have been endorsed by big employers or introduced at an institution whose graduates already have a record of success in the jobs market. They might involve classes in CV writing, interview skills, personal finance, entrepreneurship and negotiation skills, among many other topics. There can be guest lectures and demonstrations, or mock interviews, by real employers, to assess students' strengths and weaknesses. In time, these extras may turn into mandatory parts of a degree, complete with course credit.

The value of work experience

The majority of graduate jobs are open to applicants from any discipline. For these general positions, employers tend to be more impressed by a good degree from what they consider a prestigious university than by an apparently relevant qualification. Here numeracy, literacy and communications – the skills needed to function effectively in any organisation – are vitally important.

Specialist jobs, for example in engineering or design, are a different matter. Employers may be much more knowledgeable about the quality of individual courses, and less influenced by a university's overall position in league tables, when the job relies directly on knowledge and skills acquired as a student. That goes for medicine and architecture as well as computer games design or environmental management.

In virtually all fields of employment, however, work experience has become increasingly valuable. It is common for major and less major employers to hire graduates who have already worked for them, whether in holiday jobs, internships or placements. Sandwich degrees, which include extended programmes of up to a year at work, have always boosted employment prospects. Graduates – often engineers – frequently end up working where they undertook their placement. And while a sandwich year will make your course take longer, it will not be subject to a full year's fees.

Many conventional degrees now include shorter work placements that should offer some advantages in the labour market. Not all are arranged by the university – most big graduate employers offer some provision of this nature, although access to it can be competitive.

A growing (but, as yet, relatively small) number are also offering degree apprenticeships, in partnership with a wide range of universities. Even Cambridge has some at postgraduate level and is developing more. They generally take longer than a traditional degree, but there are no fees and apprentices are paid a salary. Although there is no guarantee of employment at the end of the course, employment rates from sandwich degrees suggest that companies are likely to want to retain those in whom they have invested considerable time and money.

If you opt for a traditional degree without a work placement, consider arranging your own part-time or temporary employment. The majority of full-time students now take jobs during term time, as well as in vacations, to make ends meet. But such jobs can boost your CV as well as your bank balance. Even working in a bar or a shop shows some experience of dealing with the public and coping with the discipline of the workplace. Inevitably, the more prosperous cities are likely to offer more employment opportunities than rural areas or conurbations that have been hard hit by recession.

Consider part-time degrees

Another option is part-time study. Although enrolments have fallen sharply both before and since the big 2012 increases in fees, there are now loans available for most part-time courses. Employers may be willing to share the cost of taking a degree or another relevant qualification, and the chance to earn a wage while studying has obvious attractions. Bear in mind that most part-time courses take twice as long to complete as the full-time equivalent. If your earning power is linked to the qualification, it will take that much longer for you to enjoy the benefits.

Plan early for your career

Whatever type of course you choose, it is sensible to start thinking about your future career early in your time at university. There has been a growing tendency in recent years for students to convince themselves that there would be plenty of time to apply for jobs after graduation, and that they were better off focusing entirely on their degree while at university. In the current employment market, all but the most obviously brilliant graduates need to offer more than just a degree, whether it be work experience, leadership qualities demonstrated through clubs and societies, or commitment to voluntary activities. Many students finish a degree without knowing what they want to do, but a blank CV will not impress a prospective employer.

Results of the latest High Fliers survey show that work experience schemes have become an integral part of recruiting new graduates. Students who apply for work experience in their first or second year at university go through similar selection processes to graduates, which works as a kind of pre-vetting for a job after graduation. The number of paid placements has risen sharply, reflecting the increased role of work experience in graduate recruitment. Covid-19 will have interfered with their plans, but at the time of the High Fliers survey, more than three-quarters of the country's top graduate employers had committed to paid internships for penultimate year students during the summer of 2020.

Useful websites

Prospects, the UK's official graduate careers website: **www.prospects.ac.uk**
For career advice, internships and student and graduate jobs: **www.milkround.com**
For graduate employment (and other) statistics: **www.discoveruni.gov.uk**
High Fliers research: **www.highfliers.co.uk**

4 Understanding Tuition Fees

Only two years ago England was on the cusp of reducing undergraduate tuition fees for home students, following recommendations from the Augar review into post-18 education and funding. The government-commissioned report was the first in half a century to look into the UK's post-school learning. Published in 2019, it recommended that annual tuition fees should be cut to a maximum of £7,500 per year, from £9,250, with effect from 2021–22. Universities and students were waiting with bated breath for the government to respond, some believing it a positive move, others unconvinced it would serve all parties well. But before ministers made a decision along came Covid-19, wreaking its havoc on all areas of education. In light of the pandemic, Philip Augar, the chair of the review panel, backtracked his position on its findings in May 2020, stating that such a fee cut would be too destabilising under the new conditions. At the time of writing, the government had gone quiet on the issue.

Which brings us to the candidates of 2021–22, who are back to square one, their hopes for cost savings on a degree in England dashed for the time being. What we do know is that home tuition fees for UK and Irish students in England, Northern Ireland, Scotland and Wales are not set to increase this autumn and will remain at a maximum of £9,250 for most courses, though Wales caps fees at £9,000.

The same cannot be said for students from the rest of the EU, EEA countries and Switzerland who enrol at UK universities after the summer, however. These students are losing the right to 'home' fee status in the UK, as a consequence of the end of the Brexit transition period. From the start of the 2021–22 academic year, they will have to pay much higher international tuition fees, at the rates that all other students from the rest of the world are charged. The situation for those coming to study in the UK post-Brexit is explored in greater detail in Chapter 12.

Up until 1998, tuition at UK universities was free. The £1,000 annual fees introduced that year represented a seismic shift in higher education at the time, and in British society more widely. These fees were paid upfront by students at the start of the academic year. In 2006 fees were raised to £3,000 and a new system of variable deferred fees and tuition fees loans was introduced. From 2006 fees rose gradually by inflation until 2012 when, tuition fees were raised to £9,000 per year – a move met by protest marches, campus occupations and students voting with their feet as evidenced by a downturn in applications to university. Student finance reformed at the same time, to include raising the repayment threshold to £21,000 and introducing a variable tiered rate of interest on student loans. Understanding student finance is examined in chapter seven. Fees up to £9,250 were first introduced in 2017–18 and have not gone up since. Application and enrolment numbers have regained the ground they lost in the immediate years after 2012, students appearing to have become resigned to the regime.

There are some exceptions to these upper limits; private providers are not subject to fee caps, and the maximum fee for accelerated (two-year) degree courses in England is £11,100. However, a fee loan will only be made available up to £9,250 and any shortfall must be met by the student. This applies to students undertaking accelerated degrees and those undertaking courses at providers which are not subject to a fee cap.

Most students pay the maximum fees, but tuition costs vary much more widely than the upper limits suggest for those who qualify for reductions. Bursaries and fee waivers bring down the price for students from low-income households, while merit-based scholarships – which are sometimes, but not always linked to household incomes – also make a difference.

Some universities devote substantial sums to their bursaries and scholarships programmes. The Office for Students predicts that by 2022–23, assuming the current fee levels, the lowest actual charges at mainstream universities will be at the prestigious London School of Economics and Imperial College, charging £8,144 and £8,291 respectively, thanks to their big endowments for financial assistance. Each year the LSE awards around £4 million in scholarships and financial support to its undergraduates.

The University of West London uses the surplus money it generates to effectively reduce the cost of going to university from the tuition fees rack rate of £9,250 to about £7,400 for some students. Everyone gets an annual £300 Aspire card for study essentials and Path to Success scholarships, worth £1,500 a year, are awarded to 400 entrants from households with incomes under £25,000.

This *Guide* quotes the higher headline fees, but even these will vary according to whether you are from the UK or overseas, studying full-time or part-time, and whether you are taking a Foundation degree or an Honours programme. International medical students at Imperial College London in 2021–22 will pay £45,300 a year (a figure that will rise with inflation), which for new students will include both EU and non-EU members under the post-Brexit tuition fees model. EU students already on courses before the transition period ended on 31 December 2020 will still qualify for the 'home' fees rate of £9,250 per year until the end of their course, as paid by UK students. Meanwhile British students taking a Foundation course for 2021 entry at Kingston University, not far away, will pay £5,300 to £7,800, depending on the subject and year of study.

Here we focus on full-time Honours degrees for British undergraduates, and the EU students who escaped the higher international fees by registering on courses before the end of the Brexit transition period: these students make up the biggest group on any UK campus, and are the group for whom maximum fees shot up to £9,000 in 2012 and have since risen to £9,250.

An important fact, easy to overlook, is that some universities guarantee fees will be fixed at the first-year rate for the whole of your course, while others make no such promise. In light of the financial fallout following Covid-19, along with the complications to tuition fees for EU students falling under the international category from 2021, applicants are advised to check the fees pages of individual universities closely. Reading, for example, is still guaranteeing the same rate for the duration of a degree to those enrolling in 2021. Many others, such as Bristol and UCL, warn that their fees may go up for existing students as and when the government raises the maximum it can charge.

Fees and loans

There is little sign that applicants base their degree choices on the marginal differences in fee levels and bursaries at different universities. Numbers from the poorest socio-economic groups are at record levels, although they remain severely under-represented compared with more affluent groups. Concern remains, however, over the impact on part-time courses and, in years to come, on the numbers prepared to continue to postgraduate study.

Most readers of *The Times and Sunday Times Good University Guide* will be choosing full-time undergraduate or Foundation degree courses. The fees for 2021–22 are listed alongside each university's profile in chapter 15, with a few exceptions which had yet to announce fees at the time of going to press. Details of English universities' bursaries and scholarships are on the website of the Office for Students (OfS) in the pages on access and participation plans. Universities have their own fees and funding web pages as well, which are good places to source up-to-date information regarding financial help.

Institutions in Scotland, Wales and Northern Ireland will continue to have lower charges for their own residents but will charge varying amounts to students from other parts of the UK. Only those living in Scotland and studying at Scottish universities will escape all fees, although there will be reduced fees for those normally living in Wales and Northern Ireland.

The number of bursaries and scholarships offered to reduce the burden on new students has been falling since OFFA, the former Office for Fair Access, suggested that such initiatives do little to attract students from low-income households. As a result, the Government turned the grants paid to the poorest students into loans, although it is now restoring some maintenance grants, for example for nurses.

Variations between universities

Robert Gordon University in Aberdeen is offering among the lowest full-time fees to students from the rest of the UK (RUK) in 2021–22, with prices as low as £5,000, rising to £8,500. An Honours degree in social work, for instance, studied in blended online format, costs £5,640 for RUK students, while photography, which is studied on-campus, costs £6,750. Tuition is entirely free for Scottish students, as it is at all universities north of the border for those whose homes are there too.

In Northern Ireland it is still possible to start a Foundation Degree for £2,600 a year. For Honours degrees, students from outside the province will pay £9,250 while Northern Ireland residents are charged up to £4,530. The price for international students starts at £17,238 and varies by course.

During work placements or years abroad, fees cannot exceed £1,850 (20% of the full-year fee) for work placements and £1,385 for a year abroad and are often less.

Many universities funnel a substantial proportion of the income they receive from higher fees to access initiatives, in the form of financial bursaries or investment in outreach activities. As a result, the average fee paid by a student in 2019–20 after waivers and other support was £8,836. In the case of the London School of Economics, more than half of its additional fee income above £6,000 is spent in this way, paying bursaries of up to £4,000 a year for 2020–21. A more usual figure is in the 15–30% range.

For 2020–21 at least, fees for students from other EU countries will be the same as for those from the UK, but charges will be higher, sometimes massively higher, for those from other countries.

Higher fees have had less effect on the demand for higher education than many universities dared hope in the run-up to the 2012 hike, but financial considerations will still be important to the decision-making process for many students. The impact that charging EU, EEA and Swiss students international fees will have on recruitment is yet to be seen. In the current economic circumstances, students will want to keep their debts to a minimum and are bound to take the cost of living into account. They will also want the best possible career prospects and may choose their subject accordingly.

Alternative options

Some further education colleges offer substantial savings on the cost of a degree, or of a Foundation degree, but they tend to have very local appeal, and their subject range tends to be largely vocational. The private sector may grow in popularity, following the success of two-year degrees at the University of Buckingham and BPP University in particular. Regent's University, one of the latest to be awarded that title, is charging £18,500 in 2020–21 for all students, irrespective of their place of origin, although less for some foundation years. The New College of the Humanities, also in London, now charges the standard £9,250, having originally come in at twice the price charged by mainstream institutions. The international fee is £14,000.

Impact on subject and university choice

Fee levels have had little impact on students' choices of university, but that is not the case for choices of subject. Predictions that old universities and/or vocational subjects would prosper at the expense of the rest have been shown to be too simplistic. Some, but not all, arts subjects have suffered, while in general science courses have prospered. For many young people, the options have not changed. If you want to be a doctor, a teacher or a social worker, there is no alternative to higher education. And, while there are now more options for studying post A-level, it remains to be seen whether they offer the same promotion prospects as a degree.

Even among full-time degrees, the pattern of applications and enrolments has varied considerably since the introduction of higher fees. In 2018, the big losers among disciplines included technology subjects and languages and literature, European and global. Winners included medicine and, perhaps unexpectedly, the social sciences. Notably less popular are melange degrees such as combinations of the arts, sciences and social sciences, or combined arts and sciences. Perhaps these choices seem too indecisive for the modern age. There was a small decline in applicant numbers, and less prestigious institutions felt the pinch the most. Medicine, dentistry and veterinary science have been growing in popularity and new medical schools are opening to meet the demand for more doctors.

In general terms, over the seven years since higher fees were introduced, science and business subjects have done better than the arts, as students have made their own assumptions about future career prospects. IT, engineering, physical sciences and law are ahead of 2010 application numbers and languages and linguistics are down. In the 2019 admissions cycle business courses had the most enrolments. Medicine and dentistry saw the biggest increases in popularity proportionally – as they have in other recent years. Mathematical sciences saw the largest proportional fall in acceptances in 2019.

Universities vary the courses they offer, in response to the perceived demand from students, much more frequently than they used to. A drop in applications may mean less competition for places, or it may lead universities to close courses, possibly intensifying the race for entry. The only reliable forecast is that competition for places on the most popular courses will remain stiff, just as it has been since before students paid any fees.

Two-year degrees are so far mainly the domain of the private universities. The University of Law, for example, already does degrees in this way. It charges £11,100 per year, a saving of £5,550 on a three-year course, which the same institution also offers at the standard £9,250, alongside less expensive online options. A two-year course also gets you into the workforce faster and reduces spending on living costs. However, this approach also cuts out much chance of holiday earnings and of sandwich courses or placements, where students can often get paid and gain work experience. It remains to be seen whether the idea will catch on with traditional universities and if so, whether it will be applicable to the full range of academic subjects.

Finally, there is the option of studying for a degree with no fees at all, by taking a degree apprenticeship sponsored by an employer. So far, the range of subjects in which these are available is relatively narrow – they have to go through a cumbersome accreditation procedure – but a growing number of universities are offering them, both post-1992 institutions and some of the older universities.

Many degree apprenticeships are in professional areas, such as childcare, accounting, policing and social work, but there are others in the sciences, business subjects, some social sciences and IT. On the whole students spend the majority of their time at work with their sponsoring employer – and receiving a wage, rather than having to access loans – with varying periods at university. Those on PwC's 'Flying Start' computer science or software engineering degree apprenticeships have a different experience however. Their fees at Birmingham, Leeds or Queen's Belfast universities are paid by their employer for a full BSc, and they earn a salary throughout their course. Instead of being based mostly at work, the student-trainees experience university life more traditionally and both live and study largely alongside fellow undergraduates in term time, with work placements taken in chunks throughout their degrees. A graduate scheme place awaits at the end, with a head start straight into the second year of work.

The degree versus degree apprenticeship debate is fairly even-handed. Financially, degree apprenticeships – which are known as graduate apprenticeships in Scotland – are a no-brainer; you do not pay tuition fees and you will get a salary for a job that is building experience for your future career, rather than a typical part-time role just to boost your current account. Those who last the course of up to five years will be met with immediate employment levels that are guaranteed to be excellent, and many employers pay those who complete the qualification more than traditional graduates because they will have been with them for longer and be more valuable in the short term. However, the degree apprenticeship route is too new for the long-term prospects to be certain, and it is impossible to say whether the qualification will have the same currency and be as portable as a traditional degree in mid-career.

Getting the best deal

There will still be a certain amount of variation in student support packages in 2021 and it will be possible to shop around, particularly if your family income is low. But remember that the best deal, even in purely financial terms, is one that leads to a rewarding career. By all means compare

Tuition fees by region for courses starting in 2021

Student's home region	Studying in England	Studying in Scotland	Studying in Wales	Studying in Northern Ireland
England	£9,250	Up to £9,250*	£9,000	£9,250
Scotland	£9,250	No fee	£9,000	£9,250
Wales**	£9,250	Up to £9,250	£9,000	£9,250
Northern Ireland	£9,250	Up to £9,250	£9,000	£4,395
EU & Other international	Variable	Variable	Variable	Variable

*Note that Honours Degrees in Scotland take four years and some universities charge £9,250 for each year.
**Students who live in Wales will be entitled to tuition fee loans and means-tested maintenance grants.
NB: Correct at time of going to press.
Source: UCAS

the full packages offered by individual universities but consider, too, whether marginal differences of a few hundred pounds in headline fees, repaid over 30 years, matter as much as the quality of the course and the likely advantages it will confer in the employment market. Scottish students can save themselves £27,750 by opting to study north of the border. That is a very different matter to the much smaller saving that is available to students in England, particularly if the Scottish university is of comparable quality to the alternatives elsewhere. So, it is all a matter of judgement.

The financial relief offered by means-tested bursaries may be impossible to ignore for those who qualify for them. No one has to pay tuition fees while they are a student, but you still have to find thousands of pounds in living costs to take a full-time degree. In some cases, bursaries may make the difference between being able to afford higher education and having to pass up a potentially life-changing opportunity. Some are worth up to £3,000 a year, although most are less generous than this, often because large numbers of students qualify for an award.

Some scholarships are even more valuable, and are awarded for sporting and musical prowess, as well as academic achievement. Most scholarships are not means-tested, but a few are open only to students who are both high performers academically and from low-income families.

How the £9,250 fee system works

What follows is a summary of the position for British students in late 2020. While there are substantial differences between the four countries of the UK, there is one important piece of common ground. Up-front payment of fees is not compulsory, and students can take out a fee loan from the Student Loans Company to cover them (see chapter 7). This is repayable in instalments after graduation when earnings reach £25,725 for English students, a threshold set by the Government.

Undergraduate fees are remaining unchanged at £9,250, and this is the most you can borrow to pay fees, with lower sums for private colleges (up to £6,165) and part-time study, where the cap is £6,935 at public institutions and £4,625 at private ones. There are different levels of fees and support for UK students who are not from England. From the start of the 2021–22 academic year new students enrolling at UK universities from other EU countries will pay the same rate as international students, which is usually much higher than the home rate. EU students already registered on courses before 31 December 2020 will qualify for the home rate of fees for the remainder of their course The latest information on individual university's fees at the time of going to press is listed alongside their profiles in chapter 15.

With changes, large or small, becoming almost an annual occurrence, it is essential to consult university websites for updates and those of the relevant Government agencies.

Fees in England

In England, the maximum tuition fee for full-time undergraduates from the UK will be £9,250 a year in 2021–22. As we have seen, most courses will demand fees of £9,250 or close to it.

In many public universities, the lowest fees will be for Foundation degrees and Higher National Diplomas. Although some universities have chosen to charge the full £9,250 a year for all courses, these two-year courses will remain a cost-effective stepping stone to a full degree, or a qualification in their own right, at many universities and further education colleges. Those universities that offer extended work placements or a year abroad as part of a degree course, will charge much less than the normal fee for this 'year out'. The maximum cost for a placement year is 20% of the tuition fee (£1,850), and for a full year abroad, 15%. If you spend only part of the year abroad, you will probably have to pay the whole £9,250.

Fees in Scotland

At Scottish universities and colleges, students from Scotland pay no fees directly. The universities' vice-chancellors and principals have appealed for charges to be introduced at some level to save their institutions from falling behind their English rivals in financial terms. But Alex Salmond, when he was Scotland's First Minister, famously declared that the "rocks will melt with the sun" before this happens.

Students whose home is in Scotland and who are studying at a Scottish university apply to the Student Awards Agency for Scotland (SAAS) to have their fees paid for them. Note, too, that three-year degrees are rare in Scotland, so most students can expect to pay four years of living costs.

Students from England, Wales and Northern Ireland studying in Scotland will pay fees at something like the scale that applies in England and will have access to finance at similar levels to those available for study in England. It is worth noting, however, that some courses offer considerable savings. Robert Gordon University, for example, has a fee of £6,000 per year for some four-year courses, including a BA in Accounting and Finance.

The majority of Scottish universities offer a "free" fourth year to bring their total fees into line with English universities, but Edinburgh and St Andrews charge £9,250 in all four years of their degree courses.

Fees in Wales

In previous years, Welsh universities have applied a range of fees up to £9,000, but all have now opted for £9,000. Students who live in Wales will be able to apply for a Tuition Fee Loan as well as a Tuition Fee Grant, wherever they study. You can get a combined loan and grant for up to £9,000 if you study in Wales, or £9,250 for Scotland, England or Northern Ireland, but only a loan, of up to £6,165, for study in a private institution.

Fees in Northern Ireland

The two universities of Northern Ireland are charging local students £4,530 a year for 2021–22. Students can receive a fee loan to postpone paying this until their earnings are above £19,390 for 2020–21, with an interest rate matching RPI or Bank of England base rate plus 1%, whichever is lower. For students from elsewhere in the UK, the fee is £9,250 for Queen's Belfast and for the University of Ulster.

Useful websites

The 'fees and funding' pages on university websites provide the most up-to-date information on costs of individual courses – especially for rates paid by international students, which vary. Universities also publish details of the financial help available, and how to apply.

It is essential to consult the latest information provided by Government agencies. The following websites will outline any major developments.

England: **www.gov.uk/student-finance**

Wales: **www.studentfinancewales.co.uk**

Scotland: **www.saas.gov.uk**

Northern Ireland: **www.studentfinanceni.co.uk**

Office for Students: **www.officeforstudents.org.uk**

5 Making Your Application

Students in England could receive university offers only after they have obtained their final grades, under proposals to change the current admissions system backed by the Education Secretary, Gavin Williamson. The exam chaos following the cancellation of GCSE and A-level exams in 2020 focused ongoing debate in the sector on reforms to the application and admissions process. Vice-chancellors are supporting an overhaul which would mean UK students only being offered university places once they had their A-level results.

The intention is to make the system fairer by getting rid of predicted grades, which can be unreliable and which can also work against high achievers from disadvantaged backgrounds – evidence shows their grades are more likely to be under-predicted. At the time of writing, the government had yet to confirm the change. Universities said it could be introduced as early as 2023–24, however.

Shifting to a post-qualifications admissions (PQA) model would bring the UK in line with most other countries. Our current predicted grades system is a rarity in the education sector globally, and the UK is the only developed country to organise university admissions this way. But for the applicants of 2022, the status quo remains.

The University and Colleges Admissions System, more commonly known by its acronym UCAS, makes the process of applying to university as straightforward as possible. Everything happens online and UCAS provides clear instructions, tips and suggestions about how best to navigate each section of its 'Apply' website along the way. This website becomes an applicant's new best friend, and its various stages will become part of their life until a university place has been gained. Grades will be the most important factor, but what goes on the application form is more important than many students realise. There is a knack to making the kind of application that will stand out to admissions tutors, and which will convey your knowledge of and enthusiasm for your chosen subject, preferably with supporting evidence from your school or college.

It pays to keep your eye on the ball at this stage on the journey to university. Under the current system applicants must decide on up to five choices months before they take their final exams, you do not have to use all five, but doing so gives you the best chance of success.

The application process

Almost all applications for full-time higher education courses go through UCAS, including those to the conservatoires which come with separate guidance and processes on the UCAS website.

Applications for degree apprenticeships are exceptions to the rule, however, and should be made to employers rather than universities. Deadlines differ between employers. You can apply for as many apprenticeships as you want, on top of your university applications. Many recruit through the **www.gov.uk/apply-apprenticeship** website, which also has links to vacancy information, as does UCAS at **https://careerfinder.ucas.com/**.

Some universities that have not filled all their places on conventional degrees, even during Clearing, will accept direct applications up to and sometimes after the start of the academic year, but UCAS is both the official route and the only way into the most popular courses. Apply is available 24 hours a day, and, when the time comes, information on the progress of your application may arrive at any time.

Registering with Apply

Applications kick off by registering with Apply. School and college students will be given a 'buzzword' by their tutor or careers adviser – you need this in order to login to register. It links your application to the school or college so that the application can be sent electronically to your referee (usually one of your teachers) for your reference to be attached. If you are no longer at a school or college, you do not need a "buzzword", but you will need details of your referee. More information is given on the UCAS website.

Clicking on 'Apply' begins the process for providing your personal details and generating a username and password, as well as reminding you of basic points, such as amending your details in case of a change of address. You can register separate term-time and holiday addresses – a useful option for boarders, who could find offers and, particularly, the confirmation of a place, going to their school when they are miles away at home. Remember to keep a note of your username and password in a safe place.

Throughout the process, you will be in sole control of communications with UCAS and your chosen universities. Only if you nominate a representative and give them your unique nine-digit application number (sent automatically by UCAS when your application is submitted), can a parent or anyone else give or receive information on your behalf, perhaps because you are ill or out of the country.

Video guides on the application process are available on the UCAS website. Once you are registered, you can start to complete the Apply screens. The sections that follow cover the main screens.

Personal details

This information is taken from your initial registration, and you will be asked for additional information, for example, on ethnic origin and national identity, to monitor equal opportunities

---

The main screens to be completed in UCAS Apply

» Personal and contact details and some additional non-educational details for UK applicants.
» Your course choices.
» Details of your education so far, including examination results and examinations still to be taken.
» Details of any jobs you have done.
» Your personal statement.
» A reference from one of your teachers.
» View all details to make sure they are correct and reflect your preferences.
» Pay for the application (applications for 2021 cost £26, or £20 to apply to just one course).

in the application process. UK students will also be asked to complete a student finance section designed to speed up any loan application you might make.

Choices

In most subjects, you will be able to apply to a maximum of five universities and/or colleges. The exceptions are medicine, dentistry and veterinary science, where the maximum is four, but you can use your fifth choice as a back-up to apply for a different subject.

The other important restriction concerns Oxford or Cambridge, because you can only apply to one or the other; you cannot apply to both universities in the same year, nor can you apply for more than one course there. For both universities you may need to take a written test (see page 34) and submit examples of your work, depending on the course selected. In addition, for Cambridge, many subjects will demand a pre-interview assessment once the university has received your application from UCAS, while the rest will set written tests to be taken at interview.

The deadline for Oxbridge applications – and for all medicine, dentistry and veterinary science courses – is 15 October. For all other applications the deadline is 15 January (or 24 March for some specified art and design courses). The other exceptions to this rule are the relatively small but growing number of courses that start in January or February. If you are considering one of these, contact the university concerned for application deadlines.

Most applicants use all five choices. But if you do choose fewer than five courses, you can still add another to your form up to 30 June, as long as you have not accepted or declined any offers. Nor do you have to choose five different universities if more than one course at the same institution attracts you – if you are keen on one institution in particular, applying for one course with lower entrance requirements than the other is a good way of hedging your bets. Universities are not allowed to see where else you have applied, or whether you have chosen the same subject elsewhere. But they will be aware of multiple applications within their own institution. Remember that it is more difficult to write a convincing personal statement if it has to cover two subjects.

For each course you select, you will need to put the UCAS code on the form – and you should check carefully that you have the correct code and understand any special requirements that may be detailed on the UCAS description of the course. It does not matter in what order you enter your choices as all are treated equally. You will also need to indicate whether you are applying for a deferred entry (for example, if you are taking a gap year – see page 78).

Education

This is where you provide details of the schools and colleges you have attended, and the qualifications you have obtained or are preparing for. The UCAS website gives plenty of advice on the ways in which you should enter this information, to ensure that all your relevant qualifications are included with their grades. While UCAS does not need to see qualification certificates, it can double-check results with the examination boards to ensure that no one has exaggerated their results.

In the Employment section that follows, add details of any paid jobs you have had (unpaid or voluntary work should be mentioned in your personal statement).

Personal statement

It is never too early to get cracking on your personal statement, as you will need it finished and in pristine form before making applications. Plan, write and check this statement with consideration and care. Then check it again, and once more for luck. A sloppily written personal statement is a wasted opportunity; like all elements of your UCAS form, the level of attention to detail conveys a message to its readers about the author. One statement goes to all the universities you are applying to, so do not mention any universities by name. You have between 1,000 and 4,000 characters (including spaces) over a maximum of 47 lines to make a winning case for the strength of your application, and if it comes to a tie-break in admissions departments, the strongest personal statement gives that applicant the competitive edge. Even if yours does not reach such a deal-breaking stage, it is not worth taking the chance.

While stopping short of exaggerating or out-and-out lying, this is an opportunity to promote yourself; if that makes you cringe and clam up, ask for help from your parents, friends and teachers who will be able to list your talents.

The personal statement is not the place to discuss exam grades – qualifications are covered elsewhere on your UCAS form. Academic staff in charge of admissions look for potential beyond the high grades that increasing numbers of candidates bring. They value success in extracurricular activities such as drama, sport and the Duke of Edinburgh's Award, along with more individual or unusual interests. Standing out from the crowd is a good thing; if you enjoy reading, which many people do, say which authors or books inspire you, and why. Again, ensure your account is based on lived experiences, not what you think the admissions tutor would want you to say. Your UCAS form also has your teacher's reference and your statement should be in line with their summary of your abilities and interests.

Highlight the experiences you've gained that are related to the syllabus you are applying for – clubs, lectures, visits, vlogs you have created, blogs you have written, work experience and wider reading around the subject. Practical work experience or volunteering in medical or caring settings should be included by those applying to study medicine – but don't just list what you've done, reflect on what these experiences taught you about working as a doctor and how you are suited to the training and profession. The same approach goes for other vocational degrees; explain how you see yourself using the qualification. Take advice from teachers and, if there is still time before you make your application, look for some subject-related activities that will help round out your statement. The admissions departments will understand the difficulties this year's candidates will have had in getting real-life work experience during the pandemic and will take it into consideration.

Mention the accomplishments which suggest you will turn out to be a productive member of the university and, eventually, a successful graduate. Leading activities outside your school or college are ideal, or other responsibilities you have taken on. Show the admissions tutors that you can take initiative and be self-disciplined, since higher education involves much more independent study than sixth-formers are used to.

Think hard about why you want to study your chosen subject – especially if it is one you have not taken at school or college – and align your interests and skills with the course. Showing commitment to the full course is important, so admissions officers are convinced you will get good results for its duration. Some applicants' five choices will cover more than one subject, and in this situation try to make more general comments about your academic strengths and enthusiasms and avoid focusing on just one of the courses.

If you are an international (EU and non-EU) student you should also include why you want to study in the UK, detail your English language skills, and any English courses or tests you've taken and why you want to be an international student, rather than study in your own country. Mature students can talk about any alternative entry requirements they have used – such as an Access course – that show the the skills and knowledge gained through experience.

Take advantage of the help offered by your school or college. Your teachers see personal statements every year and will have a feel for ones that have gone down well for former students. UCAS provides a checklist of themes to cover and websites such as **www.studential.com** and **www.thestudentroom.co.uk** provide tips as well. By this point in your academic career the perils of plagiarism are probably clear to you, but do not be fooled into thinking you can cut and paste from one of the personal statement help websites. UCAS and universities have software that spots plagiarism and have caught out plenty of applicants over the years.

It may be tempting to shoehorn in as much information as the space will allow but err on the side of reserve. Admissions officers will have piles of these to read and giving them a thoughtfully edited statement is likely to be looked upon kindly. Compose your statement on Word or similar and avoid kicking off with a dreary cliché. Equally, though, do not start with an overly florid introduction – the best personal statements get to the point quickly. Let someone you trust proofread your statement before you paste a copy into Apply and press send; a second pair of eyes is hugely beneficial to a piece of work like the personal statement.

References

Hand-in-hand with your personal statement goes the reference from your school, college or, in the case of mature students, someone who knows you well, but is not a friend or family member. Since 2014, even referees who are not your teachers have been encouraged to predict your grades, although they are allowed to opt out of this process. Whatever the source, the reference has to be independent – you are specifically forbidden to change any part of it if you send off your own application – but that does not mean you should not try to influence what it contains.

Most schools and colleges conduct informal interviews before compiling a reference, but it does no harm to draw up a list of the achievements that you would like to see included, and ensure your referee knows what subject you are applying for. Referees cannot know every detail of a candidate's interests and most welcome an aide-memoire.

The UCAS guidelines skirt around the candidate's right to see his or her reference, but it does exist. Schools' practices vary, but most now show the applicant the completed reference. Where this is not the case, the candidate can pay UCAS £10 for a copy, although at this stage it is obviously too late to influence the contents. Better, if you can, to see it before it goes off, in case there are factual inaccuracies that can be corrected.

UCAS tips on how to write your personal statement

Your personal statement should be unique, so there's no definite format for you to follow here – just take your time. Here are some guidelines for you to follow, but remember your personal statement needs to be 'personal'.

» Write in an enthusiastic, concise, and natural style – nothing too complex.

» Try to stand out, but be careful with humour, quotes, or anything unusual – just in case the admissions tutor doesn't have the same sense of humour as you.

» Structure your info to reflect the skills and qualities the unis and colleges value most – use the course descriptions to help you.

» Check the character and line limit – you have 4,000 characters and 47 lines. Some word processors get different values if they don't count tabs and paragraph spacing as individual characters.

» Proofread aloud, and get your teachers, advisers, and family to check. Then redraft it until you're happy with it, and the spelling, punctuation, and grammar are correct.

We recommend you write your personal statement first, then copy and paste it into your online application once you're happy with it. Make sure you save it regularly, as the site times out after 35 minutes of inactivity.

Timetable for applications for university admission in 2022

At the time of writing UCAS had not confirmed the exact dates for the application schedule. Please check the UCAS website for the most recent information.

2021

January onwards	Find out about courses and universities. Check schedule of open days.
February onwards	Attend open days.
early July	Registration starts for UCAS Apply.
mid September	UCAS starts receiving applications.
15 October	Final day for applications to Oxford and Cambridge, and for most courses in medicine, dentistry and veterinary science.

2022

15 January	Final day for all other applications from UK and EU students.
16 January–end June	New applications continue to be accepted by UCAS, but only considered by universities if the relevant courses have vacancies.
late February	Start of applications through UCAS Extra.
24 March	Final day for applications to art and design courses that specify this date.
end March	Universities should have sent decisions on all applications received by 15 January.
early May	Final time by which applicants have to decide on their choices if all decisions received by end March (exact date for each applicant will be confirmed by UCAS). **If you do not reply to UCAS, they will decline your offers.** UCAS must have received all decisions from universities if you applied by 15 January.
early June	Final time by which applicants have to decide on their choices if all decisions received by early May.
start of July	Any new application received from this time held until Clearing starts. End of applications through UCAS Extra.
early July	International Baccalaureate results published.
3 August	SQA results published. Scottish Clearing starts. (to be confirmed)
12 August	A-level results published. Full Clearing and Adjustment starts. (to be confirmed)
end August	Adjustment closes. Last time for you to meet any offer conditions, after which university might not accept you.
late October	End of period for adding Clearing choices and last point at which a university can accept you through Clearing.

Timing

The general deadline for applications through UCAS is 15 January, but even those received up to 30 June will be considered if the relevant courses still have vacancies. After that, you will be limited to Clearing, or an application for the following year. In theory – and usually in practice – all applications submitted by the January deadline are given equal consideration. But the best advice is to get your application in early: before Christmas, or earlier if possible. Applications are accepted from mid-September onwards, so the autumn half-term is a sensible target date for completing the process. Although no formal offers are made before the deadline, many admissions officers look through applications as they come in and may make a mental note of promising candidates. If your form arrives with the deadline looming, you may appear less organised than those who submitted in good time; and your application may be one of a large batch that receives a more cursory first reading than the early arrivals. Under UCAS rules, last-minute applicants should not be at a disadvantage, but why take the risk?

Next steps

Once your application has been processed by UCAS, you will receive an email confirming that it has been sent to your university choices and summarising what will happen next. The email will also confirm your Personal ID, which you can use to access 'Track', the online system that allows you to follow the progress of your application. Check all the details carefully: you have 14 days to contact UCAS to correct any errors. Universities can make direct contact with you through Track, including arranging interviews.

After that, it is just a matter of waiting for universities to make their decisions, which can take days, weeks or even months, depending on the university and the course. Some obviously see an advantage in being the first to make an offer – it is a memorable moment to be reassured that at least one of your chosen institutions wants you – and may send their response almost immediately. Others take much longer, perhaps because they have so many good applications to consider, or maybe because they are waiting to see which of their applicants withdraw when Oxford and Cambridge make their offers. Universities are asked to make all their decisions by the end of March, and most have done so long before that.

Interviews

Unless you are applying for a course in health or education that brings you into direct contact with the public, the chances are you will not have a selection interview. For prospective medics, vets, dentists or teachers, a face-to-face assessment of your suitability (social distancing measures allowing) will be crucial to your chances of success. Likewise, in the performing arts, the interview may be as important as your exam grades. Oxford and Cambridge still interview most applicants in all subjects, and a few of the top universities see a significant proportion. But the expansion of higher education has made it impractical to interview everyone, and many admissions experts are sceptical about interviews.

What has become more common, however, is the 'sales' interview, where the university is really selling itself to the candidate. There may still be testing questions, but the admissions staff have already made their minds up and are actually trying to persuade you to accept an offer. Indeed, you will probably be given a clear indication at the end of the interview that an offer is on its way. The technique seems to work, perhaps because you have invested time and nervous energy in a sometimes lengthy trip, as well as acquiring a more detailed impression of both the department and the university.

The difficulty can come in spotting which type of interview is which. The 'genuine' ones require lengthy preparation, revisiting your personal statement and reading beyond the exam syllabus. Impressions count for a lot, so dress smartly and make sure that you are on time. Have a question of your own ready, as well as being prepared to give answers.

While you would not want to appear ignorant at a 'sales' interview, lengthy preparation might be a waste of valuable time during a period of revision. Naturally, you should err on the side of caution, but if your predicted grades are well above the standard offer and the subject is not one that normally requires an interview, it is likely that the invitation is a sales pitch. It is still worth going, unless you have changed your mind about the application.

Offers

When your chosen universities respond to your application, there will be one of three answers:

» Unconditional Offer (U): This used to be a possibility only if you applied after satisfying the entrance requirements – usually if you were applying as a mature student, while on a gap year, after resitting exams or, in Scotland, after completing Highers. However, a number of universities competing for bright students now make unconditional offers to those who are predicted high grades – just how high will depend on the university. If you are fortunate (and able) enough to receive one, do not assume that grades are no longer important because they may be taken into consideration when you apply for jobs as a graduate. But see below.

» Conditional Offer (C): The vast majority of students will still receive conditional offers, where each university offers a place subject to you achieving set grades or points on the UCAS tariff.

» Rejection (R): You do not have the right qualifications or have lost out to stronger competition.

Unconditional offers have been the subject of considerable controversy over the past three years, following evidence from UCAS that applicants who received them were much more likely than others to miss their predicted grades. More than 20 universities making the highest proportions of unconditional offers were 'named and shamed' by the Education Secretary of the time, who argued that it was unethical to restrict such offers to those who made the university their first choice. Many of those on the list – and others – have now abandoned these kinds of offers. The practice was prohibited outright during the health pandemic until September 2021, but once the ban is lifted, unconditional offers are unlikely to disappear entirely, just yet.

One danger, from the student's point of view, is that an unconditional offer might tempt a candidate to lower his or her sights and accept a place that would not have been their first choice otherwise. As long as this is not the case, however, there is no reason to spurn such an offer if it comes, as long as you do not take your foot off the pedal in the run-up to exams.

If you have chosen wisely, you should have more than one offer to choose from, so you will be required to pick your favourite as your firm acceptance – known as UF if it was an unconditional offer and CF if it was conditional. Candidates with conditional offers can also accept a second offer, with lower grades, as an 'Insurance Choice' (CI). You must then decline any other offers that you have.

You do not have to make an Insurance Choice – indeed, you may decline all your offers if you have changed your mind about your career path or regret your course decisions. But most people prefer the security of a back-up route into higher education if their grades fall short. Some 35,440 took up their Insurance Choice in 2019 – a small increase on the previous year, and 15% of the total number admitted in that cycle. You must be sure that your firm acceptance is definitely your first choice because you will be allocated a place automatically if you meet the university's conditions. You cannot change your mind at this stage if you decide you prefer your Insurance Choice, because UCAS rules will not allow a switch.

The only way round those rules, unless your results are better than your highest offer (see Adjustment, below), is through direct contact with the universities concerned. Your firm acceptance institution has to be prepared to release you so that your new choice can award you a place in Clearing. Neither is under any obligation to do so but, in practice, it is rare for a university to insist that a student joins against his or her wishes. Admissions staff will do all they can to persuade you that your original choice was the right one – as it may well have been, if your research was thorough – but it will almost certainly be your decision in the end.

UCAS Extra

If things do go wrong and you receive five rejections, that need not be the end of your higher education ambitions. From the end of February until the end of June, you have another chance through UCAS Extra, a listing of courses that still have vacancies after the initial round of offers. Extra is sometimes dismissed (wrongly) as a repository of second-rate courses. In fact, even in the boom years for applications, most Russell Group universities still have courses listed in a wide variety of subjects.

You will be notified if you are eligible for Extra and can then select courses marked as available on the UCAS website. In order to assist students who choose different subjects after a full set of rejections in their original application, you will be able to submit a new personal statement for Extra. Applications are made, one at a time, through UCAS Track. If you do not receive an offer, or you choose to decline one, you can continue applying for other courses until you are successful. About half of those applying through Extra normally find a place. The numbers using Extra in 2019 declined for the third consecutive year, but it remains a valuable route for those who need it. Why wait for the uncertainty of Clearing if there are places available on a course that you want?

Results Day

Rule Number One on results day is to be at home, or at least in easy communication – this is not the day to rely on intermittent WiFi reception in a far-flung location, especially if there are complications. Not that you need to be at home to wait for the post or look for your name on a sixth-form noticeboard; Track has removed the agony of opening the envelope or scanning a results list. On the morning of A-level results day, the system informs those who have already won a place on their chosen course. You will not learn your grades until later, but at least your immediate future is clear.

The day is bound to be stressful, unless you are absolutely confident that you have achieved the required grades – more of a possibility in an era of modular courses with marks along the way.

If you get the grades stipulated in your conditional offer, the process should work smoothly and you can begin celebrating. Track will let you know as soon as your place is confirmed and the paperwork will arrive within a day or two. You can phone the university to make quite sure, but it should not be necessary, and you will be joining a long queue of people doing the same thing.

If the results are not what you hoped – and particularly if you just miss your grades – you need to be on the phone and taking advice from your school or college. In a year when results are better than expected, some universities will stick to the letter of their offers, perhaps refusing to accept your AAC grades when they had demanded ABB. Growing numbers will forgive a dropped grade to take a candidate who is regarded as promising, rather than go into Clearing to recruit an unknown quantity. Admissions staff may be persuadable – particularly if there are extenuating personal circumstances, or the dropped grade is in a subject that is not relevant to your chosen course. Try to get a teacher to support your case and be persistent if there is any prospect of flexibility. Showing commitment is a good thing.

If your results are lower than predicted, one option is to ask for papers to be re-marked, as growing numbers do each year. The school may ask for a whole batch to be re-marked, and you should ensure that your chosen universities know this if it may make the difference between whether or not you satisfy your offer. If your grades improve as a result, the university will review its decision, but if by then it has filled all its places, you may have to wait until next year to start.

If you took Scottish Highers, you will have had your results for more than a week by the time the A-level grades are published. If you missed your grades, there is no need to wait for A-levels before you begin approaching universities. Admissions staff at English universities may not wish to commit themselves before they see results from south of the border, but Scottish universities will be filling places immediately and all should be prepared to give you an idea of your prospects.

Adjustment

If your grades are better than those demanded by your first-choice university, there is an opportunity to trade up. The Adjustment period runs from when you receive your results until 31 August, and you can only use it for five 24-hour periods during that period, so there is no time to waste. First, go into the Track system and click on 'Register for Adjustment' and then contact your preferred institutions to find another place. If none is available, or you decide not to move, your initial offer will remain open. The number of students switching universities in this way has not increased as much as many observers expected, perhaps because Clearing has become much more flexible. Indeed, there was another big drop in 2019, but there were still nearly 600 successful candidates. The process has become an established part of the system and, without the previous restrictions on the number of students they could recruit, many leading universities see it as a good source of talented undergraduates. UCAS does not publish a breakdown of which universities take part, but it is known that many students successfully go back to institutions that had rejected them at the initial application stage. Even if you are eligible for Adjustment, you may decide to stick with the offer you have, but it is worth at least exploring your options.

Clearing

If results morning did not elicit a "Yay, I got in!" moment, put plan B into action and find a university place through Clearing. There will be plenty of options at a good range of universities. In 2019 over 73,000 students (more than one in seven successful applicants) found a place via this route. The process is also increasingly popular as a one-off route to a place, and nearly 20,000 candidates entered Clearing direct in 2019 without submitting an initial application. Contrary to popular belief Clearing does not open for the first time on A-level results day, it begins on 5 July, results day for the International Baccalaureate, and runs until 19 October this year. The busiest day, however, will be 24 August 2021, when this year's A-level students find out their grades. As long as you are not holding any offers and you have not withdrawn your application, you are eligible automatically. You will be sent a Clearing number via Track to quote to universities.

With recruitment restrictions lifted, universities that used to regard their absence from Clearing as a point of pride, are appearing in the Clearing vacancy lists, and candidates will see options at the coveted research-led institutions included. Certain courses have more availability than others though, and more universities are seeking to expand particularly in arts, social science and business subjects. Some subjects, such as medicine and dentistry, do not show up in Clearing as they are so oversubscribed. Only a handful of universities do not take part these days, including Oxford, Cambridge, Imperial, the LSE and St Andrews.

The most popular courses may fill up quickly, but many remain open up to and beyond the start of the academic year. And, at least at the start of the process, the range of courses with vacancies is much wider than in Extra. Most universities will list some courses, and most subjects will be available somewhere.

There are now two ways of entering Clearing: the traditional method of ringing universities that still have vacancies, or by signing up for the service in which up to five universities approach candidates with suitable grades for one of their courses. The latter, newer way of entering begins with an email from UCAS issuing a code word that universities will use when they make contact with applicants on Results Day or later. UCAS advises students to approach universities themselves in any case, but the new system may take some of the anxiety out of Clearing.

On the basis of making your own approaches, the first step is to trawl through the lists on the UCAS website, and elsewhere, before ringing the university offering the course that appeals most, and where you have a realistic chance of a place – do not waste time on courses where the standard offer is far above your grades. Universities have all hands on deck running Clearing hotlines and are adept at dealing with lots of calls in a short period, but even so you can spend a long time trying the phone while the most desirable places are beginning to disappear. If you can't get through, send an email setting out your grades and the course that interests you, but keep trying by phone, too. Schools and colleges open on Results day, and teachers should be willing to help with these calls, especially if you are in a panic. A good way of managing the calls is to let the teacher ring, get through to the university and then pass the phone to the applicant. At the end of calls do a round-up of next steps, as in the melee it is possible to misunderstand or forget things, such as requests for more information or follow-up forms to be filled out.

Wise students will not have waited for Results Day to draw up a list of possible Clearing targets. They will have had their list researched and ready to deploy, if the time comes, in advance. This way students can target the courses they know they want, without having to do so much last-minute research. Many universities publish lists of courses that are likely to be in Clearing on their websites from the start of August. Reconsider some of the courses you mulled over when making your original application, or others at your chosen universities that had lower entrance requirements. But beware of switching to another subject simply because you have the right grades – you still have to sustain your interest and be capable of succeeding over three or more years. Many of the students who drop out of degrees are those who chose the wrong course in a rush during Clearing.

In short, start your search immediately if you find yourself in Clearing, and act decisively, but do not panic. You can make as many approaches as you like, until you are accepted on the course of your choice. Remember that if you changed your personal statement for applications in Extra, this will be the one that goes to any universities that you approach in Clearing, so it may be difficult to return to the subjects in your original application.

Most of the available vacancies will appear in Clearing lists, but some of the universities towards the top of the league tables may have a limited number of openings that they choose not to advertise – either for reasons of status or because they do not want the administrative burden of fielding large numbers of calls to fill a handful of places. If there is a course that you find particularly attractive – especially if you have good grades and are applying late – it may be worth making a speculative call. Sometimes candidates holding offers drop grades and you may be on the spot at the right moment.

What are the alternatives?

If your results are lower than expected and there is nothing you want in Clearing, there are several things you can do. The first is to resit one or more subjects. The modular nature of most courses means that you will have a clear idea of what you need to do to get better grades. You can go back to school or college or try a 'crammer'. Although some colleges have a good success rate with re-takes, you have to be highly focused and realistic about the likely improvements. Some of the most competitive courses, such as medicine, may demand higher grades for a second application, so be sure you know the details before you commit yourself.

Other options are to get a job and study part-time, or to take a break from studying and return later in your career. You may have considered an apprenticeship before applying to university, but the number and variety are growing all the time, so it may be worth another look. The UCAS Progress service provides information on apprenticeship opportunities post-16 and has a search tool for higher and degree apprenticeship vacancies.

The part-time route can be arduous – many young people find a job enough to handle without the extra burden of academic work. But others find it just the combination they need for a fulfilling life. It all depends on your job, your social life and your commitment to the subject you will study. It may be that a relatively short break is all that you need to rekindle your enthusiasm for studying. Many universities now have a majority of mature students, so you need not be out of place if this is your chosen route.

Taking a gap year

The other popular option is to take a gap year. In most years, about 7% of applicants defer their entry until the following year while they travel, or do voluntary or paid work. A whole industry has grown up around tailor-made activities, many of them in Asia, Africa or Latin America. Some have been criticised for doing more for the organisers than the underprivileged communities that they purport to assist, but there are programmes that are useful and character-building, as well as safe. Most of the overseas programmes are not cheap but raising the money can be part of the experience.

Various organisations can help you find voluntary work. Some examples include vInspired **www.vinspired.com**, Lattitude Global Volunteering **www.lattitude.org.uk** and Plan my Gap Year **www.planmygapyear.co.uk**. Voluntary Service Overseas **www.vsointernational.org** works mainly with older volunteers but has an offshoot, run with five other volunteering organisations, International Citizen Service **www.volunteerics.org**, that places 18–25-year-olds around the world.

The alternative is to stay closer to home and make your contribution through organisations like Volunteering Matters **http://volunteeringmatters.org.uk** or to take a job that will make higher education more affordable when the time comes. Work placements can be casual or structured, such as the Year in Industry Scheme **www.etrust.org.uk**. Sponsorship is also available, mainly to those wishing to study science, engineering or business. Buyer beware: we cannot vouch for any of these and you need to be clear whether the aim is to make money or to plump up your CV. If it is the second, you may end up spending money, not saving it.

Many admissions staff are happy to facilitate gap years because they think it makes for more mature, rounded students than those who come straight from school. The longer-term benefits may also be an advantage in the graduate employment market. Both university admissions officers and employers look for evidence that candidates have more about them than academic ability. The experience you gain on a gap year can help you develop many of the attributes they are looking for, such as interpersonal, organisational and teamwork skills, leadership, creativity, experience of new cultures or work environments, and enterprise.

There are subjects – maths in particular – that discourage a break because it takes too long to pick up study skills where you left off. From the student's point of view, you should also bear in mind that a gap year postpones the moment at which you embark on a career. This may be important if your course is a long one, such as medicine or architecture.

If you are considering a gap year, it makes sense to apply for a deferred place, rather than waiting for your results before applying. The application form has a section for deferments. That allows you to sort out your immediate future before you start travelling or working and leaves you the option of changing your mind if circumstances change.

Useful websites

The essential website for making an application is, of course, that of UCAS:
www.ucas.com/undergraduate/applying-to-university
For applications to music conservatoires: **www.ucas.com/conservatoires**
For advice on your personal statement:
www.ucas.com/ucas/16-18-choices/search-and-apply/writing-ucas-progress-personal-statement

Gap years

For links to volunteering opportunities in the UK: **www.do-it.org**
For links to many gap year organisations: **www.yearoutgroup.org**
Also see above.

6 Where Students Come From

The impact of Covid

The drive to diversify university intakes received an unexpected boost from the Covid-19 pandemic, thanks to the way in which universities seized the initiative after the government's flawed handling of A-level outcomes in the summer of 2020. It is a boost that may well have a long-term impact on the way in which undergraduates are recruited and help towards the goal of widening participation in higher education.

From the moment the decision was taken to ditch A-level exams and their equivalents for the year, the regulator, the Office for Students (OfS), made a series of interventions to ensure that the disruption to university recruitment was minimised, that recruitment was fair and transparent and that the numbers recruited from widening participation backgrounds did not take a hit.

But it was the manifest unfairness of the Ofqual A-level algorithm – under which 40% of outcomes were downgraded from teachers' predictions – that prompted the most significant reaction. Having first backed the algorithm, the government ditched it and decided to go with Centre Assessment Grades (CAGs) – essentially teachers' predictions – instead, but only four days after Ofqual-adjusted grades had been published and shared with universities.

Universities took drastic action to ensure that those from disadvantaged backgrounds did not miss out disproportionately on places, as seemed likely. Colleges at Oxford, no less, went public after deciding to admit all those to whom offers had been made, effectively bypassing A-levels. Across the university, 350 students were admitted over and above its planned figure with a further 150 deferring entry to 2021.

Once the dust settled, it emerged that Oxford had admitted more students educated in the state sector than ever before – 68%, up from 60.6% in the 2019 admissions cycle and 55% five years ago. Oxford's lead in calling out the unfairness of the algorithm was instrumental in shoving the government towards CAGs (and also in the decision to make Oxford *The Times* and *The Sunday Times* University of the Year). The university has committed to recruiting 25% of its undergraduates from under-represented backgrounds by 2023.

"We are always going to reflect the deep socioeconomic, racial and regional inequalities in society and, alone, we can't fix that," said Prof Louise Richardson, Oxford's vice-chancellor.

"The real tragedy is how few really smart kids from deprived backgrounds are in the position to compete for the highly selective universities."

As the effects of the pandemic rumble on into the 2021 admissions cycle, the OfS has continued to flag its concern that the unevenness of the disruption to children's education in 2020–21 should be adequately captured in university admissions procedures, so that children whose grades are most at risk are not shut out of the most selective universities.

Chris Millward, the director of fair access and participation, said: "We expect admissions decisions to be fair, which means universities considering applicants on their own merits and identifying potential to succeed on a course, recognising the context in which their qualifications have been gained. This is not about dumbing down, it's about levelling up."

Change on the horizon

The OfS launched a full-blown review of the university admissions process in 2019, but this was suspended soon after the pandemic took hold. However, a parallel fair admissions review by Universities UK (UUK), the sector's lobbying group, recommended wholesale changes to the admissions process when it reported in November 2020. The key proposal was a move to post-qualifications admissions (PQA) from the 2023-24 academic year. This would see offers made to school-leavers after they have got their final year examination results. It would reduce reliance on predicted grades in the offer-making process and could significantly accelerate widening participation given that grades for children from disadvantaged backgrounds are much more often under-predicted.

The UUK report also called for greater transparency, consistency and use of standard indicators to support contextual offer-making. This sees lower offers – typically 2 A-level grades – made to students from disadvantaged backgrounds or those attending schools with a poor record of progression to higher education. Contextual offers are becoming commonplace each year, even in the more highly selective universities, with league table compilers being asked to consider dropping average tariff points from academic rankings in order to encourage further acceleration of this initiative.

Ending so-called "conditional unconditional" offers was a further key recommendation by UUK to help ensure fair admissions for all. These unconditional offers, which take effect only when the applicant makes the offering university their firm choice, had become hugely popular at some institutions in the past five years. Defenders of the practice argued it gave certainty to both universities and students, while taking the pressure off examinations; opponents said the practice was a crude attempt to put "bums on seats" in universities and demotivated students to achieve well in their A-levels. The OfS suspended the use of "conditional unconditional" offers in July 2020 through to September 2021 because of their destabilising effect on the student recruitment market at a time of increased uncertainty due to the pandemic. It now seems a good bet that they will never return.

The debate over what to do about inequalities in recruitment will run for some years yet, but after years of slow progress while spending millions of pounds in the process, significant change is afoot with the UUK proposals in play. Words are being backed up by actions. While universities cannot be expected to eradicate all the injustices embedded in society, nor will they be allowed to simply reflect them in future.

The tables

So why produce social inclusion tables? As well as providing a benchmark by which to measure change going forward, the key reason is that today's applicants want to know about the composition of the student body they will be joining – in the same way that they are interested in where their university ranks on green issues, through assessments such as that provided by People and Planet.

Our third social inclusion table shows why so much attention is being focused on the fairness or otherwise of the present admissions process. Broadly speaking, the universities at the top of our academic ranking – those with the highest entry standards, the best job prospects and most competition for places – find themselves at the bottom of our social inclusion ranking. They recruit the bulk of their students from a much narrower cross-section of British society than universities lower down our academic ranking.

The purpose of the table is not to point the finger. It is unfair to expect universities to magically overcome, through their admissions choices, the inequalities built into the education system from nursery provision upwards and present in society more widely. However, the table does accurately reflect the reality on campus, identifying those institutions with fewer students educated in comprehensives or those where BAME students will find themselves among a very small minority.

We have two social inclusion rankings; one for England and Wales, the other for Scotland which stands alone on account of its different measure of social deprivation – the Scottish Index of Multiple Deprivation (SIMD). This captures better the position in the 15 Scottish universities than the POLAR4 (Participation Of Local Areas) measure used for England and Wales, but is not directly comparable. The two universities in Northern Ireland, Queen's Belfast and Ulster, are excluded from the ranking owing to differences in their school system with a high proportion of selective grammar schools, making comparisons with the rest of the UK on social mix invalid via the methodology adopted in this guide.

We have once again resisted the suggestion to include some or all the measures contained within the social inclusion tables as part of our wider academic ranking. There is good reason for this: a university with a poor record for social inclusion may still have an excellent record for teaching and research. It might be a very good university with an outstanding global and national reputation, but with a socially-narrow recruitment profile. By using the two multi-indicator, multi-institution tables that we publish together (alongside the relevant subject table) prospective students can identify the universities which are the best fit for them academically and where they might feel most at home socially or at ease politically. The importance of that last factor will vary from applicant to applicant.

Based on the most recent data available at the time of compilation, *The Times* and *The Sunday Times* social inclusion ranking for England and Wales uses eight equally-weighted indicators covering:

» recruitment from non-selective state schools

» recruitment from all ethnic minorities

» a measurement of the black attainment gap

» recruitment from deprived areas (using POLAR4)

» a measurement of the deprived areas dropout gap

» recruitment of first generation students

» recruitment of mature students (those 21 or older on admission)

» recruitment of disabled students

For Scottish institutions, there is no measure of the deprived areas dropout gap and the deprived areas measure is based on SIMD, rather than POLAR4, as outlined above.

With the exception of the admissions data for non-selective state schools, all the other indicators are in the public domain. This social inclusion ranking is unique in combining these strands of data to build an overall picture of the social mix at each institution, and to measure university performance in the two key areas of black attainment and whether more students from the most deprived areas fail to complete their courses than those recruited from more advantaged districts.

The table is presented in a format that displays the raw data in all instances. No adjustment is made for university location, so a university with a strong, local recruitment pattern in an area of low ethnic minority population is unlikely do well on the two measures covering the ethnicity of the intake. This was most notably the case with Glyndŵr, once again the most socially inclusive university in the UK according to our ranking, but which had just 5.1% of its 2019 entrants drawn from ethnic minorities.

However, by combining the eight indicators using a common statistical technique known as z-scoring, we have ensured no single indicator has a disproportionate effect on the overall total for each university. The totals for each university were transformed to a scale with 1,000 for the top score and the performance of all universities measured relative to that of the university ranked No 1.

Just as with our academic ranking, the organisations providing the raw data for the table are not involved in the process of aggregation and are not responsible for any conclusion or inferences we have made. Every care has been taken to ensure the accuracy of the table and accompanying analysis, but no responsibility can be taken for errors or omissions.

The indicators used and what can be learned from them are outlined below.

Non-selective state school admissions

For many years, the Higher Education Statistics Agency (HESA) has published as part of its annual Performance Indicators, the proportion of students admitted to universities from all state schools. Among the entrants included in this proportion are those attending the 164 state grammars in England and the voluntary grammars in Northern Ireland. However, state school admissions to all universities stripped of the academically-selective grammar school sector are not published elsewhere. Removing the grammar school sector from the equation reveals the proportion of students admitted to each university in 2018–19 from the largely non-selective state secondary schools (comprehensives and most academies) attended by around 80% of university applicants.

At six universities – one more than last year – fewer than half the students admitted came from comprehensives and academies: Oxford (42.5%), Cambridge (43.0%), Imperial College London (43.4%), Durham (48.7%), the London School of Economics (49.0%) and University College London (49.4%). As it steps up its work to meet the target of recruiting 25% of undergraduates from previously under-represented groups by 2023, Oxford has seen those educated in comprehensives move ahead of those educated privately (now down to a still significant 39.4%) in the past year, while at Imperial, Cambridge and the LSE more than one in five students are recruited from selective grammars.

The majority of universities (94 in all, up one on last year) admit more than 80% of their students from non-selective state schools, and just 20 take less than 70% of their intake from this demographic, 15 of these being members of the Russell Group of highly-selective, research-led universities.

Ethnic minority admissions

Data gathered from the 2019 admissions cycle by UCAS shows the proportion of entrants to each university drawn from black, Asian, mixed and other ethnic minorities.

Eight London universities feature in the top 10 – all with at least 69% of their students drawn from ethnic minorities – ranking behind Aston which recruited 82.4% of its students from ethnic minorities in 2019. Bradford (78.3%), our University of the Year for Social Inclusion in 2019, is the only other non-London university in the top 10. The most ethnically diverse London universities are City, University of London (79.3%), Brunel, London (74.4%), Middlesex (73.2%), Queen Mary (70.5%), London Metropolitan (70.2%), London South Bank (70.1%), Westminster (69.8%) and East London (69.4%). Queen Mary, London is by some distance the most ethnically diverse of the Russell Group student communities.

The least ethnically diverse university is the Royal Agricultural University, in Cirencester, Gloucestershire, where 2.9% of the intake was drawn from ethnic minorities in 2019, closely followed by Harper Adams, in rural Shropshire and also specialising in predominantly land-based courses, and Bishop Grosseteste, in Lincoln, with 3%. Wrexham Glyndŵr (5.1%) is fourth bottom for ethnic diversity despite topping the overall social inclusion ranking for England and Wales for the third successive year.

Black attainment gap

One of the two university output measures in the social inclusion ranking, the data shows the percentage point difference between the proportion of black ethnic minority students and white students who achieved first class or upper second class degrees in 2019 in England, and 2018 in Scotland and Wales. This is one of the key indicators in identifying underperformance by ethnic minorities while at university, with black ethnic minority students traditionally achieving the smallest proportion of top class degrees. Ironically, the very small numbers of black ethnic students involved in the calculations make this statistic highly volatile. So, while the University of Edinburgh actually shows a higher proportion of firsts and 2:1s among its black graduates (94.7%) compared to white graduates (90.8%), this data is derived from just 19 black graduates with degree classifications, 18 of whom got a first or 2:1.

The universities with the widest negative percentage point gap for black attainment (showing low attainment by black students) were Stirling (-51.9%), Glasgow Caledonian (-46.8%), West of Scotland (-46.2%), Cardiff Metropolitan (-42.9%) and Canterbury Christ (-42.3%). Those where black students performed the best in relation to their white counterparts were Edinburgh (+4%, see caveat, above), St George's, London (-4%), Queen Mary, London (-5%), Oxford (-5.6%), LSE (-6%) and Hull (-6.5%), four of the top five places taken by Russell Group institutions, so often lagging in other areas of the social inclusion ranking.

Deprived areas

This data is drawn from the 2019 UCAS admissions cycle and looks at the home postcode of all university recruits, putting them into one of five pots, according to the level of participation in higher education. For England and Wales, this indicator records the proportion of students recruited from Quintile 1 (of POLAR4 data) – the 20% of areas that have the lowest participation rates in higher education. In Scotland, this indicator records the proportion of students recruited from postcodes which fall into the bottom 20% with the highest levels of deprivation measured by the Scottish Index of Multiple Deprivation (SIMD20)

Like all indicators, this one has limitations, chief among which is that London has relatively high participation rates in higher education, so very few London-based university entrants fall into Quintile 1, meaning that London universities score relatively poorly across the board on this measure, even if they have a socially diverse intake of students.

Teesside (29.9%) and Staffordshire (28.4%) record the highest proportions of students recruited from Quintile 1. Both institutions recruit heavily within their immediate regions, notably Teesside in the North-east, the English region with the lowest participation rate in higher education. Sunderland (26.9%), this year's University of the Year for Social Inclusion, is ranked third on this measure. City University London (2.3%), followed by the Royal Agricultural University (3%) and Queen Mary, London (3.6%) have the lowest rates of recruitment from Quintile 1.

In Scotland, the highest rates of recruitment of students falling into SIMD20 are to be found at West of Scotland (28.2%) and Glasgow Caledonian (22.6%), while the two Aberdeen universities, Aberdeen (4.4%) and Robert Gordon (6.7%) have the lowest rates.

Deprived areas dropout gap

This indicator is used in the England and Wales social inclusion ranking only. Drawing upon the same POLAR4 data as above, it measures student outcomes from each of the five social quintiles. The proportion of students dropping out who were recruited from Quintile 1 is compared to the proportion dropping out who were recruited from Quintiles 2, 3, 4 and 5. A negative score in this section of the ranking indicates a higher proportion of students is dropping out from Quintile 1 than those recruited from more advantaged areas. Already under-represented in the student population overall, this measure identifies those universities where those who do get in are more likely to fail to see their courses through.

The universities where a bigger proportion of students from the most deprived areas fail to complete their courses, compared with the rest of the student population are, Bishop Grosseteste (-8%), York (-6.6%), Bucks New (-5.9%), Worcester (-5.7%) and Falmouth (-5.2%). The universities performing most strongly here, where a smaller proportion of students from the most deprived areas drop out, compared with the rest of the student population, are Westminster (+5%), Bedfordshire and Arts London (both +4.7%) and Bolton and the University for the Creative Arts (both +4%).

First generation students

This measure records the proportion of students recruited from homes where neither parent attended university. This indicator is considered one of the most informative in assessing the overall inclusiveness of university recruitment strategies. Once again, performance varies considerably from those recruiting 60% or more first generation students – Newman (75.5%), Bradford (66.8%), Bishop Grosseteste (64.6%), Wolverhampton (63.4%), Bedfordshire (62.5%), Leeds Trinity (60.6%) and Sunderland (60.1%) – to those where fewer than 25% of students come from homes where parents did not go to university – Oxford (14%), Cambridge (14.7%), St Andrews (18%), Edinburgh (21.5%), Bristol (21.8%), Imperial (22.3%) and Durham (23.2%).

Mature students

Mature students are returners to education and often win places with "life" qualifications, rather than A-levels. This makes the group more diverse than the young entrants, who come mostly straight from school or via a gap year. The number of mature students (those aged 21 or over) on admission is expressed as a percentage of the overall number of entrants recorded by HESA in 2018–19 at each institution.

The age of the student population can have a major impact on the social scene on campus. Older students, particularly those with partners (and even children) are less likely to be found clubbing or propping up the bar late into the evening. Universities with a very small proportion of mature undergraduates – the LSE (1.8%), Loughborough (2.3%), Oxford (2.4%), Bath (2.5%)

and Birmingham (4.1%) – are likely to have a livelier campus social life than Suffolk (74.7% mature admissions) Wrexham Glyndŵr (70.8%), Bedfordshire (70.7%), Sunderland (65.5%) and London Metropolitan (63%).

Disabled students

This indicator measures the proportion of all students in higher education in receipt of Disability Support Allowance (DSA). It is part of the bigger HESA dataset on widening participation, published in February 2020 and is based on data from the 2018–19 academic year.

As with the other indicators, there is a significant difference between the universities at the top – Wrexham Glyndŵr where HESA records 21.5% of students being in receipt of DSA, Harper Adams (17.7%) and Trinity St David (17.2%) – and those at the bottom – London Metropolitan (0.2%), West of Scotland (1.5%) and Glasgow Caledonian (2.4%).

The overall picture

It is not possible to appear near the top of the social inclusion rankings if an institution is only achieving well on one or two of our eight measures. Success in the table comes from broadly-based achievement in recruiting from areas of society least represented in higher education, and then seeing those students complete their degrees and achieve well. Equally, a university that appears near the bottom is not just falling short in one or two regards; it reflects a pattern of recruitment – or poor performance – affecting swathes of society.

A different set of metrics looking at the same subject might produce a very different-looking table, which is why it is necessary to be clear about what is being measured here. Based on the measures we have chosen, the top three in the academic rankings – Cambridge, Oxford and St Andrews – appear at the bottom (or third bottom in England and Wales in Oxford's case) of our social inclusion rankings. Wrexham Glyndŵr, in the bottom 10 in the academic ranking, is top for social inclusion. Seventeen of the bottom 20 universities for social inclusion in England and Wales (and two of the bottom three in Scotland) are highly selective Russell Group universities.

Used in conjunction, our academic and social inclusion rankings provide an intriguing insight to likely academic and professional success, the quality of the student experience, and the mix of students likely to be found in lecture theatres, after-hours clubs and bars. But whatever the student recruitment profile of the university you are considering, don't rule it out on that basis. If applicants from non-traditional backgrounds don't apply to universities – all of which are now pledging to broaden their intakes – then it will only make it easier for the status quo to prevail.

Alastair McCall

Social Inclusion Ranking for England and Wales

Rank	Last year's rank	Institution	State educated (non-grammar) (%)	Ethnic (%)	Black attainment gap (%)	Deprived areas (%)	Deprived areas dropout gap (%)	First generation students (%)	Disabled (%)	Mature (%)	Total
1	1	Wrexham Glyndŵr	97.4	5.1	-25.5*	22.7	n/a	59.2	21.5	70.8	1,000
2	12	Bolton	97.9	40.0	-18.0	20.6	4.0	56.9	11.6	53.6	960
3	13	Newman	97.7	48.4	-19.0	21.3	0.0	75.5	10.3	34.9	916
4	11	Bedfordshire	98.1	63.9	-23.0	9.9	4.7	62.5	4.7	70.7	899
5	3	Bradford	93.0	78.3	-9.0	11.7	0.4	66.8	9.6	26.2	896
6	8	Plymouth Marjon	96.2	5.8	n/a	20.6	-1.0	59.9	14.8	38.7	849

7	7 Wolverhampton	97.2	56.9	-21.6	20.5	-1.8	63.4	7.9	49.3	844
8	10 Teesside	98.9	13.2	-14.3	29.9	-2.8	56.8	10.5	44.1	843
9	23 Anglia Ruskin	92.4	37.2	-10.9	15.5	1.3	54.6	5.5	61.7	836
10	9 London South Bank	95.5	70.1	-21.0	5.5	1.6	52.3	10.0	46.8	811
11	4 Sunderland	98.2	31.0	-18.8	26.9	-4.5	60.1	5.8	65.6	808
12	5 East London	97.4	69.4	-24.0	7.0	1.8	54.6	6.9	49.5	789
13	33 Staffordshire	97.0	19.6	-30.4	28.4	-1.6	57.8	11.1	35.3	771
14	37 Greenwich	93.0	59.7	-17.5	7.7	3.0	56.4	5.2	33.7	765
15	18 Leeds Trinity	96.1	35.9	n/a	19.2	-1.0	60.6	6.9	26.3	761
16	25 Kingston	94.5	64.7	-14.0	6.7	0.7	54.4	7.3	27.6	757
=17	21 Derby	96.4	24.0	-26.1	24.4	-1.8	52.3	10.2	37.5	746
=17	24 Wales Trinity Saint David	97.8	8.4	-34.4*	15.4	n/a	40.5	17.2	61.0	746
19	30 Birmingham City	96.9	56.7	-15.1	14.0	-0.7	55.7	5.6	23.6	740
20	22 Middlesex	97.1	73.2	-18.0	5.2	0.0	57.3	5.7	30.5	736
21	2 Bishop Grosseteste	95.5	3.0	n/a	23.9	-8.0	64.6	14.1	35.5	735
22	16 West London	95.3	68.1	-20.0	10.1	-5.0	52.5	7.4	58.2	727
23	43 Westminster	93.5	69.8	-25.0	4.1	5.0	55.3	5.2	21.2	726
24	15 Huddersfield	95.0	42.9	-15.0	16.0	-2.9	56.2	9.1	19.8	722
25	14 Suffolk	96.7	12.2	-29.0	18.9	-3.0	58.9	6.4	74.7	719
26	59 Arts London	91.8	31.7	-24.2	7.2	4.7	39.1	13.2	18.5	705
27	29 Goldsmiths, London	88.9	51.1	-18.0	5.0	3.0	45.6	9.3	21.3	703
=28	54 Liverpool Hope	88.4	14.1	n/a	24.0	-1.0	51.2	9.2	18.3	699
=28	6 London Metropolitan	96.8	70.2	-25.0	6.2	1.0	50.2	0.2	63.0	699
30	34 Hull	92.1	10.5	-6.5	24.1	-4.0	48.0	6.9	28.8	694
31	65 Roehampton	95.5	64.4	-26.0	4.7	-0.6	51.4	5.3	53.3	689
32	17 Central Lancashire	95.9	31.5	-26.6	14.8	-0.7	51.2	7.2	38.2	676
33	36 South Wales	95.6	10.9	-19.5*	21.8	n/a	43.3	7.2	33.2	673
34	19 Bucks New	94.2	44.9	-8.2	10.9	-5.9	48.1	2.9	62.5	671
35	40 Northampton	96.3	43.4	-20.6	14.1	-2.8	50.8	6.1	35.8	670
36	77 Gloucestershire	92.8	11.5	-27.1	15.1	1.8	47.6	10.3	24.3	665
37	27 Brunel London	90.4	74.4	-19.0	3.9	0.9	51.1	6.7	9.1	664
=38	28 Aston	84.6	82.4	-16.0	9.9	-0.5	52.3	4.7	4.9	661
=38	39 Creative Arts	93.2	21.2	-33.0	10.5	4.0	50.0	10.8	17.3	661
=40	47 Chichester	93.8	7.8	n/a	17.9	-2.0	49.6	10.1	21.6	657
=40	20 De Montfort	94.9	53.5	-25.1	14.8	-2.4	49.7	9.3	13.5	657
42	41 Edge Hill	96.6	8.0	-13.0	18.0	-3.1	55.3	6.2	24.9	656
43	50 Norwich Arts	95.7	10.4	n/a	18.0	-3.0	46.6	12.6	13.3	652
44	56 Sheffield Hallam	94.0	22.1	-25.8	20.7	-1.4	51.6	7.9	19.0	649
45	35 St Mary's, Twickenham	93.0	34.4	-13.0	5.7	-3.0	48.9	10.6	23.2	648
46	51 Queen Mary, London	80.4	70.5	-5.0	3.6	-2.0	47.8	6.5	9.1	636
47	31 City, London	87.0	79.3	-20.0	2.3	0.1	58.4	3.8	12.3	634
=48	45 Chester	93.4	10.0	-26.0	18.2	-1.5	54.3	7.5	26.9	631
=48	93 Soas, London	70.5	69.3	-13.0	4.5	n/a	42.8	9.0	23.6	631
50	78 Leeds Arts	94.2	11.0	n/a	15.4	n/a	43.0	12.4	6.4	627
51	26 Cumbria	94.9	13.5	-29.0	17.5	-5.0	54.8	8.6	47.3	626
52	46 Coventry	91.7	67.8	-20.7	11.8	-2.0	47.2	4.0	19.0	623
53	67 York St John	94.2	7.0	n/a	18.6	-0.9	46.7	7.6	12.2	611
54	60 Solent, Southampton	96.1	18.9	-26.4	17.1	-0.3	49.1	5.4	22.1	610

Social Inclusion Ranking for England and Wales cont

Rank	Last year's rank	Institution	State educated (non-grammar) (%)	Ethnic (%)	Black attainment gap (%)	Deprived areas (%)	Deprived areas dropout gap (%)	First generation students (%)	Disabled (%)	Mature (%)	Total
55	75	St George's, London	63.6	64.8	-4.0	5.3	n/a	35.4	6.8	28.6	609
56	44	Keele	86.7	34.8	-22.2	20.0	-2.1	43.6	7.1	15.2	607
=57	48	Bangor	91.0	8.8	-19.9*	12.2	n/a	41.0	10.2	28.0	605
=57	57	Canterbury Christ Church	92.2	28.6	-42.3	20.3	-2.4	59.1	6.6	35.9	605
=59	80	Northumbria	89.6	11.1	-18.5	18.1	-2.5	51.5	6.4	19.7	603
=59	42	Winchester	92.2	12.9	-31.9	14.4	-1.4	49.8	13.1	13.1	603
61	63	Lincoln	92.4	10.7	-23.7	18.6	-0.9	52.3	6.7	10.6	599
=62	52	Hertfordshire	95.6	58.7	-26.4	6.2	-1.0	49.5	4.9	22.3	598
=62	49	Portsmouth	91.0	28.5	-22.2	15.8	-3.2	49.2	8.4	14.0	598
64	72	Ravensbourne ,London	92.9	44.2	-18.0	6.2	-2.0	45.1	8.3	13.9	597
65	58	Bath Spa	90.1	9.2	-23.6	13.8	-1.4	43.3	11.8	13.8	591
=66	68	Brighton	88.7	23.0	-30.2	13.4	-1.6	46.9	10.0	22.6	584
=66	38	Salford	96.4	32.8	-27.2	15.7	-3.6	45.9	6.6	27.0	584
68	74	West of England	90.4	19.3	-26.6	14.9	-2.1	43.1	9.3	24.0	582
69	55	Plymouth	88.0	13.0	-25.6	15.3	-2.7	45.2	9.2	28.3	578
=70	61	Liverpool John Moores	89.0	12.8	-22.0	19.8	-2.8	54.2	4.9	16.7	577
=70	53	Manchester Metropolitan	94.1	37.3	-25.2	14.3	-2.0	51.2	4.4	14.3	577
=72	66	Bournemouth	88.8	17.0	-21.7	12.6	-2.1	48.4	8.1	17.7	574
=72	87	Essex	90.8	44.6	-21.3	12.3	-1.8	46.4	3.8	17.6	574
74		Hartpury	90.0	6.4	n/a	11.7	-4.0	48.8	11.0	21.5	571
75	79	King's College London	65.1	58.5	-11.2	3.7	0.5	36.4	5.9	21.8	565
76	81	East Anglia	79.1	22.2	-9.0	11.8	-1.8	39.5	6.9	12.8	563
77	62	Leicester	80.1	51.2	-19.1	9.7	0.1	39.5	5.4	9.4	560
78	64	Arts Bournemouth	94.7	11.4	n/a	12.8	-2.0	40.0	9.4	12.3	559
79	32	Worcester	95.1	13.7	-35.9	15.6	-5.7	51.1	10.5	36.4	555
80	71	Royal Holloway	74.8	43.2	-18.3	5.3	2.5	39.5	6.6	5.5	553
81	88	Harper Adams	79.3	3.0	n/a	4.7	n/a	37.5	17.7	13.6	549
82	70	Kent	90.9	39.1	-25.5	10.2	-1.4	46.4	6.1	8.2	544
83	83	Aberystwyth	90.3	7.7	-28.4*	13.8	n/a	39.9	11.3	13.3	536
84	95	Leeds Beckett	91.2	22.7	-15.0	15.6	-4.5	39.1	5.3	13.3	526
85	92	Sheffield	77.4	20.9	-11.0	9.4	-2.1	33.1	8.9	11.3	525
86	86	Cardiff Metropolitan	93.3	15.4	-42.9*	16.2	n/a	49.6	8.7	22.7	524
87	84	Sussex	78.7	25.0	-19.9	7.3	-2.0	41.4	9.4	9.7	512
=88	82	Surrey	77.9	40.7	-24.4	7.4	0.4	42.3	5.1	10.9	509
=88	89	Swansea	90.5	18.2	-17.1*	10.7	n/a	37.2	4.6	18.1	509
90	96	Loughborough	68.3	26.1	-9.8	5.7	-1.1	33.8	8.6	2.3	488
91	76	Nottingham Trent	88.2	25.5	-25.9	13.7	-4.7	43.8	6.7	10.4	481
92	98	Reading	74.8	32.5	-19.7	6.4	-1.1	36.1	7.2	7.2	474
93	91	Lancaster	78.5	17.9	-19.6	7.4	-0.4	37.0	7.0	4.2	470
94	85	Manchester	73.7	32.1	-16.6	7.3	-2.7	33.8	7.6	9.1	467
95	90	Oxford Brookes	62.9	18.2	-15.6	6.5	-3.5	39.2	9.6	17.8	463

Rank	Last year's rank	Institution									
96	106	Buckingham	76.4	43.5	-37.0	7.5	n/a	36.4	5.4	41.9	453
97	73	Falmouth	88.3	6.1	n/a	8.1	-5.2	34.5	10.3	16.6	438
98	69	Liverpool	75.4	17.2	-26.5	9.0	-0.9	41.7	5.5	8.8	436
99	94	Southampton	72.5	25.0	-20.9	7.9	-1.6	35.5	5.7	9.3	434
=100	100	Birmingham	65.0	32.6	-18.1	6.0	-0.1	28.9	5.1	4.1	412
=100	102	Royal Agricultural	57.8	2.9	n/a	3.0	n/a	36.2	12.8	26.7	412
102	97	Warwick	59.6	38.3	-14.1	4.9	-2.9	31.5	5.4	9.9	401
=103	107	Leeds	69.1	21.0	-24.2	8.1	-0.9	33.6	5.4	7.2	399
=103	104	London School of Economics	49.0	56.0	-6.0	5.1	n/a	29.5	3.8	1.8	399
105	101	Cardiff	75.7	17.1	-20.6*	9.1	n/a	31.7	5.0	11.0	395
106	112	Bath	56.9	19.7	-6.6	4.7	-1.9	25.1	5.6	2.5	376
107	105	Newcastle	64.7	14.0	-11.7	8.2	-4.0	33.7	4.4	6.5	374
108	99	Nottingham	64.8	29.1	-20.0	6.8	-2.5	30.9	4.7	7.4	371
109	103	York	69.9	13.5	-7.7	7.5	-6.6	30.3	5.7	7.2	365
110	108	University College London	49.4	50.9	-8.9	3.7	n/a	26.3	3.8	6.8	364
111	111	Exeter	52.8	11.3	-16.2	6.0	-1.6	26.9	7.5	5.9	352
112	114	Imperial College London	43.4	56.9	-7.0	4.1	n/a	22.3	2.7	7.3	340
113	110	Bristol	55.2	17.4	-12.9	5.4	-2.3	21.8	5.6	5.2	328
114	113	Oxford	42.5	22.0	-5.6	3.7	n/a	14.0	7.6	2.4	293
115	109	Durham	48.7	11.7	-14.0	5.4	-3.8	23.2	5.2	4.3	269
116	115	Cambridge	43.0	27.2	-13.5	4.2	n/a	14.7	5.2	4.3	238

* last year's data

Social Inclusion Ranking for Scotland

Rank	Last year's rank	Institution	State educated (non-grammar) (%)	Ethnic (%)	Black attainment gap (%)	Deprived areas (%)	First generation students (%)	Disabled (%)	Mature (%)	Total
1	3	Abertay	96.7	7.5	n/a	15.1	47.1	7.8	37.3	1,000
2	1	West of Scotland	98.7	8.3	-46.2	28.2	47.1	1.5	48.5	913
3	2	Queen Margaret, Edinburgh	95.7	5.8	n/a	11.7	38.7	9.2	38.0	896
4	4	Glasgow Caledonian	96.2	12.4	-46.8	22.6	44.5	2.4	39.7	886
5	8	Heriot-Watt	80.4	16.8	-10.0	10.9	31.6	5.5	23.2	823
6	6	Dundee	83.5	9.7	-6.5	16.2	39.5	3.6	24.6	776
7	7	Edinburgh Napier	93.7	8.8	-30.8	12.4	39.2	5.2	34.5	775
8	9	Robert Gordon	94.8	11.2	-16.9	6.7	34.6	5.0	32.6	766
9	5	Highlands and Islands	98.8	3.7	n/a	10.0	44.7	2.7	54.1	745
10	10	Strathclyde	90.1	11.0	-35.9	17.4	36.9	3.1	13.8	662
11	11	Stirling	87.7	6.0	-51.9	14.4	37.6	6.4*	24.9	622
12	12	Aberdeen	81.4	13.3	-16.5	4.4	29.6	4.9	15.7	601
13	13	Edinburgh	58.4	11.3	4.0	10.8	21.5	5.3	6.3	499
14	14	Glasgow	79.8	10.4	-33.0	13.3	26.2	3.1	15.4	494
15	15	St Andrews	60.6	12.3	n/a	10.6	18.0	5.4	8.1	356

* last year's data

7 Financing Your Studies

The need for enough money to live on at university and the likelihood that for the majority of students, some debt will be involved, remain constants in higher education – whatever changes in fees may be dictated by government policies and the costs of the coronavirus before the start of term in autumn 2022.

Most students take out both tuition fee and maintenance loans to cover the cost of studying and living. These are technically two types of funding, but the total amount borrowed is known as their Student Loan. Try not to focus on the scaremongering headlines you may have noticed, flagging eyewatering sums of money students owe upon graduation. Yes, there is going to be a debt and it is likely to be considerable, but (and this is a big 'but') – student loans debts are not quite like other sorts of commercial borrowing – such as on credit cards or via a mortgage. Some commentators argue they work out more like a graduate tax. Financing studies is something that needs an organised approach but it should not fill people with terror.

Each UK country has its own student finance system. The earlier sections of this chapter relate to the loans and costs incurred by students from England, while the broader content relates to students across the UK. The facts and figures for those from Northern Ireland, Wales and Scotland are detailed separately later in the chapter.

Tuition fee loans
Full-time students can borrow up to the full amount of £9,250 needed to cover tuition fees wherever they study in the UK. Those studying an accelerated (two-year) degree course could get up to £11,100. This loan is not dependent upon household income. New part-time students can apply for loans of up to £6,935 for tuition fees in an academic year.

Students never get their hands on tuition fee loans, the money is paid straight to the university. This way there is no risk of blowing the lot on something other than funding studies or running late with payments and being chased by the university.

Maintenance Loans
These are designed to help full-time home students pay for their living expenses – rent, food, travel, bills, going out, clothes, gym fees and so on. Maintenance loans are partly means-tested and the amount that can be borrowed depends on family income, whether the university is

in London or elsewhere in the UK, and whether students live at home with their family or independently.

Maximum loan amounts in 2020–21:
» £7,747 for students living at their family home during term time.
» £9,203 for students living away from home outside London.
» £12,010 for students living away from home in London.
» £10,242 for students living and studying abroad for at least one term as part of their UK course.

In general students must be under 60 on the first day of the first academic year of their course. However, in England over-60s can access a lower means-tested loan for living costs.

Maintenance Loans are paid straight into students' bank accounts in three instalments throughout the year. Budgeting to make each loan last until the next instalment is down to students. The final-year Maintenance Loan payment is a bit smaller than in the years before, because student life ends in June/July of that year, and with it the entitlement to a Student Loan.

The first loan instalment creates a bit of a heaven-and-hell moment. For most 18-year-old freshers there is the thrill of their current account probably experiencing its biggest single cash injection ever, combined with the more sobering surprise that the interest clock starts ticking on the loan from the day of the initial payment, usually the first day of the first term. It keeps ticking until the April after students finish their course, which is when repayment may or may not begin. For part-time students earning over £26,575 (this threshold increases every year for all students, and will be £27,295 from 1 April 2021) repayment starts four years after starting to receive the loan, even if they are furthering their studies then rather than working.

The most recent significant change to the student finance system, in 2016-2017, was the abolition of grants – which do not require repayment – in England for students from low-income families, and their replacement by increased maintenance loans. As with the introduction of tuition fees, there has been no immediate impact on students. Repayments begin only after graduation, and when the borrower's salary reaches £26,575. But critics have said many low and middle-income students could be put off university by having to accrue more debt.

Extra cash is also available to student healthcare workers, including doctors and dentists, teachers and social workers. From September 2020, a new £5,000 annual training grant has been available to those taking an eligible pre-registration healthcare course, following the nursing bursary's abolition in 2016–17.

Interest rates

Student loan interest rates are based on the RPI (Retail Price Index), the rate at which prices rise. While studying, until the April following graduation, students are charged RPI + 3%. From that point, interest accrues on a sliding scale of RPI plus up to 3% until they reach a salary of £47,835, after which it remains at RPI plus 3% however much they earn. As an idea of what to expect on the sliding scale, those earning a midway salary of £37,205 will accrue interest of RPI + 1.5%.

The interest rate is reduced to RPI alone if a student leaves college and gets a job paying less than £26,575. In other words, as the personal finance whiz, Martin Lewis, points out on his **www.moneysavingexpert.com** website, "Unlike other debt, the interest added ISN'T the interest paid. That depends on future earnings. Some won't repay any interest and most won't earn enough to repay close to all of it."

The interest rate changes every September, based on the RPI rate of inflation in the year to the previous March. The RPI rate was 2.6% in March 2020, so Student Loan interest is currently charged at 2.6% to 5.6%, depending on whether the student is still studying and how much they are earning. If students lose touch with the Student Loans Company, RPI plus 3% is automatically applied to their debt.

The disappearing debt

After 30 years in England (this varies a little elsewhere in the UK – please see further down this chapter), the debt is written off. Because the repayments seem modest for anyone with a qualifying income, and because of the 30-year rule, student debt is a lot more forgiving than a mortgage or a credit card, where the bills keep on coming even if you are out of work. The Student Loans Company is probably the only lender in Britain that hands out tens of thousands of pounds without a credit check.

Repaying the Student Loan

Some students may never earn the £26,575-plus per year which triggers repayments, although few go to university with that expectation. In practice, only a handful will be in that position, and they will mostly be there because of their own life decisions. At the other extreme, graduates may land such well-paid jobs that university was cheap at the price. Most will be somewhere in the middle. Contrary to the majority of debts, which are better to clear as early as possible, students should not start repaying Student Loans before the April after leaving university, as this can result in overpaying – which tens of thousands of students have done in the past and can now reclaim. From this point, students repay their loans at a rate of 9% of their earnings above £26,575, or £27,295 from 1 April 2021. In this way, the amount owed (the borrowed money plus interest) does not affect what is repaid each year.

On his website Martin Lewis the Money Saving Expert provides helpful advice to demystify Student Loan repayments, using the following example:

> **Student loan & interest: £20,000.** *Your earnings: £36,575.*
> As you repay 9% of everything above £26,575 your annual repayment is £900.

> **Student loan & interest: £50,000.** *Your earnings: £36,575.*
> As you repay 9% of everything above £26,575 your annual repayment is £900.

> **To get silly to prove a point: student loan & interest: £1 billion.** *Your earnings: £36,575.*
> As you repay 9% of everything above £26,575 your annual repayment is £900.

The Student Loans Company website **www.studentloanrepayment.co.uk** has information to guide prospective students through these arrangements and also gives examples of levels of repayment.

Affording to live

Analysis by the National Union of Students confirmed what students already knew, that the maintenance loan does not provide enough money to cover the real cost of living. Making ends meet is a constant university challenge, and students have always proved resourceful. Typically, the number one source of help is parents, whose financial assistance is implied, if not explicit, in the government's approach to student funding. Part-time jobs, savings and bursaries and scholarships also contribute to the student purse.

Scottish maintenance bursaries and loans 2020–21

Young student (under 25 at start of course)				Independent student (25+)			
Income	Loan	Bursary	Total	Income	Loan	Bursary	Total
Up to £20,999	£5,750	£2,000	£7,750	Up to £20,999	£6,750	£1,000	£7,750
£21,000–£23,999	£5,750	£1,125	£6,875	£21,000–£23,999	£6,750	–	£6,750
£24,000–£33,999	£5,750	£500	£6,250	£24,000–£33,999	£6,250	–	£6,250
Over £34,000	£4,750	–	£4,750	Over £34,000	£4,750	–	£4,750

UK Nursing and Midwifery students studying in Scotland are eligible for bursaries of £10,000 for the first three years and £7,500 for the fourth year of a course. There is a separate dental bursary scheme.

Source: Students Awards Agency Scotland

The Student Money Survey 2020 from **www.savethestudent.org** found that average undergraduate spending was £795 per month, with rent the biggest outlay at an average of £418 per month, equivalent to 73% of a maintenance loan. The survey revealed that 71% of students worried about not being able to make ends meet and that 36% had considered dropping out for that reason. Which is why savings, earnings from part-time work and help from family and friends have to be added to the pot. The annual Natwest Student Living Index for 2020 reported that 39% of all students relied on the 'Bank of Mum and Dad' to top up funds, with an average monthly contribution of £192.50.

Value for money

Most surveys suggest that, on average, a degree still offers a worthwhile return on the financial investment involved in going to university. Future salary expectations are better for graduates than those without degrees, even taking into consideration the wages that might otherwise have

Maintenance Loan entitlement, England 2020–21

Household income	Living at home	Living away from home but not in London	Living away from home and studying in London
£25,000	£7,747	£9,203	£12,010
£30,000	£7,095	£8,544	£11,340
£35,000	£6,442	£7,884	£10,670
£40,000	£5,789	£7,225	£10,000
£45,000	£5,137	£6,565	£9,330
£50,000	£4,484	£5,905	£8,659
£55,000	£3,831	£5,246	£7,989
£58,222	£3,410	£4,820	£7,557
£60,000	£3,410	£4,586	£7,319
£62,249	£3,410	£4,289	£7,017
£65,000	£3,410	£4,289	£6,649
£69,977	£3,410	£4,289	£5,981
£69,888 and over	–	–	£5,812

Source: Student Finance England

been earned while studying. Our Subject by Subject Guide in Chapter 13 delves deeper into graduate outcomes and salaries.

Budgeting

One in four freshers spend their first student loan instalment within a month, according to Endsleigh Insurance. Help is at hand to avoid such financial abandon. University websites, UCAS at **www.ucas.com/finance/managing-money/student-budgeting-tips** and many others offer guidance on preparing a budget. List all likely income (loans, bursaries, part-time work, savings, parental support) and compare this with expected outgoings. It pays to be realistic, rather than too optimistic, about both sides of the equation. With care, it should be possible to end up either only slightly in the red, or preferably far enough in the black to be able to afford some of the things you like.

Aldi, Lidl and other budget supermarkets are godsends when it comes to stretching the budget, even if shopping at one means having to get a taxi home – share with a housemate and split the cost, there will still be significant savings on the prices at the nearby Tesco Metro or Sainsbury's Local. No one is condoning binge drinking, but with 'pre-drinks' before a night out popular, great savings can be made by stocking up on Lidl et al's versions of well-known drinks and snacks. Shopping online, while not offered by the budget supermarkets, can also be cost effective if you stick to own-brand products, as the temptation of popping extra items into the trolley at will is removed and any delivery fee can be shared with housemates. Learn to cook at least a few basics and make use of leftovers in packed lunches the next day – a Tupperware

---

Funding timetable

It is vital that you sort out your funding arrangements before you start university. Each funding agency has its own arrangements, and it is very important that you find out the exact details from them. The dates below give general indications of key dates.

March/April

» Online and paper application forms become available from funding agencies.
» You must contact the appropriate funding agency to make an application. This will be the funding agency for the region of the UK that you live in, even if you are planning to study elsewhere in the UK.
» Complete application form as soon as possible. At this stage select the university offer that will be your first choice.
» Check details of bursaries and scholarships available from your selected universities.

May/June

» Funding agencies will give you details of the financial support they can offer.
» Last date for making an application to ensure funding is ready for you at the start of term (exact date varies significantly between agencies).

August

» Tell your funding agency if the university or course you have been accepted for is different from that originally given them.

September

» Take letter confirming funding to your university for registration.
» After registration, the first part of funds will be released to you.

pot is an invaluable weapon in the fight against splurging more than is affordable on daily café lunches. The same goes for a carry-cup for coffee.

More than two-thirds of 18-24-year-olds reported they received no financial education at school, according to a report by the National Association of Student Money Advisors (NASMA). Keeping track of finances is not every student's idea of a good time, but it is certain to provide greater freedom for enjoying university life. Most graduates will have to grapple with spreadsheets during their working life, and they make balancing the student budget simpler. Nobody wants any cash-machine-ate-my-card situations.

Make full use of student travel cards and shopping discounts, and shop around for the best calls and data deals on mobile phones. The 2020 Natwest Index put average monthly mobile phone spending at £12.40, while groceries and household items came in at £81.60 a month, £29.30 went on alcohol and £15.10 on books and other course-related material.

Study costs
The average student spent about £1,000 a year on costs associated with course work and studying, a survey by the NUS estimated – mainly on books and equipment. Some courses require much higher spends than others, and extra financial support may be available for certain – but not all –things. Take out library text books or buy them second-hand from students who don't need them anymore, to avoid racking up huge bills incurred by a long reading list.

Overdrafts and credit cards
These are the more expensive forms of debt, and best avoided if at all possible. Many banks offer free overdraft facilities for students but going over the limit without prior arrangement can result in high charges. Credit cards can be useful if managed properly, ideally by setting up a direct debit to pay off the full balance every month, thus avoiding any interest. To pay only the minimum charge each month can end up costing a small fortune over a long period. Those inclined to spend impulsively without keeping track are probably better off without a credit card and should stick with a debit card.

Insurance
Most students arrive at university with laptops and other goodies such as games consoles, sports equipment, musical instruments, mobile phones and bikes that are tempting to thieves. It is estimated that around a third of students fall victim to crime at some point during university. A reasonable amount of cover for these items should be found by shopping around, without it costing you an arm and a leg. It may also be possible to add this cover cheaply to parents' domestic contents policy (probably at their expense).

Scams
A number of email scams have targeted students in recent years. One offered HMRC tax refunds in an attempt to steal personal data and money, using fake university addresses or aping the GOV.UK branding or credit card companies. A phishing scam falsely using the Student Loans Company name affected home and EU students in 2020, sending emails asking people to validate their account, or provide personal security or banking details. These types of scams are especially common around student loan payment dates.

Such messages should not be clicked on, and instead forwarded to **report@phishing.gov.uk** or **phishing@slc.co.uk**.

Student loans and grants for Northern Ireland students

Maintenance loans for 2020–21 vary from a maximum of £3,750 for students living at home, £4,840 for those studying away from home and £6,780 for those studying in London. Only 25% of the loan is means-tested.

Maintenance grants range from £3,475 for students with household incomes of £19,203 or below, to zero if the figure is £41,540 or above. The maximum loan is reduced by the size of any grant received. Loan repayments of 9% of salary start once income reaches £19,390 for 2020–21, less than in England, and interest is calculated on the retail price index or 1% above base rate, whichever is lower, again less than for England. The loan will be cancelled after 25 years, also quicker than in England.

As in England, there are special funds for people with disabilities and other special needs, and for those with children or adult dependants. Students studying in the Republic of Ireland can also borrow up to €3,000 a year to pay their Irish tuition contribution and may be able to get a bursary to study there. Tuition fee loans are available for the full amount of tuition fees, regardless of where you study in the UK.

Fees for local students at the province's two universities are a lot lower than for England, Scotland or Wales, at £4,395 for 2020–21. These rates also apply to those from the Republic of Ireland. The English, Welsh and Scots will pay £9,250.

Student loans and grants for Welsh students

For 2020–21 the maximum maintenance award is £8,335 for students living at home, £9,810 for those living away from home and outside London, and £12,260 for those living in London. The cunning part is that these sums are mainly an outright grant to those from less prosperous households. So, if total household income is £18,370 or less, £8,100 of the £9,810 is a grant (and therefore does not need to be repaid) and only £1,710 a loan, but if income is over £59,200, then £8,810 is repayable and only £1,000 is a grant. The same logic applies to other levels of support, while part-time students can get a variable loan or grant that depends upon income and the intensity of their course.

Tuition fee loans are available to cover the whole £9,000 of tuition fees in Wales, or £9,250 for Welsh students in Scotland, England or Northern Ireland (£6,165 for a private provider). Those studying part-time in Wales (or at the Open University) can apply for a loan of up to £2,625. Elsewhere in the UK they can apply for up to £6,935, or for courses at private institutions, £4,625.

Repayment of loans starts once a graduate's income reaches £25,725. Interest repayments and the length of loan are as for England (see above). In addition, students in Wales are also able to apply for Welsh Government support for parents of young children, for adult learners, for those with adult dependants and for those with disabilities. This support can cover carer costs as well as equipment and general expenditure.

Student loans and grants for Scottish students

Scottish students pay no tuition fees at their own universities and can apply for up to £9,250 per year as a loan for fees elsewhere in the UK. They must reapply for this loan each year.

The Scottish Government has a commitment to a minimum income, currently £7,750, per year for students from poorer backgrounds. So, in 2020–21, students from a family with an income below £20,999 could get a £2,000 Young Students' Bursary (YSB) as well as a loan of £5,750. Unlike the other UK countries, Scotland uses a band system to calculate the combination of bursary and loan, rather than precise household income. So, for incomes from £21,000 to £23,999, the bursary is £1,125 and the loan remains the same, making a total of £6,875 and for those earning £24,000 to £33,999, the bursary is only £500, making a total of £6,250. Above £34,000, no bursary is available and the maximum loan falls to £4,750. These figures remain the same regardless of whether students live at home or where they are studying in the UK. Higher loans but more limited bursaries are available for "independent" students – those who are married, mature (25 or over) or without family support. Maintenance support loans in Scotland are not available to students aged over 55, and students must be under 60 to enrol on the first day of their course.

The Scottish government's Student Awards Agency Scotland has committed to raise the repayment threshold to £25,000 in April 2021, but at the time of writing loan repayments were triggered at incomes of £19,390-plus. Interest is linked to the Retail Price Index, as in Northern Ireland. Repayments will continue until the loan is paid off, with any outstanding amount being cancelled after 35 years, five years later than for the English, and 10 years later than in Wales.

As elsewhere in the UK, there are special funds for people with disabilities and other special needs, and for those with children or adult dependants. No tuition fee loans are required by Scottish students studying in Scotland, but such loans are available for Scottish students studying elsewhere in the UK.

Living in one country, studying in another

As each of the countries of the UK develops its own distinctive system of student finance, the effects on students leaving home in one UK nation to go and study in another have become knottier. UK students who cross borders to study, pay the tuition fees of their chosen university and are eligible for a fee loan, and maybe a partial grant, to cover them. They are also entitled to apply for the scholarships or bursaries on offer from that institution. Any maintenance loan or grant will still come from the awarding body of their home country. If you are in this position, you must check with the authorities in your home country about the funding you are eligible for. You should also contact your own government about support on offer if you are in the Channel Islands or the Isle of Man.

Following Britain's departure from the European Union, EU students from outside the UK will be charged the same tuition fees as those paid by international students, often much higher. They may be considered for some of the scholarships and bursaries offered by individual institutions.

Applying for support

English students should apply for grants and loans through Student Finance England, Welsh students through Student Finance Wales, Scottish students through the Student Awards Agency for Scotland, and those in Northern Ireland through Student Finance NI or their Education and Library Board.

Applications should be made as soon as the offer of a place at university has been received. Don't expect things to happen automatically. For instance, students have to tell the Student Loans Company to pay the tuition fees they owe to the university.

University scholarships and bursaries

Shop around for university bursaries, scholarships and other sponsorship packages, and seek other forms of supplementary support. There may be fee reductions for groups, including local students, which are usually detailed on university websites. There is funding for students with disabilities or family responsibilities; or for those taking subjects such as social work or medicine, with wide public benefit, as well as a range of charities with their own criteria.

The Scholarship Hub, a database of scholarships, suspects UK students could be missing out on funding worth up to £150million a year, as organisations offering scholarships often struggle to get enough applications. The database is free, but it requires a subscription to access advice about how to apply and enhanced search tools.

Most bursaries are means-tested, while scholarships are via open competition. Some universities offer eligible students the choice of accommodation discounts, fee waivers or cash. Most also have hardship funds for those who find themselves in financial difficulties. Many charities for specific industries or professions have a remit to support education, and many have bursaries for anyone studying a related subject. The Directory of Grant-Making Trusts lists bodies that make one-off or regular awards to all kinds of causes, often including deserving students. Only available in hard copy, a library visit may be required to see it for free.

Take note of the application procedures for scholarships and bursaries. They vary between institutions, and even from course to course within institutions. Specific awards may have specific application deadlines. In some cases, the university will work out for you whether you are entitled to an award by referring to your funding agency's financial assessment. If your personal circumstances change part-way through a course, entitlement to a scholarship or bursary may be reviewed.

Advice on scholarships and bursaries is usually included in a university's website or prospectus and many institutions also maintain a helpline. Is the bursary or scholarship automatic or conditional? When will you find out whether your application has been successful? For some awards, this won't be until after exam results.

Students with disabilities

Extra financial help is available to disabled students, whether studying full-time or part-time, through Disabled Students' Allowances, which are paid in addition to the standard student finance package. They are available for help with education-related conditions such as dyslexia, and for other physical and mental disabilities. They do not depend on income and do not have to be repaid. The cash is available for extra travel costs, equipment and to pay helpers. For 2020–21 the maximum for students in England for a non-medical helper is £23,258 a year, or £17,443 a year for a part-time student. In addition, there is a maximum equipment allowance of £5,849 for the duration of the course and £1,954 (£1,465 part-time) for general expenses a year, although the government warns that most students get less than these amounts. There is also needs-based funding for travel costs.

The National Health Service has its own Disabled Students Allowance system. The NHS Business Services Authority has a Student Services Arm which runs the NHS Learning Support Grants and the NHS Education Support Grant, again worth investigating by those planning to study health or social work.

Further sources of income

There are various types of support available for students in particular circumstances, other than the main loans, grants and bursaries.

» Undergraduates in financial difficulties can apply for help from their university's student hardship fund. These provide support for anything from day-to-day study and living costs to unexpected or exceptional expenses. The university decides which students need help and how much to award them. These funds often target older or disadvantaged students, and finalists in danger of dropping out. The sums range up to a few thousand pounds, are not repayable and do not count against other income.

» Students with children can apply for a Childcare Grant. For 2020–21 this was up to £174.22 a week for a first child and up to £298.69 for two or more children under 15, or under 17 with special educational needs, calculated on the basis of 85% of childcare costs. There was also a Parents' Learning Allowance of up to £1,766, for help with course-related costs.

» Students with a partner, or another adult family member who is financially dependent on them, can apply for an Adult Dependants' Grant of up to £3,094 a year for 2020–21.

Part-time work

A part-time term-time job is a fact of life for almost half of students. The challenge is to not let the part-time job get in the way of studying. A survey by the NUS found that 59% of students who worked felt it had an impact on their studies, with 38% missing lectures and over a fifth failing to submit coursework because of their part-time jobs.

Student employment agencies, found on many university campuses, match employers with students seeking work, sometimes offering jobs within the university itself. They also ensure both minimum wages and the maximum number of hours worked in term time, typically 15 hours a week. Students sometimes make money from freelance work and student businesses, but most take casual work in shops, restaurants, bars and call centres. Most students get a job during the holidays, including those who don't have one in the term.

Useful websites

For the basics of fees, loans, grants and other allowances: **www.gov.uk/student-finance**

UCAS provides helpful advice: **www.ucas.com/money**

For England, visit Student Finance England: **https://www.gov.uk/browse/education/student-finance**
For Wales, visit Student Finance Wales: **www.studentfinancewales.co.uk**
For Scotland, visit the Student Awards Agency for Scotland: **www.saas.gov.uk**
For Northern Ireland, visit Student Finance Northern Ireland: **https://www.studentfinanceni.co.uk/**

Office for Students: **www.officeforstudents.org.uk**

All UK student loans are administered by the Student Loans Company:
www.gov.uk/government/organisations/student-loans-company

HMRC information on the tax position of students: **www.gov.uk/student-jobs-paying-tax**

For finding out about availability of scholarships: **www.thescholarshiphub.org.uk** (requires subscription fee). Or go direct to university websites, where their scholarship and bursary provision will be detailed.

8 Finding Somewhere to Live

Starting university will be the first taste of independent living for most freshers; a milestone for new students and for their families. As the summer holidays draw to an end department stores put out their starter sets of sturdy crockery, basic pans and unfussy cutlery, fit for shared kitchens and novice cooks. The beginning of term brings social media snaps of family car boots crammed to bursting point, and bitter-sweet farewells. Safe, comfortable and affordable student accommodation is pivotal to a student's ability to settle in to all that university life has to offer. It is also the biggest financial outlay, aside from tuition fees.

The guidance in this chapter is offered on the assumption that things will be back to some sort of normal by the autumn of 2022. No one could have predicted the extraordinary new role that student accommodation would play in the midst of a global health pandemic. University teaching buildings closed, exams were cancelled and the move to blended online learning made the four walls of a student bedroom the epicentre of most campus life – even more so for those compelled to self-isolate to help stop the spread of the virus. Occupants of halls of residence flats and corridors became household 'bubbles' or 'clusters', bonded by sharing a kitchen and living area. Home-sharers off campus formed bubbles of their own, catapulted into a level of familial closeness that asked a lot of their maturity.

In the period before lockdown, students were advised by the government to return to their family homes (without using public transport), while those who had not been able to go then were later requested to stay put, and not travel. Students' anxiety about their rental contracts with landlords and universities became headline news. Did they have to pay if the government said to go home? What if they fell ill with Covid-19? Some providers waived rent for those who had vacated and for those who had stayed. Others did neither. The NUS Students and Coronavirus Survey (April 2020) showed that 72% of students were worried about their ability to pay rent during Covid-19. Never have the finer points of an Assured Shorthold Tenancy Agreement been so hotly and widely discussed.

When campuses re-opened for the 2020–21 academic year, students lived with further disruptions to normal service. On the whole they towed the line with social distancing, putting public health above the personal gratification of socialising in large groups. Smaller numbers flouted the Covid rules, turning halls of residence into unlikely makeshift nightclubs, and hosting riotous student house parties off campus – and faced stringent discipline if caught. Student housing was once again in the thick of coronavirus news reporting.

Strange and unsettling though that period was, the microscope it put student housing under will hopefully prove helpful in the long run. In the pecking order of big decisions involved in going to university, choosing somewhere to live has always been second only to selecting the right course, pandemic or no pandemic. For first-years especially, accommodation of reasonable quality in an environment conducive to meeting other students is the ideal set-up. Students spend an average of £147 a week on rent, according to the 2018 NUS/Unipol Student Accommodation Costs Survey. The 2020 National Student Accommodation Survey by www.savethestudent.org estimates a slightly lower national average of £126.42 per week, though costs can vary wildly by location. In both scenarios rent consumes the majority of even the maximum maintenance loan, which is £9,203 (for 2020–21 outside London) or £12,010 (for 2020–21 in London).

There are more student housing choices now than ever before, with a range of private providers supplementing what universities and individual landlords provide. Parents of university-age children who went to university themselves will often find little to remind them of their own experiences in today's digs. With tastes changing and the numbers going to university remaining high private student accommodation is a growth area. In 2014 two-thirds of halls of residence were provided by universities. By last year the private sector controlled more than 50% of the market. With rising rents and billions of pounds committed to residences each year, private student housing has become the property market's biggest growth area. City skylines are increasingly dotted with new-build student blocks, the speed of their construction often defying the rate of other large building projects.

Term-time accommodation of full-time and sandwich students 2018–19

University provided accommodation	351,605	18.7%
Private sector halls	160,670	8.5%
Parental home	368,475	19.6%
Own residence	316,355	16.8%
Other rented accommodation	550,880	29.2%
Other	67,250	3.6%
Not in attendance/unknown	67,915	3.6%

Source HESA 2019 (adapted)

Not all recent developments have been swiftly completed, however. Two days before they were due to move in to a new £30m development at the start of the 2019 autumn term, 200 University of Portsmouth students were asked by the private provider, Prime Student Living, if they could stay at home for the first few weeks, due to delays. Most could not, and the university rushed to find them temporary accommodation. Students started moving in from mid-October and the building was fully occupied by the end of December, but issues with lifts and hot water rumbled on. The problems in Portsmouth are not unique, many more private developments have been late completing in recent years, leaving students stranded. There is often no agreement between the provider and the university, leading vice chancellors and other stakeholders to call for the sector to be more tightly regulated.

Philip Augar's independent panel report to the Review of Post-18 Education and Funding discussed the issues and called on the Office for Students to take more interest, and Chris Skidmore, the former Minister for Universities, hosted a summit of student accommodation providers.

A report on student accommodation published in March 2020 by the House of Commons Library just before the pandemic hit, found that more than half of new undergraduates live in university or private sector halls. Demand for halls is greater than supply, but with first-years traditionally guaranteed a space by many universities it is worth paying attention to application deadlines, and meeting them. Any surplus residential rooms are allocated to postgraduates, international students in any year of study and some returning, non-first-year students. Institutions that recruit significant numbers in Clearing have rooms available late in the admissions cycle. Some universities reserve a small proportion of accommodation for students with families.

While halls are generally the preferred option for freshers, they are also the priciest – not only in private developments but in many cases in university-owned accommodation too, making affordability a sticking point. Some private blocks come with high spec interiors and swanky extras including gyms. Most developments are in big complexes, but there are also niche providers such as Student Cribs, which converts properties to a more luxurious standard than usual digs and rents them to students. It now operates in 24 cities.

Unite Students is one of the country's biggest providers and has 76,000 beds in 27 towns and cities, some provided in partnership with universities and others in developments that serve more than one institution. UPP has 36,000 residential places in operation or under construction in complexes built for 15 universities, usually on campus, and where rents are negotiated with the university, often in consultation with the students' union.

Top Ten Problems for Student Tenants

1	Noisy housemates	45%
2	Damp	35%
3	Housemates stealing food	33%
4	Lack of water/heating	32%
5	Disruptive building work	20%
=6	Rodents and pests	16%
=6	Inappropriate landlord visits	16%
=8	Dangerous living conditions	5%
=8	Break-in or burglary	5%
10	Bedbugs	3%

Source: National Student Accommodation Survey 2019

Based on 2,196 responses **www.savethestudent.org**

The 2020 National Student Accommodation Survey found that 12% of students were living in private halls, up from 8% three years ago, but university accommodation still accounts for a much higher 27% of students, while 44% have a private landlord, 12% live with their parents, and a lucky 3% own their home.

The Student Housing Awards are a new roll of honour for halls of residence, both university-owned and private. The top provider in 2019 was Host, which has accommodation in 20 UK cities. Universities, rather than private providers, came out top in the other categories; Lancaster gained the award for best halls, Derby came top for customer service and Edge Hill offered the best value for money. Service awards early in the 2020 academic year went to Ulster University for the best moving-in experience, and to Queen Margaret University for the best booking experience.

Price and location are likely to be more important to students than who owns the property, but when it comes to student accommodation: caveat emptor! Standards can be variable, prices may leave little to live on, and horror stories recounted in surveys by the NUS and Save the Student mention hot water issues, slugs, mould, mice, 'gross' common areas and dead rats under hallway floorboards.

Living at home

Almost twice as many undergraduates were living at home, the 2020 Student Accommodation Survey found, than was the case in 2019. The trend was across first-, second- and third-year students, united by the desire to save money by not moving out. The results confirm the pattern seen in recent applications. Although student loan repayments only start once graduates are earning more than the threshold, many undergraduates are understandably cautious about the debts they run up. If students live within commuting distance of a good university, the option of dodging hefty rent and household bills is tempting. This may be a permanent shift, given the rising costs of student housing and the willingness of many young people, student or not, to live with their parents well into their twenties. What effect the health pandemic has on the popularity of studying from home remains to be seen, but it would seem natural for risk-averse types to see this as a more reliable option than facing potentially chaotic situations as students did in 2020.

Stay-at-home students spend twice as long as others travelling to university, with 42-minute commutes, instead of the UK average of 21 minutes, according to the Student Accommodation Survey 2020. For the 20% of students living at home, the extra journey time is clearly a worthwhile compromise. Not only school-leavers live at home, the proportion includes mature students, many of whom live in their own homes rather than with their parents. The trend is four times more common at post-1992 universities than at older universities, reflecting the larger numbers of mature students with family responsibilities at the newer universities and a generally younger and more affluent student population at the older ones.

Before opting to stay at home based solely on the financial sense it makes, it is important to consider the relationship with your parents and the availability of quiet space in which to study. You will still be entitled to a maintenance loan, although for 2020–21 it is a maximum of £7,747 in England, rather than £9,203 if you were living away from home outside London, or £12,010 in London. There is no higher rate for anyone living at home in London, which seems unreasonable given the high cost of transport and other essentials there. There may be advantages in terms of academic work if the alternative involves shopping, cooking and cleaning as well as the other distractions of a student flat. The downside is that you may miss out on a lot of the student experience, especially the social scene and the opportunity to make new friends.

Research has found that students who live at home are less likely than others to say they are learning a lot at university, and a survey by the Student Engagement Partnership suggests that they find life unexpectedly "tiring, expensive and stressful". Issues affecting their quality of life include travel, security and the lack of their own space. But remember that you can always move on later if you think you are missing out. Many initially home-based students do so in their second year.

Living away from home

Most of those who can afford it still see moving away to study as an integral rite of passage. There is no other option for those whose chosen course is at a university further than commuting distance. Others look forward to broadening their experiences in a new, unexplored location.

For the fortunate majority, the search for accommodation will be over quickly because the university can offer a place in one of its halls of residence or self-catering flats. The choice may come down to the type of accommodation and whether or not to do your own cooking. But for others, there will be an anxious search for a room in a strange city. Most universities will help with this if they cannot offer accommodation of their own.

The practicalities of living independently loom large, all of a sudden, for students who go away to university. The location and the type of accommodation may even influence your choice of university, since there are big differences across the sector and the country in the cost and standard of accommodation, and in its availability.

How much will it cost?

Rents vary so much across the UK that national averages are almost meaningless. The 2019 NatWest Student Living Index found a range from £251 a month in Belfast and £400 in Aberdeen to £717 in London and £582 in Oxford, the next-dearest. On average though, the NatWest Living Index found that UK rent had decreased to the lowest levels since 2018 (by 6%), with only London and the South West seeing increases in the last year.

Such figures conceal a wide range of actual rents, particularly in London. This was always the case but has become even more obvious with the rapid growth of a luxury market at the same time as many students appear willing to accept sub-standard accommodation to keep costs down.

A series of recent reports suggest that the need for good Wi-Fi has overtaken reasonable rents as students' top priority in choosing accommodation. A survey by **www.mystudenthalls.com** found that a big, bright room, good Wi-Fi, friendly people, a clean kitchen and a good gym are the top things students say they value in a place to live. The same website lists a top 10 of the most Instagrammable student accommodation – won by Ernest Place, Durham with its rooftop communal areas.

Fabulous though such digs sound, being able to afford them must be a priority. Many students will not receive the full maintenance loan, because it is means-tested against household income. The 2018 edition of the NUS/Unipol Accommodation Cost survey found that in 2018–19, average rents were equal to 73% of the maximum financial support per student, up from 58% in 2011–12. The same survey raised the issue of the need for cash up front for deposits, and/or a guarantee, probably from your parents, that the rent will be paid. Most universities with a range of accommodation find that their most expensive rooms fill up first, and that students appear to have higher expectations than they used to. More than half of all the rooms in the NUS survey had ensuite facilities.

Another consideration is that both living costs and potential earnings should be factored into calculations when deciding where to live. While living costs in London are by far the highest, potential part-time earnings are, too. Taking account of both income and outgoings, the 2020 NatWest index made Manchester the most affordable student city, followed by Cambridge and Leicester. London was the dearest on this measure, ahead of Plymouth and Poole. Students were found to earn the most in Cambridge, followed by Manchester – £1,447 and £1,392 per term-time month respectively. Bottom of the league are Southampton at £820 and Glasgow on £838.

The choices you have

The NUS puts accommodation into 16 categories, ranging from luxurious university halls to a bedsit in a shared house. The choices include:

» University hall of residence, with individual study bedrooms and a full catering service. Many will have ensuite accommodation.
» University halls, flats or houses where you have to provide your own food.
» Private, purpose-built student accommodation.
» Rented houses or flats, shared with fellow students.
» Living at home.
» Living as a lodger in a private house.

Making your choice

Choosing somewhere cheap is a false economy if it ends up making you feel depressed and isolated. Financial considerations should be weighed against the value that your living environment will contribute to your enjoyment of student life. Most students who drop out of university do so in the first few months, when homesickness and loneliness can be felt most acutely.

Being warm and well-fed is likely to have a positive effect on your studies. University halls offer a convenient, safe and reliable standard of accommodation, along with a supportive community environment. The sheer number of students – especially first-years – in halls makes this form of accommodation an easy way of meeting people from a wide range of courses and making friends.

If meals are included, this extra adds further peace of mind both for students and their parents. The last NUS survey, which covered students in 2018–19, found that the difference in cost between full board and self-catering was just £37 a week on average, not unreasonable for two hot meals a day. But only 4% of places are catered, compared with 58% in the standard format of ensuite rooms and a shared kitchen. So, some basic cooking skills might help build your popularity and self-confidence when you first reach university.

Wherever you choose to live, there are some general points you will need to consider, such as how safe the neighbourhood seems to be, and how long it might take you to travel to and from classes, especially during rush hour. A survey of travel time between term-time accommodation and the university found that most students in London can expect a commute of at least 30 minutes and often over an hour, while students living in Wales are usually much less than 30 minutes away from their university.

In chapter 15, we provide details of what accommodation each university offers, covering the number of places, the costs and their policy towards first-year students.

What universities offer

You might think that opting to live in university accommodation is the most straightforward choice, especially since first-year students are given priority in the allocation of places in halls of residence, and it is possible to arrange university accommodation in advance and at a distance. Searching for private housing can often be a matter of having to be in the right place at the right time, and many potential students start the hunt in the November before they go to college. However, you may still need to select from a range of options, because most universities will have a variety of accommodation on offer. You will need to consider which best suits your pocket and your preferred lifestyle.

New student accommodation

At the top end of the market, private firms usually lead the way, at least in the bigger student cities. Companies such as UPP and Unite Students offer some of the most luxurious student accommodation the UK has seen, either in partnership with universities or in their own right. Rooms in these complexes are nearly always ensuite and with internet access and may include other facilities such as your own phone line and satellite TV. Shared kitchens are top-quality and fitted out with the latest equipment.

This kind of accommodation naturally comes at a higher price but offers the advantages of flexibility both in living arrangements and through a range of payment options.

Halls of residence

Many new or recently refurbished university-owned halls offer a standard of accommodation that is not far short of the privately-built residences. This is partly because rooms in these halls can be offered to conference delegates during vacations. Even though these halls are also at the pricier end of the spectrum, you will probably find that they are in great demand, and you may have to get your name down quickly to secure one of the fancier rooms. That said, you can often get a guarantee of accommodation if you give a firm acceptance of an offered place by a certain date in the summer.

If you have gained your place through Clearing, this option may not exist, although rooms in private halls might still be on offer at this stage. The delays experienced in development completions in recent years underline the importance of ensuring, as far as possible, that any new builds are on time and have the seal of approval (even in the absence of a formal arrangement) of the university. Cladding is a particular concern and not one that is easily assuaged. An incident in Bolton raised safety concerns as fire ripped through a relatively new hall of residence with cladding, though it appeared to have met building regulations and not be the type used on Grenfell Tower. Students were evacuated and two were treated by paramedics but fortunately none came to serious harm.

While a few halls are single-sex, most are mixed, and often house over 500 students. In student villages, the numbers are now counted in thousands and these are great environments for making friends and becoming part of the social scene.

One possible downside is that big student housing developments can also be noisy places where it can be difficult at times to get down to work. In another Unite survey, 44% of those responding identified noise as the biggest challenge in student accommodation. For those who had experienced it, peace and quiet was a higher priority than access to public transport or good nightlife. The more successful students learn, before too many essay deadlines and exams start to loom, to get the balance right between all-night partying and escaping to the library for some undisturbed study time. Many libraries, especially new ones, are now open 24 hours a day.

University self-catering accommodation

An alternative to halls offered by most universities, are smaller, self-catering properties fitted out with a shared kitchen and other living areas. Students looking for a more independent and flexible lifestyle often prefer this option, which is now often the norm. The Reality Check report found that 83% of female university applicants, and 79% of men, felt confident of their cooking abilities. The women were also more likely to say they could clean the house and cope with laundry. As well as having to feed yourself, you may also have heating and lighting bills to pay. University properties are often on campus or nearby, so travel costs should not be a problem.

Catering in university accommodation

Many universities have responded to a general increase in demand from students for a more independent lifestyle by providing more flexible catering facilities. A range of eateries, from fast food outlets to more traditional refectories, can usually be found on campus or in student villages. Students in university accommodation may be offered pay-as-you-eat deals as an alternative to full-board packages.

What to do after the first year?

After your first year of living in university residences you may well wish, and will probably be expected, to move out to other accommodation. The main exceptions are the collegiate universities, particularly Oxford and Cambridge but also others, which may allow you to stay on in college for another year or two, and particularly for your final year. Students from outside the EU are also often guaranteed accommodation. At a growing number of universities, where there is a sufficiently large stock of residential accommodation, it is not uncommon for students to move back into halls for their final year.

Practical details

Whether or not you have decided to start out in university accommodation, you will probably be expected to sign an agreement to cover your rent. Contract lengths vary. They can be for around 40 weeks, which includes the Christmas and Easter holiday periods, or for just the length of the three university terms. These term-time contracts are common when a university uses its rooms for conferences during vacations, and you will be required to leave your room empty during these weeks. Check whether the university has secure storage space for you to leave your belongings. Otherwise, you will have to make arrangements to take all your belongings home or store them privately between terms. International students may be offered special arrangements by which they can stay in halls during the short vacation periods. Organisations like **www.hostuk.org** can arrange for international students to stay in a UK family home at holiday times such as Christmas.

Parental purchases

One option for affluent families is to buy a house or flat and take in student lodgers. This might not be the safe financial bet it once appeared, but it is still tempting for many parents. Agents Knight Frank have had a student division since 2007, mostly working with new developers to sell specially adapted homes. Those who are considering this route tend to do so from their first year of study to maximise the return on their investment.

Being a lodger or staying in a hostel

A small number of students live as a lodger in a family home, an option most frequently taken up by international students. The usual arrangement is for a study bedroom and some meals to be provided, while other facilities such as the washing machine are shared. Students with particular religious affiliations or from a particular country may wish to consider living in a hostel run by a charity catering for a specific group. Most of these are in London. There are also specialist commercial providers such as Mansion Student India, which runs housing for Indian students in the UK.

Renting from the private sector

Around a third of students live in privately rented flats or houses. Every university city or town is awash with such accommodation, available via agencies or direct from landlords. Indeed, this type of accommodation has grown to the point where so-called "student ghettoes," in which local residents feel outnumbered, have become a hot political issue in some cities. Into this traditional market for rented flats and houses have come the new private-sector complexes and residences, adding to the options. Some are on university campuses, but others are in city centres and usually open to students of more than one university. Examples can be seen online; some sites are listed at the end of this chapter.

While there are always exceptions, a much more professional attitude and approach to managing rented accommodation has emerged among smaller providers, thanks to a combination of greater regulation and increasing competition. Nevertheless, it is wise to take certain precautions when seeking out private residences.

How to start looking for rented property

Start this process as soon as you have accepted a place.

Contact your university's accommodation service and ask for its list of approved rented properties. Some have a Student Accommodation Accreditation Scheme, run in collaboration with the local council. To get onto an approved list under such schemes, landlords must show they are adhering to basic standards of safety and security, such as having an up-to-date gas and electric safety certificate. University accommodation officers should also be able to advise you on any hidden charges. For instance, you may be asked to pay a booking or reservation fee to secure a place in a particular property, and there are sometimes fees for references or for drawing up a tenancy agreement. The practice of charging a "joining fee", however, has been outlawed.

Speak to older students with first-hand experience. Most universities have a clickable 'Chat to a Student' icon on their website, and **www.thestudentroom.com**, an online community of students nationwide is another helpful source of advice. Certain areas of town may be notorious among second- and third-years and you can try to avoid them.

Making a choice

Once you have made an initial choice of the area you would like to live in and the size of property you are looking for, the next stage is to look at possible places. If you plan to share, it is important that you all have a look at the property. If you will be living by yourself, take a friend with you when you go to view a property, since he or she can help you assess what you see objectively, and avoid any irrational or rushed on-the-spot decisions. Don't let yourself be pushed into signing on the dotted line there and then. Take time to visit and consider a number of options, as well as checking out the local facilities, transport and the general environment at various times of the day and on different days of the week.

If you are living in private rented accommodation, it is likely that at least some of your neighbours will not be students. Local people often welcome students, but resentment can build up, particularly in areas of towns and cities that are dominated by student housing. It is important to respect your neighbours' rights, and not to behave in an anti-social manner.

Preparing for sharing

Enjoying spending time with someone socially does not mean they will make an ideal housemate. How well you cope with some of the downsides of sharing will be partly down to the kind of person you are and where you are on the spectrum between laid back and highly strung. But it will help a lot if you are co-habiting with people whose outlook on day-to-day living is not too far out of line with your own. According to Unite Students, 31% of female students find sharing more difficult than they had expected, compared with 22% of men.

Some students sign for their second-year houses as early as November. While it is good

---

Security in Student Housing

» Before you rent, check that front and back doors have five-lever mortise locks as well as standard catch locks and use them when you go out

» Invest in a light-timer, so the house looks occupied even when you're out and don't advertise your departure on social media

» If you put your desk in a window, make sure you move your laptop, phone and any other valuable equipment away when you're not using them

» Get insurance for your valuables and take them home if you're leaving the house for any length of time. You may be able to add your valuables to your parents' home insurance

» Ask the landlord or letting agency to make sure previous tenants have returned any keys and discuss any security concerns with them

» Register your valuables (see www.immobilise.com) makes it more likely you'll be re-united if things do get stolen and invest in a good bike lock

Source: www.savethestudent.org and NUS (adapted)

to be ahead of the rush, you may not yet have met your best friends at this stage. If you have not selected your own group of friends, universities and landlords can help by taking personal preferences and lifestyle into account when grouping tenants together.

Potential issues to consider when deciding whether to move into a shared house include whether any of the housemates smokes or owns a loud musical instrument. It will also be important to sort out broadband arrangements that will work for everyone in the house, and that you will be able to access the university system. It is a good idea to agree a rota for everyone to share in the household cleaning chores from the start. Otherwise, it is almost certain that you will live in a state of unhygienic squalor, or that one or two individuals will be left to clear up everyone else's mess.

The practical details about renting

It is a good idea to ask whether your house is covered by an accreditation scheme or code of standards. Such codes provide a clear outline of what constitutes good practice as well as the responsibilities of both landlords and tenants. Adhering to schemes like the National Code of Standards for Larger Student Developments compiled by Accreditation Network UK **www.anuk.org.uk**, may well become a requirement for larger properties, including those managed by universities, now that the Housing Act is in force.

At the very least, make sure that if you are renting from a private landlord, you have his or her telephone number and home address. Some can be remarkably difficult to contact when repairs are needed or when deposits are due to be returned.

Multiple occupation

If you are renting a private house it may be subject to the 2004 Housing Act in England and Wales (similar legislation applies in Scotland and Northern Ireland). Licenses are compulsory for all private Houses in Multiple Occupation (HMOs) with three or more storeys and that house five or more unrelated residents. The provisions of the Act also allow local authorities to designate areas in which HMOs of all sizes must be licensed. The regulations may be applied in sections of university towns and cities where most students live. This means that a house must be licensed, well-managed and must meet various health and safety standards, and its owner subject to various financial regulations. There is more on this at **www.gov.uk** under Private Renting.

Tenancy agreements

Whatever kind of accommodation you go for, you must be sure to have all the paperwork in order and be clear about what you are signing up to before you move in. If you are taking up residence in a shared house, flat or bedsit, the first document you will have to grapple with is a tenancy agreement or lease offering you an 'assured shorthold tenancy'. Since this is a binding legal document, you should be prepared to go through every clause with a fine-tooth comb. Remember that it is much more difficult to make changes or overcome problems arising from unfair agreements once you are a tenant than before you become one.

You would be well advised to seek help in the likely event of your not fully understanding some of the clauses. Your university accommodation office or students' union is a good place to start. They should know all the ins and outs and have model tenancy agreements to refer to. A Citizens Advice Bureau or Law Advice Centre should also be able to offer you free advice. In particular, watch out for clauses that may make you jointly responsible for the actions of others with whom you are sharing. If you name a parent as a guarantor to cover any costs not paid by you, they may also be liable for charges levied on all tenants for damage that was not your fault. A rent review clause could allow your landlord to increase the rent at will, whereas without such a clause, they are restricted to one rent rise a year. Make sure you keep a copy of all documents and get a receipt (and keep it somewhere safe) for anything you have had to pay for that is the landlord's responsibility.

Contracts with private landlords tend to be longer than for university accommodation. They will frequently commit you to paying rent for 52 weeks of the year. Leaving aside the cost, there are probably more advantages than disadvantages to this kind of arrangement. It means you don't have to move out during vacations, which you will have to in most university halls. You can store your belongings in your room when you go away (but don't leave anything really valuable behind if you can help it). You may be able to negotiate a rent discount for periods when you are not staying in the property. The other advantage, particularly important for cash-strapped students, is that you have a base from which to find work and hold down a job during the vacations. Term dates are also not as dictatorial as they might be in halls. If you rent your own house, then you can come back when you wish.

Deposits

On top of the agreed rent, you will need to provide a deposit or bond to cover any breakages or damage. This will probably set you back the equivalent of another month's rent. The deposit should be returned, less any deductions, at the end of the contract. However, be warned that disputes over the return of deposits are common, with the question of what constitutes reasonable wear and tear often the subject of disagreements between landlord and tenant. To protect students from unscrupulous landlords who withheld deposits without good reason, the 2004 Housing Act introduced a National Tenancy Deposit Scheme under which deposits are held by an independent body. This is designed to ensure that deposits are fairly returned, and that any disputes are resolved swiftly and cheaply. There are details at citizensadvice.org.uk. You may also be asked to find guarantors for your rent payments – in practice, usually your parents.

Inventories and other paperwork

You should get an inventory and schedule of condition of everything in the property. This is another document that you should check carefully, making sure that everything listed is as described. Write on the document anything that is different. The NUS suggests taking photographs of rooms and equipment when you first move in (setting the correct date on your camera), to provide you with additional proof should any dispute arise when your contract ends and you want to get your deposit back. If you are not offered an inventory, then make one of your own. You should have someone else witness and sign this, send it to your landlord, and keep your own copy. Keeping in contact with your landlord throughout the year and developing a good relationship with him or her will also do you no harm and may be to your advantage in the long run.

You should ask your landlord for a recent gas safety certificate issued by a qualified CORGI engineer, a fire safety certificate covering the furnishings, and a record of current gas and electricity meter readings. Take your own readings of meters when you move in to make sure these match what you have been given, or make your own records if the landlord doesn't supply them. This also applies to water meters if you are expected to pay water rates (although this isn't usually the case). The NUS issues its own advice on how to keep down energy bills, at **http://studentswitchoff.org/save-energy-rented-accommodation**. The NUS says that the average student in private rented accommodation spends £500 a year on energy, so you can save money and get a glow of green virtue by cutting back.

Finally, students are not liable for Council Tax. If you are sharing a house only with other full-time students, then you will not have to pay it. However, you may be liable to pay a proportion of the Council Tax bill if you are sharing with anyone who is not a full-time student. You may need to get a Council Tax exemption certificate from your university as evidence that you do not need to pay Council Tax.

Safety and security

Once you have arrived and settled in, remember to take care of your own safety and the security of your possessions. You are particularly vulnerable as a fresher, when you are still getting used to your new-found independence. This may help explain why so many students are burgled or robbed in the first six weeks of the academic year. Take care with valuable portable items such as mobile phones, tablet computers and laptops, all of which are tempting for criminals. Ensure you don't have them obviously on display when you are out and about and that you have insurance cover. If your mobile phone is stolen, call your network or 08701 123123 to immobilise it. Students' unions, universities and the police will provide plenty of practical guidance when you arrive. Following their advice will reduce the chance of you becoming a victim of crime and help you to enjoy living in the new surroundings of your chosen university town.

Useful websites

For advice on a range of housing issues, visit:
www.nusconnect.org.uk/campaigns/welfare/housing-and-community

The Shelter website has separate sections covering different housing regulations in England, Wales, Scotland and Northern Ireland: **www.shelter.org.uk**

As examples of providers of private hall accommodation, visit:
www.upp-ltd.com
http://www.unitestudents.com/
http://thestudenthousingcompany.com
www.student-cribs.com

A number of sites will help you find accommodation and/or potential housemates, including:
www.accommodationforstudents.com
www.uniplaces.com
www.sturents.com,
www.studentpad.co.uk
www.studentcrowd.com
http://student.spareroom.co.uk
http://uk.easyroommate.com
Accreditation Network UK is at: **www.anuk.org.uk**

www.hostuk.org helps international students meet British people and families in their homes.

9 How Covid will change the university experience

As the health pandemic turned university life on its head, two things became clear: Covid-19 would not last for ever, but the blend of online and face-to-face learning was here to stay. Pre-2020 remote learning had been the preserve of mature and part-time students, but with large public gatherings off limits, the whole higher education sector pivoted to the new normal with remarkable agility, and now everyone is doing it – to some extent or other.

That said, undergraduates starting degrees in September 2020 faced a first year like no other. Universities worked hard to keep students and staff safe by implementing copious social distancing measures, while also doing their best to offer an unforgettable introduction to what are often billed as 'the best years of your life'. There were no (official) parties or nightclubs for the freshers of 2020, who lived in small household bubbles in halls. Cramming into lecture halls was out, and lecturers delivered their teaching online, while face-to-face time on campus was reduced to a practical minimum.

Almost all (circa 98%) of UK universities committed to delivering a form of blended learning in the 2020 academic year; seven in 10 of them expected their provision to be mostly online. Government guidelines aimed at reducing the spread of the virus impacted every aspect of university life, from teaching and accommodation to support services and sports.

With Downing Street's Covid-19 briefings came new statistics and more uncertainty by the day. Universities were hoping for the best but planning for the worst. Vice-chancellors across the country found themselves acting as punitive enforcers, cracking down on breaches of self-distancing regulations, linked, in some cases, to halls of residence and off-campus parties, which inevitably fuelled infection rates.

The blended future

Some academics are treating 2020 as year zero and working around a probable framework that sees the following two years continuing to be extraordinary in some way. Certainly, universities have been forced to critically review what they do and how they do it.

Even before coronavirus, lectures were being recorded for playback and online teaching was being developed to different extents. Covid-19 has pressed the fast forward button, signalling a new approach to teaching that is bolstered by readily available and user-friendly technology. Just as the majority of people moved to cashless payments without blinking an eye, and quickly became comfortable working from home, the pandemic has accelerated changes in higher education.

Digital learning environments were already burgeoning areas of investment for universities, but the onset of widespread remote learning forced them to achieve about five-years'-worth of development in around five months. Academic staff already fluent in online teaching began honing their delivery to get the most out of the medium.

The long-run view is that academics will be able to combine teaching and technology to provide a bespoke experience best-suited to individual students' learning styles. Incoming undergraduates will benefit from the increased flexibility that digital learning allows, and who knows, maybe the unholy rush to get to 9am lectures will be consigned to history.

Size is everything

Professor Andrew Wathey, vice-chancellor of Northumbria University, predicts the rise of small-group learning. "In-person lectures will not disappear, but more will be online and more academic staff time will be spent with smaller groups of students," he believes. "What has been clear for a while is that really large lectures are not necessarily very interactive learning experiences. We had begun to recognise that about five years ago and were moving in that direction. I think coronavirus will accelerate change towards blended models of this type."

To facilitate the upturn in small-group sessions many universities have extended in-person teaching hours to allow for social distancing in labs and classrooms, and students are being offered mandatory tutorials at varying times throughout the day. Such reform to traditional contact hours scheduling will become invaluable for all students over time, especially those with external commitments. Online teaching, meanwhile, gives students the option to revisit recorded content in the run-up to exams and assessments. One-to-one online sessions with tutors have also been made available, at times that suit students.

Students at Coventry University will no longer trudge in their hundreds to lectures post-Covid, says Professor Guy Daly, deputy vice-chancellor for education and students. "We have said for a number of years now that we want to have active learning based around problem-solving, as opposed to the sage on a stage, just pouring information into you assisted by a PowerPoint.

"Our response to Covid has allowed us to do that. We will not be going back to having big lecture theatres with 200 or 300 people in them. There will still be the place for the apocryphal lecture from the professor. We are not saying that TED talks are no more, they do have a place, but week in, week out, just pouring stuff into people for an hour at least per topic is not the way forward."

Students in control

The pro-vice chancellor of Cambridge, Professor Graham Virgo, has noticed certain digital learning habits emerging. "The positives are (students) can go into a lecture when they like, they can repeat it, they can slow it down, actually I know a number are speeding it up if they feel the lecturer is going a bit slowly. So, that degree of control is very interesting, and good," he explains.

The University of Northampton opened its Waterside Campus six years ago, with no lecture theatres. Teaching is instead focused on close interaction with tutors and small groups, using digital technology in and out of the classroom. "In many ways universities have changed for ever, certainly in the areas of learning and teaching," believes Professor Alejandro Armellini, the former dean of learning and teaching at Northampton and architect of the programme, who has since been headhunted by the University of Portsmouth.

There is a school of thought among many university lecturers that the coming years offer a thrilling opportunity for large-scale digital revolution; the silver lining to the coronavirus era being the opportunity to revise existing online technology and use it as a tool to empower students to take control of their own learning, to engage and challenge them.

"The world has changed, and we're seeing sector-wide agreement that we need to not just make the best of the situation, but build on it," says Paul Feldman, chief executive officer of Jisc, an education technology not-for-profit. "Students, lecturers and leaders are all saying that they wouldn't want to return to purely in-person teaching, they see what's happening now as the path to something bigger and better."

But what students themselves want to know is whether blended learning will be detrimental to their degree outcomes. Covid-19 interfered with Ewan Somerville's final year as a politics undergraduate at the University of Sheffield, but his grades were not impacted. Now a graduate, he urges prospective first-years not to be put off by the coming educational revolution, stating categorically that webcam lectures and remote learning really do work. "During lockdown I achieved some of my highest grades, including 95% for my dissertation, the best in my department," he said.

Somerville's timetable became entirely virtual in March 2020 including three-hour, live streamed tutorials. To facilitate debate, students had to press a 'hands-up' button to signal their wish to intervene in a discussion, thus avoiding a cacophony of unmuted microphones. Lecturers offered prompt and extensive essay advice on dedicated video calls and offered speedy email guidance too. "Online learning has established a unique circumstance in which we can study more flexibly, giving students a better work-life balance. After all, university is what you make of it," says Somerville.

Today's generation Z, digital natives, have no aversion to technology. In a poll by Bramble, an online tutoring platform of mostly British students, around 84% agreed that online tutoring is more valuable than, or just as effective as, being tutored in person. Institutions are taking note, recognising that the university experience of tomorrow needs to be as accessible as Netflix, offering the next generation of students access to an 'on demand' degree education that fits around their lives. Rather than entrenching old models, universities are facing the possibility of pioneering new funding structures and increasing access to higher education.

The withdrawal of traditional lectures would change the university experience of students, believes Nick Hillman, director of the Higher Education Policy Institute (HEPI), an independent think tank. "There are much more effective ways to learn than lectures, but if you take face-to-face lectures away you lose something. Learning is a social endeavour. I met my wife at university. You want it to be a free-flowing place where you don't know who the next ten people you are going to meet are. The whole point of university is you have people from lots of different backgrounds doing lots of different things."

Moves to significantly increase online learning look likely to face resistance, however tech-savvy students might be. Durham University got a flavour of the disquiet around the issue in April 2020 when it was forced to rapidly backtrack on plans to reduce the number of modules taught in person by a quarter, and provide at least 500 of them completely online by the summer of 2021.

Larissa Kennedy, president of the National Union of Students, is already concerned about the potential impact on the mental health of students. "Isolation is a key concern, the lack of community building and (the prospect of) doing university from your bedroom," she says.

Social life in a virtual world

In 2020 the University of Sheffield was quick off the mark in producing a film that showcased its social clubs to incoming students and began building an online community through Facebook. Around 2,000 students joined within the first 24 hours. Other universities at the time made similar efforts to recruit new society members. It is not far-fetched to assume that many of these efforts, like online learning, will still be in place – and improved upon – in 2022 and beyond.

But can the social side of on-campus life be replicated in a virtual world? Students have been socialising online for years and many tend to connect through social media ahead of moving into halls and starting courses. Within this context the social shift faced by students, their unions, clubs and societies may not be that substantial, after all. Furthermore, universities say measures such as sophisticated software which can assess engagement levels of students working online will help them to identify those who are struggling.

At Loughborough University, every student has a personal academic tutor to support them. "We are making sure we know whether our students are engaged with their studies because, obviously, we want to be in a position to make a timely intervention to support all of the students," says Professor Rachel Thomson, Loughborough's pro vice-chancellor of teaching.

As a result of the pandemic, "I hope our teaching and learning offer would be enhanced as there has been a sharper focus on it over the last few months and I think that will definitely benefit students coming next year," notes Thomson.

What appears most likely in the long run is that universities will do as much as possible on campus, while much of the large-scale teaching and learning activities are more likely to happen online. Students of 2022 need to be prepared for that but need not panic; universities are acclimatising quickly and have at least another year to get it right. Future undergraduates will benefit greatly from the experience gained in 2020 and 2021.

Whatever 2022 looks like, university is still the best place to be, says Nick Hillman. "One of the things the pandemic has done is actually shown the value of education. The relative benefits are as great as ever."

Online learning: making the right choices

» Do your homework. When looking at potential courses and universities find out how much content will be delivered specifically online. The university itself is not your only source of information; talk to current students and get a realistic review of the quality of delivery. This is a relatively new feature so word of mouth will be critical, and you need to look beyond prospectuses.

» Find out if the university runs digital skills workshops, and if so attend them. Do not press the snooze button on the IT induction, engage thoroughly with it and with the training offered. If you are going to be commuting in, consider the equipment you'll need – such as a laptop with a decent-sized screen and stand. If you're on a tight budget, check if you can get a student discount or whether the university loans out laptops.

» Prepare a study space for when you are working from home. A zone dedicated to university work will help create the right psychological setting to aid your productivity. No distractions, this is a place where you can focus.

» Online etiquette requires you to be aware of your surroundings and how you present yourself virtually. Mute your microphone when others are talking and don't sit with a window behind you because no one will see you. Online learning is not a duvet day; dress and present yourself as you would to attend a physical lecture.

» Students of 2020 say one of the main things they've learned is the importance of keeping to the timetable and scheduled classes as much as possible. Tempting though it is to watch recorded lectures at your leisure this is best reserved for revision. Live lessons keep you in line with the course structure and give you the opportunity to ask questions – participation is important and online doesn't mean anti-social. You may even want to attend digital lectures, seminars and tutorials together with a classmate.

» Everyone struggles from time to time. Make sure the university you choose has a dedicated student support team in place so you can ask for help.

Fees and refunds

When courses first shifted online at the start of the pandemic many undergraduates – and their parents – argued for a reduction in fees. "People chose to pay extortionate fees to attend lectures and tutorials because they want face-to-face interaction," said one student. "If things go online, the personal relationships with tutors and professors will be virtually non-existent. There will be a huge gap in learning."

The Office of the Independent Adjudicator for Higher Education (OIAHE), an independent body handling complaints for students in England and Wales, says if a university is offering 'different but broadly equivalent teaching and assessment opportunities', a reduction in fees or refund is not likely. However, if it can be proven that universities are offering fewer lectures, or the quality in online teaching is not as expected, they may be liable to repay some fees. This could particularly apply to degrees involving the development of practical skills.

A poll by Jisc in 2020 demonstrated that not all universities and their online education strategies are equal. More than one in four students said they did not feel positive about the quality of the digital teaching they received and around 11% felt they did not have access to online course materials when they needed them.

The survey of 20,500 university students suggested that 23% were unable to rate the quality of digital teaching and learning on their course as "good", "excellent" or "best imaginable". Only half (51%) said they received guidance about vital digital skills they needed for their course.

Figures from finance website Save the Student show that even before Covid-19, refunds due to substandard teaching were not uncommon. A total £650,000 compensation was awarded to 1,635 people who complained about their university in 2017. Do not expect a full refund, however, any claim will be dependent on personal circumstances.

Nick Rodrigues & Sue Leonard

10 Preparing for University Life

Tearful or jubilant, waving goodbye to their offspring as they head into halls for the first time is an emotional moment for most parents. On the one hand, university should be a brilliant experience that helps build well-rounded, self-sufficient adults. On the other, it may be their first experience of unfettered access to alcohol, drugs and relationships, and subject them to a level of academic pressure beyond that experienced at the most demanding of schools. Worries are certain to build up – even for the most chilled-out parents, let alone for today's more-intense, hands-on types, known as 'helicopter parents', who have dedicated the last 18 years to hand-rearing and educating the perfect(ish) specimen of child.

Whilst it is entirely rational to fret about how your child will cope on campus, it shouldn't absorb your every waking thought. Young people need a chance to be independent away from the parental gaze, and to make mistakes. Their university experience will be quite different to your own, so allow them space to get it wrong and be there for them when they do.

It is possible to give your child autonomy whilst also checking in with them around the major issues: drinking, taking drugs and staying safe – both physically and mentally – on campus. Even with the potentially lasting impact of coronavirus, university remains an undeniably exciting and worthwhile investment.

Another round, bartender

Much of the university social scene inevitably revolves around campus or college bars, and Freshers Week traditionally has a packed itinerary of club nights and boozy social mixer events. This extends to student accommodation, with pre-drinks ever popular among students as a cheap alternative to paying bar prices. Students gather in their kitchens for drinking games, often aiming to get sozzled enough before they go out to ensure an inexpensive night once they do. In an Alcohol Impact survey carried out by the NUS in 2018-2019, over half of the 793 respondents said they regularly drank at home or at a friend's house before a night out, and 29% stated they deliberately got drunk at pre-drinks.

Sobering thoughts

The long-term health conditions caused by regular over-consumption of alcohol are unlikely to be at the forefront of the minds of freshly independent 18-year-olds as they knock back another Jagerbomb, but the impact that the culture of student drinking can have on their social circle and academic progress may hit home more easily. Teetotal students can feel isolated, whilst those hellbent on drinking to excess can find themselves missing deadlines, involved in anti-social behaviour or letting their guard down around personal safety. Universities and student organisations have woken up to these issues and campaigns to promote responsible drinking cultures on campuses have sprung up nationwide.

Last orders

The National Union of Students (NUS) runs the Alcohol Impact programme, which partners with universities across the UK to reduce harm. Originally set up to tackle drunken antisocial behaviour, the programme had the knock-on effect of increasing student wellbeing, whilst making campus a more inclusive place for non-drinkers. It recommends 50 different actions to reduce harm around drinking, from training bar staff in helping intoxicated students, to working with the local community to ensure students get home safely from a night out. So far, 31 universities across the country have completed the scheme, and you can see if the institution you are considering applying to is part of the programme at **www.alcoholimpact.nus.org.uk**.

Among the measures used to manage student drinking are safe taxi schemes. Students can trade their ID card for a ride home and settle the fare the next day. During Freshers Weeks, there are volunteer student crews of second or third years on hand to make sure anyone who has overindulged gets back to their accommodation safely.

For non-drinkers, there may well be an active sober social scene on campus. In the 2018–19 NUS Alcohol Impact Report, 40% of the 793 students surveyed say they get drunk less than once a week, and there are an increasing number of dry societies and social events at universities for socialising without getting drunk.

Offering sober-minded advice

Michelle Hemmingfield, co-ordinator of NUS Alcohol Impact, recommends a harm reduction approach. Rather than preaching sobriety to your children, foster open conversation in which you can inform them about alcohol overconsumption. A good way to get the conversation going is by explaining how to take care of someone else who has drunk to excess. Educating them on the warning signs of alcohol overdose – such as snoring, unresponsiveness and pale skin – will not only help them but their peers as well.

In a world of coronavirus restrictions, a harm reduction approach is even more important. When bars and pubs close, hall parties become all the rage. Hemmingfield recommends buying students an alcohol measure for their accommodation, to help them more accurately keep track of the units they consume. Cringe though some students may when unpacking their drinks measure in halls kitchen, you never know, it might just work. And if having a measure does not result in your child fastidiously updating a drinks diary, it could at least make them think twice before sloshing in another huge home measure, or help them create concoctions that actually taste nice and are more likely to be savoured than inhaled.

Finally, trust them. The Alcohol Impact survey revealed 80% of respondents agreed that drinking too much can spoil a good night and cut it short. Parents who are worried about their child's drinking can find useful resources at DrinkAware online, including tips on how to facilitate conversations around alcohol.

Chasing the High

Parents cannot pull the wool over their own eyes any longer; it is easier than ever to score drugs on campus. Dealers are on the way out though, and buying through the dark web or peer hook-ups is more common and more difficult to trace. Furthermore, with Covid restrictions on bars and clubs stretching into the future, drugs are more likely to be taken at a flat or house party. This removes the limiting influence of bouncers and bar staff, along with increasing peer pressure as students try to fit in with their restricted social bubbles. It's never been more important to ensure students are equipped with harm prevention methods around drugs.

Despite being illegal, drugs are ever-present on campuses. Taking the Hit, a 2018 NUS study into drugs at university, surveyed 2,081 students at 151 institutions. It found that 39% said they currently used drugs, and 19% had used them in the past. Cannabis was the most popular, having been used at some point by 94% of respondents. It was closely followed by 'club drug' Ecstasy/MDMA, with cocaine and nitrous oxide also making the list.

'Study drugs' are also favourites on campuses across the UK, purportedly taken by students to improve concentration and keep them writing essays into the early hours. Substances such as Ritalin and Modafinil were taken by one in ten of the 2,081 respondents, utilising prescription-only medicines usually procured via other methods to keep them focused during deadlines.

Historically, universities have responded punitively to students caught with drugs. A solely disciplinary approach has limited success however, isolating students rather than aiding them. Four in ten of the respondents to Taking the Hit said they wouldn't feel comfortable disclosing their drug use to their university for fear of punishment, and as such, do not seek out help when they need it.

Changing the game

The 'abstinence only' approach to drug taking at universities is slowly changing, however. Students for Sensible Drug Policy, (SSDP) is an international grassroots organisation, led by students advocating for a change in drug policy on campuses.

Iulia Vatau, leader of the SSDP at University College London, believes in a harm reduction approach. She argues that the many reasons behind drug usage, including mental health management and peer pressure, should be acknowledged. Their team provided online Harm Prevention packs for incoming students, containing information and advice on drugs and seeking help.

Such changes are also reflected at an institutional level. Following the tragic deaths of students from drug misuse, the Newcastle University Student Union set up amnesty bins for students to dispose of any drugs, without judgement or repercussions. Similarly, at the University of the West of England, a policy promotes evidence-based information around drugs. The goal is to empower students to make informed decisions, stating that pastoral and medical needs will always be prioritised over disciplinary proceedings.

This is not to say that drugs will soon be permissible on campuses. Of the 151 institutions surveyed in the Taking the Hit report, over half took a firmer line than the law, penalising students for technically legal drug-related offences. Accommodation contracts often have an outright ban on drugs, threatening eviction if students are caught using them.

Parents

Foster open dialogue to equip your child with harm reduction knowledge. By discussing the effects of certain drugs, and what to do if someone has a bad reaction or overdoses, they'll garner information that could end up saving their life, or one of their flatmates. To facilitate such a potentially thorny chat, Hemmingfield, who also co-ordinates the NUS Alcohol and Drugs impact scheme, recommends taking a bystander approach. She advises:

"A much easier way to frame it is saying, 'your friends may take drugs, these are the risks they are undertaking.' By doing that, you make sure that they get the information for themselves whilst still not directly tackling them on it. This can make for a less awkward conversation, and it helps young people to understand the risks in a non-judgemental, safe space."

University drug policies depend on the institution, so read up on the fine print. Websites such as Talk to Frank and Volteface provide information on the effects that different substances can have and advice on how to talk to young people about drugs.

Putting it all on show

Sexual assault and violence on UK campuses is a serious problem. A sobering 2018 study by Revolt Sexual Assault found that 62% of 4,491 students surveyed had experienced sexual violence at university. Of that figure, just 2% felt able to report the incident and were satisfied with the reporting process. Women are far more likely to be victims, as are LGBTQ+ students.

Students have been increasingly vocal about sexual violence on campuses, and demanding change. An anonymous Instagram account called St Andrews Survivors became national news in July 2020, documenting St Andrews University students' first-hand accounts of sexual assault. It had gained over 200 submissions by November.

University responses have been mixed. Consent workshops, if they exist at all, often disappear after initial Welcome Week activities and some institutions received heavy criticism for using legal Non-Disclosure Agreements to prevent victims of sexual assault speaking about their experiences of university safeguarding procedures.

Turning the Tide

Initiatives across the university sector are tackling sexual harassment and consent head on. The National Union of Students launched its I Heart Consent campaign in 2014, delivering consent workshops across campuses. Sara Khan, NUS Vice President for Liberation and Equality, said she believes universities are failing on sexual misconduct, but NUS's workshops educate students and equip them to identify and act when they witness unacceptable behaviour.

Dr Nina Burns, co-founder of the Consent Collective, wants consent training to be seen as "an essential part of providing education that will set somebody up for life", not a politically correct afterthought. Her organisation provides consent training and trauma resources to universities, and students can contact them to access their latest trauma resource pack should they need to.

Universities are increasingly acting against sexual violence. Newcastle University has an online reporting tool which enables anonymous submissions and offers a sexual violence liaison officer and specialist counselling services. Canterbury Christ Church University, working with domestic abuse charity Rising Sun, trains sessional staff, postgraduate research students and students' union staff to deliver Bystander training to key members of the university's societies and sports clubs. Change is happening, but there is still more to be done.

Rethinking the Birds and the Bees chat

First and foremost, discuss consent, Burns urges, "You can have those conversations about relationships, not necessarily sexual ones, but about friendship or family relationships, consent is relevant to all of these relationships with power, communication and respect." She also encourages parents to approach universities to ask what their prevention, education and reporting procedures are directly.

Second, make them feel able to talk to you if something happens, without judgement or blame. According to the Revolt study, only 7% of students surveyed knew about their university's sexual violence policy, so go through it with your child before they leave and make sure you are both informed. Sex education in schools rarely covers issues of consent, so equip your child with practical information of the sexual support services on offer, wherever they move to.

Finally, if your child is sexually active, make sure they know how to access contraceptive services and sign up to a GP as soon as possible.

Troubled Times

The kids are not always alright, so friends and family of university students are correct to be vigilant. Jenny Smith, Policy Manager at Student Minds, is particularly concerned for new students. "The start of a new academic year is a key pressure point for many. Students may be worried about their academic capability, establishing new friendships or making ends meet financially." The onset of mental health conditions often overlaps with the age when most students go to university, so the importance of this window cannot be overestimated.

Research shows that both the number of suicides and those dropping out were increasing before the pandemic, and in 2019 mental health conditions were the second most declared disability, following a 20% increase. The mental health crisis universities were already facing is only likely to be accelerated by Covid-19.

The Resolution Foundation's Annual Intergenerational Audit found that the proportion of 19- to 29-year olds experiencing poor mental health has risen by 80% since early 2020. Depression rates across the general public have doubled, according to the Office for National Statistics, and are set to rise as unemployment, financial difficulties and housing insecurity take hold. John de Pury, mental health policy lead for Universities UK, believes that financially disadvantaged, BAME, disabled and LGBTQ+ students are most acutely at risk.

Finding your feet without sufficient funds makes things even more difficult. Part-time jobs have been squeezed as the hospitality industry has been hit hard by Covid restrictions. Over half of employed 18 to 24-year olds have been furloughed or let go since the pandemic began and universities are reporting unprecedented pressures on student hardship funds. Kingston University was forced to launch an emergency appeal, raising over £140,000 for students in financial crisis.

Tackling the load

Universities are struggling to meet demand for mental health services and long waiting times are, sadly, par for the course. Geraldine Dufour, Head of Counselling Services at Cambridge University, said: "Cambridge, the education sector and society more widely were already facing challenges in relation to meeting increasing demand for mental health services every year", a situation intensified by Covid-19.

Students aren't taking it lying down. In 2018, as part of a wider campaign, University College London students disrupted an open day, protesting the long waiting times to receive counselling. It resulted in £140,000 extra being invested in student mental health services.

There is some light on the horizon and most universities are expanding their mental health service provisions. The University of Bristol offers a ten-week Science of Happiness course to all students, which teaches exercises to improve mental wellbeing. Ten other universities will benefit from a new £1.5 million partnership between the charity Mind and Goldman Sachs investment bank to deliver wellbeing, resilience and mindfulness training over the next two years.

Manchester, home to the largest number of university students of any city region, is in the second year of a £1.6 million pilot mental health service. The scheme links psychiatrists, psychologists and mental health nurses with students from Manchester's four universities and the Royal Northern College of Music. Newcastle University's in-house approach offers cognitive behavioural therapy, delivered by trained and trainee staff and students from its School of Psychology.

Many of these support services have moved online since Covid-19, hastening a trend that was already emerging. Although this reduces face-to-face support it may make accessing services easier, both practically and psychologically, by foregoing the daunting walk there in person.

How can parents help?

The role of a parent or guardian has never been more important. Family and friends are often the first to know when students are unwell, so breaking down the stigma by talking freely about mental health will help them reach out for support when they need it.

Graham Virgo, Senior Pro-Vice Chancellor at Cambridge University urges parents to get involved: "If your prospective university student is worried about the future, tell them that they are not alone. Suggest that, while there are many things that are out of our control, they can always reach out to you with their concerns and to other people close to them at home and at university." Research what support is available to your child and spend time brainstorming helpful strategies together.

UK charity Student Minds recently launched Student Space, offering free wellbeing resources and support via phone, text, webchat or email to all university students in England and Wales. You can also contact the Parents Helpline at Young Minds for free, confidential advice if you are worried about a young person. For other resources and information visit the Student Minds parents' FAQ page at **https://www.studentminds.org.uk/supportforparents.html**.

Digital universities

This generation of students are facing the most online-based university experience to date. In the last decade higher education has increasingly seen coursework set, essays handed in and gradings taking place digitally. Lectures are recorded and placed on student interfaces. For some courses it could just about be possible to scrape through the first year without ever going to a lecture in person.

The implications of coronavirus on campus have hastened the diversion of face-to-face lectures and seminars online, and students are having to live and work in restricted 'bubbles'. Cambridge University was the first to announce that all of its lectures for the 2020–2021 academic year would be moved online as a result of the pandemic. All institutions soon followed suit, opting for a blended approach that marries mostly online lectures with some face-to-face seminars and tutorials.

These changes could potentially lead to a permanently screen-based university experience. The University of Northampton already has a digital campus, the Northampton Integrated Learning Environment (NILE). There is a NILE course for every programme offered by the university, and students engage in online activities and discussions in virtual classrooms.

Along with online learning, students should be aware of the impact their online persona has. Posting on social media and messaging online are not private affairs, and many students have been exposed in supposedly confidential group chats, or by statuses on a private profile. Once posted online – be it a compromising photo, crass opinion or cruel 'banter' – then it is there to stay. Digital footprints follow you, whether you like it or not.

Students at Durham rightly fell foul of this in September 2020, when a group chat containing multiple misogynistic, racist and discriminatory views was leaked. One student had his offer to study at Durham withdrawn. In a similar online exposure, 11 students at Warwick were suspended for making rape jokes, racist statements and anti-Semitic slurs in an online conversation.

With the popularity of social media sites on campus, where opinions can be fired off in a matter of seconds, and TikToks serving as currency, remind your child that things they post today will be taken into account not only by their university but by future employers. Caution them not to post anything online they wouldn't be comfortable having read back to them in an interview, or in front of a lecture hall of peers.

Universities have social media guidelines for students and your child will be considered to be a representative of the university, whether posting on a private page or not. Bullying, harassment and discrimination, no matter how jokily intended, won't be tolerated. Clue them up on this before they go and remind them that nothing is truly private.

Cyber Campus life

On a practical level, having a reliable laptop is going to make life a lot easier for students starting university in the next few years. If the Bank of Mum and Dad has run dry, find out what financial support is offered by your university. Anglia Ruskin University offered eligible students a £150 voucher towards the cost of a laptop for those starting in 2020, while the University of Huddersfield offered £500 to those from families with a household income of less than £25,000 per annum.

Keeping an eye online

Try not to fall into the trap of being a helicopter parent. Your child is unlikely to accept you as a friend on social media sites or share everything with you. They are entitled to their own privacy, and if you give them space, they are more likely to willingly share than if it is forced.

Make sure they are aware of the ramifications of online posting and encourage privacy settings so their posts can't be shared beyond the intended audience. This won't give them free rein to post whatever they like, but hopefully serve as damage limitation if something does go awry.

If you're concerned that they might be feeling isolated, stay in touch. As with all of the issues outlined above, the key is open dialogue and reserving your own judgement. Developing this relationship before your child goes to university will reap dividends as they navigate through their time away.

Charlie Burt & Georgie Campbell

Useful websites

For alcohol information: **https://alcoholimpact.nus.org.uk**
                                    www.drinkaware.co.uk
For information about drugs: **www.talktofrank.com**
                                    www.ssdp.org
For information around consent: **www.nusconnect.org.uk**
                                    www.revoltsexualassault.com
                                    www.consentcollective.com
For information about mental health services the first point of reference should be a university's student support services.
For more general information: **www.studentminds.org.uk**
                                    www.youngminds.org.uk

11 Going Abroad to University

Before Brexit, the option of studying abroad had long been one of the everyday freedoms UK students had been able to take for granted. Nipping on an Easyjet to an EU destination for a term, a summer, a year or your whole degree was straightforward, relatively speaking. Fees for British students choosing to study full-time at public universities on the Continent had been charged at the lower or non-existent 'home' rates granted to fellow EU students. Student visas had only been needed by those coming from further afield, outside the EU. Loans and other financial support had also been available, to varying extents.

Now that the UK has officially left the EU, the transition period having drawn to a close on 31 December 2020, changes to the mobility of UK students within EU countries have come into force. Some things, though, have stayed the same, while uncertainty is still rumbling on over certain outcomes.

Exchange students

Erasmus+, the EU's education, training and youth support programme that offers study, work experience and volunteering exchanges ranging from three months to one academic year, has been a bone of contention in withdrawal agreement negotiations. Each year around 16,000 British students travel to more than 30 countries, including non-EU members such as Norway and Serbia, via the programme. Whether or not the UK government participates in Erasmus+ in the next academic year is still being decided, leaving current and prospective exchange students worried about what to expect. Those already on them have been concerned about losing free healthcare (EHIC medical cards may no longer be valid), student finance and benefits. The Department for Education gave the following commitment to seeing through Erasmus+ programmes already on the go: "Projects successfully bid for during the current programme will continue to receive EU funding for the full duration of the project, including those where funding runs beyond 2020," a spokesperson told our *Guide*.

If Brexit does mean leaving Erasmus+, British students will get a UK-run replacement.

"We are committed to supporting international education exchanges, so we are continuing to develop a domestic alternative to Erasmus+ to ensure we are prepared for every eventuality and the 2020 Spending Review committed to fund this replacement scheme, if it is needed," said the DfE spokesperson.

Tuition fees on the Continent post-Brexit

British students already living in an EU country before the clock struck midnight on 31 December 2020 will continue to have the same educational rights as that country's nationals. UK citizens studying – or planning to study – in Ireland will continue to be covered by the Common Travel Area arrangements, which guarantees 'home' fees, lower than those charged to international students, for the future.

It is up to individual EU member states to determine their approach to tuition fees for UK nationals, post-Brexit. Some countries, such as Germany – the second most popular destination for UK students studying abroad – have always charged the same fees to students from anywhere else in the world, not just the EU, and will continue to do so post-Brexit. In other countries, such as Denmark, British citizens without permanent residency are now liable to pay university tuition fees there.

The Netherlands, which regularly promotes its universities to UK students and offers more undergraduate degrees taught in English than many other foreign destinations, had not at the time of going to press (mid-December 2020) confirmed the post-Brexit fee status for British students. Many think British students are likely to incur international fees though, which range from around €8,000 a year to €32,000 a year for medicine, compared with the standard EU tuition fees in 2020-2021 of €2,143 for most courses. Dutch tuition fee loans, available for the full amount to EU students who are resident in the Netherlands throughout their studies, will stop for UK students.

There is an onus on candidates to do their own research and keep abreast of changes. The Government has published guidance encouraging UK students starting courses after 1 January 2021 to contact their prospective university in the EU to check whether the situation, or tuition fees, are going to change. Students are also advised to consider visa requirements, healthcare and travel insurance. As negotiations continue so will the ramifications for students, so do monitor things at:

https://www.gov.uk/guidance/study-in-the-european-union
https://www.gov.uk/guidance/uk-students-in-the-eu-continuing-your-studies

Beyond Europe

But Brexit makes no difference to the situation in the most popular overseas study destination, America. Numbers of British students choosing universities in the US have been on the rise, where the fees gap has narrowed, there is no language barrier and academically broad-based degrees in charming collegiate environments beckon. This is a largely public school phenomenon for the time being, but one that is gathering steam. Australia is the third most popular destination for Brits studying abroad, and Canada the fifth.

The path less trodden

Students did not vote for Brexit and having their wings clipped by its outcomes is understandably frustrating. As a nation, however, the British are historically not prolific student-travellers. There are more than 5.3 million students worldwide pursuing their higher education abroad – which represents two out of every 100 students, according to UNESCO, but the British contingent contributes little to the global campus stampede. This is due in part to the good quality higher education at home – with UK universities second only to those in the US in all international rankings, and which at present offer enough places to meet demand. Our collectively dreadful ability to speak languages other than English also crucially limits the British taste for foreign study, unlike in most other countries where young people tend to be proficient in at least one second language by their late teens.

Cost is the third major factor that makes Britons hesitate about going abroad to study. Predictions that price would become less of a barrier once UK degrees charged £9,000-a-year from 2012, have been slow to translate into a long-term overseas applications boom. There have been flurries of activity, however; in 2013 more than 1,000 British freshers started university in the Netherlands, where fees were then around €2,000 (£1,700). The higher tuition fees at home put those charged by universities across the Atlantic into a more relatable context too.

Even taking into account grants, loans and scholarships, affordability limits access to a university abroad to those with sufficient finances to make it happen. Transatlantic flights, for instance, are pricier even than a peak return ticket on routes across our national rail network. Universities in some Continental cities, such as those in Scandinavian countries, may come with accommodation costs that are hard to swallow. Another major money concern is that although support from the Student Loans Company continues for a year abroad during a UK degree course, those studying for their whole degrees from non-UK institutions do not qualify for a loan at all.

Advantages of studying abroad

Schools, universities and students themselves are enthusiastic about studying abroad. It is exciting, it broadens horizons, offers new challenges and introduces young people to a global working environment sure to prove helpful in future careers, whatever those turn out to be. A study stint abroad on a CV shows employers that the applicant is flexible and culturally mobile, with a maturity and breadth of experience that stands out from other candidates.

Research published by Universities UK shows that students who spend time studying abroad outperform their peers in both the classroom and jobs market, being 19% more likely to graduate with a first and 24% less likely to be unemployed. British Council research has shown that one student in three is interested in some form of overseas study, and options include international summer schools and a semester or a year abroad as part of a degree, either studying or on work experience. Whatever the situation is fees-wise in EU countries, the maximum fee a UK university can charge for a year abroad is £1,385, and many charge less. The numbers going abroad as part of a UK degree have grown by 50% in recent years, topping 30,000. But France still sends three times as many, according to UNESCO. Nepal has half the UK's population but roughly the same number of students overseas.

It is possible to have your academic cake and eat it, by attending a British university in another country. Nottingham University has campuses in China and Malaysia; Middlesex can offer Dubai or Mauritius, where students registered in the UK can take part or all of their degree. Other universities, such as Liverpool, also have joint ventures with overseas institutions which offer an international experience (in China, in Liverpool's case) and degrees from both universities.

In most cases, however, an overseas study experience means a foreign university. Postgraduate degrees used to be the preferred qualification for those prepared to go abroad, and it is worth considering spending your undergraduate years in the UK before going abroad for more advanced study. Older students focused on more specialised programmes may get more out of living and studying abroad than 18-year-olds, and since first degrees in the UK are shorter than elsewhere, it could also work out cheaper.

Where do students go to?

Continental universities have been a no-brainer financially for UK students in the know, with even their generally longer courses working out less pricey than a UK degree. But the paucity of undergraduate programmes taught in English has been a barrier. Thousands of postgraduate courses are taught in English at Continental universities, though.

The obvious alternatives are American, Australian and Canadian universities, all of which are keen to attract more international students. Cost and distance are the main obstacles for these destinations. Four-year courses add considerably to the cost of affordable-looking fees, while the low exchange rate for the £ has been another disadvantage.

There is remarkably little official monitoring of how many students leave the UK, let alone where they go. But the USA remains by far the most popular student destination. The latest figures from UNESCO put Germany, Australia, Bulgaria, Canada after it, followed by Ireland, Spain, France, Denmark and the United Arab Emirates. A few British students find their way to unexpected locations, like South Korea or Slovakia, but usually for family reasons or to study the language.

Bear in mind that studying abroad can be the start of a much lengthier relocation, visa regulations allowing. University is where lots of people meet their spouses and set sail in their careers. Is the other side of the Atlantic, or the world, where you see yourself potentially settling down?

Studying in Europe

There are more than 10,000 UK students at Continental European universities and colleges, according to UNESCO. But a minority are undergraduates, because more courses are taught in English at postgraduate level.

Nearly all first degrees in France are taught in the mother tongue, though there are 100 programmes taught in English listed on the Campus France website (**www.campusfrance.org/en**) at the Licence (Bachelors equivalent) level.

Germany attracts large numbers of international students and the DAAD website (**www.daad.de/en**) lists 249 undergraduate programmes taught wholly or mainly in English. Many are at the 19 private German universities, however, like Jacobs University in Bremen, which charges €20,000 tuition fees a year. The public sector has abolished tuition fees, but you need to hunt down the courses as they are relatively scarce.

Top ten destinations for UK students studying abroad

1	United States	10,125
2	Germany	4,659
3	Australia	2,343
4	Bulgaria	2,094
5	Canada	1,781
6	Ireland	1,663
7	Spain	1,067
8	France	1,037
9	Denmark	1,007
10	United Arab Emirates	869

Source: 2019 Unesco figures

Best Student Cities in the World

1	London	United Kingdom
2	Tokyo	Japan
3	Melbourne	Australia
4	Munich	Germany
5	Berlin	Germany
6	Montreal	Canada
7	Paris	France
8	Zurich	Switzerland
9	Sydney	Australia
=10	Hongkong	China
=10	Seoul	South Korea

QS ranking 2019

Most Continental courses are longer than their UK equivalents, adding to the cost and to lost earnings from extra time at university. Travel costs will of course be higher. The cost of living varies, from lower than the UK in southern Europe, to higher in Scandinavia.

The shorter-term exchange schemes offered by Erasmus+ or its replacement, or arranged by UK universities with partners across the world, represent much less of a commitment academically, emotionally and financially than taking your whole degree abroad.

Studying in North America

For British students abroad the opportunity of carving out their own idea of the American dream at university makes the most compelling international study option. More than 10,000 UK students went to US universities in 2019, according to UNESCO, more than double the number that went to the second most common choice, Germany. The Fulbright Commission, which promotes American higher education, has seen a 30% increase in the number of Britons taking US university entrance exams. The top American universities' success in international rankings helps drive up demand, which in turn filters to universities further down the tables and across the border in Canada.

The fact that teenagers often do not know what they want to study is a driving force behind the growing popularity of American degrees, says David Hawkins, director and founder of The University Guys, which supports students and schools with university applications to the USA, Canada, Europe and beyond. "If you're admitted to Harvard you're not admitted as a biologist or a business student, you're just admitted to Harvard. Because if you go to the US you don't have to pick, and even if you major in history it's still only a third of your classes. So, there's a massive advantage there."

The chances of getting into that particular university are slim however, even for the brightest applicants, Hawkins explains: "We work with about 130 schools around the UK and if Harvard takes 15 British kids, the UK has had a good year. Harvard rejects 19 out of every 20 people that apply. Last year the Ivy League rejected more students than the total number of British 18-year-olds who went to any university in the UK." Hence the broadening out into Canada, where the University of Toronto has 60,000 undergraduates, compared with Harvard's 6,000, and to institutions such as UCLA and the University of Michigan.

British families accustomed to the fee-paying school sector find much to recommend America's top liberal arts universities, whose leafy campuses and smart facilities look similar to private schools at home. Hawkins likens many UK universities to going to a state school in the US, "It's subsidised, it's rationed, it's what you get," he says. With the UK university age demographic set to expand over the next decade, competition for places at coveted research-led universities at home will become tougher, which in turn is likely to spawn greater interest across the pond.

Tuition fees at Ivy League institutions are notoriously high – Harvard's are $51,904 in 2020–21, or $85,470 including all the costs of attendance – but generous student aid programmes mean most pay far less than the rack rate. Outside the Ivy League, the fee gap for UK students was narrowing, but fees at many state universities have shot up in the last few years as politicians have tried to balance the books. Texas A&M University, for example, ranked in the top 200 in the world, puts undergraduates' total costs at $56.290 a year. At the State University of New York, fees for out-of-state residents living on campus are $32,830. Only fees at much lower-ranked state universities compare with costs in the UK. At South Dakota State University tuition plus living costs are estimated to be less than $12,000 a year.

The state and private universities' individual systems make for big swings in the financial support open to international students. Fulbright advises students considering a US degree to assess and negotiate a funding package at the same time as pursuing their application. Otherwise, they may end up with a place they cannot afford, losing valuable time in the quest for a more suitable one.

Which countries are best?

A memorable and valuable all-round experience is up there with the need for a good course when searching for a university overseas. Location is a big deal for most students – the country and the city – as is the reputation of the institution. QS publishes an annual ranking of student cities, based on quality of life indicators as well as the number of places at world-ranked universities. London topped the ranking in 2019, followed by Tokyo, Melbourne and Munich, in that order.

Many Asian countries, such as Japan, are looking to recruit more foreign students. The high cost of living and unfamiliar language in Japan may seem hard to crack, but support for international students and courses taught in English are on the rise. As with any non-English-speaking country though, even if you are taught in English, you still need enough of the local language to get by in shops, on transport and to make friends – to sign up for an exciting study experience abroad but only mix with expats there would be a wasted opportunity.

China is worth considering, if you can get used to the dormitory accommodation that is the norm at most universities. The country's leading institutions are climbing the world rankings and improving their facilities, and the potential headstart in business offered by studying in China is hard to ignore. Until the recent disturbances, Hong Kong, which has several world-ranked universities and feels familiar for Britons, was a popular alternative to mainland Chinese universities.

Will my degree be recognised?

Even in the era of globalisation, you need to bear in mind that not all degrees are equal. Unlike the MBA, which has an international system for accrediting courses and a global admissions standard, many professional courses need a qualification recognised by the relevant professional body. It is understandable that to practise law in England, you need to have studied the English legal system. For other subjects, the issues are more about the quality and content of courses outside UK control.

Contact the National Recognition Centre for the UK (**www.naric.org.uk**), which examines the compatibility and acceptability of qualifications from around the world, or ask the UK professional body in question – an engineering institution, law society or dental council, for instance – about the qualification you are interested in.

Global rankings: which university is best?

Going abroad to study is a big and expensive decision, and you want to get it right. A university that is taken seriously around the world should be your ambition, whatever you hope to do after graduation.

At the moment, there are three main systems for ranking universities internationally. One is run by QS (Quacquarelli Symonds), an educational research company in London (**www.topuniversities.com**). Another is by Shanghai Ranking Consultancy, a company set up by Shanghai Jiao Tong University, in China, and is called the Academic Ranking of World

Top Universities in the World

Rank	(Last year)	Institution	Country
2020	**(2019)**		
1	**(1)**	Stanford University	USA
2	**(3)**	Harvard University	USA
3	**(2)**	Massachusetts Institute of Technology (MIT)	USA
4	**(4)**	University of Oxford	UK
=5	**(6)**	California Institute of Technology (Caltech)	USA
=5	**(5)**	University of Cambridge	UK
7	**(7)**	Princeton University	USA
8	**(8)**	University of Chicago	USA
9	**(9)**	Yale University	USA
10	**(=10)**	ETH Zurich (Swiss Federal Institute of Technology)	Switzerland
=11	**(=10)**	UCL (University College London)	UK
=11	**(=15)**	University of California, Berkeley (UCB)	USA
13	**(=12)**	Columbia University	USA
14	**(=12)**	Imperial College London	UK
=15	**(14)**	University of Pennsylvania	USA
=15	**(=15)**	Cornell University	USA
17	**(17)**	Johns Hopkins University	USA
=18	**(=23)**	Tsinghua University	China
=18	**(19)**	University of California, Los Angeles (UCLA)	USA
20	**(18)**	University of Michigan-Ann Arbor	USA
21	**(20)**	University of Toronto	Canada
22	**(=23)**	Northwestern University	USA
23	**(25)**	The University of Tokyo	Japan
24	**(27)**	New York University (NYU)	USA
25	**(21)**	Duke University	USA
26	**(22)**	University of Edinburgh	UK
27	**(28)**	Peking University	China
28	**(26)**	University of California, San Diego (UCSD)	USA
29	**(31)**	The University of Melbourne	Australia
30	**(=33)**	King's College London (KCL)	UK
31	**(32)**	The University of Manchester	UK
32	**(29)**	National University of Singapore (NUS)	Singapore
=33	**(=33)**	University of British Columbia	Canada
=33	**(30)**	University of Washington	USA
35	**(35)**	Kyoto University	Japan
36	**(=56)**	Université PSL (Paris Sciences & Lettres)	France
37	**(=37)**	Ecole Polytechnique Fédérale de Lausanne (EPFL)	Switzerland
38	**(=41)**	Technische Universität München	Germany
=39	**(39)**	Ludwig-Maximilians-Universität München	Germany
=39	**(=37)**	University of Wisconsin-Madison	USA
41	**(=46)**	McGill University	Canada

42	(36) Nanyang Technological University (NTU)	Singapore
43	(40) University of Texas at Austin	USA
44	(=41) Australian National University (ANU)	Australia
=45	(=44) University of Hong Kong (HKU)	Hong Kong
=45	(=46) The University of Queensland (UQ)	Australia
47	(43) Ruprecht-Karls-Universität Heidelberg	Germany
48	(54) The University of Sydney	Australia
=49	(48) Carnegie Mellon University	USA
=49	(50) Washington University in St Louis	USA
51	(=44) University of Illinois at Urbana-Champaign	USA
52	(49) London School of Economics and Political Science (LSE)	UK
53	(51) University of North Carolina, Chapel Hill	USA
54	(=52) Karolinska Institute, Stockholm	Sweden
55	(=52) The Hong Kong University of Science and Technology (HKUST)	Hong Kong
56	(64) The University of New South Wales (UNSW)	Australia
57	(=56) University of Copenhagen	Denmark
=58	(60) Seoul National University (SNU)	South Korea
=58	(=72) University of Zurich	Switzerland
60	(61) The Chinese University of Hong Kong (CUHK)	Hong Kong
=61	(82) Fudan University	China
=61	(=62) Monash University	Australia
63	(=70) Zhejiang University	China
64	(59) Sorbonne University	France
65	(=83=) Shanghai Jiao Tong University	China
66	(58) University of Bristol	UK
67	(=66) University of Southern California	USA
68	— Paris Saclay University	France
69	(=62) University of California, Santa Barbara	USA
70	— Georgia Institute of Technology (Georgia Tech)	USA
71	(55) Brown University	USA
72	(69) University of California, San Francisco	USA
=73	(65) Katholieke Universiteit Leuven	Belgium
=73	(68) University of Minnesota, Twin Cities	USA
=75	(=72) University of Amsterdam	Netherlands
=75	(=70) Utrecht University	Netherlands
77	(=83) KAIST – Korea Advanced Institute of Science and Technology	South Korea
78	(=66) Delft University of Technology	Netherlands
79	(=80) The University of Warwick	UK
80	(=76) University of Maryland, College Park	USA
=81	(75) Rockefeller University	USA
=81	(74) Boston University	USA
83	(=80) University of Colorado at Boulder	USA
=84	(=87) City University of Hong Kong	Hong Kong
=84	— University of Texas Southwestern Medical Center	USA
=84	(=78) University of Groningen	Netherlands
87	(86) Leiden University	Netherlands

Top Universities in the World cont

Rank	(Last year)	Institution	Country
2020	**(2019)**		
=88	**(100)**	University of Science and Technology of China	China
=88	**(=76)**	Erasmus University, Rotterdam	Netherlands
=90	**(=87)**	Ecole Polytechnique	France
=90	**(85)**	University of California, Davis	USA
92	**(=89)**	Tokyo Institute of Technology	Japan
=93	—	Universiti Malaya (UM)	Malaysia
=93	**(=89)**	University of Geneva	Switzerland
95	**(=92)**	University of Oslo	Norway
=96	—	National Taiwan University (NTU)	Taiwan
=96	—	Vanderbilt University	USA
98	**(=92)**	Wageningen University	Netherlands
99	—	University of Paris	France
=100	—	Universidad de Buenos Aires	Argentina
=100	—	Lomonosov Moscow State University	Russia
=100	—	Ghent University	Netherlands
=100	—	University of California, Irvine	USA
=100	**(96)**	McMaster University	Canada

Averaged from positions in the QS World University Ranking (QS); the Academic Ranking of World Universities (ARWU – Shanghai ranking) and *Times Higher Education* (THE) for 2020

Universities (ARWU) (**www.shanghairanking.com**). The third is produced by *Times Higher Education* (**www.timeshighereducation.com/world-university-rankings**), a weekly magazine with no connection to *The Times*, which published the QS version until 2010.

The QS system uses measures including academic opinion, employer opinion, international orientation, research impact and staff/student ratio to create its listing, while the ARWU takes account of Nobel Prizes and highly-cited papers, which are more related to excellence in scientific research. Times Higher Education added a number of measures to the QS model, including research income and a controversial global survey of teaching quality.

Naturally, the different methodologies produce some contrasting results – as evidenced by the three main rankings each having a different university at the top. The table on these pages is a composite of the three main rankings, which places Stanford at the top and includes two UK universities in the top ten – one less than the three that featured in our last edition, now that UCL has slipped to 11=.

In practice, if you go to a university that features strongly in any of the tables, you will be at a place that is well-regarded around the world. Even the 200th university on any of these rankings is an elite institution in a world with more than 5,000 universities.

The main international rankings focus mainly on research and tend to favour universities which are strong in science and medicine. This is why places that centre on the humanities and the social sciences, such as the London School of Economics, can appear in deceptively modest positions. It is also worth bearing in mind that the rankings look at universities as a whole and offer limited information on specific subjects. The first 26 global subject rankings that QS first published in 2011 has increased to 51.

Other options for overseas studies

A language degree will typically involve a year abroad, and a look at the UCAS website will show many options for studying another subject alongside your language of choice.

Many degrees offer a year abroad, either studying or in a work placement, even to those who are not taking a language. Shorter credit-bearing courses with partner institutions overseas are another option offered by UK universities. The best approach is to decide what you want to study and then see if there is a UK university that offers it as a joint degree or with a placement abroad. Do a background check on all the universities involved to ensure they are well-regarded, which is where the websites of global rankings will come in handy.

Useful websites

Prospects: studying abroad: **www.prospects.ac.uk/postgraduate-study/study-abroad**
Association of Commonwealth Universities: **www.acu.ac.uk**
Campus France: **www.campusfrance.org/en**
College Board (USA): **www.collegeboard.org**
DAAD (for Germany): **www.daad.de/en**
Study in Holland: **www.studyinholland.co.uk**
Education Ireland: **www.educationinireland.com/en**
Erasmus Programme (EU): **www.erasmusplus.org.uk**
Finaid (USA): **www.finaid.org**
Fulbright Commission: **www.fulbright.org.uk**
Study in Australia: **www.studyinaustralia.gov.au**
Study in Canada: **www.studyincanada.com**

12 Coming to the UK to Study

Britain's withdrawal from the European Union has brought significant change for students coming to the UK. As part of the Brexit divorce deal, students from EU countries, Iceland, Liechtenstein, Norway (EEA) and Switzerland will no longer be eligible for 'home' tuition fees of up to £9,250 in Britain. Nor can they continue to access tuition fee loans here. Instead, from the 2021–22 academic year EU, EEA and Swiss students will have to pay at the same, higher rate of 'international' tuition fees as those from the rest of the world. These vary by course and by university but were broadly in the range between £12,000 and £20,000 in 2019–20, although some cost £39,475, while medicine reached £61,435.

Students from the EU, EEA and Switzerland who have beaten the introduction of the new rules by enrolling on degrees at UK institutions before midnight on 31 December 2020 are not impacted financially by the change in status. They will remain eligible for home fees and access to student finance for the remainder of their degrees. These students are required to register with the EU Settlement Scheme by the end of June, however, as part of more stringent immigration procedures. Irish students studying in the UK will not be affected at all and will continue with the existing fee and loans status under the Common Travel Area agreement.

The change to international tuition fee rates applies to undergraduate, postgraduate and advanced learner financial support, as well as to Further Education funding for those aged 19+, and funding for apprenticeships. Its announcement by universities minister Michelle Donelan in June 2020 had been widely predicted as a consequence of Brexit, after years of uncertainty. The case for continuing to charge EU citizens lower fees than those from the rest of the world once Brexit was signed, sealed and delivered was both legally and morally wobbly. In her statement at the time, Donelan rang a positive note, saying, "EU, other EEA and Swiss students, staff and researchers make an important contribution to our universities. I want that contribution to continue and am confident – given the world-leading quality of our higher education sector – that it will."

Commentators have argued, however, that the move signals the end of a period during which UK universities have served international and academic mobility. The high quality of a

British higher education has offered good value for money to EU students at home rates, and the access to student finance has been a boon for those without wealthy families to support their study and living costs.

A decline in student numbers from Europe is expected to follow the fee increase this autumn, at least temporarily, which in turn seems likely to pose an unwelcome challenge to university finance departments attempting to balance the books. A report compiled by London Economics for the Higher Education Policy Institute (HEPI) in 2017, just before the referendum, predicted that higher fees and no further access to student loans could lead to a loss of around 31,000 EU student enrolments, representing a 57% decline at the time. Such a marked drop in students from the Continent would naturally lead to less diversity on campuses – creating a double dip of sorts, given that UK universities' reputation for diversity is one of their most highly-regarded characteristics by overseas students.

But even if fewer students do enrol at British institutions in 2021, the higher fees paid by those that still opt for UK universities should counteract the potential blow to higher education coffers. The most esteemed universities, and those which do well in league tables such as ours, are expected to experience less of an impact from fee changes than the less famed institutions. The same London Economics/HEPI report found that prestigious universities such

The top countries for sending undergraduates to the UK

EU countries	Number	%	Non-EU countries	Number	%
France	8,941	9.4	China	46,046	29.4
Romania	8,335	8.8	Hong Kong	12,867	8.2
Italy	7,802	8.2	Malaysia	11,061	7.1
Spain	6,897	7.3	India	7,795	5.0
Poland	6,888	7.3	United States	7,361	4.7
Cyprus (European Union)	6,865	7.2	Singapore	5,228	3.3
Germany	6,140	6.5	Nigeria	4,159	2.7
Bulgaria	5,258	5.6	United Arab Emirates	3,544	2.3
Greece	5,167	5.5	Kuwait	3,444	2.2
Ireland	4,700	5.0	South Korea	3,336	2.1
Portugal	4,412	4.7	Canada	3,264	2.1
Lithuania	3,900	4.1	Norway	2,912	1.9
Czech Republic	2,097	2.2	Pakistan	2,591	1.7
Belgium	2,014	2.1	Saudi Arabia	2,535	1.6
Sweden	1,966	2.1	Switzerland	2,490	1.6
Hungary	1,854	2.0	Russia	2,209	1.4
Netherlands	1,644	1.7	Qatar	2,111	1.3
Finland	1,616	1.7	Thailand	2,004	1.3
Slovakia	1,389	1.5	Egypt	1,616	1.0
Latvia	1,111	1.2	Oman	1,481	0.9
Total (all non-UK EU)	**94,697**		**Total (all non-EU)**	**156,485**	

Note: First degree non-UK domiciled students

as Cambridge and Oxford could gain about £10 million a year in fee income and some less prestigious institutions could lose about £100,000 a year through reduced student numbers.

Students from outside the EU, EEA and Switzerland are, of course, unaffected by Brexit. UK universities have long been a magnet for international students (both EU and non-EU) – only American universities attract more. More than five million people across the world travel abroad to study, according to UNESCO, and the UK's share of the world's young people who choose to study here is important to its universities and welcomed by British students.

Global surveys have shown that British universities are seen to offer high quality in a relatively safe environment, with the added bonus of students being immersed in the English language. Degree courses here, both undergraduate and postgraduate, are shorter than the average length worldwide, helping to counterbalance Britain's standing as an expensive destination. The fall in the value of the pound has added to the country's appeal lately, making a UK higher education cheaper in real terms than it has been for many years.

The underlying strength of UK universities was credited with the 9% rise in admissions from international students (those from beyond the EU) last autumn, when numbers reached a record total of 44,300. The trend defied predictions that the health pandemic would lead to financial disaster in higher education. Unease with America's reaction to Covid-19 may have contributed to the upturn in students arriving in Britain, along with the pandemic's negative impact on job vacancies, which will have painted the advantages of carrying on in education in a positive light. A CV that includes international study is seen by many as a boost to career prospects, especially in relation to jobs in global markets.

In research published by Universities UK in 2019, international students reported high rates of satisfaction. The report showed that 90% of international graduates were satisfied with the learning experience at their British university, 80% were satisfied or very satisfied with support provided during their time in the UK and 82% thought that their UK degree was worth the financial investment.

Almost three in every ten international (EU and non-EU) students at UK universities in 2019 came from China – the highest proportion from a single country by far. In light of Brexit, universities in the UK are redoubling their already proactive recruitment efforts internationally. They take part in international fairs and some have their own offices in target countries. The cultural richness that a diverse international intake of students brings is highly valued beyond their worth as a source of revenue.

Why study in the UK?

As well as the strong reputation of UK degrees and the opportunity to be taught in and soak up the English language, research shows that most international graduates are well-rewarded when they return home. A Government-commissioned report showed that graduates of UK universities earn much higher salaries than those who studied in their own country. The starting salaries of UK graduates in China and India were more than twice as high as those for graduates educated at home, while even those returning to the USA saw a salary premium of more than 10%. Students who take the plunge to travel abroad to study are likely to be bright and highly motivated, so some uplift in such students' outcomes is to be expected. Unless they have government scholarships, most international students have to be from relatively wealthy backgrounds to afford the fees and other expenses involved. The hopes of a higher salary upon graduation are likely to be part of the equation when taking on the cost of the course. But the scale of increase demonstrated in the report suggests that a UK degree remains a good investment. Three years after graduation, 95% of the international graduates surveyed were in work or further study. More than 90% had been satisfied with their learning experience and almost as many would recommend their university to others.

A popular choice

Nearly all UK universities are cosmopolitan places that welcome international students in large numbers. In many UK universities you can expect to have fellow students from more than 100 countries. Almost one student in five is from outside the UK – 6% from the EU and 14% from the rest of the world. More full-time postgraduates – the fastest-growing group – come from outside the UK than within it.

More than 90% of international students declare themselves satisfied with their experience of UK universities in surveys by i-graduate, the student polling organisation, although they are less enthusiastic in the Government's National Student Survey and more likely than UK students to make official complaints. Nevertheless, satisfaction increased by eight percentage points in four years, according to i-graduate, reflecting greater efforts to keep ahead of the global competition. International students are particularly complimentary about students' unions, multiculturalism, teaching standards and places of worship. Their main concerns tend to be financial, partly because of a lack of employment opportunities. However, from summer 2021, international students who have successfully completed an undergraduate or master's degree

The universities most popular with EU and non-EU students

Institution	EU students	Institution	Non-EU students
Coventry	3,238	University College London	5,897
University College London	2,933	Manchester	5,820
King's College London	2,819	Coventry	5,562
Aberdeen	2,514	Liverpool	5,413
Manchester	2,149	Arts London	4,731
Edinburgh	2,056	Edinburgh	4,495
Glasgow	2,015	King's College London	3,862
Warwick	2,012	Imperial College London	3,199
Arts London	1,930	Birmingham	3,092
Westminster	1,656	Sheffield	3,087
Essex	1,606	Nottingham	3,045
Bedfordshire	1,602	Warwick	2,872
Imperial College London	1,570	Leeds	2,542
Middlesex	1,501	St Andrews	2,499
Surrey	1,486	Exeter	2,480
Bath	1,407	Durham	2,459
Anglia Ruskin	1,319	Sussex	2,433
Southampton	1,302	Bristol	2,257
Queen Mary, London	1,242	De Montfort	2,249
Solent, Southampton	1,167	Portsmouth	2,179

Note: First degree non-UK domiciled students

will be able to benefit from two years' work experience in the UK upon graduation, through the new Graduate Route. Students who complete their PhD will be able to stay for three years.

The number of students taking UK degrees through a local institution, distance learning or a full branch campus of a UK university was already growing even before the health pandemic heralded widespread blended online learning. Indeed, there are now more international students taking UK first degrees in their own country than there are in Britain. The numbers grew by 70% in a decade and are likely to rise further as a result of the post-Brexit fee changes. Most branch campuses are in Asia or the Middle East, but some universities are now planning campuses in other parts of the EU. Coventry – which was the most popular UK university with EU students in 2019 – has already set up in Poland.

Where to study in the UK

The vast majority of the UK's universities and other higher education institutions are in England. Of the 132 universities profiled in this *Guide*, 107 are in England, 15 in Scotland, eight in Wales and two in Northern Ireland. Fee limits in higher education for UK and EU students are determined separately in each administrative area, which historically in some cases brought benefits for EU students, such as those who chose to study in Scotland where they paid no

The most popular subjects for international students

Subject Group	EU students	Non-EU students	Total students	% of all international students
Business Studies	14,220	26,594	40,814	16.2
Accounting & Finance	2,306	15,247	17,553	7.0
Law	4,102	10,201	14,303	5.7
Computer Science	7,123	6,625	13,748	5.5
Art & Design	4,770	7,710	12,480	5.0
Economics	2,900	7,680	10,580	4.2
Biological Sciences	4,496	3,994	8,490	3.4
Mechanical Engineering	2,061	6,074	8,135	3.2
Politics	3,858	4,060	7,919	3.2
Psychology	4,307	3,548	7,854	3.1
Mathematics	1,857	5,055	6,912	2.8
Communication and Media Studies	3,207	3,616	6,823	2.7
Electrical and Electronic Engineering	1,358	5,452	6,810	2.7
Drama, Dance and Cinematics	3,669	2,524	6,193	2.5
Medicine	1,421	4,139	5,559	2.2
Architecture	1,681	3,105	4,787	1.9
Hospitality, Leisure, Recreation & Tourism	2,548	1,981	4,529	1.8
Civil Engineering	772	3,549	4,321	1.7
Other Subjects Allied to Medicine	1,478	1,854	3,333	1.3
Aeronautical and Manufacturing Engineering	1,263	2,055	3,318	1.3
Total	**94,697**	**156,485**	**251,182**	**77.4**

Note: 22.6% of students take a range of other subjects

tuition fees. Under the new regulations however, all undergraduates from outside the UK will be charged the international rate of fees.

Within the UK, the cost of living varies by geographical area. London is home to UCL, the most popular university with non-EU students in 2019, and although it is the most expensive city, accommodation costs can also be high in many other major cities. Find out as much as you can about what living in Britain will be like. Further advice and information is available through the British Council at its offices worldwide, at more than 60 university exhibitions that it holds around the world every year, or at its Education UK website: **https://study-uk.britishcouncil.org**. Also useful for international students is the information provided by the UK Council for International Student Affairs (UKCISA) at **www.ukcisa.org.uk**.

Universities in all parts of the UK have a reputation for high-quality teaching and research, as evidenced in global rankings such as those shown on pages 130–132. They maintain this standing by investing heavily in the best academic staff, buildings and equipment, and by taking part in rigorous quality assurance monitoring. The Office for Students is the chief regulatory body for higher education in England, overseeing organisations such as the Quality Assurance Agency for Higher Education (QAA), which remains the arbiter of standards. Professional bodies also play an important role in relevant subjects.

Although many people from outside the UK associate British universities with Oxford and Cambridge, the reality at most higher education institutions is quite different. Some universities do still maintain ancient traditions, but most are modern institutions that place at least as much emphasis on teaching as on research and offer many vocational programmes, often with close links to business, industry and the professions. The table below shows the universities that are most popular with international students at undergraduate level. Although some of those at the top of the lists are among the most famous names in higher education, others achieved university status only in the last 30 years.

What subjects to study?

Strongly vocational courses are favoured by international students. Many of these in professional areas such as architecture, dentistry or medicine take one or two years longer to complete than most other degree courses. Traditional first degrees are mostly awarded at Bachelor level (BA, BEng, BSc, etc.) and last three to four years. There are also some "enhanced" first degrees (MEng, MChem, etc.) that take four years to complete. The relatively new Foundation degree programmes are almost all vocational and take two years to complete as a full-time course, with an option to study for a further year to gain a full degree. The table below shows the most popular subjects studied by international students. You need to consider the degree you wish to study and ensure that you have looked at the ranking of that university in our main league table in chapter 1 and in the subject tables in chapter 13.

English language proficiency

The universities maintain high standards partly by setting demanding entry requirements, including proficiency in English. For international students, this usually includes a score of at least 5.5 in the International English Language Testing System (IELTS), which assesses English language ability through listening, speaking, reading and writing tests. Under visa regulations introduced in 2011, universities are able to vouch for a student's ability in English. This proficiency will need to be equivalent to an "upper intermediate" level (level B2) of the CEFR (Common European Framework of Reference for Languages) for studying at an undergraduate level (roughly equivalent to an overall score of 5.5 in IELTS).

There are many private and publicly funded colleges throughout the UK that run courses designed to bring the English language skills of prospective higher education students up to the required standard. However, not all of these are Government approved. Some private organisations such as INTO **www.intostudy.com** have joined with universities to create centres running programmes preparing international students for degree-level study. The British Council also runs English language courses at its centres around the world.

Tougher student visa regulations were introduced in 2012 and have since been refined. Although under the current system, universities' international students should not be denied entry to the UK, as long as they are proficient in English and are found to have followed other immigration rules, some lower-level preparatory courses taken by international students have been affected. It is, therefore, doubly important to consult the official UK government list of approved institutions (web address given at the end of this chapter) before applying.

How to apply

The information below is best read in conjunction with that provided in chapter 5, which deals with the application process in some detail.

Some international students apply directly to a UK university for a place on a course, and others make their applications via an agent in their home country. But most applying for a full-time, first degree course do so through the Universities and Colleges Admissions Service (UCAS). If you take this route, you will need to fill in an online UCAS application form at home, at school or perhaps at your nearest British Council office. There is plenty of advice on the UCAS website about the process of finding a course and the details of the application system.

Whichever way you apply, the deadlines for getting your application in are the same. Under the regulations at the time this *Guide* went to press, for those applying from within an EU country, application forms for most courses starting in 2021 must be received at UCAS by 15 January 2021. Note that applications for Oxford and Cambridge and for all courses in medicine, dentistry and veterinary science had to be received by 15 October 2020, while some art and design courses had a later deadline of 24 March 2021. Similar dates are expected to apply for 2022 entry.

If you are applying from a non-EU country to study in 2021, you can submit your application to UCAS at any time between 1 September 2020 and 30 June 2021. Most people will apply well before the 30 June deadline to make sure that places are still available and to allow plenty of time for immigration regulations, and to make arrangements for travel and accommodation.

Entry and employment regulations

Visa regulations have been the subject of continuing controversy in the UK and many new rules and regulations have been introduced, often hotly contested by universities. Recent governments have been criticised for increasing visa fees, doubling the cost of visa extensions, and ending the right to appeal against refusal of a visa.

The current points system for entry – known as Tier 4 – came into effect in 2009. Under this scheme, prospective students can check whether they are eligible for entry against published criteria, and so assess their points score. Universities are also required to provide a Confirmation of Acceptance for Studies (CAS) to their international student entrants, who must have secured an unconditional offer, and the institution must appear as a "Tier 4 Sponsor" on the Home Office's Register of Sponsors. Prospective students have to demonstrate that, as well as the necessary qualifications, they have English language proficiency and enough money for the first year of their specified course. This includes the full fees for the first year and, currently, living costs of £1,265 a month, up to a maximum of nine months, if studying in London (£1,015 a month in the rest of the UK). Under the current visa requirements, details of financial support are checked in more detail than before.

All students wishing to enter the UK to study are required to obtain entry clearance before arrival. The only exceptions are British nationals living overseas, British overseas territories citizens, British protected persons, British subjects, and non-visa national short-term students who may enter under a new Student Visitor route. Visa fees are £348 for a Tier 4 visa, plus an annual healthcare surcharge. As part of the application process, biometric data will be requested and this will be used to issue you with a Biometric Residence Permit (BRP) once you have arrived in the UK. You will need a BRP to open a bank account, rent accommodation or establish your eligibility for benefits and services or to work part-time, for example. The details of the regulations are continually reviewed by the Home Office. You can find more about all the latest rules and regulations for entry and visa requirements at **www.gov.uk/tier-4-general-visa**.

Until now, the rules and regulations governing permission to work have varied according to your country of origin and the level of course you undertake. Those from a European Economic Area (EEA) country (the EU plus Iceland, Liechtenstein and Norway) or Switzerland have not needed permission to work in the UK, although they have been required to show an employer a passport or identity card to prove they are a national of an EEA country. However, the regulations that will apply after the UK leaves the EU are unknown at the time of writing and you will need to check for the latest information before making an application.

Students from outside the EEA who are here as Tier 4 students are allowed to work part-time for up to 20 hours a week during term time and full-time during vacations. These arrangements apply to students on degree courses; stricter limits were introduced in 2010 for lower-level courses. If you wish to stay on after you have graduated, you can apply for permission under Tier 2 of the points-based immigration system, but you will need a sponsor and the work must be considered "graduate level", commanding a salary of at least £23,000. The new work visa would offer an "unsponsored route" where universities would not need to maintain responsibility for their graduates while they try to access the jobs market.

Bringing your family

Since 2010, international students on courses of six months or less have been forbidden to bring a partner or children into the UK, and the latest reforms extend this prohibition to all undergraduates except those who are government sponsored. Postgraduates studying for 12 months or longer will still be able to bring dependants to the UK, and most universities can help to arrange facilities and accommodation for families as well as for single students. The family members you are allowed to bring with you are your husband or wife, civil partner (a same-sex relationship that has been formally registered in the UK or your home country) or long-term partner and dependent children. You can find out more about getting entry clearance for your family at **www.ukcisa.org.uk**.

Support from British universities

Support for international students is more comprehensive than in many countries, and begins long before you arrive in the UK. Many universities have advisers in other countries. Some will arrange to put you in touch with current students or graduates who can give you a first-hand account of what life is like at a particular university. Pre-departure receptions for students and their families, as well as meet-and-greet arrangements for newly-arrived students, are common. You can also expect an orientation and induction programme in your first week, and many universities now have "buddying" systems where current students are assigned to new arrivals to help them find their way around, adjust to their new surroundings and make new friends. Each university also has a students' union that organises social, cultural and sporting events and clubs, including many specifically for international students. Both the university and the students' union are likely to have full-time staff whose job it is to look after the welfare of students from overseas.

International students also benefit from free medical and subsidised dental and optical care and treatment under the UK National Health Service via a healthcare surcharge added when paying for their visas, plus access to a professional counselling service and a university careers service. EU, EEA and Swiss students have qualified for free NHS care in the past, but at the time of writing it was not known what status of healthcare provision will be offered to them after 31 December 2020. These students are advised to monitor the situation as it evolves, and check their healthcare cover.

At university, you will naturally encounter people from a wide range of cultures and walks of life. Getting involved in student societies, sport, voluntary work and any of the social activities on offer will help you gain first-hand experience of British culture, and, if you need it, will help improve your command of the English language.

Useful websites

The British Council, with its dedicated Study UK site designed for those wishing to find out more about studying in the UK:
https://study-uk.britishcouncil.org/

The UK Council for International Student Affairs (UKCISA) provides a wide range of information on all aspects of studying in the UK:
www.ukcisa.org.uk

UCAS, for full details of undergraduate courses available and an explanation of the application process:
www.ucas.com/undergraduate/applying-university/ucas-undergraduate-international-and-eu-students

For the latest information on entry and visa requirements:
www.gov.uk/tier-4-general-visa

Register of sponsors for Tier 4 educational establishments:
www.gov.uk/government/publications/register-of-licensed-sponsors-students
For a general guide to Britain, available in many languages:
www.visitbritain.com

13 Subject by Subject Guide

Recent surveys suggest that most applicants to universities take more notice of subject tables than they do of the institutional rankings that may attract more headlines. The 67 subject tables in this chapter drill down into the experience students are likely to have on their chosen course and the career prospects they might expect when they graduate. Knowing where a university stands in the pecking order of higher education is a vital piece of information, but the quality of an individual course is what matters most during one's years as a student.

The 2014 Research Excellence Framework, which was used to decide funding for each university's research, confirmed that the most modest institution may have a centre of specialist excellence, and even famous universities have mediocre departments. This chapter offers some pointers to the leading universities in a wide range of subjects. Since universities mount frequent reviews of the courses they offer, it is possible that not all institutions listed in a particular subject area will be running courses in 2022.

Many subjects, such as dentistry or sociology, have their own table, but others are grouped together in broader categories, such as "other subjects allied to medicine". Scores are not published where the number of students is too small for the outcome to be statistically reliable.

The subject tables include scores from the National Student Survey (NSS). These distil the views of final-year undergraduates on various aspects of their course, with the results presented in two columns. The teaching quality indicator reflects the average scores in the sections of the survey focusing on teaching, assessment and feedback, learning opportunities and academic support. The student experience indicator is drawn from the average of the organisation and management, learning resources, student voice and learning community sections, as well as the survey's final question, on overall satisfaction.

The three other measures used are research quality, students' entry qualifications and graduate employment prospects. The Education table uses a fifth indicator: Ofsted grades, a measure of the quality of teaching based on the outcomes of Ofsted inspections of teacher training courses. None of the measures is weighted. A full explanation of the measures is given on the next page.

Cambridge is again the most successful university. It tops 32 of the 67 tables, Oxford leads in five, Glasgow and Loughborough in four each, St Andrews and Edinburgh in three each and Birmingham and Strathclyde in two apiece. Twelve other universities are top in one subject.

Research quality

This is a measure of the quality of the research undertaken in the subject area. The information was sourced from the 2014 Research Excellence Framework (REF), a peer-review exercise used to evaluate the quality of research in UK higher education institutions, undertaken by the UK Higher Education Funding Bodies. The approach mirrors that in the main table, with the REF results weighted and then multiplied by the percentage of eligible staff entered for assessment.

For each subject, a research quality profile was given to those university departments that took part, showing how much of their research was in various quality categories. These categories were: 4* world-leading; 3* internationally excellent; 2* internationally recognised; 1* nationally recognised; and unclassified. The funding bodies decided to direct more funds to the very best research by applying weightings. The English, Scottish and Welsh funding councils have slightly different weightings. Those used by HEFCE (the funding council for England) are employed in the tables: 4* is weighted by a factor of 3 and 3* is weighted by a factor of 1. Outputs of 2* and 1* carry zero weight. This results in a maximum score of 3. In the interest of consistency, the above weightings continue to be applied this year.

The scores in the table are presented as a percentage of the maximum score. To achieve the maximum score, all staff would need to be at 4* world-leading level.

Universities could choose which staff to include in the REF, so, to factor in the depth of the research quality, each quality profile score has been multiplied by the number of staff returned in the REF as a proportion of all eligible staff.

Entry standards

This is the average UCAS tariff score for new students under the age of 21, based on A- and AS-Levels and Scottish Highers and Advanced Highers and other equivalent qualifications (including the International Baccalaureate), taken from HESA data for 2018–19. Each student's examination grades were converted to a numerical score using the UCAS tariff. The points used in the tariff appear on page 31.

Teaching quality and student experience

The student satisfaction measure is divided into two components. These measures are taken from the National Student Survey (NSS) results published in 2019 and 2020. The latest year's figures are used when only one is available, but an average of the two years' results is used in all other cases. Where the 2020 NSS data were not available, the latest available scores for Teaching Quality and Student Experience were adjusted by the percentage point change in each subject between that year and 2020. This applies mainly to Oxford and Cambridge, which last met the threshold as entire universities in 2016. The adjusted scores were used for z-scoring only, and do not appear in the final table.

The NSS covers eight aspects of a course, with an additional question gauging overall satisfaction. Students answer on a scale from 1 (bottom) to 5 (top) and the score in the table is calculated from the percentage of positive responses (4 and 5) in each section. The teaching quality indicator reflects the average scores for the first four sections of the survey. The student experience indicator is drawn from the average scores of the remaining sections and the additional question on overall satisfaction. Teaching quality is favoured over student experience and accounts for 67% of the overall student satisfaction score, with student experience making up the remaining 33%.

Graduate prospects

This is the percentage of graduates in high-skilled jobs or undertaking graduate-level study 15 months after graduation recorded in the new Graduate Outcomes survey published in June 2020 and based on 2018 graduates.

A low score on this measure does not necessarily indicate unemployment – some graduates may have taken jobs that are not categorised as professional work. The averages for each subject are given at the foot of each subject table in this chapter and in two tables in chapter 3 (see pages 52–55).

Note that in the tables that follow, when a figure is followed by *, it refers to data from a previous year.

The subjects listed below are covered in the tables in this chapter:

Accounting and Finance

Aeronautical and Manufacturing Engineering

Agriculture and Forestry

American Studies

Anatomy and Physiology

Animal Science

Anthropology and Forensic Science

Archaeology

Architecture

Art and Design

Biological Sciences

Building

Business Studies

Celtic Studies

Chemical Engineering

Chemistry

Civil Engineering

Classics and Ancient History

Communication and Media Studies

Computer Science

Creative Writing

Criminology

Dentistry

Drama, Dance and Cinematics

East and South Asian Studies

Economics

Education

Electrical and Electronic Engineering

English

Food Science

French

General Engineering

Geography and Environmental Sciences

Geology

German

History

History of Art, Architecture and Design

Hospitality, Leisure, Recreation and Tourism

Iberian Languages

Italian

Land and Property Management

Law

Librarianship and Information Management

Linguistics

Materials Technology

Mathematics

Mechanical Engineering

Medicine

Middle Eastern and African Studies

Music

Nursing

Other Subjects Allied to Medicine (see page 248 for subjects included in this category)

Pharmacology and Pharmacy

Philosophy

Physics and Astronomy

Physiotherapy

Politics

Psychology

Radiography

Russian and East European Languages

Social Policy

Social Work

Sociology

Sports Science

Theology and Religious Studies

Town and Country Planning and Landscape

Veterinary Medicine

Accounting and Finance

Strathclyde has taken the top spot in our accounting and finance table this year, up from fifth place last year. Its results in the Research Excellence Framework are second only to the LSE and it has the second-highest entry grades, which in common with other universities north of the border benefit from the conversion rate for Scottish qualifications in the UCAS tariff. Leeds (which topped the overall table last year) and Manchester have the highest entry standards of universities south of the border.

The universities further down the overall table do best in our measure of student satisfaction with teaching quality, led by 62nd-ranked Bolton, followed by Buckinghamshire New (68th) then West London (53=) – winner of our University of the Year for Student Experience 2021–22. Student satisfaction is relatively strong for accounting and finance throughout the table, however.

Accounting and finance are similar subjects that are often taken together. They differ in that accounting is a more defined topic that looks specifically at how money flows in and out of a company, while finance is broader and focuses on long-term management of assets, liabilities, and growth. Applications decreased a little in 2019 but 7,245 new students started accounting degrees, an increase on the year before. Numbers taking finance, the smaller of the two subjects, reached a new high in 2019 when 2,650 students started courses. Competition averaged at close to five applications per place for accounting while finance is more accessible, with just under two applications for each place in the 2019 cycle.

Maths A-level is not a pre-requisite, though all universities welcome it and some of the leading institutions do prefer applicants to have it. Others such as business, economics and statistics are also the kinds of A-levels worth showing talent in. Entry standards vary considerably, from well over 200 points at Glasgow and Strathclyde to under 100 at 14 universities.

Accounting and finance finished only 43rd out of 67 subject areas for the proportion of graduates who were in highly skilled jobs or study 15 months after finishing their degrees, the new Graduate Outcomes survey showed. The outlook was much more positive for those who studied at the universities at the top of our table however, led by Exeter where nearly 96% of accounting and finance graduates achieved positive work or study outcomes, followed closely by the LSE whose graduates were almost equally well-placed in their careers 15 months on from finishing their degrees.

Accounting and Finance	Teaching quality %	Student experience %	Research quality %	Entry standards (UCAS points)	Graduate prospects %	Overall score
1 Strathclyde	81.6	81.9	44.3	212	85.2	100.0
2 Leeds	86.3	88.5	39.3	179	90.2	99.3
3 London School of Economics	82.8	83.2	52.3	144	94.4	97.7
4 Bath	81.0	82.9	41.8	158	89.3	95.8
5 Glasgow	80.5	85.1	22.1	221	76.0	95.6
6 Warwick	83.9	85.5	40.4	145	88.9	95.4
7 Queen's, Belfast	81.2	84.6	32.7	157	91.8	94.7
=8 Exeter	82.5	83.9	24.4	154	95.5	93.9
=8 Loughborough	83.9	89.2	32.6	146	83.7	93.9
10 Manchester	77.4	80.2	33.3	170	84.7	93.4
11 Ulster	83.1	82.0	40.4	125	88.0	93.0

12 Lancaster	80.7	79.7	42.6	130	85.9	92.6
=13 Liverpool	89.7	90.3	20.1	140	81.5	92.4
=13 Stirling	83.9	84.4	25.2	174	71.9	92.4
15 Durham	83.0	85.5	23.1	142	89.7	92.0
16 Cardiff	75.4	73.4	32.0	165	88.9	91.9
17 Birmingham	81.6	83.1	29.1	152	80.4	91.8
18 Dundee	78.9	86.5	12.1	164	93.3	91.7
19 Southampton	79.7	83.5	24.0	147	89.1	91.5
20 Aberdeen	72.3	76.1	24.9	192	79.3	91.0
21 Nottingham	73.7	78.2	32.6	146	90.3	90.9
22 Bristol	74.5	73.2	32.1	146	92.6	90.7
23 Robert Gordon	88.4	86.9	2.6	181	72.7	90.6
24 York	82.1	80.5	24.0	151	—	90.5
25 Queen Mary, London	72.0	73.5	31.3	164	85.7	90.4
=26 Reading	76.4	78.4	29.3	132	88.8	89.7
=26 Sheffield	77.8	82.1	26.8	131	87.0	89.7
=28 Heriot-Watt	72.2	74.7	18.8	168	90.1	89.5
=28 Sussex	81.3	81.3	23.7	129	85.6	89.5
30 City, London	74.7	77.7	28.7	150	80.6	89.3
31 Swansea	81.2	83.1	22.0	123	84.2	88.7
32 Aston	81.6	82.9	19.7	132	80.6	88.5
33 Newcastle	75.8	77.4	20.7	147	81.7	88.0
34 Oxford Brookes	86.0	92.4	5.1	120	82.6	87.6
35 Glasgow Caledonian	84.9	85.6	1.8	168	67.2	87.5
36 Bangor	82.8	85.5	23.4	119	71.1	87.2
37 Edinburgh	63.5	64.1	25.8	177	85.0	87.1
38 Liverpool John Moores	90.8	88.4	—	135	72.0	87.0
39 Kent	79.3	80.2	24.8	127	72.1	86.8
=40 East Anglia	76.7	78.4	28.1	125	74.1	86.6
=40 Nottingham Trent	88.9	89.1	4.6	123	72.6	86.6
42 Aberystwyth	91.2	90.5	14.5	101	66.1	86.2
43 Hull	81.0	84.6	10.2	123	79.8	86.1
44 Portsmouth	84.7	84.3	9.5	112	74.5	85.1
45 Royal Holloway, London	74.6	74.5	27.0	124	—	84.6
46 Plymouth	83.6	86.1	13.1	104	—	84.2
47 South Wales	84.9	83.1	0.2	119	75.0	84.1
48 Surrey	71.4	73.1	15.8	142	74.2	83.9
=49 Coventry	84.3	86.9	1.6	113	72.5	83.8
=49 Leicester	71.1	73.5	24.3	125	72.8	83.8
=49 Lincoln	83.6	82.8	4.8	113	73.5	83.8
52 West of England	79.2	80.2	5.5	112	77.8	83.1
=53 Sheffield Hallam	84.2	85.0	0.6	105	73.6	82.9
=53 West London	92.7	93.3	—	121	45.8	82.9
=55 Keele	80.5	78.8	10.2	110	70.9	82.8
=55 Northumbria	81.1	83.1	4.0	134	60.9	82.8
=57 Chester	83.8	82.6	0.5	103	75.0	82.4

Accounting and Finance cont

	Teaching quality %	Student experience %	Research quality %	Entry standards (UCAS points)	Graduate prospects %	Overall score
=57 Essex	76.8	79.1	25.1	106	59.6	82.4
=57 Worcester	91.0	81.1	0.9	99	–	82.4
=60 Central Lancashire	80.9	79.1	4.4	117	68.0	82.0
=60 Manchester Metropolitan	82.6	82.2	4.7	123	59.3	82.0
62 Bolton	95.1	95.7	–	83*	53.8	81.9
63 Winchester	92.3	85.3	–	101	56.6	81.8
64 Edinburgh Napier	76.0	79.6	2.3	158	53.3	81.6
65 Cardiff Metropolitan	83.1	85.9	–	114	62.5	81.5
66 Bournemouth	75.6	76.2	8.8	104	76.8	81.4
67 Roehampton	83.6	80.8	4.5	103	–	81.2
68 Bucks New	93.9	91.6	1.8	82	52.8	81.1
69 Brighton	75.3	74.7	6.5	103	79.1	81.0
70 Huddersfield	80.7	80.1	4.1	122	58.4	80.9
71 Staffordshire	84.7	85.2	2.6	106	56.7	80.8
72 Greenwich	77.7	78.9	3.3	112	68.8	80.7
73 Hertfordshire	84.6	86.0	0.9	99	59.8	80.4
74 West of Scotland	81.0	81.3	2.9	121	52.9	80.1
75 Wolverhampton	83.2	84.1	2.4	92	61.0	79.7
=76 Derby	83.7	83.1	0.9	116	49.3	79.6
=76 Leeds Beckett	79.3	81.5	0.8	99	66.7	79.6
=76 Westminster	79.1	81.3	2.4	133	47.8	79.6
79 De Montfort	78.2	80.1	10.7	99*	57.9	79.5
80 Brunel London	69.6	73.6	23.0	106	57.1	79.1
81 Northampton	84.1	78.9	1.0	92	60.1	78.9
82 Birmingham City	80.5	79.7	1.3	109	55.6	78.8
83 Salford	71.0	77.3	5.9	119	60.5	78.6
=84 Anglia Ruskin	80.2	82.1	3.4	103	51.0	78.2
=84 Sunderland	79.8	80.8	0.4	101	56.8	78.2
86 Middlesex	76.3	77.7	10.5	109	49.5	78.1
87 East London	86.6	85.9	0.8	98	41.2	77.9
88 Teesside	74.8	72.0	2.0	112	–	77.2
89 London South Bank	82.1	85.4	2.1	99	41.1	77.0
90 London Metropolitan	81.5	82.5	0.6	63	62.7	76.7
91 Gloucestershire	81.8	74.5	–	98	50.0	76.5
92 Kingston	68.2	73.1	9.2	105	56.4	76.1
93 Edge Hill	66.5	59.5	–	122	64.3	75.0
94 Bradford	75.6	74.8	11.8	111	21.9	73.7
95 Bedfordshire	64.9	66.7	3.1	99	61.1	73.6
96 Canterbury Christ Church	63.5	63.0	–	89	58.3	71.1
=97 Kingston	74.1	78.2	9.2	116	43.9	78.0
=97 London Metropolitan	78.1	78.8	0.6	76	63.6	78.0
99 Anglia Ruskin	77.0	76.3	3.4	89	48.4	76.3

100 Canterbury Christ Church	68.3	71.6	—	103	60.5	76.0
=101 Bedfordshire	68.4	73.6	3.1	105	54.1	75.9
=101 Sunderland	66.4	66.0	0.4	104	66.7	75.9

Employed in high-skilled job	50%	Employed in lower-skilled job and studying	3%
Employed in high-skilled job and studying	11%	Employed in lower-skilled job	26%
Studying	4%	Unemployed	6%
High skilled work (median) salary	£25,000	Low/medium skilled salary	£20,000

Aeronautical and Manufacturing Engineering

Our Aeronautical and Manufacturing Engineering table is led once again by Cambridge – where strength in research, high entry grades and impressive graduate outcomes combine to create sought-after undergraduate programmes. Imperial has retained second place for the third year in a row. For student satisfaction with both teaching quality and the wider undergraduate experience 1992-founded Coventry (15th overall) is unbeaten. Of the top 10 universities third-ranked Bath does best for teaching quality, while Sheffield in 10th is best for the broader student experience. Loughborough and Strathclyde score well.

The courses under this category focus predominantly on aeronautical or manufacturing engineering, but the table also includes some degrees with the mechanical title. It is worth noting that manufacturing degrees are often called production engineering. The earn-while-you-learn degree apprenticeship route may appeal in this area, and options are offered at leading firms such as Rolls-Royce, though they do not feature in this table. Categorised by UCAS as Aerospace Engineering, both applications and enrolments rose for the seventh successive year in 2019, when 3,810 students started courses. Entry standards can be stiff: 13 of our table's universities averaged over 150 UCAS points and Cambridge achieved 220.

Almost eight in every 10 aeronautical and manufacturing engineering graduates were in highly skilled jobs or further study 15 months after finishing their degrees, the new Graduate Outcomes survey showed – ranking the subject area 25th in our graduate prospects measure.

Maths and physics A-levels are required by many universities, with further maths, computer science and chemistry among other preferred subjects.

Aeronautical and Manufacturing Engineering	Teaching quality %	Student experience %	Research quality %	Entry standards (UCAS points)	Graduate prospects %	Overall score
1 Cambridge	—	—	67.0	220	96.6	100.0
2 Imperial College London	75.3	79.7	59.6	199	90.6	95.8
3 Bath	85.8	84.1	37.4	189	89.7	94.6
4 Bristol	76.8	81.8	52.3	188	90.4	94.4
5 Strathclyde	80.1	82.0	37.2	202	87.9	93.7
6 Glasgow	70.5	76.2	47.2	217	86.9	93.2
7 Southampton	72.4	76.2	52.3	177	89.3	91.7
8 Nottingham	77.9	76.7	40.8	154	93.3	90.4
9 Loughborough	78.2	82.3	41.8	159	86.3	90.2

Aeronautical and Manufacturing Engineering cont

		Teaching quality %	Student experience %	Research quality %	Entry standards (UCAS points)	Graduate prospects %	Overall score
10	Sheffield	80.0	86.0	36.0	154	87.3	90.1
11	Leeds	75.1	75.7	40.9	176	82.4	89.1
12	Swansea	76.8	80.8	45.5	133	88.5	88.6
13	Surrey	69.7	77.2	30.8	156	94.9	87.6
14	Queen's, Belfast	72.6	71.8	36.7	148	87.0	86.2
15	Coventry	89.5	88.4	10.3	137	74.5	85.0
16	Liverpool	77.7	76.8	32.1	133	80.7	84.9
17	Birmingham	71.9	72.7	37.7	135	—	83.9
18	Plymouth	73.7	79.1	15.7	126*	88.9	83.1
19	Manchester	68.1	64.5	35.1	162	71.9	82.1
20	Aston	73.0	66.2	20.6	130	85.7	81.7
21	West of England	76.3	77.8	10.6	133	79.4	81.3
22	Central Lancashire	81.1	74.7	7.1	131	—	81.0
23	Queen Mary, London	58.7	68.5	46.7	137	74.1	80.5
24	City, London	62.4	64.1	23.1	129	90.9	80.3
25	Sheffield Hallam	69.1	67.6	17.8	116	88.2	80.0
26	Staffordshire	76.1	72.2	5.7	109	81.8	78.6
27	Wolverhampton	81.9	82.6	4.4	94	—	78.1
28	Brunel London	61.4	65.5	23.7	129	77.3	77.6
29	West of Scotland	80.8	85.1	9.0	128	52.9	77.2
30	Brighton	59.4	62.3	7.4	121	88.2	76.1
31	Teesside	58.2	64.4	5.8	145	76.9	75.4
32	Portsmouth	70.0	66.5	9.1	107	72.7	75.0
33	Hertfordshire	68.7	70.0	16.5	108	66.7	74.9
34	South Wales	76.2	72.9	—	130	56.5	74.4
35	Salford	66.7	68.4	4.4	135	61.5	73.7
36	Kingston	76.0	75.2	2.9	109	47.6	71.5

Employed in high-skilled job	66%	Employed in lower-skilled job and studying	0%
Employed in high-skilled job and studying	3%	Employed in lower-skilled job	14%
Studying	10%	Unemployed	6%
High skilled work (median) salary	£28,000	Low/medium skilled salary	£21,500

Agriculture and Forestry

Queen's, Belfast – which did best on employment and in the Research Excellence Framework – has overtaken Nottingham at the top of our Agriculture and Forestry table this year. For student satisfaction Bangor leads on both the measure of teaching quality and of the wider undergraduate experience. Reading scores well for its research, only bettered by its Northern Ireland peer.

Of the two specialist institutions that feature Harper Adams achieved significantly warmer results in the National Student Survey than its rival Royal Agricultural and ranks three places higher in the overall table.

The numbers starting degrees in agriculture increased in 2019, bringing them back above the 2,000 mark, and applications were also up on the year before. For forestry and arboriculture degrees however, both applications and enrolments fell to record lows and just 85 new undergraduates began degrees.

The two subjects have vastly improved their record on graduate prospects this year. Having been in our employment table's bottom four last year Agriculture and Forestry now ranks a much more respectable 53rd out of 67 subject areas. The new Graduate Outcomes survey showed that nearly 66% of the subjects' graduates had entered high-skilled jobs or further study 15 months after completing their degrees. Of these almost 93% of Queen's, Belfast graduates secured these top outcomes, followed by Newcastle (85.7%) and Harper Adams (77%).

Agriculture and Forestry	Teaching quality %	Student experience %	Research quality %	Entry standards (UCAS points)	Graduate prospects %	Overall score
1 Queen's, Belfast	81.5	79.5	56.3	149	92.9	100.0
2 Nottingham	86.9	81.4	36.4	140	76.5	96.7
3 Bangor	87.0	89.2	29.7	130	68.8	94.6
4 Aberystwyth	84.4	85.9	38.2	134	63.6	94.3
5 Reading	81.7	84.6	50.7	130	58.7	93.3
6 Nottingham Trent	85.1	84.4	4.1	150	51.4	92.4
=7 Harper Adams	85.1	82.0	5.7	130	77.0	92.0
=7 Newcastle	75.2	78.9	28.4	129	85.7	92.0
9 Greenwich	—	—	19.5	121	60.0	88.1
10 Royal Agricultural	75.6	71.7	2.1	122	69.1	85.8
11 Cumbria	82.1	78.1	—	115	42.9	84.1

Employed in high-skilled job	58%	Employed in lower-skilled job and studying		1%
Employed in high-skilled job and studying	3%	Employed in lower-skilled job		31%
Studying	5%	Unemployed		3%
High skilled work (median) salary	£24,000	Low/medium skilled salary		£20,000

American Studies

There are five fewer universities in this year's American Studies table compared with the previous edition of our *Guide*. The subject's popularity has been in decline, and applications for degrees have halved since their heyday before £9,000 fees were introduced. In the 2019 cycle only 290 students began American Studies degrees across all universities, though this was slightly higher than 2018's 260.

Birmingham remains the top university; it has the highest entry standards and places second for graduate prospects, bettered only by Keele – which with 95% of graduates in high-skilled work or further study 15 months after finishing their degrees has moved up to third place from 15th in the table overall this year. Manchester's second position in the table is maintained thanks in part to it achieving the best results in the Research Excellence Framework, and the third-best for student satisfaction with teaching quality.

Sussex, formerly a regular in our top-three for American Studies, has dropped to seventh place, its ranking hampered by low student satisfaction with teaching quality, as reported in the National Student Survey. For this measure Swansea leads the field, and it also scores well for student satisfaction with the wider undergraduate experience – as does Hull. American Studies does not have a history of setting our graduate prospects measure on fire, and continues the trend this year with 63% of graduates in high-skilled jobs or further study 15 months after completing their degrees, a bottom-15 result among the 67 subject groups.

Degrees classified by UCAS as American Studies include a variety of courses such as international relations and black studies. Most concentrate on the culture and politics of the USA and Canada. The opportunity of a year at an American or Canadian university as part of a four-year degree is commonly offered. The leading universities are likely to expect English or history at A-level, or in an equivalent qualification.

American Studies	Teaching quality %	Student experience %	Research quality %	Entry standards (UCAS points)	Graduate prospects %	Overall score
1 Birmingham	79.5	64.0	48.8	163	88.2	100.0
2 Manchester	84.4	76.1	49.1	146	62.9	95.7
3 Keele	77.5	77.1	29.8	n//a	95.0	93.5
4 Swansea	94.5	91.1	18.5	123	81.4	93.2
5 Nottingham	79.5	73.2	39.9	134	75.3	92.7
6 Kent	84.2	84.4	47.3	105	—	92.2
7 Sussex	74.9	70.4	45.6	144	64.3	91.6
8 East Anglia	80.5	79.3	33.1	132	71.2	90.9
9 Leicester	81.9	79.8	34.3	122	63.8	89.0
10 Hull	90.7	91.8	26.1	122	48.1	87.6
11 Goldsmiths, London	73.4	63.4	34.9	128*	—	86.2
12 Essex	77.3	75.1	46.9	96*	58.5	85.7
13 Portsmouth	80.1	66.7	32.2	111	63.9	85.5
14 Canterbury Christ Church	77.4	59.6	16.3	104	61.9	79.2

Employed in high-skilled job	47%	Employed in lower-skilled job and studying	1%
Employed in high-skilled job and studying	3%	Employed in lower-skilled job	32%
Studying	12%	Unemployed	5%
High skilled work (median) salary	£23,000	Low/medium skilled salary	£20,000

Anatomy and Physiology

Cambridge has regained the top spot in this year's table, with last year's leader St Andrews dropping to fourth place. Applications rose for the third successive year in 2019 and 5,065 students started degrees, another increase on the year before. While numbers on courses are growing, there are four fewer universities in this year's table compared with our last edition's 45.

Degrees in the fields of anatomy and physiology rank in the top 25 of our new measure of graduate prospects, which shows that 81% of graduates were in high-skilled work or further study within 15 months of finishing their courses; of these 49% were working, 53% were combining their job with further study and 27% were purely focused on academic work. Brighton has outdone all other universities for graduate prospects, with a rare 100% in high-skilled work or further study.

Led by Cambridge, which has the highest entry standards, there are four universities requiring over 200 UCAS points. Salford, Newcastle and Bangor – in that order – lead for student satisfaction with teaching quality, while Salford is top again for satisfaction with the wider undergraduate experience, a measure in which Liverpool, Glasgow and Dundee also score well. Results from the most recent Research Excellence Framework put Dundee and University College London joint-first, followed by Edinburgh, Cambridge and Oxford.

The subject table covers a broad range of courses – very few that actually have the title of anatomy or physiology – and includes the increasingly popular biomedical science degrees as well as cell biology, neurosciences and pathology. A two-science minimum at A-level usually means biology and chemistry, although just one science may be acceptable to some post-1992 universities.

Anatomy and Physiology	Teaching quality %	Student experience %	Research quality %	Entry standards (UCAS points)	Graduate prospects %	Overall score
1 Cambridge	—	—	52.5	228	91.0	100.0
2 Oxford	—	—	50.9	207	95.4	97.0
3 Dundee	84.9	88.0	55.4	190	77.6	95.4
4 St Andrews	86.7	87.9	37.6	201	80.0	94.8
5 Edinburgh	72.2	74.7	52.8	194	88.5	94.5
6 Aberdeen	82.8	87.4	34.7	191	82.2	93.5
7 University College London	76.0	75.0	55.4	182	80.8	92.6
=8 Leeds	77.9	80.3	40.9	161	88.0	92.1
=8 Swansea	82.3	81.5	44.7	144	—	92.1
10 Bristol	81.4	80.9	49.7	163	80.2	92.0
11 Glasgow	82.2	88.0	33.4	210	68.8	90.6
12 Sussex	79.6	73.3	46.8	149	81.4	89.8
13 Newcastle	89.3	87.9	47.8	164	65.0	89.7
14 Manchester	76.8	75.5	38.3	166	81.2	89.4
15 Queen's, Belfast	76.4	78.3	33.3	153	85.3	89.2
16 Brighton	80.9	79.0	4.8	128*	100.0	88.8
17 Glasgow Caledonian	85.9	83.7	8.1	119	93.8	88.4
18 Salford	94.3	89.7	12.7	125	81.6	88.2
19 Nottingham	82.5	79.8	26.5	141	81.6	87.7
20 Huddersfield	76.8	75.8	7.8	133	96.9	87.5
21 Liverpool	89.0	89.3	31.7	147	68.6	87.4
22 King's College London	74.5	75.7	38.0	146	80.7	87.3
23 Leicester	76.1	78.4	36.5	132	81.4	87.0
24 St George's, London	78.0	77.7	20.0	147	—	86.2
25 Plymouth	79.6	77.2	—	132	92.9	86.0

Anatomy and Physiology cont

		Teaching quality %	Student experience %	Research quality %	Entry standards (UCAS points)	Graduate prospects %	Overall score
26	Birmingham	69.8	67.5	31.5	158	—	85.6
=27	Bangor	89.1	87.9	—	117	83.3	85.2
=27	Reading	77.6	78.8	26.6	122	81.3	85.2
29	Derby	85.7	84.7	1.6	119	84.6	84.9
30	Westminster	85.2	79.7	21.2	105	—	84.7
31	Coventry	80.2	81.6	4.5	145	78.0	83.7
=32	Anglia Ruskin	79.7	75.5	2.2	104	90.9	83.6
=32	Queen Mary, London	70.5	77.4	26.1	143	76.5	83.6
34	Cardiff	62.4	64.5	33.3	152	—	82.8
35	Manchester Metropolitan	69.6	70.2	12.0	135	85.2	82.7
36	Oxford Brookes	73.9	79.1	21.3	117	—	82.6
=37	Keele	69.6	74.2	16.5	127	78.5	81.2
=37	Ulster	66.2	65.6	—	126	91.7	81.2
39	East London	79.5	74.5	—	96	83.3	80.3
40	Portsmouth	77.0	64.6	8.1	—	78.6	80.1
41	Middlesex	59.7	62.4	—	102	81.3	74.7

Employed in high-skilled job	49%	Employed in lower-skilled job and studying	1%
Employed in high-skilled job and studying	4%	Employed in lower-skilled job	15%
Studying	27%	Unemployed	3%
High skilled work (median) salary	£25,000	Low/medium skilled salary	£17,600

Animal Science

Now in its sixth year, we first published an Animal Science table to reflect the growing interest in this group of subjects. Extracted from the agriculture category, degree courses range from animal behaviour to equine science and veterinary nursing. Almost 2,600 students started courses in 2019 – a very similar figure to 2018. Most degrees will require biology and probably chemistry.

Across all measures Glasgow once again tops the Animal Science table, with by far the highest entry standards among the 16 universities. Reading, which received the best results in the Research Excellence Framework, has moved into second place this year, swapping with Aberystwyth which takes third position.

Animal Science traditionally sits at the bottom of our employment ranking, due to the relatively high proportion of graduates starting their careers in low-skilled jobs – as measured by the now defunct Destination of Leavers from Higher Education Survey, which assessed graduates' progress six months after finishing their degrees. The new Graduate Outcomes referenced in this edition of our *Guide* takes a census 15 months after graduates have finished their courses. The longer time frame has not lifted Animal Science subjects from the bottom of our employment ranking however, and showed that only 40% were in high-skilled jobs or further study after 15 months. More positively, just 5% of graduates were unemployed.

Some individual universities do much better, notably Nottingham where almost 80% of graduates achieved the top graduate outcomes, followed by Liverpool (77%) and Reading (70%). Worryingly, at Middlesex no graduates were in high-skilled work or further study 15 months on, and only 14% of Edinburgh Napier's cohort had achieved such an outcome.

Animal Science

		Teaching quality %	Student experience %	Research quality %	Entry standards (UCAS points)	Graduate prospects %	Overall score
1	Glasgow	81.6	84.6	42.3	200	53.8	100.0
2	Reading	86.0	84.2	50.7	146	70.0	98.2
3	Aberystwyth	83.3	86.2	38.2	134	—	91.6
4	Nottingham	76.8	77.6	36.4	127	79.6	90.9
5	Liverpool	69.1	76.6	32.9	152	76.9	90.6
6	Bristol	76.8	75.3	33.2	149	38.9	87.7
7	Nottingham Trent	86.6	85.6	4.1	140	42.3	85.5
8	Plymouth	88.5	86.4	—	135	46.4	85.2
9	Lincoln	85.5	84.7	—	140	47.1	84.9
10	Harper Adams	86.6	85.0	5.7	122	47.9	84.2
11	Royal Veterinary College	78.1	77.6	—	137	57.1	82.8
12	Greenwich	—	—	19.5	126	22.2	79.3
13	Anglia Ruskin	81.1	77.3	24.6	87	—	78.2
14	Chester	74.7	72.4	7.9	130	23.9	77.7
15	Edinburgh Napier	69.2	61.2	—	162	14.3	76.4
16	Middlesex	71.3	52.4	—	129	0.0	73.7

Employed in high-skilled job	24%	Employed in lower-skilled job and studying	4%
Employed in high-skilled job and studying	1%	Employed in lower-skilled job	55%
Studying	11%	Unemployed	5%
High skilled work (median) salary	£21,000	Low/medium skilled salary	£18,500

Anthropology

Covering the cultural and biological diversity of humans, the study of anthropology at undergraduate level has grown sharply in popularity since 2011 when tuition fees went up to £9,000. Both applications and enrolments are more than twice as high now than they were then. Applications rose to 10,220 in 2018 and were only marginally lower (10,135) in the 2019 cycle, in a year when 1,660 students started anthropology degrees – representing more than six applications for each place. Although the numbers starting degrees remain below 2,000 the number of universities in the table continues to grow and 47 universities and colleges expect to offer the subject this year.

Joint Honours degrees have contributed to the spike in student numbers, and anthropology is often paired with a wide range of degrees, from accountancy to linguistics or law. Other than that, its boom is unexplained, although television series have been mooted as possible drivers in interest. Entry requirements are broad for most degree courses and no specific subjects are needed for most degrees, although some universities favour sociology, biology or another science at A-level, or equivalent.

Our employment ranking, derived from the proportion of graduates in high-skilled jobs or further study 15 months after finishing their degrees, places anthropology 52nd out of 67 subject areas – with 65.8% of graduates achieving these top outcomes. The new Graduate Outcomes survey showed that anthropology ties with classics and ancient history, architecture and History of Art in having an 8% unemployment rate – among the highest.

Largely the preserve of old universities, anthropology is also offered by a small number of post-1992 institutions. Cambridge continues to dominate our table, though Oxford – which traditionally occupies second place – has dropped to fifth this year, overtaken by Queen's Belfast, Exeter and UCL. Birmingham had the strongest results in the Research Excellence framework and for student satisfaction with teaching quality Brunel leads the field, followed by Queen's Belfast and St Andrews.

Anthropology	Teaching quality %	Student experience %	Research quality %	Entry standards (UCAS points)	Graduate prospects %	Overall score
1 Cambridge	—	—	40.4	199	87.3	100.0
2 Queen's, Belfast	91.9	83.3	49.0	140	83.3	99.8
3 Exeter	78.4	79.3	41.0	157	100.0	99.2
4 University College London	81.4	81.9	49.3	171	76.9	98.8
5 Oxford	—	—	38.8	192	—	97.7
6 St Andrews	91.4	85.7	25.0	192	75.0	97.0
7 London School of Economics	79.9	80.2	41.3	162	· 76.2	95.2
8 Birmingham	75.2	74.2	50.9	138	—	92.8
9 Durham	76.8	70.9	29.1	172	79.2	91.9
10 Manchester	81.1	78.8	36.7	158	60.5	90.4
11 Aberdeen	76.0	78.8	31.8	160*	—	89.8
12 Edinburgh	67.4	64.0	42.2	178	58.7	88.6
13 Kent	82.4	82.3	20.5	130	75.3	87.3
14 Sussex	73.7	69.6	34.4	153	62.7	87.0
15 Roehampton	87.2	87.5	27.7	109	—	86.6
16 Brunel London	93.5	93.6	29.3	103	54.2	86.4
17 Soas, London	73.6	70.5	31.1	162	55.0	85.6
18 Goldsmiths, London	68.6	55.5	34.5	131	62.1	82.1
19 Portsmouth	79.0	76.1	32.2	113	50.0	81.9
20 Liverpool John Moores	66.6	64.2	15.1	162	65.0	81.1
21 Bournemouth	84.6	84.4	19.9	99	49.3	79.4
22 Oxford Brookes	77.8	77.7	17.3	113	54.1	78.8
23 Bristol	59.9	56.0	11.2	152	73.7	78.5
24 Leeds	80.8	69.1	—	152	55.0	78.2
25 Wales Trinity St David	76.2	65.5	17.3	96*	56.5	76.0

Employed in high-skilled job	47%	Employed in lower-skilled job and studying	1%
Employed in high-skilled job and studying	5%	Employed in lower-skilled job	26%
Studying	13%	Unemployed	8%
High skilled work (median) salary	£25,000	Low/medium skilled salary	£18,750

Archaeology and Forensic Science

As a single-honours degree archaeology had only 445 new students in 2019. Most of the students covered by this table are actually taking courses classified as forensic and archaeological science, which attracted a record 10,125 applications in 2019 and 2,320 new enrolments. As a whole, the subjects are now as in demand as they were before £9,000 fees were introduced and more than 50 universities and colleges are offering courses in them for next year. Geography, history and the sciences are all deemed relevant A-levels but there are no specific requirements. Across all universities, entry standards are relatively low – only 10 of the 53 institutions in our table average more than 150 UCAS points.

Cambridge's tenure at the top of our Archaeology and Forensic Science table continues this year, helped by it having the highest entry standards, the second-best graduate prospects and the third-strongest results in the Research Excellence Framework. Oxford has moved up to second place, replacing Dundee which has slipped to fifth and further shuffling of the top 10 has brought Glasgow up to third place and Birmingham into fourth – up from 12th last year.

Job prospects have been improving, although in the new Graduate Outcomes survey archaeology and forensic science places well outside the top 50, with 63% of graduates in high-skilled work or further study 15 months after finishing their degrees. West of England had the best outcomes, with an impressive 95% in professional roles or continuing in academia 15 months on from graduating.

Student satisfaction with teaching quality is highest at Chester, our analysis of the National Student Survey reveals, followed by Glasgow then Worcester.

Archaeology and Forensic Science	Teaching quality %	Student experience %	Research quality %	Entry standards (UCAS points)	Graduate prospects %	Overall score
1 Cambridge	—	—	47.2	198	87.3	100.0
2 Oxford	—	—	42.9	193	—	98.6
3 Glasgow	94.3	88.2	16.4	194	—	97.9
4 Birmingham	90.6	86.0	40.3	161	—	97.3
5 Dundee	85.5	87.7	55.4	160	71.4	96.8
6 University College London	93.1	87.3	51.4	162	60.0	95.8
7 Durham	88.7	82.8	41.2	161	75.9	95.5
8 Queen's, Belfast	92.8	89.9	36.9	139	—	95.0
9 Swansea	92.6	88.6	39.4	131	—	94.2
10 Southampton	86.1	79.7	43.5	135	80.6	93.2
11 York	92.8	86.0	35.1	143	70.0	92.8
12 Sheffield	83.9	79.3	31.6	145	76.2	90.9
13 Leicester	83.7	80.5	37.2	131	76.5	90.6
14 Edinburgh	77.3	67.1	20.9	192	—	90.1
15 Aberdeen	82.9	84.3	29.4	139	—	89.3
16 Nottingham	87.7	79.8	23.7	141	70.6	88.9
17 Exeter	73.4	71.0	33.6	148	79.3	88.7
18 Hull	85.6	86.5	31.7	120	—	88.6
19 Manchester	80.1	70.0	24.7	163	70.8	88.5

		Teaching quality %	Student experience %	Research quality %	Entry standards (UCAS points)	Graduate prospects %	Overall score
20	Robert Gordon	82.6	74.6	8.8	152	83.3	88.2
21	Kent	81.3	74.5	33.1	134	71.8	88.0
22	Cardiff	75.9	71.2	31.1	125	85.7	87.9
23	Reading	86.4	80.6	44.7	113	61.2	87.7
24	Worcester	93.2	88.0	8.1	101	86.0	87.6
25	Newcastle	81.7	81.4	25.8	129	70.8	87.0
26	Coventry	88.5	84.5	—	117	86.7	86.5
27	Derby	88.0	87.9	3.6	116	78.8	85.7
=28	Cumbria	91.3	84.9	1.5	134	—	85.1
=28	Lincoln	89.3	88.5	—	115	77.3	85.1
30	Wales Trinity St David	90.7	81.2	17.3	119	62.6	85.0
31	Teesside	89.3	87.1	—	136	65.4	84.6
32	Bradford	83.1	83.9	23.6	110	—	84.2
33	West of England	72.6	78.5	—	117	94.7	83.6
=34	Glasgow Caledonian	77.2	74.6	4.7	146	66.7	82.5
=34	Keele	70.6	73.2	—	143	80.8	82.5
36	Staffordshire	86.6	84.9	—	116	68.7	82.4
=37	Liverpool	77.9	70.1	33.5	139	45.9	82.2
=37	Liverpool John Moores	75.7	81.1	—	147	66.7	82.2
39	Bournemouth	78.3	79.0	19.9	112	63.7	81.8
40	Nottingham Trent	71.1	77.7	4.1	141	71.4	81.7
41	Chester	94.5	88.3	15.4	103	45.6	81.4
42	West of Scotland	80.8	81.9	—	127	62.5	80.6
43	Anglia Ruskin	71.9	68.3	24.6	112	66.7	80.5
44	De Montfort	79.6	74.5	—	115*	70.0	79.8
45	West London	80.2	83.8	—	125	57.1	79.5
46	Manchester Metropolitan	78.8	79.1	—	136*	55.8	79.4
47	Wolverhampton	77.0	77.6	—	112	70.0	79.3
48	Bangor	72.1	66.2	24.3	116	—	79.1
49	Central Lancashire	74.9	71.4	9.8	129	57.3	78.9
50	London South Bank	85.4	93.7	—	102	50.0	78.1
51	Winchester	77.1	68.0	7.5	101	68.5	78.0
52	South Wales	71.0	65.8	—	123	67.8	77.2
53	Canterbury Christ Church	88.4	82.9	16.3	98	33.5	76.7

Employed in high-skilled job	45%	Employed in lower-skilled job and studying	1%
Employed in high-skilled job and studying	2%	Employed in lower-skilled job	29%
Studying	15%	Unemployed	7%
High skilled work (median) salary	£21,000	Low/medium skilled salary	£18,000

Architecture

Bath continues its reign at the top of our Architecture table this year, thanks to its established strengths across the board from entry standards and research to student satisfaction and graduate prospects. Cambridge has been bumped from second place however, overtaken by Loughborough – which moves up to second position due in part to its perfect employment score: 100% of graduates were in high-skilled jobs or further study 15 months on from finishing their degrees.

Derived from the Graduate Outcomes survey the new measure of job prospects finds out what graduates are doing 15 months after completing their courses, in place of the now discontinued six-months-on census. The updated measure has resulted in further perfect 100% scores for fourth-ranked UCL, eighth-ranked Queen's, Belfast and 11th-ranked Arts, Bournemouth – where all graduates had entered professional work or were continuing to study. Overall, Architecture is in the top 15 for graduate prospects.

The best scores for student satisfaction with teaching quality in the National Student Survey, went to West of England, followed by Arts Bournemouth and Cardiff Metropolitan – winner of our Welsh University of the Year award 2021–22.

There were 29,790 applications to study architecture in 2019 – the highest number since 2011, and the 5,160 accepted onto courses constituted the fourth successive increase in student numbers. Competition averages a little under six applications per place.

No specific subjects are required for entry, but the leading universities prefer an art/science mix and portfolios are essential. Only 18 universities average above 150 UCAS points for entry.

The seven years it usually takes to qualify as an architect make studying the subject a considerable financial commitment, and the first degree only a step on the way. The extra £1,000 required for course materials is worth taking into account as well.

Architecture	Teaching quality %	Student experience %	Research quality %	Entry standards (UCAS points)	Graduate prospects %	Overall score
1 Bath	89.0	86.8	52.9	194	96.9	100.0
2 Loughborough	79.3	80.2	58.3	153	100.0	95.5
3 Cambridge	—	—	49.0	196	90.5	95.4
4 University College London	75.2	68.4	54.1	182	100.0	95.3
5 Cardiff	86.9	82.5	40.7	168	90.5	93.6
6 Liverpool	89.1	89.0	43.5	151	89.5	93.4
7 Sheffield	84.7	84.7	36.6	173	90.7	93.2
8 Queen's, Belfast	81.2	76.7	35.2	155	100.0	92.4
9 Edinburgh	71.7	70.0	35.1	178	95.5	90.4
10 Newcastle	80.4	80.9	43.7	169	81.6	90.3
11 Arts, Bournemouth	93.9	85.9	2.4	127	100.0	88.8
=12 Oxford Brookes	84.4	85.4	17.6	149	89.4	88.1
=12 West of England	94.8	95.0	10.6	139	84.5	88.1
14 Dundee	84.3	77.4	8.7	176	—	88.0
15 Ulster	83.9	84.4	28.6	129	87.9	87.5
=16 Kent	75.7	77.3	33.3	166	81.5	87.2
=16 Nottingham	79.0	77.2	14.8	166	89.8	87.2

Architecture cont

		Teaching quality %	Student experience %	Research quality %	Entry standards (UCAS points)	Graduate prospects %	Overall score
18	Strathclyde	65.4	61.2	23.0	198	88.2	86.4
19	Liverpool John Moores	83.8	83.5	4.9	152	88.5	86.0
20	Robert Gordon	80.6	79.1	8.3	152	90.6	85.9
=21	Manchester School of Architecture	76.7	74.6	12.6	162	84.6	84.6
=21	Nottingham Trent	85.7	84.2	3.4	130	89.4	84.6
23	Central Lancashire	88.1	83.4	3.0	128	87.5	84.2
24	Reading	68.6	66.9	40.0	128	—	83.0
25	Salford	75.5	72.9	19.6	113	91.3	82.8
26	Creative Arts	78.5	79.1	3.4	135	88.2	82.7
27	Coventry	85.5	81.4	10.3	117	—	82.6
28	Birmingham City	89.0	86.6	9.6	129	72.7	82.1
29	Plymouth	79.6	73.8	13.2	116	86.7	81.8
30	Westminster	87.7	84.3	10.7	135	70.6	81.7
=31	Cardiff Metropolitan	89.3	79.7	—	116	83.3	81.6
=31	Edinburgh Napier	65.5	70.3	5.7	150	91.7	81.6
33	Sheffield Hallam	79.7	76.0	13.4	105	86.0	81.1
34	De Montfort	65.0	67.4	35.9	109*	87.1	81.0
=35	Kingston	83.5	78.1	10.1	116	79.3	80.8
=35	Northumbria	70.3	66.3	5.9	160	82.9	80.8
37	East London	86.9	80.5	8.1	126	71.4	80.2
38	Brighton	72.8	65.6	13.1	120	87.5	80.1
39	London South Bank	73.6	66.1	19.6	109	85.7	79.9
40	Middlesex	88*	80.8*	13.3	80	—	79.6
41	Portsmouth	77.6	80.9	—	108	86.2	79.4
=42	Greenwich	87.5	78.1	2.0	118	71.4	78.5
=42	Lincoln	77.9	76.3	3.2	110	81.8	78.5
44	Solent, Southampton	80.5	73.4	—	121	78.6	78.4
45	Leeds Beckett	72.6	73.0	5.6	109	84.6	78.1
46	London Metropolitan	78.8	72.0	7.2	115	75.0	77.5
47	Anglia Ruskin	71.3	70.7	5.2	121	—	76.7
48	Wolverhampton	81.5	79.5	5.6	84	72.7	75.4
49	Huddersfield	80.0	76.1	—	126	60.0	74.3
50	Derby	77.9	85.0	6.7	113	58.3	74.1
51	Ravensbourne	55.9	53.3	—	104	85.1	71.5
=51	Lincoln	56.2	54.6	3.2	124	89.6	74.6
53	Wolverhampton	85.4	81.0	5.6	97	60.9	73.6
54	Northampton	71.4	59.9	—	102	78.6	73.0
55	Glasgow Caledonian	70.5	68.4	9.1	—	69.2	72.2
56	Ravensbourne, London	62.0	57.1	—	99	66.7	67.4

Employed in high-skilled job	74%	Employed in lower-skilled job and studying	0%
Employed in high-skilled job and studying	4%	Employed in lower-skilled job	7%
Studying	7%	Unemployed	8%
High skilled work (median) salary	£22,000	Low/medium skilled salary	£18,500

Art and Design

Results from the new Graduate Outcomes survey have shaken up the rankings in our Art and Design table. Notably Oxford, last year's top university for the subjects, has dropped to 10th overall. It registered only 50% of graduates in high-skilled work or further study 15 months after finishing their degrees – placing the academic goliath 75th for our graduate prospects measure, out of the 83 universities in the table. Oxford still leads by some distance on entry standards, but Newcastle has regained the number one position overall, which it last held jointly with Oxford two years ago.

Art and design are among the biggest recruiters in higher education, with over 118,300 applications in 2019 and nearly 25,000 new students starting courses. Design studies is much the largest area, and fine art – though it accounts for a far smaller proportion of students – still attracted 4,475 new starters in 2019.

The subjects always feature in the lower reaches of employment tables, but the trend for graduates not going straight into high-skilled jobs tends not to be a surprise to artists and designers, who accept they may have a period in low-paid self-employment early in their career. The move to finding out what graduates are doing 15 months after completing their degrees, rather than six months on, has not made a difference in this respect, and Art and Design finishes 57th for graduate prospects out of the 67 subject areas. Some universities buck the trend however, such as ninth-ranked Bournemouth which came top for graduate prospects, with 94% of graduates already in professional jobs or further study 15 months on, followed by Brunel and Glasgow Caledonian.

Further down the list Canterbury Christ Church, ranked 59th overall, received the best scores in the National Student Survey in the sections relating to teaching quality. Aberystwyth equalled that and also had the most positive overall undergraduate experience.

Most courses are at post-1992 universities, and/or the specialist arts institutions, but the older universities dominate the top 10 of our table due largely to their higher entry standards – although most artists would argue that entry grades are less significant than in other subjects. Selection rests primarily on the quality of candidates' portfolios and many undergraduates enter via a one-year Art Foundation course. Even the research-led Russell Group of universities do not require any essential A-levels, although they do advise that art and design subjects are preferred.

Art and Design	Teaching quality %	Student experience %	Research quality %	Entry standards (UCAS points)	Graduate prospects %	Overall score
1 Newcastle	85.1	84.7	37.3	207	64.5	100.0
2 Loughborough	81.4	78.5	35.3	176	80.3	98.6
3 Reading	85.2	81.7	38.9	136	81.7	97.6
4 University College London	84.3	82.5	44.7	194	53.8	97.5
5 Edinburgh Napier	88.7	86.5	—	183	75.8	95.7

Art and Design cont

	Teaching quality %	Student experience %	Research quality %	Entry standards (UCAS points)	Graduate prospects %	Overall score
6 Dundee	77.2	74.9	39.9	178	68.9	95.6
7 Ulster	75.7	68.0	57.2	134	79.3	95.5
8 Glasgow Caledonian	85.1	82.1	1.8	174	82.1	94.9
9 Bournemouth	85.3	85.3	15.0	109	94.3	94.7
10 Oxford	—	—	39.7	237	50.0	94.4
11 Lancaster	75.8	78.1	48.0	156	64.3	94.2
=12 Leeds	74.6	71.5	33.6	171	73.6	93.8
=12 Wales Trinity St David	88.0	82.0	39.2	144	55.6	93.8
14 Goldsmiths, London	79.6	74.3	25.9	177	66.0	93.3
15 Glasgow	62.3	68.1	37.2	217	—	93.2
16 Kent	79.3	72.7	44.3	135	68.5	93.0
=17 Brunel London	70.3	67.7	32.8	134	92.3	92.8
=17 Southampton	80.7	75.2	35.4	156	62.5	92.8
19 Kingston	82.9	74.7	10.1	174	71.2	92.6
20 Heriot-Watt	80.2	74.6	31.1	156	63.1	92.0
21 Northumbria	80.7	74.5	13.3	155	74.9	91.6
22 West of England	87.0	81.9	15.0	144	63.5	91.4
23 Liverpool John Moores	82.3	81.8	7.2	192	55.8	91.3
24 Plymouth	86.6	86.0	14.7	133	64.9	91.2
=25 Robert Gordon	88.7	82.8	11.5	159	52.8	90.5
=25 Teesside	88.1	82.6	2.9	123	75.0	90.5
27 Staffordshire	89.8	85.3	2.3	130	66.1	90.0
28 Edinburgh	75.5	70.4	27.9	175	55.9	89.8
29 Aberystwyth	92.4	89.3	21.6	127	44.8	89.7
=30 Nottingham Trent	80.0	79.2	4.7	145	73.4	89.6
=30 South Wales	91.7	86.1	3.3	128	61.4	89.6
=30 Sunderland	87.9	85.8	9.8	111	68.2	89.6
=33 Coventry	84.3	78.4	18.1	126	64.4	89.4
=33 Glyndŵr	87.4	79.7	7.8	107	75.0	89.4
35 Manchester Metropolitan	79.8	73.5	9.7	172	61.0	89.3
36 Sheffield Hallam	82.4	76.9	15.5	123	69.2	89.1
37 Lincoln	83.5	80.7	7.1	127	70.0	89.0
38 Bath Spa	82.1	78.6	9.6	145	63.4	88.9
39 Hull	81.3	73.8	11.2	154	—	88.7
40 London Metropolitan	89.4	82.3	4.7	120	63.6	88.6
=41 Arts, Bournemouth	83.9	78.5	2.4	149	62.5	88.4
=41 Cardiff Metropolitan	89.6	85.7	7.9	125	55.5	88.4
=41 Salford	88.5	82.1	8.0	136	55.0	88.4
=44 Central Lancashire	86.9	82.8	3.9	137	59.0	88.3
=44 Leeds Arts	83.0	78.6	—	160	60.7	88.3
=46 Brighton	78.5	69.7	13.1	147	66.8	88.1
=46 Westminster	74.2	68.3	22.5	140	68.6	88.1

48	Falmouth	83.0	77.7	3.0	138	66.0	87.9
49	West London	86.6	85.8	4.5	120	61.1	87.7
50	Bolton	90.6	82.0	—	117	60.9	87.3
=51	Huddersfield	82.8	77.2	4.8	140	58.5	86.8
=51	Portsmouth	84.8	80.8	—	123	64.6	86.8
53	Anglia Ruskin	78.5	76.1	8.5	131	65.0	86.6
54	Worcester	80.0	81.0	11.1	122	60.4	86.4
55	Arts London	79.2	71.8	8.0	143	61.0	86.3
56	Middlesex	79.4	74.8	13.3	132	57.4	86.0
=57	Abertay	80.1	68.5	—	138	67.9	85.9
=57	De Montfort	80.2	76.2	10.2	123*	61.0	85.9
59	Canterbury Christ Church	92.4	82.7	7.3	98	51.5	85.7
60	Birmingham City	79.0	72.5	9.6	132	60.7	85.6
61	Leeds Beckett	84.7	80.3	1.2	109	63.0	85.5
62	Chester	85.2	76.5	6.2	121	54.8	85.3
=63	Cumbria	80.9	74.1	6.1	130	57.7	85.1
=63	Ravensbourne	83.2	77.3	—	112	64.6	85.1
=63	Winchester	81.3	79.9	—	103	69.2	85.1
66	Oxford Brookes	74.6	73.6	10.4	148	54.2	84.8
67	Suffolk	84.0	84.5	—	106	59.3	84.7
=68	Derby	78.7	78.5	5.1	120	60.2	84.6
=68	London South Bank	82.2	79.0	12.8	109	53.6	84.6
=68	Norwich Arts	78.9	75.4	5.6	136	55.4	84.6
71	Solent, Southampton	80.0	77.7	1.6	130	56.9	84.5
72	Creative Arts	82.0	73.7	3.4	143	49.8	84.4
73	York St John	83.7	74.8	—	113	61.1	84.3
74	Wolverhampton	86.2	83.1	8.9	109	45.9	84.0
75	Northampton	85.8	74.1	2.9	114	53.3	83.8
76	East London	79.6	74.2	9.8	107	58.6	83.6
77	Gloucestershire	78.8	76.8	—	120	58.8	83.4
78	Bucks New	81.0	68.8	6.1	126	47.9	82.1
79	Hertfordshire	77.4	76.3	5.8	112	53.2	82.0
80	Greenwich	68.2	60.5	3.5	133	65.2	81.3
81	Bedfordshire	73.8	67.1	—	114	57.9	80.1
82	Liverpool Hope	79.2	70.8	—	125	40.0	79.3
83	Chichester	86.7	81.8	—	121	16.7	77.7

Employed in high-skilled job	56%	Employed in lower-skilled job and studying	1%
Employed in high-skilled job and studying	1%	Employed in lower-skilled job	31%
Studying	3%	Unemployed	7%
High skilled work (median) salary	£21,000	Low/medium skilled salary	£17,900

Biological Sciences

Cambridge is top of our Biological Sciences table for the 16th consecutive year, its tenure secured once more by the highest entry standards by some margin, along with the second-best graduate prospects. The average grades for Cambridge's Natural Sciences degree are among the highest for any subject at any university. Oxford remains in second place while St Andrews has moved up to third, bumping Dundee from the spot it held last year.

The upper reaches of our table are dominated by universities with old foundations across the UK. Eleventh-ranked Edinburgh received the highest scores in the Research Excellence Framework, followed closed by Imperial. For graduate prospects Ulster does the best out of all 120 universities, with almost 93% of its graduates working in high-skilled jobs or furthering their studies 15 months after completing their degrees. Ulster's overall ranking, though, has tumbled from 30th place last year to 78th = in this edition of our *Guide*, due to a decline in student satisfaction, on top of it not entering any academics in these subjects in the Research Excellence Framework.

For student satisfaction Lincoln – the *Sunday Times* Modern University of the Year – leads the field in both measures, of teaching quality and of the wider undergraduate experience. Of the top 25 overall universities Loughborough, Swansea and St Andrews also did well in the National Student Survey.

As a subject area the biological sciences occupy a central position within our employment ranking, in 34th place out of 67 tables. The new Graduate Outcomes survey showed that on average 43% of biological science graduates were in high-skilled jobs 15 months after finishing their degrees, 26% were engaged in further study and 3% were combining both.

Of the specialisms within the grouping, biology is the most popular – and in increasing demand – with applications that topped 40,000 and 7,300 new students in the 2019 cycle, representing more than five candidates per place. Competition for microbiology degree places was similar and though the number starting courses was only 595 it was an all-time high for the subject. Between them, molecular biology, biophysics and biochemistry also saw an upturn in applications and enrolments. Botany received only 210 applications, but this was another record, and 50 students enrolled on courses – exactly the same number as in 2018. Zoology has far more applications and places, which again saw upturns in the 2019 cycle.

Many of the leading universities will demand two sciences at A-level, or the equivalent – usually biology and chemistry – for any of the biological sciences.

Biological Sciences	Teaching quality %	Student experience %	Research quality %	Entry standards (UCAS points)	Graduate prospects %	Overall score
1 Cambridge	—	—	52.5	228	91.0	100.0
2 Oxford	—	—	50.9	199	88.7	96.0
3 St Andrews	87.2	87.1	37.6	210	82.2	95.6
4 Dundee	83.6	85.7	55.4	194	80.8	95.4
5 Strathclyde	81.2	81.0	52.2	201	84.1	95.0
6 Imperial College London	74.5	76.6	61.6	179	89.9	93.8
7 Sheffield	84.9	85.3	57.4	159	79.3	93.3
8 Durham	81.8	80.5	32.9	188	87.3	92.7
9 University College London	78.0	77.8	55.4	184	81.5	92.6
10 York	83.1	84.4	41.9	159	86.0	92.4
11 Edinburgh	74.1	76.8	62.9	186	79.8	92.2
12 Lancaster	84.3	81.2	46.5	155	83.6	92.0
13 Bristol	83.1	84.3	46.8	166	79.0	91.9
14 Exeter	83.6	84.0	39.7	164	81.8	91.6

15 Loughborough	89.7	91.0	52.1	146	69.0	91.5
=16 Glasgow	80.0	82.5	33.4	197	75.4	90.7
=16 Surrey	82.7	84.6	37.5	147	84.3	90.7
18 Manchester	81.7	78.4	38.3	168	80.5	90.3
19 Swansea	86.8	89.3	38.6	125	78.2	89.7
=20 Aberdeen	82.3	82.5	34.7	175	73.8	89.6
=20 King's College London	77.6	77.6	38.0	165	83.1	89.6
22 Leeds	75.7	77.8	40.9	160	83.9	89.4
=23 Aston	83.9	84.3	39.1	118	84.2	89.3
=23 Southampton	84.6	86.4	34.2	146	76.4	89.3
25 Royal Holloway, London	84.7	85.1	25.7	124	88.1	89.2
26 Stirling	77.0	78.0	49.0	165	74.5	89.0
27 Portsmouth	85.9	85.8	24.3	114	88.0	88.8
28 Queen's, Belfast	72.7	78.1	47.3	148	82.7	88.5
29 Sunderland	90.6	87.3	7.5	109	90.3	88.3
30 Warwick	79.7	82.7	37.1	153	75.2	88.2
31 Robert Gordon	78.2	82.0	4.9	159	90.9	87.8
32 Kent	79.6	84.0	39.1	130	77.7	87.6
33 East Anglia	83.3	81.3	38.8	130	74.5	87.4
34 Glasgow Caledonian	80.6	79.4	8.1	168	83.3	87.3
=35 Abertay	86.2	82.7	4.3	169	76.5	87.2
=35 Leicester	81.7	84.7	36.5	130	74.2	87.2
37 Birmingham	76.3	73.6	38.1	155	78.0	87.1
38 Liverpool	75.1	78.5	33.9	146	80.8	87.0
=39 Bath	71.3	75.3	31.5	167	81.3	86.9
=39 Queen Mary, London	75.1	78.5	26.1	147	83.9	86.9
41 Nottingham Trent	81.5	83.4	24.1	120	82.4	86.7
42 Sussex	78.9	76.2	46.8	152	66.7	86.5
43 Nottingham	76.8	77.1	26.5	133	84.2	86.3
=44 Hull	79.4	78.8	31.7	116	82.1	86.2
=44 Reading	84.6	84.6	26.6	123	74.0	86.2
46 York St John	90.9	88.7	—	118	80.0	86.1
=47 Keele	82.2	81.8	16.5	123	82.7	86.0
=47 Plymouth	89.3	86.3	17.4	131	69.8	86.0
49 Cardiff	74.9	74.1	33.3	150	77.8	85.9
50 Aberystwyth	85.1	85.6	38.2	118	66.3	85.8
51 Essex	84.4	84.9	17.8	97	83.7	85.6
=52 Gloucestershire	88.7	88.0	14.5	115	71.2	85.1
=52 Lincoln	91.5	91.5	—	128	70.1	85.1
=54 Coventry	84.1	81.8	4.5	105	88.0	85.0
=54 West of Scotland	88.8	81.1	29.0	134	61.5	85.0
=56 Huddersfield	85.0	85.1	7.8	116	79.3	84.9
=56 Sheffield Hallam	85.2	82.6	10.4	112	80.6	84.9
58 Oxford Brookes	76.4	77.8	21.3	114	84.5	84.6
=59 Edge Hill	85.6	85.2	6.2	111	78.7	84.4
=59 Edinburgh Napier	80.9	79.4	8.9	153	73.3	84.4

Biological Sciences cont

	Teaching quality %	Student experience %	Research quality %	Entry standards (UCAS points)	Graduate prospects %	Overall score
=59 Queen Margaret, Edinburgh	82.8	76.1	—	141	81.8	84.4
62 Heriot-Watt	78.7	76.1	26.3	161	64.4	84.1
63 West of England	85.6	86.5	8.2	110	71.9	83.3
=64 Central Lancashire	80.0	79.6	8.3	129	76.0	83.2
=64 Newcastle	72.5	78.3	28.4	146	68.3	83.2
=66 Bangor	79.0	81.8	31.5	125	63.4	83.1
=66 Liverpool John Moores	82.4	82.7	15.1	146	62.2	83.1
=66 Royal Veterinary College	74.7	77.8	—	135	84.6	83.1
69 Northampton	88.7	85.1	—	90	77.3	82.8
70 St George's, London	68.3	69.9	20.0	146	80.6	82.7
71 Worcester	83.2	83.4	10.9	103	73.4	82.6
72 Bradford	76.4	77.8	9.5	115	80.0	82.3
73 Brunel London	75.4	76.1	18.2	115	76.6	82.1
74 Manchester Metropolitan	80.7	78.6	12.0	125	68.5	81.9
75 Cardiff Metropolitan	73.8	76.7	—	122	82.9	81.6
76 Northumbria	69.6	72.2	14.0	138	77.8	81.5
77 Westminster	74.6	75.8	21.2	113	72.3	81.3
=78 Bedfordshire	76.6	78.6	25.1	97	71.0	81.2
=78 Teesside	83.4	81.9	—	133	64.7	81.2
=78 Ulster	65.6	73.1	—	120	92.9	81.2
81 Kingston	82.3	84.5	2.6	104	69.7	80.8
82 Chester	81.1	78.6	12.0	110	66.8	80.6
83 Derby	89.0	88.3	1.6	108	57.6	80.4
84 Leeds Beckett	81.5	85.8	3.5	114*	62.5	80.0
85 Roehampton	77.3	75.1	20.6	101	67.2	79.9
86 South Wales	79.2	78.5	—	122	67.5	79.7
=87 Salford	84.9	82.9	12.7	115	53.1	79.5
=87 Staffordshire	79.5	75.0	—	111	71.7	79.5
89 Bournemouth	77.9	76.2	4.7	106	70.1	79.2
90 Anglia Ruskin	78.8	78.2	2.2	98	70.9	79.1
91 Canterbury Christ Church	77.5	70.5	11.9	96	72.2	79.0
92 Hertfordshire	78.7	73.9	10.9	95	—	78.6
93 Brighton	72.7	74.8	4.8	104	70.9	78.0
=94 Bath Spa	76.9	78.5	—	96	68.0	77.7
=94 Middlesex	70.3	77.5	10.0	108	—	77.7
96 Greenwich	62.8	66.0	7.4	101	81.8	77.0
97 London South Bank	76.7	74.3	35.0	88	44.0	75.6
=98 London Metropolitan	71.6	77.7	—	111	57.9	75.2
=98 Wolverhampton	72.7	73.3	—	108	60.2	75.2

Employed in high-skilled job	43%	Employed in lower-skilled job and studying	1%
Employed in high-skilled job and studying	3%	Employed in lower-skilled job	21%
Studying	26%	Unemployed	6%
High skilled work (median) salary	£23,500	Low/medium skilled salary	£17,500

Building

Building graduates are among the country's best placed in their careers soon after finishing their degrees. The new Graduate Outcomes survey, which measures what graduates are doing 15 months after graduating, found that nearly 87% of those who had completed building degrees were in high-skilled jobs or further study – placing the subject tenth in our employment measure out of 67 subject areas. The proportion who were already in professional jobs rather than studying, 81%, puts it even higher – at eighth – behind others such as veterinary science, medicine and nursing.

Applications decreased a little in 2019, though the numbers starting courses nudged upwards, keeping the competition for places at less than four-to-one. The demand for places is down by more than a third since 2008, however. Degree apprenticeships in construction offer increasingly popular routes into the industry, which may contribute to the standalone degree's dip in popularity.

Loughborough is top of the table once again. It received the best scores in the Research Excellence Framework, and our analysis of the National Student Survey puts it second for student satisfaction with the wider undergraduate experience. West of England scored the highest on both student satisfaction measures – teaching quality and the broad experience. East London and Greenwich had the second and third strongest scores for teaching quality in a table dominated overall by post-1992 universities. However, the older institutions such as second-ranked Heriot Watt – which has overtaken University College London this year, and third-ranked Reading govern the top end of the table.

In general, entry requirements are lower than for most subjects – even the leading institutions average less than 160 points and four dropped below 100 in 2019.

Courses in this category include surveying and building services engineering, as well as construction.

Building	Teaching quality %	Student experience %	Research quality %	Entry standards (UCAS points)	Graduate prospects %	Overall score
1 Loughborough	76.5	87.6	58.3	139	95.6	100.0
2 Heriot-Watt	69.4	73.2	38.1	168	95.7	97.5
3 Reading	76.1	80.5	40.0	126	97.2	95.4
4 Oxford Brookes	82.6	86.6	17.6	119	100.0	94.0
=5 Ulster	75.5	80.4	28.6	141	89.7	93.4
=5 University College London	55.4	64.5	54.1	152	—	93.4
7 Aston	76.9	80.2	20.6	138	—	93.0
8 West of England	85.8	88.3	10.6	111	95.7	91.8
9 Coventry	81.5	86.3	10.3	124	93.8	91.7
10 Northumbria	79.1	80.5	5.9	145	89.1	91.2
=11 Edinburgh Napier	82.4	81.4	5.7	141	83.3	90.0
=11 Liverpool John Moores	77.5	78.3	4.9	138	90.4	90.0
13 Robert Gordon	79.9	79.1	8.3	128	88.9	89.5
14 Westminster	77.5	77.6	10.7	122	92.3	89.4
15 Portsmouth	76.9	80.0	—	114	100.0	89.0
16 Nottingham Trent	79.0	79.6	3.4	112	94.9	88.3
17 Nottingham	77.4	80.5	14.8	132	76.9	87.5

		Teaching quality %	Student experience %	Research quality %	Entry standards (UCAS points)	Graduate prospects %	Overall score
18	Glasgow Caledonian	74.0	71.9	9.1	144	80.5	87.4
19	Greenwich	84.0	83.8	2.0	118	81.8	87.0
20	London South Bank	73.4	73.0	19.6	114	86.7	86.9
21	East London	84.2	85.6	8.1	96*	—	86.6
22	Anglia Ruskin	76.2	78.4	5.2	110	88.9	86.0
23	Plymouth	71.7	73.9	13.2	96	95.2	85.8
24	Salford	71.4	72.4	19.6	123	78.7	85.4
25	Sheffield Hallam	75.3	73.9	13.4	106	85.7	85.3
26	Brighton	82.2	80.2	—	95	84.0	83.8
27	Kingston	67.1	70.2	—	107	93.0	83.2
28	Leeds Beckett	71.7	70.1	5.6	99	83.3	81.6
29	Central Lancashire	61.0	64.1	3.0	129	—	81.3
30	Derby	65.3	72.4	5.6	105	—	80.3
31	Wolverhampton	75.1	73.0	5.6	102	68.0	78.9
32	Birmingham City	65.6	64.3	2.7	117	70.8	78.1

Employed in high-skilled job	81%	Employed in lower-skilled job and studying		0%
Employed in high-skilled job and studying	4%	Employed in lower-skilled job		9%
Studying	1%	Unemployed		4%
High skilled work (median) salary	£28,000	Low/medium skilled salary		£20,000

Business Studies

The Business Studies table remains the biggest in our *Guide*, stretching to 120 universities. The wide choice of institutions reflects the popularity of the various branches of business and management – which between them recruit more undergraduates than any other subject area in the UK. Applications were close to 254,000 in the 2019 admissions cycle, and the numbers starting courses were just shy of 55,000. The Clearing service regularly offers a good number of places in both business and management studies courses.

St Andrews has held on to the lead in business studies that it took last year. It has the highest entry standards, the fourth-best scores for both measures of student satisfaction: teaching quality and the broad experience, and its submission in the subject area ranked fourth in the Research Excellence Framework. UCL has moved up to second place, its position boosted by excellent levels of student satisfaction; the second-highest for the broad experience and seventh-best for teaching quality. But it is West London ranked 43= and winner of our University of the Year for Student Experience award, that received the top scores for both measures in the National Student Survey (NSS). Bucks New, the only other university to receive a score over 90% in the NSS, ties with West London for teaching quality.

Some of the most famous business schools are absent from this table because they offer only postgraduate qualifications, such as MBAs and executive education, while our *Guide* details undergraduate provision. The London School of Economics (LSE), in sixth place overall, was the top scorer in the Research Excellence Framework. With 100% of LSE graduates in high-skilled work or further study 15 months after finishing their degrees the university tops our employment measure. UCL, Warwick, Oxford and Bath follow it – in that order.

Overall however the subject area finishes in the lower half of our rankings, at 42nd out of 67, with 68.7% of graduates achieving the top outcomes of a professional job or further study 15 months on from completing their degrees. The average proportion is dragged down by some particularly lowly scores, such as Bolton's 31.8% in high-skilled work or study – the bottom result in our employment ranking.

Business Studies	Teaching quality %	Student experience %	Research quality %	Entry standards (UCAS points)	Graduate prospects %	Overall score
1 St Andrews	87.4	87.6	43.8	218	90.6	100.0
2 University College London	85.3	88.8	43.9	172	95.6	97.1
3 Warwick	79.6	82.9	40.4	194	95.3	96.0
4 Bath	81.0	85.1	41.8	180	94.6	95.7
5 Oxford	—	—	32.0	204	94.7	94.8
6 London School of Economics	78.3	77.8	52.3	155	100.0	94.7
7 Strathclyde	77.7	79.8	44.3	204	76.9	93.4
8 Loughborough	81.6	86.8	32.6	150	86.9	91.3
9 Durham	80.7	81.1	23.1	164	93.3	91.1
10 Leeds	77.9	79.9	39.3	156	87.1	90.9
11 Stirling	81.5	82.2	25.2	169	81.7	90.1
12 Exeter	75.7	83.0	24.4	162	91.3	89.8
13 King's College London	68.6	79.2	38.2	180	84.2	89.7
14 Lancaster	77.2	78.5	42.6	145	81.7	89.4
15 York	81.6	80.1	24.0	144	86.5	88.7
16 Aberdeen	72.3	78.6	24.9	186	—	88.5
17 Manchester	75.0	77.5	33.3	164	79.1	88.3
=18 East Anglia	80.5	80.6	28.1	135	79.5	87.3
=18 Reading	77.8	78.6	29.3	133	85.3	87.3
=20 City, London	69.8	73.4	28.7	174	82.2	87.1
=20 Liverpool	81.1	83.4	20.1	146	77.4	87.1
=22 Queen's, Belfast	71.8	74.0	32.7	145	83.5	86.3
=22 Southampton	78.3	82.0	24.0	147	74.3	86.3
=24 Glasgow	70.4	72.1	22.1	197	72.7	86.2
=24 Heriot-Watt	74.5	78.6	18.8	163	79.4	86.2
26 Bristol	67.9	73.3	32.1	153	85.4	86.1
=27 Birmingham	70.1	72.7	29.1	152	84.8	86.0
=27 Robert Gordon	86.1	85.2	2.6	169	67.3	86.0
=27 Sussex	76.3	77.5	23.7	141	81.2	86.0
=30 Swansea	78.4	82.0	22.0	128	81.7	85.9
=30 Ulster	79.0	79.5	40.4	124	68.5	85.9
32 Newcastle	72.6	74.2	20.7	154	83.3	85.5
=33 Edinburgh	70.1	73.8	25.8	170	75.1	85.4
=33 Nottingham	67.4	72.5	32.6	145	85.4	85.4

Business Studies cont

	Teaching quality %	Student experience %	Research quality %	Entry standards (UCAS points)	Graduate prospects %	Overall score
=33 Queen Mary, London	70.2	73.5	23.5	163	80.4	85.4
36 Aston	77.4	79.3	19.7	136	78.6	85.1
37 Cardiff	68.7	70.7	32.0	155	78.6	85.0
38 Bangor	79.3	81.1	23.4	122	76.4	84.9
39 Sheffield	70.2	76.7	26.8	140	80.3	84.6
40 Soas, London	71.2	74.5	25.0	156	—	84.5
41 Royal Holloway, London	73.2	75.8	27.0	138	76.2	84.4
42 West of England	83.9	86.2	5.5	117	78.1	84.1
=43 Cumbria	83.0	78.0	5.6	118	84.2	83.9
=43 West London	91.4	91.5	—	111	69.0	83.9
=45 Glasgow Caledonian	84.0	83.7	1.8	171	55.4	83.5
=45 Kent	74.7	77.4	24.8	136	70.0	83.5
47 Harper Adams	74.4	81.9	—	143	84.6	83.3
48 Abertay	83.5	75.4	—	150	72.5	83.2
=49 Aberystwyth	83.5	86.7	14.5	121	63.0	83.1
=49 Central Lancashire	84.4	82.3	4.4	126	71.4	83.1
51 Queen Margaret, Edinburgh	80.9	77.5	—	133	80.3	82.9
52 Keele	77.1	77.1	10.2	118	83.7	82.8
53 Bournemouth	78.7	79.1	8.8	115	80.8	82.6
=54 Dundee	68.2	71.7	12.1	160	78.6	82.5
=54 Edinburgh Napier	77.2	78.3	2.3	158	69.0	82.5
=54 Nottingham Trent	79.7	81.7	4.6	124	76.4	82.5
57 Coventry	84.2	84.1	1.6	116	72.8	82.4
58 Buckingham	80.4	81.4	—	116	82.1	82.3
=59 Solent, Southampton	83.6	83.8		117	73.9	82.2
=59 Surrey	66.5	72.8	15.8	142	83.1	82.2
61 Portsmouth	78.8	79.5	9.5	116	75.3	82.0
62 Brunel London	76.2	77.9	23.0	120	65.7	81.8
=63 Plymouth	77.6	77.8	13.1	123	70.5	81.7
=63 Sheffield Hallam	80.6	79.1	0.6	110	81.6	81.7
65 Creative Arts	85.9	78.3	—	128	66.0	81.5
66 Chichester	82.5	81.6	—	100	80.0	81.4
67 Leicester	67.5	70.6	24.3	133	74.6	81.3
68 Liverpool Hope	82.1	80.6	—	112	74.2	81.1
69 Essex	73.5	76.3	25.1	105	70.9	81.0
70 Bucks New	91.4	88.5	1.8	97	57.1	80.8
=71 Northumbria	74.6	75.7	4.0	139	71.6	80.7
=71 Oxford Brookes	75.3	77.8	5.1	128	72.5	80.7
73 Lincoln	76.6	78.4	4.8	114	76.1	80.6
=74 Derby	82.6	82.0	0.9	111	68.2	80.4
=74 Worcester	82.4	78.7	0.9	105	73.8	80.4
76 Staffordshire	78.7	72.6	2.6	117	75.7	80.1

77 Liverpool John Moores	75.2	77.6	—	143	66.4	80.0
78 Chester	78.9	76.7	0.5	121	70.1	79.9
79 Leeds Beckett	79.4	79.3	0.8	102	74.9	79.7
=80 Hull	74.4	71.0	10.2	129	67.6	79.5
=80 Manchester Metropolitan	77.2	76.8	4.7	126	64.7	79.5
82 Salford	75.1	75.1	5.9	116	71.8	79.4
83 Falmouth	85.1	82.1	—	114	56.7	79.3
84 South Wales	84.7	77.2	0.2	115	58.9	79.0
=85 Bradford	77.2	82.2	11.8	113	55.7	78.9
=85 Royal Agricultural	79.5	79.8	—	121	61.5	78.9
=87 Teesside	73.6	71.1	2.0	112	79.0	78.8
=87 West of Scotland	77.4	75.7	2.9	123	63.6	78.8
89 Bath Spa	80.4	76.6	—	99	71.2	78.7
=90 Cardiff Metropolitan	76.4	76.1	—	111	71.2	78.6
=90 De Montfort	73.8	75.6	10.7	107*	68.1	78.6
=90 Wales Trinity St David	83.5	81.1	—	117	54.2	78.6
93 Gloucestershire	78.5	77.1	—	113	66.4	78.5
=94 Brighton	73.4	69.9	6.5	109	72.5	78.0
=94 Northampton	79.1	76.5	1.0	91	71.6	78.0
=94 Suffolk	78.2	76.2	—	102	69.2	78.0
97 Sunderland	82.9	80.3	0.4	98	59.1	77.8
=98 Birmingham City	77.2	75.0	1.3	114	63.2	77.7
=98 Kingston	75.1	77.9	9.2	103	62.3	77.7
100 Leeds Trinity	78.1	80.7	—	100	64.2	77.6
101 Hertfordshire	78.4	79.9	0.9	107	59.7	77.5
102 Anglia Ruskin	78.9	78.1	3.4	100	61.1	77.4
103 Bolton	89.7	84.7	—	122*	31.8	77.2
104 Huddersfield	69.1	70.8	4.1	124	66.7	76.9
105 Edge Hill	71.9	73.3	—	125	63.1	76.7
106 Westminster	71.2	74.0	2.4	127	55.6	76.0
107 St Mary's, Twickenham	80.1	78.8		101	52.2	75.9
108 Greenwich	71.4	73.2	3.3	116	57.6	75.6
109 London Metropolitan	79.8	83.3	0.6	92	49.4	75.4
110 Winchester	66.4	66.2	—	115	71.2	75.1
111 East London	78.6	78.2	0.8	111	43.4	74.9
112 Middlesex	69.2	71.4	10.5	115	51.8	74.8
=113 Bedfordshire	75.0	72.3	3.1	97	56.6	74.7
=113 Wolverhampton	78.1	76.7	2.4	97	49.0	74.7
115 York St John	77.6	71.7	0.8	88	58.5	74.6
116 Roehampton	72.7	74.7	4.5	94	54.1	74.1
117 Arts London	68.2	64.7	—	127	55.8	73.7
118 London South Bank	73.0	75.9	2.1	100	46.9	73.2
119 Canterbury Christ Church	66.3	62.7	—	96	61.0	71.6
120 Glyndŵr	63.6	64.0	—	97*	53.5	69.9

Business Studies cont

Employed in high-skilled job	60%	Employed in lower-skilled job and studying	1%
Employed in high-skilled job and studying	4%	Employed in lower-skilled job	25%
Studying	4%	Unemployed	6%
High skilled work (median) salary	£25,000	Low/medium skilled salary	£19,500

Celtic Studies

The University of Bangor in north Wales leads our Celtic Studies table this year. It recorded exceptionally high satisfaction scores in the latest National Student Survey of 98.2% for teaching quality and 96.8% for the broad experience. It is top for graduate prospects too and has the highest entry standards of any of the Welsh universities in our table. Aberystwyth did even better in the National Student survey however, receiving results closer still to 100% satisfaction in both measures.

Bangor has taken the top spot from the only English university to feature, Cambridge, which after eight years in pole position is now in second place. Cambridge received the best results in the Research Excellence Framework and its entry standards are bettered only by the Scottish universities in our table – which benefit from the generous conversion rate for Scottish secondary qualifications in the UCAS tariff.

The four universities in Wales focus predominantly on Welsh degrees, naturally enough, and those in Scotland and Ireland offer courses in Gaelic, Scottish or Irish Studies. There are three applications per place on the Anglo-Saxon, Norse and Celtic degree at Cambridge – representing much better odds than the average five-to-one ratio university-wide.

Celtic Studies degrees do not draw big crowds. Applications in the 2019 cycle stayed above 500 – just – but were lower than the year before, and 130 new undergraduates enrolled on courses.

With almost 73% of graduates in high-skilled jobs or further study 15 months after finishing their degrees, Celtic Studies is only just outside the top half of subject areas in our employment ranking.

Celtic Studies	Teaching quality %	Student experience %	Research quality %	Entry standards (UCAS points)	Graduate prospects %	Overall score
1 Bangor	98.2	96.8	39.6	176	84.4	100.0
2 Cambridge	—	—	54.0	189	—	98.9
3 Glasgow	83.9	77.9	41.1	209*	—	96.5
4 Aberystwyth	98.9	97.2	23.7	153	79.4	93.3
5 Cardiff	92.1	86.7	32.5	153	—	90.9
6 Queen's, Belfast	78.7	77.7	53.6	134	61.9	88.8
7 Edinburgh	71.7	68.2	30.3	196	—	86.7
8 Swansea	85.6	89.0	19.4	131	—	82.5
9 Ulster	83.6	79.3	35.7	108	55.9	82.2

Employed in high-skilled job	50%	Employed in lower-skilled job and studying	5%
Employed in high-skilled job and studying	2%	Employed in lower-skilled job	24%
Studying	16%	Unemployed	3%
High skilled work (median) salary	£23,000	Low/medium skilled salary	—

Chemical Engineering

Positive job prospects are an advantage of chemical engineering degrees. The subject regularly features in the top 20 for graduate prospects, and this year is no exception – it occupies 17th place. The new Graduate Outcomes survey revealed that 84.6% of chemical engineering graduates were in high-skilled work or further study 15 months after finishing their degrees, and of these, close to seven in ten were working full-time, rather than studying or combining the two.

Although applications have declined for four years in a row, including a 5% dip in the 2019 cycle, this follows significant growth in the demand for places up to 2015, and applications are still higher now than in 2010, when £9,000 tuition fees were introduced. There were nearly six applicants for each of the 2,590 places on chemical, process and energy engineering degrees in 2019.

Maths A-level, or equivalent, is usually essential, as is chemistry and often physics. Most courses offer industry placements in the final year and lead to Chartered Engineer status. Nearly half of the universities required upwards of 150 UCAS points in 2019 but only two averaged higher than 200. Contact hours are higher than most subjects, with around 20 hours a week spent in classrooms or laboratories.

Cambridge leads our table for the second consecutive year, and Imperial – which came first two years ago – is runner up once more, though there is not much between them. With a UCAS tariff of 235 Cambridge has by far the highest entry standards of the two, and it achieved the best results in the Research Excellence Framework – but Imperial's submission was scored only marginally lower. Imperial has achieved a perfect 100% score for the proportion of graduates in high-skilled jobs or further study 15 months on – the measure's top result. Cambridge chooses not to enter the National Student Survey (NSS), however, Imperial's chemical engineering degrees received glowing reviews in the most recent NSS – with students scoring their satisfaction with teaching quality 83.8% and the broad experience 86.8%. Twentieth-ranked Wolverhampton is top for student satisfaction, though, across both measures.

Further shuffling of the top 10 includes Birmingham shifting up to third and Heriot-Watt to fourth, while Nottingham has edged down to eighth and Bath to seventh. Aberdeen has entered at ninth.

Chemical Engineering	Teaching quality %	Student experience %	Research quality %	Entry standards (UCAS points)	Graduate prospects %	Overall score
1 Cambridge	—	—	62.0	235	92.3	100.0
2 Imperial College London	83.8	86.8	59.6	192	100.0	98.6
3 Birmingham	78.1	82.1	47.0	186	94.0	92.9
4 Heriot-Watt	77.5	86.0	47.8	173	93.0	92.1
5 Strathclyde	75.7	79.3	37.2	221	89.1	91.9
6 Edinburgh	68.6	73.1	50.3	192	94.2	91.3
7 Bath	78.6	85.2	37.4	175	89.7	89.9
8 Nottingham	82.3	83.3	40.8	159	87.7	89.2
9 Aberdeen	74.6	79.0	28.4	176	93.5	88.2
10 Swansea	79.8	82.7	45.5	124	91.2	87.7
11 Sheffield	78.0	80.8	36.8	144	92.0	87.5
12 Loughborough	79.6	84.5	41.8	144	83.9	86.8

	Teaching quality %	Student experience %	Research quality %	Entry standards (UCAS points)	Graduate prospects %	Overall score
13 Lancaster	76.9	77.1	41.6	147	87.5	86.7
14 Leeds	66.0	70.2	30.7	170	95.6	86.1
15 Manchester	64.3	67.6	48.4	174	84.3	85.6
16 Newcastle	73.7	80.0	30.2	138	92.7	85.3
=17 University College London	62.4	65.8	44.6	162	82.7	83.2
=17 West of Scotland	85.3	84.9	9.0	150	—	83.2
19 Greenwich	82.6	83.2	29.5	107	—	82.5
20 Wolverhampton	91.7	90.2	4.4	118	—	81.4
=21 Aston	77.9	80.6	20.6	121	81.4	80.4
=21 Surrey	69.7	71.2	30.8	132	81.8	80.4
23 Bradford	89.7	89.7	7.7	111	78.3	79.9
24 Huddersfield	84.6	76.4	10.2	118	—	79.0
25 Teesside	81.7	79.8	5.8	117	79.4	77.8
26 Chester	75.8	73.6	7.1	103	86.7	77.1
27 Hull	72.8	79.4	16.5	98	76.0	75.5
28 Portsmouth	65.5	71.5	9.1	114	78.9	74.1
29 Queen's, Belfast	45.5	47.7	36.7	153	70.4	72.9
30 London South Bank	87.7	88.7	19.6	97	50.0	72.8

Employed in high-skilled job	67%	Employed in lower-skilled job and studying	1%
Employed in high-skilled job and studying	3%	Employed in lower-skilled job	9%
Studying	14%	Unemployed	6%
High skilled work (median) salary	£30,000	Low/medium skilled salary	£22,000

Chemistry

Students of the study of matter, chemistry, tend to enjoy their degrees and satisfaction rates are generally buoyant throughout our table. They are led by 14th-ranked Lincoln, our Modern University of the Year, which achieved the best scores for both teaching quality and the broader undergraduate experience in the National Student Survey. Lincoln also scored a perfect 100% in the new measure of graduate prospects – as did Liverpool John Moores – with all graduates from both universities in high-skilled work or further study 15 months after finishing their degrees. King's College London and Oxford followed them in third and fourth place for graduate prospects. Chemistry graduates perform well in the careers landscape as a whole, and the subject ranks 16th out of the 67 subject areas.

Cambridge and Oxford have continued their reign in first and second position of our Chemistry table. Entry standards are highest at Cambridge and its submission to the Research Excellence Framework received the best results, with 97% of its work judged world-leading or internationally excellent. Oxford's research output was considered similarly excellent, and 96% of the submission was rated in the top two categories. There is international clout, too; in the 2020 QS World Rankings Cambridge ranks third for chemistry, and Oxford sixth.

In terms of the subject's popularity, three years of declining applications – which followed an extended period of rising demand for places – came to an end in the 2019 cycle, in which chemistry registered increases of around 5% in both applications and enrolments. Entry standards are pretty stiff; 21 of the 53 universities in our table averaged at least 150 UCAS points in 2019, including three of the top five which demanded more than 200 points. Chemistry A-level, or equivalent, is almost always a prerequisite and the leading universities will also look for maths and/or at least one other science – it is worth checking which second science individual universities ask for, as these may differ.

Chemistry

		Teaching quality %	Student experience %	Research quality %	Entry standards (UCAS points)	Graduate prospects %	Overall score
1	Cambridge	—	—	70.3	228	91.0	100.0
2	Oxford	—	—	63.1	206	94.7	97.1
3	Strathclyde	86.6	87.8	40.1	194	90.7	94.7
4	Durham	82.2	79.5	49.1	196	92.6	94.6
5	St Andrews	83.2	87.7	50.3	221	78.4	93.5
6	York	85.0	84.6	44.6	175	90.1	93.2
7	East Anglia	91.1	86.9	39.2	135	94.4	92.8
8	Edinburgh	76.4	75.6	48.4	191	91.5	92.3
=9	Bristol	79.3	81.0	56.6	160	87.5	91.4
=9	Warwick	82.5	84.9	50.8	152	87.8	91.4
11	Nottingham	84.5	84.1	48.5	143	88.0	91.0
12	Liverpool	79.5	80.9	55.6	147	88.1	90.7
13	Glasgow	69.8	66.9	41.1	212	90.0	90.0
14	Lincoln	95.7	95.1	—	113	100.0	89.9
=15	Loughborough	86.1	88.0	23.9	145	90.8	89.6
=15	University College London	74.1	75.7	56.0	167	85.2	89.6
17	Aberdeen	77.2	83.0	31.6	171	89.2	89.4
18	Imperial College London	69.8	70.1	54.6	157	91.2	89.0
19	Southampton	80.5	82.6	50.7	146	82.1	88.8
=20	Bath	80.9	82.6	43.0	163	81.0	88.7
=20	Heriot-Watt	79.5	77.9	34.2	167	87.0	88.7
22	Leeds	81.5	82.5	35.9	155	85.3	88.6
23	Leicester	86.5	86.1	32.8	117	88.1	88.1
24	Sheffield	76.0	78.7	38.9	155	85.7	87.6
25	Cardiff	74.0	78.7	30.9	142	92.0	87.1
26	Lancaster	88.0	88.2	37.5	147	72.7	86.8
27	Plymouth	88.3	88.4	25.3	113	85.2	86.7
=28	Birmingham	77.5	78.4	37.3	165	79.6	86.6
=28	Manchester	72.8	78.1	46.0	161	80.1	86.6
30	Liverpool John Moores	74.9	81.2	6.0	131	100.0	86.1
31	Greenwich	94.4	88.6	7.4	120	—	86.0
32	Queen Mary, London	78.5	83.0	37.0	135	80.8	85.7
33	Keele	90.5	83.6	41.1	115	74.0	85.6

		Teaching quality %	Student experience %	Research quality %	Entry standards (UCAS points)	Graduate prospects %	Overall score
34	Bangor	83.4	82.5	19.1	111	89.7	85.4
=35	Kent	73.5	69.0	27.5	125	93.6	85.0
=35	Nottingham Trent	82.2	83.1	24.1	114	85.7	85.0
37	Newcastle	75.2	81.2	28.5	136	84.1	84.8
=38	Sheffield Hallam	83.6	77.1	17.8	104	89.8	84.4
=38	Surrey	83.8	84.7	30.8	132	74.6	84.4
=38	Sussex	82.3	79.6	25.8	155	75.0	84.4
41	Aston	82.5	84.5	20.6	109	—	83.5
=42	Brighton	86.8	87.1	4.8	100	86.4	83.4
=42	Queen's, Belfast	73.2	75.6	34.7	150	76.9	83.4
44	West of Scotland	75.0	85.3	29.0	112	—	83.1
45	Manchester Metropolitan	78.7	76.9	16.3	115	85.9	82.7
46	Reading	73.2	69.2	27.3	114	87.0	82.4
47	King's College London	66.8	70.3	—	143	96.6	82.3
48	Huddersfield	83.3	77.6	11.0	134	78.4	82.2
49	Hull	73.5	80.9	24.2	112	82.9	82.1
50	Northumbria	81.7	80.8	14.0	140	74.5	81.9
51	Bradford	82.1	85.1	9.5	104	73.4	79.4
52	Central Lancashire	66.1	64.0	11.7	123	84.0	78.2
53	Kingston	81.1	82.7	2.6	101	69.4	76.8

Employed in high-skilled job	55%	Employed in lower-skilled job and studying	0%
Employed in high-skilled job and studying	3%	Employed in lower-skilled job	10%
Studying	26%	Unemployed	5%
High skilled work (median) salary	£25,000	Low/medium skilled salary	£19,500

Civil Engineering

Civil engineering graduates tend not to struggle to find professional roles soon after finishing their degrees, as reflected by the subject's consistent top-10 performance in our employment ranking. The new Graduate Outcomes survey revealed that more than nine out of every ten civil engineering graduates were in high-skilled work or postgraduate study 15 months after they had completed their undergraduate degrees, and of these almost eight in ten were in full-time work, rather than studying or combining the two. Six universities achieved perfect 100% graduate prospects scores: Anglia Ruskin, Brighton, Edinburgh, Exeter, Glasgow Caledonian and Liverpool John Moores.

The older institutions dominate the upper half of our table year-on year, albeit in slightly differing ranks, while at 22nd place Greenwich is the highest ranked of the post-1992 universities this year. Cambridge is top for the 15th year in a row. Southampton has gone from fifth up to second place and Bristol has moved into third from sixth place last year while Bath has slipped to fifth, from third. Imperial takes fourth for the second consecutive time.

For student satisfaction, however, West London, winner of our University of the Year for Student Experience, is 40th overall, but comes first in both measures: teaching quality and the wider undergraduate experience.

The numbers starting courses declined a little in 2019 for the second consecutive year but this follows increases in previous years, and both applications and enrolments are generally steady.

Some of the top degrees in civil engineering are four-year courses leading to an MEng; others are sandwich courses incorporating a work placement. The leading departments will expect physics and maths A-levels, or their equivalent. Such is the popularity of the BTEC qualification in this field, however, that fewer than half of all civil engineering undergraduates enter via A-levels.

Civil Engineering	Teaching quality %	Student experience %	Research quality %	Entry standards (UCAS points)	Graduate prospects %	Overall score
1 Cambridge	—	—	67.0	220	96.3	100.0
2 Southampton	88.9	89.1	52.3	173	94.0	98.1
3 Bristol	79.0	82.4	52.3	179	96.6	96.6
4 Imperial College London	75.8	81.1	61.5	184	92.9	96.4
5 Bath	82.3	84.4	52.9	174	92.7	96.0
6 Heriot-Watt	78.6	83.3	47.8	160	97.7	94.7
7 Strathclyde	77.2	81.1	35.7	188	94.6	94.2
8 Dundee	78.9	79.3	46.2	162	96.4	94.0
9 Leeds	86.3	89.0	32.0	171	90.3	93.8
10 Glasgow	63.1	67.3	47.2	215	94.6	93.6
11 Sheffield	80.3	84.3	43.1	153	95.2	93.3
12 Edinburgh	64.4	74.3	50.3	167	100.0	92.4
13 Nottingham	76.2	73.5	40.8	151	97.5	91.5
14 Ulster	89.7	88.5	28.6	128	93.1	91.1
=15 Loughborough	80.5	89.4	26.9	141	95.2	90.8
=15 Swansea	75.1	79.7	45.5	133	96.7	90.8
17 Cardiff	76.3	81.8	35.0	147	95.1	90.7
=18 Liverpool	78.9	82.5	32.1	139	95.7	90.4
=18 Manchester	74.6	75.1	36.4	164	92.0	90.4
20 Exeter	69.6	77.5	36.4	141	100.0	89.8
21 Aberdeen	80.4	83.1	28.4	136	—	89.0
22 Greenwich	86.5	89.5	5.5	139	—	88.0
23 Salford	84.2	83.8	19.6	137	88.4	87.9
24 Glasgow Caledonian	75.2	76.4	9.1	145	100.0	87.8
25 Newcastle	68.1	72.4	40.9	134	95.1	87.7
26 Plymouth	80.9	83.9	15.7	133	91.7	87.3
27 Birmingham	65.6	68.8	21.9	161	97.0	87.2
28 Liverpool John Moores	78.2	76.1	—	137	100.0	86.5
29 Surrey	69.3	76.2	30.8	125	93.9	85.9
30 Anglia Ruskin	77.6	80.3	5.2	117	100.0	85.8

Civil Engineering cont	Teaching quality %	Student experience %	Research quality %	Entry standards (UCAS points)	Graduate prospects %	Overall score
31 Queen's, Belfast	68.3	71.8	31.3	146	88.5	85.7
32 West of Scotland	80.2	81.8	9.0	125	92.3	85.6
33 Brunel London	69.5	70.3	23.7	140	92.3	85.3
34 Abertay	86.4	85.4	16.3	120	83.3	85.2
35 Central Lancashire	79.6	82.8	7.1	134	—	84.9
=36 Edinburgh Napier	83.0	82.9	7.7	136	84.4	84.8
=36 University College London	65.8	71.1	23.1	152	89.5	84.8
38 Nottingham Trent	83.9	84.0	3.4	114	91.2	84.6
39 Bradford	83.6	85.4	17.8	116	81.8	84.1
=40 Teesside	74.1	80.5	5.8	135	—	82.9
=40 West London	90.7	91.7	—	105	81.3	82.9
=42 Leeds Beckett	76.8	80.7	5.6	101	93.8	82.7
=42 Portsmouth	78.0	78.3	9.1	107	90.4	82.7
44 Coventry	77.3	80.8	10.3	119	84.2	82.3
=45 London South Bank	81.6	79.7	19.6	117	76.0	81.9
=45 West of England	73.5	78.7	10.6	122	—	81.9
47 Northumbria	67.2	66.9	30.7	144	75.0	81.0
48 Derby	79.9	80.4	6.7	115	80.0	80.9
49 Brighton	61.9	62.5	5.1	114	100.0	80.5
50 Kingston	76.9	73.3	2.9	125	76.2	78.9
51 East London	86.0	89.5	2.3	114	65.2	78.5
52 City, London	61.1	57.2	23.1	119	83.3	78.0
53 Bolton	70.4	72.6	—	110	70.0	74.2

Employed in high-skilled job	79%	Employed in lower-skilled job and studying	0%
Employed in high-skilled job and studying	3%	Employed in lower-skilled job	5%
Studying	8%	Unemployed	5%
High skilled work (median) salary	£27,500	Low/medium skilled salary	£19,300

Classics and Ancient History

Cambridge remains the top university in our Classics and Ancient History table for the 15th consecutive year. Oxford, in fourth position overall, averaged the highest entry standards in 2019. Durham is in second position for the third time running. In the Research Excellence Framework Cambridge's submission achieved the best scores by some margin.

For student satisfaction, though, Liverpool achieved the top results in the teaching quality sections of the National Student Survey, followed closely by Roehampton then St Andrews and Royal Holloway, which tied for third place. For satisfaction with the broader undergraduate experience three of the same universities feature in a different order: St Andrews leads the ranking, with Royal Holloway second and Liverpool tieing for third place with Swansea.

Their sharp decline as subjects taught in state schools has resulted in Latin and Ancient

Greek becoming largely the preserve of independent schools. But neither Ancient Greek nor Latin A-level – or indeed any specific subject – is a prerequisite for the study of classics at any UK university. Most that offer the subject teach it from scratch, including the Ancient Greek and Latin language elements, so it is a suitable degree for newcomers as well as those more practised in the subjects.

Several universities encompass classics and ancient history within modular degrees, but not in their own right, while most universities favour a broader offering of classical studies or classical civilisation that ranges beyond just Latin or Ancient Greek.

The number of students starting classics had been rising gradually for six years, bringing enrolments above 1,100, but the increase came to a halt two years ago and numbers have declined slightly since. There were 970 new undergraduates in 2019 – still more than when £9,000 tuition fees were introduced – and demand for places averaged just under five applications per enrolment.

The subjects fall in the lower half of our employment ranking. Of the 67.2% in the top two outcomes of professional work or further study 15 months after graduation, 18% were focused purely on study and 5% were combining a high-skilled job with academic work. Durham is top for graduate prospects with 89.7% of graduates in the top outcomes at the 15-months-on census point, followed closely by Edinburgh, St Andrews and UCL.

Classics and Ancient History	Teaching quality %	Student experience %	Research quality %	Entry standards (UCAS points)	Graduate prospects %	Overall score
1 Cambridge	—	—	65.0	206	85.6	100.0
2 Durham	86.2	80.6	54.3	197	89.7	97.1
3 St Andrews	89.1	90.6	43.2	195	88.6	96.5
4 Oxford	—	—	58.3	208	80.4	96.4
5 Exeter	82.6	75.7	45.0	160	85.5	90.5
6 University College London	77.0	73.0	42.7	171	87.8	89.6
7 Warwick	85.6	84.1	45.0	151	70.2	89.4
8 Nottingham	85.4	78.7	52.0	133	68.8	88.5
9 Liverpool	91.7	84.8	28.9	136	—	86.6
=10 Leeds	87.3	80.8	29.1	148	73.0	86.5
=10 Manchester	85.2	73.3	31.0	152	77.8	86.5
12 Reading	83.7	76.0	45.2	116	75.4	86.2
13 Bristol	74.6*	68.7*	42.2	165	70.5	85.3
14 Edinburgh	69.5	65.0	34.9	169	89.1	85.2
15 Glasgow	75.5	76.6	32.7	171	—	84.4
16 Birmingham	78.4	75.9	40.3	143	64.4	84.3
17 King's College London	79.7	71.9	43.6	158	49.1	83.6
18 Newcastle	76.7	70.7	44.7	137	54.7	82.2
19 Swansea	87.4	84.8	25.0	114	62.3	82.1
20 Royal Holloway, London	89.1	86.2	20.4	133	48.9	81.2
21 Kent	81.2	75.5	33.1	108	63.2	80.8
22 Roehampton	90.0	84.3	—	111	40.0	74.3

Classics and Ancient History cont

Employed in high-skilled job	44%	Employed in lower-skilled job and studying	1%
Employed in high-skilled job and studying	5%	Employed in lower-skilled job	25%
Studying	18%	Unemployed	8%
High skilled work (median) salary	£25,000	Low/medium skilled salary	£18,500

Communication and Media Studies

For the fourth consecutive year Loughborough is top of our Communication and Media Studies table. It has the best research scores and performs strongly in all other measures. The upper reaches of the table are dominated by the older universities, most of which featured in the top 15 last year but have since shuffled positions. Second-placed Sheffield is up from fifth, third-placed Strathclyde was formerly 11th, Stirling is fourth this year, 12th last and Warwick has risen three places to fifth. Leeds, Lancaster and Exeter have slipped a few places each and Southampton has stayed 10th.

In other shifts to the table, which stretches to 94 universities, King's College London has gained 11 places to ninth, and Northumbria has climbed 10 to rank 16th. Queen Mary, London – which was shortlisted for our University of the Year award – has risen 31 places and joined the subject's top 20, while Goldsmiths, London has gone up to 20= after poor satisfaction scores caused it to drop 57 places in our last edition. For the third year running Glasgow Caledonian is the top-ranked post-1992 university.

Plymouth Marjon comes 38th overall (its middling rank due to not entering the Research Excellence Framework) but top in our employment measure, with a rare 100% of its communication and media graduates in high-skilled jobs or postgraduate study 15 months after finishing their degrees. Kent, with 92.3% of graduates achieving the same top outcomes, is second. But as a whole communication and media studies degrees pose fairly dismal career prospects for recent graduates, and the subject area ranks 58th out of 67. Only six out of ten graduates were in professional jobs or further study when surveyed. The dearth of 'professional' entry-level jobs in the media industry is no secret, however, and is unlikely to come as a surprise to students who choose these degrees.

Enrolments in media studies declined by around 7% in 2019 and applications fell by 10% but the popular subject still registered 8,040 new undergraduates. Journalism saw a 13% drop in new student numbers, to 2,425. There are usually no required subjects for entry, even at the leading universities.

Communication and Media Studies	Teaching quality %	Student experience %	Research quality %	Entry standards (UCAS points)	Graduate prospects %	Overall score
1 Loughborough	83.2	83.8	62.3	158	85.7	100.0
2 Sheffield	86.5	85.2	37.9	145	85.7	95.8
3 Strathclyde	79.1	76.6	39.4	199	65.2	95.4
4 Stirling	85.4	79.7	36.0	169	71.2	94.4
5 Warwick	84.3	79.4	61.7	151	61.6	93.6
6 Leeds	74.4	72.6	54.5	159	75.0	93.4
7 Cardiff	78.1	72.9	55.4	149	71.7	92.5
8 Swansea	91.8	89.8	18.5	131	81.8	92.2

9 King's College London	75.5	67.6	55.8	156	70.9	92.1
10 Southampton	89.1	85.7	42.7	138	64.3	91.8
11 Exeter	84.9*	80.2*	46.2	163	53.8	91.4
12 York	81.4	80.2	26.0	140	81.8	90.9
13 Lancaster	78.3	76.2	51.4	147	61.5	89.9
14 Kent	84.5	82.1	—	134	92.3	89.6
15 Surrey	75.0	76.6	30.2	135	82.9	89.3
16 Northumbria	84.4	82.3	22.2	138	73.3	89.2
17 Newcastle	78.6	78.1	37.8	153	61.8	89.0
=18 Edinburgh Napier	86.3	83.3	9.5	151	70.7	88.9
=18 Queen Mary, London	71.1	57.5	35.1	148	84.6	88.9
=20 East Anglia	77.7	75.5	43.8	134	68.8	88.6
=20 Goldsmiths, London	67.1	60.3	60.0	141	73.1	88.6
22 Glasgow Caledonian	80.1	77.1	15.2	173	61.5	88.2
23 Queen Margaret, Edinburgh	78.9	75.9	14.0	160	70.3	88.0
24 Nottingham	76.4	78.6	45.8	121	—	87.2
25 Sussex	72.9	71.6	43.6	141	64.3	86.9
26 Bangor	88.3	82.4	24.7	120	60.1	85.5
=27 Leicester	75.1	76.9	46.1	126	58.6	85.3
=27 Royal Holloway, London	77.5	69.5	38.1	132	61.3	85.3
=27 Ulster	83.9	82.3	34.0	118	58.5	85.3
30 Bournemouth	80.3	78.8	15.1	121	73.3	84.8
31 Central Lancashire	82.4	78.5	7.9	118	77.0	84.7
32 Robert Gordon	82.0	78.0	7.5	159	54.8	84.5
33 Liverpool	78.4	77.0	27.5	128	61.8	84.3
=34 Leeds Beckett	85.0	83.4	11.0	102	76.3	84.2
=34 Salford	76.5	74.7	36.9	130	56.6	84.2
36 Keele	91.0	85.6	25.0	123	42.9	83.2
37 Westminster	78.5	73.0	28.3	113	65.4	83.1
38 Plymouth Marjon	68.5	60.4	—	116	100.0	83.0
39 Coventry	79.9	78.1	18.1	115	66.4	82.9
40 Birmingham City	86.7	80.4	6.0	119	62.9	82.7
41 Teesside	92.0	88.6	2.9	111	58.3	82.5
42 Nottingham Trent	79.3	77.4	10.0	120	68.1	82.4
43 Sunderland	83.7	80.7	13.0	108	65.0	82.1
44 Liverpool John Moores	81.0	80.2	6.2	139	54.3	81.9
=45 Manchester Metropolitan	75.2	69.4	29.0	127	56.2	81.7
=45 West of England	74.2	73.1	18.6	110	72.1	81.7
=47 Queen's, Belfast	61.2	52.3	38.3	148	—	81.6
=47 Solent, Southampton	83.0	80.4	0.8	121	64.1	81.6
49 Hull	82.0	83.8	11.2	118	57.6	81.5
=50 Canterbury Christ Church	83.2	76.3	7.3	103	70.7	81.4
=50 De Montfort	72.0	71.5	31.2	105*	68.0	81.4
=50 Kingston	71.2	70.1	15.7	107	79.2	81.4
=50 Oxford Brookes	69.5	72.1	25.3	125	63.6	81.4
54 Middlesex	79.3	77.2	11.0	103	71.7	81.3

Communication and Media Studies cont

		Teaching quality %	Student experience %	Research quality %	Entry standards (UCAS points)	Graduate prospects %	Overall score
=55	City, London	61.8	60.5	30.9	146	–	81.1
=55	Portsmouth	82.3	75.7	12.8	103	66.8	81.1
=55	Sheffield Hallam	74.3	70.4	14.4	114	71.2	81.1
58	Aberystwyth	87.9	86.0	9.2	123	46.5	81.0
59	Roehampton	80.2	82.3	26.4	98	58.3	80.9
60	Creative Arts	89.5	82.1	3.4	113	55.3	80.8
=61	Brighton	78.1	73.2	16.2	111	63.9	80.7
=61	Worcester	86.8	82.7	8.2	109	56.5	80.7
=63	Lincoln	77.2	72.6	4.0	116	69.9	80.5
=63	Ravensbourne	77.4	71.4	–	112	75.6	80.5
65	Staffordshire	84.1	81.2	6.7	107	58.8	79.9
66	Anglia Ruskin	74.9	73.4	26.4	104	60.0	79.8
67	Bucks New	79.5	80.9	–	117*	61.4	79.6
68	Gloucestershire	86.7	84.1	9.3	112	46.8	79.2
69	London South Bank	77.0	73.8	12.8	99	66.7	79.1
70	Leeds Trinity	82.8	77.7	3.9	101	61.8	78.8
71	Wolverhampton	67.9	62.8	33.2	103	63.4	78.5
=72	Chichester	75.1	75.3	–	119	62.2	78.3
=72	Falmouth	77.4	70.9	–	118	62.5	78.3
=72	Winchester	80.2	75.8	15.8	105	52.8	78.3
75	Derby	74.5	75.2	13.5	112	57.1	78.2
76	Edge Hill	78.9	79.4	10.2	126	43.1	77.9
77	West London	80.0	73.2	4.5	116	53.8	77.8
78	Brunel London	70.8	69.3	23.0	113	52.0	77.2
79	Liverpool Hope	80.9	70.4	–	114	53.3	76.8
80	Huddersfield	67.4	65.5	–	111	71.7	76.5
81	Bolton	79.7	75.2	1.6	102	–	76.2
=82	Bath Spa	74.8	70.0	13.9	107	51.7	76.1
=82	London Metropolitan	79.7	74.1	5.9	96	55.8	76.1
84	Northampton	81.7	70.2	–	102	55.8	76.0
85	Glyndŵr	71.8	68.8	7.8	109*	57.6	75.9
86	York St John	79.8	78.4	4.4	105	48.3	75.8
87	South Wales	78.0	72.6	–	114	50.0	75.6
88	West of Scotland	71.1	66.2	11.3	119	48.0	75.1
=89	Arts London	69.7	61.7	–	121	57.7	75.0
=89	Greenwich	65.7	58.8	3.5	121	61.5	75.0
91	St Mary's, Twickenham	78.4	72.7	9.1	103	45.3	74.7
92	East London	68.0	63.5	13.9	107	50.0	73.4
93	Chester	75.7	70.6	4.3	109	42.4	73.2
94	Bradford	56.9	49.5	–	109	63.1	70.4
95	Bedfordshire	72.3	64.0	8.2	83	45.5	69.8

Employed in high-skilled job	54%	Employed in lower-skilled job and studying	1%
Employed in high-skilled job and studying	2%	Employed in lower-skilled job	32%
Studying	4%	Unemployed	7%
High skilled work (median) salary	£21,000	Low/medium skilled salary	£18,000

Computer Science

The surge in popularity that computer science degrees have experienced in recent years hit a new high in 2019, with almost 97,700 applications. Our table also takes into account specialisms including artificial intelligence – which has seen applications increase by an extraordinary 376% since 2010, although this growth represents only 215 new students enrolled on degrees in the subject last autumn. Games design is another boom area; from a standing start of zero applications in 2011 it has seen demand for places increase every year, to 12,270 applications and 3,350 enrolments in 2019. Combinations within computer science saw an upturn in demand, too. A growing number of degree apprenticeships in specialisms such as cyber-security are offered by some of the leading universities, such is the demand for these skills in the workplace.

Encouraging job prospects are part of the subject's attraction, and the computer science table is 19th in our ranking of 67. On average, almost three-quarters of graduates were in professional jobs 15 months after finishing their degrees, 3% were combining high-skilled work with further study and 6% were pursuing purely postgraduate study. Fourth-ranked St Andrews and ninth-ranked Durham achieved rare 100% proportions of graduates in these top two categories. At the other end of the scale, though, only 55.6% of London Met graduates and 57.1% of London South Bank's enjoyed the same career success.

Cambridge, which has the highest entry standards, leads the table again this year while Oxford's high entry scores in 2019 have contributed to it replacing Imperial in second position. Imperial, though, received the best scores in the Research Excellence Framework, and UCL the second-best.

The upper portion of the table is dominated by the older universities, but the post-1992 institutions fare better in terms of student satisfaction. Bolton, in 68= place overall, was unbeaten for undergraduates' feelings about their teaching quality in the last National Student Survey, followed by Chester (39=) and Liverpool Hope (45). For satisfaction with the wider experience Bolton is top again, but Loughborough, Bath and Imperial also do well in this measure.

Candidates for the top courses tend to be well-qualified at entry, and five universities averaged above 200 UCAS points for entry in 2019. The leading universities will usually require maths A-level, or equivalent.

Computer Science	Teaching quality %	Student experience %	Research quality %	Entry standards (UCAS points)	Graduate prospects %	Overall score
1 Cambridge	—	—	57.1	226	94.7	100.0
2 Oxford	—	—	60.6	212	—	99.6
3 Imperial College London	76.8	83.8	64.1	206	97.4	99.0
4 St Andrews	78.4	80.1	33.4	219	100.0	96.9
5 Aberdeen	83.0	82.4	37.4	184	—	95.3
6 Glasgow	77.1	78.6	50.3	199	92.4	95.2

Computer Science cont

		Teaching quality %	Student experience %	Research quality %	Entry standards (UCAS points)	Graduate prospects %	Overall score
7	Manchester	76.2	77.2	50.7	185	94.4	94.3
8	Bath	82.8	85.1	33.3	171	94.4	93.9
9	Durham	70.5	73.1	38.8	201	100.0	93.6
10	Exeter	80.6	81.2	40.7	151	96.8	92.7
=11	Nottingham	80.0	80.1	45.4	173	87.7	92.6
=11	Warwick	68.6	69.5	54.8	187	96.1	92.6
13	University College London	71.4	76.2	62.7	169	90.7	92.5
14	Bristol	68.2	68.3	49.2	188	97.9	92.2
15	Birmingham	72.5	73.9	46.4	166	98.3	92.1
16	Sheffield	76.6	82.3	51.1	152	88.9	91.6
17	York	74.3	75.9	46.9	155	95.0	91.3
18	Swansea	79.3	79.3	47.5	136	93.7	91.2
19	Southampton	69.1	73.7	48.2	173	92.8	90.8
20	Heriot-Watt	75.1	77.7	39.5	164	90.7	90.6
21	Newcastle	69.5	76.2	49.7	146	95.9	90.1
=22	Lancaster	69.7	71.2	44.8	154	98.3	90.0
=22	Loughborough	84.7	86.3	18.7	148	89.3	90.0
24	Aberystwyth	84.4	81.2	38.4	129	85.8	89.4
25	Liverpool	75.4	78.6	40.5	146	89.7	89.3
26	Queen Mary, London	69.8	74.0	37.4	169	90.4	89.0
27	Leicester	79.3	80.3	30.2	135	91.1	88.8
=28	Edinburgh	60.5	69.4	54.3	193	84.6	88.7
=28	Leeds	66.2	66.5	41.6	173	94.1	88.7
30	King's College London	64.3	72.9	47.6	160	91.4	88.3
31	Strathclyde	71.9	74.4	21.1	185	86.7	88.0
32	Queen's, Belfast	72.0	74.8	29.5	150	92.8	87.8
33	Royal Holloway, London	73.1	73.7	35.1	134	93.9	87.6
34	East Anglia	75.0	77.3	35.9	132	88.6	87.3
35	Abertay	87.3	80.6	3.4	153	83.0	87.1
36	Dundee	73.3	77.8	29.4	158	83.1	86.9
37	Stirling	77.0	69.8	14.0	140	96.4	86.5
38	Cardiff	68.6	70.7	25.0	154	93.6	86.4
=39	Chester	88.5	82.7	1.3	117	89.5	86.2
=39	Kent	72.0	71.3	37.8	142	85.8	86.2
=41	Brunel London	75.5	75.0	25.2	137	86.4	85.8
=41	Hull	72.0	74.7	22.2	135	92.7	85.8
43	Sussex	70.2	67.8	21.6	141	94.9	85.4
44	Bangor	76.9	71.8	17.6	114	96.6	85.3
45	Liverpool Hope	88.0	77.4	8.8	121	83.3	85.2
46	Ulster	76.2	73.9	16.6	127	88.7	84.6
47	Huddersfield	79.7	77.5	7.4	132	84.8	84.3
=48	Lincoln	72.6	77.3	13.6	126	89.9	84.1

=48	Wales Trinity St David	87.7	80.8	1.0	120	81.0	84.1
=50	Bournemouth	78.6	76.6	8.5	120	88.4	84.0
=50	Edinburgh Napier	77.8	74.7	5.2	139	85.9	84.0
=50	Surrey	60.7	69.4	25.3	144	94.6	84.0
53	Edge Hill	78.2	77.7	0.3	138	85.0	83.7
54	Worcester	84.9	80.0	—	100	88.7	83.5
55	Essex	69.1	70.4	34.3	113	87.9	83.4
56	Aston	69.2	68.7	21.7	133	88.4	83.3
=57	Falmouth	83.0	82.1	—	129	78.7	83.2
=57	Plymouth	74.2	67.6	21.8	123	86.6	83.2
=59	Birmingham City	82.0	81.4	4.9	132	75.7	83.1
=59	Robert Gordon	79.0	78.2	4.3	138	79.4	83.1
=59	West of England	78.9	80.1	5.9	128	80.8	83.1
=62	Manchester Metropolitan	80.6	75.9	5.6	130	80.0	82.9
=62	Northumbria	76.2	72.5	4.0	147	81.6	82.9
=64	Salford	73.5	73.7	15.3	131	82.1	82.7
=64	South Wales	76.2	74.9	3.6	126	86.6	82.7
=64	Staffordshire	84.3	79.5	0.4	126	77.0	82.7
67	Nottingham Trent	74.4	72.8	5.2	131	84.4	82.1
=68	Bolton	93.0	88.4	—	116	63.3	82.0
=68	Leeds Beckett	76.1	74.1	0.2	113	90.2	82.0
=68	Portsmouth	79.7	78.5	7.2	111	80.7	82.0
71	Teesside	83.8	80.5	3.4	126	71.5	81.8
72	Bath Spa	78.9	81.3	13.9	92	—	81.5
=73	Glyndŵr	81.8	75.8	3.9	106	80.0	81.3
=73	Reading	67.6	63.9	16.3	126	88.9	81.3
=75	Derby	74.9	72.8	5.0	110	86.6	81.1
=75	Sheffield Hallam	74.2	71.9	14.4	120	79.2	81.1
77	Coventry	71.5	69.1	3.3	129	86.3	81.0
=78	De Montfort	70.6	71.7	13.4	111*	85.4	80.8
=78	Liverpool John Moores	73.7	73.8	3.2	154	71.8	80.8
=80	Goldsmiths, London	65.9	65.2	29.2	129	78.4	80.5
=80	West of Scotland	78.3	74.1	3.2	122	76.1	80.5
82	Greenwich	75.9	75.3	7.3	127	72.9	80.2
83	Oxford Brookes	63.8	65.0	13.0	120	89.3	79.9
=84	Cardiff Metropolitan	69.9	69.8	—	120	86.7	79.8
=84	Solent, Southampton	81.1	73.3	—	125	71.1	79.8
86	Keele	72.6	70.7	10.8	123	76.2	79.7
=87	Bradford	71.9	72.3	—	126	79.6	79.5
=87	Brighton	69.6	63.3	6.4	109	89.7	79.5
=87	City, London	66.3	69.1	21.8	120	78.0	79.5
90	Sunderland	73.0	69.6	1.8	110	84.0	79.4
91	West London	80.2	83.5	1.2	123	63.6	79.3
=92	Central Lancashire	78.9	76.1	—	126	68.3	79.1
=92	Gloucestershire	75.6	71.1	—	111	80.0	79.1
94	Anglia Ruskin	78.8	77.1	—	101	73.8	78.6

Computer Science cont	Teaching quality %	Student experience %	Research quality %	Entry standards (UCAS points)	Graduate prospects %	Overall score
95 Hertfordshire	75.5	74.1	7.8	104	73.5	78.5
96 Westminster	70.7	72.1	2.9	115	77.8	78.3
97 Wolverhampton	78.9	79.7	—	88	74.4	78.1
98 Glasgow Caledonian	73.0	70.4	4.0	145	64.3	78.0
=99 Bucks New	81.3	76.4	—	101	67.5	77.7
=99 Kingston	73.5	74.9	5.3	106	72.1	77.7
101 Suffolk	71.9	69.2	—	106	76.9	77.0
102 Middlesex	71.0	71.2	14.2	112	66.2	76.9
103 East London	65.9	65.3	2.3	109	80.5	76.5
104 Bedfordshire	68.0	67.4	9.1	104	75.0	76.4
105 Northampton	69.6	65.8	—	107	73.0	75.3
106 London South Bank	67.8	65.3	19.6	107	57.1	73.7
107 London Metropolitan	78.8	76.0	0.7	76	55.6	72.8
108 Canterbury Christ Church	56.8	57.4	—	99	60.9	68.2

Employed in high-skilled job	74%	Employed in lower-skilled job and studying	0%
Employed in high-skilled job and studying	3%	Employed in lower-skilled job	10%
Studying	6%	Unemployed	7%
High skilled work (median) salary	£27,000	Low/medium skilled salary	£18,500

Creative Writing

Warwick is top of our Creative Writing table this year. It averaged the highest entry standards in 2019 by some margin and achieved the second-best scores in the most recent Research Excellence Framework. Third-ranked Queen Mary, London – which was shortlisted for our University of the Year award – is in first place for research. Royal Holloway has moved up to second this year, from ranking fourth last, helped by a 91.8% score for student satisfaction with teaching quality, as expressed in the National Student Survey.

Worcester has done even better on student satisfaction however, achieving 96.5% for teaching quality (the top result) and 90.2% for the wider experience. London South Bank, Aberystwyth, Chester and Bournemouth also all scored above 90% for teaching quality. Aberystwyth students were the most satisfied with the broad experience of any in our table, and Worcester came a close second.

Derby, which ranks 16= overall, had the highest proportion – 88.5% – of graduates in professional jobs or further study 15 months after graduation, beating fifth-ranked Birmingham to second place in our graduate prospects measure. At the other end of the ranking only a third of St Mary's, Twickenham graduates were similarly placed in their careers.

However, the prospect of entering professional level careers immediately after finishing their degree is not necessarily the guiding motivation for all creative writing undergraduates, and some may not even be aiming for a full-time job on graduation. That is, perhaps, why many universities do not post a graduate prospects score. That said the subject is not bottom of our employment ranking, there are seven others beneath it, and across all universities 56.4% of graduates were in high-skilled work or postgraduate study after 15 months.

Demand for places declined sharply in 2019, when applications were 21% down on the year before. Enrolments also dipped significantly, but less steeply, by 15% – equalling a little over three candidates per place.

Creative Writing	Teaching quality %	Student experience %	Research quality %	Entry standards (UCAS points)	Graduate prospects %	Overall score
1 Warwick	80.6	64.6	59.8	175	—	100.0
2 Royal Holloway, London	91.8	81.8	49.9	143	—	98.6
3 Queen Mary, London	86.0	81.9	64.0	124	—	96.6
4 Nottingham	76.1	72.1	56.6	160	—	96.4
5 Birmingham	77.6	72.7	37.0	165	86.4	96.2
6 Queen's, Belfast	78.8	72.8	53.1	154	—	95.6
7 Lancaster	78.9	76.5	47.0	150	—	94.1
8 Newcastle	73.7	72.5	54.3	148	—	93.2
9 Aberystwyth	92.9	91.7	31.2	127	58.8	91.0
10 East Anglia	77.1	70.7	36.2	150	64.9	89.9
11 West of England	86.2	86.3	35.4	116	—	89.7
12 Plymouth	84.7	87.0	30.5	119	—	88.8
13 Surrey	74.2	67.5	39.1	144	—	88.6
14 Manchester Metropolitan	83.2	76.0	29.0	126	65.4	87.8
15 Liverpool John Moores	86.5	84.6	17.9	151	48.4	87.6
=16 Brunel London	79.8	75.5	30.9	122	66.7	86.9
=16 Derby	83.9	77.8	13.5	101	88.5	86.9
18 Greenwich	85.1	82.8	14.4	108	77.1	86.6
19 Hull	86.4	79.8	22.7	118*	—	86.4
20 Chichester	85.6	76.2	16.3	107	76.2	86.0
21 Bangor	74.1	70.1	46.3	120	57.9	85.7
22 Liverpool Hope	85.8	70.0	26.9	118	—	85.6
23 Worcester	96.5	90.2	8.2	118	50.9	85.3
24 Salford	84.9	83.7	7.8	127	62.9	85.2
25 Sheffield Hallam	85.7	79.1	14.6	109	68.8	84.9
26 Roehampton	87.1	82.9	20.8	107	—	84.7
27 De Montfort	81.0	70.8	24.1	111*	68.2	84.6
28 Westminster	86.1	79.0	28.9	99*	—	84.3
29 London South Bank	94.5	86.1	12.8	97*	—	84.1
30 Essex	76.0	74.0	37.7	109	—	83.9
31 Bournemouth	90.8	84.6	15.1	117	46.7	83.7
32 Kingston	82.2	84.0	15.7	115	—	83.5
33 Coventry	83.3	81.1	18.1	110	—	83.2
34 Chester	91.1	83.7	10.7	102	—	83.1
35 Bolton	88.4	87.0	14.4	94	—	82.1
36 Central Lancashire	76.3	72.3	9.9	109	70.0	81.3

Creative Writing cont	Teaching quality %	Student experience %	Research quality %	Entry standards (UCAS points)	Graduate prospects %	Overall score
37 Bath Spa	75.1	69.6	23.5	110	59.7	81.2
38 Portsmouth	74.8	70.0	17.1	101	71.1	81.1
39 York St John	88.8	84.4	9.7	102	45.5	80.1
40 Anglia Ruskin	78.4	69.0	16.3	118	47.8	79.4
41 Gloucestershire	83.7	75.8	9.3	86	61.7	78.9
42 Winchester	76.6	73.6	—	115	60.2	78.8
43 Wolverhampton	86.7	80.2	7.6	90	—	78.5
44 Edge Hill	78.8	63.8	12.1	128	40.0	78.1
45 Canterbury Christ Church	80.5	66.4	8.0	101	—	76.3
46 Falmouth	82.4	73.3	—	108	42.9	76.0
47 St Mary's, Twickenham	71.6	64.2	14.6	82	33.6	69.8
48 Northampton	54.6	47.7	15.3	109*	—	68.1

Employed in high-skilled job	42%	Employed in lower-skilled job and studying		1%
Employed in high-skilled job and studying	4%	Employed in lower-skilled job		33%
Studying	9%	Unemployed		10%
High skilled work (median) salary	£21,000	Low/medium skilled salary		£16,500

Criminology

Loughborough has retained the top spot that it took when it entered our Criminology table last year. It does not come first in any individual measure, but scores well across them all. Durham is only a hair's breadth – or 0.2%, to be more accurate – behind it and has by far the best employment record, with 95% of graduates in high-skilled jobs or further study 15 months after graduation. Kent, in 22nd place overall, had the strongest results in the Research Excellence Framework, in which Southampton's and Lancaster's submissions also did well.

Further down the table Abertay has moved into the top 25 from 39th last year, Salford has risen from 30th to 18th and Royal Holloway has gained 19 places to rank 35th this year. City, London and Canterbury Christ Church who tie at 45= this year, were 64= and 66th respectively in the previous edition of our *Guide*.

Tenth-ranked Wrexham Glyndŵr is top for both measures of student satisfaction derived from the National Student Survey: teaching quality and the wider experience. Bolton, Derby, Aberystwyth and Canterbury Christchurch also scored particularly well in terms of satisfaction. On the whole students tend to enjoy studying criminology; the subject was scored no lower than 64% in either measure at any university.

Criminology has yet to improve its record in graduate prospects however, and this year finishes second from bottom of 67 subjects for the proportion of graduates in professional employment or further study 15 months after finishing their degrees. Although the unemployment rate is a respectable 6%, more than half of graduates start out in lower-skilled work. Career opportunities further down the line are to be found in the police force, prison service, the Home Office, charities or law practice.

The data in this table previously appeared under sociology and law, but the growing demand for degrees in criminology merits a ranking of its own. Now in its fifth year the table is continuing to expand – there are three new entries this year: Bath Spa, Worcester and Solent. The growth in criminology is within traditional degrees as well as in degree apprenticeships, although the latter are not included in our table. At least 100 universities and more than 50 colleges are offering courses in criminology this year, either as stand-alone or joint honours, or as part of a broader social science degree.

Criminology	Teaching quality %	Student experience %	Research quality %	Entry standards (UCAS points)	Graduate prospects %	Overall score
1 Loughborough	83.2	82.2	40.6	148	—	100.0
2 Durham	75.3	71.3	28.7	149	95.0	99.8
3 Leeds	73.4	69.4	40.1	153	83.0	98.7
4 Stirling	83.4	77.5	33.8	179	52.4	98.1
5 Nottingham	74.7	71.5	43.5	139	76.0	96.7
6 Sussex	76.9	72.1	27.9	141	80.6	96.4
7 Sheffield	75.2	72.3	26.8	147	79.2	96.2
8 Lancaster	76.9	72.9	51.4	148	56.3	95.5
9 Southampton	73.2	71.9	52.8	142	63.5	95.4
10 Glyndŵr	92.3	88.8	—	114	78.6	95.3
11 Manchester	74.3	70.4	27.2	150	73.6	95.0
12 Aberystwyth	88.6	85.4	14.3	119	70.5	94.8
13 York	76.7	72.9	47.5	138	60.0	94.5
14 Swansea	84.7	82.7	20.4	132	63.8	94.3
15 Birmingham	72.9	68.1	40.1	146	—	93.6
=16 Essex	74.7	74.6	44.3	114	67.6	92.6
=16 Leicester	79.1	77.4	26.3	128	64.3	92.6
18 Salford	84.1	78.5	27.7	121	59.2	92.4
=19 Liverpool John Moores	82.2	79.2	5.8	145	62.9	92.3
=19 Surrey	85.3	83.2	—	135	65.7	92.3
21 Bolton	91.3	86.9	1.0	121	—	92.2
22 Kent	75.1	72.5	59.0	119	52.6	92.0
23 Edinburgh Napier	86.2	84.8	—	164	45.8	91.9
24 Abertay	86.1	77.6	5.0	135	60.0	91.4
25 Cardiff	71.7	67.9	30.8	159	53.2	91.2
=26 Northumbria	77.8	76.8	12.7	142	57.6	90.4
=26 Portsmouth	83.4	80.6	12.1	119	60.8	90.4
28 Sheffield Hallam	84.9	81.0	14.4	108	61.2	90.1
29 Bradford	79.3	79.0	10.6	131*	—	89.8
30 West of England	84.6	83.8	10.9	117	55.4	89.6
31 Greenwich	80.6	78.8	2.1	127	64.0	89.5
32 Plymouth	78.4	73.7	16.0	117	64.1	89.2
=33 Central Lancashire	80.1	75.3	11.8	130	53.9	88.6
=33 Lincoln	85.2	85.0	5.8	116	53.3	88.6
35 Royal Holloway, London	76.9	77.6	—	130	64.5	88.5

		Teaching quality %	Student experience %	Research quality %	Entry standards (UCAS points)	Graduate prospects %	Overall score
Criminology cont							
36	Nottingham Trent	82.5	79.7	5.1	115	59.8	88.4
37	Derby	87.1	86.1	2.4	111	52.9	88.3
38	Hull	80.8	77.4	14.3	123	51.9	88.2
=39	Coventry	81.8	77.4	—	116	63.5	88.1
=39	Huddersfield	81.1	77.5	9.5	120	55.8	88.1
=39	Queen's, Belfast	68.8	67.3	39.3	145	44.7	88.1
42	Keele	76.2	75.1	34.0	119	46.6	87.9
43	Liverpool	69.0	64.2	24.5	127	63.6	87.7
44	London South Bank	77.5	74.0	20.1	96	65.2	87.4
=45	Canterbury Christ Church	89.5	84.9	3.2	100	51.9	87.3
=45	City, London	71.6	69.7	20.8	130	—	87.3
=45	Manchester Metropolitan	83.0	79.8	6.9	122	48.4	87.3
48	Birmingham City	81.5	79.9	3.8	121	52.9	87.2
49	Edge Hill	78.1	76.4	12.1	127	48.4	86.8
50	Suffolk	82.6	76.0	—	86	70.0	86.1
51	Leeds Beckett	81.4	75.7	6.4	97	60.5	85.9
=52	South Wales	78.9	77.4	15.4	117	45.7	85.8
=52	Teesside	75.2	71.7	15.0	101	62.7	85.8
54	Anglia Ruskin	76.9	74.2	5.4	105	62.0	85.5
55	Solent, Southampton	82.7	83.1	—	109	49.4	85.3
56	West London	81.4	79.1	—	118	46.7	84.9
57	Worcester	76.6	67.0	—	121	58.3	84.8
58	Chester	79.4	78.5	0.3	110	51.9	84.5
59	Liverpool Hope	78.5	68.5	8.6	108	51.9	84.0
=60	Middlesex	71.6	66.9	14.9	111	54.0	83.5
=60	Westminster	81.2	78.8	—	112	44.0	83.5
62	Brighton	71.3	65.0	12.4	103	60.1	83.3
63	Bath Spa	75.0	67.9	—	103	60.3	83.0
=64	Gloucestershire	76.7	71.8	—	115	49.2	82.9
=64	London Metropolitan	76.4	73.3	8.8	91	55.6	82.9
66	Winchester	74.0	68.2	4.4	105	55.0	82.4
67	De Montfort	73.1	71.6	11.2	101*	51.4	82.3
68	Kingston	80.1	76.2	—	100	46.8	82.2
69	Roehampton	77.9	75.5	– –	95	46.3	80.8
70	Northampton	74.0	68.5		89	48.4	78.7

Employed in high-skilled job	40%	Employed in lower-skilled job and studying	1%
Employed in high-skilled job and studying	2%	Employed in lower-skilled job	43%
Studying	7%	Unemployed	6%
High skilled work (median) salary	£25,000	Low/medium skilled salary	£18,000

Dentistry

Immense demand for dentistry degrees in the 2019 admissions cycle equated to more than ten applications per place, due to a 16% increase in applications set against barely any extra enrolments. Entry standards are high and nowhere averaged fewer than 167 points on the UCAS tariff. Chemistry and biology A-levels, or equivalent, are prerequisites for most degrees, and some schools of dentistry also require maths or physics.

The career prospects offered by dentistry are a big draw, and graduates usually go straight into working as dentists, and earning commensurate salaries. The new Graduate Outcomes survey showed that nine out of ten were in professional employment 15 months after completing their degrees – a proportion bettered only by those who had studied medicine, physiotherapy, nursing and veterinary medicine. Three of our table's 15 universities – Bristol, Sheffield and Central Lancashire – had 100% of graduates in high-skilled work or further study, and none achieved lower than Birmingham's 85.7% in the top outcomes.

Glasgow has maintained its healthy lead in our Dentistry table for the fourth consecutive year. It has the highest entry standards and performs strongly in all other measures. The remainder of the top five are also unchanged since last year, unusually for a subject in which universities' positions usually fluctuate, due to their tightly packed scores. Tenth-ranked Manchester achieved the best results in the Research Excellence Framework and Central Lancashire, in 11th place overall, got the best scores in the sections of the National Student Survey that focus on teaching quality. Plymouth, which had the second-best teaching quality responses, was top for student satisfaction with the wider experience.

Degrees in dentistry last five years, or six years for those entering without the necessary scientific qualifications. A high number of mandatory modules ensure graduates are appropriately skilled to start practising as dentists but allow less flexibility than most other subjects.

Dentistry	Teaching quality %	Student experience %	Research quality %	Entry standards (UCAS points)	Graduate prospects %	Overall score
1 Glasgow	95.7	93.9	29.3	230	93.9	100.0
2 Dundee	93.5	94.4	22.1	219	97.2	94.6
3 Queen's, Belfast	94.0	92.8	50.7	172	97.0	92.1
4 Newcastle	94.3	90.3	43.6	178	95.9	91.1
5 Queen Mary, London	73.1	70.1	48.3	186	89.2	87.0
6 Bristol	77.5	74.0	47.1	173	100.0	85.1
7 Sheffield	91.5	87.4	28.5	176	100.0	84.9
8 Cardiff	77.1	71.0	36.8	186	95.3	84.6
9 Liverpool	92.1	89.6	31.7	167	95.7	84.1
10 Manchester	63.8	63.0	57.1	168	93.1	82.4
11 Central Lancashire	98.9	93.6	8.3	—	100.0	81.2
12 Plymouth	96.8	95.9	9.5	172	92.6	80.1
13 King's College London	60.7	55.4	40.9	182	91.3	79.2
14 Leeds	74.2	74.8	31.7	170	100.0	78.7
15 Birmingham	78.3	66.2	19.2	176	85.7	76.5

Dentistry cont

Employed in high-skilled job	90%	Employed in lower-skilled job and studying	0%
Employed in high-skilled job and studying	6%	Employed in lower-skilled job	0%
Studying	1%	Unemployed	3%
High skilled work (median) salary	£38,000	Low/medium skilled salary	–

Drama, Dance and Cinematics

Manchester has taken the lead in our Drama, Dance and Cinematics table this year, up from seventh place last year, thanks to a strong performance across all measures without topping any individually. Glasgow is close behind it and has the highest entry standards, while Queen Mary, London achieved the best results in the Research Excellence Framework. Central School of Speech and Drama remains in the top 10 again this year, as do Sussex, Lancaster and Exeter.

The older universities dominate the upper ranks of our table, but for student satisfaction the post-1992 institutions have the edge. They are led by ninth-ranked West London, which received the best scores in the sections of the National Student Survey that focus on teaching quality and on the wider experience – helping propel it up our table from 38th place overall last year. London Met, 54th in the main ranking, placed second in both measures of satisfaction, while Edinburgh Napier, Coventry and Staffordshire also had scores above 90% for teaching quality.

Its pairing with cinematics in the UCAS statistics means photography is also included in this table. Applications to all three subjects have declined for the past four years but are still popular enough to create a subject table stretching to 93 universities.

Queen Margaret, Edinburgh has fallen from sixth to 24th place, in spite of high rates of student satisfaction. Its ranking has been brought down by an especially poor year for graduate prospects – just 39.5% of graduates were in professional employment or further study 15 months after finishing their degrees. Only one university, Worcester, had a lower proportion in the top career outcomes. Even at the top of the employment measure, though, Birmingham registered just 75.8% of graduates in professional work or studying at the 15-months-on census point. But the creatives who opt for this group of degrees are unlikely to be surprised by the paucity of full-time professional careers waiting for them soon after graduation. Freelancing and fill-in jobs are common for those fresh from university and more than a third of drama, dance and cinematics graduates were in low-skilled work, the new Graduate Outcomes survey revealed. The subjects are 61st out of 67 in our employment ranking.

Drama, Dance and Cinematics	Teaching quality %	Student experience %	Research quality %	Entry standards (UCAS points)	Graduate prospects %	Overall score
1 Manchester	88.3	85.5	58.6	170	59.6	100.0
2 Glasgow	80.2	80.9	53.9	192	56.7	99.5
3 Lancaster	78.0	74.1	48.0	168	–	97.2
4 Birmingham	76.7	77.4	36.9	163	75.8	97.1
5 Queen Mary, London	75.0	70.5	68.4	139	75.0	96.7
6 Sussex	85.5	84.6	45.6	144	–	95.9
7 Exeter	78.5	76.9	46.3	160	66.7	95.8

8	Central School of Speech and Drama	—	—	47.7	137	67.0	95.4
9	West London	96.9	95.1	2.3	142	75.0	95.3
=10	Bristol	86.6	80.5	48.7	161	53.2	94.8
=10	Leeds	77.9	80.9	28.0	160	71.1	94.8
12	Surrey	76.9	73.9	27.2	158	74.8	94.4
13	Royal Holloway, London	79.5	74.5	50.6	145	66.5	94.2
14	East Anglia	80.5	72.3	43.8	154	64.9	94.1
15	Warwick	64.5	63.1	61.7	163	62.0	92.7
16	York	82.1	80.4	26.0	159	60.7	92.4
=17	Edinburgh Napier	91.0	89.9	37.9	161	40.6	91.9
=17	Essex	89.9	84.3	37.7	122	64.3	91.9
19	Royal Conservatoire of Scotland	88.2	82.5	11.3	128	73.9	91.2
20	Nottingham Trent	85.2	80.9	10.0	140	69.0	90.5
21	Kent	77.4	76.3	44.3	139	58.6	90.2
22	Aberystwyth	88.7	88.0	30.3	133	53.4	89.6
23	East London	87.0	82.9	11.2	128	68.4	89.4
24	Queen Margaret, Edinburgh	89.2	85.5	14.0	174	39.5	89.2
25	Edinburgh	62.4	59.6	48.0	170	54.2	88.9
26	Northumbria	86.3	81.8	13.3	143	56.3	88.3
27	Manchester Metropolitan	84.4	81.3	7.5	154	54.4	88.1
28	Central Lancashire	90.0	87.1	3.9	124	64.5	87.9
29	Hull	83.0	78.9	11.2	130	65.5	87.6
=30	Cardiff Metropolitan	89.7	85.6	—	110	72.7	87.4
=30	Leeds Arts	85.1	83.6	—	134	64.7	87.4
32	Greenwich	74.6	65.8	3.5	144	72.5	87.3
=33	Derby	87.9	81.8	5.1	121	66.7	87.2
=33	Middlesex	82.7	78.5	16.1	123	64.9	87.2
35	Coventry	90.7	83.3	18.1	121	55.6	86.9
36	Arts, Bournemouth	88.4	87.4	2.4	148	49.8	86.8
37	Bournemouth	73.8	68.2	15.1	122	73.2	86.1
38	Bedfordshire	85.5	76.1	5.6	102	75.0	85.8
39	St Mary's, Twickenham	80.7	74.5	9.1	129	61.9	85.4
40	Chichester	81.6	77.4	9.7	123	62.5	85.3
41	Bath Spa	87.2	81.7	10.7	127	52.8	85.0
=42	Chester	83.0	75.3	4.3	124	63.4	84.9
=42	Roehampton	73.6	70.8	46.6	113	56.5	84.9
44	Huddersfield	78.9	76.3	28.0	134	47.6	84.6
=45	Brighton	72.0	66.1	13.1	116	73.5	84.5
=45	Kingston	83.7	78.9	15.7	119	56.6	84.5
=45	Teesside	85.2	81.1	2.9	130*	55.6	84.5
48	Queen's, Belfast	61.5	64.5	38.3	149	51.9	84.4
49	Westminster	85.0	80.0	—	131	56.3	84.3
=50	Bolton	85.5	78.7	—	123	60.0	84.2
=50	Ulster	78.7	72.1	40.0	126	46.0	84.2
=50	West of Scotland	83.5	75.6	—	140	53.8	84.2
53	Liverpool John Moores	79.2	77.2	—	141	55.6	84.0

Drama, Dance and Cinematics cont

	Teaching quality %	Student experience %	Research quality %	Entry standards (UCAS points)	Graduate prospects %	Overall score
54 London Metropolitan	95.0	91.8	—	110	52.9	83.9
55 Northampton	87.8	77.9	—	111	63.2	83.8
=56 Staffordshire	91.9	88.5	—	117	52.3	83.7
=56 West of England	82.3	78.9	—	130	57.1	83.7
58 Norwich Arts	83.9	81.0	—	126	56.8	83.6
=59 Nottingham	56.7	51.6	45.8	124	66.7	83.4
=59 Reading	62.9	64.0	34.8	134	57.3	83.4
=59 Salford	83.3	78.9	7.2	133	50.0	83.4
62 Portsmouth	84.6	83.1	—	122	56.3	83.3
63 De Montfort	74.0	72.1	14.5	123*	60.9	83.2
=64 Lincoln	83.1	74.6	6.5	125	54.9	83.0
=64 Sheffield Hallam	79.7	74.5	14.4	127	52.2	83.0
=66 Falmouth	81.2	78.0	6.2	129	52.0	82.7
=66 Gloucestershire	81.2	74.2	—	124	59.1	82.7
=66 Plymouth	84.2	77.5	20.2	127	43.5	82.7
69 Winchester	79.1	75.6	11.2	122	54.8	82.5
=70 Edge Hill	78.3	76.8	3.8	137	50.3	82.3
=70 Sunderland	81.8	79.7	4.2	116	56.8	82.3
72 Creative Arts	79.3	72.9	3.4	129	54.5	82.1
73 Goldsmiths, London	65.3	62.7	28.3	136	52.6	82.0
74 Brunel London	71.2	69.7	32.6	125	47.8	81.7
75 Birmingham City	76.4	70.5	11.6	125	53.3	81.6
=76 Anglia Ruskin	71.0	68.8	16.9	132	51.3	81.3
=76 South Wales	78.2	74.1	6.4	123	53.2	81.3
78 Newman	77.9	69.8	9.6	121	—	80.9
=79 Hertfordshire	73.6	68.8	5.3	117	60.7	80.8
=79 Wales Trinity St David	83.7	76.4	—	132	45.1	80.8
81 London South Bank	77.0	71.2	—	110	62.7	80.6
=82 Leeds Beckett	79.6	72.1	1.7	117	55.6	80.5
=82 Wolverhampton	90.4	87.6	—	114	43.5	80.5
84 Canterbury Christ Church	78.2	75.0	15.2	101	55.9	80.2
85 Bucks New	88.2	85.8	—	115	43.0	79.8
86 York St John	78.5	71.7	10.5	112	—	79.7
87 Arts London	78.6	71.1	—	128	46.6	79.0
88 Ravensbourne	61.0	53.8	—	116	72.5	78.8
89 Solent, Southampton	76.7	74.8	—	130	43.8	78.6
90 Cumbria	76.9	71.7	—	115	51.5	78.2
91 Liverpool Hope	68.8	65.6	3.0	113	56.1	77.3
92 Worcester	75.2	73.3	3.5	123	39.2	76.3
93 Suffolk	77.6	68.3	—	95	46.2	73.9

Employed in high-skilled job	49%	Employed in lower-skilled job and studying	1%
Employed in high-skilled job and studying	2%	Employed in lower-skilled job	37%
Studying	4%	Unemployed	7%
High skilled work (median) salary	£21,000	Low/medium skilled salary	£17,500

East and South Asian Studies

The recent decline in demand for places on Chinese Studies degrees came to a halt in 2019, when applications surged by 25%. Japanese Studies already attracts bigger student numbers and it also experienced an upturn, albeit smaller, as did South Asian Studies. But the courses do not draw big crowds; in 2019, 35 new undergraduates began South Asian Studies degrees, 130 enrolled on Chinese Studies degrees and 230 started Japanese Studies degrees.

South Asian Studies is offered by only four universities at undergraduate level: Central Lancashire, Leeds, Manchester and the School of Oriental and African Studies in London (SOAS). Their small size combined with their cultural and economic significances affords these subjects extra protection by the Government.

Universities do not expect undergraduates to arrive fluent – or even experienced – in their chosen language, as most learn it from scratch, but admissions tutors do expect other modern language qualifications as proof of potential. The languages offered by SOAS in London include Burmese, Indonesian, Thai, Tibetan and Vietnamese.

Cambridge and Oxford have maintained positions one and two in our table this year, the latter being the leader on entry standards this year, and Durham has climbed to third place from 12th. Student satisfaction rates are lukewarm in comparison to many other degrees, only 12th-ranked Nottingham Trent achieved over 90% – for teaching quality, and at 84.9% it also came top in the sections of the National Student Survey that focus on the wider experience. Conversely its older neighbour, Nottingham, came bottom for both satisfaction measures.

The subjects have done better in our graduate prospects ranking this year than last, however. With 67% of graduates in professional employment or postgraduate study 15 months after finishing their degrees, East and South Asian Studies is placed 48th out of 67 subjects. Edinburgh had the highest proportion of graduates achieving the top career outcomes.

East and South Asian Studies	Teaching quality %	Student experience %	Research quality %	Entry standards (UCAS points)	Graduate prospects %	Overall score
1 Cambridge	—	—	45.0	200	—	100.0
2 Oxford	—	—	36.2	212	—	97.5
3 Durham	78.0	70.7	34.6	174	—	92.2
4 Edinburgh	64.3	64.1	30.1	185	83.3	90.8
5 Manchester	67.0	63.1	48.9	151	—	90.0
6 Leeds	77.0	72.4	30.6	153	75.5	89.6
7 Liverpool	79.5	78.5	33.4	138*	—	88.8
8 Newcastle	78.5	65.2	36.3	145	—	88.7
9 Soas, London	73.5	69.8	26.3	170	58.2	84.3
10 Hull	82.6	80.9	22.7	117*	—	84.0

East and South Asian Studies cont	Teaching quality %	Student experience %	Research quality %	Entry standards (UCAS points)	Graduate prospects %	Overall score
11 Sheffield	76.6	77.2	16.7	145	68.7	83.9
12 Nottingham Trent	90.8	84.9	10.0	123	—	83.4
13 Nottingham	58.9	50.2	27.3	135	74.5	80.5
14 Central Lancashire	71.4	70.1	—	119	58.8	72.8

Employed in high-skilled job	51%	Employed in lower-skilled job and studying	1%
Employed in high-skilled job and studying	4%	Employed in lower-skilled job	24%
Studying	11%	Unemployed	9%
High skilled work (median) salary	£25,000	Low/medium skilled salary	£20,000

Economics

Oxford has edged ahead to first place in our Economics table this year, up from fourth. It is in the top three for research quality and entry standards, and the top 10 for graduate prospects. By the narrowest of margins behind it lie Cambridge and the London School of Economics (LSE), tied in second place; the former has the highest entry standards, the latter achieved the best scores in the Research Excellence Framework. The LSE is the top-ranked UK university for economics according to QS, at 5= in the world.

Fourth-ranked Warwick has maintained its record of never having been outside the top five for economics and performs strongly across all measures without being top of any one in particular. Hertfordshire, which ranks 45th in our main table, beat all other universities for student satisfaction with both teaching quality and the wider experience. Of the top 15 universities, 12th-ranked Loughborough had the best satisfaction scores for teaching quality, followed by St Andrews.

Such is the subject's popularity that applications to study economics topped 60,000 for the first time in 2019, and in fact were closer to 61,000. It was the fifth consecutive year of record levels of demand. Competition, therefore, is fierce, at more than six applications per place.

Classified as a social science, economics encompasses the study of how people produce, use and distribute resources, and it also covers politics, marketing and geography. Those considering it as a degree should not underestimate the mathematical skills required however, and maths A-level or equivalent is usually a prerequisite of the leading universities.

When surveyed 15 months after finishing their degrees, 83.1% of economics graduates were in professional jobs or further study – the top outcomes – placing economics 20th in our employment ranking of 67 subject areas, perhaps not as high as some might expect.

Economics	Teaching quality %	Student experience %	Research quality %	Entry standards (UCAS points)	Graduate prospects %	Overall score
1 Oxford	—	—	58.0	209	91.5	100.0
=2 Cambridge	—	—	45.0	223	97.6	99.9
=2 London School of Economics	75.5	72.9	70.7	179	95.2	99.9

4 Warwick	82.1	83.0	49.6	180	95.1	99.5
5 Strathclyde	80.6	81.7	44.3	202	89.9	98.5
6 University College London	70.3	72.4	70.2	175	94.3	98.1
7 St Andrews	84.0	84.5	23.6	215	83.1	95.7
8 Bath	73.3	76.7	41.8	174	94.5	95.1
9 Glasgow	76.0	80.0	26.4	188	93.6	94.6
10 Leeds	78.0	80.7	39.3	174	86.8	94.3
11 Bristol	71.7	72.6	43.6	171	93.5	94.1
12 Loughborough	85.5	87.1	32.6	150	86.2	94.0
13 Exeter	76.4	79.3	26.9	167	91.4	92.7
14 Stirling	82.4	83.7	25.2	152	—	92.3
15 Lancaster	78.3	77.5	42.6	141	83.8	91.6
16 Durham	69.4	71.2	23.1	192	90.0	90.9
17 East Anglia	85.0	83.7	25.7	129	85.3	90.8
18 Nottingham	67.6	73.8	31.7	173	89.1	90.5
19 York	75.3	77.5	22.6	150	91.5	90.4
20 Edinburgh	68.6	69.9	30.2	178	87.7	90.0
21 Sheffield	79.4	82.1	16.6	147	87.2	89.8
22 Queen Mary, London	69.1	75.2	31.3	160	86.9	89.6
23 Liverpool	81.3	84.1	20.1	140	83.2	89.5
24 Birmingham	73.0	73.3	26.6	155	87.5	89.3
=25 Essex	85.2	86.5	43.6	98	74.9	89.2
=25 Surrey	68.8	73.2	33.0	143	90.3	89.2
27 Kent	85.2	85.9	14.6	127	84.2	89.1
28 Ulster	74.1	73.9	39.2	121	85.7	88.8
29 Manchester	72.7	74.7	26.8	165	81.6	88.7
=30 King's College London	69.4	70.9	—	183	97.0	88.5
=30 Newcastle	71.2	75.7	20.7	152	89.1	88.5
32 Southampton	76.5	80.0	23.4	140	82.2	88.1
33 Aston	74.0	75.6	19.7	125	92.2	88.0
34 Aberystwyth	83.9	85.5	14.5	116	—	87.6
=35 Queen's, Belfast	70.5	70.7	32.7	143	83.0	87.4
=35 Swansea	80.6	78.5	22.0	121	82.2	87.4
37 Soas, London	73.5	75.4	22.9	158	79.5	87.3
38 Nottingham Trent	82.5	83.8	4.6	117	85.5	86.4
39 Central Lancashire	91.1	83.6	4.4	102*	—	86.3
=40 Coventry	82.7	81.5	1.6	112	87.1	85.8
=40 Sussex	68.8	67.2	25.1	134	86.8	85.8
42 West of England	80.2	81.2	5.5	108	87.7	85.7
43 Reading	75.7	73.9	29.3	125	76.6	85.6
44 Cardiff	61.4	63.4	32.0	154	84.6	85.5
45 Hertfordshire	97.7	96.6	0.9	90	70.7	85.3
46 Bangor	75.6	85.0	23.4	97*	—	85.2
=47 Heriot-Watt	67.1	71.3	18.8	149	83.3	85.1
=47 Oxford Brookes	77.9	79.8	5.1	118	85.7	85.1
49 Dundee	78.2	79.8	12.1	157	69.2	84.7

Economics cont

	Teaching quality %	Student experience %	Research quality %	Entry standards (UCAS points)	Graduate prospects %	Overall score
=50 Aberdeen	63.0	71.5	16.0	182	77.1	84.6
=50 Royal Holloway, London	73.3	77.0	31.3	122	72.7	84.6
52 Brighton	88.6	78.3	6.5	94	—	84.4
=53 Derby	86.1	86.3	0.9	97	—	84.1
=53 Salford	83.3	79.2	5.9	109	—	84.1
55 East London	89.1	87.8	0.8	73	—	83.0
56 Keele	71.9	71.9	10.2	94	89.8	82.9
57 Hull	72.4	69.4	10.2	119	81.9	82.4
=58 Bradford	77.5	71.2	12.7	107	—	82.2
=58 Leeds Beckett	79.1	80.3	0.8	101	80.0	82.2
=58 Manchester Metropolitan	73.7	74.8	4.7	114	81.6	82.2
61 Greenwich	77.8	76.5	3.3	110	78.4	82.0
62 Sheffield Hallam	80.4	78.5	—	104	78.0	81.9
63 Portsmouth	75.4	76.0	9.5	106	76.8	81.7
=64 Leicester	63.3	71.1	21.4	128	72.5	80.5
=64 Plymouth	83.1	83.5	13.1	117	56.3	80.5
66 City, London	70.9	72.9	15.1	127	68.0	80.3
67 Goldsmiths, London	72.3	64.3	16.8	104	—	80.1
68 Anglia Ruskin	80.6	77.3	3.4	77*	71.4	78.8
69 De Montfort	75.4	74.9	10.7	94*	67.6	78.6
70 Huddersfield	75.6	73.3	4.1	109	66.7	78.3
71 Kingston	82.9	80.0	9.2	87	59.1	78.1
72 Cardiff Metropolitan	77.3	74.1	—	102	66.7	77.7
73 Brunel London	65.9	68.6	9.9	106	69.2	76.8
74 Birmingham City	68.8	72.0	1.3	101	63.6	74.8
75 Middlesex	58.9	57.8	10.5	100	—	73.5

Employed in high-skilled job	67%	Employed in lower-skilled job and studying	1%
Employed in high-skilled job and studying	7%	Employed in lower-skilled job	13%
Studying	8%	Unemployed	4%
High skilled work (median) salary	£29,000	Low/medium skilled salary	£20,000

Education

The Education table is a little different to the others in our *Guide*, due to the extra column it includes to accommodate inspection data for the universities in England by Ofsted. Eight universities, all in the top 20 overall, tie for the best scores from Ofsted.

Teacher training BEd degrees – the most common route into primary teaching – had more than 46,300 applications and 8,770 enrolments in the 2019 cycle. Academic Studies in Education degrees are also encompassed in our ranking, and garnered over 32,300 applications and 9,490 new undergraduates in the same admissions cycle. Student numbers in both declined in 2019 but remain well above the levels seen when higher fees were introduced in 2012.

Secondary school teachers are more likely to take the Postgraduate Certificate in Education, or to train through the Teach First or Schools Direct programmes, which are not included in our table's statistics. Our focus exclusively on undergraduate provision explains the absence of some of the best-known education departments, which only offer postgraduate courses. Prime examples are University College London's Institute of Education, ranked top in the world for education by QS, and Oxford, which was the top-scorer in the Research Excellence Framework in this field.

Cambridge combines the academic study of education with other subjects but does not offer Qualified Teacher Status. It takes the number one spot this year – without being first in any of the individual measures. Glasgow, which topped the table two years ago, is second this time and ties with Strathclyde in having the highest entry standards. Last year's number one university in our Education ranking, West of Scotland, takes fourth place this year. All eight Scottish institutions in the table appear in the top 18 places. They benefit from the favourable UCAS tariff conversion for Scottish secondary qualifications.

Students at tenth-ranked Sussex expressed the highest levels of satisfaction with the quality of teaching on their course in the most recent National Student Survey (NSS). Bolton, 41= overall, ranks second for satisfaction with teaching quality tieing with 54th-ranked Kingston. Students at the West of England gave the top score for the broader undergraduate experience in the NSS, followed by those at Southampton – which is 13th overall – and at Bolton, once again. Results for satisfaction all the way through the table go no lower than 69% for teaching quality and 61.7% for the broad experience, both at Bath Spa.

Only 13 of the 84 universities in our table averaged above 150 UCAS points in the 2019 cycle, and although entry standards are not generally high, demand for places is competitive, especially on BEd degrees – which attracted more than five applications per enrolment. Academic Studies in Education degrees averaged a more accessible rate of over three applications per place.

Education sits 30th in our employment ranking of 67 subjects. Variations in the demands for new primary and secondary teaching staff in different parts of the country create differing employment scores at universities. Results from the new Graduate Outcomes survey revealed that over 70% of graduates were in professional employment or further study 15 months after finishing their degrees. West of Scotland and Royal Conservatoire of Scotland did the best – 100% of their education graduates achieved the top outcomes, and universities north of the border occupy eight of the top ten places for graduate prospects. Northumbria is the top-ranked university from the rest of the UK in our employment measure, with 91% of graduates in high-skilled jobs or postgraduate study.

Education	Teaching quality	Student experience	Research quality	OFSTED Rating	Entry standards (UCAS points)	Graduate prospects	Overall score
1 Cambridge	—	—	36.6	4	186	—	100.0
2 Glasgow	82.7	77.1	32.5	—	200	91	98.0
3 Strathclyde	86.3	81.5	19.8	—	200	90	97.5
=4 Warwick	90.8	87.9	43.6	3.7	139	—	97.3
=4 West of Scotland	89.0	86.8	7.5		186	100	97.3
6 Dundee	90.0	86.8	11.7		183	94	97.0
7 Edinburgh	81.3	79.9	23.1		187	99	96.7

Education cont

		Teaching quality	Student experience	Research quality	OFSTED Rating	Entry standards (UCAS points)	Graduate prospects	Overall score
8	Birmingham	84.3	83.7	40.9	4	148	75	95.3
9	Stirling	79.0	71.8	29.2	—	182	93	94.5
10	Sussex	93.5	86.2	28.7	3.5	136	—	94.1
11	Royal Conservatoire of Scotland	80.4	74.6	—	—	193	100	94.0
12	Durham	76.1	68.8	38.9	4	151	87	93.7
13	Southampton	85.4	89.3	41.1	3	141	80	91.6
14	St Mary's, Twickenham	91.5	88.6	1.8	4	111	83	91.0
=15	Brighton	85.8	81.8	1.6	4	126	86	90.5
=15	University College London	77.6	75.9	40.2	4	129	66	90.5
17	Aberdeen	77.9	73.7	7.6	—	171	91	89.9
=18	Ulster	88.1	82.4	27.5	—	115	—	89.4
=18	Winchester	86.0	83.8	2.2	4	123	76	89.4
20	Bangor	75.5	74.7	39.6	—	132	82	89.3
21	Keele	76.8	70.2	25.0	3.5	152	81	89.2
=22	Reading	85.8	82.8	25.8	3	131	80	88.5
=22	Sheffield	81.6	81.4	32.9	3	141	77	88.5
24	Brunel London	83.6	85.1	20.4	4	114	60	88.4
25	York	78.8	75.1	43.3	3	130	78	88.0
26	Gloucestershire	85.5	84.9	—	3.7	125	72	87.3
=27	Cardiff	73.3	71.2	35.3	—	172	58	87.2
=27	Liverpool John Moores	88.9	88.8	3.0	3.5	134	62	87.2
=27	Northumbria	84.2	79.8	—	3	147	91	87.2
=27	Plymouth Marjon	90.8	88.5	—	3.3	123	76	87.2
31	Derby	87.6	86.2	1.1	3.4	128	71	86.7
32	West of England	91.0	89.7	5.3	3	117	73	85.8
33	Birmingham City	86.2	85.0	1.8	3	121	83	85.5
34	West London	86.8	85.2	7.6	—	116	—	85.4
=35	Liverpool Hope	90.1	88.1	7.3	3	121	65	85.1
=35	Newcastle	77.5	71.6	33.1	3.1	125	69	85.1
37	Teesside	85.9	81.6	15.0	—	110	69	85.0
38	Chester	74.6	75.1	1.4	3.7	124	79	84.9
39	Wales Trinity St David	86.1	81.7	—	—	150	56	84.8
40	Sheffield Hallam	78.3	72.7	2.0	3.7	120	74	84.6
=41	Bolton	92.1	89.2	3.1	—	105	64	84.5
=41	South Wales	83.5	81.9	—	—	122	74	84.5
=43	Bedfordshire	89.2	84.0	3.1	3.1	110	71	84.3
=43	Worcester	86.5	86.0	2.5	3	117	74	84.3
=43	York St John	83.1	82.9	1.5	3.3	108	78	84.3
46	Coventry	79.3	68.8	18.1	—	132	—	84.2
47	Leeds	74.7	70.7	31.6	3	143	62	84.1
48	Plymouth	82.5	80.8	9.4	3	123	73	84.0
=49	Greenwich	81.3	76.6	0.8	3.3	128	71	83.8

=49	Roehampton	78.2	77.0	20.2	3	108	79	83.8
51	Nottingham Trent	82.6	82.2	2.6	3.3	123	64	83.7
52	Cumbria	84.3	79.5	0.4	3	117	78	83.5
53	Huddersfield	84.3	78.6	5.9	3.1	127	64	83.4
54	Kingston	92.1	83.4	—	3	110	65	83.3
55	Edge Hill	80.4	79.3	1.4	3	126	77	83.2
56	Staffordshire	87.5	82.3	7.6	3	128	55	83.1
57	Anglia Ruskin	90.4	88.0	0.8	3	107	63	83.0
58	Chichester	75.4	74.4	—	3	125	89	82.9
=59	Hull	85.2	81.1	5.0	3	129	60	82.8
=59	Leeds Beckett	84.0	78.9	2.3	3	111	75	82.8
=59	Newman	84.6	83.5	2.2	3	116	69	82.8
62	Manchester Metropolitan	81.1	79.6	5.8	3	128	66	82.7
=63	Wolverhampton	83.9	80.3	1.9	3	118	69	82.5
=63	Bishop Grosseteste	83.2	79.8	1.4	3	113	74	82.5
=65	Canterbury Christ Church	82.0	76.5	2.8	3	111	77	82.4
=65	Hertfordshire	85.2	82.0	—	3	112	70	82.4
=65	Middlesex	79.8	74.6	14.9	3	118	67	82.4
=68	Central Lancashire	79.5	81.3	—	—	122	67	82.0
=68	Oxford Brookes	75.2	72.3	3.3	3	122	82	82.0
70	Northampton	83.0	78.6	1.8	3	110	71	81.8
71	Leeds Trinity	80.9	78.8	—	3	113	73	81.6
72	Sunderland	79.0	77.1	3.8	3	119	68	81.4
73	East Anglia	74.6	75.0	27.2	3	123	50	80.9
74	Bath Spa	69.0	61.7	3.2	3.7	102	78	80.8
75	Aberystwyth	84.3	84.5	—	—	120	50	80.6
76	Cardiff Metropolitan	75.7	71.1	—	—	121	71	80.1
77	Portsmouth	80.5	74.5	—	3.3	118	51	80.0
78	De Montfort	73.4	73.1	11.2	—	120*	60	79.4
79	London South Bank	83.6	81.9	—	3	109	48	79.0
80	East London	84.2	80.8	2.8	3	119	39	78.9
81	Suffolk	77.1	70.1	—	—	106	69	78.7
82	London Metropolitan	81.8	76.2	3.3	3.1	113	38	77.9
83	Glyndŵr	77.2	68.4	—	—	122	56	77.8
84	Goldsmiths, London	78.7	73.1	17.4	3	99	42	77.7

Employed in high-skilled job	61%	Employed in lower-skilled job and studying	1%
Employed in high-skilled job and studying	2%	Employed in lower-skilled job	26%
Studying	6%	Unemployed	4%
High skilled work (median) salary	£24,000	Low/medium skilled salary	£17,100

Electrical and Electronic Engineering

Imperial College has closed the gap on top-ranked Cambridge this year, partly through a perfect 100% score for graduate prospects, with all of its electronic and electrical engineering graduates being in professional employment or postgraduate study 15 months after finishing their courses.

Cambridge has the highest entry standards by a clear margin though, and its submission to the Research Excellence Framework achieved the top scores. The QS rankings rate Cambridge in the top four globally, and Imperial only three places lower.

Southampton is in third place of our table for the second year running, with strong performances in all measures. Exeter has re-entered the top ten, having slipped to 18th last year, and Aberdeen has shot up from 40th to ninth place, helped by the fifth-highest entry standards. Bristol has also joined the top 10 at seventh, up nine places.

In the sections of the National Student Survey (NSS) that focus on teaching quality 27th-ranked Derby came out top, and others further down the overall table also did well, notably Westminster, at 46th= and West of England, 40th – which came second and third respectively. Cardiff, fourth for teaching quality, was unbeaten in the sections of the NSS relating to the broader undergraduate experience.

UCL and Surrey tied with Imperial in having 100% of graduates in the top career outcomes of high-skilled work or further study. Across all universities more than seven out of every ten electrical and electronic engineering graduates were in professional-level jobs, the new Graduate Outcomes survey showed. A further one in ten was engaged in postgraduate study or combining it with a high-skilled job. The outcomes add up to a healthy 23rd place out of the 67 subject areas in our employment ranking, although the subject placed 14th last year.

The 2019 application cycle saw a resurgence in the demand for places, following recent years in which applications have dipped. With over five applications per place competition is stiff, but a bit less so than in other branches of engineering. Maths A-level or equivalent is required by the leading universities, as is a second science such as physics, electronics or chemistry.

Electrical and Electronic Engineering	Teaching quality %	Student experience %	Research quality %	Entry standards (UCAS points)	Graduate prospects %	Overall score
1 Cambridge	—	—	67.0	220	96.3	100.0
2 Imperial College London	74.4	78.5	65.0	193	100.0	97.7
3 Southampton	77.0	81.5	53.3	173	97.6	95.4
4 Heriot-Watt	79.5	82.5	47.8	174	95.7	95.1
5 Strathclyde	76.7	77.5	41.7	211	91.3	94.9
6 Queen's, Belfast	84.0	80.7	47.3	152	93.8	93.9
7 Bristol	74.5	81.2	52.3	172	93.5	93.7
8 Exeter	82.4	86.1	36.4	151	95.7	93.1
9 Aberdeen	81.0	78.9	28.4	187	—	93.0
10 Leeds	76.1	80.5	41.8	180	91.7	92.9
=11 Nottingham	84.6	87.2	40.8	145	87.0	92.1
=11 University College London	69.5	74.1	59.0	149	100.0	92.1
13 Surrey	77.7	80.2	36.3	145	100.0	91.8
14 Glasgow	71.3	72.4	47.2	204	83.8	91.6
15 Cardiff	86.1	88.2	30.2	139	87.5	90.9
16 Manchester	77.9	77.1	37.0	167	87.2	90.5
17 Loughborough	80.5	82.7	23.8	150	89.8	89.5
18 Edinburgh	74.2	81.8	50.3	164	77.3	89.4
19 Bath	70.6	77.8	28.6	163	95.8	89.3
=20 Aston	73.5	77.9	25.8	169	86.7	88.2

=20	Robert Gordon	83.0	83.9	8.8	145	90.3	88.2
=20	Sheffield	77.7	85.4	42.6	127	82.9	88.2
23	Swansea	79.7	81.6	45.5	122	81.8	88.0
24	Lancaster	69.0	76.8	41.6	156	—	87.9
25	York	75.7	77.7	21.4	136	95.2	87.5
26	Liverpool	79.3	82.2	30.4	125	—	87.1
27	Derby	90.4	86.7	6.7	128	81.8	86.9
=28	Birmingham	67.5	68.7	32.1	157	92.4	86.8
=28	Newcastle	71.6	81.4	39.4	135	84.0	86.8
30	Queen Mary, London	67.4	69.0	41.9	134	93.5	86.5
31	Northumbria	78.0	86.1	30.7	145	73.3	86.3
32	Coventry	82.2	82.9	10.3	121	85.7	85.3
33	Liverpool John Moores	79.6	72.6	8.7	155	82.4	85.1
34	Essex	75.7	73.0	34.3	123	—	84.9
35	Kent	73.9	75.4	27.3	131	84.1	84.8
36	Hull	75.9	81.8	16.5	133	—	84.6
37	Sussex	72.7	77.1	24.0	138	—	84.5
38	Bangor	81.8	85.0	31.9	110	72.4	84.4
39	Solent, Southampton	83.6	80.4	—	128	83.3	84.2
40	West of England	86.4	82.8	10.6	129	68.4	83.3
41	Huddersfield	77.6	77.2	10.2	126	82.6	83.2
=42	Central Lancashire	74.0	77.2	11.7	130*	83.3	83.0
=42	Ulster	71.9	70.0	22.8	116	88.2	83.0
44	London South Bank	75.4	74.8	19.6	124	—	82.9
45	Salford	84.2	78.2	4.4	133	73.0	82.7
=46	City, London	73.3	67.1	23.1	127	82.6	82.6
=46	Westminster	86.7	81.0	2.9	110	76.9	82.6
=48	Brunel London	75.6	73.4	26.4	135	71.4	82.5
=48	Plymouth	69.7	74.2	13.3	124	88.9	82.5
50	Manchester Metropolitan	74.3	71.4	16.3	125	82.6	82.4
51	Reading	71.2	71.2	16.3	—	84.2	82.1
52	Birmingham City	80.4	77.8	—	144	71.5	81.8
=53	Portsmouth	74.7	74.0	7.2	103	89.1	81.5
=53	Sheffield Hallam	77.8	79.5	17.8	116	71.8	81.5
55	Teesside	80.9	78.9	5.8	133	68.2	81.1
56	Brighton	73.0	72.7	7.4	115*	81.8	80.3
57	Glasgow Caledonian	76.0	74.7	4.7	148	64.5	79.7
58	Greenwich	74.3	72.6	7.5	109	—	78.8
59	Chester	75.9	72.4	7.1	103*	—	78.6
60	Staffordshire	72.8	74.1	5.7	111*	—	78.4
61	Hertfordshire	74.9	80.2	16.5	103	63.6	78.0
62	De Montfort	57.0	58.7	12.5	112*	—	72.2

Employed in high-skilled job	71%	Employed in lower-skilled job and studying	0%
Employed in high-skilled job and studying	2%	Employed in lower-skilled job	12%
Studying	8%	Unemployed	6%
High skilled work (median) salary	£28,350	Low/medium skilled salary	£20,850

English

In the latest reshuffle of our English table, Oxford has come out top. Unlike many other subjects where the same university hangs on to the number one spot for years on end, the front runners in English change frequently. Oxford has not outdone all universities on any one measure, but a strong set of results across them all includes a top-three score for graduate prospects and the fifth highest entry standards. Durham was first last year and takes third this, while St Andrews was first two years ago and remains in second position in our current edition.

Strathclyde has climbed from 32nd to fifth place this year, a huge leap that is down to much improved graduate prospects and slightly higher entry standards. Queen Mary, London – which was shortlisted for our University of the Year award – was the top scorer in the Research Excellence Framework, but its mid-range entry standards hold it back from featuring higher up the main table.

Applications to study English have been declining and fell again in 2019 for the ninth time in a decade. They are more than a third lower than in 2010. The drop in enrolments has been less steep, but still significant, at around 25% over the same period. But English is still one of UK higher education's biggest recruiters, as reflected in the length of our table – which stretches to more than 100 universities.

The subject offers graduate prospects that typically occupy the lower end of our employment ranking, as they do this year, in 51st place out of 67 subject areas. Bishop Grosseteste, though, which ranks 22nd= overall, had 90.6% – the highest proportion – of graduates in professional work or postgraduate study when the Graduate Outcomes survey conducted its census 15 months after they had finished their degrees. Aston, 33rd in the table, came second in this measure.

At 15th Edinburgh Napier is the highest-ranked post-1992 university, but Solent (78=) got the highest scores in the sections of the National Student Survey that focus on teaching quality, in which Bolton and Bishop Grosseteste came second and third – in that order. Aberystwyth (20=) leads the field for student satisfaction with the broader undergraduate experience.

Entry standards are generally high at the leading universities, and 24 institutions averaged 150 UCAS points or more among 2019's intake of new undergraduates – although only St Andrews had higher than 200 points. At the other end of the scale 15 universities in our table averaged scores lower than 100 in the UCAS tariff in the same recruitment round. English literature A-level or equivalent is usually required by the leading universities.

English	Teaching quality %	Student experience %	Research quality %	Entry standards (UCAS points)	Graduate prospects %	Overall score
1 Oxford	—	—	50.7	194	87.0	100.0
2 St Andrews	89.6	85.8	60.4	205	63.0	99.1
3 Durham	81.1	72.7	57.9	197	82.6	98.7
4 York	89.2	82.6	61.5	155	74.0	97.2
5 Strathclyde	83.0	76.9	39.4	198	82.2	97.0
6 Cambridge	—	—	50.0	195	82.5	96.9
7 Glasgow	80.3	79.3	52.0	185	75.0	95.8
8 University College London	74.8	62.9	61.7	179	84.4	95.6
9 Exeter	82.1	78.8	46.2	166	80.9	95.2

10 Loughborough	87.9	85.9	32.4	143	85.2	94.7
11 Warwick	79.1	70.5	59.8	168	76.2	94.6
12 Lancaster	81.7	78.9	47.0	151	81.6	94.2
13 Nottingham	77.9	72.9	56.6	150	81.8	93.9
14 King's College London	79.6	69.2	47.6	165	78.0	93.0
15 Edinburgh Napier	93.0	89.7	37.9	159	59.1	92.7
16 Manchester	79.2	72.9	49.1	163	73.8	92.4
=17 Dundee	87.6	85.9	32.8	170	64.1	92.1
=17 Liverpool	78.6	71.2	47.8	134	84.8	92.1
=17 Southampton	86.2	81.1	38.4	144	73.7	92.1
=20 Aberystwyth	94.9	94.6	31.2	135	63.6	91.9
=20 Birmingham	80.3	77.9	37.0	156	77.7	91.9
=22 Bishop Grosseteste	95.0	86.8	6.7	115	90.6	91.8
=22 Royal Holloway, London	83.2	76.9	49.9	132	75.0	91.8
=24 Hull	89.6	87.1	22.7	126	81.8	91.7
=24 Stirling	86.8	79.1	29.8	173	67.4	91.7
26 Surrey	80.8	80.9	39.1	141	77.6	91.4
27 Sussex	77.8	73.0	45.6	139	80.7	91.2
28 Bangor	84.2	82.9	46.3	119	74.0	91.0
29 Queen Mary, London	75.0	70.6	64.0	134	71.8	90.6
30 Swansea	80.1	77.5	43.6	133	74.8	90.3
31 Leeds	77.5	73.0	38.6	157	74.3	90.2
32 Bournemouth	88.3	83.4	15.1	120	84.2	90.0
33 Aston	79.9	78.7	23.4	124	88.8	89.8
34 Sheffield	73.4	71.7	42.2	150	78.0	89.7
35 Aberdeen	81.5	79.7	46.3	174	52.2	89.5
36 Queen's, Belfast	74.3	69.1	53.1	152	68.9	89.4
37 Newcastle	74.5	69.5	54.3	141	71.2	89.3
38 Edinburgh	72.6	67.9	43.6	183	64.4	88.9
39 Bristol	72.6	64.6	30.0	169	79.3	88.8
40 Bedfordshire	86.6	82.8	45.8	101	66.7	88.5
41 Leicester	81.3	77.7	45.4	125	66.7	88.4
42 Edge Hill	90.5	88.2	12.1	121	73.2	88.3
43 Huddersfield	85.1	75.5	29.9	109	78.2	88.2
44 Ulster	88.0	84.1	35.1	113	65.1	88.1
45 Teesside	90.9	88.0	15.6	106	73.9	87.9
=46 Kent	77.3	73.3	47.3	135	64.6	87.6
=46 Reading	79.5	75.6	36.3	119	74.1	87.6
48 East Anglia	77.6	73.1	36.2	147	67.5	87.5
49 Oxford Brookes	85.3	82.2	27.8	117	68.8	87.3
50 Essex	76.4	73.0	37.7	113	78.4	87.2
=51 Brunel London	86.4	85.0	30.9	97	69.4	86.9
=51 Cardiff	78.3	70.1	35.1	145	66.7	86.9
=53 Birmingham City	85.1	80.6	30.9	117	64.6	86.6
=53 Nottingham Trent	89.6	84.6	30.0	113	59.6	86.6
55 Liverpool Hope	86.9	82.6	26.9	103	68.2	86.3

English cont

	Teaching quality %	Student experience %	Research quality %	Entry standards (UCAS points)	Graduate prospects %	Overall score
=56 London South Bank	94.5	86.1	12.8	97*	—	86.0
=56 Roehampton	87.2	86.4	20.8	99	69.6	86.0
58 Bolton	95.3	93.7	14.4	80	—	85.9
=59 Coventry	83.5	79.8	18.1	113	72.3	85.6
=59 Northumbria	88.2	79.6	27.2	126	56.3	85.6
=59 West of England	85.7	83.1	35.4	108	58.6	85.6
=62 Buckingham	89.2	84.5	—	106	76.7	85.4
=62 Kingston	84.2	74.3	15.7	102	79.0	85.4
64 Sheffield Hallam	82.9	79.5	14.6	104	77.0	85.2
=65 Manchester Metropolitan	82.9	79.5	29.0	119	60.8	85.0
=65 Plymouth	90.8	87.4	30.5	120	46.3	85.0
67 Derby	88.5	79.1	13.5	115	—	84.9
=68 Central Lancashire	84.2	79.2	9.9	110	72.3	84.3
=68 Westminster	83.3	79.0	28.9	103	63.2	84.3
=70 Keele	82.7	79.3	29.8	111	60.2	84.2
=70 York St John	92.3	87.3	9.7	97	62.8	84.2
72 Portsmouth	88.6	86.4	17.1	105	59.6	84.1
73 Chester	90.2	87.2	10.7	113	57.8	83.9
74 Worcester	87.2	80.8	8.2	108	67.4	83.8
75 De Montfort	80.0	80.5	24.1	104*	64.8	83.4
=76 Leeds Trinity	81.9	81.8	6.2	94	76.9	83.3
=76 Liverpool John Moores	82.7	81.1	17.9	137	53.6	83.3
=78 Greenwich	82.4	82.1	14.4	104	66.4	83.0
=78 Solent, Southampton	95.8	87.6	—	106	56.5	83.0
80 Northampton	82.3	85.1	15.3	104	—	82.9
=81 Lincoln	85.1	82.1	16.2	119	54.7	82.6
=81 Newman	89.0	84.5	9.6	103	58.8	82.6
83 Salford	85.9	80.9	7.8	109	60.8	82.0
84 Bath Spa	80.2	69.3	23.5	108	63.1	81.9
=85 Cardiff Metropolitan	84.9	78.5	—	100	68.4	81.4
=85 Sunderland	80.3	67.2	15.3	103	68.4	81.4
=87 Middlesex	81.6	85.9	11.0	95	—	81.0
=87 Winchester	81.8	77.7	—	110	67.0	81.0
=89 Anglia Ruskin	83.7	77.6	16.3	99	54.8	80.2
=89 Chichester	75.0	68.1	16.3	104*	67.6	80.2
91 Goldsmiths, London	70.4	59.9	34.9	116	60.4	80.1
92 Wolverhampton	81.8	80.0	7.6	88	63.6	79.9
93 Leeds Beckett	84.9	77.7	11.0	94	53.4	79.1
94 Canterbury Christ Church	79.4	71.0	8.0	97	60.7	78.3
95 Suffolk	89.6	83.0	—	97	46.4	78.1
96 Gloucestershire	75.7	70.2	9.3	92	63.8	77.8
97 Hertfordshire	81.5	80.0	7.8	97	46.6	76.8

98 South Wales		77.4	73.6	12.8	117	42.9	76.5
99 Falmouth		82.1	74.4	—	114	42.3	75.6
100 Brighton		68.7	60.4	16.2	104	57.3	75.4
101 St Mary's, Twickenham		63.4	70.6	14.6	88	—	72.5

Employed in high-skilled job	48%	Employed in lower-skilled job and studying	1%
Employed in high-skilled job and studying	4%	Employed in lower-skilled job	28%
Studying	13%	Unemployed	6%
High skilled work (median) salary	£23,000	Low/medium skilled salary	£18,125

Food Science

Degrees in food science range from nutrition and dietetics – many of which offer opportunities to study alongside doctors, nurses and other health professionals in hospitals – to food manufacturing and professional cookery. London South Bank offers a baking science and technology degree. The subject is consistently inside the top 30 of our employment ranking, where is has landed comfortably at 26th place this year.

Glasgow has retained its position at the top of the Food Science table, having entered at number one last year. Its entry standards are much the highest, and Glasgow is the only university whose entrants averaged more than 200 UCAS points in 2019. Only eight universities averaged 150 points or more, seven of which are in the table's top ten. The older institutions dominate the upper end of the main ranking – with the exception of Glasgow Caledonian, the top-ranked post-1992 university, in third place.

Abertay achieved stellar scores in the sections of the National Student Survey that focus on teaching quality and on the wider undergraduate experience – and comes top of both measures by a long chalk. Student satisfaction is generally high in food science, with more than half the universities in our table achieving scores above 80% for teaching quality and the wider experience.

In terms of academic research into food science, Queen's Belfast, Reading and King's College London had the leading scores – in that order – in the Research Excellence Framework.

Food Science	Teaching quality %	Student experience %	Research quality %	Entry standards (UCAS points)	Graduate prospects %	Overall score
1 Glasgow	79.2	86.1	42.3	214	—	100.0
2 Surrey	83.5	88.3	37.5	160	90.0	93.5
3 Glasgow Caledonian	88.7	83.7	8.1	188	—	92.6
4 Leeds	82.4	88.3	36.8	166	82.8	92.3
=5 Queen's, Belfast	76.7	81.9	56.3	150	83.3	91.8
=5 Reading	82.6	81.3	50.7	133	89.7	91.8
7 King's College London	68.9	68.2	46.8	157	100.0	90.9
8 Ulster	84.3	88.2	42.5	135	80.6	90.1
9 Newcastle	75.5	78.9	28.4	134	93.2	87.4
10 Abertay	99.7	98.6	—	154	63.0	87.1
11 Robert Gordon	81.5	84.1	4.9	146	91.7	86.7

Food Science cont	Teaching quality %	Student experience %	Research quality %	Entry standards (UCAS points)	Graduate prospects %	Overall score
=12 Manchester Metropolitan	84.4	84.0	12.0	134	85.7	86.2
=12 Plymouth	78.8	80.5	17.4	132	91.5	86.2
14 Chester	79.1	82.3	12.0	119	100.0	86.1
15 Nottingham	73.4	70.2	36.4	122	87.8	85.0
=16 Bournemouth	91.1	89.7	4.7	122	77.8	84.6
=16 Liverpool John Moores	84.8	81.5	6.0	146	76.9	84.6
18 Coventry	80.4	79.7	—	128	96.2	84.5
19 Oxford Brookes	81.2	83.3	3.0	113	94.4	83.7
20 Sheffield Hallam	87.9	88.3	3.7	118	78.5	83.4
21 Northumbria	75.5	76.2	14.0	133	84.6	83.3
22 Hertfordshire	76.2	78.6	14.8	114	88.2	82.7
=23 Cardiff Metropolitan	77.7	73.6	—	127	89.5	81.8
=23 Queen Margaret, Edinburgh	76.4	67.7	—	171	72.4	81.8
25 Roehampton	87.5	86.9	20.6	117	56.5	81.4
26 Greenwich	70.6	75.9	19.5	130*	—	80.9
27 Leeds Beckett	83.9	80.7	—	113	78.1	80.5
28 Harper Adams	85.0	81.4	5.7	96	77.8	80.0
29 Edge Hill	82.9	84.2	—	135	60.7	79.5
30 Huddersfield	89.2	93.2	—	129*	44.6	78.4
31 St Mary's, Twickenham	57.3	65.8	—	125	93.2	76.9
32 Bath Spa	81.7	82.7	—	91	63.2	75.3
33 Westminster	72.2	75.9	—	89	73.9	74.3

Employed in high-skilled job	66%	Employed in lower-skilled job and studying		0%
Employed in high-skilled job and studying	3%	Employed in lower-skilled job		17%
Studying	11%	Unemployed		4%
High skilled work (median) salary	£24,000	Low/medium skilled salary		£18,500

French

French remains the most popular language at degree level. It has not been immune to the continuing long decline of modern languages, however. Only 275 students began French degrees in autumn 2020, a record low and 60% fewer than in 2012 when £9,000 tuition fees were introduced. Our French table has contracted in size, from 48 universities in our previous edition to 42 this year.

The falling numbers have not caused entry standards to slip or competition to cool off. There were more than six applications to the place in 2019. More than half of the table's universities averaged above 150 UCAS points among their 2019 student intake, and three averaged at least 200. Candidates often come from high-achieving independent schools. Almost all undergraduates arrive with French A-level, or equivalent, although many universities will teach the language from scratch, especially if it forms part of a joint honours degree.

In a year of major reshuffles to our French table the gap has closed between Cambridge at the top and the rest of the universities. Strathclyde has moved into second place, just one percentage point behind Cambridge, its position boosted from 4= last year by averaging the second-highest entry standards. Cambridge still leads on research, but its entry standards fell below 200 UCAS points and rank fourth. Aberdeen has shot up 31 places to fifth and Southampton has also joined the top ten, tying with Warwick in sixth place. Last year's runner up, Surrey, has dropped to 22nd this year, while Sheffield has gone from 6th to 28th and Exeter has moved down from ranking ninth last year to 20th this year.

Bangor, 16= overall, leads on the sections of the National Student Survey that focus on satisfaction with teaching quality, followed closely by 19th-ranked Leicester – which came top for student satisfaction with the broader experience.

Durham had the best-employed graduates in the new Graduate Outcomes survey, with 91% in professional jobs or postgraduate study 15 months after finishing their French degrees. Oxford and Liverpool universities also had over 90% of graduates engaged in the top two career outcomes. As a subject French falls in the upper half of our employment ranking, in 32nd place.

French	Teaching quality %	Student experience %	Research quality %	Entry standards (UCAS points)	Graduate prospects %	Overall score
1 Cambridge	—	—	54.0	197	86.8	100.0
2 Strathclyde	87.7	81.1	42.0	217	84.6	99.0
3 Oxford	—	—	41.3	194	90.1	96.9
4 St Andrews	93.4	89.8	26.4	207	80.5	96.8
5 Aberdeen	91.7	91.8	29.3	181	—	96.1
=6 Southampton	89.8	84.0	42.7	158	78.8	94.5
=6 Warwick	82.8	79.2	45.2	164	84.4	94.5
8 Queen's, Belfast	82.3	79.3	53.6	155	71.7	92.5
9 Manchester	78.9	71.2	48.9	156	82.6	92.4
10 University College London	74.4	66.9	43.7	171	88.9	92.3
=11 Durham	73.5	68.5	34.6	185	91.0	92.0
=11 Liverpool	81.9	83.7	33.4	139	90.0	92.0
13 Bath	84.9	82.4	27.4	153	86.0	91.6
14 Glasgow	77.5	80.4	26.3	220	73.9	91.4
15 Royal Holloway, London	79.5	73.8	48.3	147*	—	91.2
=16 Bangor	95.8	94.4	39.6	113	67.6	90.9
=16 York	84.8	82.7	37.3	142	—	90.9
18 Bristol	80.4	74.6	36.0	160	79.7	90.3
19 Leicester	95.2	95.5	16.9	132	—	90.1
20 Exeter	79.7	79.0	35.1	156	78.2	89.9
21 Stirling	84.5	77.9	29.8	157	—	89.7
22 Surrey	79.9	82.0	39.1	138	—	89.4
23 Lancaster	75.3	71.9	47.0	148	—	89.3
24 Newcastle	80.2	79.0	36.3	155	74.0	89.2
=25 Birmingham	74.7	73.1	33.7	177*	77.8	89.1
=25 Nottingham	75.2	71.8	39.4	137	85.3	89.1

French cont

		Teaching quality %	Student experience %	Research quality %	Entry standards (UCAS points)	Graduate prospects %	Overall score
27	Reading	80.6	80.3	41.7	124	—	88.7
=28	King's College London	79.4	75.7	42.1	161	65.8	88.4
=28	Sheffield	77.6	78.9	41.2	151	70.5	88.4
30	Leeds	84.7	82.0	30.6	161	66.3	88.3
31	Heriot-Watt	81.7	85.2	26.3	156	67.2	87.0
32	Kent	87.1	84.9	41.9	110	62.5	86.9
33	Queen Mary, London	80.8	82.3	35.1	133	68.6	86.8
=34	Aberystwyth	88.7	84.9	16.6	122*	—	85.5
=34	Cardiff	77.6	77.9	32.5	144	67.3	85.5
36	Aston	85.4	84.0	23.4	116	—	85.4
37	Edinburgh	68.8	67.6	30.3	184	69.2	85.1
=38	Manchester Metropolitan	82.8	77.2	29.0	100	—	83.5
=38	Swansea	83.0	76.7	22.8	116*	—	83.5
40	Nottingham Trent	82.3	80.4	7.6	107	—	79.1
41	Chester	79.9	83.5	17.3	98	55.8	78.1
42	Westminster	74.6	73.4	2.0	114	—	74.9

Employed in high-skilled job	54%	Employed in lower-skilled job and studying	1%
Employed in high-skilled job and studying	4%	Employed in lower-skilled job	22%
Studying	14%	Unemployed	5%
High skilled work (median) salary	£25,000	Low/medium skilled salary	£19,500

General Engineering

For the second year running Bristol has pipped Cambridge to the post in our General Engineering table. The margin of victory is a slim 0.2% and the two universities are so evenly matched that they have been swapping first and second position for the last four editions of this *Guide*. Bristol received glowing feedback from students in the National Student Survey, it topped the measure for the overall student experience with 86% and scored 85.4% for teaching quality, tieing for second place in that measure with its neighbour West of England. Cambridge has the highest entry standards, better graduate prospects and achieved higher scores in the Research Excellence Framework – although third-ranked Oxford's submission was judged better still.

Coventry, ranked 26th overall, leads on teaching quality satisfaction and Bradford – one place below in the main table, also achieved excellent scores in the National Student Survey.

The subject is growing in popularity and numbers starting general engineering degrees topped 5,000 for the first time in 2019. The high spot follows a series of incremental rises over recent years, bar a minor dip in 2018. Students opting for the general strand of the subject gain the flexibility that the broad study of engineering allows in their future careers, while they also have the opportunity to specialise in a specific area of interest. Men still outnumber women at degree level, but the study of general engineering is more evenly split between the genders than the other engineering disciplines.

Maths and physics A-levels, or the equivalent, are usually required. Five universities averaged above 200 points in the UCAS tariff, and Cambridge went as high as 220 points. Entry is far more accessible at the other end of the table though. Aston, which ranks 19th overall and in the top ten for graduate prospects, averaged only 104 UCAS tariff points in 2019's intake.

The subject is a regular fixture at the upper end of our employment ranking, where it occupies 11th place this year. Of the engineering stable only civil did better, ranking eighth. More than 90% of graduates at ten universities (all of them in the top 20 overall) had secured professional jobs or were engaged in postgraduate study 15 months after finishing their degrees.

General Engineering

		Teaching quality %	Student experience %	Research quality %	Entry standards (UCAS points)	Graduate prospects %	Overall score
1	Bristol	85.4	86.0	52.3	213	90.9	100.0
2	Cambridge	73.3	79.9	67.0	220	96.3	99.8
3	Oxford	73.4	75.1	68.7	214	96.3	99.1
4	Imperial College	77.3	79.4	60.1	180	94.1	96.6
5	Heriot-Watt	78.8	77.7	47.8	181	—	94.6
6	Durham	72.9	74.5	39.4	207	93.4	93.9
7	Swansea	74.0	80.8	45.5	175	92.9	93.4
8	Warwick	72.1	73.4	47.2	163	92.8	91.4
9	Sheffield	76.0	80.9	51.4	171	77.8	91.3
10	Cardiff	74.6	79.9	30.2	160	95.0	90.8
11	King's College London	70.7	80.7	56.6	146	—	90.7
12	Loughborough	72.7	70.9	41.8	159	93.9	90.5
13	Liverpool	78.1	80.9	32.1	156	—	89.7
14	Lancaster	73.9	77.5	41.6	156	—	89.5
15	Glasgow	56.6	61.8	47.2	214	89.5	88.9
=16	Dundee	68.4	70.8	34.1	185	—	87.9
=16	Aberdeen	72.1	76.6	28.4	173	—	87.9
18	Surrey	74.6	72.5	30.8	163	—	87.7
19	Aston	80.0	80.0	20.6	104	92.3	86.5
20	Leicester	80.9	81.4	34.4	131	71.2	86.2
21	Ulster	74.9	79.3	22.8	131	86.8	86.1
22	West of England	85.4	85.0	10.6	121	—	85.8
23	Nottingham Trent	83.9	82.1	20.1	110	—	85.5
24	Exeter	67.5	65.9	36.4	160	80.0	85.1
25	Queen Mary, London	59.0	65.7	46.7	164	—	84.2
26	Coventry	86.1	82.5	10.3	105	—	84.1
27	Bradford	84.1	85.6	7.7	128	71.0	83.7
=28	Liverpool John Moores	76.1	79.5	14.2	149	70.0	83.1
=28	London South Bank	73.0	75.6	19.6	136	—	83.1
30	Strathclyde	78.1	77.1	—	166	70.0	82.5
31	Hull	76.1	76.7	16.5	111	—	81.5
32	Bournemouth	78.6	81.8	8.5	105	—	81.2
33	Glasgow Caledonian	70.2	68.7	4.7	148	80.0	81.0

General Engineering cont	Teaching quality %	Student experience %	Research quality %	Entry standards (UCAS points)	Graduate prospects %	Overall score
34 City	67.8	64.5	23.1	116	77.1	79.5
35 Edinburgh Napier	70.1	72.1	–	134	74.6	78.7
36 Greenwich	75.8	75.2	5.5	101	–	78.2
37 West of Scotland	72.9	64.9	9.0	–	68.8	77.1
38 Wolverhampton	77.7	72.8	–	98	55.6	74.2
39 Northampton	64.1	57.4	–	99	66.7	71.3

Employed in high-skilled job	71%	Employed in lower-skilled job and studying	0%
Employed in high-skilled job and studying	3%	Employed in lower-skilled job	8%
Studying	11%	Unemployed	6%
High skilled work (median) salary	£29,000	Low/medium skilled salary	£21,500

Geography & Environmental Sciences

Applications to study degrees in the science of aquatic and terrestrial environments recorded a new high in 2019, having increased by 10% on the year before. Enrolments went up a little more still, by 11%, to equal their highest point since 2007. The spotlight that Greta Thunberg, David Attenborough and others have shone on climate change is perhaps beginning to translate into greater interest in the subjects among young people. Physical geography did not follow the same pattern however, and both applications and enrolments declined – but only by a small margin. Human and social geography degrees had almost the same number of new students in 2019 as in the year before.

The top four universities in our table have swapped positions this year. Cambridge has regained the top spot it last held three years ago, while St Andrews – which has the highest entry grades – has dropped from first to fourth place. Durham and Oxford have each risen by one rank. UCL and Dundee have joined the top ten, helped by much improved satisfaction scores. Fifth-ranked LSE is unbeaten on graduate prospects this year, and sixth-ranked Bristol was the top scorer in the Research Excellence Framework.

Coventry, in 32= place overall, received the best results in the sections of the National Student Survey that focus on teaching quality. Chester's scores were close behind on the same measure, as were those for West of England – which came top for student satisfaction with the wider experience.

Geography and environmental sciences are just outside the top 30 of our employment measure. The new Graduate Outcomes survey showed that 54% of graduates were in professional jobs 15 months after finishing degrees, 15% had entered postgraduate study and 3% were combining the two. Twenty-two per cent had started out in lower-skilled jobs.

A science or maths A-level – as well as geography – is preferred for physical geography courses. For environmental science most of the leading universities will ask for two from biology, chemistry, maths, physics and geography A-levels or equivalent. The different branches make for varying entry scores.

Geography and Environmental Sciences	Teaching quality %	Student experience %	Research quality %	Entry standards (UCAS points)	Graduate prospects %	Overall score
1 Cambridge	—	—	57.3	199	94.9	100.0
2 Durham	84.9	83.4	55.0	182	85.9	97.8
3 Oxford	—	—	41.1	190	88.2	97.6
4 St Andrews	89.5	89.0	44.2	209	68.5	96.1
5 London School of Economics	78.5	79.3	46.9	165	95.3	95.8
6 Bristol	81.2	80.9	61.3	166	80.8	95.2
7 University College London	78.1	80.8	52.3	169	81.3	93.6
8 Glasgow	84.1	83.6	42.4	195	70.6	93.5
9 Manchester	80.5	82.4	36.6	164	84.3	92.9
10 Dundee	85.5	84.1	28.3	175	79.2	92.8
=11 Leeds	79.9	80.8	42.3	151	84.2	92.4
=11 Southampton	81.2	84.0	45.8	147	80.4	92.4
13 Royal Holloway, London	85.7	85.1	45.8	135	77.9	92.2
14 Lancaster	82.2	80.6	46.5	152	77.2	91.9
15 Stirling	83.5	83.7	30.3	171	77.0	91.8
16 Aberdeen	77.9	80.7	38.2	180	77.1	91.6
17 Exeter	80.5	81.1	43.7	159	76.5	91.5
=18 Edinburgh	76.7	76.0	38.2	180	78.8	91.1
=18 Newcastle	79.3	81.5	43.1	141	81.2	91.1
20 Cardiff	81.7	84.0	36.8	136	81.5	91.0
=21 Leicester	82.9	84.1	29.7	127	84.7	90.5
=21 Loughborough	84.3	89.0	24.3	142	79.1	90.5
=23 Nottingham	81.4	82.7	39.6	133	79.1	90.3
=23 Swansea	84.0	85.9	39.4	125	77.3	90.3
25 Birmingham	75.1	73.3	42.0	146	84.8	90.1
26 East Anglia	81.3	81.2	47.4	132	71.5	89.3
27 Hull	87.8	86.3	31.7	108	76.8	89.2
28 Sheffield	82.3	83.6	31.1	147	71.9	88.9
=29 Aberystwyth	86.2	86.5	38.6	122	67.4	88.4
=29 King's College London	75.4	76.5	40.0	152	75.0	88.4
=29 Salford	89.4	79.5	16.7	111	82.4	88.4
=32 Coventry	92.5	87.2	2.0	113	81.1	88.1
=32 Keele	87.2	87.1	16.4	120	77.2	88.1
34 Plymouth	87.0	88.0	25.8	119	71.0	87.9
=35 Chester	92.2	89.8	6.4	105	76.5	87.4
=35 Worcester	87.3	90.0	8.1	104	81.3	87.4
37 Northumbria	82.2	84.4	15.4	134	76.4	87.2
38 Ulster	87.7	85.6	17.2	117	72.8	87.0
=39 Liverpool	79.1	82.6	26.3	132	74.0	86.9
=39 Reading	77.0	75.8	35.0	122	77.9	86.9
=39 York	76.9	78.9	23.9	145	75.6	86.9
=42 Gloucestershire	88.5	87.3	14.5	108	73.2	86.5

Geography and Environmental Sciences cont	Teaching quality %	Student experience %	Research quality %	Entry standards (UCAS points)	Graduate prospects %	Overall score
=42 Northampton	87.7	83.3	7.7	87	85.4	86.5
44 Bangor	82.6	83.1	31.5	119	67.3	86.1
45 West of England	91.7	91.3	6.4	101	70.5	85.8
46 Manchester Metropolitan	86.4	83.3	14.9	108	72.1	85.4
47 Queen Mary, London	68.1	72.1	45.1	127	74.8	85.1
48 Bournemouth	80.9	77.7	19.9	93	76.9	84.1
49 Portsmouth	86.3	82.5	14.9	97	69.5	84.0
=50 Oxford Brookes	79.8	81.0	17.3	117	69.3	83.7
=50 Queen's, Belfast	64.9	68.5	36.9	139	74.5	83.7
=50 Sussex	71.0	72.3	35.8	140	66.7	83.7
53 Derby	88.1	87.9	3.6	103	66.4	83.4
54 Sheffield Hallam	83.1	83.0	13.4	106	67.1	83.1
55 Hertfordshire	82.6	80.1	—	78	78.9	81.9
56 Liverpool John Moores	87.2	87.8	—	120	56.7	81.6
57 Nottingham Trent	85.1	85.4	4.1	106	59.6	81.0
58 Brighton	79.1	73.2	5.1	101	69.4	80.1
59 Cumbria	82.5	78.1	1.5	113	57.9	79.3
60 Liverpool Hope	86.6	77.5	1.6	109	54.2	79.1
61 Leeds Beckett	80.0	82.6	5.6	94	60.0	79.0
62 Edge Hill	75.3	73.1	6.2	111	64.8	78.9
63 Kingston	81.1	74.9	6.9	81	62.8	78.2
64 Bath Spa	69.6	67.0	—	90	76.8	77.5
65 Staffordshire	82.5	79.9	—	94	50.0	76.3
66 Winchester	72.4	64.2	7.5	97	—	75.7

Employed in high-skilled job	54%	Employed in lower-skilled job and studying	1%
Employed in high-skilled job and studying	3%	Employed in lower-skilled job	22%
Studying	15%	Unemployed	5%
High skilled work (median) salary	£24,000	Low/medium skilled salary	£19,000

Geology

Cambridge has taken the lead in our Geology table, bumping Imperial down to second place this year. Cambridge averaged 228 points in 2019's UCAS tariff – an extraordinarily high rate, but lower than it has achieved in the last two years, when geology at Cambridge attracted among the highest UCAS points of any subject at any university. Imperial, though, has the best results from the Research Excellence Framework and outdid Cambridge on our graduate prospects measure. It also received excellent scores in the National Student Survey, for both teaching quality and the wider experience. Cambridge chooses not to enter the survey.

Two more Scottish universities have joined St Andrews in the top ten; Glasgow, at fifth, which has gained seven places since our previous edition, and ninth-ranked Edinburgh, up from

21st. They have taken the places of Royal Holloway, which has fallen to 18th this year, and East Anglia – which has tumbled 15 places from 10th last year.

Aberystwyth, which does consistently well on student satisfaction across the subjects, comes top for teaching quality in geology. Students throughout the universities in our table tend to enjoy their degrees; scores were above 90% for teaching quality at four institutions, and only one achieved under 70%, just (UCL, 69.5%). Hull, in 19th place overall, beat all others in the sections of the National Student Survey that focus on the wider experience.

The numbers starting degrees, which have never hit the 2,000 mark, continued a downward trajectory in the 2019 cycle when only 1,140 new students enrolled – a new low. Applications were 40% lower than they were in 2014, the highest point in the last decade, but there are still 40 institutions planning to offer the subject in 2022.

Jobs-wise, results from the new Graduate Outcomes survey were strong enough to place geology in the top 30 of our employment ranking. Fifty-two per cent of graduates were in full-time professional jobs 15 months after finishing their degrees, the survey found, and just under a quarter – one of the higher proportions – had entered postgraduate study full-time, while 2% were combining both.

Geology

		Teaching quality %	Student experience %	Research quality %	Entry standards (UCAS points)	Graduate prospects %	Overall score
1	Cambridge	—	—	58.0	228	91.0	100.0
2	Imperial College London	89.3	90.6	59.6	181	93.8	99.5
3	St Andrews	86.6	88.4	44.2	204	94.4	98.1
4	Oxford	—	—	52.1	205	89.5	97.7
5	Glasgow	88.3	92.2	38.5	201	88.2	96.8
6	Exeter	92.7	91.1	45.7	134	91.4	95.4
7	Bristol	87.1	85.2	55.8	170	76.5	93.8
8	Durham	88.1	86.5	42.2	170	82.1	93.5
9	Edinburgh	76.9	76.9	38.2	193	94.6	93.1
10	Southampton	80.5	84.9	58.3	137	85.5	92.6
11	Leeds	81.0	82.3	41.9	157	91.4	92.5
12	Leicester	88.2	88.8	37.2	126	84.6	91.3
13	Bangor	89.4	90.3	31.5	137*	—	91.2
14	Birmingham	81.8	82.7	38.6	137	88.0	90.5
15	Newcastle	78.6	88.8	35.4	123	92.3	90.2
16	Aberystwyth	93.4	89.4	34.9	116	73.3	89.4
17	University College London	69.5	79.1	47.9	146	85.7	88.6
18	Royal Holloway, London	83.3	84.7	43.4	125	75.0	88.5
19	Hull	91.0	94.8	31.7	97	74.7	88.3
20	Plymouth	89.3	89.4	25.3	118	77.8	88.2
21	Cardiff	87.8	86.4	21.3	134	77.4	87.8
22	Aberdeen	72.3	75.6	38.2	158	82.6	87.6
23	Manchester	75.6	74.5	44.5	151	77.1	87.5
24	Portsmouth	90.4	85.3	19.8	106	78.8	86.7
25	East Anglia	81.8	81.9	47.4	131	64.3	86.5
26	Keele	85.7	86.5	12.2	109	83.1	85.9

Geology cont	Teaching quality %	Student experience %	Research quality %	Entry standards (UCAS points)	Graduate prospects %	Overall score
27 Liverpool	75.1	76.9	30.3	131	80.0	85.3
28 Brighton	87.1	87.0	5.1	93	80.0	83.8
29 Derby	89.2	88.0	3.6	98	72.3	82.9
30 Kingston	88.6	80.9	6.9	105*	47.1	77.7

Employed in high-skilled job	52%	Employed in lower-skilled job and studying	0%
Employed in high-skilled job and studying	2%	Employed in lower-skilled job	16%
Studying	24%	Unemployed	6%
High skilled work (median) salary	£24,000	Low/medium skilled salary	£18,000

German

The number one university to study German is still Cambridge, the most regular incumbent of our table's top spot. Every other university in the ranking has shifted positions since last year, however. St Andrews has gone from second to 12th, King's College London was fourth last year and is 22nd this and Lancaster – third last year and a former leader – does not feature at all in our current edition. UCL has gained 26 places to rank sixth this year and Bangor has moved into ninth from 26=.

German attracts small student numbers on courses, which in turn create fluctuations in the rankings. The subject's decline has been ongoing for around 20 years, and the 2019 recruitment cycle brought numbers to their lowest point yet. Applications tumbled by a further 16% and there were only 85 new enrolments in autumn 2020 – the first time fewer than 100 undergraduates have begun German studies degrees at UK universities. German has suffered more than other modern languages with dwindling take-up at sixth-form level. The steep decline in its learning is a worldwide trend and a cause of alarm to the German government, academic linguists and employers.

Graduate prospects are not the issue though, with German ranking a respectable 37th out of 67 subject areas this year – one place below social work and one above politics. Fifty-five per cent of graduates were in professional jobs 15 months after finishing their German degrees, the Graduate Outcomes survey found, and a further 15% were in postgraduate study full-time or combining it with high-skilled work.

Entry standards are pretty stiff; around two-thirds of the universities in our table average above 150 UCAS tariff points, and two average above 200. Nottingham Trent, one of the few post-1992 universities in the table, got the best satisfaction scores for both teaching quality and the wider experience in the National Student Survey.

Our German table has shrunk by another nine universities this year, but there are still plenty of places to study the language, either as a single honours degree or in combination with a wide range of subjects including law, film, accountancy and other languages. Most universities in the table offer German from scratch as well as catering for those who took it at A-level.

German

	Teaching quality %	Student experience %	Research quality %	Entry standards (UCAS points)	Graduate prospects %	Overall score
1 Cambridge	—	—	54.0	197	86.8	100.0
2 Warwick	86.1	82.5	45.2	167	91.4	96.7
3 Southampton	92.9	83.1	42.7	159*	—	95.5
4 Oxford	—	—	41.3	193	80.5	93.8
5 Glasgow	84.5	85.3	26.3	204	—	92.7
6 University College London	81.1	74.2	43.7	163	—	91.6
7 Sheffield	83.8	77.1	41.2	157	—	91.3
8 Durham	73.5	68.5	34.6	185	91.0	91.1
9 Bangor	87.9	83.3	39.6	137	—	90.6
=10 Bristol	80.9	74.4	36.0	167	79.4	89.9
=10 Newcastle	82.8	82.8	36.3	155	—	89.9
12 St Andrews	77.3	77.0	26.4	202	—	89.3
13 Exeter	79.7	79.0	35.1	156	78.2	88.8
14 Manchester	76.2	66.1	48.9	157	70.8	88.6
15 Kent	89.1	85.7	41.9	103	—	88.5
16 Leeds	81.9	71.8	30.6	153	80.0	87.5
17 Reading	80.2	84.4	41.7	119	—	87.3
18 Nottingham	83.5	75.0	39.4	145	67.0	87.0
=19 Edinburgh	73.7	72.3	30.3	181	—	86.6
=19 Heriot-Watt	81.7	85.2	26.3	156	72.7	86.6
21 Birmingham	74.7	73.1	33.7	153	77.8	86.4
22 King's College London	76.2	70.2	42.1	169	60.4	86.1
23 Bath	77.8	76.6	27.4	144	—	83.5
24 Queen Mary, London	70.2	71.3	35.1	130	—	81.5
25 Cardiff	69.4	66.1	32.5	138	70.3	81.4
26 Nottingham Trent	94.9	93.3	7.6	115*	—	81.2
27 Portsmouth	87.9	80.3	32.2	99	55.3	80.6
28 Liverpool	67.6	66.6	33.4	139	—	80.5

Employed in high-skilled job	55%	Employed in lower-skilled job and studying	1%
Employed in high-skilled job and studying	3%	Employed in lower-skilled job	22%
Studying	12%	Unemployed	7%
High skilled work (median) salary	£24,000	Low/medium skilled salary	£19,500

History

The London School of Economics has entered our History table's top five, boosted from 17th place in our previous edition by virtue of the best graduate prospects this year. Its arrival has led a shake-up among the leading five universities, which were unchanged for the past two years. Durham, Oxford and St Andrews have also swapped positions this year and Sheffield has moved from fifth to ninth place.

Cambridge is unmoved in the top spot however, its lead extended further by graduate prospects second only to the LSE's as well as the best results in the Research Excellence Framework. St Andrews has the highest entry grades, and is the only university of 90 in our table to average above 200 points in the UCAS tariff.

Led by 40th-ranked Newman in the sections of the National Student Survey that focus on teaching quality, and Suffolk (73=) for the wider experience, the post-1992 universities are the top scorers for student satisfaction. In spite of this the universities with older foundations continue to dominate the main table's top 20.

History is one of the most popular subjects in higher education, but both applications and enrolments fell for the fourth year in a row in 2019. Uninspiring graduate prospects may be to blame. The subject ranks 14th from bottom in our employment ranking, with nearly three in every ten graduates in low-skilled jobs 15 months after finishing their degrees. The proportion in professional employment at the 15-month census point was only 43% – which is among the lowest in our ranking, though the 16% in postgraduate study plus the 3% combining it with a high-skilled job improves history's standing somewhat.

History	Teaching quality %	Student experience %	Research quality %	Entry standards (UCAS points)	Graduate prospects %	Overall score
1 Cambridge	—	—	56.3	199	91.4	100.0
2 St Andrews	87.9	85.4	46.7	204	80.0	96.7
3 Oxford	—	—	56.1	196	86.1	96.1
4 Durham	81.9	72.8	41.4	196	85.3	93.6
5 London School of Economics	76.5	71.6	46.8	171	91.6	92.6
6 Glasgow	82.4	76.7	47.7	187	71.5	91.4
7 University College London	78.0	70.4	51.9	175	75.4	90.4
8 Warwick	76.9	68.5	51.7	161	82.0	90.3
9 Sheffield	78.6	78.6	53.7	151	75.5	89.7
10 Exeter	79.0	75.2	45.6	167	76.4	89.5
11 Birmingham	79.5	72.3	48.8	154	76.7	88.9
12 Strathclyde	85.7	82.0	42.0	197	53.4	88.6
13 Leeds	79.8	72.7	43.6	166	74.1	88.5
14 York	78.3	69.4	43.3	154	81.5	88.4
15 Southampton	80.3	75.6	50.6	141	74.3	88.1
=16 Edinburgh	69.4	65.4	46.9	175	77.9	87.6
=16 Lancaster	82.4	77.0	37.0	153	75.7	87.6
18 Aberdeen	84.0	80.7	36.1	172	65.3	87.5
=19 King's College London	76.9	66.0	45.3	158	74.1	86.8
=19 Sussex	79.8	72.6	41.3	140	78.1	86.8
=21 Loughborough	85.4	84.3	22.5	138	83.1	86.6
=21 Queen Mary, London	84.3	80.0	43.7	131	71.2	86.6
23 East Anglia	80.3	73.7	47.4	141	70.7	86.5
24 Dundee	86.5	81.5	30.4	172	61.4	86.2
=25 Bristol	74.5*	68.6*	40.6	165	71.7	85.7
=25 Stirling	84.9	79.7	28.5	165	65.8	85.7

27 Nottingham	81.0	73.7	36.9	143	73.6	85.6
28 Manchester	77.2	67.5	39.8	155	72.3	85.4
=29 Liverpool	81.2	75.6	38.9	134	72.2	85.1
=29 Reading	80.9	75.1	35.4	121	80.6	85.1
31 Royal Holloway, London	82.3	79.2	40.6	132	65.5	84.5
32 Aberystwyth	90.4	83.5	19.5	125	75.0	84.2
33 Cardiff	81.1	73.5	31.4	145	69.6	83.9
=34 Kent	83.3	77.2	41.3	126	63.0	83.5
=34 Lincoln	88.7	82.5	25.9	113	72.9	83.5
=34 Queen's, Belfast	73.1	64.5	46.3	142	68.8	83.5
37 Soas, London	86.0	75.7	20.8	148	68.2	83.2
38 Derby	90.1	85.1	13.5	109	79.8	83.0
39 Swansea	84.7	79.7	25.0	122	72.9	82.9
40 Newman	98.8	93.7	12.0	99	71.4	82.8
41 Wales Trinity St David	92.9	80.5	17.3	129	66.7	82.6
=42 Greenwich	94.9	88.2	8.6	107	75.9	82.4
=42 Teesside	76.6	79.1	27.9	99	85.7	82.4
44 Northumbria	87.6	83.4	30.7	133	56.3	82.3
45 Newcastle	74.2	67.5	29.0	147	73.0	82.2
46 Ulster	87.1	80.0	24.0	111	71.9	82.1
47 Plymouth	95.3	91.0	22.6	104	61.3	81.9
48 Hull	85.9	85.1	26.1	115	65.6	81.8
=49 Oxford Brookes	77.9	76.0	35.0	110	72.4	81.7
=49 Roehampton	88.3	87.0	21.4	102	71.4	81.7
51 Keele	79.6	77.0	32.8	116	68.8	81.5
52 Liverpool John Moores	91.4	86.9	15.9	134	58.6	81.3
53 Huddersfield	89.6	79.1	22.3	107	67.8	81.0
=54 Essex	83.0	80.8	34.8	108	61.5	80.8
=54 Sheffield Hallam	79.2	75.3	38.3	101	67.8	80.8
56 Leicester	76.9	72.9	34.3	122	65.0	80.5
57 Liverpool Hope	89.5	81.0	15.7	108	67.6	80.0
58 Hertfordshire	81.9	80.0	46.7	97	53.5	79.9
59 Edge Hill	86.2	78.7	23.6	117	59.6	79.5
60 Bangor	83.4	76.6	24.3	120	60.0	79.2
61 St Mary's, Twickenham	97.1	88.4	11.0	89	—	79.0
62 Brunel London	88.2	79.2	32.4	110	50.0	78.9
63 Central Lancashire	86.4	80.9	12.0	105	69.0	78.7
=64 Canterbury Christ Church	93.6	86.2	16.3	95	56.4	78.0
=64 West of England	88.3	77.7	28.9	108	50.0	78.0
66 Manchester Metropolitan	85.3	79.9	18.0	117	57.3	77.9
67 Coventry	88.7	82.9	5.6	111	64.7	77.8
68 De Montfort	84.1	75.9	23.4	105*	57.5	77.3
69 Chichester	87.4	79.2	15.8	102	60.0	77.2
70 Nottingham Trent	82.1	76.1	17.5	108	62.1	77.0
71 Wolverhampton	78.8	78.8	18.8	103	64.9	76.9
72 Salford	92.0	86.2	—	115	58.5	76.8

	Teaching quality %	Student experience %	Research quality %	Entry standards (UCAS points)	Graduate prospects %	Overall score
=73 Anglia Ruskin	87.3	79.2	15.3	111	54.3	76.6
=73 Suffolk	97.8	96.9	—	96	54.2	76.6
75 Winchester	83.8	77.2	19.1	105	55.1	76.0
76 Portsmouth	76.7	67.7	32.2	106	53.2	75.5
77 Bishop Grosseteste	88.9	85.0	7.0	90	59.2	75.3
78 Leeds Beckett	87.9	87.5	11.0	98	45.0	73.6
79 Goldsmiths, London	71.0	66.0	34.5	112	45.3	73.3
=80 Bath Spa	79.9	77.4	8.3	101	55.9	73.0
=80 Brighton	79.4	74.6	13.1	94	—	73.0
82 York St John	86.6	80.7	—	93	55.0	72.4
83 Northampton	82.6	74.4	21.5	91	39.4	71.2
84 Chester	81.6	75.7	9.1	107	43.5	71.1
85 Westminster	80.7	75.6	11.8	101	44.1	71.0
86 South Wales	71.1	65.7	15.8	93	48.9	69.0
87 Gloucestershire	66.1	58.0	11.2	116	—	68.7
88 Sunderland	54.2	41.0	7.7	115	68.8	67.5
89 Worcester	58.2	58.0	19.5	109	39.5	65.3
90 Leeds Trinity	68.4	51.9	10.3	85*	—	64.9

Employed in high-skilled job	43%	Employed in lower-skilled job and studying	1%
Employed in high-skilled job and studying	3%	Employed in lower-skilled job	29%
Studying	16%	Unemployed	6%
High skilled work (median) salary	£24,000	Low/medium skilled salary	£18,500

History of Art, Architecture and Design

Cambridge's tenure at the top of our table remains secure for the sixth year running, due to its strength across the measures rather than it topping any individually. St Andrews has moved into second place in a similar manner, and achieves among the best results in all measures – including student satisfaction (unlike Cambridge which boycotts the National Student Survey). Fourth-ranked Oxford has the edge in entry standards, in a subject that attracts generally high UCAS point averages. Though no universities have reached 190 points in the UCAS tariff, more than half the table averages above 150 points and none goes below 100.

The best results in the Research Excellence Framework (REF) were produced by the eighth-ranked Courtauld Institute, which had 95% of its submission classed as world-leading or internationally excellent. An independent college of the University of London based in Somerset House, the Courtauld has previously topped our table and been the only specialist institution to do so in any of the subject rankings in our *Guide*.

The most satisfied history of art students are at Plymouth, in 13th place overall, which comes top for both teaching quality and the wider experience in the relevant sections of the National

Student Survey. Birmingham is in second place for both measures – propelling it into third place overall this year.

East Anglia had the highest proportion of graduates (76.9%) in professional-level work or postgraduate study 15 months after finishing their degrees. History of art as a whole is in our employment ranking's bottom ten subjects of 67, and only 41% of graduates were in high-skilled jobs 15 months on, though there were also 17% in postgraduate study, or combining it with a professional-level job. The 8% unemployment rate is among the highest, however.

History of art has largely withstood the fluctuations in student numbers that the humanities have experienced over recent years, and 85 universities and colleges are offering it in 2021, often as part of broader liberal arts, design or art degrees.

History of Art, Architecture and Design	Teaching quality %	Student experience %	Research quality %	Entry standards (UCAS points)	Graduate prospects %	Overall score
1 Cambridge	—	—	49.0	181	—	100.0
2 St Andrews	86.3	85.7	42.1	185	68.2	98.6
3 Birmingham	94.5	90.6	43.7	140	73.1	98.3
4 Oxford	—	—	39.7	189	—	96.6
5 Sussex	86.9	85.8	25.2	151	75.0	95.0
6 Exeter	79.1	75.0	35.1	185	—	94.8
7 Warwick	77.7	82.3	53.0	160	65.9	94.7
8 Courtauld	73.3	59.5	66.0	168	65.2	94.4
9 Kent	91.8	86.1	44.3	129*	—	94.3
10 Glasgow	80.9	73.4	37.2	171	68.6	94.2
11 York	80.1	73.2	53.2	144	68.3	93.7
12 East Anglia	78.2	78.9	36.9	138	76.9	93.5
13 Plymouth	96.8	92.3	14.7	137	—	91.4
14 Leicester	87.3	67.8	42.0	135*	—	91.2
15 Manchester	79.0	71.4	54.0	158	57.1	90.9
16 Leeds	78.1	76.1	30.0	159	65.6	90.3
=17 Edinburgh	77.4	69.3	27.9	165	65.6	89.9
=17 University College London	78.8	74.2	44.7	182	50.9	89.9
19 Bristol	74.6*	68.7*	28.3	161	66.7	89.3
20 Soas, London	79.9	73.8	40.9	130	—	88.7
21 Manchester Metropolitan	87.4	69.9	9.7	155	—	87.4
22 Nottingham	80.6	68.6	30.9	135	62.5	86.9
23 Liverpool John Moores	91.7	88.6	7.2	126*	—	86.3
24 Goldsmiths, London	76.8	64.4	25.9	141	63.6	86.0
25 Oxford Brookes	79.9	80.8	35.0	126	56.9	85.5
26 Brighton	71.0	58.5	13.1	103	68.0	79.8

Employed in high-skilled job	41%	Employed in lower-skilled job and studying		1%
Employed in high-skilled job and studying	3%	Employed in lower-skilled job		33%
Studying	14%	Unemployed		8%
High skilled work (median) salary	£22,000	Low/medium skilled salary		£19,000

Hospitality, Leisure, Recreation & Tourism

A wide variety of courses are encompassed in this table, all of them directed towards management in the leisure and tourism industries. They include degrees in management, international hospitality management and adventure tourism management. The UK's modern universities take precedence in these fields and occupy by far the lion's share of our table.

But it is Birmingham, which was founded at the turn of the 20th century, that has now taken the lead for five consecutive years. It achieved the best results in the Research Excellence Framework by far and averaged the sixth-highest UCAS tariff points in 2019. Ninth-ranked Edinburgh has the highest entry standards, and along with Glasgow Caledonian and Edinburgh Napier – fellow Scottish institutions, which benefit from a favourable conversion rate in the UCAS tariff – is one of only three universities in the table to average more than 150 points. Elsewhere entry standards are modest, though only six out of 56 universities average under 100 UCAS points.

Sunderland achieved resoundingly the best results in the National Student Survey for both measures included in our ranking – student satisfaction with teaching quality and the wider experience. Lincoln, Central Lancashire and Edge Hill also all received scores over 90% in both satisfaction measures.

Applications and enrolments dipped for the fifth year in a row in 2019, but numbers – which also include sports studies students, according to UCAS's tally – are still buoyant, and nearly 7,500 new undergraduates enrolled on courses last autumn.

Four in ten graduates were employed in jobs categorised as 'low-skilled' 15 months after finishing their degrees, due to the entry-level positions graduates in these fields often start out in. Only a slightly higher proportion, 48%, were in 'high-skilled' professional work, and collectively the subjects finish fourth from bottom in our employment ranking.

Hospitality, Leisure, Recreation and Tourism	Teaching quality %	Student experience %	Research quality %	Entry standards (UCAS points)	Graduate prospects %	Overall score
1 Birmingham	73.3	73.2	63.7	146	—	100.0
2 Liverpool John Moores	85.4	83.9	45.3	147	61.8	96.9
3 Edge Hill	92.1	92.5	7.7	147	—	92.4
4 Glasgow Caledonian	86.3	84.2	15.2	155	61.0	91.7
5 Canterbury Christ Church	86.3	89.5	19.0	115	68.6	88.8
6 Surrey	74.4	76.8	33.6	133	58.1	88.5
7 Arts, Bournemouth	85.6	81.6	—	144	70.6	88.4
8 Lincoln	94.4	91.0	11.4	115	61.1	87.5
9 Edinburgh	49.4	58.4	26.1	178	—	86.9
10 Coventry	82.7	82.3	1.6	131	73.3	86.8
11 Edinburgh Napier	80.2	79.9	2.3	153	59.4	86.5
12 Central Lancashire	93.4	90.6	5.1	123	58.1	86.3
13 Bournemouth	80.6	79.8	9.0	121	71.5	85.9
=14 Manchester	80.0	76.7	—	136	71.4	85.7
=14 Portsmouth	88.2	91.0	8.1	114	63.3	85.7
=14 Queen Margaret, Edinburgh	84.6	82.6	—	136	64.0	85.7

17 Huddersfield	81.1	81.0	—	137	66.5	85.5
18 Leeds Beckett	89.1	88.7	12.6	111	59.3	85.3
19 Cardiff Metropolitan	79.1	82.1	7.7	129	62.7	84.8
20 Robert Gordon	83.7	80.2	2.6	139	56.4	84.6
=21 Solent, Southampton	82.1	81.3	0.6	136	60.6	84.4
=21 Ulster	83.2	85.1	31.0	124	35.3	84.4
23 Plymouth	75.1	75.3	13.1	125	64.7	84.3
24 Aberystwyth	77.0	84.1	14.5	123*	—	84.0
25 Staffordshire	76.1	78.4	19.1	120	—	83.9
26 Oxford Brookes	74.1	72.6	5.1	125	70.6	83.2
27 Liverpool Hope	85.9	87.5	10.9	108	—	83.1
28 Greenwich	79.3	74.9	3.3	118	68.6	82.8
29 Manchester Metropolitan	80.2	79.1	4.7	133	52.2	82.5
30 Falmouth	84.9	78.1	—	112	65.5	82.0
31 Sheffield Hallam	79.3	80.2	8.5	113	59.8	81.9
32 St Mary's, Twickenham	77.9	72.2	4.8	131*	—	81.6
33 Chester	78.0	75.5	6.6	127	53.8	81.5
34 Derby	86.6	85.7	0.9	123	48.8	81.4
=35 Gloucestershire	78.0	75.9	6.0	109	63.3	80.7
=35 Sunderland	95.9	96.3	2.4	108	39.5	80.7
37 Westminster	75.3	71.0	10.7	122	53.9	80.6
=38 East London	87.3	86.5	0.8	93	61.9	80.0
=38 South Wales	81.6	83.1	10.8	102	—	80.0
40 West London	88.3	89.1	—	117	41.9	79.6
41 Northampton	84.5	79.9	—	107	52.8	78.8
42 Wales Trinity St David	83.0	77.3	—	129	39.4	78.5
43 Hertfordshire	82.1	82.7	0.9	115	45.2	78.3
=44 Brighton	66.5	62.7	10.9	108	64.3	78.1
=44 Bucks New	77.3	72.6	0.9	98	65.5	78.1
46 Leeds Trinity	81.5	83.5	0.8	104	—	77.7
47 Chichester	77.4	77.3	—	107	51.9	76.8
48 London South Bank	70.1	70.3	35.0	98	33.3	76.6
49 Salford	64.8	67.8	5.9	112	57.1	76.2
50 Wolverhampton	66.9	59.5	5.6	102	62.5	75.3
51 West of Scotland	68.3	65.8	9.1	107	46.2	74.3
52 Anglia Ruskin	81.9	80.4	3.4	78	—	72.9
53 York St John	70.2	66.7	5.5	98	—	72.2
54 Middlesex	75.5	73.6	10.5	102	20.0	70.7
55 London Metropolitan	62.4	65.7	—	102	37.5	68.5
56 Bedfordshire	64.8	64.5	6.7	92	23.1	65.8

Employed in high-skilled job	48%	Employed in lower-skilled job and studying	1%
Employed in high-skilled job and studying	2%	Employed in lower-skilled job	40%
Studying	3%	Unemployed	6%
High skilled work (median) salary	£22,000	Low/medium skilled salary	£19,000

Iberian Languages

Applications to study Spanish have taken another hit of 12%. The decline in enrolments was steeper still, with only 210 students beginning degrees in autumn 2020, 60 fewer than in the year before. Applications have fallen by 35% since 2012, when the higher rate of tuition fees was first introduced, and the numbers starting Spanish degrees are 48% lower. Those statistics do not capture the much larger numbers who study Spanish as part of broader modern language degrees, however; courses that welcomed 2,260 new undergraduates in 2019.

Portuguese, the Iberian partner to Spanish, is included in the table, too – but not one student has enrolled on a single honours course in the subject since 2012. Portuguese can still be studied though, and 22 universities are offering it as part of modern languages degrees and in joint honours degrees, combined with diverse subjects from archaeology and classics to Danish and Czech.

The gap between first-placed Cambridge and its closest competitor in our table has widened this year. Oxford takes the runner-up spot, it has the best graduate prospects and has gained seven places on its previous rank. Aberystwyth finished second last year but no longer offers Iberian studies degrees. There have been lots of other shake-ups to the rankings, including Glasgow's fall from fifth to 22nd and Strathclyde's climb from 10= to third place. A drop in student satisfaction scores have contributed to St Andrews slipping outside the top ten, but it averaged the highest entry standards in 2019. Students tend to arrive at university well-qualified for Iberian studies degrees, and half of the table averaged above 150 points in the UCAS tariff; three of them more than 200.

Satisfaction rates were highest at Bangor for teaching quality, results from the National Student Survey showed, and at Chester for the wider undergraduate experience. In 33rd place out of 67 subject areas the languages are in the top half for overall graduate prospects – an improvement on our previous edition – with on average 73.1% of graduates in professional employment or postgraduate study 15 months after finishing their degrees. This proportion went as high as 93.2% of Oxford graduates, and 91% of those from Durham.

Iberian Languages	Teaching quality %	Student experience %	Research quality %	Entry standards (UCAS points)	Graduate prospects %	Overall score
1 Cambridge	—	—	54.0	197	86.8	100.0
2 Oxford	—	—	41.3	192	93.2	96.5
3 Strathclyde	86.0	82.0	42.0	207	75.0	95.5
4 Southampton	89.1	84.8	42.7	161	76.7	93.6
5 Warwick	81.6	79.9	45.2	167	—	93.5
6 York	88.5	84.2	37.3	155	—	93.1
7 Queen's, Belfast	80.8	79.3	53.6	148	79.9	93.0
8 Surrey	88.3	86.9	39.1	141	—	92.4
9 Aberdeen	83.0	88.9	29.3	176	—	91.9
=10 Bangor	94.3	90.4	39.6	106*	—	91.6
=10 Durham	73.5	68.5	34.6	185	91.0	91.6
12 St Andrews	76.9	75.1	26.4	211	79.4	90.9
13 Nottingham	82.4	72.2	39.4	138	87.3	90.8

=14 Exeter	79.7	79.0	35.1	156	78.2	89.3
=14 Lancaster	75.7	72.9	47.0	150	—	89.3
=14 Manchester	77.3	68.8	48.9	154	74.3	89.3
=17 Edinburgh	74.8	69.9	30.3	177	83.5	89.0
=17 Stirling	88.8	86.3	29.8	165	65.3	89.0
19 University College London	69.1	66.3	43.7	166	82.5	88.8
20 Newcastle	80.2	80.9	36.3	152	74.2	88.7
21 King's College London	74.8	70.8	42.1	154	78.6	88.6
22 Glasgow	74.2	80.9	26.3	207	70.5	88.5
23 Cardiff	81.2	82.2	32.5	134	80.0	88.3
=24 Bath	78.8	79.5	27.4	159	77.8	87.8
=24 Royal Holloway, London	75.0	65.4	48.3	144*	—	87.8
26 East Anglia	81.0	78.6	33.1	144	—	87.7
27 Sheffield	76.3	74.1	41.2	144	75.2	87.6
28 Heriot-Watt	81.7	85.2	26.3	156	72.7	87.5
29 Bristol	74.1	69.7	36.0	154	78.8	87.1
30 Birmingham	74.7	73.1	33.7	149	77.8	86.6
=31 Manchester Metropolitan	85.7	83.5	29.0	116	—	86.1
=31 Reading	77.5	73.6	41.7	123	—	86.1
33 Chester	91.2	92.9	17.3	101	75.4	85.4
34 Coventry	90.0	79.9	18.1	125*	—	85.1
35 Nottingham Trent	87.5	82.2	7.6	110	87.8	85.0
36 Leeds	75.9	74.3	30.6	152	68.6	84.6
37 Swansea	84.3	85.5	22.8	112	—	83.9
38 Liverpool	80.2	78.9	33.4	133	61.4	83.6
39 Queen Mary, London	71.7	62.6	35.1	148	—	83.4
40 Kent	75.7	73.2	41.9	105	66.1	82.5
41 Leicester	79.7	75.7	16.9	127*	—	81.0
42 Portsmouth	84.4	84.5	32.2	99	52.1	80.3
43 Aston	82.6	79.0	23.4	111	58.1	79.9
44 Westminster	78.2	76.0	2.0	129*	—	77.0

Employed in high-skilled job	57%	Employed in lower-skilled job and studying	1%
Employed in high-skilled job and studying	3%	Employed in lower-skilled job	21%
Studying	11%	Unemployed	6%
High skilled work (median) salary	£24,000	Low/medium skilled salary	£19,500

Italian

Italian attracts few students – just 15 new undergraduates in 2019, to be precise – but those who study it enjoy their degrees. In the sections of the National Student Survey that focus on teaching quality, Italian studies received scores no lower than 72.1% (at Glasgow), and up to 92.1% – (at Nottingham Trent). Italian's decline in student numbers is in common with other modern language degrees. The latest enrolments were 10 students fewer than in the year before and applications also fell to a record low of 125.

Tiny though the student numbers are, they represent a highly competitive eight applicants per place and entry standards are high; the majority of the table averaged more than 150 points in the UCAS tariff, and Glasgow's intake averaged 218 points. The subject is largely the preserve of older universities, with only Portsmouth and Nottingham Trent representing the post-1992 foundations.

Most of the 33 universities offering Italian at degree level do so in combination with another subject as a joint honours degree, or as part of a wider modern languages programme, but it is still being offered as a single honours degree by a handful of institutions. Most undergraduates in the language have no previous knowledge of Italian, although the leading universities usually require another language at A-level, or equivalent qualification.

Cambridge was the top scorer in the Research Excellence Framework and continues to lead the table by a clear margin. The small student cohorts make for a volatile ranking and most other universities have changed position. Oxford has moved into second place from third, while there were bigger shifts for third-ranked Edinburgh (up from 12th) and tenth-ranked Leeds (formerly 15th).

Durham had far and away the best results in the new Graduate Outcomes survey, which showed that 15 months after finishing their degrees 91% of the subject's graduates were in professional employment or postgraduate study. The subject has scraped into the top 50 of our employment measure with, on average, 66.6% achieving these top outcomes 15 months on.

Italian	Teaching quality %	Student experience %	Research quality %	Entry standards (UCAS points)	Graduate prospects %	Overall score
1 Cambridge	—	—	54.0	197	86.8	100.0
2 Oxford	—	—	41.3	195	—	93.9
3 Edinburgh	83.0	84.0	30.3	180	—	92.8
4 Durham	73.5	68.5	34.6	185	91.0	91.9
5 Manchester	77.7	72.2	48.9	149*	—	91.3
6 Exeter	79.7	79.0	35.1	156	78.2	90.6
7 Glasgow	72.1	78.2	26.3	218	—	90.4
8 University College London	74.2	66.4	43.7	178	—	90.3
9 Warwick	75.7	66.4	45.2	159*	—	89.6
10 Leeds	80.3	77.4	30.6	152	—	88.4
11 Bristol	81.0	78.7	36.0	148	65.5	88.2
12 Bath	83.0	82.6	27.4	144	70.8	88.1
13 Birmingham	74.7	73.1	33.7	153*	77.8	88.0
=14 Cardiff	77.9	80.0	32.5	133	73.3	87.3
=14 Reading	80.2	72.7	41.7	115	—	87.3
16 Portsmouth	89.1	82.6	32.2	99	56.3	84.9
17 Nottingham Trent	92.1	85.7	7.6	115*	—	84.4

Employed in high-skilled job	51%	Employed in lower-skilled job and studying	0%
Employed in high-skilled job and studying	4%	Employed in lower-skilled job	27%
Studying	12%	Unemployed	7%
High skilled work (median) salary	£24,000	Low/medium skilled salary	£22,864

Land and Property Management

The career opportunities posed by degrees in land and property management are a big selling point for the subject. More than 80% of graduates were in professional employment 15 months after finishing their degrees – a proportion bettered only by six others in our employment measure. Two universities, Reading and Sheffield Hallam, achieved rare 100% proportions of graduates in these top outcomes 15 months on.

Courses under the table's heading vary from real estate degrees – the biggest recruiters – to woodland ecology, surveying and conservation. Cambridge's land economy degree encompasses law and economics along with aspects of the environment, business finance and resource management. It attracted six applicants per place in 2019, and the university's entry standards – by far the highest in the table – help it secure the number one spot again this year. Cambridge also got the best results in the Research Excellence Framework.

Students were most satisfied at third-ranked Ulster, however, which received the warmest reviews in both sections of the National Student Survey included in our table: teaching quality and the broader undergraduate experience.

The 'Pathways to Property' widening participation programme, held at Reading's Henley Business School for Year 12 pupils, is funded by property firms. Its aim is to attract more state school-educated applicants into studying real estate, an area that has traditionally recruited disproportionate numbers from independent schools.

Land and Property Management	Teaching quality %	Student experience %	Research quality %	Entry standards (UCAS points)	Graduate prospects %	Overall score
1 Cambridge	—	—	49.0	203	—	100.0
2 Reading	77.2	77.8	40.0	141	100.0	91.5
3 Ulster	86.5	86.1	28.6	124	—	91.3
4 Sheffield Hallam	81.6	79.3	13.4	99	100.0	85.7
5 Nottingham Trent	74.5	74.0	3.4	108	97.2	82.3
6 Birmingham City	75.9	74.4	2.7	117	—	81.7
7 Greenwich	68.9	70.2	2.0	126*	—	80.3
8 Leeds Beckett	68.9	69.1	5.6	89	—	77.2
9 Westminster	56.1	55.3	10.7	121	84.8	74.9

Employed in high-skilled job	83%	Employed in lower-skilled job and studying	0%
Employed in high-skilled job and studying	10%	Employed in lower-skilled job	2%
Studying	2%	Unemployed	3%
High skilled work (median) salary	£26,500	Low/medium skilled salary	—

Law

The gap between the runner-up in our law table, University College London, and the winner, Cambridge, is closer this year than it was last. Neither university comes top in any of the five individual measures, but both are among the best for research, entry standards and graduate prospects. UCL also performed strongly in the sections of the National Student Survey that focus on teaching quality and the wider experience.

The LSE was the top scorer in the Research Excellence Framework, but Oxford outdoes all other UK universities in the QS World Rankings 2020. Eighth-ranked Edinburgh has the highest entry standards in our table, which benefit from the favourable conversion rate for Scottish secondary qualifications in the UCAS tariff as all institutions north of the border do. The law students at Solent in Southampton, which is placed 48 overall, are the most satisfied with both their teaching quality and the wider experience.

The rising demand for places to study law is showing no signs of slowing down. More than 28,000 students started degrees in 2019, the fifth consecutive year that enrolments have increased. Entry standards signify the subject's popularity; eight of the table's 101 universities averaged 200 points or more in 2019's UCAS tariff and almost a third averaged over 150 points. At the other end of the scale though, nine universities averaged fewer than 100 UCAS points – four more than last year – reflecting the now extensive range of providers.

Royal Holloway, which ranks 24= overall, is top for graduate prospects. A rare 100% proportion of its law graduates were in professional work or postgraduate study 15 months after they had finished their degrees. On the whole though, immediate graduate prospects are not law's main attraction; the subject occupies a modest 30th place in our employment ranking, out of 67. Only about half of all graduates go on to practise law, and training contracts for those that do keep pay in graduate-level jobs relatively low. There is a strong case for the delayed career gratification posed by law however, and recent surveys suggest that the average law graduate almost doubles their salary within a decade.

Law graduates who want to become solicitors in England progress to the Legal Practice Course, while those aiming to be barristers take the Bar Vocational Course. In Scotland, most law courses are based on the distinctive Scottish legal system, which also has different professional qualifications.

Law

		Teaching quality %	Student experience %	Research quality %	Entry standards (UCAS points)	Graduate prospects %	Overall score
1	Cambridge	—	—	58.7	201	94.1	100.0
2	University College London	82.6	79.6	57.7	208	93.6	99.2
3	London School of Economics	80.8	74.6	64.5	176	97.2	97.9
4	Oxford	—	—	51.8	200	88.7	95.8
5	Glasgow	77.8	81.2	33.8	220	89.6	94.7
=6	Durham	76.2	70.0	32.8	189	89.5	90.7
=6	Leeds	80.5	80.1	40.1	167	81.8	90.7
8	Edinburgh	65.0	67.3	40.8	221	86.9	90.5
=9	Aberdeen	77.5	80.4	20.9	201	83.7	90.1
=9	King's College London	70.1	68.4	39.2	198	87.2	90.1
11	Strathclyde	77.0	78.9	29.4	203	79.0	90.0
12	Dundee	79.8	82.3	16.3	175	89.7	89.7
13	Kent	80.7	79.8	43.9	143	81.3	89.5
14	Sheffield	77.9	77.5	31.9	153	87.7	89.1
15	Bristol	69.0	62.7	50.5	174	85.3	88.8
16	Stirling	86.0	79.1	19.4	191	73.1	88.6
17	Glasgow Caledonian	87.8	89.8	1.8	202	73.5	88.5

=18 Exeter	74.3	75.9	21.4	168	89.2	87.9
=18 Queen Mary, London	69.2	67.1	23.7	187	92.2	87.9
=18 Ulster	81.8	76.8	48.5	128	75.9	87.9
=21 Queen's, Belfast	68.1	68.1	40.3	156	90.7	87.8
=21 York	75.6	72.7	30.3	168	83.8	87.8
23 Swansea	82.7	81.9	20.4	129	89.1	87.7
=24 Nottingham	70.5	70.1	45.2	161	80.7	87.3
=24 Royal Holloway, London	81.0	81.6	—	135	100.0	87.3
=26 Birmingham	71.4	71.5	33.6	159	86.5	87.2
=26 Warwick	67.5	66.1	41.9	170	84.8	87.2
28 Lancaster	74.8	68.5	38.9	141	84.3	86.7
29 Edinburgh Napier	84.3	87.0	—	166	80.4	86.3
30 Reading	80.0	79.6	31.2	132	78.9	86.2
31 South Wales	90.2	88.5	—	118	87.0	86.1
32 Abertay	84.1	80.4	1.2	169	—	85.8
33 Aston	82.3	79.0	19.7	135	80.0	85.5
34 Newcastle	71.3	67.3	25.4	152	87.0	85.1
35 Manchester	67.2	63.2	27.2	173	85.3	85.0
36 Leicester	76.8	73.3	26.4	134	80.9	84.6
=37 Cardiff	68.9	68.3	27.2	157	83.3	84.4
=37 Portsmouth	78.7	76.6	32.2	125	75.5	84.4
=39 East Anglia	72.4	72.5	26.5	149	78.8	84.1
=39 Roehampton	91.5	90.6	—	104	80.0	84.1
=41 Aberystwyth	81.5	84.1	14.3	123	77.8	83.8
=41 Bangor	79.3	81.2	12.0	134	79.8	83.8
43 Southampton	76.7	73.9	18.2	150	77.0	83.7
44 Lincoln	80.4	81.5	5.0	117	85.8	83.4
=45 Bolton	92.5	91.2	—	93	76.9	83.0
=45 Soas, London	72.2	70.2	26.7	149	75.3	83.0
47 Liverpool	73.1	71.5	19.6	139	80.3	82.8
48 Solent, Southampton	95.9	94.1		99	68.2	82.5
=49 Keele	73.3	71.4	30.5	113	78.6	82.2
=49 Northumbria	80.0	77.6	2.5	136	79.3	82.2
=49 Plymouth	81.8	79.9	16.0	126	71.0	82.2
52 Robert Gordon	75.8	72.5	3.9	168	72.3	81.4
53 Edge Hill	76.2	78.7	12.1	123	76.1	81.2
=54 Salford	78.7	76.5	5.9	116	79.2	80.9
=54 Sussex	72.1	65.6	23.3	139	73.9	80.9
56 Heriot-Watt	62.3	64.1	18.8	181*	—	80.8
57 Buckingham	80.4	79.4	—	106	81.8	80.7
58 Chester	77.8	76.0	—	116	82.2	80.5
59 West London	85.7	87.6	—	111	68.8	80.2
=60 Bradford	74.7	79.0	11.8	118	74.2	80.1
=60 Sheffield Hallam	75.8	66.9	14.4	107	80.9	80.1
62 Nottingham Trent	81.4	77.6	2.3	119	73.1	79.9
63 Coventry	78.9	76.6	5.6	112	75.6	79.8

Law cont

	Teaching quality %	Student experience %	Research quality %	Entry standards (UCAS points)	Graduate prospects %	Overall score
=64 Bournemouth	73.4	74.9	8.8	105	81.3	79.6
=64 Manchester Metropolitan	77.2	77.4	14.9	121	67.6	79.6
66 London Metropolitan	84.8	81.5	0.3	96	73.5	79.5
=67 Essex	70.6	72.9	31.6	103	70.0	79.2
=67 Liverpool John Moores	74.8	72.5	2.7	130	75.9	79.2
69 Oxford Brookes	74.3	72.6	5.1	107	80.8	79.1
=70 Hull	75.6	74.3	12.6	122	69.1	79.0
=70 Surrey	62.6	65.2	8.5	132	86.7	79.0
72 Westminster	76.7	75.3	7.5	111	73.1	78.8
73 West of England	75.7	76.1	3.5	112	75.0	78.6
74 London South Bank	82.7	82.3	20.1	95	58.8	78.5
75 Huddersfield	72.6	70.1	—	121	79.4	78.3
76 Gloucestershire	78.7	74.3	—	102	76.2	78.2
=77 Brunel London	66.6	66.5	20.3	114	75.0	77.9
=77 Teesside	82.1	79.6	15.0	105	58.8	77.9
=79 Anglia Ruskin	76.5	78.5	5.2	96	72.9	77.7
=79 Birmingham City	78.1	75.5	2.8	111	69.9	77.7
=81 Derby	79.6	76.2	2.4	108	68.8	77.6
=81 St Mary's, Twickenham	78.6	74.0	—	93	76.7	77.6
=81 Sunderland	80.6	80.9	0.7	103	67.7	77.6
84 De Montfort	75.8	76.2	5.2	102*	71.4	77.3
85 Hertfordshire	72.6	74.0	—	105	77.5	77.2
=86 Staffordshire	82.1	75.4	—	111	65.0	77.1
=86 Wolverhampton	85.5	85.1	2.7	101	57.7	77.1
88 Winchester	70.4	63.7	—	106	83.6	77.0
=89 Brighton	65.9	63.0	6.5	99	85.3	76.7
=89 Leeds Beckett	73.2	76.1	—	100	75.0	76.7
=91 City, London	62.1	63.4	9.1	142	73.6	76.4
=91 Greenwich	67.9	66.4	2.1	118	77.7	76.4
=91 Northampton	71.3	71.5	—	91	80.8	76.4
94 Canterbury Christ Church	80.3	74.6	3.2	105	61.1	75.8
95 West of Scotland	80.4	76.6	—	131	53.6	75.5
96 Middlesex	71.2	74.6	21.4	106	56.6	75.2
=97 Bedfordshire	81.6	78.3	3.6	99	56.3	75.0
=97 Central Lancashire	74.0	74.0	5.3	121	58.7	75.0
99 East London	72.8	66.2	8.6	104	64.5	74.5
100 Kingston	75.9	78.3	—	101	56.4	73.3
101 Liverpool Hope	75.8	72.2	—	107	50.0	71.5

Employed in high-skilled job	53%
Employed in high-skilled job and studying	6%
Studying	13%
High skilled work (median) salary	£22,000

Employed in lower-skilled job and studying	1%
Employed in lower-skilled job	20%
Unemployed	6%
Low/medium skilled salary	£19,000

Librarianship and Information Management

Traditional librarianship requires some postgraduate training after a first degree in order to enter the profession, and it has practically disappeared at undergraduate level. The courses in this category mainly focused on broader information services and had dwindled to a table of only three universities two years ago. We therefore changed the parameters of our Librarianship and Information Services ranking last year and gave universities the option of appearing here rather than in the table for computer science. A ranking that includes degrees classified by UCAS under information systems should be more valuable to prospective students. Some universities chose not to make the switch, but others agreed that this category offers a better reflection of the content of their programmes.

Loughborough was top of the old table for five consecutive years and has retained the lead of our new version for the second time running, by a clear margin. It has the highest entry standards and was the only university to average more than 150 UCAS points among the 2019 intake of students. It also secured the best scores in the Research Excellence Framework and received the most glowing reviews from students in both the teaching quality and wider experience sections of the National Student Survey.

East Anglia has entered the table in second place, helped by having the second-best research results. Third-ranked Brunel London achieved a rare 100% of graduates in professional employment or postgraduate study 15 months after finishing their degrees, as did Gloucestershire which is ranked 10=. Wolverhampton has moved into the top ten from 18th last year, and Manchester Metropolitan – which also featured in our old-style table, has gained ten places to enter this year's top ten. Northumbria, another such entrant, has moved into fourth position from seventh last year.

As a subject area Librarianship and Information Management does well in our employment ranking – at 29th place out of 67 subject areas, with more than three-quarters of graduates in professional jobs or further study 15 months on.

Librarianship and Information Management	Teaching quality %	Student experience %	Research quality %	Entry standards (UCAS points)	Graduate prospects %	Overall score
1 Loughborough	90.5	92.3	45.1	158	78.3	100.0
2 East Anglia	73.6	74.1	43.8	137	—	92.4
3 Brunel London	79.5	81.0	23.0	128	100.0	91.9
4 Northumbria	73.5	70.0	21.0	142	82.6	87.9
5 Edinburgh Napier	87.2	83.9	9.5	128	77.3	87.4
6 Wolverhampton	73.6	70.8	33.2	—	77.3	86.9
7 De Montfort	69.9	72.6	31.2	113*	89.7	86.4
8 Derby	85.0	79.2	13.5	139*	62.5	86.2

Librarianship and Information Management cont	Teaching quality %	Student experience %	Research quality %	Entry standards (UCAS points)	Graduate prospects %	Overall score
9 Manchester Metropolitan	84.9	86.2	4.7	134	64.3	84.9
=10 Birmingham City	77.6	82.6	6.0	126	—	83.6
=10 Gloucestershire	73.4	70.0	—	117	100.0	83.6
12 Aberystwyth	82.9	83.4	9.2	—	66.7	83.3
13 Portsmouth	79.6	77.4	12.8	110	78.4	83.2
14 Bradford	78.1	79.2	—	114	83.8	82.4
=15 East London	87.3	87.2	13.9	104	57.1	81.7
=15 Sheffield Hallam	74.5	73.9	14.4	112	74.7	81.7
17 Leeds Beckett	75.6	74.4	11.0	107	77.8	81.2
18 Westminster	62.4	67.6	28.3	122	60.9	80.0
19 London Metropolitan	69.6	70.4	5.9	93	54.5	72.6

Employed in high-skilled job	68%	Employed in lower-skilled job and studying	1%
Employed in high-skilled job and studying	4%	Employed in lower-skilled job	16%
Studying	3%	Unemployed	9%
High skilled work (median) salary	£26,000	Low/medium skilled salary	£20,500

Linguistics

In its pure form, linguistics examines how language works, and can lead to work in speech therapy or in teaching English as a foreign language – a growing field. Our table includes some degrees in English language and large numbers that pair linguistics with other subjects.

Oxford has maintained its lead in our table, despite having lower scores than Cambridge in the three measures in which they publish figures: research quality, entry standards and graduate prospects. Cambridge has moved up to second position from fourth last year, with the highest entry standards as well as an unbeaten proportion (91.7%) of graduates in high-skilled work or further study 15 months after graduation. This looks like a statistical anomaly, but as in other subjects, neither university reached the required 50% response rate in the National Student Survey (NSS). So, because Cambridge had the lowest scores in the entire table on the last occasion that a score could be produced, this has been enough to keep Oxford at the top.

Fifth-ranked Edinburgh received the best scores in the Research Excellence Framework, while for student satisfaction York St John was unbeaten in the NSS sections that focus on both teaching quality and the wider undergraduate experience.

Generally, there are no specific subjects required for entry, but standards are fairly high, and close to a third of the table averaged more than 150 points in the UCAS tariff among their 2019 intake of students. The subject has weathered the 2012 introduction of £9,000 tuition fees well, and both applications and enrolments have increased since then, though they have declined a little over recent years. Linguistics is just inside the top 50 in our employment ranking, an improvement on last year. The new Graduate Outcomes survey showed that two-thirds of graduates were working in professional-level jobs or engaged in postgraduate study 15 months after finishing their degrees.

Linguistics

	Teaching quality %	Student experience %	Research quality %	Entry standards (UCAS points)	Graduate prospects %	Overall score
1 Oxford	—	—	41.3	193	89.3	100.0
2 Cambridge	—	—	54.0	208	91.7	98.0
3 Aberdeen	84.7	82.1	46.3	162	—	95.8
4 Lancaster	85.3	82.0	47.0	159	76.9	95.0
5 Edinburgh	68.9	68.2	57.7	183	—	94.9
6 Warwick	86.5	79.5	45.2	148	—	93.9
7 King's College London	78.5	78.6	42.1	168	73.3	92.3
8 University College London	77.7	83.1	43.7	160	73.4	92.2
9 Cardiff	88.8	88.6	35.1	136	—	91.9
10 Newcastle	83.0	77.3	36.3	149	—	90.6
11 York	80.3	77.2	37.3	145	75.0	89.9
12 Queen Mary, London	80.7	79.1	50.3	141	64.3	89.4
13 Leeds	73.0	68.4	30.6	155	78.6	88.0
14 Essex	86.5	83.5	36.0	114	—	87.9
15 Kent	80.3	77.0	41.9	119	73.1	87.8
=16 Manchester	73.1	74.1	48.9	156	59.6	87.3
=16 Sheffield	68.8	71.1	42.2	150	—	87.3
18 Bangor	79.4	73.4	39.6	110	76.1	86.8
19 Huddersfield	86.8	73.9	29.9	123*	—	86.2
20 York St John	95.6	92.5	9.7	93	76.7	85.1
21 Nottingham Trent	91.5	84.0	10.0	114	75.0	84.9
22 Wolverhampton	93.8	90.2	12.8	96	71.0	83.9
23 Central Lancashire	93.6	82.3	15.2	125	61.5	83.6
24 Roehampton	80.9	89.0	21.8	94	70.0	82.3
25 Hertfordshire	88.2	86.8	—	100	77.7	82.1
26 Manchester Metropolitan	85.8	81.2	29.0	112	48.2	79.9
27 Reading	56.2	63.4	25.8	138*	66.7	78.5
28 West of England	78.9	75.2	9.5	106	—	77.1
29 Ulster	72.5	78.0	22.4	122	50.0	77.0
30 Westminster	75.5	71.7	2.0	104*	—	73.6
31 Brighton	67.3	57.9	16.2	104	—	72.8

Employed in high-skilled job	49%	Employed in lower-skilled job and studying	1%
Employed in high-skilled job and studying	3%	Employed in lower-skilled job	29%
Studying	14%	Unemployed	5%
High skilled work (median) salary	£23,000	Low/medium skilled salary	£18,000

Materials Technology

Courses in this category cover four distinct areas: materials science, mining engineering, textiles technology and printing, and marine technology. The various subjects are highly specialised and attract relatively small numbers. Degrees in materials science alone have been growing in demand however, with both applications and enrolments seeing a 30% upturn in 2019. This hike – while significant in percentage terms – still amounted to just 65 new enrolments.

Maths and physics are usually required by the leading universities for materials science, while chemistry and/or design technology A-level or equivalent may also be pre-requisites – depending on the specialism within the broader grouping.

Cambridge's lead in our table is secure again this year. It was the top scorer in the Research Excellence Framework in which only 3% of its submission was deemed less than world-leading or internationally excellent. Cambridge also has the highest entry standards out of a strong field; eight of the 13 universities in the table average more than 150 points in the UCAS tariff. Fourth-ranked Birmingham received the best results for the sections of the National Student Survey that focus on teaching quality, and fifth-placed Loughborough came top for student satisfaction with the wider undergraduate experience.

Sheffield has moved up a place to third this year – helped by equalling Oxford's record in our graduate prospects measure; 100% of graduates were in professional employment or further study 15 months after finishing their degrees. As a whole the materials technology subject area falls in the upper third of our 67-strong employment ranking, with 59% of graduates in high skilled jobs, 20% in postgraduate study (one of the highest proportions out of all subject areas) and 3% combining the two.

Materials Technology	Teaching quality %	Student experience %	Research quality %	Entry standards (UCAS points)	Graduate prospects %	Overall score
1 Cambridge	—	—	78.3	228	91.0	100.0
2 Oxford	—	—	70.8	214	100.0	97.8
3 Sheffield	81.9	84.4	41.0	168	100.0	96.6
4 Birmingham	83.8	84.1	49.3	164	86.5	93.9
5 Loughborough	81.9	85.7	41.8	152	86.7	92.3
6 Imperial College London	66.3	72.1	62.3	155	92.9	91.1
7 Exeter	75.4	72.6	36.4	153	93.3	90.6
8 Manchester	80.5	81.4	36.4	168	76.5	89.0
9 Swansea	76.3	76.9	45.5	113	85.2	88.0
10 Queen Mary, London	64.4	79.0	40.0	131	81.3	84.9
11 Huddersfield	74.1	73.1	10.2	126*	—	83.4
12 De Montfort	75.4	72.2	12.5	91*	81.8	81.8
13 Sheffield Hallam	70.5	69.1	17.8	96	—	80.6

Employed in high-skilled job	59%	Employed in lower-skilled job and studying	0%
Employed in high-skilled job and studying	3%	Employed in lower-skilled job	13%
Studying	20%	Unemployed	4%
High skilled work (median) salary	£28,000	Low/medium skilled salary	£19,500

Mathematics

The top three universities in our Maths table remain the same this year as they were last – in the same order. Entry standards at top-ranked Cambridge reached an average of 237 UCAS points in the 2019 admissions round, higher than at any other institution, including those in Scotland which benefit from a favourable conversion rate in the UCAS tariff. Oxford though, in second place overall, had the better results in the Research Excellence Framework. St Andrews, in third place, has a strong set of results across all five of our measures, without finishing first in any individually.

There have been some remarkable shifts further down the table, however. Notably South Wales has gained 16 places to rank 15th overall, its position boosted by being the top university for graduate prospects this year. When surveyed 15 months after finishing their degrees, a rare 100% of South Wales maths graduates were in professional employment or postgraduate study. South Wales also comes second for student satisfaction with teaching quality, but that measure is bested by Aberystwyth and Northumbria – which tie at the top. The same two universities take first and second place – in alphabetical order – for the sections of the National Student Survey that focus on the wider experience. East Anglia has seen the biggest rise of all though, from 50= last year to 19th, while Heriot-Watt has re-entered the top ten at sixth, having placed just outside it at 11th last year.

There was a significant decline in the demand for places to study maths in the 2019 admissions cycle. Both applications and enrolments fell by 10% – adding up to over 4,800 fewer applicants and 815 fewer new undergraduates beginning maths degrees, compared with the year before. The dip in popularity follows several years of boom however, during which maths A-level overtook English as the most popular in the UK, and maths undergraduate degrees enjoyed levels of enrolments as high as the era pre-2012, when £9,000 fees were introduced. Including statistics and joint honours degrees there were still more than 46,000 applications in 2019.

Entry standards are high; 30 out of the maths table's 71 universities averaged 150 UCAS points or more among their 2019 intake, and six averaged higher than 200. The leading universities will usually require further maths, as well as maths, at A-level or equivalent.

Graduate prospects are encouraging for those with a maths degree; the subject ranks 21st out of 67 subject areas, with 82.5% of graduates in professional employment or postgraduate study 15 months after graduation.

Mathematics	Teaching quality %	Student experience %	Research quality %	Entry standards (UCAS points)	Graduate prospects %	Overall score
1 Cambridge	—	—	60.7	237	97.6	100.0
2 Oxford	—	—	67.5	213	98.6	98.3
3 St Andrews	88.0	86.8	44.2	233	92.2	97.7
4 Imperial College London	77.0	77.1	59.7	193	91.1	93.7
5 Warwick	76.9	77.0	55.8	199	89.3	93.0
6 Heriot-Watt	85.2	81.4	42.3	180	89.9	92.4
7 Durham	75.5	73.9	44.0	215	90.6	92.0
8 University College London	80.1	80.8	42.0	176	93.1	91.7
9 Edinburgh	74.6	77.8	43.7	208	87.1	91.0
10 Manchester	77.8	78.2	44.3	177	90.9	90.7
11 Bristol	75.5	73.0	57.3	187	82.0	90.1

Mathematics cont

	Teaching quality %	Student experience %	Research quality %	Entry standards (UCAS points)	Graduate prospects %	Overall score
12 Bath	76.9	76.4	35.7	189	90.5	89.8
13 Glasgow	73.9	76.0	41.4	210	83.8	89.6
14 Strathclyde	71.9	74.1	34.6	191	94.4	89.3
15 South Wales	92.1	86.0	10.1	130	100.0	89.1
16 Birmingham	83.5	81.2	34.1	172	83.6	89.0
17 Southampton	79.3	79.2	41.9	157	87.5	88.9
18 Lancaster	80.8	80.5	45.8	157	82.3	88.8
19 East Anglia	85.6	84.1	33.7	139	87.9	88.7
=20 Exeter	78.2	79.7	37.9	163	88.0	88.6
=20 Loughborough	85.9	88.1	31.0	159	81.3	88.6
22 Nottingham	77.4	76.2	44.8	172	82.6	88.4
23 Aberdeen	81.0	80.3	32.0	165	—	87.9
24 Northumbria	94.3	93.1	16.7	128	84.3	87.8
25 Leeds	75.8	76.2	42.0	169	80.0	86.9
26 London School of Economics	74.0	69.4	28.7	168	91.6	86.3
27 Liverpool	81.4	82.1	29.8	141	82.9	86.0
28 Reading	81.1	79.6	35.3	125	84.4	85.8
=29 Cardiff	72.5	74.1	31.6	158	88.2	85.6
=29 Nottingham Trent	88.9	88.8	18.4	115	84.7	85.6
31 King's College London	75.8	71.4	37.1	163	80.3	85.3
=32 Aberystwyth	94.3	93.6	19.4	127	70.6	85.1
=32 Central Lancashire	91.2	87.8	19.8	107	—	85.1
34 York	79.7	77.3	27.0	151	81.5	84.9
35 Queen's, Belfast	73.7	74.0	25.0	165	85.7	84.8
36 Leicester	73.0	73.7	25.0	131	95.2	84.6
37 Surrey	76.5	77.1	31.5	150	80.1	84.5
38 Stirling	84.0	82.1	14.0	161	77.8	84.4
39 Sheffield	73.7	76.9	34.0	146	81.1	84.2
40 Dundee	65.8	66.2	48.2	159	—	83.9
41 Middlesex	91.0	86.6	14.2	107*	—	83.8
42 Royal Holloway, London	73.7	74.5	35.5	133	80.5	83.2
43 Newcastle	70.6	76.3	32.0	149	79.1	82.9
=44 Greenwich	91.6	91.6	5.1	105	77.9	82.5
=44 Sheffield Hallam	85.3	85.3	17.8	110	77.4	82.5
46 Keele	85.5	83.3	19.5	117	74.6	82.3
47 Salford	89.9	88.2	4.4	109	—	82.1
=48 Aston	73.9	70.2	21.7	122	88.8	82.0
=48 Lincoln	80.6	84.4	—	114	90.9	82.0
50 Kent	74.9	74.4	28.2	126	80.1	81.9
51 Queen Mary, London	71.2	72.6	30.3	147	73.1	80.9
52 City, London	76.8	77.8	30.2	121	71.6	80.8
53 Liverpool John Moores	78.1	82.0	3.2	134	81.4	80.7

54 Derby	88.5	90.1	5.0	94	75.2	80.4
55 Swansea	77.9	76.3	20.7	123	74.3	80.3
56 Coventry	74.4	75.4	9.4	121	84.2	79.9
=57 Brighton	81.9	73.9	6.4	95	86.2	79.8
=57 Wolverhampton	83.7	74.2	—	88	90.5	79.8
59 Portsmouth	80.3	77.3	11.2	105	79.7	79.7
=60 Plymouth	81.1	77.2	9.3	119	74.9	79.4
=60 West of England	87.8	87.5	10.6	110	64.7	79.4
62 Hull	88.1	77.7	24.2	125	56.0	79.2
63 Sussex	74.3	71.5	28.5	143	64.8	79.1
64 Chester	77.9	83.5	7.1	107	76.2	78.7
65 Liverpool Hope	80.3	75.0	8.8	113	—	78.3
66 Essex	77.8	81.0	34.3	113	50.7	76.9
67 Manchester Metropolitan	80.5	73.7	5.6	111	69.8	76.7
68 Oxford Brookes	68.3	67.7	13.9	135*	—	76.4
69 Hertfordshire	77.2	82.2	20.2	94	61.3	76.1
70 Brunel London	67.3	68.8	25.8	112	68.9	75.9
71 Kingston	68.0	71.6	—	97	76.0	73.4

Employed in high-skilled job	62%	Employed in lower-skilled job and studying		0%
Employed in high-skilled job and studying	7%	Employed in lower-skilled job		12%
Studying	13%	Unemployed		5%
High skilled work (median) salary	£27,000	Low/medium skilled salary		£19,000

Mechanical Engineering

Of all the strands of engineering, mechanical is the most in demand. It attracts more than twice as many applications as any other engineering specialism. The introduction of £9,000 tuition fees in 2012 focused the minds of applicants looking for a degree that offered secure career prospects; for mechanical engineering this led to a surge in applications rather than numbers tailing off as they did in many other subjects. Enrolments in 2019, even after three consecutive years of small declines, were more than 30% higher than they were a decade before.

Applicants are wise to recognise the job prospects that engineering degrees offer. With 84% of graduates in high-skilled employment or postgraduate study 15 months after finishing their degrees, mechanical engineering is 18th in our employment ranking this year. Civil, general and chemical engineering did even better – in that order – but only civil engineering had a higher proportion of graduates in full-time professional jobs (79%), not including further study, than mechanical engineering (72%).

Led by Cambridge, which has the best Research Excellence Framework results and the highest entry standards, the top three universities are unchanged this year. Helped by strong results in the National Student Survey (NSS), Imperial has closed the gap that opened between it and Cambridge last year, however. The two universities shared the top spot two editions of our *Guide* ago.

Ulster has moved into the top 20, in a shift accelerated by coming top for graduate prospects. One hundred percent of the university's mechanical engineering graduates were in professional work or postgraduate study 15 months on – a rare achievement. Elsewhere in the table Manchester has entered the top 15, up from 33rd place last year, and Sussex has gained 21 positions to 22=.

London South Bank, which ranks 25th overall, has the highest rates of student satisfaction for the second year running, both with teaching quality – by far – and also in the sections of the NSS that focus on the wider experience.

There were just under six applications per place in 2019 and entry standards are generally high; four universities averaged more than 200 points in the UCAS tariff and only three averaged below 100 points. Maths and physics A-levels, or equivalent, are usually essential.

Mechanical Engineering	Teaching quality %	Student experience %	Research quality %	Entry standards (UCAS points)	Graduate prospects %	Overall score
1 Cambridge	—	—	67.0	220	96.3	100.0
2 Imperial College London	85.6	88.5	59.6	205	95.1	98.5
3 Bristol	78.1	85.6	52.3	181	96.3	93.9
4 Bath	80.6	82.7	37.4	184	97.3	92.5
5 Strathclyde	74.0	78.4	37.2	217	91.7	92.0
=6 Leeds	82.4	82.5	40.9	194	81.0	90.6
=6 Southampton	77.0	78.5	52.3	164	91.9	90.6
8 Sheffield	83.2	87.2	36.0	156	90.1	89.6
9 Loughborough	80.0	82.0	41.8	159	90.2	89.5
10 Heriot-Watt	74.7	79.1	47.8	185	80.0	88.7
11 Edinburgh	63.7	67.5	50.3	178	96.8	88.4
=12 Lancaster	72.7	77.4	41.6	153	94.2	87.7
=12 Swansea	77.8	79.3	45.5	135	92.0	87.7
=14 Glasgow	61.5	72.2	47.2	210	82.5	87.4
=14 Manchester	73.1	76.7	35.1	169	91.0	87.4
16 Exeter	73.5	75.4	36.4	154	95.4	87.2
17 Nottingham	80.7	80.6	40.8	152	78.7	86.3
=18 Birmingham	70.3	68.0	37.7	156	95.3	86.0
=18 Ulster	80.8	81.5	22.8	122	100.0	86.0
20 Queen's, Belfast	66.8	72.3	36.7	154	97.3	85.9
21 University College London	68.7	71.1	44.6	171	82.0	85.4
=22 Cardiff	74.5	77.3	30.2	142	88.9	84.5
=22 Sussex	76.8	78.4	24.0	135	92.9	84.5
24 Liverpool	75.0	80.9	32.1	137	86.3	84.4
25 London South Bank	91.2	89.7	19.6	117	81.0	84.3
26 Surrey	73.5	76.3	30.8	148	85.0	83.9
27 Robert Gordon	71.8	75.8	8.8	163	94.4	83.5
28 Newcastle	69.0	73.2	30.2	146	89.2	83.2
29 Aberdeen	63.6	69.6	28.4	157	91.3	82.7
30 Northumbria	69.1	76.0	30.7	148	81.0	82.1
31 Solent, Southampton	85.7	82.5	—	126	88.0	81.8
32 Greenwich	86.5	86.0	29.5	118	66.7	81.3
33 Dundee	61.9	67.6	34.1	161	81.4	81.2

=34 Hull	76.5	82.7	16.5	122	82.9	80.8
=34 Teesside	82.3	82.8	5.8	139	78.1	80.8
36 West of Scotland	78.5	79.0	9.0	128	84.6	80.5
37 Lincoln	79.2	81.3	—	114	92.3	80.3
38 Queen Mary, London	55.9	65.1	46.7	138	83.6	80.0
=39 Central Lancashire	81.3	81.5	7.1	141	74.1	79.9
=39 Coventry	73.9	71.7	10.3	134	87.0	79.9
41 Brunel London	66.6	67.1	23.7	128	86.1	79.0
=42 Glasgow Caledonian	73.5	73.7	4.7	149	—	78.7
=42 Harper Adams	82.7	84.4	—	112	80.6	78.7
=42 Plymouth	77.6	76.7	15.7	119	77.2	78.7
=42 Portsmouth	78.7	79.9	9.1	108	82.1	78.7
46 Huddersfield	69.9	70.2	10.2	117	92.0	78.6
47 Bradford	81.7	83.8	7.7	109	76.9	78.5
48 West of England	78.2	80.6	10.6	121	75.6	78.4
=49 Aston	69.4	69.7	20.6	132	77.1	77.9
=49 Liverpool John Moores	77.4	73.2	4.7	132	77.9	77.9
=49 Sheffield Hallam	65.6	68.7	17.8	113	90.4	77.9
=49 Wales Trinity St David	87.8	84.4	1.0	121	67.6	77.9
53 Northampton	89.7	80.4	4.1	88	—	77.8
54 Anglia Ruskin	78.1	81.7	9.1	107	—	77.7
55 Manchester Metropolitan	71.6	69.9	16.3	123	77.2	77.1
56 Chester	78.1	81.8	7.1	103	—	76.9
57 Birmingham City	67.2	68.5	—	127	89.5	76.6
58 Oxford Brookes	66.1	66.9	13.9	114	81.8	75.5
59 City, London	73.9	70.5	23.1	117	64.1	75.4
60 Hertfordshire	68.4	72.0	16.5	106	76.2	75.1
61 Salford	78.0	86.2	4.4	125	56.0	74.3
62 Derby	64.9	63.7	6.7	119	80.0	73.9
63 Kingston	80.3	80.0	2.9	107	61.4	73.6
64 Brighton	69.6	68.3	7.4	95	79.3	73.5
65 Sunderland	77.8	78.9	8.8	98	62.5	73.3
66 De Montfort	63.0	69.0	12.5	107*	72.4	72.3
67 Staffordshire	63.6	59.8	5.7	112	42.9	64.5

Employed in high-skilled job	72%	Employed in lower-skilled job and studying	0%
Employed in high-skilled job and studying	3%	Employed in lower-skilled job	11%
Studying	8%	Unemployed	5%
High skilled work (median) salary	£28,000	Low/medium skilled salary	£21,500

Medicine

It remains to be seen whether the health pandemic and ensuing spotlight on the NHS have any effect on applications to study medicine. The number of places at Britain's medical schools, which are tightly restricted by the government, were already in the process of being expanded even before the cap was lifted last summer in order to honour more offers following the A-level marking debacle. The new medical schools at Edge Hill, Lincoln and Sunderland that opened in 2019 have already had their allocations of places enlarged, another new medical school at Kent welcomed its first students in the autumn and others have also been granted more places.

Applications increased by 7% in 2019, on top of a 10% hike the year before, bringing numbers close to 81,000 – their highest in five years. Enrolments were still below 1,000, equalling more than eight applications to the place. Only one university averaged less than 167 UCAS points in its 2019 intake, and eight averaged more than 200. The career opportunities offered by medicine contribute to its unique cachet. It is consistently top of our employment ranking, which it has achieved again this year – without sharing the honour as in recent years, and virtually all graduates become junior doctors or researchers. The assuredness of graduate prospects means we do not use the measure to help calculate our rankings (although they are still shown for guidance) to avoid small differences distorting positions.

For the tenth consecutive year Oxford is top of our Medicine table, with strong scores across the board. There have been significant changes among the rest of the top five though. Glasgow has moved into runner-up position and Swansea has climbed 23 places back to third place, the position it last held two years ago. Edinburgh has dropped from second to fourth and Bristol has entered in fifth position. Cambridge meanwhile has slipped outside the top five to eighth this year.

Brighton and Sussex has moved into the top 10 on the back of rave reviews in the National Student Survey, which place it top for satisfaction with teaching quality and second for the wider experience – the measure in which St Andrews has the best scores. Ninth-ranked Lancaster was the top-scorer in the Research Excellence Framework, though only by a whisker and there was little to choose between the best submissions.

Nearly all schools demand chemistry and biology, while physics or maths is required by some, either as an alternative or addition to biology. Candidates need to show commitment to the subject through work experience or volunteering. Almost all schools interview candidates, and several use one of the two specialist aptitude tests (see chapter 2). Undergraduates should be prepared to work long hours, particularly towards the end of the course, which will usually be five years long. Many students are now opting for the postgraduate route into the medical profession instead, although this is even longer.

Medicine	Teaching quality %	Student experience %	Research quality %	Entry standards (UCAS points)	Graduate prospects %	Overall score
1 Oxford	—	—	48.9	217	99.2	100.0
2 Glasgow	80.8	83.7	42.3	236	99.3	96.7
3 Swansea	88.0	81.8	44.7	—	97.3	96.1
4 Edinburgh	80.3	80.3	49.8	221	100.0	95.9
5 Bristol	89.1	84.6	47.5	188	99.0	95.4
=6 Aberdeen	88.3	91.7	20.2	240	100.0	95.2
=6 Dundee	84.9	87.8	25.1	245	98.9	95.2
8 Cambridge	78.9	74.3	52.0	217	97.4	94.4
9 Lancaster	88.9	81.2	55.2	168	100.0	94.1
10 Brighton and Sussex Medical School	92.9	94.1	34.3	178	100.0	93.3
11 Queen Mary, London	83.2	83.2	40.2	209	98.8	93.2
12 Newcastle	85.8	82.8	44.8	184	99.2	92.3

=13 Keele	85.6	85.0	50.0	170	98.5	92.2
=13 St Andrews	90.5	95.1	19.8	207	96.3	92.2
15 Exeter	82.6	86.4	41.6	192	100.0	91.7
16 Imperial College London	75.4	78.8	54.6	195	99.5	91.6
17 Queen's, Belfast	88.4	88.8	34.6	183	99.1	91.3
18 Leeds	88.2	89.1	32.1	181	97.5	90.3
19 University College London	72.8	76.4	53.3	196	97.3	89.7
20 Cardiff	82.1	84.4	34.5	196	100.0	89.6
21 Sheffield	85.8	84.1	36.5	179	100.0	89.4
22 East Anglia	85.8	88.3	31.8	171	100.0	87.6
23 King's College London	76.9	73.5	48.3	181	98.5	87.5
=24 Hull-York Medical School	84.9	76.7	36.2	167	98.6	86.0
=24 Liverpool	81.7	84.5	31.7	177	100.0	86.0
26 Birmingham	79.7	80.7	31.5	186	98.9	85.6
27 Leicester	80.8	79.5	33.3	175	99.0	84.9
28 Manchester	79.1	74.2	34.6	182	98.9	84.6
29 Southampton	76.1	74.9	35.6	179	100.0	83.4
30 Nottingham	72.2	66.6	36.8	182	98.8	81.0
31 Plymouth	77.7	80.1	23.1	171	97.9	80.2
32 St George's, London	75.7	76.6	22.4	183	99.3	80.1
33 Warwick	78.1	75.1	26.2	—	97.8	79.8
34 Central Lancashire	84.3	78.9	8.3	120	—	71.4

Employed in high-skilled job	91%	Employed in lower-skilled job and studying	0%
Employed in high-skilled job and studying	6%	Employed in lower-skilled job	0%
Studying	2%	Unemployed	0%
High skilled work (median) salary	£34,000	Low/medium skilled salary	—

Middle Eastern and African Studies

One of the smallest categories in our *Guide*, Middle Eastern and African studies are afforded some official protection because they are classified as 'vulnerable' and of national importance. Applications for African Studies dwindled to just 30 in 2019, and no enrolments were registered at all. Middle Eastern studies has fared better, in spite of the higher rate of tuition fees since 2012, and 90 new students began degrees in the autumn. Larger numbers of students will have included modules from this group in a broader area studies degree.

It is all change – almost – in our rankings this year. Cambridge has ousted St Andrews from the number one spot, helped by having the highest entry standards, while Manchester – which had the best rates of student satisfaction for both teaching quality and the wider experience – has moved into second place from sixth. St Andrews has slipped to third position. Fourth-ranked Birmingham (which was ninth last year) received the best results in the Research Excellence Framework. The small student numbers have created volatility to the positions of every university except for Westminster, which remains in 11th place.

The subjects rank 41st in our employment table, with 70% of graduates in professional jobs or postgraduate study after 15 months. The tiny numbers on courses at individual universities means that many did not have a sufficient cohort to meet the threshold of responses to be included in our analysis of the new Graduate Outcomes survey.

Middle Eastern and African studies	Teaching quality %	Student experience %	Research quality %	Entry standards (UCAS points)	Graduate prospects %	Overall score
1 Cambridge	—	—	45.0	200	—	100.0
2 Manchester	88.4	91.5	48.9	163	75.6	99.2
3 St Andrews	74.3	74.8	46.7	187	—	96.8
4 Birmingham	79.8	77.8	50.9	138	—	94.9
5 Durham	73.5	68.5	34.6	194*	—	93.3
6 Exeter	71.4	75.4	36.0	156	80.0	92.2
7 Oxford	—	—	36.2	197	—	91.5
8 Edinburgh	76.0	72.2	30.1	182	65.0	88.6
9 Leeds	72.4	67.5	30.6	152	—	87.5
10 Soas, London	68.0	60.4	26.3	156	77.8	87.4
11 Westminster	66.9	69.7	11.3	102	—	75.9

Employed in high-skilled job	54%	Employed in lower-skilled job and studying	0%
Employed in high-skilled job and studying	7%	Employed in lower-skilled job	24%
Studying	8%	Unemployed	6%
High skilled work (median) salary	£25,000	Low/medium skilled salary	£18,000

Music

The style and course content of degrees in music vary considerably, from the practical and vocational programmes in conservatoires to the more theoretical degrees in some of the older universities, and everything from creative sound design and new media to sonic arts elsewhere. As a whole, the subject has enjoyed a boom in popularity lately, and applications in 2019 were nearly 30% higher than a decade ago. The numbers starting courses have surged even more sharply and are close to double the level of 10 years ago.

Our Music table stretches to 76 universities this year, such is the extent of provision. Entry standards are as high as 217 UCAS points at Durham – which takes first place overall this year – while three institutions average under 100 points, and more than half of those listed average less than 150 points.

Music grades and the quality of auditions tend to carry more weight than exam grades in winning places, although most degree applicants take A-levels – with music expected among them by most universities. They may accept a distinction or merit in Grade 8 music exams, however.

Last year's winner Manchester has moved into second place this year and fourth-ranked Southampton, which has slipped from third, was the top scorer in the Research Excellence Framework. Chester ranks 46th overall but is placed first for student satisfaction with teaching quality, while Manchester Metropolitan – which came second for teaching quality – got the best scores in the sections of the National Student Survey that focus on the wider experience.

The Royal Conservatoire of Scotland leads for graduate prospects, and 97.2% of its music graduates were in professional employment or further study 15 months after finishing their degrees, the new Graduate Outcomes survey found. Music invariably finishes ahead of the other performing arts in the employment table and is placed 45th out of 67 subject areas this year.

Music

		Teaching quality %	Student experience %	Research quality %	Entry standards (UCAS points)	Graduate prospects %	Overall score
1	Durham	86.6	77.5	64.9	217	76.2	100.0
2	Manchester	88.4	89.2	56.3	199	81.9	99.6
3	Oxford	—	—	66.3	198	82.4	99.1
4	Southampton	92.3	86.4	70.7	174	74.3	98.2
5	Royal Holloway, London	80.4	73.2	55.0	181	90.7	96.1
6	Sheffield	87.8	87.3	60.0	159	77.8	94.8
7	Edinburgh	73.9	73.6	48.0	199	85.2	94.4
8	Bristol	86.6	82.4	48.0	172	80.7	94.1
9	Birmingham	75.5	71.1	50.7	180	84.6	92.7
=10	Cardiff	90.0	90.6	47.0	169	66.7	92.2
=10	Leeds	81.8	80.9	44.2	188	72.0	92.2
12	Cambridge	—	—	48.0	196	87.5	92.1
13	Soas, London	90.2	83.3	60.0	122*	—	91.6
14	Glasgow	68.3	67.7	46.0	204	79.4	91.5
15	King's College London	81.6	72.2	43.5	161	82.4	90.5
16	Aberdeen	86.4	86.6	32.0	171	72.7	90.3
17	Surrey	85.6	81.8	27.2	178	74.7	89.9
18	Newcastle	81.1	75.6	40.8	161	80.0	89.8
19	Nottingham	83.6	79.4	55.4	141	71.2	89.1
=20	Edinburgh Napier	91.5	88.4	—	183	77.3	88.8
=20	Royal Conservatoire of Scotland	81.3	76.5	11.3	158	97.2	88.8
22	York	87.0	83.5	37.1	161	64.7	88.0
23	Goldsmiths, London	80.0	72.4	51.1	123	81.5	87.2
24	Queen's, Belfast	70.4	69.1	38.3	157	80.0	86.1
25	Royal Academy of Music	78.3	76.9	23.9	130	90.6	85.8
26	Ulster	80.2	78.6	40.0	129	75.6	85.6
27	Bangor	89.1	83.8	24.7	129	73.3	85.1
28	Salford	86.2	84.4	7.2	135	80.4	84.0
29	Manchester Metropolitan	95.9	95.6	7.5	—	61.1	83.6
30	Kent	72.9	69.9	44.3	132	73.1	83.5
31	Sussex	70.4	58.5	30.2	154	80.0	83.4
32	Birmingham City	86.2	77.5	11.6	125	82.4	83.3
=33	East London	93.6	91.1	11.2	120	—	83.1
=33	Royal Northern College of Music	78.5	76.7	12.3	130	86.7	83.1
35	Liverpool	73.3	67.3	31.4	152	68.6	82.5
36	Middlesex	74.9	71.2	16.1	116	92.4	82.2
37	Royal College of Music	78.6	77.7	10.9	122	85.7	82.0
38	Sunderland	86.2	84.5	4.2	—	72.2	81.8

Music cont

		Teaching quality %	Student experience %	Research quality %	Entry standards (UCAS points)	Graduate prospects %	Overall score
39	Winchester	95.8	93.8	11.2	128	54.5	81.3
40	Leeds Beckett	83.7	84.6	1.7	116	81.8	80.9
41	Coventry	86.9	76.9	18.1	121*	66.7	80.6
=42	Chichester	86.8	82.7	9.7	129	64.8	80.3
=42	Huddersfield	73.9	71.1	28.0	131	68.9	80.3
=44	Brighton	88.5	83.3	13.1	112	—	79.8
=44	Lincoln	86.8	81.8	6.5	127	—	79.8
46	Chester	96.0	89.7	4.3	126	54.2	79.6
=47	London South Bank	94.2	83.7	12.8	96	—	79.2
=47	Westminster	74.2	74.4	22.5	116	73.3	79.2
=49	De Montfort	80.3	80.6	14.5	118*	—	78.2
=49	Kingston	88.9	79.1	—	113	69.2	78.2
=49	South Wales	80.6	76.0	6.4	120	70.9	78.2
=49	West London	77.7	76.2	2.3	134	70.2	78.2
53	Greenwich	76.9	56.5	—	157	70.5	78.1
=54	Hull	87.7	84.8	11.2	113	57.9	77.8
=54	West of Scotland	78.1	76.4	11.3	140	58.6	77.8
56	Liverpool Hope	76.9	64.9	15.5	121	70.4	77.6
57	Derby	87.6	84.8	6.7	98	—	76.5
58	Anglia Ruskin	78.2	69.0	16.9	112	63.2	76.0
59	Bath Spa	76.3	72.5	10.7	123	61.5	75.9
60	Canterbury Christ Church	75.6	64.2	15.2	108	69.4	75.7
=61	Wolverhampton	82.9	82.6	—	107	64.1	75.5
=61	York St John	83.9	77.4	10.5	94	64.3	75.5
=63	Hertfordshire	78.9	76.7	5.3	112	64.3	75.4
=63	Solent, Southampton	87.1	83.3	—	121	52.1	75.4
=65	Falmouth	80.2	74.6	6.2	111	61.4	74.9
=65	Keele	60.1	55.2	41.7	122	59.4	74.9
=65	Oxford Brookes	71.6	76.5	30.2	114	50.0	74.9
68	Bedfordshire	83.2	73.0	5.6	107	—	74.7
=69	City, London	63.6	62.7	34.0	134	50.0	74.4
=69	Plymouth	82.5	76.1	20.2	137	33.3	74.4
71	Gloucestershire	82.3	69.5	—	122	52.0	73.0
72	Edge Hill	70.8	68.4	3.8	141	39.3	70.2
73	Central Lancashire	67.2	58.7	3.9	111	57.6	69.4
74	Staffordshire	74.4	70.3	—	120	33.3	67.2
75	Plymouth Marjon	47.2	49.0	—	114	50.0	62.0
76	Cumbria	44.7	40.3	—	134	43.5	61.4

Employed in high-skilled job	55%	Employed in lower-skilled job and studying	1%
Employed in high-skilled job and studying	4%	Employed in lower-skilled job	27%
Studying	8%	Unemployed	5%
High skilled work (median) salary	£22,000	Low/medium skilled salary	£17,500

Nursing

Applications to study nursing are beginning to recover from the two-year, 30% dent they experienced when loans replaced bursaries in England in 2017, and they increased a little in 2019. Nursing attracts such big numbers, though, that even with 72,000 fewer applications across those two years, enrolments barely dipped. Unpopular though the move to scrap bursaries was with many, recruitment numbers reached a new record in the 2019 admissions cycle, with almost 30,400 student nurses beginning courses. The landmark in popularity further cements nursing's status as by far the most popular degree in the UCAS system. What – if any – effect the health pandemic will have on nursing student numbers remains to be seen.

Edinburgh is secure at the top of our table for the second year running, its lead well clear of the other 71 universities – including second-ranked Glasgow, with which it has a history of rivalry. Edinburgh achieved the highest scores in the sections of the National Student Survey (NSS) that focus on the wider undergraduate experience, and 100% of its graduates were in high-skilled jobs or postgraduate study 15 months after finishing their degrees. This is a rare feat in most other subjects, but one in which Edinburgh ties with ten other universities in our nursing table, due to the subject's strong employability record. Only medicine and physiotherapy degrees outdo nursing in our employment ranking, with 93% of nursing graduates in professional jobs 15 months after completing their studies, 3% combining graduate-level work with postgraduate study and 1% solely furthering their studies.

Seventeenth-ranked Southampton received much the best results in the Research Excellence Framework, while Glasgow was the only university to average 200 UCAS points among 2019's intake. In third place overall Queen Margaret, Edinburgh, makes it a clean sweep for Scottish universities in our top three. It has risen from seventh place last year, buoyed by the top score for teaching quality in the NSS. York has moved into fourth place this year, from 11th, and Stirling is in the top 15 – a rise of 20 places. Abertay has gained even more ranks, from 59= last year to 10th this – driven up by much improved satisfaction scores.

Considering the high levels of demand for places, entry levels are relatively low. Almost two-thirds of nursing students arrive without A-levels, many of them upgrading other health-related qualifications.

Nursing	Teaching quality %	Student experience %	Research quality %	Entry standards (UCAS points)	Graduate prospects %	Overall score
1 Edinburgh	95.6	96.0	53.4	176	100.0	100.0
2 Glasgow	83.3	81.8	42.3	200	94.1	96.2
3 Queen Margaret, Edinburgh	97.8	92.0	1.5	177	100.0	94.7
4 York	86.9	85.2	40.2	149	100.0	93.6
5 Manchester	83.9	81.9	57.1	144	97.8	93.3
6 Liverpool	91.9	91.8	35.3	137	100.0	93.0
7 Cardiff	77.7	72.1	36.8	167	99.4	92.5
8 Surrey	83.8	80.8	37.5	149	98.6	91.9
9 Birmingham	83.5	77.3	37.0	140	97.8	90.3
10 Abertay	93.8	87.1	—	146*	100.0	90.2
11 Hull	84.1	77.4	16.7	148	100.0	90.0

Nursing cont

		Teaching quality %	Student experience %	Research quality %	Entry standards (UCAS points)	Graduate prospects %	Overall score
12	Bangor	78.5	69.2	34.7	146	99.0	89.8
13	Queen's, Belfast	82.0	79.6	34.7	138	97.4	89.7
14	West of Scotland	88.7	84.2	29.0	137	94.9	89.5
15	Stirling	82.8	79.0	34.1	128	98.7	89.2
16	Leeds	76.2	71.0	31.7	146	98.8	89.1
17	Southampton	66.0	59.0	65.7	144	95.9	89.0
=18	Keele	87.1	81.8	20.9	125	100.0	88.7
=18	Ulster	81.2	81.8	27.7	139	96.2	88.7
=20	Dundee	82.9	81.5	22.1	136	97.1	88.3
=20	East Anglia	78.7	74.1	24.9	137	99.3	88.3
22	King's College London	70.0	63.3	34.6	148	98.9	88.2
23	Lincoln	77.6	76.4	22.6	135	100.0	88.1
24	Northumbria	78.9	72.0	14.0	152	97.7	88.0
25	Coventry	90.3	85.5	4.5	137	96.6	87.9
26	Portsmouth	78.4	77.1	24.3	129	100.0	87.8
27	Manchester Metropolitan	82.4	80.1	12.0	136	98.8	87.7
28	Huddersfield	82.1	78.0	13.2	138	98.3	87.6
29	Liverpool John Moores	75.1	75.1	6.0	157	98.1	87.5
30	City, London	83.6	80.1	20.5	140	93.4	87.3
31	Derby	83.6	76.9	7.3	137	98.8	87.2
32	Wolverhampton	80.7	72.8	11.0	142	98.0	87.1
33	Plymouth	83.8	74.6	9.5	139	96.7	86.8
34	Edinburgh Napier	85.2	81.1	5.3	126	99.5	86.7
35	Staffordshire	89.2	83.0	—	122	100.0	86.6
=36	South Wales	84.2	79.6	2.2	140	96.5	86.5
=36	Swansea	75.9	72.4	14.5	148	95.7	86.5
=38	Greenwich	85.9	82.4	2.2	127	98.5	86.3
=38	Nottingham	68.2	57.9	31.4	140	99.1	86.3
=38	Worcester	86.0	80.9	2.6	128	98.4	86.3
41	Kingston/St George's, London	85.2	84.7	2.6	129	97.1	86.1
42	Chester	81.7	80.1	12.0	129	96.6	86.0
43	West of England	83.2	78.9	8.2	127	97.6	85.9
44	Brighton	77.6	74.4	4.8	136	99.2	85.8
=45	Glasgow Caledonian	81.0	77.1	8.1	122	99.0	85.4
=45	Sheffield Hallam	79.1	74.7	3.7	133	98.4	85.4
47	West London	89.0	87.9	2.5	138	89.8	85.3
=48	Birmingham City	80.8	75.0	1.5	134	97.3	85.2
=48	Robert Gordon	85.3	82.4	4.9	126	95.4	85.2
=50	Anglia Ruskin	82.9	79.1	3.1	126	96.9	84.9
=50	Bradford	72.5	68.3	9.5	143	96.7	84.9
=50	Canterbury Christ Church	80.4	73.0	2.2	131	97.7	84.9
53	Northampton	80.6	74.3	1.6	128	98.2	84.8

54 Hertfordshire	84.9	83.2	4.0	116	97.1	84.7
55 Middlesex	84.5	81.6	10.0	127	92.3	84.6
56 London South Bank	79.3	76.7	13.7	125	94.9	84.5
57 Essex	85.3	78.9	—	109	100.0	84.3
58 Sunderland	80.7	71.5	7.5	129	—	84.2
=59 Bedfordshire	74.8	64.9	25.1	117	97.0	84.1
=59 De Montfort	75.5	71.0	13.0	128*	95.9	84.1
61 Teesside	79.9	72.3	2.4	127	97.0	84.0
62 Leeds Beckett	81.4	80.8	3.5	122	95.2	83.9
63 Cumbria	79.5	73.1	0.7	131	95.4	83.7
64 Salford	69.4	63.3	3.8	141	96.2	83.1
65 Edge Hill	70.7	67.9	2.0	136	95.5	82.6
66 Oxford Brookes	72.6	66.5	3.0	129	94.4	81.8
67 East London	77.5	67.5	7.6	119	—	81.7
=68 Central Lancashire	60.7	58.1	8.3	143	94.4	81.3
=68 Suffolk	75.9	72.0	—	103	99.0	81.3
=70 Bournemouth	67.0	58.5	4.7	114	99.2	80.7
=70 Bucks New	80.9	81.8	1.0	104	92.5	80.7
72 Bolton	82.8	79.0	—	124	63.3	72.5

Employed in high-skilled job	93%	Employed in lower-skilled job and studying	0%
Employed in high-skilled job and studying	3%	Employed in lower-skilled job	2%
Studying	1%	Unemployed	1%
High skilled work (median) salary	£24,000	Low/medium skilled salary	£17,500

Other Subjects Allied to Medicine

Our table for the group of subjects 'allied to medicine' encompasses a wide range of degrees. They include audiology, complementary therapies, counselling, health services management, health sciences, nutrition, occupational therapy, optometry, ophthalmology, orthoptics, osteopathy, podiatry and speech therapy. Physiotherapy and radiography have rankings of their own. Not all the universities that feature in this table offer all of the subjects that fall under the broad 'allied to medicine' heading, and performance in our ranking is naturally influenced by which specialisms are offered.

Strathclyde, which takes first place in the table for the fifth year in a row, has degrees in speech and language, prosthetics and orthotics, and pathology. In the most recent National Student Survey it received rave reviews in the sections that focus on teaching quality and on the wider experience, which have outdone all other universities on both measures. Southampton has moved up to second place this year and was the top scorer in the Research Excellence Framework. Cambridge, confined to fifth place overall because it did not enter the Research Excellence Framework in the relevant category, has the highest entry standards.

Elsewhere in the table Aston and East Anglia have moved into this year's top ten while poor student satisfaction rates have sent Leeds from tenth place last year to 28= and Newcastle from 11th to 21st.

Early career prospects are good. Four universities achieved rare 100% proportions of graduates in professional employment or further study 15 months after finishing their degrees; Plymouth – which has moved into 11th place from 24=, Sunderland, Bedfordshire and Northampton. As a grouping the subjects are placed 15th in our 67-strong employment ranking, and almost three-quarters of graduates were working full-time in professional-level jobs 15 months on from graduation.

Applications in virtually all the subjects in this group were impacted by the withdrawal of NHS bursaries, but increased offer rates have kept enrolments steady and 2019 saw increases in most of the subjects, including anatomy, physiology and pathology and opthalmics, as well as the much larger 'others' grouping.

Other Subjects Allied to Medicine	Teaching quality %	Student experience %	Research quality %	Entry standards (UCAS points)	Graduate prospects %	Overall score
1 Strathclyde	93.3	96.3	52.2	208	93.5	100.0
2 Southampton	81.1	81.3	65.7	164	93.3	93.6
3 Dundee	83.0	82.4	31.3	218	84.6	92.7
4 Lancaster	83.0	82.6	55.2	152	96.8	92.6
5 Cambridge	—	—	—	228	91.0	91.6
=6 Aston	87.0	86.0	39.1	139	97.4	90.9
=6 Cardiff	81.1	81.3	36.8	165	96.5	90.9
8 East Anglia	85.4	85.8	24.9	152	98.4	90.2
9 Robert Gordon	92.6	92.0	4.9	157	94.4	89.5
10 University College London	72.7	80.9	48.4	159	—	89.3
11 Plymouth	87.0	83.9	9.5	155	100.0	89.0
12 Exeter	78.8	78.3	41.1	166	86.9	88.6
13 Manchester	72.0	67.7	57.1	158	91.8	88.4
14 Reading	81.7	76.7	42.3	144	91.7	88.3
15 Glasgow Caledonian	84.9	82.9	8.1	173	92.2	88.2
=16 Birmingham	82.9	82.3	31.5	151	90.2	88.1
=16 Liverpool	86.0	84.0	35.3	129	92.7	88.1
=16 Swansea	82.1	77.3	44.7	136	91.7	88.1
19 Surrey	74.2	79.7	37.5	156	93.8	88.0
20 City, London	82.2	80.1	20.5	141	95.3	86.7
21 Newcastle	77.2	79.7	47.8	156	78.8	86.6
22 Hull	83.3	81.0	16.7	153	—	86.4
23 Northumbria	81.9	77.7	14.0	145	95.8	86.1
24 Wolverhampton	88.5	84.7	11.0	139	—	86.0
25 Sheffield	80.9	81.1	38.3	151	77.4	85.5
=26 King's College London	74.3	71.4	34.6	152	—	85.4
=26 Nottingham	87.5	73.2	31.4	123	—	85.4
=28 Leeds	78.5	75.2	31.7	141	—	85.3
=28 Sunderland	79.4	79.1	7.5	139	100.0	85.3
30 Warwick	82.7	86.3	25.3	151	78.5	85.2
31 Northampton	87.3	79.3	1.6	119	100.0	84.6
=32 Bournemouth	83.5	80.6	4.7	151	88.9	84.5

=32	Brighton	86.6	80.5	4.8	129	94.1	84.5
34	Bedfordshire	75.4	68.3	25.1	122	100.0	84.0
35	South Wales	85.1	76.4	2.2	139	92.6	83.9
36	Oxford Brookes	76.4	74.3	3.0	143	97.6	83.4
=37	Cumbria	81.9	76.5	0.7	131	95.5	83.1
=37	Ulster	75.6	76.2	27.7	139	84.1	83.1
39	Cardiff Metropolitan	84.5	82.3	3.6	134	87.0	82.9
40	Teesside	83.7	79.3	2.4	127	89.3	82.2
=41	Huddersfield	83.4	79.3	13.2	126	82.8	81.9
=41	Queen Margaret, Edinburgh	76.4	68.7	6.7	172	80.0	81.9
43	Lincoln	88.7	86.2	22.6	124	69.0	81.7
=44	Sheffield Hallam	79.9	76.7	3.7	128	90.3	81.6
=44	West of England	83.8	84.9	8.2	123	82.0	81.6
46	Greenwich	75.6	76.0	2.2	129	94.4	81.4
47	Bradford	76.8	75.7	9.5	136	86.2	81.3
48	Manchester Metropolitan	84.5	83.0	12.0	127	76.7	81.2
49	Queen Mary, London	53.8	71.6	48.3	142	—	80.7
=50	Salford	86.0	83.6	3.8	130	75.4	80.5
=50	York St John	84.5	80.5	1.9	114	85.7	80.5
52	Coventry	77.4	71.6	4.5	123	90.8	80.3
53	Anglia Ruskin	79.4	78.7	3.1	114	89.1	80.2
54	Liverpool John Moores	73.0	78.1	6.0	145	81.5	80.1
=55	Birmingham City	75.5	72.6	1.5	130	88.4	79.7
=55	Leeds Beckett	79.7	81.8	3.5	109	86.7	79.7
=55	Portsmouth	78.0	70.6	24.3	119	78.8	79.7
58	London South Bank	77.5	72.4	13.7	128	80.0	79.6
=59	Brunel London	62.5	69.8	18.2	123	94.3	79.4
=59	Central Lancashire	75.8	70.8	8.3	139	80.4	79.4
=61	Essex	79.1	80.4	—	94	93.9	79.2
=61	Roehampton	76.2	75.5	20.6	109	—	79.2
63	Bangor	70.1	64.2	34.7	110	84.2	79.1
64	West of Scotland	84.3	83.9	29.0	122	59.3	78.9
65	Hertfordshire	80.6	78.2	4.0	108	84.1	78.8
66	Chester	77.8	75.6	12.0	112	81.5	78.7
=67	Bucks New	80.8	81.7	1.0	105	—	77.8
=67	St Mary's, Twickenham	77.1	75.7	4.8	121	78.8	77.8
69	De Montfort	77.4	78.5	13.0	112*	73.1	77.1
=70	Canterbury Christ Church	71.8	65.2	2.2	117	86.9	76.8
=70	Derby	79.2	75.4	7.3	123	69.8	76.8
72	Glyndŵr	80.2	74.1	3.6	110	75.0	76.5
73	Gloucestershire	73.7	57.7	6.0	133	—	76.4
74	Middlesex	69.4	69.1	10.0	112	79.9	75.6
75	Worcester	72.0	75.8	2.6	129	65.2	74.2
76	East London	75.2	73.6	7.6	110	67.6	74.1
77	Edge Hill	62.2	63.2	2.0	137	—	73.7

Employed in high-skilled job	67%	Employed in lower-skilled job and studying	1%
Employed in high-skilled job and studying	4%	Employed in lower-skilled job	12%
Studying	13%	Unemployed	3%
High skilled work (median) salary	£24,000	Low/medium skilled salary	£17,500

Pharmacology and Pharmacy

The disciplines of pharmacology and pharmacy are entirely different courses, that lead to different careers. Pharmacology is a branch of medicine concerned with drugs, their uses, effects and how they interact with the human body. Pharmacy degrees are designed to train and license individuals to dispense prescription medicines and become pharmacists. This table also includes toxicology, which is similar to pharmacology but focuses on the toxic – rather than healing – properties of venoms, poisons and drugs.

Pharmacology and pharmacy courses are evenly split between universities in England, and few cover both. The MPharm degree is the only direct route to professional registration as a pharmacist and takes four years, while pharmacology is available as a three-year BSc or as an extended course. Thirty institutions are offering the MPharm course in 2021–22, and a further nine are running a BSc in pharmaceutical science or as part of a broader degree. Chemistry and another science or maths A-levels or the equivalent are usually required.

Applications to the group of three degrees increased by 7% in 2019, putting a halt to nine consecutive years of downturns during which numbers had fallen by around 25%. As in other health subjects, increased offer rates have maintained enrolments at a steady rate even as applications dipped. Entry standards are not as stiff as they were in 2011, when there were seven applications to the place, but with more than five candidates per enrolment in 2019 they are not a walkover, either.

Cambridge averaged the highest entry standards in the UCAS tariff in 2019, contributing to its continued position at the top of the table. It shares first place with Dundee this year, which also averaged entry standards above 200 UCAS points, and performs strongly across the board. Third place is another draw, between Strathclyde and Queen's, Belfast; and the latter of the two achieved the best results in the Research Excellence Framework.

Three universities scored higher than 90% in the sections of the National Student Survey that focus on teaching quality; London Metropolitan, Westminster and Sussex – in that order. London Met also came top in the sections relating to the wider experience.

Ulster, Leeds and Queen Margaret, Edinburgh all had 100% of graduates in professional employment or further study 15 months after finishing their degrees. The subjects have maintained their top ten position in our employment ranking this year, with just under 90% in the top outcomes, of these 72% were working in high-skilled jobs, 5% were combining such work with study and 12% were solely engaged in postgraduate study.

Pharmacology and Pharmacy

	Teaching quality %	Student experience %	Research quality %	Entry standards (UCAS points)	Graduate prospects %	Overall score
=1 Cambridge	—	—	52.5	228	91.0	100.0
=1 Dundee	80.8	84.3	55.4	201	—	100.0
=3 Queen's, Belfast	85.8	86.9	60.0	159	98.1	98.8
=3 Strathclyde	76.3	80.8	52.2	220	96.2	98.8
5 Ulster	87.9	88.8	42.5	159	100.0	98.0
6 Cardiff	87.6	87.2	36.8	157	97.6	96.3
=7 Bath	80.3	85.1	56.2	154	95.8	96.0
=7 Nottingham	82.4	83.8	51.2	147	98.4	96.0
9 Glasgow	81.0	86.9	33.4	199	85.7	94.3
10 Bristol	89.3	89.9	47.0	155	81.3	93.8
11 East Anglia	84.6	85.5	38.1	129	97.4	93.7
=12 Leeds	75.2	77.3	40.9	152	100.0	93.2
=12 University College London	78.5	80.3	51.3	169	86.9	93.2
14 Manchester	77.1	79.6	57.1	152	89.7	93.1
15 Newcastle	80.9	77.7	47.8	146	89.8	92.3
16 Robert Gordon	85.9	80.1	4.9	188	90.2	91.8
17 Reading	82.8	81.3	34.2	126	90.9	90.5
18 Bradford	89.6	92.0	9.5	133	88.5	90.3
19 Queen Margaret, Edinburgh	88.1	79.4	1.5	127*	100.0	90.2
20 Liverpool	76.9	80.4	31.7	156	87.9	90.1
21 Westminster	91.5	88.8	21.2	105	—	89.9
22 Aberdeen	75.6	81.1	34.7	183	79.3	89.8
23 Birmingham	82.0	81.5	19.2	148	89.0	89.7
=24 Glasgow Caledonian	89.0	91.0	8.1	167	76.9	89.2
=24 Lincoln	81.2	82.7	22.6	130	90.3	89.2
26 King's College London	68.8	74.4	46.8	145	90.1	89.1
27 Nottingham Trent	85.7	85.5	24.1	113	—	88.9
28 Keele	83.5	80.2	20.9	134	87.8	88.8
29 Swansea	77.4	74.3	44.7	120	—	88.5
30 Sussex	90.2	81.4	8.0	125	—	88.3
31 Aston	77.9	79.1	39.1	119	86.0	88.0
32 Huddersfield	75.7	75.8	13.2	125	97.8	87.7
33 Portsmouth	86.3	84.2	24.3	100	85.5	87.4
=34 Kent	73.1	62.1	42.3	132		86.2
=34 Sunderland	73.5	76.5	7.5	120	97.2	86.2
36 London Metropolitan	95.1	92.1	5.2	118*	73.3	86.1
37 Liverpool John Moores	74.8	78.9	6.0	140	88.9	85.8
38 De Montfort	77.2	75.5	13.0	115*	91.1	85.6
39 Coventry	81.5	85.2	4.5	120*	—	85.4
40 Queen Mary, London	82.1	86.0	40.2	143	60.0	84.7
41 Chester	80.9	79.6	12.0	102	—	83.8
42 Greenwich	72.8	80.3	2.7	126	86.9	83.7

Pharmacology and Pharmacy cont	Teaching quality %	Student experience %	Research quality %	Entry standards (UCAS points)	Graduate prospects %	Overall score
43 East London	80.0	81.5	7.6	105	—	83.5
44 Hertfordshire	79.6	82.0	10.9	107	81.1	83.4
45 Wolverhampton	73.9	71.9	11.0	124	82.1	82.5
46 Kingston	74.7	74.4	2.6	112	86.7	82.4
47 Brighton	73.1	76.9	4.8	108	84.7	81.8
48 Central Lancashire	61.6	66.7	8.3	141	88.4	81.7
49 Anglia Ruskin	76.5	70.7	3.1	83*	—	78.2

Employed in high-skilled job	72%	Employed in lower-skilled job and studying	0%
Employed in high-skilled job and studying	5%	Employed in lower-skilled job	5%
Studying	12%	Unemployed	6%
High skilled work (median) salary	£30,000	Low/medium skilled salary	£19,500

Philosophy

St Andrews has edged ahead of Oxford in this year's Philosophy table, securing the top spot. It performs strongly across the board, without coming first in any individual measures. Oxford has had a good run at number one; it still has the highest entry standards and was the top scorer in the Research Excellence Framework. St Andrews' position has been boosted by improved satisfaction scores, but Oxford continues to boycott the National Student Survey (NSS), as does fourth-ranked Cambridge. Warwick, which has the best graduate prospects, has moved up the table to third from ninth place last year.

Thirty-third-ranked West of England outdoes all others for student satisfaction for both teaching quality and the wider undergraduate experience. Gloucestershire and St Mary's, Twickenham also topped 90% in the sections of the NSS related to teaching quality.

Applications declined in 2019 for the second year running. The dip follows five years of increases however, which had brought numbers to levels last seen before £9,000 fees were introduced. The latest drop has brought applications a little lower than that now, but enrolments were exactly the same in 2019 as they were in 2011: 1,660.

Under the new Graduate Outcomes measure, which takes a census 15 months after graduates have finished degrees, Warwick was the only university with more than 90% in professional-level jobs or further study, though the London School of Economics came close. As a whole, the subject ranks 44th in our employment table, with 68.6% of graduates achieving the top two outcomes 15 months on.

Relatively few philosophy undergraduates took the subject at A-level, and some departments actively discourage it. Degrees involve more maths skills than many candidates expect, especially when the syllabus has an emphasis on logic.

Philosophy

	Teaching quality %	Student experience %	Research quality %	Entry standards (UCAS points)	Graduate prospects %	Overall score
1 St Andrews	88.8	87.5	52.7	202	80.0	100.0
2 Oxford	—	—	61.3	209	87.8	99.6
3 Warwick	82.4	79.1	47.7	173	92.0	96.7
4 Cambridge	—	—	51.6	195	76.5	96.2
5 University College London	75.1	70.9	55.6	180	87.6	94.8
6 London School of Economics	77.0	72.3	48.6	172	89.2	94.0
=7 Durham	78.1	70.6	30.1	196	87.5	92.8
=7 King's College London	73.7	68.7	53.9	174	83.9	92.8
9 Birmingham	80.3	69.9	52.8	157	80.2	92.4
10 Lancaster	78.5	74.7	53.0	146	80.6	91.8
11 Bristol	75.3*	69.3*	40.9	176	84.7	91.6
=12 Aberdeen	79.7	79.4	39.1	164	—	91.0
=12 Exeter	75.8	74.5	41.0	175	78.4	91.0
=14 Dundee	88.5	84.6	27.7	149	—	90.9
=14 Newcastle	75.6	71.0	54.3	137	84.6	90.9
=14 Stirling	87.4	78.9	22.7	171	—	90.9
17 Southampton	89.9	86.4	31.7	139	65.7	89.2
18 Edinburgh	67.8	65.5	49.7	177	76.6	89.1
=19 Royal Holloway, London	86.3	83.7	30.5	130	—	88.7
=19 York	81.9	75.8	30.7	145	77.9	88.7
21 Nottingham	83.2	77.4	28.2	141	75.4	88.0
22 Glasgow	82.1	77.8	18.9	169	72.2	87.9
23 Sussex	79.1	72.4	34.2	138	79.1	87.8
24 Sheffield	79.8	74.2	48.3	145	62.0	87.6
25 Manchester	75.3	70.9	31.9	159	77.2	87.5
26 Leeds	73.5	71.1	39.5	157	69.6	86.7
27 East Anglia	80.3	75.4	28.6	129	76.7	86.5
28 Cardiff	78.7	76.1	36.3	139	68.2	86.4
29 Essex	77.9	75.8	44.0	106	73.5	85.9
=30 Liverpool	79.3	73.2	28.4	129	69.9	84.6
=30 Reading	82.9	78.9	28.6	123	64.1	84.6
32 Manchester Metropolitan	88.2	82.5	12.5	117	67.6	84.1
33 West of England	92.9	92.9	18.6	105	54.5	84.0
34 Gloucestershire	91.9	90.2	6.9	103	—	83.9
35 Queen's, Belfast	65.6	62.7	40.3	139	72.6	83.0
36 Hertfordshire	81.9	73.2	32.9	96	—	82.6
37 St Mary's, Twickenham	91.9	86.7	7.0	94*	—	82.4
38 Kent	73.6	73.3	31.0	124	64.0	82.1
39 Nottingham Trent	87.4	81.3	10.0	116	54.5	80.8
40 Brighton	81.4	76.6	13.1	100	69.3	80.7
41 Bangor	88.4	90.3	—	129	45.0	79.6
42 Oxford Brookes	80.9	76.6	8.4	108	61.2	78.9

Philosophy cont	Teaching quality %	Student experience %	Research quality %	Entry standards (UCAS points)	Graduate prospects %	Overall score
43 Keele	72.3	73.0	23.7	115	48.4	76.8
44 Hull	79.2	71.4	10.5	111	44.1	75.2

Employed in high-skilled job	48%	Employed in lower-skilled job and studying	1%
Employed in high-skilled job and studying	5%	Employed in lower-skilled job	26%
Studying	14%	Unemployed	6%
High skilled work (median) salary	£25,000	Low/medium skilled salary	£18,500

Physics and Astronomy

Sky high entry grades are often a hallmark of physics and astronomy degrees, which attract some of the heftiest UCAS tariff scores of any subject. Six universities in this year's table average at least 200 UCAS points and another 11 average more than 170. Only three institutions drop below 110 points, the equivalent of BBC at A-level. Most degree courses in both physics and astronomy demand physics and maths A-level. Physics is much the larger subject of the two, attracting almost six applications to the place, while astronomy edged towards seven applications per enrolment in 2019.

The so-called 'Brian Cox effect' has been credited with the recent upturn in popularity of both physics and astronomy, in recognition of the Manchester University professor of particle physics' frequent television work. Their ninth successive increase brought applications to study physics to a record number in 2019. Astronomy applications declined slightly but have been on such an upward trajectory that 2019's numbers were still approaching double those that applied ten years ago.

Cambridge has overtaken St Andrews at the top of our table this year. Cambridge's entry standards beat all others and its submission to the Research Excellence Framework achieved the best results. St Andrews is behind only by 0.3% though, its position buoyed by consistently high scores for student satisfaction, along with strong performance in all other measures. West of Scotland, in 32nd place overall, has the highest rates of student satisfaction for both teaching quality, 92.7%, and the wider experience, 92.5%, though the latter is equalled by Royal Holloway in 14th place.

Oxford leads for graduate prospects with close to 97% in professional-level work or further study 15 months after graduation. The new Graduate Outcomes survey showed that 28% stay on for a postgraduate course, rising to nearly a third including the 4% who combine graduate-level work with part-time study. The high proportion that continues in academia helps the subjects to place 12th in our employment ranking, even though only 54% of graduates were in full-time professional jobs.

Physics and Astronomy	Teaching quality %	Student experience %	Research quality %	Entry standards (UCAS points)	Graduate prospects %	Overall score
1 Cambridge	—	—	55.7	228	91.0	100.0
2 St Andrews	88.7	88.3	51.0	224	89.0	99.7
3 Oxford	—	—	52.1	215	96.9	98.0
4 Durham	80.5	79.9	46.2	216	93.8	96.9

5	Heriot-Watt	89.5	89.4	44.1	173	87.2	95.3
6	Manchester	80.2	78.0	44.9	197	92.3	94.9
7	Lancaster	91.6	88.5	37.6	169	88.5	94.6
8	Warwick	82.5	79.8	46.1	183	90.1	94.4
9	Edinburgh	75.9	75.3	48.7	197	92.2	94.3
10	Bath	81.5	82.8	40.0	178	93.4	94.0
11	Leicester	92.0	91.1	40.8	135	88.7	93.5
=12	Birmingham	78.7	79.7	33.8	192	91.9	92.3
=12	Exeter	81.0	84.3	42.4	175	85.2	92.3
14	Royal Holloway, London	90.0	92.5	31.5	140	89.5	92.2
15	University College London	69.7	76.2	45.1	181	93.7	91.9
16	Surrey	82.2	82.5	39.6	145	92.4	91.8
=17	Queen's, Belfast	85.5	85.0	44.4	157	81.5	91.7
=17	Strathclyde	80.5	80.8	45.3	191	79.0	91.7
19	Southampton	80.9	79.3	44.1	156	87.1	91.3
=20	Imperial College London	61.8	64.5	49.6	201	95.1	91.2
=20	Nottingham	78.7	78.9	48.3	162	84.1	91.2
22	York	82.1	80.1	35.8	154	91.1	91.0
23	Leeds	85.2	81.2	41.8	160	81.4	90.9
24	Glasgow	74.8	77.6	42.0	200	81.5	90.7
25	Bristol	77.8	78.3	43.7	177	82.5	90.6
26	Sheffield	79.1	79.1	36.8	152	91.0	90.3
27	Cardiff	85.2	87.6	34.9	146	83.2	90.0
=28	Sussex	78.7	76.9	24.7	149	96.8	89.1
=28	Swansea	85.1	86.8	33.0	115	89.1	89.1
=30	Aberdeen	77.1	81.5	32.0	173	—	89.0
=30	Liverpool	80.4	79.2	31.5	145	90.1	89.0
32	West of Scotland	92.7	92.5	19.1	134	—	88.9
33	Hull	87.2	84.7	24.2	110	88.4	87.3
34	Loughborough	82.9	83.1	19.0	144	86.7	86.9
35	King's College London	71.6	69.7	35.8	149	88.1	86.6
36	Dundee	75.6	71.6	34.1	160	—	86.5
37	Kent	82.0	79.3	30.7	119	84.4	86.3
38	Northumbria	87.3	85.7	30.7	133	70.7	85.7
39	Nottingham Trent	92.0	88.8	20.1	107	76.4	85.0
40	Keele	86.5	84.6	31.8	115	66.7	83.5
41	Salford	89.0	88.3	4.4	116	80.0	82.9
42	Portsmouth	81.7	77.9	21.8	101	80.0	82.4
43	Aberystwyth	82.6	86.8	12.4	115	73.7	81.2
44	Central Lancashire	78.2	74.5	19.8	128*	73.7	81.0
45	Queen Mary, London	70.6	72.0	27.6	140	72.4	80.9
46	Hertfordshire	84.9	82.9	20.2	107	59.3	78.7

Employed in high-skilled job	54%	Employed in lower-skilled job and studying	0%
Employed in high-skilled job and studying	4%	Employed in lower-skilled job	9%
Studying	28%	Unemployed	5%
High skilled work (median) salary	£28,000	Low/medium skilled salary	£19,000

Physiotherapy

Only medicine has outdone physiotherapy in our employment ranking this year, across all 67 subject areas. The new Graduate Outcomes survey revealed that 94% of physiotherapy graduates were already working in professional-level jobs 15 months after completing their degrees, while a further 2% were juggling high-skilled work with postgraduate studies. Only 1% had started out in jobs deemed 'low-skilled' and the same proportion was unemployed. Nineteen of our table's 36 universities achieved 100% graduate prospects scores, and none had less than 84% of graduates in the top career outcomes.

Rates of pay at the same 15-months-on point do not rank as high as the levels of professional employment however, and 33 subjects outdid the £24,000 median salaries earned by physiotherapy graduates.

The physiotherapy table is now in its eighth year, having been extracted from our 'other subjects allied to medicine' ranking. Southampton, one of the institutions with perfect graduate prospects scores, remains clear at the top with the best results in the Research Excellence Framework and good student satisfaction scores. The highest entry standards are at Robert Gordon, which has been a close second to Southampton for a number of years. It has top five satisfaction rates in both the teaching quality and wider experience measures but is held back overall by a low score for research.

Physiotherapy students at Worcester, ranked 16=, awarded it unbeaten scores for teaching quality in the National Student Survey, that were only 1.2% shy of full marks. Worcester also equalled Robert Gordon in coming top for the wider experience. Satisfaction rates are generally high for physiotherapy degrees, with 15 universities achieving above 90% for teaching quality and nine for the broad experience.

Entry standards go no lower than 112 UCAS points, and half of the table average above 150. More than 60 universities and colleges are offering degree courses in physiotherapy, or a related subject such as osteopathy or chiropractic, starting in 2021. The majority are post-1992 institutions, four of which feature in our top ten.

Physiotherapy	Teaching quality %	Student experience %	Research quality %	Entry standards (UCAS points)	Graduate prospects %	Overall score
1 Southampton	88.9	91.4	65.7	165	100.0	100.0
2 Robert Gordon	94.6	95.3	4.9	204	100.0	98.2
3 Liverpool	94.4	88.6	35.3	156	100.0	96.6
4 Nottingham	91.5	89.3	40.6	149	100.0	96.2
5 Birmingham	78.9	70.8	63.7	169	96.0	96.0
6 Northumbria	93.7	90.9	14.0	151	100.0	94.1
7 Glasgow Caledonian	89.8	88.9	8.1	203	92.9	93.9
8 Cardiff	87.9	86.7	36.8	165	93.9	93.7
9 Salford	95.6	92.9	3.8	154	100.0	93.6
10 Plymouth	87.4	87.5	9.5	156	100.0	93.2
11 Manchester Metropolitan	87.5	87.5	12.0	149	100.0	92.8
12 Central Lancashire	91.1	87.8	8.3	148	100.0	92.7
13 Teesside	79.8	78.6	2.4	170	100.0	92.4
14 Coventry	91.1	88.0	4.5	148	100.0	92.3

15 Wolverhampton	92.9	86.1	11.0	147	—	92.1
=16 Leeds Beckett	90.5	94.3	3.5	143	100.0	92.0
=16 Worcester	98.8	95.3	2.6	132	100.0	92.0
18 Brunel London	94.1	92.7	18.2	132	97.7	91.7
=19 Bradford	92.2	88.7	9.5	161	94.1	91.2
=19 Hertfordshire	91.4	89.6	4.0	134	100.0	91.2
=21 Brighton	93.6	86.8	4.8	128	100.0	90.8
=21 Ulster	75.4	68.7	27.7	151	97.1	90.8
=23 Keele	87.3	88.9	20.9	136	95.1	90.1
=23 King's College London	59.6	50.8	34.6	150	100.0	90.1
=23 Oxford Brookes	85.1	90.5	3.0	132	100.0	90.1
=26 Huddersfield	76.3	78.6	13.2	143	97.0	89.1
=26 West of England	78.2	82.0	8.2	139	98.0	89.1
28 York St John	94.7	88.2	1.9	136	95.2	89.0
=29 Bournemouth	95.9	94.5	4.7	132	94.4	88.9
=29 Sheffield Hallam	83.1	82.0	3.7	135	98.1	88.9
31 Kingston/St George's, London	73.2	76.8	2.6	154	96.7	88.4
=32 Canterbury Christ Church	69.5	63.7	2.2	167	—	88.2
=32 East London	83.0	82.2	7.6	112	100.0	88.2
34 Cumbria	72.4	70.1	0.7	138	100.0	88.1
35 East Anglia	88.4	87.4	24.9	151	84.6	86.6
36 London South Bank	61.4	47.1	13.7	159*	—	86.5

Employed in high-skilled job	94%	Employed in lower-skilled job and studying	0%
Employed in high-skilled job and studying	2%	Employed in lower-skilled job	1%
Studying	0%	Unemployed	1%
High skilled work (median) salary	£24,000	Low/medium skilled salary	—

Politics

Brexit has not dimmed young people's enthusiasm for politics degrees. Applications to study the subject have been in the ascendant for the past decade and continued to climb after the 2016 referendum. Even though they dipped a little in 2019, there were still nearly 14,000 more candidates than had applied ten years before. Enrolments have managed to keep up with the pace of demand due to considerable expansion of provision; there are 120 universities and colleges offering politics in 2021 as single and/or joint honours programmes. Competition remains stiff at just under six applications per place in the 2019 admissions round.

Few universities have sat still in our Politics table since last year. The state of flux starts from the top, where St Andrews has ousted former winner Warwick, which has slipped to fourth. St Andrews has the highest entry standards and performs strongly across all other measures. Oxford, bucking the trend of change, remains in second place, while Cambridge has slipped one place to fifth. The London School of Economics – which is top for graduate prospects – has moved into third, from seventh. The top ten has four new (or re-)entrants; Stirling in seventh, King's College London, Bath, and Durham which have all improved from top 25 positions. Loughborough is among those that have moved in the opposite direction, going from tenth place last year to 28th this, due to lower scores in most measures. Essex – which is well ahead in the Research Excellence Framework – has moved out of the top five to rank 13th.

As is the case in many subjects, the best rates of student satisfaction are found at a university further down the table, in this case in 47= place at Salford, which received the highest scores in the sections of the National Student Survey relating to teaching quality. Aberystwyth (14th) was not far behind. West of England, in 30th, is in front on the measure of the wider student experience.

Entry standards offer something for a wide range of candidates; over a quarter of universities average more than 150 points in the UCAS tariff, and a similar proportion average under 110.

Politics ranks a modest 38th in our employment table, with 70.9% of graduates in professional employment or pursuing postgraduate studies 15 months after finishing their degrees. Earnings-wise the subject fares better though, in 19th place, with median salaries of £26,000 for those working in the desirable 'high-skilled' category of jobs.

Politics	Teaching quality %	Student experience %	Research quality %	Entry standards (UCAS points)	Graduate prospects %	Overall score
1 St Andrews	87.8	81.8	38.4	219	84.8	100.0
2 Oxford	–	–	61.1	209	87.9	98.9
3 London School of Economics	77.2	73.5	54.6	175	94.5	97.8
4 Warwick	80.5	79.5	52.7	182	81.6	96.8
5 Cambridge	–	–	38.2	198	87.3	95.7
6 University College London	69.6	68.3	57.0	187	–	94.0
7 Stirling	87.9	81.3	33.8	159	77.9	93.4
8 King's College London	75.5	72.7	29.0	185	91.2	93.1
9 Bath	78.4	75.1	27.4	164	93.5	92.8
10 Durham	73.1	69.2	27.0	188	90.9	91.9
=11 Lancaster	77.8	74.0	53.0	141	77.8	91.8
=11 Strathclyde	77.3	76.0	41.6	195	67.6	91.8
13 Essex	76.6	77.2	69.6	106	74.2	91.3
14 Aberystwyth	90.0	86.1	40.2	108	72.7	90.7
15 Exeter	76.9	76.4	29.8	165	80.5	90.4
16 Sheffield	77.5	71.5	48.3	151	71.7	90.1
=17 Southampton	78.0	74.9	37.0	134	82.2	89.7
=17 York	78.2	74.5	36.9	146	78.3	89.7
19 Edinburgh	65.3	65.9	44.5	188	76.5	89.5
20 Glasgow	73.8	69.0	30.5	190	72.9	89.1
21 Nottingham	75.7	69.8	30.8	147	83.2	88.7
22 Surrey	86.5	83.6	12.5	143	76.7	88.4
23 Soas, London	78.4	75.8	30.5	173	65.9	88.3
24 Manchester	73.5	70.1	28.4	161	80.3	88.2
=25 East Anglia	78.3	77.6	35.5	128	74.9	88.0
=25 Leeds	73.7	69.9	25.1	163	81.4	88.0
27 Bristol	71.7	66.8	30.4	165	79.8	87.9
28 Loughborough	83.7	82.3	22.5	138	71.2	87.7
29 Northumbria	89.2	81.6	12.7	131	–	87.6

30 West of England	89.5	88.1	13.8	106	77.8	87.4
=31 Aberdeen	78.8	80.2	18.4	179	65.1	87.3
=31 Newcastle	77.4	76.0	22.0	148	77.1	87.3
=33 Birmingham	72.7	68.4	31.1	150	78.6	87.1
=33 Brunel London	81.8	73.1	32.4	97	82.7	87.1
35 Aston	75.4	73.0	38.6	118	77.7	87.0
36 Sussex	76.2	71.0	33.6	148	70.9	86.9
37 Royal Holloway, London	78.0	77.5	30.5	124	73.0	86.4
38 Greenwich	83.4	86.2	8.6	104	85.0	86.2
39 Cardiff	73.1	69.9	30.4	140	75.3	85.8
40 Oxford Brookes	74.2	75.0	17.8	112	90.0	85.7
41 Swansea	83.1	83.9	18.5	116	70.8	85.4
42 Portsmouth	84.4	82.0	32.2	103	63.3	85.2
43 Chichester	85.9	82.9	15.8	106	—	85.0
=44 Kent	76.4	71.8	27.8	121	73.5	84.7
=44 Queen Mary, London	71.3	68.7	28.1	146	72.8	84.7
46 Coventry	83.5	80.3	5.6	103	82.6	84.5
=47 Queen's, Belfast	65.4	65.8	35.0	147	73.5	84.3
=47 Salford	91.9	83.1	4.8	107	69.6	84.3
49 Dundee	76.8	73.6	10.8	170	65.9	84.2
50 Manchester Metropolitan	86.7	81.5	18.0	120	59.6	83.8
51 Canterbury Christ Church	87.8	83.0	3.2	93	76.3	83.4
52 Huddersfield	85.8	78.7	9.5	110	—	83.3
=53 De Montfort	84.3	78.0	10.7	100*	72.5	82.9
=53 Leicester	75.1	72.6	20.0	121	72.0	82.9
=55 Bradford	71.6	69.4	12.7	114*	85.7	82.8
=55 Derby	80.0	80.7	13.5	113	—	82.8
57 Sheffield Hallam	86.4	80.1	14.4	106	61.9	82.4
=58 Keele	74.6	74.0	24.0	111	68.8	82.2
=58 Reading	69.1	67.7	37.0	118	66.4	82.2
60 Plymouth	78.5	70.5	25.8	111	64.3	82.1
61 City, London	67.6	70.4	24.6	129	71.0	81.9
62 London Metropolitan	84.0	78.8	1.2	102*	73.5	81.7
63 Liverpool	76.6	76.1	12.0	135	63.8	81.6
64 Lincoln	82.9	81.2	7.7	111	60.0	80.6
=65 Hull	83.0	76.1	10.8	113	56.0	79.8
=65 Winchester	85.3	71.5	—	106	66.7	79.8
=67 East London	78.9	71.0	13.7	97	—	79.3
=67 West of Scotland	81.8	73.7	—	124	60.9	79.3
69 Nottingham Trent	81.9	77.6	5.1	108	57.3	78.7
70 Liverpool Hope	78.0	66.9	7.0	109	—	78.1
71 Westminster	79.0	76.5	14.3	104	51.6	77.9
72 Chester	76.0	73.6	—	100	68.8	77.8
73 Bournemouth	71.0	69.4	15.1	104	—	77.5
74 Goldsmiths, London	67.3	62.5	16.8	109	67.5	77.3
75 Brighton	68.6	53.4	13.1	96*	77.3	77.1

Politics cont

	Teaching quality %	Student experience %	Research quality %	Entry standards (UCAS points)	Graduate prospects %	Overall score
76 Leeds Beckett	83.5	77.9	—	95	54.5	76.8
77 Ulster	72.5	66.8	20.9	112	49.0	76.2
78 Central Lancashire	89.1	79.9	12.0	110	28.6	76.1
79 Kingston	83.2	81.7	—	68	50.4	74.3
80 Middlesex	60.6	55.0	14.9	99	—	71.1

Employed in high-skilled job	52%	Employed in lower-skilled job and studying	1%
Employed in high-skilled job and studying	4%	Employed in lower-skilled job	23%
Studying	13%	Unemployed	6%
High skilled work (median) salary	£26,000	Low/medium skilled salary	£19,500

Psychology

Psychology commands the second-biggest table in our *Guide*; only business is larger. It is just as big a hitter in terms of applications – outdone by nursing alone – and demand is continuing to grow. The 2019 admissions cycle heralded new highs in applications and enrolments, which both increased by 6% to nearly 128,800 and almost 24,400 respectively. Over 50% more students started psychology degree courses last autumn than did so a decade ago, pre-£9,000 tuition fees.

The growing popularity of psychology A-level may go some way to explaining the undergraduate boom, though potential students are advised not to underestimate the amount of data collection and statistics involved in the subject at degree level. Graduate prospects are unlikely to be the driving force for the undergraduate boom; psychology is sixth from the bottom of our employment ranking – with 39% of graduates in low-skilled jobs 15 months after finishing their degrees, and 6% unemployed. Only 36% of graduates were in full-time professional employment, earning median salaries of £23,000 (49 subjects recorded higher pay).

Oxford, which has the best graduate prospects, is secure at the top of the overall table, as is Cambridge in runner-up position and St Andrews – with the highest entry standards – in third once again. Ninth-ranked Loughborough received the best results in the Research Excellence Framework and Aberystwyth (53=) came top in the sections of the National Student Survey that focus on teaching quality, in which it was the only university to reach 90%. Tenth-ranked York has the best rates of satisfaction with the wider undergraduate experience.

Most undergraduate programmes are accredited by the British Psychological Society, which ensures that key topics are covered, but the clinical and biological content of courses still varies considerably. Some universities require maths and/or biology A-levels among three high-grade passes, but others are much less demanding. Entry standards range from three universities that average 200 points or more in the UCAS tariff, to 24 others that average higher than 150, down to 30 that average less than 110 UCAS points. The older foundation universities dominate the upper third of the table and Plymouth, in 30th place, is the highest-ranked post-1992 university.

Psychology

	Teaching quality %	Student experience %	Research quality %	Entry standards (UCAS points)	Graduate prospects %	Overall score
1 Oxford	—	—	58.6	200	84.1	100.0
2 Cambridge	—	—	57.5	199	84.0	96.9
3 St Andrews	81.1	85.3	45.4	214	72.5	94.1
4 Bath	75.9	81.1	56.2	193	77.4	93.1
5 University College London	77.5	80.5	57.0	177	79.8	92.7
6 Glasgow	79.5	87.0	52.9	201	65.0	92.4
7 Cardiff	81.6	83.3	55.7	162	74.8	91.8
8 Newcastle	79.9	81.2	50.0	157	82.7	91.7
9 Loughborough	81.3	86.9	62.3	152	69.8	91.3
=10 King's College London	77.0	79.7	54.1	179	73.3	91.1
=10 York	86.3	88.1	46.7	155	70.4	91.1
12 Durham	78.4	77.0	37.1	186	78.2	90.5
13 Warwick	81.4	83.9	43.1	148	76.8	89.7
14 Aberdeen	81.4	84.3	38.7	165	72.3	89.6
15 Edinburgh	71.8	73.5	52.8	199	67.4	89.2
16 Royal Holloway, London	82.5	86.9	37.8	147	71.8	88.7
17 Exeter	73.4	77.3	43.3	170	75.0	88.3
18 Manchester	76.7	78.4	44.9	153	73.5	87.8
19 East Anglia	82.7	82.5	33.2	144	71.2	87.3
20 Birmingham	68.2	70.0	55.8	157	77.3	87.1
21 Strathclyde	82.7	84.4	23.5	190	56.3	86.9
22 Southampton	78.7	81.6	47.8	153	61.3	86.6
23 Nottingham	73.6	76.0	36.4	155	75.8	86.3
24 Stirling	80.5	74.4	40.1	158	64.3	86.2
25 Sussex	75.6	75.1	42.3	144	72.9	86.1
26 Sheffield	79.2	79.9	38.8	143	64.2	85.4
27 Bangor	85.4	87.1	32.0	120	63.6	85.1
28 Kent	72.8	77.2	38.8	146	70.4	85.0
29 Bristol	58.3	62.9	49.4	168	81.5	84.7
30 Plymouth	81.4	81.0	33.8	126	65.7	84.5
31 Swansea	73.9	78.0	44.7	131	67.7	84.4
32 Surrey	75.4	76.9	22.0	148	73.8	84.3
33 Lancaster	78.1	79.7	38.5	148	58.2	84.2
34 Chichester	89.8	87.6	10.3	117	66.7	84.0
35 Nottingham Trent	86.0	85.0	19.3	124	62.6	83.6
36 Dundee	75.1	77.2	22.7	170	61.1	83.5
37 Aston	74.0	74.2	39.1	121	72.0	83.3
38 Liverpool	74.2	74.2	34.6	143	65.5	83.2
39 Leeds	66.9	70.7	33.0	159	68.8	82.6
40 Portsmouth	82.2	82.0	21.0	121	63.7	82.5
=41 Abertay	86.0	80.9	15.1	146	51.4	82.0
=41 Northumbria	80.4	78.4	18.7	136	61.5	82.0

Psychology cont

	Teaching quality %	Student experience %	Research quality %	Entry standards (UCAS points)	Graduate prospects %	Overall score
43 Glasgow Caledonian	82.9	82.1	8.1	166	50.0	81.8
=44 Reading	70.8	70.8	42.3	132	63.5	81.7
=44 Salford	84.7	82.9	3.8	119	67.5	81.7
46 Edinburgh Napier	79.6	82.2	5.3	171	52.4	81.6
47 Queen's, Belfast	68.0	67.8	40.2	149	62.5	81.4
48 Heriot-Watt	75.9	68.9	26.9	162	54.8	81.3
49 Essex	75.3	75.4	41.0	107	63.1	81.2
=50 Bournemouth	81.8	81.1	13.0	109	66.8	81.1
=50 Lincoln	82.7	84.0	7.9	126	60.8	81.1
52 Greenwich	73.3	78.3	6.7	124	76.8	81.0
=53 Aberystwyth	90.8	87.7	—	117	55.7	80.9
=53 Liverpool John Moores	81.7	79.6	7.8	137	59.4	80.9
55 Wales Trinity St David	88.5	87.0	—	118	57.9	80.8
56 Teesside	75.3	71.5	15.0	101	79.8	80.5
57 Keele	75.8	75.4	17.7	122	66.6	80.4
=58 Leicester	71.1	74.9	29.6	130	61.2	80.2
=58 Manchester Metropolitan	80.3	81.0	12.0	127	58.0	80.2
60 Chester	85.6	84.5	7.9	107	59.0	80.1
61 Hull	77.6	75.6	26.8	117	58.9	80.0
=62 Brunel London	70.1	71.9	26.6	113	71.5	79.9
=62 Sunderland	83.9	80.4	7.5	108	62.5	79.9
=64 Coventry	78.3	76.0	7.8	115	68.8	79.8
=64 Edge Hill	73.6	74.7	18.8	126	64.7	79.8
66 West London	83.1	84.7	7.6	117	56.1	79.7
67 West of England	84.4	82.5	8.2	117	54.9	79.6
68 Bolton	87.0	81.8	3.6	97	61.8	79.4
69 Ulster	71.8	74.6	23.2	131	59.2	79.2
70 Derby	85.5	81.4	8.4	107	55.6	79.1
=71 Birmingham City	85.5	82.4	—	113	56.6	78.9
=71 Staffordshire	85.1	80.8	8.2	111	54.2	78.9
73 Huddersfield	79.5	77.0	9.5	120	58.5	78.8
=74 Oxford Brookes	79.6	77.2	18.1	120	52.6	78.7
=74 Queen Mary, London	68.9	73.0	26.1	150	52.6	78.7
76 Hertfordshire	80.4	76.2	6.0	103	64.9	78.5
=77 Glyndŵr	88.8	80.0	3.6	—	46.7	78.3
=77 Sheffield Hallam	81.1	76.1	3.7	113	60.8	78.3
79 St Mary's, Twickenham	82.7	87.1	4.8	97	56.3	78.1
80 De Montfort	78.0	76.9	11.2	109*	59.7	78.0
81 City, London	69.8	70.4	24.1	132	56.5	77.9
82 Cumbria	79.7	74.5	—	134	54.5	77.7
83 Winchester	75.5	72.2	6.5	101	67.7	77.3
=84 East London	74.3	73.8	8.3	103	66.0	77.2

=84 Westminster	74.7	78.7	9.3	104	61.5	77.2
=86 Central Lancashire	72.2	71.8	12.2	123	59.7	77.1
=86 York St John	82.4	80.7	11.0	110	46.7	77.1
88 Cardiff Metropolitan	79.3	77.5	—	116	55.8	76.8
89 Kingston	70.0	70.3	6.5	98	73.4	76.6
90 London Metropolitan	79.7	80.8	—	83	64.2	76.5
91 Suffolk	75.5	65.7	—	105	69.4	76.4
=92 Gloucestershire	80.0	78.0	—	114	52.7	76.3
=92 Worcester	78.3	80.7	7.1	110	50.2	76.3
=94 London South Bank	79.3	76.9	8.6	103	52.5	76.2
=94 Roehampton	76.8	76.9	26.4	100	46.3	76.2
=96 Goldsmiths, London	65.3	66.0	40.4	124	49.0	76.1
=96 Leeds Beckett	81.2	81.2	6.5	105	47.4	76.1
=96 South Wales	82.8	76.8	0.9	112	48.8	76.1
99 Solent, Southampton	87.3	83.8	—	112	37.9	75.8
100 West of Scotland	77.8	78.0	9.4	125	41.7	75.6
101 Leeds Trinity	78.0	80.6	—	102	53.2	75.4
102 Middlesex	72.8	70.9	7.6	109	58.1	75.3
103 Liverpool Hope	75.5	77.5	5.5	106	52.9	75.2
104 Newman	77.9	77.7	0.8	108	47.1	74.3
105 Bradford	75.7	74.6	9.5	116	42.5	74.1
=106 Bedfordshire	72.2	69.7	25.1	97	46.8	74.0
=106 Bucks New	79.4	76.0	—	104	46.7	74.0
108 Anglia Ruskin	68.8	69.1	12.6	111	53.0	73.8
109 Queen Margaret, Edinburgh	71.3	64.7	8.6	134	45.0	73.6
110 Northampton	78.7	74.8	0.4	95	47.0	73.1
111 Wolverhampton	76.4	75.3	—	104	43.3	72.6
112 Brighton	74.5	71.4	12.4	108	37.0	72.2
113 Bath Spa	67.9	67.5	—	98	56.8	71.7
114 Canterbury Christ Church	73.6	69.2	2.2	100	44.6	71.3
115 Bishop Grosseteste	72.0	72.0	—	103	42.3	70.8

Employed in high-skilled job	36%	Employed in lower-skilled job and studying	2%
Employed in high-skilled job and studying	4%	Employed in lower-skilled job	39%
Studying	13%	Unemployed	6%
High skilled work (median) salary	£23,000	Low/medium skilled salary	£18,000

Radiography

Robert Gordon, *The Sunday Times* Scottish University of the Year 2021, tops our Radiography table. A stellar set of results includes achieving the highest rates of student satisfaction for both measures – teaching quality and the wider experience – in the National student Survey, along with an unbeatable employment score: 100% of graduates were in professional-level jobs or further study 15 months after finishing their degrees. Sixth-ranked Glasgow Caledonian has higher entry standards, though there are only four UCAS tariff points in it. Third-ranked Exeter was the top scorer in the Research Excellence Framework. Leeds, last year's top university for radiography, takes second place this year, while Ulster has shot up the table to join the top ten, from 23rd.

This is the eighth year we have published a dedicated ranking for radiography degrees, which were previously listed among 'other subjects allied to medicine' in the *Guide*. Diagnostic courses usually involve two years of studying anatomy, physiology and physics followed by further training in sociology, management and ethics, and the practice and science of imaging. The therapeutic branch covers much of the same scientific content in the first year, but follows this with training in oncology, psycho-social studies and other modules. Degrees require at least one science subject, usually biology, among three A-levels or the equivalent. Entry grades are tightly packed, ranging from an average of 172 UCAS points to 115.

Robert Gordon was one of eight universities to achieve perfect 100% employment scores, and as a subject radiography ranks sixth for graduate prospects. The new Graduate Outcomes survey showed that an impressive 92% of graduates were in professional jobs 15 months after finishing their degrees, and a further 3% were studying or combining it with high-skilled work. Just 2% were employed in jobs deemed 'low-skilled', while the same small proportion was unemployed. The subject has slipped further down the earnings table however, and salaries of £24,000 in those professional jobs rank a more modest 34th=.

Radiography	Teaching quality %	Student experience %	Research quality %	Entry standards (UCAS points)	Graduate prospects %	Overall score
1 Robert Gordon	91.1	90.0	4.9	168	100.0	100.0
2 Leeds	76.2	71.2	31.7	156	100.0	99.1
3 Exeter	75.2	74.7	42.4	149	96.8	98.3
4 Liverpool	87.5	80.1	35.3	133	97.1	97.6
5 Cardiff	70.8	66.8	36.8	155	97.5	97.5
6 Glasgow Caledonian	89.1	88.1	8.1	172	90.7	96.3
7 Bangor	53.6	36.8	34.7	166	100.0	95.5
8 Salford	83.6	76.8	3.8	146	100.0	95.2
9 Ulster	79.4	81.0	27.7	143	93.5	95.0
10 Keele	83.8	86.2	20.9	130	–	94.7
=11 Cumbria	88.3	82.6	0.7	130	100.0	93.9
=11 Portsmouth	77.0	64.6	24.3	135	97.2	93.9
13 Teesside	85.1	83.9	2.4	130	100.0	93.8
=14 Queen Margaret, Edinburgh	82.5	76.2	1.5	157	94.1	93.5
=14 West of England	85.7	85.3	8.2	120	100.0	93.5
16 Birmingham City	75.1	70.0	1.5	137	100.0	92.2
17 Sheffield Hallam	78.4	78.9	3.7	136	95.9	91.5
18 Hertfordshire	84.9	80.8	4.0	122	95.6	90.8
19 Suffolk	84.4	83.9	–	115	97.1	90.2
20 London South Bank	74.5	71.6	13.7	130	92.3	89.6
21 Bradford	59.1	63.6	9.5	157	91.3	89.1
22 Derby	72.2	68.7	–	147	91.7	89.0
=23 Canterbury Christ Church	77.6	68.7	2.2	126	93.8	88.4
=23 City, London	86.3	86.5	20.5	126	82.9	88.4
25 Kingston/St George's, London	72.6	65.3	2.6	130	90.6	86.6

Employed in high-skilled job	92%	Employed in lower-skilled job and studying	0%
Employed in high-skilled job and studying	2%	Employed in lower-skilled job	2%
Studying	1%	Unemployed	2%
High skilled work (median) salary	£24,000	Low/medium skilled salary	—

Russian and Eastern European Languages

Applications and enrolments in Russian and Eastern European languages were exactly the same in 2019 as in 2018: 210 and 35 respectively. The subjects have been in decline over recent years but even in 2010 – their highest point in a decade – there were only 575 applications and 100 new undergraduates. The small numbers still make for stiff competition though, at six applications per place. Many other students are learning Russian as part of broader modern languages programmes, and although these, too, have suffered a decline in demand they remain much bigger areas.

Cambridge has maintained its lead in the table for the sixth consecutive year, with the second highest entry standards and the best results in the Research Excellence Framework. Oxford takes third place, having been ousted from second by Manchester, which in the most recent National Student Survey topped 90% for the sections that focus on teaching quality – by far the highest result. Fifth-ranked Bristol was the top scorer in the sections relating to the wider undergraduate experience.

The tiny student cohorts make for exaggerated swings in statistics, as evidenced by our earnings rankings. The median graduate salary for those in professional-level jobs was £21,000 last year but has leapt to £26,000 this year – boosting the subjects to a top 20 place. Rates of graduate employment are prone to big changes too, although they have stayed steadier this year, and Russian ranks 28th in this measure. Fifteen months after finishing their degrees 64% of graduates were in professional employment, 2% were combining this level of work with postgraduate study and 12% were solely engaged in further study. UCL is first for graduate prospects, with 92.6% in these top career outcomes.

Most undergraduates learn Russian or another Eastern European language from scratch. Entry standards are pretty demanding; eleven of the 15 universities in our table average above 150 points in the UCAS tariff, one of them more than 200, and only two average beneath 130.

Russian and Eastern European Languages	Teaching quality %	Student experience %	Research quality %	Entry standards (UCAS points)	Graduate prospects %	Overall score
1 Cambridge	—	—	54.0	197	86.8	100.0
2 Manchester	90.8	85.4	48.9	160	—	97.7
3 Oxford	—	—	41.3	184	—	92.2
4 University College London	75.7	75.2	43.7	169	92.6	92.0
5 Bristol	84.6	87.2	36.0	152	—	89.6
6 Durham	73.5	68.5	34.6	185	91.0	89.0
7 Glasgow	76.1	74.8	26.3	206	—	87.6
8 Exeter	79.7	79.0	35.1	156	78.2	86.9
9 Queen Mary, London	82.6	74.3	35.1	146	—	86.3

Russian and Eastern European Languages cont	Teaching quality %	Student experience %	Research quality %	Entry standards (UCAS points)	Graduate prospects %	Overall score
10 Nottingham	83.9	70.9	39.4	128	—	86.1
11 Sheffield	73.8	62.4	41.2	146*	—	84.7
12 Birmingham	74.7	73.1	33.7	153	77.8	84.4
13 Edinburgh	70.5	60.0	30.3	169	—	81.4
14 Leeds	72.8	56.5	30.6	159	—	80.7
15 Portsmouth	89.1	82.6	32.2	99	56.3	79.8

Employed in high-skilled job	64%	Employed in lower-skilled job and studying	0%
Employed in high-skilled job and studying	2%	Employed in lower-skilled job	17%
Studying	12%	Unemployed	5%
High skilled work (median) salary	£26,000	Low/medium skilled salary	—

Social Policy

The London School of Economics has returned to its accustomed spot at the top of the Social Policy table, following a year's hiatus in the previous edition of our *Guide*. Its submission to the Research Excellence Framework achieved the best results by far, and a formidable 96% of work was deemed world-leading or internationally excellent. The LSE also leads on graduate prospects – again by a clear margin – with more than 95% of its social policy graduates in professional-level work or postgraduate studies 15 months after their degrees. QS ranks the LSE second only to Harvard globally for social policy , although it calls its table 'social sciences management'. Last year's winner, Strathclyde, has the highest entry standards and takes second place this year. Edinburgh moved up eight places to third this year, helped by much improved satisfaction scores.

Students at fifth-ranked Bangor are the most satisfied with the quality of the teaching, with Swansea the only other university to also achieve 90%. Bangor came top again in the sections of the National Student Survey that focus on the wider experience.

Graduates in professional-level jobs were being paid median salaries of £24,000 15 months after finishing their degrees, a wage that ranks social policy 34= in our earnings table. The subject does much worse for graduate prospects however, finishing third from bottom, because 40% of graduates – one of the highest proportions in the *Guide* – work in jobs categorised as 'low-skilled', for which median salaries are £17,750. Only marginally more, 41%, had secured professional-level employment.

Applications edged up a little in 2019, for the fifth time in a row, which has brought them close to the level they were at before £9,000 tuition fees were introduced. There are fewer than four applications to the place and entry standards are modest; only five universities average more than 150 points in the UCAS tariff and none averages more than 195. Our table this year is smaller by 11 universities than last year's, but 82 universities and colleges plan to offer the subject in 2021, either as single or joint honours degrees, or as part of wider social sciences programmes.

Social Policy

	Teaching quality %	Student experience %	Research quality %	Entry standards (UCAS points)	Graduate prospects %	Overall score
1 London School of Economics	78.0	76.0	74.9	164	95.2	100.0
2 Strathclyde	86.0	85.7	31.9	195	—	98.3
3 Edinburgh	75.9	73.6	53.4	188	—	96.4
4 Glasgow	79.7	75.4	41.8	175	82.1	94.5
5 Bangor	91.9	88.6	39.6	130*	—	92.7
6 Leeds	74.9	74.1	47.6	150	80.7	91.0
7 Loughborough	83.1	83.5	40.6	140	—	90.7
8 Bath	79.0	70.9	43.4	137	84.2	90.2
9 Kent	81.4	75.1	59.0	112	77.4	89.7
10 Nottingham	75.9	73.3	43.5	149*	—	88.6
11 Bristol	70.9	66.2	47.9	146	79.1	88.4
12 Stirling	73.5	73.5	33.8	165*	—	88.2
13 Swansea	90.0	83.8	22.7	122	—	86.8
=14 Salford	82.6	77.7	27.7	133	61.9	85.4
=14 Ulster	82.6	83.9	39.2	110	62.8	85.4
16 Birmingham	66.8	60.1	40.1	147	77.4	85.3
17 Chester	86.5	81.3	0.3	123	72.0	83.2
18 Aston	72.1	77.7	38.6	133	50.0	82.3
19 Wales Trinity St David	88.9	80.3	—	142	48.1	81.8
20 Liverpool Hope	86.2	76.6	8.6	117	62.1	81.6
21 Edge Hill	79.5	81.1	5.7	130	—	80.6
22 Central Lancashire	86.0	79.0	11.8	124	46.9	80.5
23 York	71.5	70.5	47.5	128	36.7	80.1
24 Middlesex	77.7	74.2	14.9	116	—	78.8
25 De Montfort	70.8	68.0	11.2	124*	66.7	78.6
26 South Wales	78.9	77.4	15.4	100	—	77.4
27 Wolverhampton	86.7	83.8	—	111	41.9	77.2
28 Cardiff	63.2	55.2	30.8	135	—	77.0
29 London Metropolitan	79.7	79.3	8.8	97	52.8	76.4
30 Bedfordshire	78.7	76.8	16.3	97	39.1	74.8
31 Brighton	75.8	68.3	12.4	105	46.7	74.7
32 Lincoln	72.5	71.7	5.8	102	—	72.6
33 Anglia Ruskin	62.7	47.2	5.4	95	—	64.6

Employed in high-skilled job	41%	Employed in lower-skilled job and studying	2%
Employed in high-skilled job and studying	3%	Employed in lower-skilled job	40%
Studying	8%	Unemployed	6%
High skilled work (median) salary	£24,000	Low/medium skilled salary	£17,750

Social Work

Edinburgh has the highest entry standards in our Social Work table, and has returned to its top this year, while last year's number one university Stirling has moved into second place. Kent achieved the best results in the Research Excellence Framework, and has been propelled by much improved satisfaction scores into the top five, from 21st place last year. Students at 16th-ranked Oxford Brookes are the most satisfied with the teaching quality on social work degrees – as they were last year – while those at Sheffield Hallam (30=) rate their wider undergraduate experience the highest.

The Frontline fast-track training scheme, modelled on Teach First, is trying to attract graduates of other subjects to train as social workers, but for the time being social work degrees are still the main route into the profession. Applications fell by 10% in 2019, bringing numbers to not far off half the rate they were a decade ago. But enrolments are actually higher now than they were then, and the offer rate more accessible at less than four applications to the place, compared with seven-to-one in 2010.

Social work graduates were earning median salaries of £28,000 when the Graduate Outcomes survey took its census 15 months after they finished their degrees – a top-ten wage out of the 67 subject areas. Graduate prospects vary considerably by university, from rare 100% scores at eight universities – Lancaster, Stirling, London South Bank, Bedfordshire, Bournemouth, Glyndŵr, Essex and West of England, to 24.1% at Liverpool John Moores. The highs and lows even out at 36th place in our employment table, with 63% of graduates in professional employment, a further 4% combining this level of work with postgraduate study and the same proportion studying full-time. Unemployment was only 4% while 24% of graduates were in jobs deemed 'low-skilled' at this juncture in their careers, and 1% were combining this type of work with postgraduate study.

Social Work	Teaching quality %	Student experience %	Research quality %	Entry standards (UCAS points)	Graduate prospects %	Overall score
1 Edinburgh	77.2	70.3	53.4	174	77.4	100.0
2 Stirling	87.5	83.9	33.8	—	100.0	99.7
3 Lancaster	75.3	70.1	51.4	148	100.0	98.9
4 York	83.6	67.7	47.5	143	94.1	98.1
5 Kent	87.8	76.2	59.0	127	82.5	97.0
6 Strathclyde	87.2	82.3	31.9	156	77.4	96.7
7 Dundee	82.0	82.2	31.1	148	90.9	96.5
8 Bath	79.7	74.2	43.4	150	81.8	96.1
9 Queen's, Belfast	72.8	72.3	39.3	152	90.7	95.5
10 West of England	88.7	83.9	10.9	132	100.0	93.9
11 Leeds	70.0	68.2	47.6	153	78.4	93.8
=12 Bedfordshire	87.0	78.3	16.3	131	100.0	93.7
=12 Bournemouth	82.7	75.0	4.7	151	100.0	93.7
14 East Anglia	76.5	56.2	45.8	133	94.1	93.5
15 Teesside	83.3	84.8	15.0	135	96.0	93.1
16 Oxford Brookes	96.5	91.1	—	133	91.7	93.0
17 Plymouth	78.9	73.1	16.0	158	84.2	92.9
18 Nottingham	73.9	65.3	43.5	136	85.0	92.1

19	Birmingham	69.0	59.8	40.1	145	88.2	92.0
20	Swansea	81.4	76.7	22.7	140	83.3	91.8
21	London South Bank	77.2	66.3	20.1	136*	100.0	91.7
22	Glyndŵr	91.5	82.7	—	124	100.0	91.2
23	Glasgow Caledonian	83.2	81.5	8.1	130	96.9	91.0
=24	Hull	81.8	79.1	14.3	140	82.1	90.5
=24	Ulster	77.7	77.8	39.2	123	80.0	90.5
26	Robert Gordon	86.7	82.8	18.0	120	87.5	90.2
27	Coventry	88.1	85.6	5.6	132	83.7	90.0
28	Anglia Ruskin	89.0	86.0	5.4	120	91.7	89.7
29	Greenwich	87.3	81.1	2.2	172*	51.1	89.6
=30	Central Lancashire	81.2	71.0	11.8	144	77.5	89.0
=30	Sheffield Hallam	93.4	93.1	—	129	76.2	89.0
32	Brighton	85.6	75.6	12.4	120	90.9	88.9
33	Manchester Metropolitan	83.0	82.9	6.9	139	75.0	88.4
34	Salford	78.3	72.4	27.7	127	78.2	88.3
35	Middlesex	77.5	72.6	14.9	123	93.3	88.1
=36	East London	81.7	76.1	10.6	115	96.3	87.8
=36	Keele	67.3	60.4	25.0	134	90.9	87.8
38	Essex	87.0	73.8	—	113	100.0	87.5
39	Lincoln	81.1	76.0	5.8	—	87.5	87.3
40	Solent, Southampton	86.1	86.0	—	112	94.1	87.1
41	Cardiff Metropolitan	81.2	75.8	—	130	87.5	86.9
42	Hertfordshire	73.7	65.6	4.0	131	96.9	86.8
43	West London	87.8	84.8	—	120	82.4	86.7
44	Liverpool Hope	71.3	66.0	8.6	134	92.3	86.6
45	Winchester	86.5	77.7	—	121	85.5	86.4
46	Sussex	59.7	48.1	27.9	145	86.4	86.3
47	Huddersfield	85.5	82.8	9.5	136	59.3	86.0
48	Northumbria	82.0	74.9	12.7	144	56.9	85.9
49	De Montfort	80.5	77.2	11.2	119*	81.3	85.8
50	West of Scotland	80.6	78.1	9.4	131	70.5	85.6
51	Edge Hill	84.9	81.0	5.7	127	68.8	85.3
=52	Chichester	92.4	91.5	—	109	72.6	84.7
=52	Worcester	88.4	90.8	—	114	73.7	84.7
54	Leeds Beckett	84.0	81.2	6.4	110	79.2	84.4
=55	Derby	85.6	80.9	5.6	124	62.3	83.8
=55	Kingston/St George's, London	85.5	83.7	—	115*	75.0	83.8
57	Portsmouth	67.4	54.1	12.1	124	92.6	83.7
58	South Wales	80.5	72.7	15.4	117	69.5	83.6
59	Birmingham City	77.8	78.6	3.8	124	73.5	83.4
60	Suffolk	74.2	67.1	—	122*	87.1	83.0
61	Nottingham Trent	82.0	81.7	5.1	123	60.6	82.4
62	Gloucestershire	81.1	73.1	—	119	73.0	82.1
63	Cumbria	78.8	78.2	—	125*	67.4	82.0
64	Goldsmiths, London	74.5	59.7	13.5	108	81.8	81.5

Social Work cont

	Teaching quality %	Student experience %	Research quality %	Entry standards (UCAS points)	Graduate prospects %	Overall score
65 Bucks New	68.9	61.0	—	117	90.9	81.1
66 Staffordshire	69.8	66.2	—	124	79.7	81.0
67 Chester	82.1	75.6	0.3	113	69.0	80.9
68 Liverpool John Moores	91.7	91.7	5.8	132	24.1	80.6
69 Bradford	63.0	63.6	10.6	126	65.4	78.7
70 Bangor	85.9	75.7	—	104	55.6	77.7
71 Plymouth Marjon	91.3	88.3	—	82	60.0	77.4
72 London Metropolitan	67.3	59.8	8.8	99	79.5	77.1
73 Newman	80.0	76.3	2.2	111	50.0	77.0
74 Northampton	66.3	65.4	—	111	72.9	76.6
75 Sunderland	72.2	70.7	1.9	114	56.4	76.4
76 Wolverhampton	78.1	75.2	—	112	49.6	76.2
77 Bishop Grosseteste	65.8	58.6	—	111	72.7	75.9
78 Canterbury Christ Church	63.8	64.4	2.2	99	68.9	73.6

Employed in high-skilled job	63%	Employed in lower-skilled job and studying	1%
Employed in high-skilled job and studying	4%	Employed in lower-skilled job	24%
Studying	4%	Unemployed	4%
High skilled work (median) salary	£28,000	Low/medium skilled salary	£17,535

Sociology

More than 9,000 new undergraduates began sociology degrees in autumn 2020, a record number and the seventh consecutive increase. Applications have been in line with the growth in enrolments, going up each of the past seven years to reach nearly 45,000 in 2019. The subject studies human social life and covers topics such as work, families, gender roles, multiculturalism, media and culture, and globalisation. Its popularity is reflected in our table's extensive 92 entries, and 139 universities and colleges are offering sociology in the coming academic year either as single honours programmes, or as joint honours degrees often with criminology, less frequently with psychology, or others.

Sociology tends not to bring immediate gratification in terms of graduate prospects, and it regularly occupies the lowest rungs of our employment table. This year it is fifth from bottom, with 40% of graduates in professional-level jobs 15 months after their degrees and almost the same proportion, 39%, working in jobs categorised as 'low-skilled'. Postgraduate study accounts for 11% of graduates' outcomes, and a further 3% combined study with high-skilled work. Graduates in professional-level jobs earn median salaries of £23,000, ranking sociology 50= in our earnings table.

Cambridge, which has retained the top spot in the table again this year, does the best on graduate prospects with 87.3% in professional employment or further study 15 months on. Cambridge also has the highest entry standards, and with an average of 198 points in the UCAS tariff it is one of only 15 universities to average 150 points or more. Surrey has shot up our rankings into second place, from 24th last year, helped by much improved graduate prospects as well as better satisfaction scores. Glasgow Caledonian has risen even more places, from 33rd to seventh. Kent, in 17= place overall, received the best results in the Research Excellence Framework, where its submissions were favoured over those from universities with more prominent reputations, such as Cambridge and the LSE. The best rates of satisfaction with teaching quality are at Canterbury Christ Church, at 54= overall, while Derby students, at 23rd, rate their wider undergraduate experience the most highly.

Sociology	Teaching quality %	Student experience %	Research quality %	Entry standards (UCAS points)	Graduate prospects %	Overall score
1 Cambridge	—	—	39.2	198	87.3	100.0
2 Surrey	84.6	83.1	30.2	129	86.5	94.9
3 Bristol	76.2	75.7	46.7	152	79.5	94.8
4 Edinburgh	73.7	68.0	48.8	177	67.8	93.7
5 Glasgow	78.5	72.2	41.8	182	58.8	93.4
6 Leeds	72.9	68.7	47.6	150	78.7	92.8
7 Glasgow Caledonian	85.9	81.6	12.7	171	64.4	92.6
8 London School of Economics	74.5	71.9	45.2	159	69.2	92.5
=9 Manchester	75.6	71.0	50.4	152	63.4	91.7
=9 Stirling	78.8	73.6	33.8	164	63.4	91.7
11 Bath	69.7	69.3	43.4	141	83.9	91.4
12 York	73.7	69.7	45.1	138	76.5	91.3
13 Loughborough	82.5	82.1	40.6	138	57.1	91.2
14 Nottingham	72.7	74.8	43.5	138	75.0	91.1
15 Warwick	78.8	74.9	31.7	143	71.2	91.0
16 King's College London	74.3	71.4	42.2	152	—	90.7
=17 Kent	74.2	73.0	59.0	114	71.1	90.6
=17 Lancaster	74.5	69.7	51.4	144	63.3	90.6
19 Exeter	72.9	68.5	41.0	155	66.7	90.2
20 Edinburgh Napier	86.2	84.8	5.3	153	63.1	90.1
21 Southampton	67.6	68.4	52.8	134	76.1	90.0
22 Newcastle	72.7	71.7	30.3	135	80.0	89.5
23 Derby	88.4	87.1	13.5	108	71.1	89.4
24 Durham	78.8	74.6	28.7	150	60.6	89.3
25 Salford	82.3	77.4	27.7	121	68.0	89.1
26 Sheffield	72.2	73.4	26.8	145	74.5	89.0
27 Sussex	77.5	73.0	29.7	139	66.7	88.9
28 Aston	76.0	72.9	38.6	121	69.4	88.5
29 Aberdeen	72.8	75.6	31.0	176	45.5	87.7
30 Lincoln	86.3	86.7	—	113	71.4	87.4
31 Bradford	82.6	83.1	10.6	105	75.0	87.3
32 Cardiff	70.5	66.1	30.8	146	68.0	87.2
33 Bangor	80.5	79.6	39.6	119	49.8	87.1
34 Queen's, Belfast	75.2	70.2	26.2	143	58.7	86.4

Sociology cont

		Teaching quality %	Student experience %	Research quality %	Entry standards (UCAS points)	Graduate prospects %	Overall score
35	Leicester	83.3	82.5	18.4	123	52.3	86.1
36	Essex	71.4	70.2	44.3	110	65.9	86.0
=37	Abertay	86.1	77.6	5.0	132	56.0	85.9
=37	Portsmouth	83.1	80.1	32.2	101	53.6	85.9
39	Robert Gordon	83.0	80.3	4.9	151	48.0	85.7
40	Birmingham City	81.5	79.9	3.8	119	65.9	85.2
41	Birmingham	74.1	66.9	31.1	139	53.8	85.1
=42	Chester	80.8	80.5	6.4	108	68.7	85.0
=42	Manchester Metropolitan	81.1	78.8	14.9	129	51.6	85.0
44	Newman	87.9	82.5	2.2	107	—	84.6
=45	Northumbria	75.4	75.8	12.7	135	59.3	84.5
=45	Sheffield Hallam	84.8	81.1	14.4	109	52.5	84.5
=47	Huddersfield	79.6	77.1	9.5	112	64.7	84.3
=47	Liverpool	69.0	64.2	24.5	128	69.6	84.3
=49	Hull	79.1	78.3	14.3	106	60.1	83.7
=49	West of England	83.6	82.9	10.9	114	48.6	83.7
51	Coventry	80.9	75.8	5.6	114	61.3	83.6
=52	Brunel London	77.7	77.3	26.0	106	52.9	83.5
=52	Suffolk	82.6	76.0	—	116	61.2	83.5
=54	Canterbury Christ Church	90.5	86.0	—	94	52.4	83.3
=54	Plymouth	78.4	74.9	16.0	114	—	83.3
56	Edge Hill	77.8	77.2	5.7	117	61.9	83.2
=57	Bucks New	84.3	83.9	—	122	47.4	83.0
=57	Westminster	84.6	82.5	—	113	52.9	83.0
59	Roehampton	77.9	75.5	24.9	96	55.6	82.8
60	Anglia Ruskin	77.0	74.3	26.4	105	51.5	82.6
=61	Central Lancashire	78.4	74.4	11.8	113	55.3	82.4
=61	Nottingham Trent	82.7	80.4	5.1	106	53.2	82.4
=61	Queen Margaret, Edinburgh	77.7	72.3	—	132	57.1	82.4
64	Liverpool John Moores	82.2	79.2	5.8	138	37.2	82.3
65	Oxford Brookes	75.3	75.4	17.8	112	—	82.2
66	Teesside	75.2	71.7	15.0	101	63.6	82.0
=67	Bedfordshire	74.6	73.6	16.3	106	58.4	81.8
=67	South Wales	78.9	77.4	—	105	62.8	81.8
=67	Staffordshire	80.2	77.4	—	113	56.2	81.8
70	London South Bank	76.6	75.3	20.1	93	57.6	81.7
71	Bournemouth	81.9	75.6	4.7	106	—	81.6
72	Keele	77.1	75.7	25.0	111	42.0	81.4
73	Ulster	77.3	73.1	39.2	113	30.2	81.3
74	Liverpool Hope	78.7	69.1	8.6	112	—	80.8
=75	Gloucestershire	76.7	71.8	14.5	113	47.9	80.6
=75	Goldsmiths, London	69.2	58.9	33.4	113	53.7	80.6

=75	Leeds Beckett	80.8	75.1	6.4	95	54.4	80.6
78	Greenwich	79.3	75.3	—	116	50.0	80.5
79	Sunderland	81.7	76.4	1.9	104	50.0	80.4
80	Middlesex	74.4	69.9	14.9	107	51.7	80.0
81	City, London	74.8	69.1	20.8	122	34.6	79.2
82	East London	74.7	62.0	13.7	105	52.9	79.0
83	St Mary's, Twickenham	78.0	67.8	—	95*	53.0	77.8
=84	West of Scotland	67.0	60.3	9.4	114	58.6	77.7
=84	Winchester	71.6	67.6	4.4	105	54.0	77.7
=84	Wolverhampton	83.4	73.7	—	101	37.0	77.7
87	Worcester	75.9	66.5	—	110	45.5	77.1
88	Kingston	78.2	72.9	—	90*	47.0	76.9
89	Bath Spa	75.0	67.9	13.9	90	42.9	76.6
90	Northampton	71.2	64.7	—	89	55.4	75.3
91	Brighton	71.6	66.1	12.4	104	33.3	74.8
92	London Metropolitan	69.4	68.2	—	88*	43.3	73.0
90	Northampton	71.2	64.7	—	89	55.4	75.3
91	Brighton	71.6	66.1	12.4	104	33.3	74.8
92	London Metropolitan	69.4	68.2	—	88*	43.3	73.0

Employed in high-skilled job	40%	Employed in lower-skilled job and studying	2%
Employed in high-skilled job and studying	3%	Employed in lower-skilled job	39%
Studying	11%	Unemployed	6%
High skilled work (median) salary	£23,000	Low/medium skilled salary	£18,500

Sports Science

Glasgow has overtaken its sports science rivals to lead our table this year, in a leap from 6= last year. There is not much in it between the top five (less than two percentage points) but the highest entry grades have helped Glasgow secure the top spot. Last year's winner Loughborough – the most famous name in university sport – takes third position and fellow sporting big hitter Bath takes second. All the universities at the top of the table have excellent sports facilities and successful teams, but these do not come into play in the context of our table, which is concerned with the quality of degree courses, research and career prospects. Eighth-ranked Birmingham has the best results in the Research Excellence Framework but Winchester, much further down the table at 50= has the best record for graduate prospects this year. Robert Gordon is first for student satisfaction with both teaching quality and the wider experience, its resounding results in these measures having propelled it into the top six from 17th.

There is a wide range of specialisms within the UCAS category of sport and exercise science, from sports performance and sports global management to sports coaching, sports rehabilitation and sport psychology. Some candidates may be surprised at how much more science and how much less physical activity many courses contain. The leading universities usually require two A-levels or equivalent from a list of maths, biology, chemistry, physics, physical education and psychology.

Sports science has been one of UK higher education's big growth areas, with a 50% increase in undergraduate entrants at the highest point over the last decade. Following some dips in demand in recent years, this has dropped to 35% more enrolments in 2019 than a decade before, and 12% more applications. Sports and exercise science is still among the top ten subjects for applications however, and 157 universities and colleges are offering courses starting in 2021. Offer rates have become more favourable, contributing to the buoyant numbers starting courses, rising from more than five applications per place in 2010 to just over four to the place in 2019.

Sports scholarships are offered by many universities for elite performers, who do not have to study a particular course in order to qualify for one, and officially at least, these do not mean that the degree's normal entry requirements are any different.

Half of graduates were in professional employment 15 months after their sports science degrees, 5% were combining this level of career with further study and 12% were entirely focused on postgraduate study – ranking the subject 46th in our employment table. Unemployment was a low 4%. Sport and exercise science features in a similar position (50=) for earnings, with graduates in high-skilled jobs commanding median salaries of £23,000.

Sports Science	Teaching quality %	Student experience %	Research quality %	Entry standards (UCAS points)	Graduate prospects %	Overall score
1 Glasgow	81.0	86.6	42.3	199	—	100.0
2 Bath	84.6	85.5	54.0	160	85.4	98.4
3 Loughborough	84.1	88.1	52.1	157	84.6	97.8
4 Exeter	86.4	87.6	50.8	155	82.2	97.5
5 Aberdeen	83.5	80.3	34.7	183	—	96.7
6 Robert Gordon	93.9	94.1	4.9	171	82.6	96.2
7 Durham	89.1	84.8	28.7	166	80.0	95.8
8 Birmingham	76.7	77.9	63.7	154	83.2	95.6
9 Nottingham	83.2	86.3	31.4	145	—	92.4
10 Liverpool John Moores	82.1	81.2	45.3	159	66.2	92.2
11 Ulster	84.7	85.7	31.0	142	75.7	92.0
12 East Anglia	87.7	83.3	27.2	150	70.8	91.8
=13 Coventry	88.4	85.5	4.5	149	81.4	91.5
=13 Swansea	84.7	86.8	38.8	128	74.5	91.5
=15 Edinburgh	76.1	78.9	26.1	179	72.0	91.2
=15 Leeds	78.0	82.4	50.5	145	69.2	91.2
17 Surrey	81.4	82.9	33.6	141	—	91.1
18 Brunel London	79.4	76.1	46.4	132	78.4	91.0
=19 Aberystwyth	89.8	87.4	23.5	125	—	90.9
=19 Strathclyde	84.6	72.7	—	184	76.5	90.9
21 Stirling	81.5	78.7	33.6	158	65.5	90.1
=22 Hull	88.5	86.3	14.2	140	70.5	89.8
=22 Manchester Metropolitan	88.4	87.1	12.0	140	71.4	89.8
24 Essex	79.3	80.3	25.8	125	85.2	89.7
25 Chester	91.2	91.8	6.6	126	72.9	89.4
26 Edge Hill	88.7	87.5	7.7	143	69.5	89.3
=27 Abertay	92.7	91.4	8.9	149	57.6	89.0
=27 Anglia Ruskin	88.1	89.8	—	113	85.7	89.0

=27 Bangor	83.6	84.1	30.6	133	67.2	89.0
30 Chichester	84.7	85.3	15.2	130	72.5	88.4
31 Bucks New	91.4	92.9	0.9	110	76.4	88.1
32 Lincoln	87.8	89.4	11.4	128	67.6	88.0
33 London South Bank	84.8	86.3	35.0	100	—	87.9
=34 Brighton	84.1	80.6	10.9	127	77.1	87.8
=34 Oxford Brookes	90.4	87.3	3.0	123	72.2	87.8
=36 Central Lancashire	87.4	85.8	5.1	122	75.1	87.7
=36 Northumbria	87.2	85.9	4.4	150	63.5	87.7
=36 Salford	88.3	85.0	3.8	141	66.7	87.7
=39 Cardiff Metropolitan	81.2	83.3	7.7	142	73.6	87.6
=39 York St John	90.4	88.2	5.5	107	76.4	87.6
41 Nottingham Trent	85.0	82.2	7.3	136	71.5	87.5
42 South Wales	87.3	86.1	10.8	122	70.4	87.4
43 Plymouth Marjon	90.1	89.5	—	117	73.0	87.3
=44 Cumbria	88.2	86.5	3.2	123	72.2	87.2
=44 Sheffield Hallam	86.8	84.2	8.5	128	69.9	87.2
46 London Metropolitan	87.3	80.4	—	111	83.3	87.1
=47 Bradford	82.5	83.2	9.5	—	73.3	86.9
=47 Canterbury Christ Church	86.4	84.4	19.0	109	70.9	86.9
49 Liverpool Hope	80.7	85.0	10.9	110	81.4	86.8
=50 Portsmouth	84.6	84.0	8.1	127	70.6	86.6
=50 Winchester	82.2	83.9	—	110	85.9	86.6
52 Staffordshire	79.2	76.5	19.1	129	73.0	86.4
53 Leeds Beckett	83.2	83.3	12.6	115	73.6	86.3
=54 Gloucestershire	83.5	81.5	6.0	127	72.2	86.2
=54 Newman	87.4	81.3	2.8	114	75.0	86.2
=54 Worcester	84.2	84.8	4.9	123	72.4	86.2
=57 Bolton	82.7	80.4	—	118	80.5	86.0
=57 Kingston	90.9	88.9	2.6	115	65.6	86.0
=57 Middlesex	85.4	85.8	10.0	120	67.3	86.0
60 Teesside	86.3	84.6	2.4	120	70.7	85.9
61 Bournemouth	78.8	80.6	9.0	120	76.7	85.5
62 Solent, Southampton	84.8	84.5	0.6	132	65.5	85.3
63 Leeds Trinity	78.3	77.7	0.8	111	85.6	85.0
=64 Roehampton	76.5	73.5	20.6	101	81.3	84.7
=64 West of Scotland	80.2	77.9	9.1	127	69.5	84.7
66 East London	83.0	82.1	7.6	114	70.0	84.6
67 Suffolk	90.7	88.6	—	112	61.1	84.4
68 Kent	76.5	75.1	21.0	138	60.2	84.1
69 Bedfordshire	76.2	75.3	6.7	106	82.5	83.9
70 St Mary's, Twickenham	79.4	78.2	4.8	119	70.2	83.5
71 Sunderland	78.4	80.4	2.4	111	73.3	83.1
72 Edinburgh Napier	78.9	81.2	5.3	160	47.9	83.0
73 Wolverhampton	81.2	80.8	5.6	111	66.0	82.7
=74 Hertfordshire	79.5	77.5	0.9	117	66.2	82.0

Sports Science cont		Teaching quality %	Student experience %	Research quality %	Entry standards (UCAS points)	Graduate prospects %	Overall score
=74	Wales Trinity St David	82.3	76.9	—	131	57.1	82.0
76	Greenwich	68.3	62.3	7.4	131	76.2	81.5
77	Northampton	78.7	73.9	—	102	69.8	80.6
78	Derby	74.7	75.7	1.7	123	59.3	79.8
79	Huddersfield	74.6	76.6	—	137	47.3	78.5
80	Glyndŵr	73.0	62.1	3.6	127	30.8	72.7

Employed in high-skilled job	50%	Employed in lower-skilled job and studying		1%
Employed in high-skilled job and studying	5%	Employed in lower-skilled job		29%
Studying	12%	Unemployed		4%
High skilled work (median) salary	£23,000	Low/medium skilled salary		£17,750

Theology and Religious Studies

The number of students starting theology and religious studies degrees has followed a similar pattern to the size of congregations filling pews on Sundays. Less than 800 started degrees in autumn 2020, representing a 40% decline in the past decade. Applications have fallen more sharply still, by 50% in the same period. The 2019 admissions cycle saw demand for places drop beneath four applications to the enrolment. But there are still 47 universities and colleges offering the subjects, many of them as part of a broader degree. Often paired with philosophy in joint honours programmes, religion joins other wide-ranging subjects including Oriental studies at Oxford, film and media at Stirling and popular music at West London.

The top two universities are unchanged from last year, with Cambridge maintaining first place by performing strongly across the board without topping any individual measures, followed by Durham which produced the best results in the Research Excellence Framework. Three Scottish universities feature in the top six, led by St Andrews in third place, with the highest entry standards. Rates of student satisfaction are highest at Chester, at 23= overall, which received the best scores in the sections of the National Student Survey dealing with both teaching quality and the wider undergraduate experience. Gloucestershire, which ties in 23= with Chester, also scored above 90% in both satisfaction measures.

Not all those who take theology or religious studies degrees go to work for the Church, but the vocation does help to maintain relatively healthy graduate employment records, and the subjects rank 40th in our jobs table this year. Fifteen months after finishing their degrees, 45% of graduates were in full-time professional employment, 17% had gone on to a postgraduate course and a further 7% were juggling both. The subjects rank a little higher in our earnings table, at 34= with median salaries of £24,000 for those in graduate-level work.

Theology and Religious Studies

	Teaching quality %	Student experience %	Research quality %	Entry standards (UCAS points)	Graduate prospects %	Overall score
1 Cambridge	—	—	44.6	193	85.7	100.0
2 Durham	85.1	77.7	56.6	165	83.5	97.9
3 St Andrews	87.0	77.7	28.9	204	—	97.6
4 Oxford	—	—	46.7	176	91.7	96.0
5 Edinburgh	78.1	78.6	43.2	155	92.2	94.7
6 Glasgow	87.5	86.9	21.4	180*	—	94.3
7 Exeter	84.5	83.9	38.9	155	81.1	93.8
8 Manchester	88.3	87.7	37.2	142	78.1	93.1
9 Lancaster	73.9	60.0	53.0	155	—	90.5
10 Birmingham	81.5	69.6	36.2	145	79.1	89.9
=11 Bristol	79.4	74.2	36.0	149	75.8	89.4
=11 Kent	85.3	80.2	44.1	119	72.0	89.4
13 Leeds	77.0	73.6	44.4	146	69.4	88.6
14 Wales Trinity St David	88.3	81.0	30.0	111*	—	87.7
15 Winchester	85.9	80.8	18.0	103	87.5	86.9
16 Soas, London	77.6	67.8	34.1	142*	—	86.8
17 Nottingham	73.4	63.8	43.9	135	74.5	86.7
18 Queen's, Belfast	91.8	88.7	—	149	70.2	86.6
19 Liverpool Hope	91.9	85.1	17.7	110	—	86.4
20 King's College London	72.1	60.7	37.1	152	71.4	85.8
21 St Mary's, Twickenham	80.3	76.5	9.4	107	90.6	84.6
22 Newman	84.9	81.6	3.5	107*	84.6	84.0
=23 Chester	94.7	90.3	11.1	111	58.7	83.7
=23 Gloucestershire	91.9	90.2	6.9	103	—	83.7
25 Sheffield	71.0	66.8	25.3	147*	—	83.0
26 Roehampton	88.1	88.8	24.3	104	51.9	82.1
27 Leeds Trinity	88.9	82.7	9.9	99*	—	81.9
28 York St John	87.7	86.9	4.8	96	64.0	80.1
29 Canterbury Christ Church	88.8	76.4	16.3	86	56.5	78.9
30 Bath Spa	83.2	68.1	8.3	107	—	78.5
31 Cardiff	67.7	63.8	33.5	131	48.6	77.7

Employed in high-skilled job	45%	Employed in lower-skilled job and studying	1%
Employed in high-skilled job and studying	7%	Employed in lower-skilled job	25%
Studying	17%	Unemployed	5%
High skilled work (median) salary	£24,000	Low/medium skilled salary	£17,000

Town and Country Planning and Landscape

Cambridge has regained its lead in our table, after two years of UCL pipping it to the post. Entry standards are by far the highest at Cambridge, but UCL performs strongly in all other measures – including student satisfaction – without topping any individually. The best results in the Research Excellence Framework were produced by 11th-ranked Loughborough, however. Glasgow Caledonian's propulsion into third place from 12th last year is down to superb rates of satisfaction; it is top in the sections of the National Student Survey relating to teaching quality, and in second place under those concerning the wider experience – with scores around 95% for both measures. Students at Ulster, though, are more satisfied still with the broad undergraduate experience, awarding a score over 96%.

Newcastle has moved up 11 places to the top five this year, and all of its graduates in the subjects were in professional-level jobs or postgraduate study 15 months after finishing their degrees – a rare achievement. As a whole, town and country planning and landscape have a strong record in our graduate employment ranking, where they place 13th this year. Nearly three-quarters were in professional-level work 15 months after their degrees. The subjects are just outside the top 20 for earnings, and graduates in those high-skilled jobs earn median salaries of £25,000.

Degrees in planning include surveying techniques, computer-aided design, plan drawing, report writing and negotiation skills. Various planning courses being offered in 2021 include urban studies, sustainable development, land economy and rural enterprise management. In spite of a slight dip in applications, demand for places is still a bit higher than it was a decade ago before £9,000 fees came in, and competition has got stiffer – going from less than four applications to the place in 2010 to nearly five-to-one in 2019.

Entry standards are lower on landscape and garden design degrees, where there are three applications per place. Demand declined in the 2019 admissions cycle, with fewer than 600 applications and under 200 enrolments. But there are still more than 45 universities and colleges offering courses in landscape and/or garden design in 2021, many of them as part of broader degrees in conservation, architecture and archaeology, among others.

Town and Country Planning and Landscape	Teaching quality %	Student experience %	Research quality %	Entry standards (UCAS points)	Graduate prospects %	Overall score
1 Cambridge	–	–	49.0	203	–	100.0
2 University College London	82.6	83.5	54.1	162	90.0	96.9
3 Glasgow Caledonian	94.1	95.6	9.1	160	92.3	94.7
4 Sheffield	87.0	85.2	36.6	147	87.7	93.5
5 Newcastle	70.1	69.5	43.7	128	100.0	91.3
6 Manchester	74.9	73.0	36.5	162	85.2	90.5
7 Liverpool	86.1	83.7	26.3	133	–	90.0
8 Cardiff	78.5	77.2	36.8	133	88.2	89.8
9 Leeds	79.0	79.9	32.0	141	–	89.7
10 Heriot-Watt	77.5	77.3	38.1	163	76.9	89.3
11 Loughborough	73.8	80.5	58.3	150	72.7	89.1
=12 Queen's, Belfast	77.6	78.3	35.2	132	86.7	89.0

=12 Reading	73.4	71.2	40.0	145	—	89.0
14 Ulster	92.2	96.0	28.6	116	78.6	88.9
15 Dundee	77.2	75.2	8.7	166*	—	87.4
16 West of England	87.7	86.9	10.6	114	88.2	87.3
17 Oxford Brookes	76.5	79.8	17.6	120	91.7	86.9
18 Birmingham	71.3	74.0	42.0	141	76.2	86.0
19 Gloucestershire	81.3	73.6	20.6	106	90.0	85.9
20 Leeds Beckett	87.3	86.3	5.6	106	86.7	85.3
21 Edinburgh	65.3	63.0	35.1	145	—	84.8
22 Greenwich	81.4	76.0	2.0	161*	72.7	83.7
23 Birmingham City	89.6	74.7	2.7	101	—	81.5
24 Westminster	70.8	70.6	10.7	122	—	80.0

Employed in high-skilled job	74%	Employed in lower-skilled job and studying	1%
Employed in high-skilled job and studying	4%	Employed in lower-skilled job	10%
Studying	7%	Unemployed	4%
High skilled work (median) salary	£25,000	Low/medium skilled salary	£21,000

Veterinary Medicine

For such a prominent profession, veterinary medicine is offered by very few universities. The UK's eighth vet school opened at the University of Surrey in 2013, and while it has swelled student numbers, there is still insufficient data to include it in this table. A ninth launched in 2020, in a joint venture between Keele and Harper Adams universities, whose data will also be included in our table once it is sufficient. The extra places will not be hard to fill, in a subject where the numbers are centrally controlled. Applications increased for the second time running in 2019, by 11%, and exceeded 10,000, while more than 1,400 new students started courses.

Successful candidates average 189 points in the UCAS tariff – just one point below the average for medicine this year. Securing a place to study veterinary science is famously competitive and in the 2019 admissions round there were more than seven applications to the place.

The rankings in our table are largely static compared with last year. Edinburgh, which has the best scores in the Research Excellence Framework, has maintained the top spot, while Glasgow is runner up again, and has the highest entry standards. Nottingham has moved up to third place, helped by having the best rates of satisfaction in both teaching quality and the wider undergraduate experience.

Most courses demand high grades in chemistry and biology, with some accepting physics or maths as one alternative subject. Cambridge also sets applicants its own admissions assessment and candidates applying to the Royal Veterinary College take a science aptitude test also used by a number of medical schools. Evidence of practical commitment to the subject through work experience in veterinary practices or laboratories is the norm. Most degrees take five years, but the Cambridge course takes six years and both Bristol and Nottingham offer a 'gateway' year. Edinburgh and the Royal Veterinary College also run accelerated four-year courses for graduates. Neither Wales nor Northern Ireland has a vet school, nor do any post-1992 universities, although a number offer veterinary nursing.

Only dentistry and medicine (in that order) do better than veterinary medicine for starting salaries; newly qualified vets were earning median annual incomes of £31,000 when the Graduate Outcomes survey conducted its census 15 months after their degrees. The subject comes fourth in our graduate prospects measure and 96% – the highest proportion – of graduates were in professional employment 15 months on from graduation. Though still shown in the table, employment scores have been removed from the calculations that determine universities' positions, because they are so tightly bunched that small differences could distort the overall ranking.

Veterinary Medicine	Teaching quality %	Student experience %	Research quality %	Entry standards (UCAS points)	Graduate prospects %	Overall score
1 Edinburgh	90.1	85.6	46.8	206	97.2	100.0
2 Glasgow	84.6	84.7	42.3	221	100.0	97.7
3 Nottingham	95.0	93.6	36.4	165	98.6	91.3
4 Cambridge	—	—	43.1	199	91.4	90.9
5 Royal Veterinary College	81.2	79.3	40.8	174	97.2	88.2
6 Bristol	85.0	85.3	33.2	184	96.8	87.7
7 Liverpool	86.0	84.2	32.9	179	98.5	87.0

Employed in high-skilled job	96%	Employed in lower-skilled job and studying	0%
Employed in high-skilled job and studying	0%	Employed in lower-skilled job	2%
Studying	1%	Unemployed	1%
High skilled work (median) salary	£31,000	Low/medium skilled salary	—

14 Applying to Oxbridge

The two ancient universities of Oxford and Cambridge – or Oxbridge as they are collectively known – bring academic prestige on an international scale unparalleled by any other UK universities. Oxford is top in the world, according to the latest *Times Higher Education* global ranking, where Cambridge sits seventh. Both feature in the QS World Rankings top ten.

But that is not why they merit a separate chapter in this *Guide*. If you want to apply to Oxbridge, the process starts earlier than at other universities and the deadline – 15 October at 6pm – is three months before the rest. You also need to decide which of the two you want to apply to, as you cannot apply to both in the same year. Also unique to Oxbridge is that selection is down to each university's colleges rather than handled centrally, although you can make an open application if you are happy to go to any college.

Both universities have made efforts to create more user-friendly application processes over recent years, so as to debunk the procedure for those without school or family experience to give them an advantage. Cambridge has reintroduced 'pre-interview written assessments' in most subjects, with tests on the day of interview – social distancing measures allowing – in the rest. Oxford also has tests in about ten subject areas. Both universities have changed the way applicants are matched to the colleges too, and candidates are now distributed around colleges more efficiently, regardless of the choices they make initially.

While a formidable number of successful (and even unsuccessful) applicants have the maximum possible grades, talented students should not be put off applying. Both universities have fewer applicants per place than many less prestigious universities, and admissions tutors are always looking to broaden the range of schools and colleges they recruit from. For academic high achievers, there is little to lose by applying to Oxbridge, except the possibility of one wasted space out of five on the UCAS application.

Choosing to go to Oxbridge tends not to be a point of regret for most. While the universities, somewhat confoundingly, choose to boycott the National Student Survey, research by the Higher Education Policy Unit found Oxbridge students were more satisfied than those at other Russell Group universities. Three-quarters, compared with less than half elsewhere, felt their course was good value for money. They worked harder and received better and more timely feedback from academics.

The career and networking prospects offered by Oxbridge are renowned historically and continue to be worth their salt. In the new Graduate Outcomes survey, which measures what graduates are doing 15 months after finishing their degrees, more than nine out of ten Oxbridge graduates were in high-skilled jobs or further study – the top outcomes.

Oxford is our University of the Year 2021–22 in recognition of its response to the Covid-19 pandemic, as well as its commitment – and recent action – on social diversity. Scientists at the university's Jenner Institute and the Oxford Vaccine Group were early leaders in the race to protect mankind from the worst health pandemic since the Spanish flu 100 years ago. The university led from the front again when 2020's A-level results were corrupted by Ofqual's deficient algorithm, offering clemency to 300 students who it felt had been adversely affected. Worcester College announced it would admit all offer holders, so little faith did it hold in the official results. Further pandemic-induced tumult allowing, there should be no such circumstances for those applying to enter in 2022.

Cambridge meanwhile has pipped Oxford to the post at the top of our league table for the eighth successive year. It also comes first in 32 of our 67 subject tables. It has a higher spend on services and facilities, even better completion rates than Oxford and slightly higher entry standards. The international rankings – which place greater emphasis on research than we do in our domestic table – put Oxford just ahead.

One of the big questions posed by potential applicants is: what are my chances of getting in? The quick answer is: on average about five-to-one at Cambridge and about six-to-one at Oxford. Applications to both universities increased in the 2019 cycle, despite a continuing decline in the 18-year-old population. There are big differences between subjects and colleges, however. As the tables in this chapter show, competition is particularly fierce in subjects such as medicine and law, but those applying to read earth sciences or modern languages have a much better chance of success. The pattern is similar across other universities, although the high degree of selection (and self-selection) that goes before an Oxbridge application means that even in the less popular subjects, candidates will be strong.

Cambridge: The Tompkins Table 2019

College	2019	2018	2017	2016	College	2019	2018	2017	2016
Christ's	1	1	2	3	Gonville & Caius	16	14	11	19
Trinity	2	3	1	1	Fitzwilliam	17	19	21	23
Pembroke	3	2	4	2	Magdalene	18	18	16	9
Peterhouse	4	4	10	8	Murray Edwards	19	26	29	25
Churchill	5	7	5	11	Girton	20	23	24	27
Queens'	6	13	7	6	Robinson	21	24	25	22
Emmanuel	7	9	6	4	Newnham	22	22	23	21
Selwyn	8	11	9	15	Downing	23	20	20	12
St Catharine's	9	10	19	17	Clare	24	16	13	18
Trinity Hall	10	12	15	13	Hughes Hall	25	25	26	29
Corpus Christi	11	15	12	10	Homerton	26	27	28	24
King's	12	5	8	14	Wolfson	27	29	27	20
Sidney Sussex	13	17	17	16	St Edmund's	28	21	22	28
Jesus	14	6	14	7	Lucy Cavendish	29	28	18	26
St John's	15	8	3	5					

Both universities are at pains to shake off their exclusive image, but many sixth-formers still fear that they might be out of their depth at them, socially as well as academically. In fact, the state sector produced about 61% of 2019's entrants to Oxford and 65% at Cambridge – although the high proportion that progress from selective grammar schools means only 43% at both universities came from non-selective schools. The kinds of scenes depicted in *Brideshead Revisited* bear little resemblance to today's Oxford (punting aside), and though the activities of the still-present, elite drinking societies are well-publicised, actually belonging to one is considered uncool by many. Most Oxbridge students are hard-working high achievers with the same concerns as their counterparts on other campuses.

Diversity

Efforts to encourage applications from state school students are extensive, and many colleges have launched their own campaigns. Cambridge has two Stormzy Scholarships for black students, funded by the grime musician, which have prompted an increase in black applicants since their introduction in 2018. The total of 91 black students admitted in 2019 was a record. However, this followed years in which six Cambridge colleges admitted fewer than ten black British students between 2012-16, and the university finishes bottom of our social inclusion table again this year. Oxford, which had a quarter of colleges fail to admit even one black student in three years, is only two places higher in our social inclusion ranking. However, its work to make places available to the students let down by 2020's A-levels fiasco resulted in the university greeting its biggest intake yet from the state sector in 2020 – 68%, which should lift its social inclusion ranking in our next *Guide*.

Some colleges set relatively low standard offers to encourage applicants from the state sector whose potential may shine at interview. Some admissions tutors will give the edge to well-qualified candidates from comprehensive schools over those from highly academic

Oxford: The Norrington Table 2019

College	2019	2018	2017	2016	College	2019	2018	2017	2016
Merton	1	4	2	1	Brasenose	16	7	7	7
New College	2	5	1	18	Pembroke	17	25	3	13
Magdalen	3	2	11	3	St Hilda's	18	=13	28	27
St Catherine's	4	3	26	10	Exeter	19	18	25	25
Mansfield	5	20	15	29	Wadham	20	8	13	6
St John's	6	1	6	12	Lincoln	21	26	30	19
Queen's	7	19	5	30	Somerville	22	22	23	16
Oriel	8	12	20	2	Keble	23	23	12	17
Balliol	9	9	10	8	Worcester	24	=13	4	9
Jesus	10	6	18	14	St Peter's	25	16	29	28
Harris Manchester	11	30	27	11	Trinity	26	10	9	5
Corpus Christi	12	15	16	15	Lady Margaret Hall	27	21	14	23
University	13	17	8	4	St Anne's	28	24	19	26
Hertford	14	27	22	20	St Edmund Hall	29	29	24	21
Christ Church	15	11	17	24	St Hugh's	30	28	21	22

Oxford applications and acceptances by course

Arts	Applications 2019	Applications 2018	Applications 2017	Acceptances 2019	Acceptances 2018	Acceptances 2017	Success rate % 2019	Success rate % 2018	Success rate % 2017
Ancient and modern history	94	104	92	24	18	23	26	21	22
Archaeology and anthropology	103	108	94	22	26	19	21	24	20
Classical archaeology and ancient history	110	88	85	17	22	22	15	25	26
Classics	278	308	293	115	115	116	41	37	40
Classics and English	40	38	37	12	10	13	30	26	35
Classics and modern languages	9	28	26	3	6	7	33	38	28
Computer science and philosophy	149	121	82	13	12	14	9	10	17
Economics and management	1,529	1,449	1,317	85	90	80	6	6	6
English	1,058	983	938	223	236	224	21	24	24
English and modern Languages	104	132	85	24	32	20	23	24	24
European and Middle Eastern languages	51	42	63	18	13	16	35	31	25
Fine art	231	231	246	26	27	28	11	12	11
Geography	538	321	405	84	81	77	16	25	19
History	1,127	1,036	971	223	231	214	23	22	22
History and economics	168	121	121	19	16	16	11	13	13
History and English	110	91	89	13	14	16	12	15	18
History and modern languages	98	109	109	19	19	28	19	21	26
History and politics	403	383	417	36	44	52	9	11	12
History of art	131	138	126	14	12	14	11	9	11
Law	1,566	1,541	1,501	178	202	192	11	13	13
Law with law studies in Europe	303	333	278	30	31	28	10	9	10
Mathematics and philosophy	137	142	108	13	18	16	9	13	15
Modern languages	414	423	436	156	157	159	38	37	36
Modern languages and linguistics	96	79	74	32	29	26	33	37	35
Music	198	204	175	70	75	69	35	37	39
Oriental studies	205	177	155	40	40	44	20	23	28
Philosophy and modern languages	78	62	48	23	22	17	29	35	35
Philosophy and theology	149	155	141	30	28	32	20	18	23
Physics and philosophy	179	156	131	17	13	13	9	8	10
Philosophy, politics and economics (PPE)	2,338	2,219	1,983	242	239	249	10	11	13
Theology	92	110	99	35	37	30	38	34	30
Theology and oriental studies	7	8	8	2	4	2	29	50	25
Total Arts	**12,093**	**11,388**	**10,747**	**1,858**	**1,919**	**1,876**	**15.4**	**16.6**	**17.4**

independent schools, because they consider the former to have made a greater achievement in the circumstances. Others stick with tried and trusted sources of good students. The independent sector still enjoys a degree of success out of proportion to its share of the school population.

Oxford applications and acceptances by course cont

Sciences	Applications			Acceptances			Success rate %		
	2019	2018	2017	2019	2018	2017	2019	2018	2017
Biochemistry	752	689	731	96	101	108	13	15	15
Biological sciences	700	575	568	110	109	113	16	19	20
Biomedical sciences	418	438	370	39	41	37	9	9	12
Chemistry	637	585	601	179	179	184	28	31	31
Computer science	693	592	427	44	36	36	6	6	8
Earth sciences (Geology)	116	127	122	35	38	31	30	30	25
Engineering sciences	1,040	1,055	904	174	169	170	17	16	19
Experimental psychology	427	395	295	56	53	51	13	13	17
Human science	186	159	185	30	31	30	16	19	16
Materials science	188	148	167	47	40	31	25	27	19
Mathematics	1,656	1,567	1,371	184	177	185	11	11	13
Mathematics and computer science	424	371	306	40	46	33	9	12	11
Mathematics and statistics	225	202	190	12	13	13	5	6	7
Medicine	1,795	1,667	1,544	161	150	152	9	9	10
Physics	1,405	1,324	1,231	185	181	178	13	14	15
Psychology and philosophy (PPL)	265	233	189	30	26	42	11	11	22
Total Sciences	**10,0927**	**10,127**	**9,191**	**1,422**	**1,390**	**1,394**	**12.9**	**13.9**	**15.1**
Total Arts and Sciences	**23,020**	**21,515**	**19,938**	**3,280**	**3,309**	**3,270**	**14.1**	**15.2**	**16.4**

Choosing the right college

In terms of winning a place at Oxford or Cambridge, choosing the right college is not quite as important as it used to be. Both universities have got better at assessing candidates' strengths and finding a suitable college for those who either make an open application or are not taken by their first-choice college. At Oxford, subject tutors from around the university put candidates into bands at the start of the selection process, using the results of admissions tests as well as exam results and references. Applicants are spread around the colleges for interview and may not be seen by their preferred college if the tutors think their chances of a place are better elsewhere. More than a quarter of successful candidates are offered places by a college other than the one to which they applied.

Cambridge relies on the "pool", which gives the most promising candidates a second chance if they were not offered a place at the college they applied to. Those placed in the pool are invited back for a second round of interviews early in the New Year. The system lowers the stakes for those who apply to the most selective colleges – typically around 20% of offers come via the pool. Cambridge still interviews about 80% of applicants, whereas the system at Oxford has resulted in more immediate rejections in some subjects. Overall, fewer than half of Oxford applicants are interviewed, but there is great variation by subject.

Most Oxbridge applicants still apply direct to a particular college, however. This may maximise

Cambridge applications and acceptances by course

Arts, Humanities and Social Sciences	Applications			Acceptances			Success rate %		
	2019	2018	2017	2019	2018	2017	2019	2018	2017
Anglo-Saxon, Norse and Celtic	60	47	49	19	17	19	31.7	36.2	38.8
Archaeology	58	51	56	22	18	26	37.9	35.3	46.4
Architecture	455	438	430	53	35	37	11.6	8.0	8.6
Asian and Middle Eastern studies	143	133	114	43	47	32	30.1	35.3	28.1
Classics	134	141	172	66	63	84	49.3	44.7	48.8
Classics (4 years)	57	54	50	21	20	18	36.8	37.0	36.0
Economics	1,143	1,094	1,005	156	167	155	13.6	15.3	15.4
Education	153	112	95	42	34	34	27.5	30.4	35.8
English	766	780	763	189	187	212	24.7	24.0	27.8
Geography	297	241	324	93	95	90	31.3	39.4	27.8
History	616	576	591	174	176	181	28.2	30.6	30.6
History and Mod Lang	92	78	77	25	23	20	27.2	29.5	26.0
History and Politics	223	210	195	41	44	40	18.4	21.0	20.5
History of art	122	120	109	26	30	23	21.3	25.0	21.1
Human, social and political sciences	1,089	932	1,070	185	167	166	17.0	17.6	17.8
Land economy	314	312	276	50	58	56	15.9	18.6	20.3
Law	1,498	1,357	1,161	221	202	219	14.8	14.9	18.9
Linguistics	100	112	96	24	31	33	24.0	27.7	34.4
Modern and medieval languages	417	408	404	159	158	180	38.1	38.7	44.6
Music	172	157	136	65	63	65	37.8	40.1	47.8
Philosophy	251	275	270	47	46	45	18.7	16.7	16.7
Theology and religious studies	124	99	91	39	35	39	31.5	35.4	42.9
Total Arts, Humanities and Social Sciences	**8,284**	**7,746**	**7,396**	**1,760**	**1,716**	**1,774**	**21.2**	**22.2**	**24.4**

Sciences	2019	2018	2017	2019	2018	2017	2019	2018	2017
Computer science	1,330	1,157	867	116	133	105	8.7	11.5	12.1
Engineering	2,250	2,299	2,296	329	330	334	14.6	14.4	14.5
Mathematics	1,518	1,597	1,456	253	234	257	16.7	14.7	17.7
Medicine	1,584	1,474	1,341	281	265	257	17.7	18.0	19.2
Medicine (graduate course)	552	–	–	43	–	–	7.8	–	–
Natural sciences	2,922	2,810	2,809	608	611	629	20.8	21.7	22.4
Psych and behavioural sciences	527	461	379	71	69	75	13.5	15.0	15.6
Veterinary medicine	392	357	248	67	71	59	17.1	19.9	23.8
Total Science and Technology	**11,075**	**10,155**	**9,396**	**1,768**	**1,713**	**1,700**	**16.0**	**16.5**	**18.1**
Total	**19,359**	**17,901**	**16,792**	**3,528**	**3,429**	**3,474**	**18.2**	**18.9**	**20.7**

Note: the dates refer to the year in which the acceptances were made.
Mathematics includes mathematics and mathematics with physics.

their chances of getting in, knowing that they will be living and socialising there as well as learning. To the uninitiated most colleges may look the same, but there are important differences. Famously sporty colleges, for example, might be trying for those in search of peace and quiet. Note that neither the Tompkins table at Cambridge, nor the Norrington table at Oxford, which rank colleges, were updated in 2020 because of the pandemic.

Finding the right college requires thorough research. Personal contact is essential; even within colleges, different admissions tutors may have different approaches. The tables in this chapter give an idea of the relative academic strengths of the colleges, as well as the varying levels of competition for a place in different subjects. But only individual research will suggest where you will feel most at home. For example, women may favour one of the few remaining women-only colleges (Murray Edwards, Newnham and Lucy Cavendish at Cambridge). There are no men-only colleges at either university.

The applications procedure

Both universities will have a UCAS deadline of 15 October 2021 (at 6pm) for entry in 2022 or deferred entry in 2023. For Cambridge, you may then take admissions tests at the beginning of November – usually at your school or college, or other authorised centre. Other subjects will continue to administer tests when you attend for interview. The Cambridge website lists the subjects setting the pre-interview assessments, which may include a reading comprehension, problem-solving test, or thinking skills assessment, in addition to a paper on the subject itself.

At Oxford, a number of subjects (but not all) also require applicants to take a written test, either before or at the time of interview. In addition, once Cambridge receives your UCAS form, you will be asked to complete an online Supplementary Application Questionnaire (SAQ) by 22 October in most cases. For international applications to Cambridge, you must also submit a Cambridge Online Preliminary Application (COPA), by 20 September or 19 October, depending on where interviews are held; check the Cambridge website for full details.

For short-listed international candidates, Cambridge holds some interviews overseas while Oxford holds some over the internet, though medicine interviewees must come to Oxford (again, restrictions permitting), as must EU interviewees. Applicants will receive either a conditional offer or a rejection early in the new year.

For more information about the application process and preparation for interviews, visit **www.undergraduate.study.cam.ac.uk/** or **www.ox.ac.uk/admissions/undergraduate**.

Oxford College Profiles

Balliol

Oxford OX1 3BJ   01865 277777   www.balliol.ox.ac.uk
Undergraduates: 383   Postgraduates: 369   undergraduate@balliol.ox.ac.uk

As the oldest academic site in the English-speaking world that was co-founded by a woman, Balliol has maintained its reputation since 1263. The current Master, Dame Helen Ghosh, is expanding both the early career fellowship programme – which gives young academics a springboard to teaching careers – and a new outreach scheme that offers children aged 11 to 14 an inspiring experience of Balliol and Oxford. The college was named after John de Balliol, who, following a row with the Bishop of Durham, was ordered by Henry III to perform a substantial act of charity. He founded the 'House of the Scholars of Balliol' and after his death its continuation was guaranteed by endowments established by his wife Dervorguilla. Home to many prominent post-war politicians, including Prime Minister Boris Johnson, Balliol is usually well represented in the Union. The college typically features in the top ten of the Norrington Table – where it currently ranks ninth. Alongside its academic focus, Balliol is the only Oxford college with the impressive triple 'threat' (to students' focus on their studies) of a student-run bar, popular café and excellent theatre – the Michael Pilch Studio. Run by an elected officer known as Lord or Lady Lindsay, the bar's imaginative cocktails and impromptu pub sports tournaments are renowned. Its community goings-on help create Balliol's close-knit and cross-year cosmopolitan atmosphere. The college has surprisingly spacious grounds for its Broad Street location, with elegant traditional buildings and the occasional concrete block. Its impressive medieval library hosts 70,000 books and periodicals. Undergraduates are guaranteed college accommodation for their first and final years, while graduate students are typically lodged in beautiful Holywell Manor.

Brasenose

Oxford OX1 4AJ   01865 277830   www.bnc.ox.ac.uk
Undergraduates: 356   Postgraduates: 204   admissions@bnc.ox.ac.uk

In a prime location opposite the Radcliffe Camera, the entrance to Brasenose contains a blackboard celebrating its well-known reputation as the happiest Oxford college. Student welfare is a particular focus, perhaps explaining the college's excellent student satisfaction results. Weekly yoga classes and welfare walks, a baking fund and a secret welfare cookie fairy are among many provisions for student support. Diversity is also a priority, with Brasenose celebrating cultural events like St. David's Day and Holi – and putting up portraiture of BAME, LGBTQ+ and female alumni. Popular extracurriculars include the newfound cross-country club and active history and debating societies. The sporting community is equally thriving and includes Brasenose's prestigious boat club – one of the oldest in the world. The annual sports day involves both staff and students, while Arts Week attracts undergraduates and graduates from across the university. Food at Brasenose is known for being delicious and affordable and is served in the beautiful sixteenth-century dining hall. The Brazen Nose door knocker, after which the college is named, was placed on the wall in 1890 and hangs above the high table. David Cameron and William Golding are among a long list of famous alumni. Sixteenth in the Norrington Table, Law, PPE, and History are traditional strengths. College accommodation is guaranteed for all undergraduates – with first and third years housed in college; and second and fourth years in either the Frewin or Hollybush Row annexes nearby.

Christ Church

Oxford OX1 1DP   01865 286583 (admissions)   www.chch.ox.ac.uk
Undergraduates: 443   Postgraduates: 216   admissions@chch.ox.ac.uk

Adjacent to beautiful Christ Church meadow, 'ChCh' is one of the largest and most traditional Oxford colleges. Founded by Cardinal Wolsey in 1525 its chapel is also the Cathedral of the Oxford diocese. Chiming 'Tom Tower', the main entrance, has long been a symbol of both the gleaming spires of the university and the wider city. Boasting the largest quad in Oxford, Christ Church's scale and religious foundations continue to attract students, academics and tourists alike to this impressive, though at times seemingly austere, college. Bowler-hatted porters, a listed eighteenth-century library, daily formal dining and wooden-panelled shared sets (double rooms) for students, still characterise the overall feel of student life here. The infamous 'Harry Potter' Hall hosts two servings every evening, one informal and one formal. Students can choose between two student bars, The Buttery (open daily) and The Undie (open Wednesday to Saturday). Christ Church 'bops' (big organised parties) have a university-wide reputation as some of the best, though they have had to be restricted to college members only due to high demand. The summer months see students strolling along the riverbank beside rowing teams, local walkers and even a herd of English Longhorn cows. Accommodation ranges from the modern Blue Boar 1960s concrete block (typically for first-years), to the beautiful quad-facing rooms in Peck quad (usually inhabited by second-years) and the impressive Meadows and Old Library rooms (mostly snapped up by third- and fourth-years). Offsite options are all ten minutes from the main college.

Corpus Christi

Oxford OX1 4JF   01865 276693 (admissions)   www.ccc.ox.ac.uk
Undergraduates: 267   Postgraduates: 93   admissions.office@ccc.ox.ac.uk

Corpus Christi prides itself on inclusivity: as one of the smallest Oxford colleges, its tight-knit community and friendly atmosphere are nurtured within beautiful buildings. Nestled between Christ Church meadow and the High Street, Corpus has an enviable location. Extracurriculars are a strong focus: the large and modern MBI Al-Jaber Auditorium is used for music, drama, art exhibitions and film screenings. Corpus's drama club, The Owlets, is highly regarded. The college hosts a charity tortoise fair every summer, when crowds gather for the famous inter-college tortoise race, plus live music. Academic expectations are high; Medicine, English, Classics and PPE are especially well-established. Corpus also provides one of Oxford's most generous set of bursary schemes which bestows travel, book and vacation grants at an almost unparalleled level. The college was founded in 1517 by Richard Fox, Bishop of Winchester, and at its heart is an impressive sixteenth-century library. The original bookstacks sit alongside more modern reading rooms, which contain 70,000 volumes. Founder Bishop Fox's focus on humanist learning had a strong influence on the former trilingual library (Latin, Greek and Hebrew), and recent library exhibitions have showcased Corpus's very own Magna Carta and King James Bible manuscripts.

Exeter

Oxford OX1 3DP   01865 279668 (admissions)   www.exeter.ox.ac.uk
Undergraduates: 346   Postgraduates: 227   admissions@exeter.ox.ac.uk

One of Exeter's many envy-inspiring features is its spectacular view from the Fellows' Garden, which overlooks beautiful Radcliffe Camera and impressive All Souls' College. The college is situated in the heart of town on Turl Street, between the High Street and Broad Street, and has occupied its current site since 1315 – one year after it was founded. Most undergraduates are guaranteed in-college accommodation, although many second years choose to live out. The 2017 Cohen Quad development, located on Walton Street and nearer Worcester college, provides 90 ensuite bedrooms in an attractive modern building. Exeter counts many prominent twentieth-century writers among its alumni including Martin Amis, Alan Bennett, Phillip Pullman and JRR Tolkien. Arts-based extracurriculars are strong: the John Ford Society runs dramatic projects, while the annual Arts Festival (in partnership with neighbours Lincoln and Jesus) provides a week of live music, theatre and poetry during Hilary (second) term. The student-run charity, ExVac, is a big part of Exeter's strong and lively JCR community. The college maintains a focus on access and equality, compiling anti-racist literature and holding racial equality seminars. The college has signed the Oxfordshire rough sleeping charter, which commits to ending homelessness in the region. The 2020 Exeter Plus residential bridging programme provides transitions for prospective students from secondary school to university.

Harris Manchester

Oxford OX1 3TD   01865 271009 (admissions)   www.hmc.ox.ac.uk
Undergraduates: 115   Postgraduates: 142   admissions@hmc.ox.ac.uk

Known for its inclusivity and openness, Harris Manchester attracts students from across the globe. It is perhaps one of the less famous colleges but is unique as the only one solely for mature students – who must be 21 or over at the start of their course. All members of the MCR (middle common room) are also members of the JCR (junior common room), which creates a close-knit community across the student body. The college was originally founded in Manchester in 1786 to provide education for non-Anglican students and after stints in both York and London, Harris Manchester finally settled in Oxford in 1889. Since 1996 the college has been established in central Oxford with beautiful buildings and grounds just off Holywell Street. All accommodation is on the main site and rooms are available for the first and final years. Most accommodation has been renovated and a new student building opened in 2017, providing eight more ensuite rooms, a lecture hall, music practice rooms and a gym. Close to the Bodleian, Harris Manchester's own library is excellent, and boasts the best student-to-book ratio of any college. Its small size means Harris Manchester's degree course offering is relatively limited, and many sports teams join other colleges. Its international community hosts a range of extracurriculars, though, centred around diversity, including weekly language nights over dinner; a liberations working group relating to BAME, LGBTQ+, women and disability communities and a refugee language programme which provides tutoring and companionship to a number of Syrian families.

Hertford

Oxford OX1 3BW   01865 279404 (admissions)   www.hertford.ox.ac.uk
Undergraduates: 418   Postgraduates: 239   undergraduate.admissions@
hertford.ox.ac.uk

Known as 'the college with the bridge', the breathtaking Bridge of Sighs links two of Hertford's buildings opposite the Bodleian Library, and the college prides itself on building bridges for prospective students, regardless of their backgrounds. Although it history is deep-rooted, Hertford is one of the most socially progressive colleges and prioritises access, outreach and funding across its large undergraduate and postgraduate communities. Established in 1282, tenants at 'Hart Hall' were among the majority belonging to halls – rather than to the few more elite and restrictive colleges. Granted full college status in 1740, Hertford now provides means-tested bursaries to UK undergraduates studying for a first degree. It also partners with Opportunity Oxford, which supports talented offer-holders from under-represented backgrounds. John Donne, Jonathan Swift and Evelyn Waugh are among a long list of historic Hertfordians. The new principal, Tom Fletcher (a Hertford alumnus and foreign policy adviser to three Prime Ministers) announced the highest number of undergraduates this year – 80% of them from state schools. The college provides undergraduate accommodation across all years: first-years live on the main site, while second- and third-years are in catered halls near Folly Bridge or spacious house shares in north Oxford. Hertford's strong music scene includes a jazz band, wind band, choir and orchestra. The college's popular open mic nights and lunchtime recitals contribute to a fun reputation, and the 'Entz' (entertainment) reps often hire entire nightclubs for 'bops'.

Jesus

Oxford OX1 3DW   01865 279721 (admissions)   www.jesus.ox.ac.uk

Undergraduates: 357   Postgraduates: 200   admissions.officer@jesus.ox.ac.uk

Jesus is one of the friendliest Oxford colleges and consistently ranks highly for student satisfaction. Tucked away on a small site off Turl Street, Jesus houses a 24-hour library, music rooms and a bar. Offsite it has squash courts and extensive playing fields with hockey, cricket, football and rugby pitches, grass tennis courts, netball courts, a boathouse and a sports pavilion. The college maintains strong links with Wales, having been founded by Elizabeth I at the request of a Welsh churchman in 1571. It runs a flagship summer school programme to encourage Welsh state school students to apply to Oxford and Welsh dragons sit proudly at the entrances to staircases in Second Quad. Jesus is home to the only Professorship in Celtic at an English university. To mark its 450th anniversary the college will open its transformed Northgate site in 2021 with new teaching facilities, communal spaces, a café and exhibition space, plus new postgraduate accommodation. Jesus' range of generous bursaries and grants include book and vacation grants. A series of online events for black history month in 2020 included exhibitions, live talks, films and a vital written exploration of the college's colonial connections throughout its 450-year history. It holds a shared ball with Somerville every three years.

Keble

Oxford OX1 3PG   01865 272708 (admissions)   www.keble.ox.ac.uk

Undergraduates: 423   Postgraduates: 426   admissions@keble.ox.ac.uk

With an impressive Victorian Gothic brick façade that looks onto University Parks, Keble is one of the most distinctive colleges – and one of the largest. It claims the university's Museum of Natural history and the Pitt Rivers Museum, and its dining hall is said to be the longest in Oxford – which is fitting in light of Keble's 1870s foundation around the idea that students should eat together regularly. Aside from formal and informal hall (available three and four days of the week respectively), Café Keble is open all day – as is the Red Brick Oven, the college pizza bar. Student productions run from the O'Reilly Theatre every fortnight during term, making Keble one of the best places for drama. Alumni have set up the Keble Association to provide study grants for arts and humanitarian projects. Undergraduates are offered college accommodation for three years, and some students live out in their second or fourth year. The graduate community is based a short distance from the main site at the new H B Allen Centre, which opened in 2019. With a sports ground for football, cricket and tennis 15 minutes' walk away, as well as shared squash courts and a boat house, the sporting facilities and record are exemplary. The annual Keble Ball is arguably the hottest ticket and the best value of Oxford's black-tie events.

Lady Margaret Hall

Oxford OX2 6QA   01865 274310 (admissions)   www.lmh.ox.ac.uk

Undergraduates: 404   Postgraduates: 259   admissions@lmh.ox.ac.uk

Lady Margaret Hall (LMH) sits just north of the city centre. Much like St Hugh's, LMH has an enviable expanse of green space compared to more central colleges. Beautiful gardens back onto the Cherwell River and the grounds include a punt house and tennis courts. LMH's comparative isolation and large undergraduate population create a strong community feel. Originally Oxford's first women-only college, established in 1879, LMH has been co-educational from 1978. Since the first nine women arrived in the nineteenth-century LMH has been a pioneer. In 2016 it became the first Oxbridge college to establish a Foundation Year to encourage access by students from under-represented groups. The initiative has paved the way for Foundation Oxford, a new university-wide scheme. With Alan Rusbridger (former editor-in-chief of *The Guardian*) as principal since 2015, LMH has a strong arts scene and its library has extensive collections in the arts and humanities. It also has a fine reputation in PPE (philosophy, politics and economics) and Nobel Peace Prize winner Malala Yousafzai was among the college's 2020 PPE graduates. Benazir Bhutto, the former Prime Minister of Pakistan, was also an alumna. Accommodation is guaranteed for first-, second- and third-year students in the Pipe Partridge, a graceful neo-classical building with 64 ensuite bedrooms, the theatre and JCR (junior common room).

Lincoln

Oxford OX1 3DR   01865 279836 (admissions)   www.lincoln.ox.ac.uk
Undergraduates: 304   Postgraduates: 298   admissions@lincoln.ox.ac.uk

Lincoln is one of Oxford's smaller colleges, located centrally on Turl Street – next to Exeter and Jesus. It prides itself on being a friendly and dynamic college, with both academic and extracurricular focus. Ivy-covered medieval buildings distinguish Lincoln, and it is home to arguably the most beautiful library in Oxford, a converted Queen Anne Church. The warmth of the community means that many of Lincoln's staff members have considered it home for many years. At the close of Michaelmas term the fire is lit in Hall and the Christmas tree decorated for various 'Oxmas' celebrations. City centre accommodation is provided for all undergraduates, while graduate students are housed nearby in Bear Lane or Little Clarendon Street. Drama and music are popular: the Oakeshott room in the recently refurbished Garden Building is a well-used venue for screenings and performances – especially during the Turl Street Arts festival. College food is excellent; the dining hall serves three meals a day during term time – a rarity amongst older colleges. Deep Hall, the college bar, is popular with students and serves lighter food. Lincoln rewards undergraduates who perform well in examinations and has one of the largest number of scholarships available for graduate students. Prominent alumni include the writers John le Carré and Dr Seuss.

Magdalen

Oxford OX1 4AU   01865 276063 (admissions)   www.magd.ox.ac.uk
Undergraduates: 408   Postgraduates: 178   admissions@magd.ox.ac.uk

CS Lewis is said to have dreamt up Narnia while strolling around the beautiful grounds of Magdalen college. Renowned for its stunning bell tower, from which choir boys sing to mark May Day, Magdalen rivals Christ Church in terms of fame, scale and breathtaking grounds, and has its own deer park and riverside walkway among its attractions. Such renown can lead to feelings of 'imposter syndrome' for some students, and the porters are notoriously unfriendly to undergraduates visiting outside approved hours. But lately Magdalen has worked harder than many of the older colleges to shake off its traditional, public school image. Its current diversity initiatives include a partnership with the House of Commons to encourage BAME leaders to stand for political office by 2022. Perhaps due to its consistently strong position in the Norrington Table, currently fourth, Magdalen tends to attract students who have rarely dropped a grade. Aside from its academic reputation, Magdalen has enjoyed success on the river in recent years. The punting house is popular with tourists and students alike during the summer months. The Magdalen Players also host a production in the gardens every summer. All undergraduates have access to beautiful in-college rooms over their course. More than a quarter of students receive some sort of financial support during their studies – from funding for creative projects to travel grants.

Mansfield

Oxford OX1 3TF   01865 282920 (admissions)   www.mansfield.ox.ac.uk
Undergraduates: 241   Postgraduates: 164   admissions@mansfield.ox.ac.uk

Mansfield is proud to have the highest state sector intake of all Oxford colleges, along with a growing reputation for academic excellence: it currently occupies fifth place in the Norrington Table. Opened in Oxford in 1886, the college was previously located in Birmingham and known as Spring Hill College. Mansfield's original purpose – to provide educational training to nonconformist ministers – is echoed in its current ethos: to champion equality, diversity and access, while fostering academic excellence in a strong community. Known for its high-quality teaching, central location and small, friendly and fun feel, Mansfield maintains the perfect balance between active scholarship and a tangibly relaxed atmosphere. Undergraduates live in college accommodation throughout their degree, either onsite in Victorian buildings or in an East Oxford annexe. With four 24-hour libraries, the popular Crypt Café and the sun terrace open during Trinity term, Mansfield has estimable facilities considering its relatively small size. The new Hands Building is home to the Law faculty's Bonavero Institute of Human Rights and also provides a new lecture space and additional accommodation with 73 ensuite rooms. Proximity to University Parks puts the college's sporting enthusiasm into action. Welfare provisions are strong, with designated tutors for women, students with disabilities, LGBTQ+ and BAME students.

Merton

Oxford OX1 4JD   01865 286316 (admissions)   www.merton.ox.ac.uk
Undergraduates: 302   Postgraduates: 223   undergraduate.admissions@
                                          merton.ox.ac.uk

Merton's reputation for academic excellence is reflected in its consistently high position on the Norrington Table, which it currently heads for the second time in a row. Founded in 1264 by Walter de Merton (Bishop of Rochester and Chancellor of England), Merton is one of Oxford's oldest and most prestigious colleges. It houses Europe's oldest academic library in continuous use. Fellow librarian Dr Julia Walworth recently released *Merton College Library* to shed light on the library's 700-year history, exploring the collections, buildings, scholars and staff who have shaped and looked after the texts. Walworth revealed that medieval Mob Quadrangle, the oldest quad in the university, was almost replaced with undergraduate accommodation in the nineteenth-century. Merton's luminous roll of alumni includes Nobel Prize winners: poet T. S. Eliot, physicist Sir Anthony Leggett, zoologist Nikolaas Tinbergen and Chemist Frederick Soddy – not to mention the former Emperor of Japan, Naruhito; and creator of Lord of the Rings, JRR Tolkien. Merton's wide range of subjects goes some way to explaining its breadth of achievment. Some of the cheapest accommodation across Oxford colleges is guaranteed for all three years of study. The college also provides generous bursaries and grants. Although commonly deemed 'where fun goes to die' by its own undergraduates, extracurriculars at Merton hold a growing reputation and include the Merton Floats drama society and the Bodley Club for literary speakers. Merton's Winter Ball is popular across the university.

New College

Oxford OX1 3BN   01865 279272 (admissions)   www.new.ox.ac.uk
Undergraduates: 415   Postgraduates: 295   admissions@new.ox.ac.uk

Despite its academic prestige, New College has a more fun and relaxed community than some of its Norrington Table rivals (it ranks third in the current edition). The college has one of the largest sites in central Oxford, though its expansive buildings are essentially hidden from view. Founder William of Wykeham was the first to build a college as an integrated complex in 1379 – set with Hall, Chapel, Library and Muniment Tower – and New became a model for the Oxford college layout. Grounds extend from the original gatehouse, tucked away on New College Lane, to the larger entrance on Holywell Street. Well-preserved 13th-century city walls enclose New's garden, with its famous ornamental mound. One of the few colleges with its own sports ground and pavilion, just five minutes' walk from the main site, New has football, rugby and hockey pitches, as well as all-weather netball and basketball courts. Both music and drama are prominent, aided by practice music rooms, a well-equipped band room and a 120-seat, 14th-century performance space, the Long Room. Since completion in 2019, the new Clore Music Studios on Mansfield Road have been used by the orchestra, chamber groups and a world-class male choir which sings a Choral Evensong six nights a week during term. In Michaelmas term, the ante-chapel holds opera performances, and in Trinity term productions take place in the ancient cloisters – which feature in *Harry Potter and the Goblet of Fire*. All first-, second- and fourth-year students can live in college (90% of rooms are ensuite) and most third years live out in private accommodation.

Oriel

Oxford OX1 4EW   01865 276522 (admissions)   www.oriel.ox.ac.uk
Undergraduates: 327   Postgraduates: 198   admissions@oriel.ox.ac.uk

Oriel undergraduates have maintained a strong presence in the Union and Conservative Association over the years. The college's central location and unusual portico, which leads directly to the immaculate main quad, are particular favourites of students. Oriel's acclaimed 'strong crew spirit' reflects its rowing achievements. Its notorious reputation also includes the controversial Cecil Rhodes statue, which looks out from the main façade onto the High Street. After motions by the Junior and Middle Common Rooms to take down the statue, prompted by 'Rhodes Must Fall' protests from locals and students, the college set up a commission of enquiry due to report in 2021 on the statue's future. Yet Oriel's beautiful surroundings continue to attract tourists and students alike. Formal dinner in its small yet impressive medieval hall is a popular feature of the undergraduate experience, with Latin grace providing a traditional atmosphere. Facilities include a sports ground, multiple gyms, a boathouse and squash courts. Accommodation is guaranteed for the duration of study, graded from A* to D, with varying rents. Graduate housing is off the popular Cowley Road a mile away and includes several recently renovated flats. The college usually places at the upper end of the Norrington Table, and currently sits in the top ten.

Pembroke

Oxford OX1 1DW   01865 276412 (admissions)   www.pmb.ox.ac.uk
Undergraduates: 363   Postgraduates: 203   admissions@pmb.ox.ac.uk

Home to a lively and ambitious intellectual community, Pembroke offers an array of joint honours undergraduate courses – from PPL (psychology, philosophy and linguistics) to European and Middle Eastern languages. Located just off St Aldates, Pembroke sits opposite Christ Church in a quieter part of the city centre. It was founded by King James I in 1624 and the current site is based around four quads: Old, Chapel, North and The Rokos. There are five recently developed buildings and two new quadrangle spaces, with a footbridge linking Chapel

Quad with the new area. Tributes to the Pembroke fallen include war memorial plaques in the Damon Wells Chapel and just outside it a three-figure sculpture, the Mourning Women. History is a strong subject, though Pembroke regularly sits in the lower half of the Norrington Table. Sir Ernest Ryder, a former Lord Justice of Appeal, became college Master in July 2020. Applicants from disadvantaged and non-traditional backgrounds are encouraged to apply to Pembroke, and its outreach work targets London and north-west England. The McGowin Library's special collections include works by alumnus Samuel Johnson. Rowing is strong, as are talks and panels by high-profile media figures. Living onsite requires pre-payment for a minimum of six dinners a week, representing one of the biggest student outlays on food among the colleges.

Queen's

Oxford OX1 4AW   01865 279161   www.queens.ox.ac.uk
Undergraduates: 343   Postgraduates: 173   admissions@queens.ox.ac.uk

Located just off the High Street, Queen's neo-classical buildings and bell tower create an imposingly beautiful entrance to the college. Facilities are excellent, with accommodation offered throughout undergraduate courses – some in annexes around central Oxford and others on the main site, mostly ensuite. The lecture theatre is used for concerts and screenings, while the two refurbished squash courts are said to be the best in Oxford. Sport, drama and music are all important parts of the community, particularly the Trinity Term garden play. A budget of £90,000 is set aside each year for student support, with grants and loans awarded by a student finance committee – made up of undergraduate and postgraduate welfare representatives. Music awards (including choral, organ and instrumental) are given annually to undergraduate offer-holders following auditions. Queen's student-run debating club, the Addison Society, was founded in 1883 by a group of mathematicians to improve cultural understanding – and still runs today. The beer cellar is popular and JCR facilities are extensive; afternoon tea is a daily highlight. The college is fully catered, providing three subsidised meals a day. Its Upper Library is known as one of the most beautiful reading rooms in Oxford and the impressive New Library was finished in 2017.

St Anne's

Oxford OX2 6HS   01865 274840 (admissions)   www.st-annes.ox.ac.uk
Undergraduates: 437   Postgraduates: 339   admissions@st-annes.ox.ac.uk

Like its motto, 'consulto et audacter' (purposely and boldly), St Anne's purpose-built complex is boldly modern. The college has a friendly and down-to-earth atmosphere, encouraging applicants from every background to become part of its diverse community. St Anne's has focused on widening access since 1879, when it was founded as the Society of Oxford Home-Students to allow women to study in affordable halls around Oxford – without having to pay for college membership. More of a manifesto than a location, the Society espoused a progressive conviction to educate any student, whatever their financial situation. St Anne's gained full college status in 1952. The college is particularly strong for music, with a student-led society encompassing various ensembles. The termly showcase gives students of every level a chance to perform, and usually stars STAcapella – the non-auditioning, informal acapella group – alongside the non-auditioning orchestra, ANNIE. St Anne's Swingers perform jazz, swing and soul. The college Arts Week, held in Trinity term, includes drama, talks, film and even dance classes. Although closer to Jericho (north of the city) than central Oxford, the college is conveniently near University Parks. Many students cycle to the university sports ground, though there is an onsite gym and nearby sports field with rugby, hockey, football and cricket pitches. Rooms are decided by a yearly ballot and accommodation is guaranteed over three-year courses. With 2,000 books added every year, the new library and academic centre on Woodstock Road is a point of pride.

St Catherine's

Oxford OX1 3UJ 01865 271703 (admissions) www.stcatz.ox.ac.uk
Undergraduates: 495 Postgraduates: 364 admissions@stcatz.ox.ac.uk

'Catz' has the most undergraduates of any Oxford college. It is characterised by a laid-back atmosphere within its spacious site just outside the city centre, right by the English, law and social science faculties. Established in 1962, its modern design and progressive JCR appeal to those who prefer a less traditional experience. Facilities include a theatre, onsite boathouse, squash courts, gym (free after a one-off £3 induction) and even a car park – a rare feature among Oxford colleges. St Catherine's offers 36 undergraduate subjects and houses more than 60,000 books in its modern and spacious library. With the largest bar in Oxford, Catz has a reputation as a sociable college and hosts popular 'bops' four times a term. Increased welfare support in recent years has seen the appointment of a college counsellor and a fund for transgender students. Catz's strength in student numbers brings strength in extracurriculars – particularly in men's rugby, women's football and drama. Extensive sporting funds mean Catz is the college of choice for many university athletes. The annual Cameron Mackintosh Chair of Contemporary Theatre has seen visiting Professorships held by Arthur Miller, Sir Ian McKellen and Sir Tom Stoppard. Rooms are small but tend to be warmer than in older colleges – and are now available onsite for first-, second- and third-years.

St Edmund Hall

Oxford OX1 4AR 01865 279009 (admissions) www.seh.ox.ac.uk
Undergraduates: 391 Postgraduates: 299 admissions@seh.ox.ac.uk

The undergraduate community at Teddy Hall is known for being tight-knit, lively and social. The sporting culture is renowned and the college has enjoyed repeat successes in the Cuppers basketball and rugby tournaments. Located just off the High Street on the quieter Queen's Lane, students can easily access university facilities. Teddy Hall is among the oldest colleges, dating back to 1317 – and likely to the 1190s when its namesake, St Edmund of Abingdon, taught on the site. Its library is in a converted church, St Peter in the East, complete with a book-filled tower and stained-glass windows. Although often at the lower end of the Norrington Table it offers a wide range of scholarships and prizes – from volunteering and travel bursaries, to academic scholarships and an annual personal academic expense grant. The Masterclass Awards offer up to £1,000 to support extracurricular development, from cricket coaching to music lessons. Exchange partnerships with Lingnan University, China, provide opportunities for international study. Teddy Hall has a burgeoning reputation for creative writing, and hosts a writer in residence, journalism prizes, weekly student-run writers' workshops and an annual publication. The two-part college bar is home to the Buttery, a meeting place for sports teams or societies, while the much busier Well Bar features competitive darts matches. Undergraduate accommodation is offered for two years; offsite rooms are at Norham Gardens, close to the University Parks. All first-years live in the medieval college quads, minutes from the Bodleian library. College food is excellent, although fairly expensive.

St Hilda's

Oxford OX4 1DY   01865 286620 (admissions)   www.st-hildas.ox.ac.uk
Undergraduates: 398   Postgraduates: 187   admissions@st-hildas.ox.ac.uk

Its location just beyond Magdalen bridge towards Cowley contributes to St Hilda's campus feel. Founded in 1893 as an all-female college, St Hilda's started admitting men in 2006 and now has an equal gender split. Excellent facilities include an exceptionally well-stocked library, one of the busiest JCR-run student bars, and beautiful gardens – instead of the more typical Oxford quads – which lead straight onto the River Cherwell. The idyllic riverside setting is ideal for punting season, when students can make full use of St Hilda's own punts. The college also has a purpose-built music building and recording studio, and the drama society puts on termly plays in the theatre. With a two-phase building project underway, 52 new student bedrooms have just been finished. The new riverside pavilion will replace Milham Ford by 2021. Second-year students typically live out, but onsite undergraduate accommodation will be available for the full three years once the building project completes. St Hilda's prides itself on an inclusive atmosphere. The college introduced the post of 'class liberation officer' to represent those who self-identify as being from working class backgrounds, it has its own multi-faith room and the Hilda's ball is Oxford's most affordable.

St Hugh's

Oxford OX2 6LE   01865 274900 (admissions)   www.st-hughs.ox.ac.uk
Undergraduates: 426   Postgraduates: 381   admissions@st-hughs.ox.ac.uk

With 14 acres of green space and extensive on-site facilities St Hugh's makes the cycle into the city centre largely unnecessary. Like St Hilda's, it has more of an independent campus feel than that of a traditional Oxford college – and was also women-only at its foundation in 1886. When it began admitting men 100 years later, St Hugh's was criticised by students – although there is now an equal ratio of men and women. The architecture combines listed red-brick Edwardian buildings with more recent additions such as the modern Maplethorpe building. Undergraduate accommodation is guaranteed; the new Dickson Poon building houses 63 lucky graduates in ensuite bedrooms. Also functioning as the University's China Centre, the Dickson Poon has five spacious floors, 60,000 volumes, a lecture theatre, language laboratory and an ecologically efficient roof terrace. St Hugh's Howard Piper Library is one of the best in Oxford, containing over 70,000 volumes and seven reading rooms. The college's slightly more relaxed approach to academia means it often falls at the bottom of the Norrington Table, though its site (north of the city centre) enjoys proximity to the Science and Maths departments. The food is excellent and Hall costs are subsidised; brunch at weekends is popular and there is also a café. Other Hugh's highlights include themed formal dinners on special occasions, a croquet lawn and tennis courts, as well as areas for frisbee and football.

St John's

Oxford OX1 3JP   01865 277317 (admissions)   www.sjc.ox.ac.uk
Undergraduates: 406   Postgraduates: 242   admissions@sjc.ox.ac.uk

The richest Oxford college by some distance, St John's has a reputation for academic and sporting success. Occupying a large site off St Giles the college is ideally placed – just a few minutes' walk from the Bodleian and the High Street. A shortcut via Lamb and Flag Passage leads to Parks Road and University Parks. Founded by wealthy London merchant tailor, Sir Thomas White, in 1555, the college traditionally produced Anglican clergymen – and in its early history was known for medicine and law. Expanding to the Arts and Humanities over the last half-century, St John's alumni include poets AE Housman and Philip Larkin. Subsidised accommodation is guaranteed over undergraduate degrees and for first-year graduate students. The college also provides generous academic prizes and book grants. The unique St John's discount scheme is the envy of other colleges and gives students money off at many nearby eateries. St John's sits in sixth place in the Norrington Table and came first in 2018. The college buildings combine traditional limestone quadrangles (the Front and Canterbury Quads) with modern accommodation blocks (Kendrew Quad) and the spacious new Library and Study Centre – which doubled library seating and shelving capacity. Women's rowing is a particular sporting strength. Other extracurriculars include a chapel choir, drama society and orchestra. Unsurprisingly, entry is competitive.

St Peter's

Oxford OX1 2DL   01865 278863 (admissions)   www.spc.ox.ac.uk
Undergraduates: 359   Postgraduates: 196   admissions@spc.ox.ac.uk

St Peter's was founded as St Peter's Hall in 1929 to offer an Oxford education to students with limited financial means. A medium-sized college it is small enough to create an intimate and caring environment, though large enough to be diverse. Close to the new Westgate shopping centre, St Peter's is centrally located and near Oxford's main facilities. Granted college status in 1961, it has since fostered an open community. Welfare provisions are excellent. The college is averse to pomposity and stuffiness, but dabbles in more typical Oxford traditions from time to time – including Formal Hall, which is held twice a week. Its buildings are an eclectic mix of medieval, Georgian and nineteenth-century styles. St Peter's generally sits in the middle of the Norrington Table and keeps busy in university extracurriculars. Facilities are impressive, although it is one of the least endowed colleges. The recently renovated JCR and popular student-run bar are favourite haunts. Undergraduate accommodation is available for first- and third-years and ranges from traditional to purpose-built rooms – the latter a few minutes' walk away. Music is well represented, with the JCR hosting popular open mic nights every two weeks and a particularly tuneful college choir. Rugby and rowing contribute to Peter's sporting reputation.

Somerville

Oxford OX2 6HD   01865 270600 (admissions)   www.some.ox.ac.uk
Undergraduates: 425   Postgraduates: 212   secretariat@some.ox.ac.uk

Somerville is one of the most diverse and international colleges, located just off St Giles and close to the Ashmolean Museum – as well as the beautiful Taylor Institution language library. Named after Mary Somerville, the astronomer and pioneering academic, Somerville was one of the first two Oxford colleges (along with Lady Margaret Hall) founded in 1879 to admit women – and also, in Somerville's case, students of diverse beliefs. Somerville started admitting men in 1994 and retains its pioneering and inclusive ethos. Access and outreach are priorities, as evidenced by Somerville's Twitter page which aims to demystify the undergraduate application process and promote the college's activities with state school applicants, which are focused on the south east. The atmosphere is friendly and fun, with strong extracurriculars. There is an excellent chapel choir, a baking society and boat club, while the new arts budget funds creative projects – including one of the best Arts Week programmes in Oxford. Somerville students are prominent in both journalism and drama. Food is particularly good value and there are independent student kitchens in all buildings. College rooms are provided for three years to most undergraduates and all first-year postgraduates. Somerville typically falls towards the lower half of the Norrington table, although it has one of the largest libraries with over 100,000 volumes.

Trinity

Oxford OX1 3BH   01865 279860 (admissions)   www.trinity.ox.ac.uk
Undergraduates: 297   Postgraduates: 128   admissions@trinity.ox.ac.uk

Trinity has the highest student-to-grass ratio in Oxford and its lawns are a point of pride for this small, popular college. The tight-knit and friendly community begins from the moment of entry with welcoming and helpful porters. Located on Broad Street – minutes from the Bodleian Library, Radcliffe Camera, High Street and Cornmarket – Trinity is in the heart of the city, though its long drive and expansive green spaces make it a peaceful haven. Strong biochemistry, maths, English and history departments create an academic focus – although Trinity has fallen towards the Norrington Table's nether reaches recently. Since Dame Hilary Boulding was appointed President in 2017, access and outreach have gained momentum to balance Trinity's traditionally high public-school intake. The boat club and the chapel choir are the largest societies. Journalism is also popular and students produce the Broadsheet termly newsletter, while Trinity Arts Week has gained momentum. During Trinity term, the lawns off Garden Quad fill with students from across the university, along with croquet players practising for the Cuppers tournament. The Trinity Players stage a garden play every summer. First- and second-years live in college, with second-year 'sets' (double rooms) popular due to their views over Garden Quad. Third- and fourth-years mostly live out, either in 'Stav' on Woodstock Road or in privately rented Cowley properties. The food is some of the best – with Monday's steak and brie night and weekend brunches a feature. Formal Hall is held three times a week. Taking place once every three years, Trinity's big budget Commemoration Ball sells out in minutes.

University

Oxford OX1 4BH   01865 276677 (admissions)   www.univ.ox.ac.uk
Undergraduates: 410   Postgraduates: 227   admissions@univ.ox.ac.uk

The High Street location, musical talent and recent focus on access are central to University College's identity. The college is working hard to shake off its private-school image and an extra 10% of undergraduate spaces introduced under its Opportunity Programme are reserved exclusively for applicants from low-income backgrounds. Baroness Valerie Amos, a Labour life peer and former UN official, became Oxford's first black head of house when she was appointed Master of 'Univ' in 2019. The generally accepted legend that Univ was founded by King Alfred in 872 makes it the oldest Oxford college – although, more likely, its origins lie with William of Durham who died halfway through the thirteenth century. It began with small funds; only enough to support four theologians. Its intellectual activity has grown since the 18th century and Univ remains one of the largest and most academic colleges. Strong across the board it excels in the sciences, PPE and law – although dropped outside the top 10 to 12th in the latest Norrington Table. A generous bursary scheme includes travel grants for study trips abroad. First- and third-years live in college, with second-years housed in a comfortable annexe near Summertown. Both men's and women's rowing have excelled in recent years. College members have access to a chalet in the foothills of Mont Blanc. Multiple 24-hour libraries and proximity to the Bodleian make Univ ideal for book lovers. Beyond the libraries, the chapel choir is excellent, and students put on a popular comedy revue every Hilary Term.

Wadham

Oxford OX1 3PN   01865 277545 (admissions)   www.wadham.ox.ac.uk

Undergraduates: 474   Postgraduates: 215   admissions@wadham.ox.ac.uk

One of the larger Oxford colleges in terms of size, student intake and even college stereotype, Wadham occupies an imposing and attractive site opposite Trinity on Parks Road. The college's overt leftist politics and activism (the sincerity of which is questioned by some) creates a liberal atmosphere. Its reputation for being the coolest college appeals to some undergraduates, while others find it daunting. The JCR has rebranded itself as a student union (combining the JCR and MCR) and prioritises welfare for minority groups, while the Wadham Human Rights Forum attracts national figures to speak at the college each term. Wadham contributes to the local community through a new scheme which delivers food not eaten in hall to a local homeless centre. Partly due to its successful Student Ambassador Scheme, the college has a strong state school intake. Queerweek – a celebration of LGBTQ+ culture – is a highlight of Wadham's social calendar and Wadstock – its open-air music festival in Hilary (spring) term – has become a university-wide event. The Holywell Music Room is the oldest purpose-built European music room, while the Sir Claus Moser Theatre stages many student plays. Wadham's beautiful gardens host Shakespeare performances each summer. The college offers more languages than any other. Weekday dinners are served in the 17th century hall, although Wadham is the only college with no gowned formal sittings. Undergraduates are guaranteed onsite rooms in their first and final years; other years are offered modern accommodation in two college-owned complexes about a mile away.

Worcester

Oxford OX1 2HB   01865 278391 (admissions)   www.worc.ox.ac.uk

Undergraduates: 437   Postgraduates: 176   admissions@worc.ox.ac.uk

Worcester is one of Oxford's most popular colleges, with beautiful grounds and both a strong academic reputation and student satisfaction rate. The college has its own lake and the architecture ranges from medieval cottages to Baroque and modern buildings. Worcester's horticulture is the subject of a blog by its gardeners, and croquet on the extensive lawns is a popular summer activity. With its sports grounds uniquely in college, Worcester attracts university athletes. Art and humanities lovers enjoy its popular Arts Week and annual summer Shakespeare performances by the Buskins dramatic society. The new Sultan Nazrin Shah Centre provides extra lecture theatres and rehearsal space. Accommodation is guaranteed across all three years and is uniquely close to the heart of college – either within the grounds or close by in comfortable rooms with kitchen access. Good food is served at the nightly formal hall, where students stand at the entrance and exit of tutors and Latin grace is said, creating a traditional dining experience. Worcester in the Park is a highlight of the social calendar, featuring music and Pimm's. The college is among those that host a popular Commemoration Ball every three years.

Cambridge College Profiles

Christ's

Cambridge CB2 3BU	01223 763983	www.christs.cam.ac.uk
Undergraduates 433	Postgraduates 256	admissions@christs.cam.ac.uk

Backing onto the lovely Christ's Pieces park, the college is a stone's throw from the city centre's shops and cafés. It has earned a reputation for being something of an academic hothouse, having topped the Tompkins Table in both 2018 and 2019, with more than 40% of students awarded a first in 2019. The pandemic meant there was no table in 2020. Around three-quarters of Christ's 2019 student intake came from the state sector – one of the highest proportions in Cambridge. Its recently launched Bridging Programme run jointly with King's, provides new students from under-represented backgrounds with further academic support and an introduction to university life. Rooms are allocated by ballot, but students with first-class exam results get preference, as Christ's is one of the few remaining colleges to run a 'Scholar's Ballot'. Mere steps from Ballare, the staple nightclub (better known to students as Cindie's), Christ's is well-positioned for downtime socialising. The Visual Arts Centre and Yusuf Hamied Theatre host student productions and keep Christ's culturally vibrant. Sports-wise Christ's has plenty of active teams, with women's badminton finishing top of the latest intercollegiate league. The swimming pool at Christ's, a rarity at Oxbridge colleges, is thought to be the oldest still in use in the UK. Most undergraduates live in, although a few are in row houses on King's Street and Jesus Lane. About 40% of rooms are ensuite. This includes small, single bedrooms in the Modernist 'Typewriter' building (New Court) and large, double bedrooms in Second Court. More traditional rooms and sets (a study room and bedroom) are in First Court. Alumni range from Charles Darwin to John Milton and Sacha Baron Cohen.

Churchill

Cambridge CB3 0DS	44 01223 336202	www.chu.cam.ac.uk
Undergraduates 499	Postgraduates 346	admissions@chu.ac.uk

Known to some for its brutalist architecture and STEM-heavy student cohort, Churchill has much more to offer than many realise. A little way out of the city centre it is the college closest to the West Cambridge Site, home to many of the university's science departments. One of Cambridge's largest campuses, Churchill has some of the best facilities: a gym, theatre-cum-cinema, music room and recording studio, squash and tennis courts, grass pitches and the university's largest dining hall. College sport is popular, and in 2019 a number of teams (including men's badminton, rugby, lacrosse and netball) all made it to the finals of intercollegiate cuppers. A new court, housing 68 ensuite rooms, is reputed to be the university's plushest undergraduate accommodation, and was completed in 2016, along with a new boathouse. More graduate accommodation opened in 2019 and has already been shortlisted for an award. More than 40% of rooms are now ensuite. Churchill is one of the least traditional colleges: students are welcome to walk on the grass and they don't wear academic gowns when dining formally in hall. It is also one of the few not to charge a fixed bill for catering in addition to meal charges – a move popular with Churchillians. Churchill often has one of Oxbridge's highest state undergraduate intakes – 74% last year – and, for the first time, half its intake was women, up from 42% in 2019.

Clare

Cambridge CB2 1TL   01223 333246   www.clare.cam.ac.uk
Undergraduates 519   Postgraduates 289   admissions@clare.cam.ac.uk

Eye-pleasing and centrally located, Clare is next to King's College chapel, with an ornate gate and bridge opening onto the Backs. The second oldest college in Cambridge, founded in 1326, it has a strong reputation for music, a world-renowned choir and regular recitals. The popular student bar is in Clare Cellars, an atmospheric venue often host to DJ and live music nights that draw students from across the university. For accommodation, Old Court offers a traditional experience, while Memorial Court, across the river, is close to the University Library and both humanities and science departments. Students in their second year often live at 'Clare Colony', closer to the boathouse on the slopes of Castle Hill. The Colony's large, old houses and more modern buildings are around a 13-minute walk from the main site. However, Old Court is being extensively updated ready for the college's 700th anniversary, with plans to build a new River Room Café with terrace views onto the Cam. All freshers live in Memorial, Thirkill or Lerner Court (a modern living space opened in 2008). The college has an enthusiastic boat club, and very good sports facilities just beyond the botanic garden (a ten-minute cycle ride). Clare has a good gender split – almost 50:50 among undergraduates. An arts-heavy list of notable alumni includes David Attenborough and the journalist Matthew Parris. There is also a popular Politics Society, drawing high-profile speakers and a student-run newspaper, *Clareification*.

Corpus Christi

Cambridge CB2 1RH   01223 338056   www.corpus.cam.ac.uk
Undergraduates 294   Postgraduates 259   admissions@corpus.cam.ac.uk

One of Cambridge's smallest colleges, with an undergraduate population that hovers just below 300, Corpus Christi is also one of the most tight-knit. The only Oxbridge College founded by townspeople (in 1352), it is home to the oldest court in either university. In 2019, Corpus committed to creating ten new student places a year specifically for undergraduates from under-represented backgrounds over the following three years, along with a three-week 'bridging course' for these students before they matriculate. Some students are housed in ancient rooms, others are accommodated away from, but close to, the main site, in the Beldam, Bene't Street and Botolph Court buildings. The college has its own gym, playing fields and an open-air swimming pool, located at Leckhampton, just over a mile away. All undergraduates are guaranteed accommodation, although some rooms are allocated based on exam results, which is not always popular. Many in Cambridge know Corpus for its unusual clock, donated by alumnus and inventor John C Taylor in 2008 and displayed on the outside of the eponymous Taylor Library in Kwee Court, where the cosy underground bar is also housed. The recently unveiled renovations to the medieval Old Hall were shortlisted for a RIBA award. To expand the sports offering, Corpus joins with King's and Christ's Colleges to form collaborative 'CCK' teams. Its small but much-used theatre, the Corpus Playroom, is where students university-wide stage plays and comedy nights. Corpus fought its way to the 2020 final of *University Challenge*.

Downing

Cambridge CB2 1DQ   01223 334826   www.dow.cam.ac.uk
Undergraduates 463   Postgraduates 382   admissions@dow.cam.ac.uk

Downing students are sometimes considered the envy of those at other colleges, enjoying some of Cambridge's most comfortable accommodation and summer terms spent relaxing on the Paddock lawn. It offers more than creature comforts, however, and its students throw themselves into plenty of extra-curriculars. On the sports front, Downing is known as a fearsome opponent on both the rugby pitch and the river. For arts and culture there is the 160-seat Howard Theatre, a vibrant drama society that hosts a festival of student writing each year, and the 2016-opened Heong Gallery – dedicated to modern and contemporary art. Downing also has its own termly student-run magazine, *The Griffin*. The advantage of Downing's double beds and ensuite bedrooms is reflected in relatively high rents. A lively social scene centres on the comfy Butterfield Café and Bar, which hosts pub quizzes and live music in the evenings, and makes a casual study space during the day. The college was originally founded for the study of law and natural sciences, and while it is still popular with scientists, lawyers and geographers thanks to its fall-out-of-bed-and-into lectures proximity to their faculties, it is now home to an eclectic body of students studying all subjects.

Emmanuel

Cambridge CB2 3AP	01223 334290	www.emma.cam.ac.uk
Undergraduates 512	Postgraduates 206	admissions@emma.cam.ac.uk

Visit Emmanuel and you might spot some of the college ducks among the students in the beautiful gardens. Nicknamed 'Emma', students love the college for its central location, bustling and cheap bar, relatively affordable rents (which include a weekly load of washing) and friendly atmosphere. The large Paddock lawn is a space to study and socialise, while the open-air swimming pool is a boon in the summer. Emma regularly ranks in the top 10 of the Tompkins Table, and has fielded a couple of successful *University Challenge* teams. Founded by Puritans in the 1580s, Emma strives to maintain a forward-thinking and egalitarian atmosphere. It has a relatively even gender split and more than three-quarters of 2019's new students came from state schools. At last count, around 67% of students studied STEM subjects. Societies and sports focus more on inclusion than competition and activities are diverse. Among Emma's sporting successes, though, are its 2019 runner-up Cricket Cuppers team, and Emma students regularly feature in university Blues teams. The elegant Christopher Wren chapel hosts concerts organised by the music society. As one of the better-endowed colleges, Emmanuel offers a number of bursaries and scholarships.

Fitzwilliam

Cambridge CB3 0DG	01223 332030	www.fitz.cam.ac.uk
Undergraduates 486	Postgraduates 413	admissions@fitz.cam.ac.uk

The walk up Castle Hill to 'Fitz' is worth it to students who enjoy the community atmosphere and some space away from the city centre. Founded in the 19th century to increase access to Cambridge, Fitzwilliam is proud of its heritage as a college committed to widening participation. Nearly three-quarters of its intake came from the state sector in 2019, one of the highest figures in Cambridge. It moved to its current location in the grounds of a Regency estate in 1963, and while it lacks the archetypal ancient architecture, Fitzwilliam's gardens are among Cambridge's most beautiful and its dining hall boasts an eye-catching lantern roof. Students are accommodated throughout their degrees in one of 400 rooms or in houses minutes from the campus. A friendly feel is enshrined at the busy coffee shop where homemade cakes are legendary among students and staff. There have been extensive renovations to the Central Building, dining hall and accommodation. All first-year rooms are semi ensuite, equipped with a shower and washbasin, and most student kitchens include ovens – a step-up compared with many of the older colleges whose basic 'gyp rooms' have only fridges and hobs. Fitz's Winter Ball at the end of Michaelmas term has been popular lately. The college ranked 17th in 2019's Tompkins Table and its sporting champions include the men's football and cricket teams (for three and four consecutive years, respectively) in the inter-college Cuppers. In 2020, the women's netball team topped the league, as did the athletics team. Fitz has a new gym and well-kept pitches five minutes' away.

Girton

Cambridge CB3 0JG   01223 338972   www.girton.cam.ac.uk
Undergraduates 516   Postgraduates 292   admissions@girton.cam.ac.uk

Girton is as far to the west of Cambridge as Homerton is to the east. The distance out of town has its own appeal and can offer students a break from the hustle and bustle of central Cambridge. Its 50 acres include lawns, orchards, sports pitches and courts along with majestic brick buildings and an indoor swimming pool. Girton students can live on its tranquil campus, in rooms that range from atmospheric Victorian bedrooms to modern ensuites in Ash Court. Off-site accommodation is in college-owned houses or the recently opened Swirles Court, located on the university's new North West Cambridge Development at Eddington. One accommodation corridor is reserved for women and non-binary students in the main building. Founded as a women's College in 1869, Girton was the first to go co-educational. Being out of town fosters a familial feel and many would consider themselves Girtonian first and Cambridge students second. In the most recent Tompkins Table the college was placed 20th. Girton has its own museum and a vibrant artsy extra-curricular scene – supported by a dark room for photography and permanent 'Peoples' Portraits' exhibition. Alumni include the Supreme Court President Lady Hale and Sandi Toksvig.

Gonville & Caius

Cambridge CB2 1TA   01223 332413   www.cai.cam.ac.uk
Undergraduates 602   Postgraduates 247   admissions@cai.cam.ac.uk

Gonville and Caius' beautiful library in the Cockerell Building is one of the grandest in Cambridge, and previously served as the university's main library. The college is more tranquil than its location at the end of King's Parade would suggest. Founded as Gonville Hall in 1348, Caius is one of the oldest colleges and its undergraduate population is among the largest, at just over 600. Unlike other colleges, Caius has Formal Hall – a three-course meal served in the ancient dining hall – every night of the week. Students must wear the Caius blue formal gown to attend, though often with jeans or sports kit underneath. A unique dining policy obliges undergraduates to pay for 36 dinners a term (around four per week) in advance. Though unpopular with some, this tradition creates a strong community of students returning to the main site for meals they have already paid for. The Stephen Hawking Building offers modern, ensuite rooms, named in honour of the physicist who was a Fellow for more than 52 years. More traditional rooms and sets are in the central, historic Old Courts, steps away from King's Parade. A new boathouse and gym have been welcomed by rowers. Events for potential applicants include Caius' pioneering Women in Economics day. New academic prizes for sixth formers were launched in 2017. However, in 2019 only around 55% of new undergraduates were from the maintained sector, the lowest of any non-mature college. Caius generally sits in the upper half of the Tompkins table (although 16th in 2019). It elected its first female master, Dr Pippa Rogerson, in 2017.

Homerton

Cambridge CB2 8PH   01223 747252   www.homerton.cam.ac.uk
Undergraduates 594   Postgraduates 645   admissions@homerton.cam.ac.uk

Homerton's sprawling size and distance from the central colleges creates the atmosphere of a self-contained village. It gained full college status in 2010 – making it Cambridge's youngest – although it was founded more than 250 years ago. It is also the university's largest college, with around 1,200 students. Close to the railway station, a 15-minute cycle ride brings students into town. The benefit of space means accommodation is mainly ensuite study bedrooms of a high standard. The college also has tennis courts, a gym, a squash court and a football pitch. There is an orchard and extensive lawns that can be walked on – contributing to the friendly and unpretentious atmosphere. A striking new £8m dining hall, which will also hold kitchens and a buttery is under construction. A new auditorium and 18 ensuite bedrooms in North Wing have been added recently. The gym has been revamped as has Homerton's well-used bar. One of the few colleges to have a near 50:50 gender split among undergraduates, Homerton also has the most education Tripos students, in line with its history as a teacher training college. The arts abound and honorary fellows include Dame Carol Ann Duffy, Sir Andrew Motion and Dame Evelyn Glennie.

Hughes Hall

Cambridge CB1 2EW   01223 334897   www.hughes.cam.ac.uk
Undergraduates 150   Postgraduates 711   admissions@hughes.cam.ac.uk

Hughes Hall sits in a unique location near Mill Road, famous for its Cambridge 'village' atmosphere and quirky, independent shops and restaurants. Founded in 1885, Hughes is the oldest graduate college in the University of Cambridge. Undergraduates aged over 21 are also welcomed in all subjects. Thirty-eight per cent of undergraduates come from outside the UK, and around 57% study humanities – the highest proportion of any college. Hughes enjoys a peaceful setting around the University's cricket ground, although it is close to the busy high street, and has two terraces above the dining hall which provide a great view of cricketing action. It is also close to the main city sports centre, and Hughes Hall has a strong record on the sports pitch and the river. In 2017, four students competed at the World Rowing Championships. The year before, one of them took gold in the Rio Olympics. First-years are generally given rooms in the central college site. In 2016, 85 single ensuite rooms were built along with a bike store and study rooms in the new Gresham Court building. The college also has a number of flats and studios for student couples in established long-term relationships, but these tend to be in high demand. The Porter's Lodge is newly located in a repurposed shipping container.

Jesus

Cambridge CB5 8BL   01223 339455   www.jesus.cam.ac.uk
Undergraduates 513   Postgraduates 411   undergraduate-admissions@jesus.cam.ac.uk

Its spacious grounds near both the river and the centre of town make Jesus an enviable college. Many of its red brick buildings date back to Jesus's founding in the 1500s, while the chapel is believed to be the oldest university building in Cambridge. There are modern facilities too, such as the West Court development which has student common rooms, a games room, a swanky café that doubles as a popular bar in the evenings and a terrace. Jesus also has on-site pitches for football, rugby and cricket, as well as squash and tennis courts. As one of the biggest colleges, it is home to an eclectic student population known for being as strong in sports as in music and art.

All undergraduates are accommodated for every year of their degree, not just the first three – a feature especially welcome for medical students. Jesus's new master, former media executive Sonita Alleyne, is the first black woman to lead an Oxbridge college. Since taking over she has underlined her wish to preserve Jesus's community spirit. The much-loved grounds are often punctuated by modern sculpture exhibitions, and the college's own collection contains work by Antony Gormley and John Bellany, among others. Students are permitted to roam on most – but not all – of the grass. The hotly touted May Ball is particularly popular with first-years. The college tumbled down the Tompkins Table in 2019, to 14th place, having finished sixth the year before.

King's

Cambridge CB2 1ST   01223 331255   www.kings.cam.ac.uk

Undergraduates 442   Postgraduates 284   undergraduate.admissions@kings.cam.ac.uk

The view of King's Chapel and the Backs conjures the quintessential image of time-honoured Cambridge, yet King's grand buildings house one of the university's least traditional and most progressive colleges. Tours of the chapel – home to the famous Carol service broadcast on Christmas Eve – make King's popular with tourists for good reason, while its central location on King's Parade appeals to students of all subjects. The college is known for a political student body, as well as for holding an 'Affair' instead of a May Ball, focused on alternative music with elaborate costumes and a left-field theme. There is a popular cafe that doubles as an informal study space, while the bar has been given a recent make-over. King's state school intake (77% in 2019) is one of the highest of any college, aided by a campaign to seek out students from disadvantaged settings. A bridging programme run with Christ's provides further academic support and an introduction to Cambridge life for those from under-represented backgrounds. The split between Arts and STEM students is relatively even. King's has its own punts for students to rent, and art studio space for them to use. Accommodation ranges from archetypally Cambridge (think mullioned windows overlooking the river) to ensuite rooms in newer hostels. First-years tend to live on the main site in the more modern Keynes building or older Webb's Court, and in the Spalding hostel by Market Square. The 1950's Garden Hostel, beside the Fellows' Garden on the other side of the river, has been extensively renovated. In 2020, the back lawn was transformed into a beautiful wildflower meadow for the first time in hundreds of years.

Lucy Cavendish

Cambridge CB3 0BU   01223 330280   www.lucy-cav.cam.ac.uk

Undergraduates 120   Postgraduates 320   admissions@lucy-cav.cam.ac.uk

Traditionally a college only for women aged over 21, Lucy Cavendish caused a stir in 2019 when it announced its intention to become mixed-gender and to accept students from age 18. Those plans have since been accelerated, and this year younger female undergraduates were accepted, while co-education is to come in 2021. The aim is to increase student numbers and make space for those from widening participation backgrounds. Accommodation is provided for all undergraduates for at least three years, subject to availability. Housing is either in college or in nearby houses, close to those of fellow 'hill' colleges, St Edmunds and Fitzwilliam. There is also an attractive apartment complex in Histon Road. Women-only housing for cultural or religious reasons will be an option once the college goes co-ed. Lucy Cavendish has a growing reputation for sport and has players on many of the university's first teams. It has provided two consecutive captains for Cambridge's female rugby team, football players and four rowers in the

Blues Boat. Internally, sport is also strong, and the Lucy Cavendish Boat Club persuades a third of students to give rowing a try. The college's Fiction Prize, in its tenth year in 2020, has helped launch the publishing career of many successful authors, including Gail Honeyman and Laura Marshall. Its first Literary Festival in 2019 sold out. Lucy is known for a slightly more staid and studious atmosphere than other colleges, but one that is highly supportive. Students come from a wider range of backgrounds than at many others, with at least a third of each year's first-time undergraduates having undertaken access diplomas and qualifications other than A-levels.

Magdalene

Cambridge CB3 0AG   01223 332135   www.magd.cam.ac.uk
Undergraduates 382   Postgraduates 190   admissions@magd.cam.ac.uk

Magdalene students have the picturesque 'beach' to revise on during the summer exam term – a gentle grassy slope that leads to the river and an advantage of being the college with the longest river frontage. Magdalene is also renowned for its ancient and beautiful grounds. Being one of the smaller colleges means that students tend to know each other. Magdalene has a more traditional reputation than some: it famously hosts one of the university's few white-tie balls every two years, and has one of the cheapest formal halls in Cambridge. It also has its own punts – a popular fixture in the summer term. The sports pitches are shared with St John's (both colleges have a sporty reputation) and Magdalene also has its own Eton Fives court. Students either live in the main courts, in the 'village' on the other side of Magdalene Street, or in college-owned houses a few minutes' walk away. Students from different year groups are housed together, which helps with socialising. The college's most famous alumnus, Samuel Pepys, is immortalised in the Pepys Building that houses a collection of 3,000 of the diarist's books and manuscripts preserved on their original shelves. A new library is being built next to the Pepys building, however, which will host an archive centre and an art gallery, as well as vastly increasing the amount of available study space. Magdalene's master is the former Archbishop of Canterbury, Rowan Williams.

Murray Edwards

Cambridge CB3 0DF   01223 762229   www.murrayedwards.cam.ac.uk
Undergraduates 376   Postgraduates 189   admissions@murrayedwards.cam.ac.uk

Of Cambridge's colleges for women, Murray Edwards (often shortened to 'Medwards') is possibly the most gregarious. It is an informal, relaxed place whose students spend as much time mingling with those from other colleges as taking advantage of their calm and spacious campus at the top of Castle Hill. Its May Week garden party is renowned, and the Saturday brunch, served in The Dome dining hall – which rises above the college's brutalist buildings – has been voted best in Cambridge. Among a range of work-focused activities Murray Edwards runs the Gateway weekly programme on academic leadership and career development. It also has a strong population of women in STEM subjects. The laid-back atmosphere extends to the gardens where students can grow herbs and vegetables, as well as walk on the grass – a rare privilege among Cambridge colleges. Sport is strong and everything from climbing to hockey is catered for. The college often provides Blues players to the university teams. Murray Edwards is also home to the second largest collection of women's art in the world, including work by Barbara Hepworth, Tracey Emin and Paula Rego. It has some of the highest rents, however, and has faced pressure from students who want them reduced.

Newnham

Cambridge   CB3 9DF 01223 335783   www.newn.cam.ac.uk
Undergraduates 416   Postgraduates 290   admissions@newn.cam.ac.uk

Newnham has a long tradition of allowing women to find their feet at Cambridge and to make the most of their potential. It was founded in 1871 so female students could attend lectures, well before they could become members of the University. Its 'Old Labs', now an arts centre, were built in 1879 so women could study science subjects before they were permitted to use the University's main laboratories. Alumni include Mary Beard, who is a fellow and still teaches, Sylvia Plath, Diane Abbott and Emma Thompson. For arts students, Newnham is ideally located for the Sidgwick Site and for those who like to socialise, Newnham often joins up with nearby Selwyn College for socials, formals and the choir. Newnham does not have its own chapel. The grounds stretch across 18 acres and feature sports pitches, tennis courts and beautiful gardens. Upgrades to the estate mean that Newnham students can now enjoy 90 new ensuite rooms, as well as a new porters' lodge, gym, café and some of the plushest student kitchens in Cambridge. Rooms for conferences and supervisions are in the Dorothy Garrod building, named after Cambridge's first-ever female professor. The new cafe, Iris, is a light-filled space whose popular sandwiches create a daily lunchtime rush of students, fellows and visitors from other colleges. One criticism, however, is that Newnham's rents are among the highest. All rooms cost the same, although there are large variations in quality. The college has made rent bursaries automatic and reduced proposed increases.

Pembroke

Cambridge CB2 1RF   01223 338154   www.pem.cam.ac.uk
Undergraduates 475   Postgraduates 285   admissions@pem.cam.ac.uk

Set amid tranquil gardens just off busy Trumpington Street, Pembroke is Cambridge's third-oldest college. Given its central position, it is surprisingly large, and its extensive grounds include a bowling green, wild orchard area and the first chapel designed by Christopher Wren. Its food is famed among students – brunch draws crowds from across the university and formal dinner is served every night. Most well-known for its poet alumni, such as Ted Hughes and Edmund Spenser, Pembroke has also educated a number of actors, including Naomie Harris and Tom Hiddleston. Pembroke students praise the relatively cheap rents (though reports suggest the price reflects the quality of some rooms) and facilities that include an on-site gym. Renovations to the Mill Lane site across the road, due to complete by 2023, will enlarge the college's footprint by a third. Most first-years live in the modern Foundress Court and in New Court. Second years tend to move further afield to Selwyn Gardens behind the Sidgwick Site, or to Lensfield Road near the train station, while some move as far as Grantchester Meadows. Many desirable third-year rooms are in attractive terraced houses on Fitzwilliam Street. Pembroke performs well academically – it came third in 2019's Tompkins Table – and also fields a strong extra-curricular ethos. Dozens of clubs and societies include the Music Society, the Stokes Scientific Society, Pembroke Politics and *Pembroke Street* magazine. The Pembroke Players group regularly takes productions to the Edinburgh Festival and is considered one of the most active drama societies.

Peterhouse

Cambridge CB2 1RD   01223 338223   www.pet.cam.ac.uk

Undergraduates 292   Postgraduates 178   admissions@pet.cam.ac.uk

Cambridge's oldest college, and with fewer than 300 undergraduates one of its smallest, Peterhouse retains some traditional idiosyncrasies. It hosts a white tie ball every other year and Formal Hall dinners glow atmospherically by candlelight. The college welcomed its first female Master, the journalist Bridget Kendall in 2016. It is one of Cambridge's wealthier colleges and as such can offer a roster of travel grants and academic awards, and high-standard accommodation. Students are housed either on site or not more than five minutes away for all years of their degree. Rooms are allocated on a points-based system that rewards both academic and extra-curricular achievements. The practice means students can end up with a hectic schedule of committees, plays and sports in the quest for a better room. Most freshers live in St Peter's Terrace – grand Georgian houses on Trumpington Street, or in the William Stone building, an eight-floor high-rise dating from the 1970s. Though it shares sports grounds with Pembroke, Peterhouse has its own squash court and a modern gym. It also has one of Cambridge's wilder outdoor spaces, known as the Deer Park – where no deer but plenty of students roam in summer. Peterhouse is well located for both the science and arts faculties and is particularly strong in the arts. It has two libraries, the Perne and the Ward, which provide plenty of quiet learning space away from the busier faculty libraries.

Queens'

Cambridge CB3 9ET   01223 335540   www.queens.cam.ac.uk

Undergraduates 521   Postgraduates 500   admissions@queens.cam.ac.uk

Queens' – not to be confused with its Oxford counterpart, Queen's – is a bustling college in a central location spanning both sides of the River Cam. The Mathematical Bridge, attributed to Sir Isaac Newton, joins the two. The college's lively, outgoing feel is especially felt in the new courts. The active BATS dramatic society puts drama centre stage and sport is also strong – Queens' tends to field a number of Blues team players and its own clubs cover everything from chess to water polo. Its biennial May Ball is a popular fixture that welcomes big-name bands. An annual Arts Festival features work from both inside the college and outside, along with a range of events. It has an eclectic mix of architecture that reflects its long history, spanning its founding in 1448 to the present day. First-year students are housed in the Cripps Building, while second- and third-years are allocated accommodation through a ballot system. Queens' is also one of the few colleges to host all undergraduates onsite for three years, while postgraduates tend to live off-site in shared houses or hostels. Rents, though, are expensive. Students have the option of sharing a set of rooms, rather than having their own single bedsit, which can prove awkward if students have to pass through another's room to reach their own. Accommodation in the Dokett building includes ensuite facilities. Queens' is particularly strong in the sciences (thanks partly to a roster of bursaries and awards) and performs well at Tripos, generally ranking within the upper half of the Tompkins Table – where it finished sixth in 2019.

Robinson

Cambridge CB3 9AN   01223 339143   www.robinson.cam.ac.uk

Undergraduates 412   Postgraduates 252   apply@robinson.cam.ac.uk

Robinson may not be the most architecturally beautiful college, but the 'red-brick fortress' has an active social scene and a relaxed atmosphere that creates fierce loyalty among its students. A rolling programme of refurbishment has also resulted in very good facilities, and cyclists enjoy the short ride into town. Robinson's Brickhouse student-run theatre company is one of Cambridge's most popular, and it hosts a full line-up of shows over the course of term. The red-brick chapel is renowned for its fantastic acoustics and organ. The college prides itself on the quality of its food and 'The Garden Restaurant' canteen is renowned. Conveniently situated just behind the University Library, Robinson is minutes from the arts faculties on the Sidgwick Site and the maths, physics and materials science buildings. On the sports front, Robinson often fields strong football, netball and rugby teams. The sports grounds, shared with Queens', Selwyn and King's, are less than a mile from the main site. It is also very close to the University Rugby Ground and five minutes from the University Sports Ground. Robinson tends to rest in the bottom half of the Tompkins Table (it was 21st in 2019). It has recently faced criticism for having a particularly low intake of students from state schools, with only 41.3% of those accepted in 2018 coming from the maintained sector, the lowest of any college, although this increased to 56.3% in 2019. The 2018 Big Cambridge Survey gave Robinson the dubious honour of having some of the highest rents of all.

Selwyn

Cambridge CB3 9DQ   01223 335896   www.sel.cam.ac.uk
Undergraduates 419   Postgraduates 249   admissions@sel.cam.ac.uk

Arts students can get out of bed five minutes before lectures begin if they live in Selwyn – which has an entrance to the Sidgwick Site by the Seeley Historical Library and Faculty of Divinity. The college sits on the other side of the River Cam from the city centre, near Newnham and Wolfson. The ten-minute walk to the nearest cash point and supermarket is a point of consternation, though. It was among the first colleges to admit women and typically has an even gender balance – the undergraduate student body was around 52% women at last count. In 2019, Selwyn accepted a larger proportion of its intake from the state sector than any other non-mature college, around 78%. All the students are accommodated for every year of their degree in what is likely to be an ensuite room, thanks to extensive refurbishments. A successful fundraising campaign has resulted in a brand new library, and an auditorium is being built on Ann's Court. The sleek, newly-renovated bar buzzes in the evenings and makes a popular study space during the day. Selwyn has a strong musical tradition, and the chapel choir has recorded numerous albums and toured the world. Long-standing sports clubs known as the Hermes and Sirens fund grants for various teams and the college recently christened a new rowing boat.

Sidney Sussex

Cambridge CB2 3HU   01223 338872   www.sid.cam.ac.uk
Undergraduates 380   Postgraduates 247   admissions@sid.cam.ac.uk

Founded in 1596, Sidney Sussex has a range of attractions to today's undergraduates, among them its convenient location opposite the entrance to the city centre's main supermarket. The river can be reached by a short bike ride, the ADC main student theatre is two-minutes away, and students arrive at the natural science faculties after a five-minute walk. Sidney is one of the smaller colleges by population, and its compact site means many students are housed in one of 11 nearby hostels. However, there are some atmospheric rooms to be had in the main buildings, a few of which even include ensuite facilities. Sidney is a musical college with an award-winning chapel and a recently inaugurated organ. More bizarrely, it is also where the head of Oliver Cromwell is buried, the Lord Protector and ruler of the English Commonwealth having been among the college's first students. The bar is a social hub, thanks to its affordability and rowdy 'bops' – which are cheesy dance nights held every other Friday in term time. The chefs scooped numerous awards in the 2017 university-wide culinary competition. Sidney Sussex is undergoing renovations that will add a new kitchen and servery. Sports teams are more enthusiastic than wildly competitive, and grounds are shared with Christ's, a ten-minute cycle ride away.

St Catharine's

Cambridge CB2 1RL   01223 338319   www.caths.cam.ac.uk
Undergraduates 481   Postgraduates 287   undergraduate.admissions@caths.cam.ac.uk

Catz is right in the middle of town, and unlike most colleges its street-facing front court is open – giving visitors a chance to peek inside without passing through the gates. This openness is reflected in what many students find to be a friendly atmosphere. The mid-size Catz has two libraries, having been founded by benefactor Robert Woodlark in 1473 with a library of 84 manuscripts and three printed books. A high state school intake is the norm, and in the 2019 application cycle around three-quarters of new students came from the maintained sector. Catz students live on-site in their first year before moving out to the popular St Chad's complex in second year, where accommodation is split into flats with octagonal bedrooms. St Chad's is near the Sidgwick Site – useful for arts students looking to wake up as late as possible before lectures. Recent improvements include the McGrath Centre, which houses an auditorium, junior common room and bar, plus a refurbished boathouse and hockey pitch. St Catharine's came ninth in the 2019 Tompkins table, and 10th the year before. Its students are enthusiastic on the extra-curricular front. There are strong rowing and hockey teams and the college's literary society, the Shirley Society, is Cambridge's oldest. Catz holds a May Ball every other year, and students can attend one at Corpus during the 'off' years. The David and Claudia Harding Foundation made a £25m donation to Catz in 2019 – one of the largest in Cambridge's history – which will support postgraduates and encourage applications by students from under-represented backgrounds. Catz has planning permission for extensive renovations to the central site, which will give the buildings' interiors a new look.

St Edmund's

Cambridge CB3 0BN   01223 336086   www.st-edmunds.cam.ac.uk
Undergraduates 121   Postgraduates 452   admissions@st-edmunds.cam.ac.uk

Students looking to join a vibrant, international community of graduates and mature undergraduates aged over 21, would do well to end up at St Edmund's. Known as 'Eddies', the college enjoys one of the university's most global reputations, and students hail from almost 80 different countries, though the gender split is male-heavy. It is renowned for providing sportsmen and women to the University's Blues teams. In 2017 a team of four broke the world record for the longest continual row. Based on the 'hill' near Fitzwilliam and Murray Edwards, Eddies is a tight-knit, friendly community. The bar is entirely student-run, adding to its social aspect. The college also prides itself on being family-friendly with partners and spouses welcome at formal dinners. Lunches for families are hosted on Sundays. After climbing to 21st in the Tompkins Table in 2018, Eddies dropped to 28th in 2019. Accommodation and food can be pricy as St Edmund's doesn't enjoy the big endowments of some of the larger colleges. The variety of rooms is good, though, from ensuites in the Brian Heap building to maisonettes a short walk away, available to couples and small families. The new Mount Pleasant Halls opened next door in September 2019 and provide 136 comfortable ensuite bedrooms and 64 studio flats. St Edmund's is unique among Cambridge colleges for having a Catholic chapel and takes a relaxed approach to traditions. There is no Fellows' high table in hall, and students and academics at all stages of their careers are encouraged to mingle. In 2019, St Edmund's had the university's highest intake of undergraduates from state sector schools and colleges, 83.3%.

St Johns

| Cambridge CB2 1TP | 01223 338703 | www.joh.cam.ac.uk |
| Undergraduates 658 | Postgraduates 319 | admissions@joh.cam.ac.uk |

Few things in Cambridge are as idyllic as lounging on the St John's lawns by the Cam in the summer months. Students live around stunning buildings – such as the iconic Bridge of Sighs that played film set for the *Theory of Everything*. St John's and Trinity enjoy a friendly rivalry, which sparks partly from being next-door neighbours. A large and wealthy college, St John's is renowned for its prowess on the sports field. The 'Red Boys' team is the dominant force in inter-college rugby – they won the league for the fourth time in five years in 2018 – and 'Maggie', as the boat club is known, is another force to reckon with. General knowledge aficionados may be impressed that St John's won *University Challenge* in 2018. Its sizeable endowments support a wide range of activities, from launching its own record label in recognition of the strong music scene (the Gentlemen of St John's singers tour worldwide) to financial initiatives that help students from low-income backgrounds, such as the St John's College Studentships. The Picturehouse is the college's own student-run cinema, with weekly screenings. Academically ambitious types may earn grants by achieving first-class results. Only 59% of St John's new undergraduates in 2019 came from state schools, one of the lowest proportions at Cambridge. The college says far more students arrived from the maintained sector in 2020 though. Accommodation standards are high and food in the buttery is delicious and well subsidised. St John's May Week Ball is known as one of the most fabulous. On the night, punts fill the river near the college to watch the legendary fireworks display.

Trinity Hall

| Cambridge CB2 1TJ | 01223 332535 | www.trinhall.cam.ac.uk |
| Undergraduates 376 | Postgraduates 226 | admissions@trinhall.cam.ac.uk |

Study at Trinity 'Tit' Hall and you have to try not to be distracted by one of the best library views in Cambridge. The Jerwood Library overlooking the Cam and Garret Hostel Bridge enjoys a stunning river frontage, while students might find tourists trying to peer through the windows. The college's small size, tucked between Trinity and Clare, allows its undergraduates to get to know each other quickly. It is also ideally located for a wander into town or to the Sidgwick Site for the arts faculties and the University Library. Thanks to its endowments, Tit Hall is one of the richer colleges, which means accommodation is at the cheaper end and facilities are good. All first-years are housed on the central site, where the cafeteria, coffee shop, bar, library, chapel and main music room are also located. The new off-site accommodation, WYNG Gardens, is a swanky block with double ensuite rooms. The rooms at the Wychfield Site (a ten-minute walk away) have been refurbished. Both sporty and musical, the college has a chapel choir whose recordings are well-received, and off-site there are squash and tennis courts, plus football, hockey, rugby, cricket and netball facilities. The boathouse has benefited from a refurb. Trinity Hall also has a relatively even gender split and rose to 10th place in the 2019 Tompkins Table. Alumni include the scientists Stephen Hawking and David Thouless, actress Rachel Weisz and Olympic medal-winning cyclist Emma Pooley.

Trinity

Cambridge CB2 1TQ   01223 338422   www.trin.cam.ac.uk
Undergraduates 722   Postgraduates 332   admissions@trin.cam.ac.uk

Trinity is arguably Cambridge's most famous college, with its vast grounds on the Cam and an alumni list that ranges from Sir Isaac Newton to Eddie Redmayne. The riverbank Wren Library is renowned and houses tomes from the Capell collection of Shakespeariana to the earliest manuscript of Winnie-the-Pooh. Founded in 1546, Trinity has more undergraduates than any other college. It is also the wealthiest, which allows it to provide high-quality and well-priced accommodation, and bursaries. It accepted 64% of its intake from the state sector in 2019, and at last count around 63% of its undergraduates were studying STEM subjects. Trinity's student population is 68% male – the highest proportion of any Cambridge college. The Tudor-Gothic buildings of New Court have been renovated to provide 169 student rooms, and nearly half the accommodation is now ensuite. A two-storey gym is minutes from the main gate, along with pitches for netball, football, rugby and cricket. Their proximity makes it easy to enjoy sport, and there are also hockey pitches and courts for badminton, tennis and squash. The punts are popular on summer afternoons. The famed chapel choir enjoys an ambitious tour programme, which visited New York in 2019, and plans to take in Australia in 2022. Following a revamp, the JCR (Junior Common Room) now boasts a 65-inch television complete with Sky Sports and Netflix. It's a wonder work gets done, but students say the college takes on a studious atmosphere in exam term. Known as one of the most academically-intense places, Trinity topped the Tompkins Table for seven consecutive years, before slipping to third place in 2018 and second place the year after.

Wolfson

Cambridge CB3 9BB   01223 335918   www.wolfson.cam.ac.uk
Undergraduates 180   Postgraduates 832   ugadministrator@wolfson.cam.ac.uk

As a modern college mainly for graduates – plus an intake of around 50 mature undergraduates every year – Wolfson has a relaxed and unstuffy atmosphere and a friendly student community. It prides itself on its egalitarian traditions, with little distinction between fellows and students (there is no 'high table' in hall, for example) and a President rather than a Master. The current President is biophysical scientist Professor Jane Clarke. Similarly, its mature students – aged from 21 to their sixties – bring a wide range of life experiences (the average age is 25). Founded in 1965, Wolfson's buildings are not the city's most beautiful, but its gardens are an oasis of calm. It also offers easy access to the Sidgwick Site and the University Library, though the city centre is a 20-minute walk. Wolfson's 'Howler' comedy nights three times a term are popular across the university and attract professionals from the stand-up circuit as well as student talent. The college has one of the university's best gyms as well as a basketball-cum-tennis court. Wolfson raised £7 million in donations when it celebrated its 50th anniversary in 2015, and students are seeing the benefit in grants and modernisations. Such was the success of Wolfson's inaugural May Ball in 2018 – said to be as much fun and better value than many others – that another followed in 2019.

15 University Profiles

The UK's departure from the European Union has brought changes to tuition fees for EU students in the UK. If you are from a country in the EU, the European Economic Area (the EU plus Iceland, Liechtenstein and Norway) or Switzerland, and you are thinking of starting to study in the UK from 2021, you now have to pay international student fees. These vary by institution and degree but are consistently higher than the home fees EU students had to pay before Brexit. EU students who started courses in 2020 or earlier will continue to pay the home rate for the remainder of their courses. The tuition fee changes do not apply to students from Ireland, whose rights to study and access benefits in the UK have been preserved.

The rising price of a British university education for EU students will inevitably have a knock-on effect on the numbers who want – or can afford – to study here, which in turn will create a new playing field for home students, too. Combined with the flux to higher education provision caused by the health pandemic there has perhaps never been a more important time to carefully and thoroughly weigh up your prospective university and degree options.

This chapter provides profiles of all 131 universities that feature in *The Times and Sunday Times* league table. The Open University, which supplies more part-time degrees than anywhere else, is also profiled although its lack of physical facilities excludes it from our main league table. Similarly, a profile for evening course specialist Birkbeck, University of London is included, although the university has withdrawn from our rankings due to feeling at a disadvantage compared with its traditional, residential peer institutions. University College Birmingham withheld data for our table and is therefore not profiled, although it is listed at the end of the book.

Specialist colleges, such as the Royal College of Music (**www.rcm.ac.uk**) or institutions that only offer postgraduate degrees, such as Cranfield University (**www.cranfield.ac.uk**), are omitted. This is not a reflection on their quality and is simply due to their particular roles. A number of additional institutions with degree-awarding powers are listed at the end of the book with their contact details.

Dating back to 1836, the University of London (**www.london.ac.uk**) is Britain's biggest conventional higher education institution by far, with more than 120,000 students [https://london.ac.uk/ways-study/study-campus-london/member-institutions]. A federal university, it consists of 17 self-governing colleges and the majority of students are based in the capital. Further afield it also offers degrees at the Institute in Paris, and its global prestige attracts more than 50,000 students in 190 countries to take University of London degrees via distance learning. Its School of Advanced Study comprises nine specialist institutes for research and postgraduate education (**details at www.sas.ac.uk**).

The university does not have its own entry in this chapter but the following colleges do:

Birkbeck, City, Goldsmiths, King's College London, London School of Economics and Political Science, Queen Mary, Royal Holloway, SOAS, St George's and University College London. Contact details for its other constituent colleges are given on page 586.

Guide to the profiles

Our extensive survey of UK universities provides detailed, up-to-date information for their profiles. The latest campus developments, results from the National Student Survey, trends in application and social data, financial help available to undergraduates, research reputation and findings from the government's Teaching Excellence Framework inform their content. You can also find contact details for admission enquiries along with postal addresses. In the light of social distancing measures open days have had to go online and any physical dates are liable to change. So, we recommend prospective students consult a university's website for the most recent and relevant information on how best to visit – virtually or in person.

We also include data under the heading 'Where do the students come from?' This is taken from our revamped table on social inclusion that gives details of student recruitment and the socio-economic and ethnic mix of each institution. The methodology for its data can be found on pages 82–86.

In addition, each profile provides information under the following headings:

» ***The Times and Sunday Times* rankings:** For the overall ranking, the figure in bold refers to the university's position in the 2022 *Guide* and the figure in brackets to the previous year. All the information listed below the heading is taken from the main league table. (See chapter 1 for explanations and the sources of the data).
» **Undergraduates:** The number of full-time undergraduates is given first followed by part-time undergraduates (in brackets). The figures are for 2018–19 and are the most recent from the Higher Education Statistics Agency (HESA).
» **Postgraduates:** The number of full-time postgraduates is given first followed by part-time postgraduates (in brackets). The figures are for 2018–19 and are the most recent from HESA.
» **Mature students:** The percentage of undergraduate entrants who were 21 or over at the start of their studies in 2019. The figures are from UCAS.
» **International students:** The number of undergraduate overseas students (both EU and non-EU) as a percentage of full-time undergraduates. The figures are for 2018–19 and are from HESA.
» **Applications per place:** The number of applications per place for 2019, from UCAS.
» **Accommodation:** The information was obtained from university accommodation services, and their help is gratefully acknowledged.

Tuition fees

Details of tuition fees for 2021–22 are given wherever possible. At the time of going to press, a number of universities had not published their international fees for 2021–22. In these cases, the fees for 2020–21 are given. Please check university websites to see if they have updated figures.

It is of the utmost importance that you check university websites for the latest information. Every university website gives details of the financial and other support available to students, from scholarships and bursaries to study support and hardship funds. Some of the support will be delivered automatically but most will not, and you must study the details on the websites, including methods of applying and deadlines, to get the greatest benefit. In addition, in England the Office for Students (**www.officeforstudents.org.uk**) publishes "Access Agreements" for every English university on its website. Each agreement outlines the university's plans for fees, financial support and measures being taken to widen access to that university and to encourage students to complete their courses.

University of Aberdeen

In its Aberdeen 2040 vision, the UK's fifth-oldest university has set out a 20-year strategy to be inclusive, interdisciplinary, international and sustainable. Aberdeen brings more than five centuries of history to its future-facing outlook, and its estate reflects the blend of tradition and modernity. The Hogwarts-esque King's buildings of the Old Aberdeen campus are complemented by developments such as the Sir Duncan Rice Library, opened by the Queen in 2012 and winner of design plaudits.

A new £37.5m science teaching hub is on the horizon, due to open in 2022. Dedicated to science laboratories, the facility will house digitised and flexible teaching spaces and multi-function areas intended to encourage public engagement. It will be another development in the university's programme of regeneration, allied to that of the wider city in partnership with the region's businesses and councils.

In July 2020, Aberdeen's business school announced two new international accreditations, one with a platform that is supported by the United Nations to raise the profile of sustainability across the world; the other with the global, non-profit European Foundation for Management Development. It also plans to move the business school to its own site in anticipation of doubling recruitment over the next decade. Business students already have access to the Bloomberg virtual trading floor software platform.

Our Scottish University of the Year for 2019, Aberdeen organises its teaching across 12 schools, located at the Old Aberdeen and Foresterhill campuses — the latter housing Europe's largest health campus, shared between the university and NHS Grampian.

As is the norm in Scotland, undergraduate degrees last four years. Aberdeen builds in opportunities to follow special interests during a course, allowing students to add contrasting studies to their main degree. Studying abroad is encouraged too, either via the European or International Exchange programmes, with the academic credits gained overseas counting towards degrees.

Aberdeen is the first UK university to operate a dedicated campus in Qatar, where it is teamed with AFG College and offers bachelor's degrees in accounting and finance and business management. It also has partnerships in Sri Lanka and an alliance with Curtin University in Western Australia.

Around 70% of Aberdeen students come from Scotland. Enrolments fell marginally in 2020, a drop the university attributed to demographics. Entry requirements and the applications per place remain highly competitive. To widen participation, Aberdeen makes lower offers to applicants who qualify on "contextualised information" that takes into account a broad range of socioeconomic factors,

King's College
Aberdeen AB24 3FX
01224 272 000
study@abdn.ac.uk
www.aberdeen.ac.uk
www.ausa.org.uk
Open days:
see website

The Times and The Sunday Times Rankings
Overall Ranking: 27 (last year: 27)

Teaching quality	78.4%	=84
Student experience	80.3%	=25
Research quality	29.9%	43
Entry standards	183	9
Graduate prospects	79.8%	36
Good honours	86.2%	=14
Expected completion rate	88.9%	=41
Student/staff ratio	16.2	=74
Services and facilities	£2,517	60

and includes these entry standards alongside the standard grades in the university prospectus.

The university's prominence in academic research is underlined by its association with five Nobel laureates in the fields of chemistry, medicine, physics and peace. In the most recent Research Excellence Framework, three-quarters of the work submitted by Aberdeen was rated world-leading or internationally excellent. For environmental and soil science the university was top in the UK, and it was ranked in the top three for psychology and English.

Located in Europe's energy capital, Aberdeen has strong links with the oil and gas industries. The university is home to the National Decommissioning Centre and renowned for its expertise in offshore oil and gas decommissioning. At the Oceanlab research facility, just north of Aberdeen, engineers test subsea equipment.

Each new first-year student is buddied with a peer mentor under the Students4Students scheme to help them settle in, plus everyone has a personal tutor who offers general support throughout their time at the university. Aberdeen also operates a free counselling service.

The tremendous sports facilities at the Aberdeen Sports Village are a resource for the northeast of Scotland, and are even up to scratch for Olympic athletes, who have used them for training. Facilities include a 150-station gym, an Olympic-size swimming pool, a diving pool, indoor and outdoor athletics arenas and a full-size indoor football pitch.

The King's Pavilion has outdoor playing fields, tennis courts and an artificial cricket wicket. The Hillhead Centre houses the sports stadium owned and managed by the university and its shinty club is the oldest in the world, dating back to 1861. The Scottish game, similar to field hockey, is played at Balgownie. Aberdeen has a rowing club boathouse on the River Dee and a climbing bothy in Royal Deeside.

All new students are guaranteed one of the university's 2,181 residential spaces, and accommodation is located in or near the King's Head campus, Hillhead Student Village and the city centre. A catered hall has 588 rooms where meals are included, but most students self-cater.

Aberdeen enjoys long summer days, when daylight lasts until 11pm and the city's latitude even offers the chance of seeing the Northern Lights. Opportunities to get active outdoors include skiing and snowboarding at Glenshee Ski Centre, nature-spotting in the Cairngorms National Park and watersports along the 150 miles of coastline and in the lochs.

Tuition fees

- » Fees for Scottish students   £0–£1,820
  RUK fees   £9,250 (capped at £27,750 for 4-year courses)
- » Fees for International students 2020–21   £17,200–£19,800
  Medicine   £43,500
- » For scholarship and bursary information see
  www.aberdeen.ac.uk/study/undergraduate/finance.php
- » Graduate salary   £26,000

Student numbers		
Undergraduates	9,707	(477)
Postgraduates	3044	(1,548)
Applications/places	19,065/2,475	
Applications per place	7.7	
Overall offer rate	70.8%	
International students – EU	19.6%	
Non-EU	15.8%	

Accommodation

University provided places: 2,181
Catered costs: £147 per week
Self-catered: £90–£148 per week
First years guaranteed accommodation
www.abdn.ac.uk/accommodation

Where do the students come from?				Social inclusion ranking (Scotland): 12	
State schools (non-grammar)	81.4%	First generation students	29.6%	Black attainment gap	-16.5%
Grammar schools	2.9%	Deprived areas	4.4%	Disabled	4.9%
Independent schools	15.7%	All ethnic minorities	13.3%	Mature (over 21)	15.7%

Abertay University

Abertay is our University of the Year for Teaching Quality after a second successive year of stellar results in the National Student Survey. Small class sizes and integrated student support facilitate personalised learning, with the students ranking Abertay second in the UK for satisfaction with teaching quality in 2020, up from ninth place in 2019.

Awarded silver in 2017's Teaching Excellence Framework, assessors praised Abertay for embedding employability within the curriculum, which had benefited from institution-wide reform to include more choice and flexibility. The panel also highlighted course design and assessment, which provides scope for high levels of stretch, and teaching that encourages students to be engaged and committed to their learning and study.

With fewer than 4,000 students at Abertay, undergraduates get a more personal experience than they would at most larger universities.

The university's new cyberQuarter hub opened for the start of the 2020 academic year, designed to oil the cogs of collaboration between academia and industry in cyber-security. With £11.7m investment from the Scottish and UK governments through the Tay City Deal, the centre features a secure cloud-based, virtual ethical hacking lab and has funding to develop innovative digital products and services. The university aims to seed new companies and to help existing ones grow locally, nationally and globally.

The facility builds on Abertay's ground-breaking reputation in the sector – it was the first in the world to offer degrees in ethical hacking, where students are trained in offensive cyber-security and taught to think like hackers.

The city of Dundee is widely regarded as an international hub for the gaming industry and at Abertay's School of Design and Informatics a new £5.5m videogames and cyber-security resource opened in 2019, housing an Emergent Technology Centre for teaching and research into the latest mixed-reality technologies. The space includes a development studio for experimental games design and hacking projects, eye-tracking equipment, specialist cameras and an extended reality lab with room-scale virtual reality.

Abertay leads InGAME (Innovation for Games and Media Enterprise), an R&D project which aims to increase the value and scale of the Dundee videogames cluster through creative experimentation, exploiting innovation and sector intensification. Partners include the BBC, Biome Collective, Microsoft, Outplay Entertainment and V&A Dundee.

In 2019 the university launched a scholarship with Ninja Kiwi Europe, offering financial support and a work placement with the international

Kydd Building
Bell Street
Dundee DD1 1HG
01382 308 080
sro@abertay.ac.uk
www.abertay.ac.uk
www.abertaysa.com
Open days:
see website

The Times and The Sunday Times **Rankings**
Overall Ranking: =80 (last year: =98)

Teaching quality	87%	2
Student experience	81.2%	=14
Research quality	5.1%	=91
Entry standards	148	40
Graduate prospects	67.3%	104
Good honours	75.8%	61
Expected completion rate	74.3%	122
Student/staff ratio	21.2	128
Services and facilities	£1,853	113

games company. A large intake of students from China is attracted by Abertay's global reputation in computer arts and games design.

Sony, which chose Abertay as the site for the largest teaching laboratory in Europe for its PlayStation consoles, has forged closer links through the new Emergent Technology Centre, where PlayStation development tools are used within the labs. The university also hosts the national Centre for Excellence in Computer Games Education. All games students become members of UKIE (UK Interactive Entertainment) and gain access to a bespoke programme of industry mentorship and support. Graduates include David Jones, creator of the hit Grand Theft Auto videogames.

But there is more than tech at multi-faculty Abertay. The university's School of Applied Sciences has secured new research projects to investigate sustainable foods and child learning, and in a partnership with Queen Margaret University and Scotland's Rural College, it is co-creating the Thrive entrepreneurship programme for food and drink students and graduates.

Abertay has reshaped its curriculum in recent years by introducing mandatory interdisciplinary courses for all undergraduates, plus Scotland's first accelerated degrees – which last three years rather than four.

Abertay tops our social inclusion table of Scottish universities. Its strength in widening participation is illustrated by being the first university in Scotland to implement access thresholds, a key recommendation of the Commission on Widening Access. This contextual admissions policy allows applicants from disadvantaged educational backgrounds to be offered a place at university with lower tariff scores than the standard requirement.

The university hosts the Dundee Academy of Sport, launched in partnership with Dundee and Angus College – a venture using sport as a vehicle for learning across the school curriculum and throughout life. There is a new strength and conditioning laboratory for sports science students and an exercise studio on campus is open to the public. A 580-bed student village allows all first-years who apply for accommodation to be guaranteed a place.

Scotland's fourth-largest city, on the north bank of the River Tay, has a rollcall of claims to fame. Dundee is credited as the birthplace of marmalade, described as "Britain's coolest little city" in GQ magazine, and 2019's Best Place to Live in Scotland by *The Sunday Times*. The V&A Museum of Design is an architectural triumph and the centrepiece of the historic waterfront's regeneration.

Tuition fees

» Fees for Scottish students	£0–£1,820
RUK fees	£9,250
» Fees for International students 2021–22	£14,000–£15,500
» For scholarship and bursary information see	
www.abertay.ac.uk/study-apply/money-fees-and-funding/	
» Graduate salary	£22,000

Student numbers

Undergraduates	3,676	(255)
Postgraduates	218	(208)
Applications/places		5,485/1,065
Applications per place		5.2
Overall offer rate		84.9%
International students – EU		12.1%
Non-EU		3.5%

Accommodation

University provided places: 500
Self-catered: £65–£132 per week
www.abertay.ac.uk/accommodation

Where do the students come from?

State schools (non-grammar)	96.7%	First generation students	47.1%	Black attainment gap	n/a
Grammar schools	0.1%	Deprived areas	15.1%	Disabled	7.8%
Independent schools	3.1%	All ethnic minorities	7.5%	Mature (over 21)	37.3%

Social inclusion ranking (Scotland): 1

Aberystwyth University

Aberystwyth topped our analysis of 2020's National Student Survey for both satisfaction with teaching quality and with the wider university experience. It ranked second in the UK on both measures in 2019 and has been the top Welsh university for student satisfaction for five successive years.

It is rare for a university to achieve this double success in student satisfaction scores – although St Andrews managed it in 2019 – and all the more so given that Aberystwyth was struggling to make the top 100 on both measures as recently as 2015.

It's not just the students who think the teaching is good; the university was awarded gold in the government's Teaching Excellence Framework. Its panel found "outstanding levels of stretch" ensuring that all students were significantly challenged to achieve their full potential. Substantial investment in e-learning was another plus point, as was the integrated approach to Welsh-language teaching.

Our Welsh University of the Year in 2019, Aberystwyth is due to open the first school of veterinary science in Wales in September 2021. The new five-year bachelor of veterinary science (BVSc) degree will be offered jointly by Aber and the Royal Veterinary College (RVC). Students will spend the first two years on the Welsh coast followed by three at the RVC's Hawkshead campus in Hertfordshire.

A new veterinary education centre is being created on Aber's Penglais campus, together with an EU-backed veterinary hub containing high-specification laboratories and office space. The Bovine Tuberculosis Centre of Excellence will be based at the new facility.

There are more developments taking place on campus. In September 2020, the Pantycelyn hall of residence reopened after a £16.5m makeover. The iconic hall, first opened in 1951 and used by Prince Charles when he studied at Aber, provides ensuite accommodation for 200 students who want to live in a Welsh-speaking environment or wish to learn Welsh. About a third of students come from Wales and Welsh-medium teaching is flourishing.

Two new study facilities also opened in 2019–20 in the Hugh Owen Library on the Penglais campus, as part of a £1m refurbishment, increasing the number of study places. There is no shortage of books around here: the Penglais campus is also home to the National Library of Wales, one of the UK's copyright libraries.

The university's Old College, a grade I listed building on the seafront, has secured a £10m National Lottery grant that will help pay for its transformation into a centre for culture, heritage, discovery, learning and enterprise. A £40.5m Innovation and Enterprise Campus (AberInnovation) was also opened on the university's Gogerddan

Penglais Campus
Aberystwyth SY23 3FL
01970 622 021
ug-admissions@aber.ac.uk
www.aber.ac.uk
www.abersu.co.uk
Open days:
see website

The Times and The Sunday Times **Rankings**
Overall Ranking: 42 (last year: 45)

Teaching quality	87.3%	1
Student experience	86.4%	1
Research quality	28.1%	45
Entry standards	123	=76
Graduate prospects	66.9%	=106
Good honours	70.7%	=104
Expected completion rate	82.8%	=78
Student/staff ratio	16.8	=86
Services and facilities	£2,493	62

site, focusing on food, bio-refining and agri-tech research and development.

Scores in the 2014 Research Excellence Framework showed improvement on Aberystwyth's previous assessments, with the best scores in international politics, geography and earth science. There was also recognition for the Institute of Biological, Environmental and Rural Sciences, which serves 1,500 undergraduate and research students, and offers the UK's widest range of land-related courses.

Aber was the first university in the world to be given Plastic Free University status. The award was made by the marine conservation charity Surfers Against Sewage in recognition of the institution's campaign to reduce the use of single-use plastics such as bottles, coffee cups and straws. The university's green credentials have been further enhanced with the introduction of six new degrees in climate change, combining its study with biology, business, economics or English.

More than a third of undergraduates receive some financial support, which includes Rashid Domingo bursaries worth £12,000 over three years and open to students in biological, rural and environmental sciences who went to secondary school in Wales and require financial assistance. There are also about 70 scholarships and 250 merit awards each year, worth up to £2,000 for each year of a course, based on the outcomes of two exams set by the university and taken in January.

Separate academic excellence studentships worth £2,000 in the first year are offered to candidates who excel in the A-level, BTec, IB or other specified examinations.

All first-year students – including those who sign up through clearing and adjustment – are guaranteed university-owned accommodation, which houses more than half of all Aber's undergraduates.

The students' union has the region's largest entertainment venue, while sports facilities are good and well used. There is a women-only area and designated strength zone in a refurbished fitness centre, while outdoor facilities include a swimming pool, 400-metre running track, 50 acres of playing fields and specialist facilities for water sports. You can even bring your horse to university and all students in halls get free unlimited access to the sports centre.

The attractive seaside location remains a draw for applicants, although travel to other parts of the UK is slow. The two campuses are about a mile apart, with teaching facilities and residential accommodation within walking distance of each other.

Tuition fees

- » Fees for UK students £9,000
- » Fees for International students 2021–22 £14,000–£16,000
- » For scholarship and bursary information see www.aber.ac.uk/en/undergrad/before-you-apply/fees-finance/
- » Graduate salary £21,000

Student numbers

Undergraduates	5,711	(1,024)
Postgraduates	591	(519)
Applications/places		7,780/1,470
Applications per place		5.3
Overall offer rate		96.1%
International students – EU		11.5%
Non-EU		5.9%

Accommodation

University provided places: 3,610
Catered costs: £167 per week
Self-catered: £85–£147 per week
First years guaranteed accommodation
www.aber.ac.uk/en/accommodation

Where do the students come from?

State schools (non-grammar)	90.3%	First generation students	39.9%	Black attainment gap	-28.4%
Grammar schools	4.4%	Deprived areas	13.8%	Disabled	11.3%
Independent schools	5.3%	All ethnic minorities	7.7%	Mature (over 21)	13.3%

Social inclusion ranking: 83

Anglia Ruskin University

Anglia Ruskin University (ARU) has invested £115m in campus developments over the past five years – opening a new science centre, law clinics and a gym as well as the first School of Medicine in Essex. Another £200m over the next 10 years is earmarked for digital learning options and activities beyond the classroom, designed to boost employability and enhance the student experience.

The business school's new curriculum now features more shared modules in the first year. It will also increase active learning through "live briefs", setting students a task to create, test and launch a fresh concept. The focus on employability is clear at ARU's Arise innovation hub in Chelmsford, where start-up businesses in the health, wellbeing and performance sectors work alongside students and academics to develop new products. Due to its success, another Arise innovation hub is now open in Harlow.

The university scored well in the new Graduate Outcomes survey, which showed more than 73% were in high-skilled employment or postgraduate study 15 months after completing their courses. Practice interviews are part of a range of careers support. Year-long undergraduate work placements with local and national businesses have increased by 50% and more than 2,000 students are signed up for work experience through bureaux at the Cambridge and Chelmsford campuses.

The university also has bases in Peterborough and the City of London and a partnership with University Centre West Anglia allows about 10,000 students to take ARU degree courses in King's Lynn and Milton, on the outskirts of Cambridge.

As the largest provider of health, social care and education courses in the east of England, ARU has a strong record in training the region's essential workers. It was chosen to develop a new nursing training and education facility for the North Anglia NHS Foundation Trust, and the *Nursing Times* has shortlisted ARU for its Pre-registration Provider of the Year award in both 2019 and 2020.

At the height of the coronavirus pandemic more than 400 ARU nursing and midwifery students joined the NHS front line as part of a national initiative.

ARU is again among the top universities in our social inclusion table, gaining 14 places to move into the top 10 in England and Wales. The university is committed to widening access, making a lower conditional offer (ABB at A-level) to disadvantaged students applying to ARU's new £20m medical school in Chelmsford.

Across the university, more than 92% of

Bishop Hall Lane
Chelmsford CM1 1SQ
01245 686 868
answers@aru.ac.uk
www.aru.ac.uk
www.angliastudent.com
Open days:
see website

Edinburgh
Belfast
CAMBRIDGE
CHELMSFORD
Cardiff
London

The Times and The Sunday Times Rankings
Overall Ranking: 117 (last year: 120)

Teaching quality	80%	=62
Student experience	78.1%	=61
Research quality	5.4%	=89
Entry standards	113	=106
Graduate prospects	73.8%	64
Good honours	75.6%	=63
Expected completion rate	78.1%	=110
Student/staff ratio	17.7	=101
Services and facilities	£1,525	127

ARU's intake comes from non-selective state schools and almost two-thirds of students are aged at least 21 at entry. The focus of extensive outreach initiatives is on care-leavers and applicants with disabilities. Personal development tutors and mentors provide tailored assistance to new students. ARU's silver award in the Teaching Excellence Framework drew attention to its strong support for students at risk of dropping out. The latest figures show around one in seven fail to complete their course, significantly lower than the expected level.

ARU is one of the UK's leading providers of degree apprenticeships. In partnership with more than 350 employers across a range of industries, the university operates 19 programmes with about 1,800 students enrolled. New degree apprenticeships are planned for roles including operating department practitioner, paramedic and laboratory scientist, which will boost numbers to 2,500 by September 2021.

Degrees in professional policing, finance and economics, business with entrepreneurship and dual awards in nursing (adult and mental health), and in nursing (child and mental health) are joining the curriculum.

Applications increased about 6% in 2019 and enrolments stepped up by 11% after a two-year decline when they dropped by a third. In our overall ranking, ARU remains outside the top 100, and results in this year's National Student Survey saw falls in both our measures covering student satisfaction with teaching quality and the wider experience.

In Cambridge, accommodation in a university bedroom is guaranteed for all new first-year students who apply by the end of June. The Chelmsford campus has residential spaces, too, as well as the new Old Factory gym, featuring fitness mod cons including sled tracks, a multi-purpose rig and a spin studio. The Cambridge campus has a gym, fitness studio and tennis court. Students also get discounted membership at the Kelsey Kerridge Sports Centre nearby.

Tuition fees

- » Fees for UK students   £9,250
- » Fees for International students 2021–22   £13,900–£16,200
- » For scholarship and bursary information see www.aru.ac.uk/student-life/help-with-finances
- » Graduate salary   £24,000

Student numbers	
Undergraduates	17,370 (2,260)
Postgraduates	2,057 (2,803)
Applications/places	15,170/2,350
Applications per place	6.5
Overall offer rate	60%
International students – EU	6.3%
Non-EU	8.1%

Accommodation

University provided places: 2,128
Self-catered: £146–£430 per week
First years accommodated on first-come-first-served basis
www.aru.ac.uk/student-life/accommodation

Where do the students come from?

State schools (non-grammar)	92.4%	First generation students	54.6%	
Grammar schools	3.6%	Deprived areas	15.5%	
Independent schools	4%	All ethnic minorities	37.2%	

Social inclusion ranking: 9

Black attainment gap	-10.9%
Disabled	5.5%
Mature (over 21)	61.7%

Arts University Bournemouth

Banksy expert, television presenter and artist Professor Paul Gough is the new principal and vice-chancellor at Arts University Bournemouth (AUB). He took over a flourishing institution in January 2020 following the retirement of Stuart Bartholomew after 27 years. This small, specialist art, design, media and performance institution packs a big punch in terms of student satisfaction with teaching quality and the wider university experience, together with good staffing levels and a high degree completion rate.

The university offers more than 20 undergraduate degrees in architecture, dance and event management as well as art and design, acting and film subjects. Courses contain practical elements that are designed to give students an edge in a competitive world, some incorporating live briefs that students carry out for local and national businesses.

AUB brings in professionals from the creative industries as visiting tutors — a practice that impressed the panel awarding the university gold in the Teaching Excellence Framework. Recent guest lecturers include the director and AUB alumni Edgar Wright (*Baby Driver*, *Ant-Man* and *Spaced*), Peter Lord, the co-founder of Aardman Animations, and the ballerina Darcey Bussell.

Only 12 staff were entered for the 2014 Research Excellence Framework but 43% of their work was rated as world-leading or academically excellent.

Bournemouth Film School, part of the university, is the largest outside London, running nine courses covering all aspects of filmmaking. Its students make more than 50 films a year, partly through crowdfunding.

All undergraduate courses have their own studio space but students are encouraged to work together across disciplines on the single campus, learning the networking skills that will prove useful during an arts career.

The university is proud of its inspiring architecture, housing industry-standard technology. Students have access to laser-cutting and 3D printing equipment, and tuition fees include the cost of standard materials on most courses. The library's Museum of Design in Plastics showcases more than 12,000 examples of mass-produced design icons from the past 120 years of popular culture.

The CRAB drawing studio is the first to be built at an art school for more than a century. Designed by the architect Sir Peter Cook, another AUB alumnus, it was opened in 2016 by Dame Zaha Hadid, who said: "I simply love this building."

A striking Innovation Studio, also designed by Cook, will provide a hub for start-up businesses set up by AUB students and alumni. The Photography Building

Wallisdown
Poole BH12 5HH
01202 363 228
admissions@aub.ac.uk
www.aub.ac.uk
www.aubsu.co.uk
Open days: see website

The Times and The Sunday Times **Rankings**
Overall Ranking: 54 (last year: 43)

Teaching quality	86.5%	4
Student experience	83.2%	5
Research quality	2.4%	118
Entry standards	147	41
Graduate prospects	57.3%	=128
Good honours	68.3%	113
Expected completion rate	91.4%	=30
Student/staff ratio	14.5	=37
Services and facilities	£1,745	120

has flexible teaching spaces and IT suites and TheGallery is AUB's own exhibition space, where the work of students and other contemporary artists is showcased.

Environmental sustainability is the watchword for development at AUB and the campus holds an EcoCampus Platinum award after cutting waste and achieving a 59% recycling rate. All courses bear in mind environmental impact and for a recent production of *Treasure Island*, AUB costume and performance design students sourced recycled fabrics.

Rooftop solar panels will help power the new Campus Halls development, where 299 rooms in three blocks of studios and cluster flats are due to open in 2021.

More than 200 staff have been trained in mental health first aid, and the students' union runs The Small Things Matter, a campaign offering mindful self-care tools, tips and encouragement to improve mental wellbeing, from plant re-potting and cups of tea to how best to connect via social media.

A low dropout rate of about half the expected level is a point of pride for AUB. Applications nudged upwards in 2019 and competition for places was slightly stiffer, with offers made to 52% of applicants, compared with 56% in 2018.

Accommodation is modern and the housing office allocates rooms in waves from March to June to avoid any first-come, first-served scrum, and all first-year full-timers can live in. Rents are from £150 a week up to £205 a week in a brand new penthouse studio.

For £2 an hour, the students' union offers social sports sessions such as yoga, jogging and football through the Give It A Go programme (regular attendees get a free hoodie). AUB does not have its own sports facilities but a subsidy allows students to share the neighbouring Bournemouth University's extensive gym, courts, pitches and fitness studios. An Olympic-sized velodrome 10 minutes away is free for students to use.

Tuition fees

» Fees for UK students	£9,250
Foundation years	£5,421
» Fees for International students 2021–22	£16,950
» For scholarship and bursary information see www.aub.ac.uk/fees/undergraduate	
» Graduate salary	£21,000

Student numbers

Undergraduates	3,239	(0)
Postgraduates	87	(61)
Applications/places	6,575/1,185	
Applications per place	5.5	
Overall offer rate	52.1%	
International students – EU	6.8%	
Non-EU	9.7%	

Accommodation

University provided places: 1,000
Self-catered: £150–£205 per week
www.aub.ac.uk/accommodation

Where do the students come from?

State schools (non-grammar)	94.7%	First generation students	40%
Grammar schools	2.3%	Deprived areas	12.8%
Independent schools	3%	All ethnic minorities	11.4%

Social inclusion ranking: 78

Black attainment gap	n/a
Disabled	9.4%
Mature (over 21)	12.3%

University of the Arts London

For the second year in a row in 2020, University of the Arts London (UAL) was ranked by QS as second in the world for art and design, behind only the Royal College of Art, a postgraduate institution. One university comprised of six distinct colleges, UAL's appeal is enduring. The stellar subject ranking has driven up applications from European and international students – and overall recruitment was up more than 8% in 2019. There was a further 11.5% surge in applications in the 2020 admissions cycle.

The university's chancellor, the Turner prize-winning artist Grayson Perry, said of its international accolade: "It's great to see UAL shoot up the rankings to claim the No 2 spot in the world for art and design. It's a testament to the incredible talent of UAL that has shaped the visionaries, renegades and pioneers that fuel the world's need for creativity. It's a brilliant result."

When it became a university in 2004, UAL hung on to the unique identities of each constituent college: Camberwell College of Arts, Central Saint Martins, Chelsea College of Arts, London College of Communication, London College of Fashion and Wimbledon College of Arts. Building on their long histories (all were founded in the 19th or early 20th centuries), UAL has established a reputation for innovation across the creative fields and has produced more than half of the nominees for the Turner prize since its inception in 1984.

Two pilot projects are pushing forward UAL's influence in the creative sector. The Decolonising Arts Institute aims to prompt a rethink of art and design practice, and the UAL Social Design Institute hopes to reshape the international research agenda for sustainability through design.

The London College of Fashion (LCF) has campuses across the city from Shoreditch to Oxford Circus. Part of a £4m grant in March will go towards developing its new campus at Queen Elizabeth Olympic Park in Stratford, east London, where the college will join creative organisations including the BBC, Sadler's Wells and the V&A at London's new East Bank hub. Building work was forced to pause during the coronavirus outbreak, pushing back the move, planned for 2022.

LCF has also earmarked grant money for its outreach projects with female prisoners and ex-offenders, designed to boost confidence and wellbeing as well as providing skills and qualifications.

In south London, Camberwell College of Arts (CCA) has opened The Playground, a new community space for workshops and multi-arts events designed for age groups from 11 to the over-60s. The college campus, where facilities include workshops and a

272 High Holborn
London WC1V 7EY
020 7514 6000
http://enquiries.arts.ac.uk
www.arts.ac.uk
www.arts-su.com
Open days:
see website

modern library, offers about 1,600 design and fine art courses from foundation to postgraduate level and plays a big part in the area's lively art scene. Camberwell graduates have opened local galleries and art and design studios.

UAL's £200m development of a former King's Cross granary into the award-winning Central Saint Martins (CSM) campus was an integral part of the area's hugely successful regeneration, and students benefit from modern facilities in architecturally striking buildings, opening on to Granary Square.

Theatrical courses at Wimbledon College of Arts are expanding. The college offers acting, costume, theatre, film and television programmes and has introduced BA degrees in creative technical theatre and technical arts for theatre and performance.

LFC has added a BA course in fashion media practice and criticism, and in the 2021 academic year the London College of Communication (LCC) will begin a music production BA. A course in fine art: computational art will begin at CCA. All new courses are subject to UAL'S validation process, which means their content and structure may be tweaked if necessary.

In a prescient move, UAL took steps towards a "virtual campus" even before social distancing measures caused upheaval during the coronavirus crisis. Shared Campus is a collaboration with art and design institutions in Zurich, Singapore, Taipei, Kyoto and Hong Kong, connecting their shared interests to form a cross-cultural digital university.

In the shifting jobs landscape, creative industries are growing at a higher-than-average rate in the UK. In this context UAL graduates should fare well, though that has yet to trickle through to our graduate prospects score, where the university sits four places off the bottom of the table. Budding entrepreneurs receive enterprise development support and in 2017–18 UAL students began 240 start-up businesses. Jobs and paid internships, part-time work, freelance contracts and full-time opportunities in the creative sector are posted on the jobs board.

Links with global brands are built into teaching programmes, requiring students to respond to "live" industry briefs or undertake work placements or other projects. A five-year investment by the fashion giant Kering, owner of Gucci, Balenciaga, Alexander McQueen and Stella McCartney, to develop UAL's sustainability curriculum is the flagship partnership among the institution's industry-funded consultancy projects.

Tuition fees

» Fees for UK students	£9,250
Foundation courses	from £5,420
» Fees for International students 2021–22	£22,920
» For scholarship and bursary information see www.arts.ac.uk/study-at-ual/student-fees-funding	
» Graduate salary	£21,400

Student numbers

Undergraduates	14,951	(62)
Postgraduates	3,445	(638)
Applications/places	27,100/4,410	
Applications per place	6.1	
Overall offer rate	41.9%	
International students – EU	12.8%	
Non-EU	37.9%	

Accommodation

University provided places: 3,200
Self-catered: £140–£407 per week
No accommodation guarantee
www.arts.ac.uk/study-at-ual/accommodation

Where do the students come from?

State schools (non-grammar)	91.8%	First generation students	39.9%	Black attainment gap	-24.2%
Grammar schools	1.6%	Deprived areas	4.7%	Disabled	13.2%
Independent schools	6.6%	All ethnic minorities	31.7%	Mature (over 21)	18.5%

Social inclusion ranking: 26

Aston University

The popularity of Aston University reached new heights in the 2019 recruitment cycle, when the Birmingham university famed for turning out work-ready graduates received a record number of applications, up 22% on the previous year. Enrolments also jumped 16%.

A successful track record offering practical degrees paired with careers guidance and work experience has built Aston an enduring reputation in the graduate employment market. It ranks in the top 20 UK universities for the proportion of graduates (81%) in high-skilled employment or postgraduate study within 15 months of completing their courses.

Aston's extensive and active connections with business and industry create opportunities for students to get a foot in the door when it comes to the graduate jobs market. More than 160 companies vie for the best candidates at its recruitment events, and Aston has links with thousands of firms of all shapes and sizes, many of which offer placements as well as possible jobs.

Every Aston degree has either a placement year or work-based modules within its design. About 70% of students choose a placement year, paying an average £16,000, which comes in handy for student finances and gives them a head start on networking and work experience. The university careers and placements team also helps students who want to study overseas or start their own business. A scheme called Languages for All allows students to learn a language alongside or as part of their degree.

Awarded gold in the Teaching Excellence Framework (TEF), Aston scored highly for the way employability skills are embedded in degrees, as well as the involvement of professional bodies and employers in course design and delivery. The TEF report noted the outstanding personalised provision and highest levels of engagement and commitment, including bookable personal tutoring sessions. Course design and assessment stretched and engaged students, assessors found.

Once a college of advanced technology, the university remains strong in engineering and the sciences but has other strings to its bow. Undergraduate courses are arranged under five schools: business, medical, engineering and applied science, life and health sciences and languages and social sciences.

More than 80% of Aston students are from ethnic minority backgrounds, the largest proportion of any UK university. Its success in our social inclusion table, ranked in the top 40 in England and Wales, is even better when viewed in the context of fellow pre-1992 universities, among which Aston sits in the top 10.

Seven new degrees will be added from 2021, most of them building on Aston's engineering expertise by including an environmental

---

Aston Triangle
Birmingham B4 7ET
0121 204 3030
ugadmissions@aston.ac.uk
www.aston.ac.uk
www.astonsu.com
Open days:
see website

The Times and The Sunday Times **Rankings**
Overall Ranking: 43 (last year: 48)

Teaching quality	77.8%	96
Student experience	77.9%	=68
Research quality	25.8%	48
Entry standards	128	=60
Graduate prospects	81.3%	=30
Good honours	81.9%	=31
Expected completion rate	89.9%	=36
Student/staff ratio	16.1	=72
Services and facilities	£2,126	91

element, such as chemical engineering with sustainability and civil engineering with sustainability. Business enterprise development is joining the curriculum too.

Aston pioneered degree apprenticeships in the UK through a partnership with Capgemini, a global consulting, technology and outsourcing company, training the first degree apprenticeship graduates in the country. Today there are 850 students on 17 programmes in engineering, business, transport, audiology and technology roles. The numbers are expected to increase to 1,500 by September 2021, with eight new programmes set to be offered under the same umbrella of subjects.

In the latest Research Excellence Framework in 2014, life and health sciences produced Aston's best results and the proportion of work placed in the top two categories doubled to nearly 80%. New research centres in enterprise, healthy ageing, Europe, and neuroscience and child development have proved their worth. Pharmacy, another of the university's strengths, was awarded a prestigious Regius Professorship to celebrate the Queen's 90th birthday.

Based near the centre of Birmingham on a 60-acre self-contained site, Aston prides itself on offering a campus experience within a big city. The recently built students' union is at the heart of the campus and a long-running programme of improvements has opened up green spaces and remodelled Chancellor's Lake.

Teaching facilities are modern and the Main Building is gaining additional social learning facilities. Redevelopment has created an impressive library and a new home for the highly-rated business school, the base for almost half of all Aston's students.

The Sir Doug Ellis Woodcock Sports Centre on campus has a gym with more than 100 stations plus a women-only gym, a swimming pool and a sports hall with indoor courts and team facilities. Six miles from campus, the Outdoor Recreation Centre has pitches for football, cricket and hockey.

The Unibuddy scheme allows prospective students to message current ones to find out what life at Aston is really like. Student accommodation is on campus and the university's 1,500 rooms allow for all first-years – undergraduate and postgraduate – to be guaranteed a space if they apply in time. Campus catering outlets offer a termly meal deal.

Birmingham is one of the country's leading student cities with something to suit every undergraduate tribe.

Tuition fees

» Fees for UK students	£9,250
» Fees for International students 2021–22	£15,950–£19,800
Medicine	£42,750
» For finance information see www.aston.ac.uk/study	
» Graduate salary	£25,000

Student numbers

Undergraduates	10,948	(1,318)
Postgraduates	1,263	(1,461)
Applications/places	17,120/2,355	
Applications per place	7.3	
Overall offer rate	82.5%	
International students – EU	4.9%	
Non-EU	11.5%	

Accommodation

University provided places: 1,500
Self-catered: £138–£144 per week
www2.aston.ac.uk/accommodation/

Where do the students come from?

State schools (non-grammar)	84.6%	First generation students	52.3%		
Grammar schools	9.7%	Deprived areas	9.9%		
Independent schools	5.7%	All ethnic minorities	82.4%		

Social inclusion ranking: =38

Black attainment gap	-16%
Disabled	4.7%
Mature (over 21)	4.9%

Bangor University

With Snowdonia National Park on one side and the Menai Strait on the other, Bangor University offers one of the UK's most scenic settings for student life. It has performed consistently well in the annual National Student Survey and although it fell back somewhat in 2020 for teaching quality and student experience, it still ranked in the top 40 for both.

Bangor was the only university in Wales to be awarded gold in the 2014 Teaching Excellence Framework. Assessors commended the personalised support for students and strategic approach to assessment plus bilingual learning in Welsh and English, coupled with very good physical and virtual learning resources.

Undergraduate provision is distinguished by a successful work experience programme. Year-long placements are offered at the end of the second year for almost all degree programmes and there are voluntary two-week placements too. Students have gained valuable experience in their field with companies such as Santander Bank, Coutts, Welsh Rugby Union, BBC Cymru and the adventure business ZipWorld.

There is also an international exchange programme, offering the option of studying overseas for an extra year. The Bangor Employability Award accredits activities such as volunteering, learning a new language and part-time work, all valued by employers, and graduates can take paid internships within Bangor's own academic schools and services.

There is some ground to make up on Bangor's dropout rate: at more than one in seven it is significantly higher than the expected rate of 10.7% based on the social and academic background of its students.

University buildings are located throughout the small coastal town of Bangor in Gywynedd, the county with more Welsh speakers than any other. The university recruits Welsh and English students in similar proportions, and about 20% speak Welsh. Peer guides help all newcomers settle in and personal tutors provide advice and support for the duration of each student's time at Bangor.

The institution was in the top 50 universities in the latest Research Excellence Framework in 2014. Half of its faculties were rated in the top 20 in the UK, led by leisure and tourism, languages and psychology. The School of Ocean Sciences is highly rated and a £20m science park on the island of Anglesey brings together businesses from the ICT, science and research sectors with staff and students from the university.

Twelve new degree programmes include a suite of business management degrees plus medical biochemistry, marketing with psychology, Welsh history and archaeology,

College Road
Bangor LL57 2DG
01248 383 717
applicantservices@bangor.ac.uk
www.bangor.ac.uk
www.undebbangor.com
Open days:
see website

The Times and The Sunday Times **Rankings**
Overall Ranking: 62 (last year: 70)

Teaching quality	81.1%	=40
Student experience	79.6%	=36
Research quality	27.2%	47
Entry standards	125	=70
Graduate prospects	73.2%	66
Good honours	72%	=90
Expected completion rate	83.8%	=70
Student/staff ratio	15.7	=67
Services and facilities	£1,932	106

and politics and economics. Banking with financial technology and business analytics, financial technology are also being introduced, subject to validation.

Bangor has expanded its portfolio of degree apprenticeships from five roles in cyber-security, mechanical and electrical engineering, data science and software engineering to include four further engineering and IT programmes, and a professional policing practice programme.

Applications dropped by 13% in 2019, and enrolments were down by 8% – continuing a trend since 2016 recording falling applications (down 30%) and enrolments (down 18%). In 2019, 15% of Bangor's intake came through clearing.

Financial support for Welsh students is via the Welsh Government Learning Grant, worth up to £1,500. For English students, the university offers its own bursaries and scholarships, and nearly half of English admissions qualify for some form of financial assistance. Bangor's Talent Opportunities Programme raises aspirations for more than 2,000 pupils in years 9–11 at schools across north Wales.

Both student villages, St Mary's and the larger Ffriddoedd, are within walking distance of university buildings. Accommodation is guaranteed for first-years and prices are at the more affordable end of the scale. One hall of residence is reserved for Welsh speakers and those learning the language, and quiet accommodation or alcohol-free areas can also be requested.

An arts and innovation centre called Pontio – which means "to bridge" – houses the students' union and links the university with the town. It has a cinema, theatre and lecture theatres and places to eat and drink. Membership to all clubs and societies is free and there are about 200 sports and other activities to choose from.

The university sports centre, Canolfan Brailsford (named after the cycling coach Sir Dave Brailsford, who grew up nearby) at Ffriddoedd has two sports halls, three gyms, a multi-route climbing wall, outdoor grass pitches and a floodlit synthetic pitch. There is also a fitness room at the St Mary's student village and gym membership is included in the fees for halls.

Bar Uno at Ffriddoedd is the main campus hangout and the beaches of Anglesey are popular with students.

Tuition fees

- » Fees for UK students — £9,000
- » Fees for International students 2020–21 — £14,500–£16,800
- » For scholarship and bursary information see www.bangor.ac.uk/studentfinance/Info/Index.php.en
- » Graduate salary — £21,000

Student numbers

Undergraduates	7,415	(395)
Postgraduates	1,636	(748)
Applications/places		7,765/1,860
Applications per place		4.2
Overall offer rate		84.5%
International students – EU		5.3%
Non-EU		14%

Accommodation

University provided places: 2882
Self-catered: £100–£197 per week
First years guaranteed accommodation
www.bangor.ac.uk/studentlife/accommodation.php.en

Where do the students come from?

State schools (non-grammar)	91%	First generation students	41%
Grammar schools	4.6%	Deprived areas	12.2%
Independent schools	4.4%	All ethnic minorities	8.8%

Social inclusion ranking: =57

Black attainment gap	-19.9%
Disabled	10.2%
Mature (over 21)	28%

University of Bath

A new building for the School of Management is under construction at the University of Bath. The £70m development's open layout is designed to encourage effective teamwork between students, academics and employers and it features eight lecture theatres and a 250-seat auditorium.

Awarded gold in the Teaching Excellence Framework (TEF), and an eminent research institution, the university moves back into our top 10 this year for the first time since 2014, and earns a shortlisting for our University of the Year award. The TEF panel recognised Bath for its high-quality physical and digital resources as well as students' engagement with developments at the forefront of research and the university's strong employment orientation. Professional accreditation is embedded extensively across the curriculum.

The university continues to be a very popular choice for students, offering courses in engineering, humanities, management, science and social science from an attractive campus at Claverton Down just outside the Unesco World Heritage-listed city.

Student numbers are on an upward trajectory – rising by 12% between 2018 and 2019 – and applications for 2020 admissions rose by 8%. More students than usual came through clearing in 2019 (9%), but the university expects this proportion to decrease.

New options in beginner's French, German, Spanish, Russian and Mandarin have been added to the modern languages curriculum and can be combined with international politics. Students can now study computer science and artificial intelligence and a degree in maths, statistics and data science is being introduced in 2021.

Bath's work placement scheme has links with more than 3,000 organisations around the world and two thirds of undergraduates spend a placement year in the private, public or not-for-profit sectors. The careers service hosts up to 400 employer visits a year. Just five universities beat Bath's record of 89.9% employment in high-skilled jobs or further study 15 months after graduation.

Bath excelled in the latest Research Excellence Framework in 2014. Almost a third of the work submitted was assessed as world-leading and 87% was in the top two categories. Research grants and contracts won by the university are worth more than £130m and there are 25 international strategic partnerships with top-ranked institutions worldwide.

Significant funding has been received to develop Bath's Institute for Advanced Automotive Propulsion Systems, which

Claverton Down
Bath BA2 7AY
01225 383 019
admissions@bath.ac.uk
www.bath.ac.uk
www.thesubath.com
Open days:
see website

The Times and The Sunday Times Rankings

Overall Ranking: 9 (last year: 11)

Teaching quality	79.1%	=74
Student experience	80.9%	18
Research quality	37.3%	24
Entry standards	174	12
Graduate prospects	89.4%	6
Good honours	89%	9
Expected completion rate	96.2%	5
Student/staff ratio	14.9	=49
Services and facilities	£2,736	42

links research and teaching in mechanical and automotive engineering with the global industry developing ultra-low emissions vehicles and driverless cars. Bath is also the base for the UK's Institute of Coding, a consortium creating new courses for diverse groups of people seeking digital careers.

Bath has its work cut out in broadening its intake of students, however, more than 40% of whom arrive from independent or selective grammar schools. Outreach initiatives are organised at schools across the country and at the university, aimed at helping pupils to make successful applications. A research project with potential students teaches time management and extended writing skills, and student ambassadors provide positive role models.

Any pupil who qualifies under the widening participation scheme has their application flagged up to the admissions department and each person's potential is considered within the context of their background. There is a range of income-related scholarships and bursaries, notably the Gold Scholarship Programme, which awards £5,000 a year, except during paid placement years, to 50 disadvantaged students each year. About 15% of admissions qualify for some form of financial assistance.

Winner of the *Sunday Times* Sports University of the Year 2018, Bath has world-class facilities – matched by the quality of its sport, health and exercise science degrees. The on-campus Sports Training Village (STV) is a £35m multi-sport centre open to students, staff and the public. As well as providing a home for all clubs in Team Bath, it is a national training centre for several Olympic and Paralympic sports. The Team Bath Gym and Fitness Centre has been expanded to offer 200 workout stations and two exercise studios, hosting 100 classes weekly.

Among the STV's superb resources are extensive indoor and outdoor tennis courts, a legacy swimming pool from the London 2012 Olympics, a fencing hall and the UK's only bobsleigh and skeleton push-start track. There are more than 20 games pitches for football, hockey, rugby and cricket. Access to most of the facilities is free with the Student Sport Pass, included in tuition fees, so there is no excuse to duck out.

A room in university accommodation is guaranteed for all first-years and about 1,000 of the 4,700 residential spaces are catered – a rare feature today. Most undergraduates move out to the city from their second year, where a thriving social scene is on their doorstep.

Tuition fees

» Fees for UK students	£9,250
» Fees for International students 2021–22	£18,900–£23,400
» For scholarship and bursary information see www.bath.ac.uk/topics/tuiton-fees	
» Graduate salary	£29,000

Student numbers

Undergraduates	13,296	(117)
Postgraduates	3,090	(1,563)
Applications/places	27,205/3,605	
Applications per place	7.5	
Overall offer rate	74.9%	
International students – EU	10.1%	
Non-EU	20.7%	

Accommodation

University provided places: 4,773
Catered costs: £140–£178 per week
Self-catered: £72–£215 per week
First years guaranteed accommodation
www.bath.ac.uk/professional-services/student-accommodation/

Where do the students come from?

State schools (non-grammar)	56.9%	First generation students	25.1%	Black attainment gap	-6.6%
Grammar schools	17.3%	Deprived areas	4.7%	Disabled	5.6%
Independent schools	25.9%	All ethnic minorities	19.7%	Mature (over 21)	2.5%

Social inclusion ranking: 106

Bath Spa University

Bath Spa University's arts and design campus on Locksbrook Road opened to students in 2019. With views over the River Avon, the city centre building features technical workshops, flexible studio spaces and social areas in a redeveloped factory. It is especially convenient for those living in nearby Lower Bristol Road and Oldfield Park student accommodation.

Locksbrook is Bath Spa's fourth campus. Headquarters are at Newton Park four miles outside the Unesco World Heritage City, in an attractive country setting with grounds landscaped by Capability Brown. Newton Park's imposing Georgian manor house is owned by the Duchy of Cornwall, and some classes take place in the 14th-century gatehouse. Reflecting the university's substantial investment in 21st-century facilities, the Commons building and the purpose-built Michael Tippett concert hall provide modern learning spaces.

The Sion Hill campus, which has also recently been updated, is within walking distance of Bath city centre. It houses studios and workshops for fashion and textiles, and a specialist art and design library. Corsham Court, another historic manor house, is the university's postgraduate centre near Chippenham.

A snapshot of the applications cycle at the end of March 2020 showed a 4% dip in numbers, which the university attributes to fewer EU applications combined with its discontinuation of more than 70 combination courses. Only 8% of students entered via clearing in September 2019.

Bath Spa has stopped its 3, 2, 1, Go! admissions scheme, which guaranteed offers to students based on their performance at interview, audition or through their portfolio in arts subjects – regardless of exam results.

The curriculum gained four new degrees in 2020 including honours programmes in law, and game art. A further 14 courses across a broad subject range are being added from 2021, including educational psychology, film-making, politics, philosophy and economics, and wildlife conservation. The university plans to offer more degree apprenticeships beyond the MBA leadership programme currently offered.

The Teaching Excellence Framework (TEF) awarded Bath Spa silver, praising its course design and assessment practices "that provide high levels of rigour and stretch". Assessors also noted the personalised teaching, the availability of a personal tutor, peer mentoring, and independent study at Bath Spa.

Work-based learning is built into courses wherever possible. The music and performing arts school, for example, uses work placements and live briefs with industry partners such as the Bath Festival and the National Theatre to enhance students'

Newton Park
Newton St Loe
Bath BA2 9BN
01225 876 180
admissions@bathspa.ac.uk
www.bathspa.ac.uk
www.bathspasu.co.uk
Open days:
see website

The Times and The Sunday Times Rankings		
Overall Ranking: =104 (last year: 110)		
Teaching quality	77.5%	98
Student experience	73.1%	=119
Research quality	7.9%	=73
Entry standards	112	=109
Graduate prospects	62.4%	=119
Good honours	80.1%	36
Expected completion rate	84%	=68
Student/staff ratio	17.2	=93
Services and facilities	£2,165	88

learning and graduate prospects. The school of sciences has links with the Yeo Valley food business and the Avon and Somerset police; the business school with H&M and Oracle. There is also a strategic partnership with Santander.

Bath Spa received funding from the Office for Students government body to finance the GradTalent Agency, a careers service pairing graduates from the southwest of England with the region's small and medium-sized businesses. However, the university has more work to do to turn around its graduate prospects score in our league table, where it has finished in the lower reaches for several years in a row. Just over 60% of students are in high-skilled jobs or postgraduate study 15 months after graduation, according to a new survey.

Poor scores for graduate prospects help to keep Bath Spa out of our top 100 overall, but modest improvements in student satisfaction this year have at least helped the university to climb six places. Student views on teaching quality lift Bath Spa into the top 100 on this measure, but remain a long way short of the 6= ranking the university earned as recently as 2015. It is in the bottom 10 for satisfaction with the wider student experience.

In 2014 an assessment under the Research Excellence Framework rated more than half of the university's relatively small submission world-leading or internationally excellent – leading to an 86% increase in research funding.

Bath Spa finishes in the middle reaches of our social inclusion table. Its outreach programme with children aged nine to 19 – called Be Inspired! – is designed to widen participation. The admissions process takes into account the varying experiences of applicants who may have followed non-traditional paths to higher education.

Sports facilities including a gym, netball courts and games pitches are dotted around the campuses at present. The Bath Spa Sports ground is being developed close to the city and will offer a cricket pitch, tennis courts and floodlighting. The university fields 15 teams in the BUCS (British Universities and Colleges Sport) league.

There are nearly 2,200 university-owned or managed residential places, enough to guarantee one for all first-years who apply by the deadline. The allocation process gives all applicants an equal chance of getting their first preference, rather than relying on a first come, first served system.

Tuition fees

»	Fees for UK students	£9,250
	Foundation courses	£7,950
»	Fees for International students 2020–21	£13,700–£15,300
»	For scholarship and bursary information see www.bathspa.ac.uk/students/student-finance	
»	Graduate salary	£20,000

Student numbers

Undergraduates	5,944	(115)
Postgraduates	922	(787)
Applications/places	11,940/2,245	
Applications per place	5.3	
Overall offer rate	81.5%	
International students – EU	3%	
Non-EU	4.4%	

Accommodation

University provided places: 2,196
Self-catered: £70–£252 per week
First years guaranteed accommodation
www.bathspa.ac.uk/be-bath-spa/accommodation/

Where do the students come from?

State schools (non-grammar)	90.1%	First generation students	43.3%	Black attainment gap	-23.6%
Grammar schools	3.4%	Deprived areas	13.8%	Disabled	11.8%
Independent schools	6.5%	All ethnic minorities	9.2%	Mature (over 21)	13.8%

Social inclusion ranking: 65

University of Bedfordshire

Bedfordshire's new campus at Aylesbury opened in early 2020. A partnership with Buckinghamshire Healthcare NHS Trust, it is located at Stoke Mandeville Hospital, home to the highly regarded National Spinal Injuries Centre. Healthcare students have a new three-storey building on the hospital site with a specialist skills room set out as a ward, complete with audiovisual technology.

Six classrooms, a library, social learning spaces and computing facilities add to the provision, and students also gain experience at the specialist, acute and community services trust.

The Aylesbury campus is Bedfordshire's fifth base. It follows a £40m new building for Stem (science, technology, engineering and maths) subjects that has added 6,000 square metres of high-tech teaching space at the university's main campus in Luton. There are computer laboratories and workshops for automotive engineering, cyber-security and robotics, along with large teaching labs, specialist containment labs and an outreach centre to promote Stem subjects to the community.

More future-facing initiatives for Bedfordshire include a year-long Target Zero campaign to reduce carbon emissions by 510 tons and increase recycling by 12% across all campuses. *There's Gonna Be a Storm* is a tornado-shaped tower of plastic bottles installed at the university, to highlight the extreme weather effects of climate change and plastic pollution. Sustainability is embedded in the curriculum and Bedfordshire was the first university in England to stop investing in the fossil fuel industry, following a national student campaign, and is Fairtrade-accredited.

This level of responsiveness to student concerns might go some way to helping Bedfordshire improve its scores in future National Student Surveys. It has fallen out of the top 100 for satisfaction with teaching quality this year and has dropped even further for contentment with the overall experience – finishing in the bottom 10 UK universities for this measure, having ranked as high as 44= in 2018.

Along with one third of students failing to complete their degrees – far in excess of the expected level of 22.8% based on the social and academic background of Bedfordshire's intake – this has contributed to the university's decline to the foot of our academic ranking, a position it last occupied in the first edition of the *Sunday Times* University Guide in 1998. A rise in our social inclusion ranking to fourth place offers some consolation.

The government's Teaching Excellence Framework awarded Bedfordshire a silver

University Square
Luton LU1 3JU
0300 330 0073
admissions@beds.ac.uk
www.beds.ac.uk
www.bedssu.co.uk
Open days:
see website

The Times and The Sunday Times Rankings
Overall Ranking: 131 (last year: 128)

Teaching quality	76.8%	=104
Student experience	72.4%	=122
Research quality	7.0%	=77
Entry standards	103	=127
Graduate prospects	70.1%	=91
Good honours	65.6%	=124
Expected completion rate	58.5%	131
Student/staff ratio	19.7	=121
Services and facilities	£2,043	96

rating. The university was praised for its successes in widening participation, not only in enrolling students from groups that are under-represented in higher education, but also in helping them to achieve good results.

Fifteen courses are joining the roster of degrees, among them behavioural science in health, clinical exercise therapy, interior design and environmental health science. Football degrees with four specialisms of business, coaching, development and science are also being added.

Bedfordshire offers 14 higher and degree apprenticeships in midwifery, social work, cyber-security, associate project management and registered nursing among others. There are plans to develop programmes in Stem-related occupations and the university expects numbers to grow from 300 to between 350 and 400 by September 2021.

Bedfordshire offers students who enter with fewer than 112 UCAS tariff points, or equivalent, a bursary worth £1,500 over three academic years – in recognition that it is often the least qualified students who need the most support, financially and generally, to successfully complete their studies. Merit scholarships worth £2,400 over three years are awarded to those achieving more than 112 UCAS tariff points

The university's biggest campus, in the centre of Luton, is the site of a £40m seven-floor library with 900 study spaces and laptops for loan. The second campus in Bedford is home to the education and sport faculty and has more than 2,000 students, making it one of the UK's largest providers of physical-education teacher training, as well as a national centre for other subjects. Students here also take subjects such as performing arts, law and business management. The campus is in a leafy setting 20 minutes' walk from the town centre and has a 280-seat auditorium and a students' union.

Tuition fees

»	Fees for UK students	£9,250
	Foundation courses	£6,165
»	Fees for International students 2020–21	£12,650
»	For scholarship and bursary information see www.beds.ac.uk/howtoapply/money/fees/	
»	Graduate salary	£24,000

Student numbers

Undergraduates	9,511	(1,889)
Postgraduates	1,722	(802)
Applications/places	9,160/1,275	
Applications per place	7.2	
Overall offer rate	79.7%	
International students – EU	12.4%	
Non-EU	12.6%	

Accommodation

University provided places: 1,369
Self-catered: £109–£199 per week
www.beds.ac.uk/accommodation

Where do the students come from?

State schools (non-grammar)	98.1%	First generation students	62.5%
Grammar schools	1.5%	Deprived areas	9.9%
Independent schools	0.4%	All ethnic minorities	63.9%

Social inclusion ranking: 4

Black attainment gap	-23%
Disabled	4.7%
Mature (over 21)	70.7%

Birkbeck, University of London

The introduction of more than 50 full- and part-time degrees offering a foundation year to ease students into their higher education is Birkbeck's latest initiative to widen educational access, the cause around which it has been built. Courses last six years part-time and four years when taken full-time.

Full-time at Birkbeck means for the most part studying in the evening. "All of our facilities and support services are geared around evening study. Evenings are when we really come to life," the university prospectus says. It was founded nearly 200 years ago to provide higher education to working Londoners, and that remains true today, with many students fitting in their studies around work and/or family life. Classes are held between 6pm and 9pm.

Birkbeck withdrew from our league table in 2019 because it felt that, in comparison with traditional, residential universities, our measures placed it at a disadvantage. It has a point. The university's decision to join the rankings was prompted by a rapid increase in full-time courses – albeit taught in the evening – which made comparisons with other universities more valid than before. While that process will accelerate with the start of a raft of new degree programmes with a foundation year, the nature of the student experience at Birkbeck remains part-time.

Unlike other institutions that withhold their data from this publication, we continue to include Birkbeck in our listings due to its unique mission and place in British higher education, where it does more to widen participation than the vast majority of universities.

Birkbeck remains in the international rankings, where it does much better because they are based mainly on research and reputation. In the QS World University Rankings, Birkbeck is 344= and placed among the UK's top-40 institutions, and seventh in London.

It has been expanding its teaching reach across the capital from its base in Bloomsbury. A partnership with the University of East London established a presence in Stratford, close to the Olympic Park, and a new teaching facility is soon to open in Euston Road.

The Wohl Wolfson ToddlerLab in Torrington Square will be the world's first purpose-built centre dedicated to studying brain development in toddlers as they interact with their natural environment. It will build on the globally-renowned research conducted in Birkbeck's BabyLab. As well as studying typically developing toddlers, it is hoped the new lab will advance understanding in the development of toddlers with conditions such as autism, ADHD, Fragile X and Williams Syndrome.

The university was in the top 30 in the 2014 Research Excellence Framework, when

Malet Street
London WC1E 7HX
020 3907 0700
studentadvice@bbk.ac.uk
www.bbk.ac.uk
www.bbk.ac.uk/su
Open days: see website

The Times and The Sunday Times **Rankings**
Overall Ranking: n/a
No data available

more than 80% of its eligible academics were entered. Almost three-quarters of the work submitted was rated world-leading or internationally excellent, with psychology and environmental science in the top six.

Birkbeck earned a silver rating in the Teaching Excellence Framework (TEF). Assessors were impressed by the range of initiatives to help students who would not otherwise be in higher education to graduate successfully. Programmes supported students from diverse backgrounds, the TEF panel said, enabling them to achieve their full potential through a curriculum that is at the forefront of research.

The university offers undergraduate degree apprenticeships in chartered management and digital and technology solutions and a postgraduate option in management practice. There are plans for further degree apprenticeships and Birkbeck is investigating new modes of delivery, including online, to support this.

Birkbeck graduates enjoy high average starting salaries – among the best in the sector – partly because two-thirds are mature students, many of them returning to already successful careers. The college has a wide range of links with the City, including businesses such as JP Morgan, Santander, Facebook and PwC.

Industry partnerships support students, helping them gain business skills, work experience and internships while studying, and growing their professional networks and improving job prospects, regardless of the stage in their career at which they opt to study at Birkbeck. Its recruitment service, Birkbeck Talent, links students and recent graduates with leading employers. Since its launch in 2015, it has found jobs or internships for almost 400 students.

The college welcomes applications from people without the usual qualifications and continues to attract non-traditional learners of all ages and backgrounds. Those who have taken A-level or equivalent qualifications recently are made offers based on the UCAS tariff, but others are assessed by the college on the basis of interviews and/or short tests. The My Birkbeck student centre brings together all of the college's student support services.

Most Birkbeck students already live in the capital but full-time students looking for accommodation can apply for places in intercollegiate halls, as well as those in private purpose-built study bedrooms run by Unite Students. A gym, swimming pool and other facilities are available at Student Central, the former University of London students' union, which is next door to the Bloomsbury campus.

Tuition fees

- » Fees for UK students — £9,250
- » Fees for International students 2021–22 — £14,280
- » For scholarship and bursary information see www.bbk.ac.uk/student-services/financial-support
- » Graduate salary — n/a

Student numbers

Applications/places	5,530/755
Applications per place	7.3
Overall offer rate	n/a

Accommodation

University provided places: 152
Catered costs: £156–£314
Self-catered costs: £152–£283
www.bbk.ac.uk/student-services/accommodation

Where do the students come from?

No data available

University of Birmingham

Not since its original redbrick buildings were completed in 1909 has the University of Birmingham experienced such transformation. Britain's first "civic" university will have spent £600m on an ambitious 10-year development programme by the time it completes in 2026.

The plan has already produced a collaborative teaching laboratory, opened in 2018 and incorporating a wet lab, dry lab and e-lab, which has enabled the university to rethink how Stem (science, technology, engineering and maths) subjects are taught. There are new 500-seat and 250-seat lecture theatres, seminar rooms and learning spaces to house 1,000 students.

Work has begun on a new School of Engineering, which will bring together Birmingham's extensive engineering disciplines and house a centre of excellence in rail innovation, drawing on the city's industrial heritage. Part of the building is already open at the 260-acre campus in leafy Edgbaston, where the clocktower – Old Joe, 100 metres high – is a local landmark.

In the city centre on Broad Street, the university has begun developing the site of the former municipal bank into the Exchange, which will be a hub for public engagement, regional and national policy development, and skills and leadership training.

Dentistry is already based in the city. A health innovation campus in Selly Oak, formerly Birmingham Life Sciences Park, will open in 2022, a mile from the City South campus at Edgbaston. Here Birmingham plans to deliver the full cycle of medical treatments from drug development to real-world studies. Drama is also located in Selly Oak, where students have the opportunity to take placements at the BBC Drama Village, which shares the campus.

Birmingham is the first Russell Group university to open a campus in Dubai. The second intake of students enrolled there in 2019 taking courses in business, economics, computer science, mechanical engineering and teacher training.

A pioneer of unconditional offers, which guaranteed students a place regardless of A-level grades if they named the institution as their first choice, Birmingham put an end to the scheme before the Office for Students abolished it during the Covid-19 pandemic. Instead it has introduced "attainment offers" which set a minimum grade requirement (lower than standard entry grades) for high-achieving students who make Birmingham their first, firm choice.

The record levels of applications the university has experienced in recent years dipped slightly in 2018, and again the following year. Even so, the number of enrolments rose slightly in 2019 in a

Edgbaston
Birmingham B15 2TT
0121 414 3344
www.birmingham.ac.uk
www.guildofstudents.com
Open days:
see website

The Times and The Sunday Times **Rankings**
Overall Ranking: 19 (last year: 14)

Teaching quality	76.4%	=110
Student experience	74.9%	108
Research quality	37.1%	26
Entry standards	159	=22
Graduate prospects	84.7%	=13
Good honours	86.2%	=14
Expected completion rate	94.6%	=11
Student/staff ratio	14.1	=27
Services and facilities	£3,331	13

recruitment round when 5% of first-years arrived through clearing.

Birmingham eclipsed several other Russell Group universities to be awarded gold in the Teaching Excellence Framework. The panel praised a strategic focus on the development and delivery of relevant, research-informed teaching.

Only one university (Manchester) did better than Birmingham in the 2020 High Fliers report, which looks at whose graduates are the most targeted by top employers. Undergraduates can build work experience through research assistant roles and summer internships, with advice from alumni mentors. Bursaries are available to help fund internships, and scholarships for travel projects that are not linked to the student's main degree help bring opportunities to life.

Two of Birmingham's degree apprenticeships – computer science with digital technology – run in partnership with PwC and Vodafone, are taking the earn-and-learn route to the next level. The employers pay their apprentices' tuition fees as well as salaries throughout the four-year course. Apprentices study and live full-time as students for the first two years, undertaking work experience outside term time. The entire third year is spent in the workplace, after which they return to university for the fourth year. A graduate job awaits at the end, subject to performance.

In our social inclusion table, Birmingham outperforms the majority of other Russell Group universities but is still in the bottom 20 overall. Its Pathways to Birmingham programmes for year 12 and 13 school pupils encourages applications from under-represented backgrounds, and provides bursaries that do not need to be repaid.

Birmingham's success in the 2014 Research Excellence Framework – which rated 80% of its submission world-leading or internationally excellent – placed it in the top five for philosophy, history, classics, theology and religion, area studies, chemical engineering and sport, exercise and rehabilitation studies.

The university boasts world-class sports facilities. The £55m sports centre in Edgbaston's arena, seating 800, has been earmarked for use in the 2022 Commonwealth Games.

Catered places account for 19% of the 7,003 rooms endorsed by the university. Prices for self-catered rooms start at £89 per week. A guarantee scheme for first-years secures them a space via random selection from a set of six preferences.

Tuition fees

- » Fees for UK students — £9,250
- » Fees for International students 2021–22 — £19,740–£24,600
  Medicine & dentistry — £42,000
- » For scholarship and bursary information see www.birmingham.ac.uk/undergraduate/fees/index.aspx
- » Graduate salary — £26,000

Student numbers

Undergraduates	22,208	(732)
Postgraduates	7,628	(4,877)
Applications/places	53,050/6,260	
Applications per place	8.5	
Overall offer rate	73.2%	
International students – EU	4.4%	
Non-EU	21.3%	

Accommodation

University provided places: 7,003
Catered costs: £130–£208 per week
Self-catered: £89–£271 per week
First years guaranteed accommodation
www.birmingham.ac.uk/accommodation

Where do the students come from?

State schools (non-grammar)	65%	First generation students	28.9%		
Grammar schools	14.8%	Deprived areas	6%		
Independent schools	20.2%	All ethnic minorities	32.6%		

Social inclusion ranking: =100

Black attainment gap	-18.1%
Disabled	5.1%
Mature (over 21)	4.1%

Birmingham City University

A Victorian factory is being transformed into a £60m centre for businesses, artists and academics at Birmingham City University (BCU). The derelict Belmont Works site, which once manufactured bicycles, will become the headquarters of BCU's STEAMhouse project encouraging collaboration on Steam (science, technology, engineering, arts and maths) subjects, allowing start-ups to tap into the latest teaching and research.

It is part of a £340m programme of developments at BCU, where the canalside city centre campus is at the heart of a wider Eastside regeneration programme. University buildings look out on Eastside City Park, Birmingham's first new urban green space for more than 130 years, and will be close to the HS2 rail terminus.

Student services and a library are based here, as are courses such as music, business, English, social sciences, acting and media. Music students have the benefit of the Royal Birmingham Conservatoire's 500-seat concert hall, rehearsal rooms and teaching spaces on campus.

The Sir Lenny Henry Centre for Media Diversity, a new research centre, has the backing of the comedian – who is BCU's chancellor – to work towards accurate representation of all sections of society across contemporary UK media.

The current STEAMhouse site, opened in 2018, is creating a new £3.4m virtual reality and technology hub.

The City South campus in Edgbaston has had a £41m extension to update resources for health, education and life sciences courses. Sport, currently also offered at City South, is relocating to the city's revamped Alexander Stadium once Birmingham has finished hosting the 2022 Commonwealth Games. The three-storey Western Stand will allow for up to 1,000 students, with facilities such as anti-gravity treadmills and environmental chambers.

BCU's world-renowned School of Jewellery, founded in 1890, is based in the city's Jewellery Quarter. Further afield is the Birmingham Institute of Fashion and Creative Art in Wuhan, China, in partnership with Wuhan Textile University.

Degrees in accounting and Islamic finance, immersive media and youth and community are joining the curriculum from 2021. Midwifery with public health is also being introduced as an integrated master's degree, which counts as an undergraduate course. Practical experience is built into courses and work placements are available on most programmes of study.

The 15-strong portfolio of higher and degree apprenticeships will begin training diagnostic radiographers and midwives in 2021 and programmes in operating

University House
15 Bartholomew Row
Birmingham B5 5JU
0121 331 6295
admissions@bcu.ac.uk
www.bcu.ac.uk
www.bcusu.com
Open days:
see website

The Times and The Sunday Times **Rankings**
Overall Ranking: =90 (last year: =96)

Teaching quality	80.3%	=57
Student experience	76.7%	=86
Research quality	4.3%	=98
Entry standards	123	=76
Graduate prospects	71.4%	80
Good honours	74.4%	74
Expected completion rate	84%	=68
Student/staff ratio	16.6	83
Services and facilities	£2,102	92

department and advanced clinical practice will be offered. A number of four-year nursing degree apprenticeships are in the pipeline, covering specialisms in adult, child, learning disability and mental health nursing and leading to registered nurse status.

More than 70% of graduates were in high-skilled jobs or postgraduate study within 15 months of finishing their courses, but this was not enough to retain BCU's place among the top half of UK universities on this measure.

Applications increased by about 6% and enrolments by nearly 8% in 2019, having dropped in 2018 after a very strong run. Since its name change from the University of Central England in 2007, BCU's enrolments increased for seven years in a row, and the intake of undergraduates increased by a quarter.

"Meet or beat" scholarships offer £1,000 incentives for students to match or exceed published entry requirements, with £850 cash and £150 credit towards course materials.

BCU is one of the UK's most successful universities in terms of diversity and has achieved a top-20 finish in our social inclusion table, up more than 10 places. Initiatives to widen participation among non-traditional groups encompass student mentors under the Aimhigher scheme, summer schools and interactive workshops. Through links with more than 200 schools and colleges, BCU reached nearly 18,000 young people in the last academic year, delivering more than 400 activities such as one-to-one talks, study skills sessions and literacy tutoring at primary school level.

Awarded silver in the Teaching Excellence Framework (TEF), BCU's consistency in retaining students most at risk of dropping out was recognised. The TEF panel also praised personalised learning and the use of peer mentors, including a black and minority ethnic support scheme. The university's dropout rate (11.4%) is better than the 13.3% benchmark expected on the basis of its intake's social and academic background.

BCU managed only a relatively small submission to the Research Excellence Framework in 2014, of which 60% gained the top two categories of world-leading or internationally excellent work.

Just over 2,500 residential spaces in student accommodation are endorsed by the university, enough to guarantee a place for all full-time first-years who come from more than 10 miles away, if they apply by the deadline.

Dyed-in-the-wool Brummies and outsiders alike have the city's thriving social scene on their doorstep.

Tuition fees

- » Fees for UK students £9,250
- » Fees for International students 2021–22 £13,200
- » For scholarship and bursary information see www.bcu.ac.uk/student-info/finance-and-money-matters
- » Graduate salary £23,000

Student numbers

Undergraduates	18,463 (2,015)
Postgraduates	2,860 (2,519)
Applications/places	35,760/5,235
Applications per place	6.8
Overall offer rate	63.8%
International students – EU	2.9%
Non-EU	8.5%

Accommodation

University provided places: 2,564
Self-catered: £119–£165 per week
First years (except local students) guaranteed accommodation
www.bcu.ac.uk/student-info/accommodation

Where do the students come from?

State schools (non-grammar)	96.9%	First generation students	55.7%	Black attainment gap	-15.1%
Grammar schools	0.7%	Deprived areas	14%	Disabled	5.6%
Independent schools	2.3%	All ethnic minorities	56.7%	Mature (over 21)	23.6%

Social inclusion ranking: 19

Bishop Grosseteste University

The small size of Bishop Grosseteste University (BGU) is one of its biggest assets and the university takes pride in the family feel that its students enjoy. Based in historic Lincoln, BGU has inhabited the same attractive, leafy campus since 1862, when it was founded as an Anglican teacher training college for women.

Named after a theologian and scholar who was bishop of Lincoln in the 13th century, these days the university welcomes men and women of all faiths and none. Teacher training remains BGU's biggest focus but many other courses are offered.

Awarded gold in the Teaching Excellence Framework, BGU was commended for an outstanding learning environment and a personalised approach with high-quality support maximising retention, attainment and progression. Course design and assessment were highlighted for providing outstanding levels of stretch, ensuring students are consistently challenged and engage with developments from the forefront of research, scholarship or working practice.

Significant improvements in student satisfaction in 2020 carry BGU into the UK top 10 for satisfaction with teaching quality under our analysis of the National Student Survey, and have contributed to the joint biggest rise — 38 places — of any university in our academic ranking overall.

Satisfaction with the wider undergraduate experience earns BGU a top-20 national ranking, while high degree completion rates put the university in the top 40 on this measure — both contributing to BGU's exceptional rise in our wider league table, which is based on nine key areas of performance.

Although only 11 staff entered the 2014 Research Excellence Framework under three subject areas, some of their work was classed "world-leading" in education, history and English.

BGU's teaching degrees incorporate a wide range of specialisms and many degrees have foundation years built in. Drama, archaeology and sport are among the options and from 2020 the curriculum is offering degrees in counselling, music and musicianship, health and social care and a one-year top-up in business.

The university has introduced four new degree apprenticeships: operational department manager, chartered manager, business-to-business sales professional and a senior leader master's degree apprenticeship.

The campus has been gearing up for a larger intake. One of the two on-site halls of residence has new teaching and learning facilities attached and a £2.2m extension

Longdales Road
Lincoln LN1 3DY
01522 583 658
enquiries@bishopg.ac.uk
www.bishopg.ac.uk
www.bgsu.co.uk
Open days: see website

The Times and The Sunday Times Rankings
Overall Ranking: 64 (last year: =102)

Teaching quality	84.7%	8
Student experience	81.2%	=14
Research quality	2.1%	120
Entry standards	109	=117
Graduate prospects	71%	=83
Good honours	70.7%	=104
Expected completion rate	89%	40
Student/staff ratio	18.4	115
Services and facilities	£2,445	67

doubled the teaching space three years ago. An extended library houses student advice and learning development teams.

The Venue, at the heart of the campus, is used primarily as a theatre during the daytime by drama and performing arts students, then turns into a cinema with Dolby surround sound and the latest releases (Covid-19 restrictions permitting).

Applications dropped for the fourth consecutive year in 2019, when they fell by 12%, while enrolments were down 6%. The chances of being accepted are encouraging for applicants, however: 95% were offered places in 2019, much higher than the 67% offer rate of five years earlier.

BGU has fallen 19 places in our social inclusion table to rank just outside our top 20. When considering applicants, the university conducts interviews on campus or over the phone and takes into account their work experience and qualifications that may not count towards tariff points, alongside predicted grades.

The First Steps initiative for school pupils in years 9–11 invites them to campus for skills booster sessions and Next Steps helps sixth-formers develop independent learning skills, while advice for potential applicants is provided by staff and student ambassadors. The programme has proved successful in encouraging students from disadvantaged backgrounds or with challenging personal circumstances to enter higher education, offering contextual offers at a lower UCAS tariff than standard applications. BGU's residential summer schools also help to raise aspirations among year 10 and year 12 pupils.

Financial help is available for those with a low household income, care leavers, single parents and mature students. BGU expects to award about 500 bursaries a year.

The 365 university-owned or endorsed residential spaces allow all first-years to be guaranteed a room. BGU's sports facilities include a sports hall, gym and acres of outdoor fields, offering opportunities to take part in activities from fitness classes and indoor tennis to hockey, volleyball and rugby. The campus grounds have a peace garden where students can relax in tranquillity.

Tuition fees

»	Fees for UK students	£9,250
	Foundation courses	£6,935
»	Fees for International students 2020–21	£12,200
»	For scholarship and bursary information see www.bishopg.ac.uk/apply-now/fees-funding/	
»	Graduate salary	£23,000

Student numbers

Undergraduates	1,657	(7)
Postgraduates	393	(202)
Applications/places		1,365/520
Applications per place		2.6
Overall offer rate		92.2%
International students – EU		0.4%
Non-EU		0.3%

Accommodation

University provided places: 365
Self-catered: £88–£143 per week
First years guaranteed accommodation
www.bishopg.ac.uk/student/accommodation/

Where do the students come from?

					Social inclusion ranking: 21	
State schools (non-grammar)	95.5%	First generation students	64.6%	Black attainment gap	n/a
Grammar schools	3.2%	Deprived areas	23.9%	Disabled	14.1%
Independent schools	1.3%	All ethnic minorities	3%	Mature (over 21)	35.5%

University of Bolton

Bolton in Greater Manchester has a reputation as one of Britain's friendliest towns, mirrored in its university's welcoming approach to students. Across all measures of widening participation to higher education, Bolton exceeds expected rates. Its proportion of students drawn from areas without a tradition of sending pupils on to higher education (21.3%) is one of the biggest for any UK university and it outperforms most others on part-time student numbers. Almost all students arrive from non-selective state schools.

The university was founded as one of the country's first mechanics institutes 195 years ago, and after a series of mergers and developments gained university status in 2005. It merged with Bolton College in 2018 and has a strategic link with Alliance Learning, which provides apprenticeships, foundation degrees and training courses.

Bolton's first university centre in Manchester has been established through a partnership with a training provider. Overseas, the university has a branch campus at Ras al-Khaimah near Dubai, in the United Arab Emirates, which offers undergraduate and postgraduate courses identical to those taught in Bolton, with space for 700 students.

Enrolments swelled by 9% in 2019 in a recruitment round that drew 42% of its intake via the clearing process. Applications for 2020 admission increased by a huge margin of 24% compared to the year before. The university credits the upturn to its expanding curriculum and encouraging earlier applications.

Having introduced nine new degrees in 2020, including physiotherapy, midwifery and social work, 10 more will start in 2021 – including degrees in urban and contemporary music, and another in hip hop, as well as environmental engineering, paramedic practice and cloud computer science.

There will also be new degree apprenticeships in district nursing, environmental or civil engineering, construction project management, electrical vehicle technology and a postgraduate engineering programme, on top of 26 existing options. These additions will bring apprentice numbers to about 850, from the current 620. Masters courses in careers development have also been launched.

Bolton was awarded silver in the Teaching Excellence Framework (TEF), commended for an institutional culture that facilitates, recognises and rewards excellent teaching, as well as providing excellent support for students from disadvantaged backgrounds. The TEF panel blamed "the student demographic and the challenging local employment context" for the university's above-benchmark dropout rate and relatively poor graduate employment record, and praised Bolton's initiatives to address these areas.

Deane Road
Bolton BL3 5AB
01204 903 394
study@bolton.ac.uk
www.bolton.ac.uk
www.boltonsu.com
Open days:
see website

The Times and The Sunday Times **Rankings**
Overall Ranking: 118 (last year: 125)

Teaching quality	85.6%	6
Student experience	81.3%	=11
Research quality	2.9%	114
Entry standards	114	=102
Graduate prospects	64.2%	114
Good honours	60.4%	=129
Expected completion rate	72.2%	127
Student/staff ratio	14.4	=33
Services and facilities	£2,179	87

Bolton is still near the bottom of our academic league table despite this year's seven-place rise – not least because of its projected dropout rate, one of the highest in the country at about one in five. However, it is close to the top of our social inclusion ranking, climbing 10 places this year to rank second.

The university is a hit with its students for the quality of teaching, ranking sixth on this measure in our analysis of the National Student Survey. For the wider student experience, Bolton is 11th. Tuition fees include extras such as course materials, compulsory trips, uniform and equipment, and a printing allowance.

Bolton's distinctive research facilities include the Centre for Islamic Finance and the National Centre for Motorsport Engineering, opened in 2017, which incorporates the renowned Centre for Advanced Performance Engineering (Cape) training base. The university helps to run a professional motor racing team in conjunction with a motorsports company and students work and learn alongside its engineers and mechanics as they study for a degree in automotive performance engineering or motorsport technology.

General engineering was one of two subject areas which had most of their work rated as world-leading or internationally excellent in the 2014 Research Excellence Framework. The best results were in English, and almost a third of the university's small submission reached the top two categories overall.

Bolton has bought 1,000 bicycles and safety helmets for its new Student Bike Loan scheme. Any student may use one to commute to classes and between campuses under the scheme, brought in to cut down potential exposure to Covid-19 on public transport.

The Bolton One development, a £31m leisure centre on the Deane campus, developed with the council and local NHS, has a fitness suite and swimming pool. Students can also keep fit at a multi-use sports hall and indoor climbing wall. The Anderton Centre, eight miles away, is available for outdoor adventure activities and students have access to football pitches at Ladybridge FC, four miles away.

There are 381 rooms in Orlando Village, endorsed by the university. Most rooms cost less than £100 per week and there are enough to guarantee first-years a room, as so many students live locally.

If Bolton's entertainments don't do the trick, Manchester is only 20 minutes away.

Tuition fees

» Fees for UK students	£9,250
» Fees for International students 2020–21	£12,450
» For scholarship and bursary information see www.bolton.ac.uk/study/undergraduate/feesfunding/	
» Graduate salary	£20,000

Student numbers

Undergraduates	4,827	(777)
Postgraduates	576	(765)
Applications/places		5,105/980
Applications per place		5.2
Overall offer rate		62.5%
International students – EU		2.5%
Non-EU		6%

Accommodation

University provided places: 381
Self-catered: £99–£125 per week
www.bolton.ac.uk/student-life/accommodation/

Where do the students come from?

State schools (non-grammar)	97.9%	First generation students	56.9%		Black attainment gap	-18%
Grammar schools	1.1%	Deprived areas	20.6%		Disabled	11.6%
Independent schools	1.0%	All ethnic minorities	40%		Mature (over 21)	53.6%

Social inclusion ranking: 2

University of Bournemouth

Bournemouth University has opened two new Gateway Buildings – one on each of its campuses. Poole Gateway, on the university's Talbot campus, has 5,000 square metres of space for industry-standard facilities for Bournemouth's flagship media courses. As well as two television studios with ultra-high definition cameras, there is a film studio and sound stage, green screen, edit suites and a motion capture studio for animation.

The university hosts the National Centre for Computer Animation and graduates have worked on films such as *Blade Runner 2049*, *Dunkirk*, *The Avengers* and *Solo: A Star Wars Story*. For music and sound production there are two recording studios with mixing desks, three surround-sound studios and two post-production studios. Students also have access to Games PC and Mac laboratories, a critical listening lab and seminar and workshop facilities.

On the main Lansdowne campus in Bournemouth, the newly opened Gateway Building hosts the Faculty of Health and Social Sciences. Its simulation suites replicate an operating theatre, hospital wards, a birthing room and a residential flat, where students can learn to provide care at a patient's home. It also has an MRI scanner to train local medical staff as well as students.

There are 120 undergraduate courses to choose from in 16 subject areas at Bournemouth. Degree courses in accounting, finance, sport coaching and sport and exercise science accepted their first students in 2020. New to the curriculum from 2021 are honours programmes in virtual and augmented reality, immersive media, multimedia sports journalism and photography.

Bournemouth is in the top 40 universities – and ranked top among modern universities founded since 1992 – for the proportion of graduates (79%) who end up in high-skilled jobs or postgraduate study within 15 months of leaving. The university builds the option of a work placement – in the UK or abroad – into every degree, an opportunity that has proved popular with students. The internships have translated into graduate jobs for almost three in 10 students.

The successful placement system helped the university to gain silver in the Teaching Excellence Framework (TEF). Assessors also highlighted Bournemouth's peer-assisted learning, ensuring all first-years are offered advice and mentoring from students who are further along in their chosen course.

Applications in 2019 dropped by about 4% compared with the previous year, and since 2016 have fallen by more than a quarter. Enrolments, however, increased a little in 2019, during a recruitment round where nearly nine out of 10 school-leavers who applied were offered places.

Fern Barrow
Talbot Campus
Poole BH12 5BB
01202 961 916
futurestudents@bournemouth.ac.uk
www.bournemouth.ac.uk
www.subu.org.uk
Open days:
see website

The Times and The Sunday Times **Rankings**
Overall Ranking: 68 (last year: 94)

Teaching quality	78.3%	=89
Student experience	76.2%	=93
Research quality	9.0%	=64
Entry standards	115	=100
Graduate prospects	79%	38
Good honours	78.8%	=45
Expected completion rate	84.3%	=62
Student/staff ratio	17.6	100
Services and facilities	£2,455	=65

The AccessBU contextual offer system makes allowances for applicants' personal circumstances, which may qualify them for entry at lower than published grades. Outreach initiatives aim to raise aspirations and attainment among disadvantaged pupils. In the past four years, one in four students has received a bursary or scholarship.

Although the university's subject mix and the upwardly hip trajectory of the city appeal to more middle-class students than many other post-1992 universities, just under nine out of 10 students come from non-selective state schools. It slips six places in our social inclusion table this year to rank in the lower middle reaches.

Bournemouth has a long track record in raising its technology game and introduced the Brightspace virtual learning environment in 2017, giving students access to a range of services and enabling academics to track their progress. The £6m investment seems prescient as all institutions scramble to increase their distance learning capacity as a result of the Covid-19 pandemic.

Bournemouth had one of the best results of any post-1992 universities in the 2014 Research Excellence Framework, with 60% of its entry assessed as world-leading or internationally excellent. However, although it has made up some ground in the latest National Student Survey, it still ranks surprisingly low for both teaching quality and the wider student experience in our analysis, despite excellent graduate outcomes and a beguiling seaside location.

Bournemouth has recently bought the 65-acre Chapel Gate sports facility, near the airport, where university teams and clubs have been training and playing for a number of years. The site is used for football, rugby, hockey, cricket, squash, table tennis, archery and rifle shooting. Bournemouth has fitness and spin studios, a sports hall, treatment rooms and dance studios which host more than 50 group fitness classes each week.

In the BUCS (British Universities and Colleges Sport) league, Bournemouth ranked 23rd out of 153 institutions during the most recent completed season in 2018–19. In a bid to edge into the top 20 it has identified three focus sports: golf, tennis and volleyball, which will benefit from extra investment, coaching and competitive opportunities.

The university guarantees accommodation to all undergraduate applicants who have made it their firm choice and applied online by the deadline. They can also select and book their own room online, rather than the more common university allocation system.

Tuition fees

» Fees for UK students	£9,250
Foundation courses	£8,200
» Fees for International students 2021–22	£14,100–£15,000
» For scholarship and bursary information see	
www.bournemouth.ac.uk/study/undergraduate/fees-funding	
» Graduate salary	£24,000

Student numbers

Undergraduates	**13,286**	**(1,415)**
Postgraduates	**1,675**	**(1,502)**
Applications/places		**19,460/3,875**
Applications per place		**5**
Overall offer rate		**78.7%**
International students – EU		**4.2%**
Non-EU		**8.1%**

Accommodation

University provided places: 3,400
Self-catered: £128–£201 per week
First years guaranteed accommodation
www.bournemouth.ac.uk/why-bu/accommodation

Where do the students come from?

State schools (non-grammar)	88.8%	First generation students	48.4%	
Grammar schools	5%	Deprived areas	12.6%	
Independent schools	6.3%	All ethnic minorities	17%	

Social inclusion ranking: =72

Black attainment gap	-21.7%
Disabled	8.1%
Mature (over 21)	17.7%

University of Bradford

Lady Hale, former president of the Supreme Court, opened a mock court named after her in January 2020 at the University of Bradford, where she is an honorary graduate. Law students can hone their professional skills at the new facility.

Bradford teamed up with the University of Leeds and Bradford Teaching Hospitals NHS Foundation Trust to open the Wolfson Centre for Applied Health Research in 2019. Combining the expertise of academic researchers, doctors and nurses, the multi-million-pound centre at Bradford Royal Infirmary hopes to put its findings rapidly into practice to improve health outcomes across the generations.

Advanced health, innovative engineering and sustainable societies are the strategic themes at Bradford, a former college of advanced technology which became a university in the 1960s. Bradford's highly regarded School of Management has long been regarded as its flagship department, its distance learning MBA ranked the best value for money in the world in 2019.

Our University of the Year for Social Inclusion in 2019, Bradford ranks in the top five again this year on the diversity of its intake and their subsequent success – far outdoing any other pre-1992 university.

More than 130 nationalities are represented within a student population of 11,000. The proportion from ethnic minority backgrounds is one of the highest of any UK institution, accounting for 78.3% of entrants in 2018–19.

Bradford gained silver in the Teaching Excellence Framework (TEF), receiving praise for "strategic and systematic commitment to diversity and social mobility that enables the majority of students, including a very high number from black, Asian and minority backgrounds, to achieve excellent outcomes".

The TEF panel commended the curriculum for stretching students to achieve their full potential and acquire the knowledge, skills and understanding valued by employers, and for its work-based learning. The physiotherapy and sport rehabilitation team was singled out for recognition with a teaching excellence award from Advance HE in 2019.

Bradford has a strong record for graduate jobs, where it finishes just outside the top 50 this year for the proportion of graduates who gain high-skilled jobs or go into postgraduate study within 15 months of leaving. Work experience or placements are offered within many degrees and course curriculums are often designed with input from industry partners such as the BBC, the NHS, Jaguar Land Rover, Wm Morrison Supermarkets and the global IT company Fujitsu.

Funding for resuscitation training equipment will add new resources for students

Richmond Road
Bradford BD7 1DP
01274 233 0815
enquiries@bradford.ac.uk
www.bradford.ac.uk
www.bradfordunisu.co.uk
Open days:
see website

The Times and The Sunday Times **Rankings**
Overall Ranking: 106 (last year: 105)

Teaching quality	76.5%	109
Student experience	76.3%	=89
Research quality	9.2%	=62
Entry standards	125	=70
Graduate prospects	75.6%	55
Good honours	79.9%	=37
Expected completion rate	82.5%	=80
Student/staff ratio	18	=108
Services and facilities	£2,217	84

taking a paramedic science degree, whose course also includes a paid placement year with the Yorkshire Ambulance Service. Students from other subjects allied to health courses will also be able to practise with the new equipment.

Bradford's seven degree apprenticeships cover roles in health, outside broadcasting, chemistry and management. The university's new academy membership under a programme run by Amazon Web Services (AWS) will help students learn the technology skills necessary for careers in the IT cloud. A new degree in applied artificial intelligence has been introduced, as have MNurse qualifications – which lead to eligibility as a registered nurse at master's level – in both adult and child mental health.

The world-renowned Peace Studies and International Development department has more than 40 years' experience and collaborates with governments and organisations such as the United Nations, the UK Ministry of Defence and the China Development Bank. Its research was part of Bradford's submission to the Research Excellence Framework in 2014. Across all subjects, less than a quarter of eligible academics were entered, but almost three-quarters of work submitted reached the top two categories. Allied health, management and archaeological science led the way.

The university has received European Commission funding, in spite of Brexit, for a chemical manufacturing project to help small and medium-sized enterprises in Yorkshire

gain access to the latest technology to grow their businesses.

About 60% of students receive some form of financial assistance. A range of workshops and summer schools target schools and colleges where progression to higher education is uncommon in the push to widen participation.

Bradford has four venues for sport. At Unique Fitness and Lifestyle, on the city centre campus, there is a swimming pool, climbing wall and squash courts and students can also have a beauty therapy after training. The campus has a multi-use games area and 3G five-a-side pitch too. A full-size football pitch can be used at Bradford Sports Park, a five-minute walk away, plus tennis courts and a conditioning suite, while the Woodhall sports ground has more pitches, four miles from the city campus.

Bradford endorses accommodation at the student village on campus, the Green, near the students' union and library. It has more than 1,000 spaces, allocated on a first come, first served basis. Rents are some of the most affordable in the country.

Tuition fees

» Fees for UK students	£9,250
» Fees for International students 2021–22	£16,895–£20,843
Foundation years	£12,800
» For scholarship and bursary information see www.bradford.ac.uk/money/fees/	
» Graduate salary	£23,000

Student numbers

Undergraduates	6,920	(517)
Postgraduates	826	(1,401)
Applications/places		11,205/1,635
Applications per place		6.9
Overall offer rate		82.3%
International students – EU		4.1%
Non-EU		10.5%

Accommodation

University provided places: 1,026
Self-catered: £75–£90 per week
www.bradford.ac.uk/accommodation/

Where do the students come from?

State schools (non-grammar)	93%	First generation students	66.8%	
Grammar schools	4.4%	Deprived areas	11.7%	
Independent schools	2.6%	All ethnic minorities	78.3%	

Social inclusion ranking: 5

Black attainment gap	-9%
Disabled	9.6%
Mature (over 21)	26.2%

University of Brighton

The University of Brighton has transformed its Moulsecoomb campus at the gateway to the city. From the 2021–22 academic year, students will benefit from the university's masterplan development at the largest of Brighton's four campuses, where a new academic building, 800 student bedrooms in new halls of residence, a new students' union and fitness facilities will come on stream.

At the city centre campus on Grand Parade, the Brighton Centre for Contemporary Arts opened in 2019. Open to all and free to enter, the galleries showcase a year-round programme of contemporary arts practices and research at the university.

Brighton's campus along the coast in Eastbourne – which has a modern library, extensive leisure and sports facilities and 354 ensuite student rooms – has also gained from the university's upgrade of teaching and learning spaces. A multi-professional skills simulation suite opened in 2020, to help healthcare students develop their techniques in real-life scenarios.

Brighton holds silver in the government's Teaching Excellence Framework (TEF). The judging panel praised its close working relationships with professional bodies, employers and local community groups and its personalised learning and support, particularly for first-year students. Brighton is also in the top tier of the People and Planet league of environmental performance, ranked 25th in the UK in 2019. It holds bronze Athena Swan gender equality and Race Equality Charter awards, and ranks in Stonewall's top-100 employers for LGBT people.

The university's record in the Research Excellence Framework is especially noteworthy, and among the most successful of the post-1992 institutions. In the 2014 assessments two-thirds of work submitted was placed in one of the top two categories, indicating world-class or international excellence.

Winner of our inaugural University of the Year award in 1999, Brighton has dropped down our league table in recent times. However, it scores well in the new Graduate Outcomes survey with 76% of graduates in high-skilled employment or postgraduate study within 15 months of leaving – ranking the university just outside the top 50. All courses have an element of work-related experience. These include long or short placements, assessed voluntary work and live project briefs. However, at 17.1% its dropout rate is significantly higher than the projected level of 12.2% based on the social and academic backgrounds of its intake.

Applications dropped by 10% in 2019 compared with the year before, and have fallen by around 26% over the past three years – despite a rising offer rate. The decline in enrolments has been less steep, but the numbers arriving in 2019 were still down

Mithras House
Lewes Road
Brighton BN2 4AT
01273 644 644
enquiries@brighton.ac.uk
www.brighton.ac.uk
www.brightonsu.com
Open days:
see website

The Times and The Sunday Times **Rankings**

Overall Ranking: 120 (last year: 122)

Teaching quality	76.8%	=104
Student experience	72.4%	=122
Research quality	7.9%	=73
Entry standards	114	=102
Graduate prospects	76.2%	=52
Good honours	67.8%	114
Expected completion rate	80.7%	96
Student/staff ratio	17.5	=98
Services and facilities	£2,003	98

for the fourth consecutive year.

Nine new degrees have joined the courses offered, including fine art, English literature with drama, strength and conditioning and an honours degree in law with an integrated foundation year. Those applying for courses beginning in 2021 will also have the option of degrees in entrepreneurship (team enterprise and innovation), and in fashion accessories with business studies.

Brighton is expanding further its degree apprenticeship portfolio. Four new programmes are offered from 2021, covering roles in education, construction and environment, business, and health and science. The university anticipates that by the end of the 2021–22 academic year it will have about 800 apprentices on programmes, more than twice the number it had in 2019–20.

In a long-standing partnership with the University of Sussex, Brighton runs one of the first medical schools awarded to a post-1992 university. Based at the Sussex campus in Falmer, a few miles outside Brighton, the medical school accepts 200 trainee doctors each year.

At Brighton's own Falmer campus nearby, students take education and applied sciences courses, and sports facilities include a hall, synthetic and grass pitches, an artificial outdoor cricket wicket and a pavilion. A privately-run gym offers special swimming deals for students.

The university has more international students than most post-1992 universities, and although its UK student profile is more middle-class than most, almost nine out of 10 undergraduates enrol from non-selective state schools and colleges.

Brighton earmarked around £3.5m of financial support for lower-income students for 2020, including £2.3m for bursaries. The investment is part of its efforts to widen the intake. There are cash bursaries of £500 a year for those with a household income of under £25,000, and larger awards for care leavers and those estranged from their families. Scholarships awarded on academic and sporting merit are offered too, and about 40% of undergraduates qualify for some form of financial assistance. Brighton also has well-established progression partnerships with schools in the region.

There is a guaranteed place for all first-years in one of the 2,653 residential spaces the university owns or endorses. Brighton's seaside location, hip atmosphere and renowned social life (DJ Norman Cook, aka Fatboy Slim, is a Brighton alumnus) are a compelling combination for students.

Tuition fees

» Fees for UK students	£9,250
» Fees for International students 2020–21	£13,416–£14,604
Medicine	£35,517
» For scholarship and bursary information see www.brighton.ac.uk/studying-here/fees-and-finance/index.aspx	
» Graduate salary	£24,000

Student numbers

Undergraduates	14,100	(2,661)
Postgraduates	1,644	(2,063)
Applications/places		25,915/3,550
Applications per place		7.3
Overall offer rate		72.6%
International students – EU		4.8%
Non-EU		8.4%

Accommodation

University provided places: 2,653
Catered costs: £168–£188 per week
Self-catered: £131–£205 per week
First years guaranteed accommodation
www.brighton.ac.uk/accommodation-and-locations/Index.aspx

Where do the students come from?

State schools (non-grammar)	88.7%	First generation students	46.9%	Black attainment gap	-30.2%
Grammar schools	5.7%	Deprived areas	13.4%	Disabled	10%
Independent schools	5.5%	All ethnic minorities	23%	Mature (over 21)	22.6%

Social inclusion ranking: =66

University of Bristol

Few Russell Group universities have undergone the expansion seen at Bristol since the lifting of the cap on student recruitment. The number of enrolments is up 23% since 2014 and the number of applications has risen by 32% over the same period.

As the whole university grows, a new campus is being created to accommodate an expanded range of activities. The Temple Quarter Enterprise Campus will open in 2023 and focus on digital, business and social innovation. It will bring together academic, industrial and entrepreneurial expertise on a car-free campus as part of an extensive city redevelopment close to Temple Meads railway station.

Around 3,000 students will study there, 800 academics, business and community partners will work there and just under 1,000 students will live there in a new student village. New courses will be created and delivered with industry partners, offering flexible degrees and courses with evening and weekend delivery. Three research centres will be based on the Temple Quarter site, alongside the Centre for Entrepreneurship and Innovation and a new management school.

The aim is to produce a generation of students capable of developing their studies beyond undergraduate level or ready to join the workforce in an increasingly digital world. Bristol graduates are already sought after: the university ranks fourth in the 2020 High Fliers table of the universities targeted most by the largest number of leading employers.

The new Graduate Outcomes survey found more than 83% of Bristol graduates were in high-skilled jobs or postgraduate study 15 months after graduation, putting the university back in the UK top 20 on this measure.

Preparing students for work is embedded into campus culture. About 20 degree programmes offer a year in industry or work placements as part of the course and a professional liaison network engages social science and law students with companies relevant to their academic study through mentoring and internships. The Industrial Liaison Office performs a similar role for students in the faculty of engineering and the UoB Internship Scheme provides paid work experience with SMEs across the UK.

However, continued poor scores for student satisfaction with teaching quality (down again in the 2020 National Student Survey) and the wider university experience prevent Bristol from reclaiming its place in the UK top 10 despite a two-place rise in our new academic ranking.

Upgraded facilities should enhance the student experience over the coming years. A new humanities hub features a lecture theatre, social learning zone, gallery space, virtual

Beacon House
Queens Road
Bristol BS8 1QU
0117 394 1649
choosebristol-ug@bristol.ac.uk
www.bristol.ac.uk
www.bristolsu.org.uk
Open days:
see website

The Times and The Sunday Times Rankings
Overall Ranking: 13 (last year: 15)

Teaching quality	76.4%	=110
Student experience	75%	107
Research quality	47.3%	6
Entry standards	169	15
Graduate prospects	83.6%	=16
Good honours	90.1%	7
Expected completion rate	95%	=8
Student/staff ratio	13.3	=13
Services and facilities	£2,548	58

museum and a cinema room. The refurbished Senate House building at the heart of the university campus will feature a new food court and students' union café and bring together student-focused services.

Bristol has been a pioneer of contextual offers, now the norm across the university sector, making offers two grades lower than standard to students who come from low-achieving schools and postcodes where progression to higher education is low. The university's bursary and scholarships help up to a quarter of students. Provision includes a bursary of up to £2,060 for students from households with income as high as £42,875. The more generous Access to Bristol and Bristol Scholars awards are reserved for local students.

However, the university has slipped into the bottom four in our social inclusion table for England and Wales and barely one in 20 students are recruited from the most deprived parts of the country, still below the benchmark figure for the university.

About 20 new degrees were introduced in 2020, mostly integrated master's options. These include chemistry with scientific computing, economics with innovation, psychology and neuroscience, social policy with innovation and physics with scientific computing. There are also new BA options in international business management with French, German or Spanish.

Results in the 2014 Research Excellence Framework were outstanding. Bristol was rewarded for entering more than 90% of its eligible staff – a higher proportion than Oxford – with 83% of its research rated world-leading or internationally excellent. Geography, sport and exercise sciences were judged the best in the country overall. Bristol's full submissions in clinical medicine, health subjects, economics and sport and exercise sciences were placed in the top categories for their impact.

The university has 6,300 residential places for undergraduates, a quarter in catered halls – enough for almost all first-years who want to live in. An impressive sports complex with a well-equipped gym is at the heart of the university precinct, where the careers centre has been refurbished. The students' union houses one of the city's biggest live music venues plus a café, bars, theatre and swimming pool.

As one of Britain's most prosperous cities, Bristol offers job opportunities to students and graduates alike. Staying on after graduation is common, the city's charms outweighing its relatively high living costs.

Tuition fees

- » Fees for UK students £9,250
  Foundation years £5,150
- » Fees for International students 2021–22 £20,100–£24,700
  Dentistry £38,000; Medicine £35,000; Veterinary science £32,000
- » For scholarship and bursary information see
  www.bristol.ac.uk/study/undergraduate/fees-funding/
- » Graduate salary £27,500

Student numbers

Undergraduates	18,614	(367)
Postgraduates	5,726	(1,248)
Applications/places	52,525/6,360	
Applications per place	8.3	
Overall offer rate	69.8%	
International students – EU	5%	
Non-EU	20%	

Accommodation

University provided places: 6,300
Catered costs: £187–£217 per week
Self-catered: £111–£209 per week
First years guaranteed accommodation
www.bristol.ac.uk/accommodation/undergraduate/

Where do the students come from?

State schools (non-grammar)	55.2%	First generation students	21.8%	Black attainment gap	-12.9%
Grammar schools	12.4%	Deprived areas	5.4%	Disabled	5.6%
Independent schools	32.4%	All ethnic minorities	17.4%	Mature (over 21)	5.2%

Social inclusion ranking: 113

Brunel University, London

Brunel University, London's new medical school will welcome its first intake of students in 2021, following five-year undergraduate Bachelor of Medicine, Bachelor of Surgery degrees. To start with, the medical school will be open only to students from outside Britain. The university could not be keener to extend applications to UK students as soon as possible, though, and is opening discussions with Health Education England and the Office for Students about accepting local applicants.

The self-contained campus that Brunel occupies to the west of the capital at Uxbridge is rare among London universities, which are more commonly spread across different locations. Students can get from A to B on Brunel's campus within 10 minutes, wherever their start and finish points are, and public transport gets them to the West End within 45 minutes.

A new learning and teaching centre is due to open in 2022. Designed to make an architectural statement on the Quad at the heart of the campus, the building will incorporate spaces for individual and group study and feature the latest teaching facilities.

Founded in 1966, Brunel has long aimed to be the UK's leading technological university. A stark decline in scores for student satisfaction has sent it into the bottom half of our main league table since 2018, however. National Student Survey results recovered slightly in 2020, but remain in the bottom 20 for student experience and the bottom 10 for teaching quality.

Three-quarters of students land high-skilled jobs or go into postgraduate study within 15 months of graduating, according to the latest national statistics on graduate employment – putting Brunel just outside the top 50 UK universities. Applications edged upwards by about 2% in 2019, though the number of students starting courses was about 8% lower than the year before.

Practical learning is embedded in all courses, taught in hands-on settings such as laboratories, the theatre or clinical simulation suites. Almost all degrees have the option of work placements for a few weeks or up to a full academic year. Via the Blackboard Learn virtual platform, students can access recordings of all lectures and find out about relevant materials, learning resources and reading lists.

The Teaching Excellence Framework (TEF) panel awarded Brunel silver, praising high levels of employer engagement and opportunities for work experience. Assessors also highlighted the university's analytical approach to addressing attainment gaps within its diverse student body.

The curriculum has gained 10 new degrees including suites of anthropology courses and theatre options, electronic and electrical engineering (artificial intelligence) and physical education, coaching and sport development.

Kingston Lane
Uxbridge
UB8 3PH
01895 265 265
admissions@brunel.ac.uk
www.brunel.ac.uk
https://brunelstudents.com/
Open days:
see website

UXBRIDGE

The Times and The Sunday Times **Rankings**
Overall Ranking: 88 (last year: 100)

Teaching quality	73.9%	122
Student experience	73.9%	=115
Research quality	25.4%	49
Entry standards	119	=92
Graduate prospects	75.0%	=57
Good honours	75.6%	=63
Expected completion rate	87.5%	=50
Student/staff ratio	17.7	=101
Services and facilities	£1,945	105

Degree apprenticeship provision is expanding too. Brunel is increasing the number of students on its three established programmes, which cover healthcare assistant, nurse associate and advanced clinical practitioner roles. A policing programme was added in 2020 and from 2021 a level 7 specialist community and public health nurse course will be offered, and a level 7 physician associate.

There are some well-known figures on staff, such as the performance poet Benjamin Zephaniah as chair of creative writing, and the author Will Self, professor of contemporary thought. Brunel alumni and comedians Jo Brand and Lee Mack have helped establish the Centre for Comedy Studies.

In the top 40 overall for social inclusion, Brunel is in the top five among universities created before 1992. About three-quarters of undergraduates are from black and ethnic minority backgrounds – many from the local Asian communities in northwest London. Almost a third of students are from low-income households, and half are the first members of their family to go university.

In 2019 the university awarded more than 500 scholarships and bursaries to the new intake of students, a number likely to be similar in 2021. The HeadStart programme helps students from under-represented groups transition to Brunel by giving them a sense of what to expect and introducing them to the support services available.

The university is superbly equipped for sports, and boasts a multi-million-pound Indoor Athletics Centre with a 32-metre straight sprint, pole vault, high jump and long/triple jump facilities. There is also a bespoke strength and conditioning gym for elite student athletes. The Brunel University London Athletics Club has produced athletes who have gone on to represent Great Britain at World Championships and Olympic Games.

The Sports Park opposite campus hosts all outdoor facilities, such as an FA-registered 3G pitch and a floodlit international standard rugby pitch. There are sports scholarships for elite student athletes – and all students are encouraged to get involved. Brunel was the first university to introduce a sports hijab for its female Muslim students, long underrepresented in competitive sport.

Student accommodation is in plentiful supply, existing halls having been refurbished and new ones built. First-year students – including those who come from the local area – are guaranteed a space in one of the 4,549 on-campus rooms.

Tuition fees

» Fees for UK students	£9,250
» Fees for International students 2021–22	£16,335–£19,855
Medicine	£40,000
» For scholarship and bursary information see	
www.brunel.ac.uk/study/undergraduate-fees-and-funding	
» Graduate salary	£25,000

Student numbers

Undergraduates	10,917	(207)
Postgraduates	2,743	(923)
Applications/places		20,710/2,135
Applications per place		9.7
Overall offer rate		76.2%
International students – EU		6%
Non-EU		21.7%

Accommodation

University provided places: 4,609
Self-catered: £119–£202 per week
First years guaranteed accommodation
www.brunel.ac.uk/life/accommodation

Where do the students come from?

State schools (non-grammar)	90.4%	First generation students	51.1%	Black attainment gap	-19%
Grammar schools	5.4%	Deprived areas	3.9%	Disabled	6.7%
Independent schools	4.3%	All ethnic minorities	74.4%	Mature (over 21)	9.1%

Social inclusion ranking: 37

University of Buckingham

The University of Buckingham's two-year undergraduate degrees first disrupted the higher education landscape more than four decades ago. Instead of the usual 26 to 30 weeks of teaching over three years, as is the norm across UK universities, most Buckingham students have 40 weeks per year over two years. The subtle shift in pattern is a big draw for students, who graduate with a year's head start on their peers in the jobs market.

Applications have boomed in recent years, during a period when many other universities have struggled with recruitment. After a 25% increase in 2019 there had already been 18% more applications by the end of March 2020 compared with the same point the year before.

Helping to accommodate this expansion is Buckingham's new Crewe campus, which opened at the start of 2020, 120 miles from the university headquarters. A joint venture with Indian private healthcare company Apollo Hospitals, the campus has kicked off with medicine and podiatry courses, with a view to adding other medical and allied health degrees in future.

The medical school programme is one of Buckingham's biggest draws. It has seen a sharp increase in applicants from home and overseas, having started out catering mainly for international students. The UK's first private not-for-profit medical school offers a 4½-year course modelled on Leicester University's MB ChB programme. Its first cohort graduated in 2019, the same year it received full accreditation from the General Medical Council.

To meet demand, from January 2021 the MB ChB course will be offered at both the Buckingham and Crewe campuses. Fees for medicine are £37,000 a year, but in other subjects UK and EU undergraduates have been paying a total of £25,200 for their two-year course – marginally less than three-year degrees in other universities, while also saving a year's living costs. Buckingham students on two-year courses qualify for up to £900 per year additional Student Loans support to account for the extra weeks at university.

The extended academic year consists of four nine-week terms and undergraduates still get 12 to 13 weeks off. They also have the option of beginning their courses in September or in January – when nearly 10% of the intake is transfer students making a fresh start after being unhappy with their original university. Buckingham also offers three-year degrees in the humanities, and other schools are beginning to follow suit. Just over half of the students are from overseas, but the proportion from Britain is growing.

Under a new school of computing and centre for artificial intelligence (AI), Buckingham's portfolio of degrees in these areas is expanding. An Institute for Ethical

Hunter Street
Buckingham MK18 1EG
01280 820 227
admissions@buckingham.ac.uk
www.buckingham.ac.uk
www.buckingham.ac.uk/student-life/the-students-union/
Open days: see website

The Times and The Sunday Times **Rankings**

Overall Ranking: 108 (last year: =92)		
Teaching quality	82.5%	=22
Student experience	81%	17
Research quality	n/a	
Entry standards	121	=84
Graduate prospects	74.7%	61
Good honours	63.5%	127
Expected completion rate	83.1%	75
Student/staff ratio	15	=51
Services and facilities	£805	131

AI has been set up to explore how education interfaces with AI. Degree apprenticeships are under consideration to train AI (data specialists) and bioinformatics scientists.

Five new degrees launched in 2020, including English literature, international relations and flexible honours in modern languages. Four more are coming on stream from 2021: psychology with an integrated foundation, sociology, accounting and finance.

The government's Teaching Excellence Framework awarded Buckingham gold, its highest standard. Assessors praised personalised learning, due to teaching in small groups, and rigorous attendance monitoring, making for the best rates of retention, attainment and progression. Physical and digital resources are outstanding, the panel noted, encompassing one-to-one IT support as needed and extensive access to online journals.

Buckingham is a former winner of our University of the Year for Teaching Quality. However, student satisfaction scores slumped into the middle of the rankings for teaching quality in 2019, triggering a hefty drop in our league table, where it had previously been a regular top-50 performer. Although 2020's results derived from the National Student Survey have bounced back, the improvement is not reflected in Buckingham's overall ranking due to movements at other institutions.

The £8m Vinson Building opened in 2018 housing the Centre for Economics and Entrepreneurship. Buckingham is launching a new MA in political economy in association with the Institute of Economic Affairs in London. The building is also home to the university's biggest lecture theatre as well as an enterprise hub for the region and a coffee shop.

Buckingham is moving toward needs-based financial awards and students can access bursaries and tuition fee discounts of £1,000 to £2,000, depending on household incomes. High-achiever scholarships of £2,000 are open to students who achieve AAB in their A-levels, or equivalent.

The leafy main campus is the safest in the southeast, according to a study in 2016. It has a bar and fitness facilities, and university and external events are hosted at the Radcliffe Centre nearby. Buckingham's 548 student bedrooms provide enough spaces for all first-years who want to live in.

The surrounding town is pretty and rural, offering a social life that centres more around pubs and eateries than all-night raves.

Tuition fees

» Fees for UK students (Two-year degrees)	£12,600
Foundation years	£9,450
» Fees for International students 2021–22	£17,800
Medicine	£37,000
» For scholarship and bursary information see www.buckingham.ac.uk/admissions/fees	
» Graduate salary	£24,000

Student numbers

Undergraduates	1,476	(49)
Postgraduates	1,265	(278)
Applications/places		1,195/130
Applications per place		9.2
Overall offer rate		n/a
International students – EU		4.2%
Non-EU		24.4%

Accommodation

University provided places: 548
Self-catered: £95–£237 per week
First years guaranteed accommodation
www.buckingham.ac.uk/life/accommodation

Where do the students come from?

State schools (non-grammar)	76.4%	First generation students	36.4%	
Grammar schools	2.5%	Deprived areas	7.5%	
Independent schools	21.1%	All ethnic minorities	43.5	

Social inclusion ranking: 96

Black attainment gap	-37%
Disabled	5.4%
Mature (over 21)	41.9%

Buckinghamshire New University

Bucks New's focus on serving the public sector as well as the creative and cultural industries runs through the reshaping of its curriculum. Over the past three years almost 60 new courses have been added. Fresh for 2020–21 were eight degrees, ranging from architectural technology and a pre-join professional policing programme to criminology and forensics, media production with industry partner Creative Media Skills (CMS) and a nursing degree specialising in disability.

There are big plans for degree apprenticeship provision, too. The university is doubling the number of apprentices from 550 to 1,100 by September 2021, and adding six new programmes. The current portfolio of 11 options covers roles including police constable, academic professional, digital and technology solutions professional and social worker. Joining the stable from 2021 are level 6 courses for paramedic, physician associate and construction site management roles, and level 7s for district nurses, specialist community and public health nurses and postgraduate engineers.

The expanded course options have had a positive impact on student numbers. Enrolments in 2019 saw a 14% upturn on the previous year, though they have yet to climb back up to 2017's high. Applications for the 2020 cycle also showed a 14% increase.

Awarded university status in 2007, Bucks New has its main campus in High Wycombe, which has benefited from £100m in site developments over the past decade. Its prize-winning Gateway Building is a focal point in the town centre. The university has a second base in Uxbridge, northwest London. Its newest campus is in Aylesbury, where nursing and other healthcare courses are taught.

The university was one of the first to offer a degree in policing and is also among the leading providers of nursing qualifications in the southeast offering adult, child and mental health pre-qualifying nursing, as well as post-registration courses. Social work courses are professionally accredited and Bucks New works with local health authorities, NHS trusts and primary and healthcare organisations in London and the Home Counties to develop and provide training courses for students, as well as work opportunities.

Just under 70% of graduates were in high-skilled employment or postgraduate study within 15 months of finishing their courses, the latest Graduate Outcomes survey revealed – ranking Bucks New just inside the top 100 UK universities for this measure.

The university's suite of film and television degrees has the advantage of teaching on location from industry professionals at nearby Pinewood Studios, home of the James Bond movies and other film and television

Queen Alexandra Road
High Wycombe HP11 2JZ
0330 123 2023
admissions@bucks.ac.uk
www.bucks.ac.uk
www.bucksstudentsunion.org
Open days: see website

The Times and The Sunday Times Rankings
Overall Ranking: =112 (last year: 113)

Teaching quality	82.5%	=22
Student experience	79.8%	34
Research quality	1.5%	123
Entry standards	109	=117
Graduate prospects	69.6%	95
Good honours	58.2%	131
Expected completion rate	79.3%	=102
Student/staff ratio	16.5	=80
Services and facilities	£2,796	37

productions. Courses are run via Bucks New's partnership with Pinewood's CMS training platform. The university is upgrading teaching facilities there, and installing a cinema-standard viewing room and new equipment for film workshops.

There are links with other local businesses and private sector employers, who help to shape course design as well as provide placements. Travel and aviation courses include the opportunity to study for a professional pilot's licence while working towards a degree.

The government's Teaching Excellence Framework (TEF) upgraded an initial bronze award to silver for Bucks New in the second round of assessments. The judging panel was impressed by the university's small class sizes and individual action plans to support students into work, as well as its active engagement with the student body, and the "live briefs" co-designed with students to address real-world problems.

The university was less successful in the Research Excellence Framework, where it entered only 24 staff in the 2014 assessments and is ranked in the bottom 10 in our research quality table.

For social inclusion however, Bucks New regularly finishes in the upper reaches of our ranking. Nearly two out of three students are aged 21 or more and just under half of the student community comes from ethnic minority backgrounds. Nearly half are the first in their family to go to university.

Bursaries and scholarships are being repackaged so more students who need help may access it, and the university expects a larger proportion of 2021's intake to benefit.

Bucks New takes pride in having an active students' union, which gives everyone its Big Deal package of freebies to use in entertainment, recreation and sport. The university runs one of only five swimming performance centres approved by Swim England. There are more than 30 sports clubs and links with professional clubs in the region.

The university gym is a local highlight, featuring app-based cardio machines and interactive exercise equipment. The Human Performance, Exercise and Wellbeing Centre has a three-lane running track with 3D motion-capture technology, with sports injury and physiotherapy clinics.

Bucks New owns or endorses 885 student bedrooms, enough for all first-years who want to live in to be guaranteed a space. London is within easy reach of High Wycombe, which has its own student pubs and clubs too.

Tuition fees

» Fees for UK students	£9,250
» Fees for International students 2021–20	£13,750
» For scholarship and bursary information see www.bucks.ac.uk/applying-to-bucks/undergraduate/fees-and-funding	
» Graduate salary	£24,000

Student numbers

Undergraduates	8,210	(1,496)
Postgraduates	412	(885)
Applications/places		5,970/1,490
Applications per place		4
Overall offer rate		80%
International students – EU		6.5%
Non-EU		0.8%

Accommodation

University provided places: 885
Self-catered: £118–£186 per week
First years guaranteed accommodation
www.bucks.ac.uk/life-at-bucks/accommodation

Where do the students come from?

State schools (non-grammar)	94.2%	First generation students	48.1%		
Grammar schools	2.5%	Deprived areas	10.9%		
Independent schools	3.3%	All ethnic minorities	44.9%		

Social inclusion ranking: 34

Black attainment gap	-8.2%
Disabled	2.9%
Mature (over 21)	62.5%

University of Cambridge

The gap has narrowed, but Cambridge remains the top university in Britain for the eighth successive year. Oxford and St Andrews have both eaten into Cambridge's lead since our last ranking, but its ability to attract the best qualified school-leavers and see more of them through to complete their degrees than at any other university help Cambridge to hold off its nearest UK rivals.

Cambridge also spends more on services and facilities than its principal foe, Oxford, but continues to lag behind it in international rankings. Cambridge is placed seventh in the latest QS World University Rankings, two places adrift of Oxford. Global rankings have a greater emphasis on research and academic citations, while domestic tables like ours focus more on the undergraduate student experience. Cambridge is top in 32 of our 67 subject tables, five more than in 2019.

The traditional locations are a large part of the Oxbridge appeal. Cambridge University dominates its city, a much smaller and more intimate location than Oxford. The 31 colleges – housed in a mixture of old and new buildings – support a student community of around 20,000 undergraduates and postgraduates.

Colleges usually provide rooms for students in college-owned accommodation throughout their three-year courses (and for a fourth year where relevant). Some rooms overlook the quads for which the university is famed; others are in modern blocks, often in the grounds nearby. The porters may be able to tell you of your room's illustrious former occupants: Stephen Hawking's or Rachel Weisz's old haunt at Trinity Hall anyone?

The colleges vary considerably in size, age, intake and character, so it pays to take a view to maximise your chances of success rather than submit an open application to the university. Some admit many more state school-educated students than others; some are much more socially diverse. Statistics are available covering most admissions information.

However, Cambridge is at the bottom of our social inclusion ranking, well below Durham and Oxford, when measured across eight metrics. Cambridge has promised to admit one in six students from the 40% of postcodes with the lowest participation rates in higher education by 2024–25 and draw 69.1% of students from state schools.

Student financial support is extensive. The Cambridge Bursary is paid to all students from households where income is less than £43,620, beginning at £300 a year and rising to £3,500 a year for students from homes where the household income is less than £25,000. The bursary rises to £5,600 a year for care leavers.

Without doubt, the two Stormzy Scholarships, each worth £18,000 paid over a year to cover tuition fees and maintenance,

---

Cambridge Admissions Office
Student Services Centre
New Museums Site
Cambridge CB2 3BT
01223 333 308
admissions@cam.ac.uk
www.cam.ac.uk
www.cambridgesu.co.uk
Open days:
see website

The Times and The Sunday Times Rankings
Overall Ranking: 1 (last year: 1)

Teaching quality	n/a	
Student experience	n/a	
Research quality	57.3%	1
Entry standards	212	1
Graduate prospects	91.4%	3
Good honours	92.9%	2
Expected completion rate	98.7%	1
Student/staff ratio	11.2	=4
Services and facilities	£3,828	5

have attracted the most attention. They were funded by the grime musician to support black students at Cambridge. Publicity surrounding the scholarships prompted an increase in black applicants and the total of 91 black students admitted in 2019 was a record, taking the number of black undergraduates at the university past 200 for the first time. That record was broken again with October 2020's intake.

For those applying to Cambridge, competition doesn't get much tougher. More than 84% of admissions exceeded A*AA at A-level or equivalent in the most recent intake analysis. Even to get through the first stage of the selection process, applicants must be predicted A*AA at A-level in arts subjects and A*A*A in the sciences – although lower offers may be made where a candidate's school or personal circumstances may disadvantage them. Cambridge also sets its own entrance tests, taken either on the day of an interview or in advance.

Applications must be in by October 15. At that point candidates receive a supplementary application questionnaire seeking greater detail on their academic record. Unlike most Russell Group institutions, Cambridge has not expanded its undergraduate intake significantly, with around 2,600 places available each year.

For the few who make it through the doors, the workload is high, with a demanding schedule crammed into eight-week terms. Cambridge was awarded gold in the Teaching Excellence Framework. Its tutorial system enabled students to engage with world-leading scholars, said assessors, and to receive personalised feedback on their academic progress.

Renowned worldwide for its research, Cambridge entered 95% of eligible academics for the Research Excellence Framework – the highest proportion of any institution in the UK – and 87% of their work was rated as world-leading or internationally excellent. The university got the best results in the country for aeronautical and electronic engineering, business and management, chemistry, classics and clinical medicine.

Among the abundance of extra-curricular opportunities, sports facilities are excellent at individual colleges and at the university's £16m sports centre, which features a large sports hall and a strength and conditioning wing.

What do students make of it all? Sadly, we don't know at present. Students at Cambridge have not seen fit to complete the National Student Survey in sufficient numbers to register results for the past four years.

Tuition fees

» Fees for UK students	£9,250
» Fees for International students 2021–22	£22,227–£33,825
Medicine and veterinary science	£58,038
» For scholarship and bursary information see	
www.undergraduate.study.cam.ac.uk/fees-and-finance	
» Graduate salary	£30,000

Student numbers

Undergraduates	12,267	(346)
Postgraduates	6,912	(1,367)
Applications/places		19,625/3,415
Applications per place		5.7
Overall offer rate		28.5%
International students – EU		12.6%
Non-EU		22.6%

Accommodation

See: http://www.undergraduate.study.cam.ac.uk/why-cambridge/student-life/accommodation
College websites provide accommodation details

See Chapter 14 for individual colleges

Where do the students come from?

State schools (non-grammar)	43%	First generation students	14.7%		
Grammar schools	22.3%	Deprived areas	4.2%		
Independent schools	34.7%	All ethnic minorities	27.2%		

Social inclusion ranking: 116

Black attainment gap	-13.5%
Disabled	5.2%
Mature (over 21)	4.3%

Canterbury Christ Church

As Canterbury Christ Church (CCCU) hits a new low in our rankings – five places off the bottom of the table – it has something big to celebrate with the opening of a new medical school, in partnership with the University of Kent.

The first 100 students began their studies at the Kent and Medway Medical School in September 2020, bringing together centres of excellence in health and medical education provided by both universities and offering a medical training to students drawn from local communities and beyond. Along with the Brighton and Sussex medical school, it plugs a notable gap in provision in the region.

Falls in student satisfaction and a dropout rate running at more than double the expected level are the chief reasons for CCCU's decline in our rankings. Although it was in the UK top 50 for satisfaction with teaching quality in 2019, the university barely made the top 75 in the latest results, while dissatisfaction with the wider student experience saw it fall into the bottom 20 on this measure.

However, it is CCCU's dropout rate that draws most attention, with more than one in four students (28.4%) failing to complete their courses – more than double the expected level (13.7%) taking into account the social and subject mix at the university. It falls more significantly short of its benchmark than any other university.

The university has a strong record for attracting students from groups that are under-represented in higher education. Just over 20% of admissions in 2018–19 came from postcodes with the lowest participation rates and there are partnership programmes with more than 50 schools and colleges in Kent and Medway.

A new BA in product design will be offered from September 2021, while several new engineering degrees were introduced in September 2020 at both MEng and BEng level. These include product design engineering, biomedical engineering, and mechanical engineering with specialisms in systems, building services or advanced manufacture.

The engineering courses, with their accent on problem-solving and real-world applications, were developed jointly with employers. They will be delivered in a new £65m science, technology, health, engineering and medicine building on the main Canterbury campus, and in centres of excellence across the region with links to engineering and technology businesses where students may seek work.

The numbers starting degrees remained close to the 3,500 mark in 2019 as a new building opened for the schools of media, art and design, and music and performing arts, with specialist teaching facilities including performance space and design studios. The project marked the start of a £150m plan to develop its main

North Holmes Road
Canterbury CT1 1QU
01227 928 000
courses@canterbury.ac.uk
www.canterbury.ac.uk
https://ccsu.co.uk
Open days:
see website

The Times and The Sunday Times **Rankings**
Overall Ranking: 127 (last year: 118)

Teaching quality	79.2%	73
Student experience	73.5%	118
Research quality	4.5%	97
Entry standards	106	124
Graduate prospects	70.9%	85
Good honours	66.7%	=119
Expected completion rate	67.3%	129
Student/staff ratio	15.6	66
Services and facilities	£1,904	109

campus in Canterbury over 15 years.

There are plans for about 500 students to enrol on an expanding portfolio of higher and degree apprenticeships. Subject to validation, there will be new degree apprenticeships for academic professionals, manufacturing engineers, and science industry process/plant engineers to add to existing courses for police constables, chartered managers and occupational therapists, among other options.

The university has campuses in Chatham and Broadstairs and a postgraduate centre in Tunbridge Wells. The purpose-built Broadstairs site offers subjects ranging from commercial music to digital media, photography, and early childhood studies, while the recently expanded Medway campus at Chatham's historic dockyard specialises in education and health programmes.

A life sciences industry liaison laboratory at Discovery Park in Sandwich provides students with first-class facilities for research, and acts as a resource for local businesses.

Most students, however, are based in Canterbury, on a world heritage site where CCCU has a prize-winning library and student services centre. All campuses are interconnected by a high-speed data network.

The former Church of England college achieved university status in 2005 and is one of the region's largest providers of courses and research for the public services. Its teacher training courses are highly rated by Ofsted and there are strong programmes in health and social care, nursing and policing. The university remains a Church of England foundation and has the Archbishop of Canterbury as its chancellor, but admits students of all faiths and none.

The university has a silver rating in the Teaching Excellence Framework, recognising the gains made by students from disadvantaged backgrounds, ethnic minority communities and those with disabilities, who achieve good degrees at the same rate as other students and have good long-term employment prospects.

Almost half of CCCU's submission to the 2014 Research Excellence Framework was placed in the top two categories, resulting in one of the biggest percentage increases in funding at any university. It has since established the UK Institute for Migration Research and the Institute of Medical Sciences, which builds on the university's work in stem cell research and minimally invasive surgery.

Sports facilities are good for those on the Canterbury campus and there is enough residential accommodation to guarantee a place for first-years who apply by the end of July.

Tuition fees

»	Fees for UK students	£9,250
	Foundation courses	£7,050
»	Fees for International students 2021–22	£13,000
	Medicine (2020–21)	£45,000
»	For scholarship and bursary information see	
	www.canterbury.ac.uk/study-here/fees-and-funding/	
»	Graduate salary	£23,700

Student numbers

Undergraduates	9,290	(2,011)
Postgraduates	1,115	(1,757)
Applications/places	10,560/2,745	
Applications per place	3.8	
Overall offer rate	84.5%	
International students – EU	3.4%	
Non-EU	1.8%	

Accommodation

University provided places: 1,825
Self-catered: £118–£167 per week
First years guaranteed accommodation
www.canterbury.ac.uk/study-here/student-life/accommodation

Where do the students come from?

					Social inclusion ranking: =57	
State schools (non-grammar)	92.2%	First generation students	59.1%		Black attainment gap	-42.3%
Grammar schools	5.6%	Deprived areas	20.3%		Disabled	6.6%
Independent schools	2.2%	All ethnic minorities	28.6%		Mature (over 21)	35.9%

Cardiff University

The biggest campus upgrade for a generation is under way at Wales's only Russell Group university, Cardiff. The Centre for Student Life, a £50m development designed to transform the way the university supports students, is due to open in 2021. The new hub will locate student services, including those for wellbeing and mental health, at the heart of the Cathays Park campus. A partnership with the students' union, the centre will add study spaces, quiet contemplation areas, consultation rooms and a 550-seat auditorium.

Top-ranked in Wales for the first time in three years, Cardiff has more capital projects on the horizon as part of its £600m masterplan. A joint new home for the schools of science and informatics, and mathematics should open in 2021–22, as will the Cardiff Innovation Campus at Maindy Park. An innovation centre at the campus will house student start-ups and graduate entrepreneurs, which in turn will open up work placement opportunities. The university's social science research park – sbarc|spark – is the first of its kind globally, and another feature of the innovation campus.

The highly rated School of Journalism, Media and Culture is next door to BBC Cymru Wales, boosting industry links and student employability by providing direct access to leading media organisations. Across the university lecture theatres, classrooms and seminar rooms are also being refurbished.

Cardiff medical students can now complete their whole degree at Bangor University in north Wales, in a collaboration designed to produce doctors with a deep understanding of the region. Additional routes into medicine and increased diversity within the medical profession are also intended as part of the programme.

The university's Data Science Academy welcomed its first students in September 2019. Focusing on growth areas such as data science, artificial intelligence and cyber-security, the academy's courses are all postgraduate programmes.

Applications for 2020 admissions were 15% higher than the year before, following an already healthy 2019 in which the number of students enrolled on courses reached a record level. Postgraduate applications for this research goliath saw a huge 41% increase in 2020.

In the government's Teaching Excellence Framework, Cardiff was awarded silver, thanks in part to the support that personal tutors provide and the direct engagement of students with developments at the forefront of research, scholarship and professional practice.

Cardiff's research pedigree is renowned. The university counts two Nobel Prize winners and 15 Royal Society Fellows on staff and in 2019 it made record research income of just over £116m. Cardiff achieved excellent results in the

Cardiff
CF10 3AT
029 2087 4455
enquiry@cardiff.ac.uk
www.cardiff.ac.uk
www.cardiffstudents.com
Open days:
see website

The Times and The Sunday Times **Rankings**
Overall Ranking: 34 (last year: 34)

Teaching quality	76.9%	103
Student experience	75.8%	98
Research quality	35%	34
Entry standards	154	=27
Graduate prospects	83.1%	20
Good honours	81.7%	33
Expected completion rate	91.8%	28
Student/staff ratio	14.3	=30
Services and facilities	£2,581	53

2014 Research Excellence Framework, but entered only 62% of eligible staff – the lowest proportion at any Russell Group university. This depressed its position in our research ranking (which rewards quantity as well as quality), but 87% of the submission was rated as world-leading or internationally excellent, and Cardiff was in the UK's top three for the impact of its research. Civil and construction engineering was rated top in the exercise.

Most academic schools are based at the Cathays Park campus, where the university's elegant pale stone buildings sit within tree-lined avenues in the city's civic centre. The healthcare schools share a 53-acre campus at Heath Park with the University Hospital of Wales. The £18m Cochrane Building provides teaching and learning facilities for all healthcare schools based there. The School of Dentistry is the only one in Wales and offers students some of the UK's most modern training facilities, including a simulation suite.

Residential summer schools, roadshows, community-based courses and on-campus activities are some of the widening participation programmes that target those from areas where few apply to university, care leavers and those with autism. Contextual admissions are considered using a weighted scale based on the disadvantages and advantages of each candidate.

Certain subjects award £3,000 scholarships over three years to students arriving with AAA results, and Coleg Cymraeg Cenediathol scholarships are for students completing their courses in Welsh. The schools of engineering and music also offer awards based on merit.

Once a well-kept secret, Cardiff's Russell Group experience within a vibrant, relatively affordable city is now well and truly out of the bag. Its live music scene, bars and clubs are buzzing enough to earn Cardiff a party town reputation. Combined with its cultural heritage, the Millennium Stadium, arts venues, urban green spaces and proximity to the great outdoors in the Brecon Beacons and on the coast, the city offers something for most students.

Sports facilities include a three-floor fitness centre at Senghennydd Road, the Sports Training Village at the Talybont campus with floodlit outdoor courts and pitches and two sports halls, 33 acres at the university sports fields in Llanrumney and a studio on Park Road that offers more than 100 fitness classes a month.

Cardiff owns or endorses 5,346 rooms for undergraduates, enough to guarantee a space for every first-year.

Tuition fees

» Fees for UK students	£9,000
» Fees for International students 2021–22	£17,700–£21,950
Medicine	£34,450
» For scholarship and bursary information see www.cardiff.ac.uk/study/undergraduate/funding	
» Graduate salary	£24,000

Student numbers

Undergraduates	19,949 (4,012)
Postgraduates	6,233 (2,996)
Applications/places	34,465/5,495
Applications per place	6.3
Overall offer rate	72.5%
International students – EU	4.3%
Non-EU	21.7%

Accommodation

University provided places: 5,346
Catered costs: £155–£164 per week
Self-catered: £104–£144 per week
First years guaranteed accommodation
www.cardiff.ac.uk/study/accommodation

Where do the students come from?

State schools (non-grammar)	75.7%	First generation students	31.7%	Black attainment gap	-20.6%
Grammar schools	9.6%	Deprived areas	9.1%	Disabled	5%
Independent schools	14.7%	All ethnic minorities	17.1%	Mature (over 21)	11%

Social inclusion ranking: 105

Cardiff Metropolitan University

Our Welsh University of the Year is designed for hands-on learning. The Cardiff School of Technologies recently moved to its new building at Cardiff Metropolitan University and plans to expand to host more than 2,000 students by 2022. It has sophisticated laboratories for robotics, data science and artificial intelligence, games design, cyber-security and electronic systems.

Cardiff Met's ethos is to provide practice-focused, professionally-oriented education on its Llandaff and Cyncoed campuses near the city centre. Over the past two years, 37 new degrees have been offered, with additions in 2020 ranging from early years education to law. Courses in applied entrepreneurship and innovation management, aviation management, digital health and management and leadership will accept their first students in 2021.

The degree apprenticeship in data science plans to treble its places to 65 in 2021, rising to 85 as the Cardiff School of Technologies adds programmes for software engineering and cyber-security.

The expanded curriculum has pushed up application figures for 2020, which were 7% higher at the end of March than at the same point the year before. The upturn is good news for Cardiff Met after a 2019 recruitment round that saw the number of applicants and enrolments dip to their lowest point since 2014.

Cyncoed, where first-years tend to settle into student social life, packs a big punch in sport, the university's best-known feature. Its facilities live up to its strong sporting record and support the portfolio of sports degrees. The £7m National Indoor Athletics Centre has a six-lane 140m straight and competition-standard long jump, high jump and pole vault pits. Other features include fully equipped physiotherapy and sports medicine facilities. Cyncoed also hosts an archery arena, fitness centre, grass and 3G pitches, a swimming pool, a sprung-floor gym and an indoor centre.

Elite sport scholarships offer tailored support worth up to £5,000 a year. A free sport and fitness membership encourages first-years to follow the example of more than 300 past and present students who have competed at international level in 30 sports. In recent years the university has had British university champions in sports ranging from archery and gymnastics to weightlifting, squash and judo. Cardiff Met teams also take part in competitions including the WRU Championship and Uefa Europa League.

The university prioritises civic engagement and social responsibility in its strategy to

200 Western Avenue
Llandaff
Cardiff CF5 2YB
029 2041 6010
askadmissions@cardiffmet.ac.uk
www.cardiffmet.ac.uk
www.cardiffmetsu.co.uk
Open days: see website

The Times and The Sunday Times **Rankings**
Overall Ranking: 79 (last year: 112)

Teaching quality	81.1%	=40
Student experience	80.2%	=27
Research quality	3.9%	107
Entry standards	128	=60
Graduate prospects	72.2%	74
Good honours	70.6%	108
Expected completion rate	80.1%	99
Student/staff ratio	18.1	=111
Services and facilities	£2,561	57

put Cardiff Met at the heart of life in the city, sharing its resources with staff, students and local communities to comply with the Wellbeing of Future Generations Act (Wales).

Cardiff Met was one of only four Welsh universities awarded silver in the government's Teaching Excellence Framework (TEF). Assessors noted that its personalised learning secured high levels of commitment from students, including those studying in the Welsh language. An enhanced personal tutor system gives students greater access to academic guidance.

The TEF panel said that course design was informed by a significant focus on employability, producing good outcomes for a range of student groups, including those from black and minority ethnic communities, disadvantaged and mature students.

About a fifth of students are estimated to qualify for bursaries and scholarships and the university expects financial aid to hold steady at that level in 2021. A £10 travel incentive bursary for local applicants — or £20 for those living further afield — helps prospective students get to the university for interviews or open days. Coleg Cymraeg Cenedlaethol scholarships are worth £3,000 over three years to students studying eligible courses in Welsh.

Each academic school has its own careers consultants with sector-specific knowledge, and students can access professional help without an appointment. Graduate start-ups

are on the rise, and support is offered through the Centre for Entrepreneurship.

The university entered only 35 academics for the 2014 Research Excellence Framework out of 381 who were eligible — the third smallest submission. However, 80% of the work submitted was rated in the top two categories. The university has since received a Queen's Anniversary Prize for the use of design and related 3D digital scanning technologies used in maxillofacial reconstructive surgery.

The ZERO2FIVE Food Industry Centre supports food businesses with expertise and modern facilities while PDR, an international centre for design and research, has forged partnerships with Panasonic, Virgin Atlantic, Rolls-Royce, Bosch and Skype, among others, to improve product design and development.

Cardiff Met owns almost 1,000 halls of residence spaces, and endorses a further 624 rooms — enough for all first-years who apply by the end of May. The city's student delights have earned Cardiff a strong reputation as a go-to undergraduate destination.

Tuition fees

» Fees for UK students   £9,000
» Fees for International students 2021–22   £13,000
» For scholarship and bursary information see www.cardiffmet.ac.uk/study/finance/Pages/default.aspx
» Graduate salary   £21,000

Student numbers

Undergraduates	7,619	(754)
Postgraduates	1,493	(808)
Applications/places		8,790/1,990
Applications per place		4.4
Overall offer rate		84.4%
International students – EU		2.5%
Non-EU		10.1%

Accommodation

University provided places: 1,570
Catered costs: £168–£179 per week
Self-catered: £118–£127 per week
www.cardiffmet.ac.uk/accommodation/Pages/default.aspx

Where do the students come from?

State schools (non-grammar)	93.3%	First generation students	49.6%	
Grammar schools	1.0%	Deprived areas	16.2%	
Independent schools	5.7%	All ethnic minorities	15.4%	

Social inclusion ranking: 86

Black attainment gap	-42.9%
Disabled	8.7%
Mature (over 21)	22.7%

University of Central Lancashire

The University of Central Lancashire's (UCLan) footprint in its home town of Preston is growing. The £35m Engineering Innovation Centre (EIC) opened in the 2019–20 academic year, bringing modern facilities for research and teaching in engineering-related projects. Designed to give students real-world experience, the EIC engages directly with industry partners and its resources range from a 3D printing lab and an advanced manufacturing workshop to a motorsports and air vehicles laboratory and a flight simulator suite.

A £60m student centre and pedestrianised public square in the heart of the Preston campus will be the next development to open – due at the start of the 2021–22 academic year. It will house student mental health services and careers advice alongside communal areas and a rooftop garden. It is set to form a gateway to the town and will be open to the community and businesses as well as to UCLan students.

The university is already one of Britain's biggest, and has expanded its presence in nearby Burnley, too, with its collaboration with Cisco Systems for advanced manufacturing. UCLan aims to increase its student population there tenfold by 2025 to 4,000 – an enormous hike that will be in part supported by the new accommodation and car parking that is planned.

The capital developments are part of a £200m campus masterplan that has already added a multi-faith centre and two social spaces. The UCLan School of Medicine was granted degree-awarding powers in 2020 by the General Medical Council. The school has been open for five years, at first only to international students, with British trainee doctors starting from 2019.

The Westlakes campus in West Cumbria focuses on nursing and other health subjects and UCLan has an outpost in Cyprus, which has a wide range of courses and offers the opportunity of a year abroad for UK students, although without access to student loans for that period.

Among 13 new courses offered from 2020 are ophthalmic dispensing, football studies, social work, and physical activity, health and wellbeing. Thirty-four degree apprenticeships are offered across diverse roles in the fields of engineering, professional services and health and wellbeing. More are planned and the university anticipates it will have over 3,000 degree apprentices by September 2021.

Awarding silver to UCLan in its 2019 assessment, the Teaching Excellence Framework (TEF) panel commended it for embedding employability skills in all curricula and for extensive engagement with local employers. All students can take advantage of work placements and other opportunities to boost their work-readiness at graduation. There is also a strong focus on entrepreneurship,

---

Preston PR1 2HE
01772 892 400
cenquiries@uclan.ac.uk
www.uclan.ac.uk
www.uclansu.co.uk
Open days:
see website

The Times and The Sunday Times **Rankings**
Overall Ranking: 87 (last year: 75)

Teaching quality	78.4%	=84
Student experience	75.7%	=99
Research quality	5.6%	=86
Entry standards	127	=65
Graduate prospects	72.5%	72
Good honours	72.3%	88
Expected completion rate	76.2%	119
Student/staff ratio	13.3	=13
Services and facilities	£2,629	48

supported by a range of business incubation facilities for students and graduates.

The university finishes just outside the top 30 of our social inclusion table and continues to build on its enduring commitment to widening participation in higher education. All undergraduate courses have the option of a foundation entry year, an initiative designed to ease the transition to university for those who arrive with non-traditional qualifications. The UCLan financial bursary of £2,000 is widely taken up by students from households with incomes of less than £20,000.

The university promotes Stem (science, technology, engineering and maths) subjects at its flagship Lancashire Science Festival for 12,000 primary and secondary school pupils and families. The event was cancelled in 2020 because of the coronavirus pandemic but celebrates its 10th anniversary in 2021. In another Stem initiative, UCLan opened the Young Scientist Centre at the Darwin Building in Preston in partnership with the Royal Institution, where children from key stages 2 to 5 take part in practical science workshops in a fully kitted out laboratory.

UCLan's exceptionally broad curriculum includes astrophysics, which has the bonus of a longstanding collaboration with Nasa. The partnership led to UCLan recently unveiling the highest-ever resolution images of the sun from Nasa's solar sounding rocket mission. The Dental School was one of the few to open in 100 years and the university's architecture degree was the first introduced at a British university for a decade.

UCLan's link with the BBC and MediaCityUK meant students on courses including fashion, acting and television and media production were granted permission to recreate a lost 1960's episode of Doctor Who.

World-leading research was found in all 16 subject areas assessed in the 2014 Research Excellence Framework. UCLan academics have been involved in sector-leading stroke research with the Department of Health and work on nutritional science with the Bill and Melinda Gates Foundation. The undergraduate research internship scheme enables students from all disciplines to work on research projects for up to 10 weeks.

Facilities for sport are excellent, both on campus and at the UCLan Sports Arena, two miles away. Preston offers a generally safe student environment and lower cost of living than Liverpool or Manchester.

Tuition fees

»	Fees for UK students	£9,250
	Foundation courses	£5,550
»	Fees for International students 2021–22	£13,000–£14,000
	Foundation courses	£7,800–£8,800
	Medicine (2020–21)	£40,500
»	For scholarship and bursary information see www.uclan.ac.uk/study_here/fees_and_finance/index.php	
»	Graduate salary	£23,000

Student numbers

Undergraduates	15,525 (1,981)
Postgraduates	2,369 (3,287)
Applications/places	19,525/3,790
Applications per place	5.2
Overall offer rate	70.7%
International students – EU	2.4%
Non-EU	9.3%

Accommodation

University provided places: 1,150
Self-catered: £77–£125 per week
First years guaranteed accommodation on Preston campus
www.uclan.ac.uk/accommodation/index.php

Where do the students come from?

State schools (non-grammar)	95.9%	First generation students	51.2%	Black attainment gap	-26.6%
Grammar schools	2.7%	Deprived areas	14.8%	Disabled	7.2%
Independent schools	1.4%	All ethnic minorities	31.5%	Mature (over 21)	38.2%

Social inclusion ranking: 32

University of Chester

Students from the University of Chester have helped to design recent campus developments ranging from the students' union building and bar to seminar spaces, laboratories and lecture theatres. Chester students also pitched in with ideas for shops, a student information point and outdoor seating areas – and contributed to plans for a grandstand at the all-weather pitch gifted to the university's Parkgate Road campus by Chester Hockey Club.

It is a point of pride for Chester that its students are known by name within the friendly communities at each of its seven sites. Today, Chester, which gained university status in 2005, continues to reflect its origins as a Church of England teacher training college established by William Gladstone, among others, in 1839, predating all other English universities except Oxford, Cambridge, Durham and London. Two of the modern campuses have chapels as well as facilities for other faiths, and teacher training has been rated outstanding by Ofsted.

Teaching is now just one of more than 20 subject areas covered by Chester at four bases in its home town and outposts in Warrington, Thornton and Shrewsbury. The original Parkgate Road campus has a 32-acre site just a 10-minute walk from the city centre, and the Queen's Park campus, once the wartime headquarters of the Army's Western Command, now houses the Chester Business School.

At the Riverside campus, the Faculty of Health and Social Care's new interprofessional simulation facility was the first used to train nursing students to join the coronavirus front line in the northwest. Courses in education and children's services are also based at Riverside, in the former County Hall, and the Riverside Innovation Centre hosts business start-ups generated by Chester students and graduates.

The university has invested £750,000 in digital resources, providing 600 laboratory computers and extra laptops for loan to students – likely to pay dividends in future with the post-pandemic emphasis on online teaching. An extra 200,000 e-resources were added in March 2020 to facilitate virtual learning and the Kingsway creative campus, housing arts and media courses, has added 150,000 e-books to its collection.

When Chester's engineering school opened in 2014, in the former Shell research facility at the Thornton Science Park campus, it was the first new such faculty in the UK for two decades. The Energy Centre shares the site, near Ellesmere Port, bringing industry and academia together to work on new intelligent energy technologies. The Warrington campus focuses on the creative industries and public services, with high-quality production facilities and links with the BBC in Salford.

The university is giving the curriculum a thorough shake-up, offering a raft of new

Parkgate Road
Chester CH1 4BJ
01244 511 000
admissions@chester.ac.uk
www.chester.ac.uk
www.chestersu.com
Open days:
see website

The Times and The Sunday Times **Rankings**
Overall Ranking: 69 (last year: =79)

Teaching quality	82.4%	=26
Student experience	80.1%	=30
Research quality	4.1%	=101
Entry standards	116	=97
Graduate prospects	67.8%	103
Good honours	71.5%	96
Expected completion rate	79.7%	=100
Student/staff ratio	15.1	=55
Services and facilities	£2,879	29

courses across its campuses from 2020. An integrated nursing master's degree has been introduced, with six specialisms relating to adult and children's general health, mental health and learning disabilities.

Among 24 new degrees in a diverse range of subjects are business management (with a placement year), childhood studies and applied psychology, and marine biology. In line with Chester's commitment to widening participation, 14 courses come with foundation years – including theology, English language, medical genetics and biochemistry. Students joining in 2021 will have the added options of applied sports studies, adult nursing and professional policing.

Chester's focus on workplace learning chimes with the breadth of its degree apprenticeship programme. Another five options will be added to the current nine, more than doubling the number of apprentices to more than 1,000 by 2021. New subjects will include roles in digital technology solutions, digital user experience, cyber security, laboratory science and serious and complex crime investigation.

Chester's silver award in the Teaching Excellence Framework (TEF) brought praise for its students' employability skills. About two-thirds of undergraduates take work-based learning modules. The TEF panel said Chester had an "embedded culture of valuing, recognising and rewarding good teaching".

More than two-thirds of the academic staff hold Higher Education Academy fellowships. Evening classes in a foreign language are offered to all students.

All but one of 15 subject areas entered in the 2014 Research Excellence Framework had some research that was judged world-leading.

There are 1,615 residential places for students in Warrington and Chester, some catered in full or in part. Accommodation guarantees vary between campuses but with many students living at home, new students seeking accommodation are almost always successful.

There are extensive sports facilities at Warrington and especially on the Parkgate Road campus, which has tennis courts, a 100-metre sprint track and a floodlit 3G multi-use sports pitch. Shrewsbury students are entitled to free membership at the town's sports village.

Chester's quaint walled city is a regional tourist attraction, and the bright lights of Liverpool and Manchester are within striking distance.

Tuition fees

» Fees for UK students	£9,250
Foundation courses	£7,850
» Fees for International students 2021–22	£12,750
Foundation courses	£9,250
» For scholarship and bursary information see http://www1.chester.ac.uk/finance	
» Graduate salary	£22,000

Student numbers

Undergraduates	8,990 (1,140)
Postgraduates	1,360 (3,081)
Applications/places	16,005/2,095
Applications per place	7.6
Overall offer rate	75.8%
International students – EU	1.3%
Non-EU	5.5%

Accommodation

University provided places: 1,615
Catered costs: £146–£150 per week
Self-catered: £88–£149 per week
www1.chester.ac.uk/departments/residential-living

Where do the students come from?

				Social inclusion ranking: =48	
State schools (non-grammar)	93.4%	First generation students	54.3%	Black attainment gap	-26%
Grammar schools	3.9%	Deprived areas	18.2%	Disabled	7.5%
Independent schools	2.7%	All ethnic minorities	10%	Mature (over 21)	26.9

University of Chichester

It may one day be worthy of a good quiz question. A University Challenge "starter for 10" even: what did the Duke and Duchess of Sussex do on their first – and as it has turned out so far, only – visit to the county from which they drew their royal titles? Answer: open the Tech Park at the University of Chichester.

The £35m development on the Bognor Regis campus is something of a departure for a university best known for its strong arts and teacher training bias. The Tech Park brings together degree courses in Steam (science, technology, engineering, arts and mathematics) subjects including creative and digital technologies.

The venture is supported by more than 40 companies, including Rolls-Royce (based at nearby Goodwood), Sony and a number of small and medium-sized enterprises with skill shortages. It is part-funded by an £8m grant from the south coast Local Enterprise Partnership.

Engineering students at the Tech Park have access to a machinery workshop with welding floor, fabricating laboratory, specialist 3D printers and an engineering centre. This has been built alongside a department of creative digital technologies with a 300 square-metre television production studio, a 100 square-metre special effects room and a 400 square-metre media operations centre.

The new facilities and the courses offered there have reversed several years of declining applications and enrolments at Chichester, down 24% and 23% respectively between 2014 and 2019. Now the numbers have bounced back with applications for the 2020 admission cycle up by 17%. The broader range of options should help the university to achieve its plans for gradual growth. The new engineering degrees, for example, which took their first students in 2018, have an industry-led curriculum on the CDIO (conceiving, designing, implementing, operating) model that is being adopted by a growing number of universities.

Also bouncing up is the university's ranking. A 23-place gain last year has been followed by a further 25-place improvement in our latest institutional league table as Chichester breaks into the top 50. Student satisfaction levels are the best they have been in the past three years with the university securing top-20 rankings both for satisfaction with teaching quality and the wider student experience.

The buoyant student mood is reflected in one of the lowest dropout rates in British higher education, an ongoing pattern that has earned Chichester our University of the Year for Student Retention title on three occasions. The latest figures show a dropout rate of 5.7%, less than half its benchmark figure (12.9%).

Bishop Otter Campus
College Lane
Chichester PO19 6PE
01243 816 002
admissions@chi.ac.uk
www.chi.ac.uk
www.ucsu.org
Open days:
see website

The Times and The Sunday Times **Rankings**
Overall Ranking: =46 (last year: 71)

Teaching quality	83.8%	14
Student experience	81.1%	16
Research quality	6.4%	81
Entry standards	122	=80
Graduate prospects	69.5%	96
Good honours	75.6%	=63
Expected completion rate	90.5%	35
Student/staff ratio	14.4	=33
Services and facilities	£1,926	107

Bursary support is less generous than at many institutions with just £300 a year on offer to students from homes with less than £25,000 annual income, and around a quarter benefit from some financial assistance. To help broaden the intake, Chichester is developing two bridging courses – health and social care, and maths for engineering for students who lack the qualifications to begin a degree in those areas.

New programmes are coming on stream. Degrees in computer science; criminology and forensic psychology; educational psychology; dance, aerial and physical theatre; dance education and teaching; football development; games design and development; physical education and secondary years QTS; and physiotherapy saw their first intakes in 2020. In September 2021 the curriculum will gain criminology; law with criminology; sociology; and sociology with criminology.

The university traces its history back to 1839 as a teacher training college set up in memory of William Otter, Bishop of Chichester, for whom the development of education was a passion. In 1873 it became a women-only college and although male students were accepted from 1957, women still hold two-thirds of the places today.

The university entered a quarter of its eligible staff for the Research Excellence Framework in 2014 and did well in music, drama and performing arts, English and sport. The Mathematics Centre has an international reputation and has become a focal point for curriculum development in England and elsewhere.

The 1,125 residential places are roughly equally divided between the Bognor Regis and Chichester (Bishop Otter) campuses, and Chichester guarantees accommodation to offer holders who make it their first choice. There is a university bus service linking the two centres, and students' union bars at each.

A £2m investment programme has matched the university's excellent sports provision with world-class facilities. The university runs a programme for gifted athletes who will use a new running track on the Chichester campus. A sports dome has been built as part of the Tudor Hale Centre for Sport, which allows for all-weather teaching for sports courses. As well as tennis and netball courts, the centre has laboratories and a sports injury clinic.

The small cathedral city of Chichester is best known for its theatre and as a yachting venue, while Bognor is said to have the longest stretch of coastline in the south, where all types of water sports are available.

Tuition fees

» Fees for UK students	£9,250
Foundation courses	£5,500
» Fees for International students 2020–21	£13,500
» For scholarship and bursary information see www.chi.ac.uk/study-us/fees-finance	
» Graduate salary	£22,000

Student numbers

Undergraduates	3,960	(414)
Postgraduates	456	(639)
Applications/places	5,665/1,270	
Applications per place	4.5	
Overall offer rate	74.8%	
International students – EU	1.8%	
Non-EU	1.3%	

Accommodation

University provided places: 1,125
Catered costs: £159–£177 per week
Self-catered: £118–£152 per week
First years guaranteed accommodation
www.chi.ac.uk/accommodation

Where do the students come from?

State schools (non-grammar)	93.8%	First generation students	49.6%	
Grammar schools	2.2%	Deprived areas	17.9%	
Independent schools	4%	All ethnic minorities	7.8%	

Social inclusion ranking: =40

Black attainment gap	n/a
Disabled	10.1%
Mature (over 21)	21.6%

City, University of London

Journalism students at City, University of London have a new facility modelled on a broadcast newsroom designed for multiple channels. They can learn their trade in a setting where breaking stories and background material are integrated across television, radio, online and print, using a radio studio and television booth.

City has a long tradition of educating students to go into business and the professions. The institution has been rooted in the heart of London since its foundation more than 125 years ago with the help of the livery companies of the City of London. Today, its courses span a wide range including law and the arts.

The university's School of Law was the first in London to offer programmes from undergraduate to professional courses. The opening of its new seven-storey building, delayed as a result of the coronavirus pandemic, will consolidate the university's legal facilities in Clerkenwell and provide up-to-date facilities such as a mock court room and a pro bono law clinic, open to the public.

Construction is following exacting sustainability criteria at City, named as London's greenest university by the student campaign network People & Planet in 2019. The law school will have solar panels and a ground source heat pump to save energy, and the university is planning a vegetable garden to add to its green roof, where the student bee team looks after hives producing 10kg-20kg of honey each year.

Most of City's investment in development, totalling more than £140m since 2012, has gone on improvements to the main campus at Northampton Square in Clerkenwell. A coffee shop, seating areas and exhibition space have augmented the main entrance area and the building also has a 240-seat lecture theatre, students' union facilities, a cafeteria and multifaith area.

Once a college of advanced technology, City joined the University of London in 2016. It was awarded silver in the Teaching Excellence Framework thanks to strong engagement with students and the students' union, as well as the university's excellent assessment and feedback.

The course profile pays dividends in the employment market, with 77% of graduates in high-skilled jobs or postgraduate study within 15 months of leaving – ranking the university in the UK's top 50. City's Micro-Placements programme aims to improve social mobility by arranging summer work experience for three to five weeks for students from under-represented backgrounds. Another scheme, Gradvantage is funded by Santander, providing 10-week internships with small and medium-sized enterprises – leading to a permanent job in some cases.

Northampton Square
London EC1V 0HB
020 7040 8716
ugadmissions@city.ac.uk
www.city.ac.uk
www.citystudents.co.uk
Open days:
see website

The Times and The Sunday Times **Rankings**
Overall Ranking: 82 (last year: 73)

Teaching quality	71.7%	=126
Student experience	72.1%	124
Research quality	22.6%	51
Entry standards	136	=48
Graduate prospects	76.7%	49
Good honours	75.6%	=63
Expected completion rate	87.5%	=50
Student/staff ratio	17.3	=95
Services and facilities	£2,709	44

City has dropped the Cass name from its Business School. It took the name of the 18th-century MP, merchant and philanthropist Sir John Cass, a key figure in the early development of the transatlantic slave trade, as recently as 2002 after a donation from the Sir John Cass Foundation, an educational charity. The school's MBA has been ranked fifth in the world for entrepreneurship by the *Financial Times* and attracts high-profile visiting lecturers.

Located on the doorstep of the capital's digital start-up hub, the university's own City Launch Lab runs a three-month accelerator programme to kickstart new businesses, providing mentoring and free desk space for student and graduate entrepreneurs. The incubator created over 1,000 jobs, secured £13.6m in investment and generated £23.74m of revenue in 2018–19.

Some of the worst scores in the country for student satisfaction with teaching quality and the wider student experience continue to depress City's overall standing in our academic ranking, but it finishes in the top half of our social inclusion table for England and Wales, in eighth place among pre-1992 universities. Nearly nine out of 10 City students come from a non-selective state school, more than half are the first from their family to go to university and more than three-quarters come from ethnic minority backgrounds.

City's outreach work won Higher Education Institution of the Year at the 2019 Neon awards for its commitment to increasing access to higher education. The widening participation team offers maths and English tutoring as well as careers guidance.

Integrated foundation years are being added to a number of established degrees in 2021, such as maths, computer science and data science. A new degree in business management with social purpose will also accept its first students in 2021.

The university entered just over half of its eligible academics in the 2014 Research Excellence Framework, but three-quarters of its submission was rated as world-leading or internationally excellent. The best results were in music and business.

City only has 729 residential places, though this is enough to guarantee accommodation for new entrants who accept an offer by the end of June.

The redeveloped sports centre, between the campus and the business school, has 3,000 square metres of facilities available to students, staff and the local community. Its Saddlers sports hall seats 400 spectators.

Tuition fees

» Fees for UK students	£9,250
» Fees for International students 2021–22	£15,160–£19,500
» For scholarship and bursary information see www.city.ac.uk/study/fees-and-funding	
» Graduate salary	£26,000

Student numbers

Undergraduates	9,748 (1,274)
Postgraduates	6,743 (2,446)
Applications/places	24,440/2,675
Applications per place	9.1
Overall offer rate	54.5%
International students – EU	9.7%
Non-EU	25.8%

Accommodation

University provided places: 741
Catered costs: £268–£276 per week
Self-catered: £156–£223 per week
First years guaranteed accommodation
www.city.ac.uk/accommodation/undergraduate

Where do the students come from?

State schools (non-grammar)	87%	First generation students	58.4%	Black attainment gap	-20%
Grammar schools	6.1%	Deprived areas	2.3%	Disabled	3.8%
Independent schools	7%	All ethnic minorities	79.3%	Mature (over 21)	12.3%

Social inclusion ranking: 47

Coventry University

 One of the most dynamic and innovative modern universities, Coventry moves up our table again this year and earns a shortlisting for our University of the Year award, having been named our Modern University of the Year three times between 2014 and 2016 and University of the Year for Student Experience in 2018.

Its latest success as one of the five contenders for University of the Year is reward for its proactive approach to widening participation and a portfolio of careers-focused courses that led to excellent results in the first Graduate Outcomes survey published in 2020.

Coventry University is now something of an educational brand with campuses in Coventry, Scarborough and two in London (in the City and Dagenham) in the UK and campuses and collaborations in Poland, Egypt and Morocco.

Degree fees from £6,500 are obvious attractions at the Coventry University Group's two "no frills" colleges in Scarborough and Dagenham, east London. Students sacrifice some facilities for a lower-cost degree. Elsewhere, the usual £9,250 tuition fee applies.

Coventry has one of the largest degree apprenticeship programmes of any university with just under 1,000 enrolled across 19 undergraduate and three postgraduate programmes based in Coventry, Scarborough and London. New options for project manager, supply chain leadership professional, environmental practitioner, rail and rail systems senior engineer, and accountancy/taxation professional will expand the portfolio further.

Recent campus improvements in Coventry have seen the central Lanchester library completely refurbished. The new Beatrice Shilling Building for the faculty of engineering, environment and computing opened in autumn 2020, and includes a gaming and virtual reality studio, a 3D printing and rapid prototyping area, a laser facility, and physics and electronics laboratories.

In London, the university has added a second campus building in the City, Cutlers Exchange, with state-of-the-art teaching facilities that include Bloomberg terminals, computer laboratories and a Standard & Poor's market intelligence suite.

These additions should add further lustre to Coventry's scores in the National Student Survey, which this year saw levels of satisfaction with teaching quality improve sufficiently to lift the university back into the UK top 30. Scores for satisfaction with the broader student experience slipped back a little but were still good enough to rank Coventry in the top 25.

The university's excellent showing in the new Graduate Outcomes (GO) survey is explained by academic collaborations such as the Institute for Advanced Manufacturing and

Priory Street
Coventry CV1 5FB
024 7765 2222
ukadmissions@coventry.ac.uk
www.coventry.ac.uk
www.cusu.org
Open days: see website

The Times and The Sunday Times Rankings
Overall Ranking: =46 (last year: 50)

Teaching quality	82.4%	=26
Student experience	80.5%	23
Research quality	3.8%	=108
Entry standards	122	=80
Graduate prospects	78.6%	40
Good honours	74.6%	72
Expected completion rate	81.8%	88
Student/staff ratio	13.9	25
Services and facilities	£2,625	49

Engineering (AME), run with the Unipart manufacturing group. AME is a working factory that doubles as an academic base, providing students with real-world experience and the skills to address domestic shortages while they study. The GO survey showed 78.6% of Coventry's graduates to be in high-skilled employment or postgraduate study 15 months after leaving the university, a result that places it second among the post-1992 universities.

Other notable industrial partnerships involve Coventry's National Transport Design Centre and the Centre for Advanced Low Carbon Propulsion Systems.

Working with the University of Warwick and the West Midlands Combined Authority – and supported by the mental health charity, Mind – Coventry has been studying the link between workplace productivity and the mental health of employees. A £6.8m government grant is bringing together academics, health professionals and business leaders to tackle poor mental health in the workplace, an issue compounded by the Covid-19 pandemic. Over the next three years, the project aims to engage with 1,600 businesses, 45,000 staff and offer a free online resource to one million people.

The university was awarded gold in the government's Teaching Excellence Framework, whose judging panel found "consistently outstanding" student support services, especially for those from disadvantaged backgrounds.

The range of degrees is expanding at each campus. In Coventry, among new options are global journalism and media, creative writing, banking and finance, computer science with AI and sports coaching. At Coventry University London (City campus), there is a new degree in global events management, while at CU London (Dagenham) oil and gas management, and sport and leisure management recruited their first students. CU Scarborough has gained applied psychology.

Pandemic-enforced changes to teaching will accelerate the move to greater online delivery of courses via Coventry's Aula social learning hub, piloted in pre-Covid times by more than 2,000 students. The pilot found that student engagement improved significantly, with learners three times more likely to engage with course materials on a daily basis. Applicants who make Coventry their firm choice and request accommodation by mid-July are guaranteed one of the 4,700 rooms owned or endorsed by the university. Coventry has a relatively low cost of living and the city is not short of student-oriented nightlife.

Tuition fees

»	Fees for UK students	£9,250
	Foundation courses	£7,500
»	Fees for International students 2020–21	£13,900–£15,600
	Foundation courses	£11,000
»	For scholarship and bursary information see	
	www.coventry.ac.uk/study-at-coventry/finance/	
»	Graduate salary	£24,000

Student numbers

Undergraduates	26,347 (2,659)
Postgraduates	3,885 (2,093)
Applications/places	34,845/5,915
Applications per place	5.9
Overall offer rate	72.8%
International students – EU	10.5%
Non-EU	23.8%

Accommodation

University provided places: 4662
Catered costs: £99–£130 per week
Self-catered: £110–£199 per week
First years guaranteed accommodation
www.coventry.ac.uk/life-on-campus/accommodation

Where do the students come from?

State schools (non-grammar)	91.7%	First generation students	47.2%		
Grammar schools	4.8%	Deprived areas	11.8%		
Independent schools	3.5%	All ethnic minorities	67.8%		

Social inclusion ranking: 52

Black attainment gap	-20.7%
Disabled	4%
Mature (over 21)	19%

University for the Creative Arts

More student accommodation will be added in 2021 at the University for the Creative Arts (UCA), where applications leapt by 18% last year. The extra 252 spaces will be snapped up at the Farnham campus as UCA continues to attract more international students during a period when many universities are struggling with low recruitment.

The specialist arts institution has also developed its first overseas campus: the Institute of Creativity and Innovation in China. Opened in September 2020 in partnership with Xiamen University, it expects 300 students in its first cohort in the coastal city in southeast China, taking undergraduate programmes in digital media technology, visual communication design, advertising, and environmental design. The courses will be taught jointly and comply with UK higher education standards.

Our Modern University of the Year for 2018–19, UCA jointly reached the then highest position achieved by a post-1992 institution. A dip in student satisfaction scores in the 2020 National Student Survey, however, has toppled UCA from such lofty heights, although its satisfaction with teaching quality remains well above the level of most other specialist arts institutions.

UCA fared worse in the new Graduate Outcomes statistics, with only 54% in high-skilled jobs or postgraduate study within 15 months of completing their degrees, the worst rate in the country. Considering the course profile, its ranking is not wholly unexpected, and there is a concerted attempt to improve employability.

Of the 11 new courses introduced in 2020, ranging from arts and festival management, product and furniture design, and digital media to music business and management, 10 include the option of a professional practice year. Many staff are practitioners as well as academics, and UCA has plenty of successful role models among its alumni such as the artist Tracey Emin and the fashion designers Karen Millen and Zandra Rhodes, its former chancellor.

A gold award in the Teaching Excellence Framework reflects UCA's outstanding levels of stretch for students, driving them to achieve their full potential. The TEF panel also hailed "significant contact with employers that frequently engages students in developments from the forefront of professional practice".

UCA offers some four-year degrees incorporating a foundation year. Students can also take a two-year extended diploma that can be topped up to produce an honours degree. Students are encouraged to collaborate with their peers and to develop an international perspective.

Teaching is split on four campuses – Farnham, Epsom, Canterbury and Rochester – while UCA also offers distance learning

UCA Farnham
Falkner Road
Farnham GU9 7DS
01252 892 960
admissions@uca.ac.uk
www.uca.ac.uk
http://ucasu.com
Open days:
see website

The Times and The Sunday Times **Rankings**

Overall Ranking: 71 (last year: 42)

Teaching quality	81.9%	35
Student experience	74.5%	111
Research quality	3.4%	112
Entry standards	136	=48
Graduate prospects	54.2%	131
Good honours	73.5%	=82
Expected completion rate	84.8%	59
Student/staff ratio	13.7	=20
Services and facilities	£2,775	39

degree and diploma courses through the Open College of the Arts, which became part of the university in 2016.

More than 2,000 students are based at Farnham, the biggest site, where subjects range from advertising, animation and computer games technology to film production, journalism, music composition and technology. The £4m Film and Media Centre opened in 2019, consolidating UCA's strong reputation in the industry, underlined by Oscar and Bafta nominations for its alumni.

The Epsom campus specialises in fashion, graphics, music and business programmes. Its Business School for the Creative Industries is the first of its kind in the UK, focusing on the growing creative employment sector. Courses include event and promotion management and international buying and merchandising.

Epsom also offers further education courses in general art, design and media. At Rochester, where the purpose-built campus overlooks the River Medway, there is a full range of art and design courses, covering fashion, photography, computer animation and jewellery-making. Students taking UCA's popular television production course are based at Maidstone TV Studios, the largest independent studio complex in the UK.

The Canterbury School of Architecture is a rarity, one of only two such faculties remaining within a specialist art and design institution – promoting collaboration between student architects, designers and fine artists. On a modern site close to the city centre, the Canterbury campus also hosts degree courses in fine art, interior design, graphic design, and illustration and animation.

From UCA's small submission to the Research Excellence Framework, almost two thirds was rated world-leading or internationally excellent and 90% reached the top two categories for its impact.

For social inclusion measures, UCA reaches the top 40 in our table, one of only two specialist arts institutions to do so. It offers travel bursaries and provides art materials and equipment on its school outreach programmes to make sure disadvantaged pupils are not excluded. About 10% of students qualify for some form of financial assistance.

There are no sports facilities but the students' union operates a variety of clubs using outside facilities. When the new accommodation is open at Farnham there will be 1,330 residential spaces for 2021–22, as the university aims to improve on the average of 52% of first-years who are offered a room across all sites.

Tuition fees

»	Fees for UK students	£9,250
»	Fees for International students 2021–22	£16,270
	Foundation courses	£12,810
»	For scholarship and bursary information see www.uca.ac.uk/life-at-uca/fees	
»	Graduate salary	£20,000

Student numbers

Undergraduates	4,492	(1,672)
Postgraduates	317	(136)
Applications/places		5,520/965
Applications per place		5.7%
Overall offer rate		88.2%
International students – EU		7%
Non-EU		9.3%

Accommodation

University provided places: 1,078
Self-catered: £1012–£170 per week
www.uca.ac.uk/life-at-uca/accommodation

Where do the students come from?

State schools (non-grammar)	93.2%	First generation students	50%	Black attainment gap	-33%
Grammar schools	3.6%	Deprived areas	10.5%	Disabled	10.8%
Independent schools	3.2%	All ethnic minorities	21.2%	Mature (over 21)	17.3%

Social inclusion ranking: =38

University of Cumbria

With seven sites in and around the Lake District – plus one in east London – Cumbria is one of the country's youngest universities, established in 2007. Its campus in Ambleside lies in a national park and offers the UK's biggest programme of outdoor education courses as well as conservation and forestry degrees.

The university has improved its position in our rankings for the second year running, though still has a way to go before breaking into the top 100. Student satisfaction with teaching quality (ranked 44th) is a contributing factor and there was also an improvement in satisfaction with the wider experience, although Cumbria remains in the bottom 25 on this measure.

With 75% of graduates in high-skilled jobs or postgraduate study within 15 months of finishing their degree, Cumbria is just outside the top 50 UK universities for graduate prospects. It has also done well on completion rates, with fewer students dropping out than the expected level based on the social and academic backgrounds of the intake.

Student numbers have been in decline, however. Applications were down about 5% early in the 2020 recruitment cycle, which the university blamed on the withdrawal of a small number of courses. In 2019 alone they fell by 17% and since 2014 they have decreased by nearly 50% as Cumbria has struggled to fill places. The decline in enrolments has been less steep but still significant, falling nearly 37% from 2014–19.

The university has extensive plans to redevelop its main campus in Lancaster following the addition of the £9m Sentamu teaching and learning building with a 200-seat lecture theatre. The parkland campus, a short walk from the city centre, has a gymnastics centre and fitness suite as well as modern accommodation and a restaurant with panoramic views towards Morecambe Bay. The library has bookable study rooms, individual booths and laptops available for loan. A living centre is being built on the site of former tennis courts to include 11 flats for wheelchair users.

The Workington campus has dedicated facilities for its graduate programme providing specialist courses in decommissioning, reprocessing and managing nuclear waste. The university is a partner in both the National College for Nuclear and the Project Academy for Sellafield. Cumbria's base in Barrow is at Furness College, specialising in nursing and health practitioner courses. The London campus, in the East End, is now in its 13th year and provides an urban setting for the training of teachers, police officers and health professionals. The university also has two campuses in Carlisle.

Cumbria was one of 11 universities awarded bronze in the government's Teaching

Head Office
Fusehill Street
Carlisle CA1 2HH
0845 606 1144
UoCAdmissions@cumbria.ac.uk
www.cumbria.ac.uk
www.ucsu.me
Open days: see website

The Times and The Sunday Times Rankings
Overall Ranking: 114 (last year: 121)

Teaching quality	81%	44
Student experience	75.4%	106
Research quality	1.2%	124
Entry standards	120	=97
Graduate prospects	75%	=57
Good honours	63.9%	126
Expected completion rate	82.9%	=76
Student/staff ratio	15.7	=67
Services and facilities	£1,760	119

Excellence Framework in 2017. However, although it was marked down for a low graduate employment rate in high-skilled jobs, the university pointed out such roles are in short supply in the region compared with the national average. As our graduate prospects measure shows, Cumbria is now doing much better on employability. Among its academic staff, 76% held teaching qualifications when surveyed in 2016, compared with a national average of 44%.

There are 12 degree apprenticeship programmes training students for roles in health, business and industry. Cumbria hopes to add another five programmes: nurse associate, diagnostic radiographer, registered nurse, district nursing and engineering, and to increase the numbers from 250 to about 900 in 2021.

Cumbria is among the UK's more socially inclusive universities, ranking just outside the top 50 in England and Wales across the eight measures included in our table. More than half its students are the first in their family to go to university, almost half are mature and more than one in six come from deprived areas.

The creative arts produced by far the best results in the 2014 Research Excellence Framework, with 90% of the submission assessed as world-leading or internationally excellent. Overall, Cumbria is just two places off the bottom of our research ranking, having entered only 27 academics (8% of those

eligible) for assessment. Almost 30% of the work of this small group was placed in the top two categories, however.

First-years are guaranteed student accommodation on campus in the university's supply of 607 residential places, plus 174 endorsed rooms in privately-owned accommodation. Some halls of residence at the Ambleside campus are in attractive stone cottages, complementing the Lake District setting.

Tuition fees

»	Fees for UK students	£9,250
	Foundation courses	£6,000
»	Fees for International students 2020–21	£10,500–£15,500
	Foundation courses	£7,500
»	For scholarship and bursary information see	
	www.cumbria.ac.uk/study/student-finance/undergraduate/	
»	Graduate salary	£24,000

Student numbers

Undergraduates	4,375	(1,488)
Postgraduates	770	(960)
Applications/places		4,370/940
Applications per place		4.6
Overall offer rate		78.2%
International students – EU		3.2%
Non-EU		1.5%

Accommodation

University provided places: 781
Catered costs: £91–£118 per week
Self-catered: £70–£120 per week
First years guaranteed accommodation
www.cumbria.ac.uk/student-life/accommodation/

Where do the students come from?

State schools (non-grammar)	94.9%	First generation students	54.8%	Black attainment gap	-29%
Grammar schools	1.9%	Deprived areas	17.5%	Disabled	8.6%
Independent schools	3.2%	All ethnic minorities	13.5%	Mature (over 21)	47.3%

Social inclusion ranking: 51

De Montfort University

In the run-up to its 150th anniversary in 2020, De Montfort University (DMU) produced an economic impact report to examine how it had contributed to the local coffers in Leicester.

The findings support DMU's belief in the power of a modern university as a catalyst for economic growth. The university adds £500m to the UK economy each year, half of which is spent in Leicestershire, the report said. Researchers reported that one in 30 jobs in Leicester can be traced back to DMU and 80% of nursing graduates take up their first post in the region. Student volunteers logged 33,400 hours in a year to support the university's longstanding commitment to community projects under its successful Square Mile programme.

Our inaugural University of the Year for Social Inclusion for 2018–19, DMU opened in 1870 as an art school, providing education and training for workers from Leicester's booming industries. Today one in 10 working-age Leicester residents studies at DMU, the impact report showed. The university's transformative programme of campus developments has amounted to £24m of investment per year since 2007.

The Vijay Patel Building, which brought all art and design courses together for the first time, includes the city's largest display space – and was named the region's best new educational building. The restoration of Leicester Castle, where the university's business school occupies the Great Hall, won an East Midlands construction award.

More than half of DMU students are from black, Asian and minority ethnic (BAME) backgrounds, and just under half are from families where neither parent went to university. The university is determined to reduce the attainment gap between BAME students and their white peers. It was awarded £230,000 funding from the Office for Students to support Leicester Future Leaders, a three-year programme with national industry partners to increase the number of ethnic minority graduates securing internships, jobs and senior roles in the region's businesses. The university also has a strong reputation for supporting disabled students.

The magazine publisher and radio giant Bauer Media has formed a partnership with DMU to deliver a master's degree for senior leaders, helping to build high-performing teams in the creative sector. Natwest bank has also collaborated with De Montfort to give budding entrepreneurs a leg-up through its flagship pre-accelerator programme, introduced in Leicester.

The economic impact report also found that DMU has the eighth highest number of graduate start-ups of any UK university. Its successful graduate employment record contributed to a gold award in the Teaching Excellence Framework, whose panel also

The Gateway
Leicester LE1 9BH
0116 270 8443
enquiry@dmu.ac.uk
www.dmu.ac.uk
www.demontfortsu.com/
Open days: see website

The Times and The Sunday Times **Rankings**
Overall Ranking: 119 (last year: 74)

Teaching quality	75.2%	119
Student experience	74.6%	110
Research quality	8.9%	=67
Entry standards	111	=111
Graduate prospects	71%	=83
Good honours	72.5%	87
Expected completion rate	81.4%	=90
Student/staff ratio	19.8	=123
Services and facilities	£2,407	70

commended "optimum" levels of contact time between students and staff and "outstanding" support for learning. However, in the new Graduate Outcomes survey, only 71% of graduates had high-skilled jobs or had entered postgraduate study within 15 months of leaving university, placing the university in the bottom half of our ranking on this measure.

Building on its teaching strength, DMU has launched a dedicated Centre for Academic Innovation (CAI), providing lecturers and students with a physical and virtual space to develop new and disruptive learning methods. There was a dip in applications in 2019, but only by 7%. Enrolments fell by 12%. There are 10 higher and degree apprenticeship programmes including policing, architecture, digital and technology solutions, cyber-security and hearing aid dispensing.

The university's #DMUglobal programme broadens horizons for all students by providing opportunities to spend time abroad or learn new languages on campus. In partnership with the United Nations, DMU acts as an ambassador for 17 sustainable development goals and incorporates them in its teaching, research and student activities.

Almost 60% of the university's research was rated world-leading or internationally excellent in the 2014 Research Excellence Framework. Longstanding partnerships with Hewlett-Packard and Deloitte illustrate strong links with business and industry, which feed into innovative training and research collaborations. The Stephen Lawrence Research Centre is one recent example, established to promote social justice on a local, national and global scale.

The university has 4,600 rooms in 14 halls of residence, but only international students are guaranteed a place if they apply by the end of July. The excellent sports facilities include a 25-metre swimming pool and an £8m leisure centre. Outdoor pitches, five miles to the north and served by free buses, have had a £3.4m upgrade.

Almost £1m has been spent on coaching and support for DMU's sports teams and there are partnerships with Leicester City football club, Leicester Tigers rugby club, Leicestershire County Cricket Club and Leicester Ladies' Hockey Club.

One of the UK's most diverse cities, Leicester has benefited from £3bn in regeneration funds since the millennium. Private-sector rents are low and most university accommodation is within walking distance of the city centre.

Tuition fees

» Fees for UK students	£9,250
Foundation courses	£6,165
» Fees for International students 2021–22	£14,250–£14,750
» For scholarship and bursary information see www.dmu.ac.uk/study/fees-and-funding/index.aspx	
» Graduate salary	£22,000

Student numbers

Undergraduates	20,436	(1,316)
Postgraduates	2,573	(1,487)
Applications/places	23,235/4,815	
Applications per place	4.8	
Overall offer rate	82.3%	
International students – EU	4.5%	
Non-EU	15.9%	

Accommodation

University provided places: 4,100
Self-catered: £99–£197 per week
www.dmu.ac.uk/study/undergraduate-study/accommodation/index.aspx

Where do the students come from?

State schools (non-grammar)	94.9%	First generation students	49.7%	Black attainment gap	-25.1%
Grammar schools	2.8%	Deprived areas	14.8%	Disabled	9.3%
Independent schools	2.3%	All ethnic minorities	53.5%	Mature (over 21)	13.5%

Social inclusion ranking: =40

University of Derby

Teaching and learning at Derby enjoys a strong reputation. The university holds gold – the highest accreditation – in the government's Teaching Excellence Framework, whose judging panel praised Derby's personalised learning and support. Its high standards were also recognised with a Times Higher Education Teaching and Learning Strategy Award in 2018. Rankings in the top 25 for student satisfaction with both teaching quality and the wider student experience back up the official findings.

The university's commitment to furthering teaching quality is ongoing. Its Learning and Teaching Strategy is based on three pillars: student employability, teaching quality and research in the curriculum. A progressive approach to feedback and assessment methods – often a bone of contention in student satisfaction surveys – aims to lead the higher education sector by deploying practices such as self- and peer-evaluation.

Derby was the first university to sign the Student Success Framework memorandum with Advance HE, which promotes excellence in higher education, and has focused especially on the digital offering lately. All undergraduates have access to one-to-one academic tutor sessions whenever they need them, and the university's Centre for Excellence in Learning and Teaching works with staff and students on all aspects of learning, teaching, assessment and digital practice.

More than £200m has been invested in modern facilities over the past decade. Students experience hands-on learning in "real-world" simulation environments such as a crime scene house for forensic science students, a replica crown court, a Bloomberg financial markets lab and an NHS-standard hospital ward. Hospitality courses benefit from industry-standard kitchens and a fine dining restaurant. The Devonshire spa is an award-winning commercial day spa that doubles as a classroom for spa management students.

A shuttle bus links the university's three bases in Derby. Kedleston Road is the biggest campus, home to the students' union, multi-faith centre and the main sports facilities. Most teaching subjects are hosted here, too, as well as clinical skills facilities such as a full-body iDXA scanner, which measures body fat and muscle mass to help top-level athletes achieve peak condition.

The Markeaton Street site hosts arts, design, engineering and technology courses, while courses including fine art and social care are based at Britannia Mill, 10 minutes' walk away. The 550-seat Derby Theatre is in the city centre and there are ambitious plans to create a university quarter. A plan to develop a new business school on a car park site purchased in 2018 has been mooted.

Nursing has a school of its own in the market

Kedleston Road
Derby DE22 1GB
01332 590 500
admissions@derby.ac.uk
www.derby.ac.uk
www.derbyunion.co.uk
Open days: See website

The Times and The Sunday Times **Rankings**

Overall Ranking: =94 (last year: 91)

Teaching quality	83%	=19
Student experience	80.4%	24
Research quality	2.5%	117
Entry standards	118	94
Graduate prospects	68.7%	98
Good honours	66.9%	=116
Expected completion rate	78.3%	109
Student/staff ratio	14.6	=39
Services and facilities	£1,957	101

town of Chesterfield, in a former girls' school, to accommodate the growing demand for places and to keep teaching up to date. Engineering and IT is also taught in Chesterfield, and the university has an innovation centre there.

In the spa town of Buxton, the university's operations are based in the Devonshire Dome, formerly the Devonshire Royal Hospital, where courses include hospitality management.

Accelerated degrees in professional policing and in law welcomed their first cohort of students in 2020. Courses in biomedical health and in environmental sustainability are joining the curriculum in 2021.

Derby also offers degree apprenticeships in 19 subject areas including nursing and allied health, digital technology, civil engineering and policing. The university is working with the NHS to develop apprenticeships in prosthetics and orthotics, and podiatry. There will be about 1,400 apprenticeship students by September 2021.

Bursary and scholarship provision is exceptionally broad, and about three-quarters of admissions received a financial award of some sort in 2020. Bursaries are paid according to household income, starting with £100 e-cards for study resources, up to £900 cash plus the £100 e-card. Academic achievement awards of £1,000 are made in the first year to students with upwards of BBB/120 UCAS tariff points, or ABB/128 points for certain health courses.

Derby monitors the results of its dedicated programme of outreach activities to widen participation. In September 2019 there were 1,176 students who enrolled from target schools and colleges. Nearly a third of them were from the most disadvantaged areas. The university moves up four places in our social inclusion ranking into the UK top 20.

Links with local industry include work placements at Microsoft and IBM and internships at car manufacturers including Porsche, Bentley, Rolls-Royce and the locally-based Toyota. The new Graduate Outcomes data, which measures the proportion of graduates in high-skilled jobs or postgraduate study 15 months after leaving, put Derby at 62.4%, just outside the top 100.

Only 19% of Derby's eligible academics were entered for the 2014 Research Excellence Framework, although nearly 30% of the university's submission was placed in the top two categories.

All first-years are guaranteed accommodation following a £30m, five-year investment to offer nearly 3,000 places. The sports centre has a 70-station fitness gym, squash courts, sports hall, climbing wall and adjacent outdoor pitches.

Tuition fees

- » Fees for UK students — £9,250
- » Fees for International students 2020–21 — £14,045–£14,700
- » For scholarship and bursary information see www.derby.ac.uk/study/fees-and-finance/
- » Graduate salary — £22,000

Student numbers

Undergraduates	11,894 (2,882)
Postgraduates	1,605 (2,766)
Applications/places	16,825/2,785
Applications per place	6
Overall offer rate	80.7%
International students – EU	4.6%
Non-EU	4.7%

Accommodation

University provided places: 2,999
Self-catered: £110–£162 per week
First years guaranteed accommodation
www.derby.ac.uk/life/accommodation/

Where do the students come from?

State schools (non-grammar)	96.4%	First generation students	52.3%	Black attainment gap	-26.1%
Grammar schools	1.6%	Deprived areas	24.4%	Disabled	10.2%
Independent schools	2%	All ethnic minorities	24%	Mature (over 21)	37.5%

Social inclusion ranking: =17

University of Dundee

The University of Dundee has initiated the Eden Project Scotland proposal with Dundee city council and the Eden Project, to investigate whether it would be feasible to host an outpost of the Cornish gardens and biomes. The university has experience in attracting landmark cultural developments to the region, having played a founding role in bringing the V&A to Dundee. The architectural masterpiece on the city's River Tay waterfront is widely considered a resounding success.

The university is world-renowned for its strength in the life sciences, and Dundee is leading the Tay Cities Biomedical Cluster with NHS Tayside. The Scottish government has earmarked £25m initial funding through the Tay Cities Deal for the project, which will feature an innovation hub for new life sciences companies and a medical device research and development facility, and is designed to promote growth in the region.

Dundee's school of life sciences and medicine was awarded the Gold Watermark in 2017 for its public engagement work. During the Covid-19 outbreak it pivoted its focus to work on developing vaccines and treatments for the coronavirus and future infections.

The first students on Dundee's new double degree in biomedical engineering at the Northeastern University in Shenyang, China, started their courses in autumn 2019. Academic staff from the two partner universities are delivering teaching and students will complete the final year of the four-year programme in Dundee. The course is anticipated to grow from the initial cohort of almost 120 students to 500, who will be skilled in ultrasound, CT and MRI scanning, as well as image-guided surgery.

Outstanding student satisfaction scores were the driving force behind our Student Experience award for Dundee in 2019–20, and it finished in the elite top 20 again in 2020 for the wider student experience. The teaching quality score given by students has slipped back more significantly, but still ranks in the UK top 50.

Dundee has spent £200m redeveloping its campus, partly designed by the leading architect, Sir Terry Farrell. The £50m Discovery Centre encourages interaction between different disciplines. Away from the city centre, the medical school is on a 20-acre site, while nursing and midwifery students are 35 miles away in Kirkcaldy. The highly-rated design courses are taught at the Duncan of Jordanstone College of Art, which has become one of the university's 10 schools.

Dundee was one of just three Scottish universities to be awarded gold by the Teaching Excellence Framework (TEF) panel. Assessors commended the opportunities students have to develop work-ready skills and knowledge, and said courses encourage ideal levels of stretch and student engagement. Students from all

Nethergate
Dundee DD1 4HN
01382 383 838
contactus@dundee.ac.uk
www.dundee.ac.uk
www.dusa.co.uk
Open days: see website

The Times and The Sunday Times **Rankings**
Overall Ranking: =23 (last year: 24)

Teaching quality	80.9%	45
Student experience	80.7%	=19
Research quality	31.2%	41
Entry standards	176	10
Graduate prospects	84.4%	15
Good honours	76.5%	56
Expected completion rate	87.7%	48
Student/staff ratio	14.3	=30
Services and facilities	£2,779	38

backgrounds achieve outstanding outcomes at Dundee, the TEF report found.

The university's global reputation continues to grow, and undergraduate applications from overseas for admission in September 2020 had surged by 35% before the Covid-19 pandemic.

In the 2014 Research Excellence Framework Dundee was top for biological sciences and the university attracts students from all over the world in this area. It also offers a joint degree with the National University of Singapore. However, excellence runs much wider: Dundee was in the top three in the UK for research in civil engineering and in the top 10 for maths and general engineering.

Dundee's research in the field of male fertility is working towards developing a male pill, among other projects. Dr Sarah Martins da Silva from the medical school was named on the BBC's 100 Women list in 2019 in recognition of her inspirational and influential work to solve the problem of male infertility.

There is also the Leverhulme Research Centre for Forensic Science, a £10m, 10-year research centre drawing on forensic scientists, legal practitioners and members of the public to improve the use and understanding of science in the justice system. It received the Gold Watermark for public engagement in 2019.

Bursaries of £2,000 a year are available for students from low-income families. Academic excellence scholarships encourage top entry standards, awarded to applicants from the rest of the UK (at £3,000 per year of study) and to international students (at £5,000 per year of study, capped at £25,000). There are also scholarships for refugees. Dundee's scholarships and bursaries spend is more than £1.5m for overseas students alone, an outgoing the university expects to remain the same in 2021.

Ranking sixth in Scotland for social inclusion, Dundee does well to attract applications from students from disadvantaged backgrounds. Outreach activities in schools and communities combine with support for access students as they prepare for higher education. The university's summer schools have helped more than 3,000 students who otherwise might not have considered higher education.

Sports facilities are excellent and the university has one of Scotland's most active students' unions. Dundee has a lot to offer for student life, with low rents, a lively social scene and the buzz of a city in the ascendant.

Tuition fees

- » Fees for Scottish students   £0–£1,820
  RUK fees   £9,250
- » Fees for International students 2021–22   £18,950–£22,950
  Medicine £46,380; Dentistry £49,200 (clinical years)
- » For scholarship and bursary information see
  www.dundee.ac.uk/study/tuition-fees/
- » Graduate salary   £24,000

Student numbers

Undergraduates	9,938 (1,489)
Postgraduates	2,186 (2,301)
Applications/places	21,985/2,635
Applications per place	8.3
Overall offer rate	48.8%
International students – EU	5.6%
Non-EU	10.8%

Accommodation

University provided places: 1,587
Self-catered: £128–£158 per week
First years guaranteed accommodation
www.dundee.ac.uk/accommodation

Where do the students come from?

State schools (non-grammar)	83.5%	First generation students	39.5%
Grammar schools	5.7%	Deprived areas	16.2%
Independent schools	10.7%	All ethnic minorities	9.7%

Social inclusion ranking (Scotland): 6

Black attainment gap	-6.5%
Disabled	3.6%
Mature (over 21)	24.6%

Durham University

Durham is a university in transition on several fronts. It is expanding rapidly to welcome 21,500 students by 2027 within the small cathedral city, while opening new colleges and teaching buildings to accommodate them, and working hard to diversify its intake. Applications hit a new high in 2019, cresting 30,000 for the first time, with admissions also at record levels.

The fruits of this strategy are becoming more visible with South College opening its doors for the first time in September 2020 and John Snow College moving into new buildings next door, having operated previously in the university's now-closed outpost in Stockton-on-Tees. Further new colleges are planned as the university works towards its target of housing half of all students in university-owned accommodation.

The opening of a new teaching and learning centre in September 2019 proved timely. Its classrooms allow students to share courses in real time with their peers around the world, a facility that will come in particularly useful in the post-Covid world. By 2027, Durham is aiming for 35% of students to be international. Durham's Encore system means lectures were already being recorded ahead of the pandemic for students to replay at their convenience and the university's IT systems are benefiting from a £25m upgrade.

Two new degrees – in accounting, and mathematics and statistics – recruited their first students in September 2020. A £40m new building for mathematical sciences and computer science is nearing completion and there are plans for a new business school on the banks of the River Wear within the university's wider estates masterplan. A £32m upgrade of sports facilities has also come on stream.

The third-oldest university in England, Durham is one of the few collegiate universities in the UK. The colleges are social rather than academic groupings, of vastly differing sizes and atmospheres. They range from Collingwood, one of the modern so-called hill colleges on the south side of the city, which has more than 1,500 students, to St Chad's College, a much more intimate community of 550 students, located in historic buildings next door to the cathedral.

All the colleges are within comfortable walking distance of each other and students make frequent use of the bars and leisure facilities at colleges other than their own. Students can express a preference of college on their applications, but college principals have far less say in who goes where nowadays, with places largely allocated according to an algorithm. Wherever they end up, students seem to enjoy their time here, with just

---

The Palatine Centre
Stockton Road
Durham DH1 3LE
0191 334 1000
www.durham.ac.uk/study/askus
www.dur.ac.uk
www.durhamsu.com
Open days: see website

The Times and The Sunday Times **Rankings**
Overall Ranking: 6 (last year: 7)

Teaching quality	79%	=76
Student experience	76.2%	=93
Research quality	39%	16
Entry standards	188	7
Graduate prospects	87%	7
Good honours	91.7%	4
Expected completion rate	95.6%	6
Student/staff ratio	14.7	=41
Services and facilities	£3,498	9

2.7% predicted to drop out, well below the expected level.

When they leave, 87% end up in a high-skilled job or postgraduate study, according to the new Graduate Outcomes survey, published for the first time in 2020, helping the university gain a place in the top 10 on this measure. And the longstanding High Fliers survey of the leading graduate employers ranks Durham as the 11th most-targeted university.

A member of the research-led Russell Group since 2012, Durham reached the top five in a quarter of the subject areas submitted to the Research Excellence Framework in 2014 – English, classics, chemistry, law, anthropology, archaeology, education, physics, theology and music – and 80% of its academics' work was judged world-leading or internationally excellent.

Durham has set out its stall in its access and participation plan to shed its image as one of the bastions of middle- and upper-class privilege in the higher education sector. Next to bottom in our social inclusion ranking, 10 students are recruited from places with the highest participation in higher education for every one recruited from those with the lowest participation rates. The university is aiming to cut that ratio to 3:1 by 2024–25.

It also aims to recruit 100 more UK-domiciled black students by the same time, addressing a longstanding issue. The proportion of students recruited from private schools is down from 38.7% to 34.3% in the latest figures, the lowest proportion in the history of this guide but still the seventh highest in the UK.

The university's Durham Grant Scheme offers £2,000 a year to students from homes where the household income is less than £25,000, with a sliding level of support offered up to £42,875. A recent donation of £2m from cash-and-carry millionaire alumnus Charles Wilson was specifically targeted at recruiting more students to the university from poorer backgrounds in the northeast.

Sport is played regularly by around three-quarters of all students, partly as a result of often intense college rivalries. However, elite sport flourishes too, and Durham has established itself as one of Britain's leading sporting universities. Former England cricket captains Andrew Strauss and Nasser Hussain are Durham graduates. There are national centres of excellence in cricket, fencing, lacrosse, rugby union, tennis and rowing.

Tuition fees

» Fees for UK students £9,250
» Fees for International students 2021–22 £21,730–£27,350
» For scholarship and bursary information see www.dur.ac.uk/student.finance/
» Graduate salary £27,000

Student numbers

Undergraduates	14,208	(113)
Postgraduates	3,539	(1,165)
Applications/places	30,710/4,485	
Applications per place	6.8	
Overall offer rate	76.6%	
International students – EU	5.6%	
Non-EU	24.6%	

Accommodation

University provided places: 6,479
Catered costs: £202–£215 per week
Self-catered: £142–£154 per week
First years guaranteed accommodation
www.dur.ac.uk/experience/colleges/accommodation/

Where do the students come from?

State schools (non-grammar)	48.7%	First generation students	23.2%
Grammar schools	16.9%	Deprived areas	5.4%
Independent schools	34.3%	All ethnic minorities	11.7%

Social inclusion ranking: 115

Black attainment gap	-14%
Disabled	5.2%
Mature (over 21)	4.3%

University of East Anglia

The University of East Anglia (UEA) opened its New Science Building in 2019, with cutting-edge equipment on four floors to encourage collaboration across disciplines on the campus on the edge of Norwich. The £30m, 7,000 square-metre development has been designed to have some of the most accessible Stem (science, technology, engineering and maths) facilities in the country, with wheelchair-friendly laboratories and hearing loops in all teaching spaces.

Focusing on student engagement and wellbeing, the university has rolled out a new continuous improvement platform, the Enlitened App. A forum for students to access tailored information and to submit ideas for improvements, the app is designed by The Student Room, the widely used national online student community. Every faculty now has student services embedded within it, to make it easier for students to get help with their studies, student life and the UEA community.

The introduction of the app and the embedded faculty teams, which work closely with central student services and academic advisers, come after a petition signed by 5,000 students calling for better mental health services. The moves have contributed to improvement in scores in the 2020 National Student Survey, notably those parts measuring satisfaction with teaching quality.

Twenty-five new degree courses were introduced for 2020, most adding the option of a year abroad, working in industry or a foundation year to existing programmes. An even bigger tranche of 34 new courses joins the curriculum in 2021, again adding new options to established courses such as geophysics, and meteorology and oceanography with placement years. There are plenty of standalone new courses as well, ranging from film and television production to law with criminology.

UEA achieved gold in the government's Teaching Excellence Framework (TEF), earning praise for its "strategic approach to personalised learning, which secures high levels of commitment to studies". The TEF panel also noted that investment in high-quality physical and digital resources have had a demonstrable impact on the learning experience. These include a media suite in the arts and humanities faculty, a £19m Biomedical Research Centre for medical students and the Enterprise Centre, dedicated to supporting entrepreneurial skills.

Work experience opportunities are built into most degrees and recent graduates can tap into UEA's paid internship programme, taking placements at businesses in the eastern region for periods of between four weeks and a year. The university is in the top 40 in the country for graduate prospects according to the latest Higher Education Statistics Agency figures, with 80% in high-skilled jobs or postgraduate study 15 months after finishing their courses.

Norwich Research Park
Norwich NR4 7TJ
01603 591 515
admissions@uea.ac.uk
www.uea.ac.uk
www.uea.su
Open days: see website

The Times and The Sunday Times **Rankings**
Overall Ranking: 21 (last year: 23)

Teaching quality	80.7%	=48
Student experience	79.1%	47
Research quality	35.8%	32
Entry standards	138	47
Graduate prospects	79.6%	37
Good honours	84.7%	21
Expected completion rate	87.8%	=46
Student/staff ratio	13.5	19
Services and facilities	£2,924	23

Of the six degree apprenticeships offered, five cover health sector roles – a focus UEA hopes to expand. The university expects to have between 600 and 650 degree apprentices on programmes by September 2021.

Environmental science has long been recognised as UEA's flagship subject area. Its Climatic Research Unit and the Tyndall Centre for Climate Change Research, funded by a consortium of universities and the Chinese government, are among the leading investigators of climate change.

In the 2014 Research Excellence Framework, social work and pharmacy led UEA's results, and 82% of all work submitted was placed in one of the top two categories. The £75m Quadram Institute based on Norwich Research Park has joined UEA's research facilities, with the remit of improving health and preventing disease through innovations in microbiology, gut health and food.

The Sainsbury Centre for the Visual Arts houses a priceless collection of modern and tribal art in a building designed by Sir Norman Foster.

More bursaries were expected to be paid in 2020 than in 2019, when 22% of undergraduates received one. Awards are £800 or £1,300 per year of study depending on household income, or £2,500 for care leavers. Students receive them mainly as fee waivers, though accommodation discounts or cash grants are available. Bright spark scholarships of £3,000 over three years are awarded to new entrants who have gone above and beyond their entry requirements.

UEA makes contextual offers or guarantees interviews to applicants from widening participation programmes.

UAE is a 1960s campus university set in 320 acres of parkland on the edge of Norwich, England's first Unesco City of Literature and named one of the best places to live by *The Sunday Times* in 2020. Many of the original campus buildings are listed, including the iconic Denys Lasdun-designed Ziggurat accommodation blocks. There are 4,226 residential spaces, enough for all first-years to be guaranteed a room.

UEA's Sportspark and Colney Lane Sports Pavilion have extensive on-site facilities including an Olympic-sized swimming pool and fitness centre, five sports halls, a climbing wall and pitches for rugby, cricket and football. The students' union hosts more than 200 clubs and societies, and organises the unique Pimp My Barrow event, where students parade and race customised wheelbarrows to raise money for charity.

Tuition fees

» Fees for UK students £9,250
» Fees for International students 2021–22 £17,100–£19,800
  Medicine £33,500
» For scholarship and bursary information see
  www.uea.ac.uk/study/fees-and-funding/funding-options/
» Graduate salary £24,000

Student numbers

Undergraduates	12,799	(418)
Postgraduates	3,231	(1,479)
Applications/places		21,905/3,870
Applications per place		5.7
Overall offer rate		80.9%
International students – EU		4.8%
Non-EU		16.4%

Accommodation

University provided places: 4,226
Self-catered: £79–£171 per week
First years guaranteed accommodation
www.uea.ac.uk/uea-life/accommodation

Where do the students come from?

State schools (non-grammar)	79.1%	First generation students	39.5%	Black attainment gap	-9%
Grammar schools	10.2%	Deprived areas	11.8%	Disabled	6.9%
Independent schools	10.8%	All ethnic minorities	22.2%	Mature (over 21)	12.8%

Social inclusion ranking: 76

University of East London

Under its Vision 2028 strategy, the University of East London (UEL) is forging ahead to position itself as a university fit for the fourth industrial revolution, where students learn the skills, emotional intelligence and creativity needed in today's evolving careers landscape. A contemporary logo supports the rebranding, incorporating the phoenix from UEL's traditional coat of arms with an Olympic torch – in honour of its connection to London's 2012 Games – and cogs symbolising the university's role in the community and its links with industry.

UEL's ambition is to become the UK's leading careers-focused, enterprising university – while operating sustainably and inclusively. Underpinning this is a Professional Fitness and Mental Wealth programme which inserts a module promoting cognitive intelligence, digital proficiency and developing cultural capital into each year of study. Some skills are validated externally by companies such as Amazon and Microsoft; others managed internally by UEL's employment hub. Designed to help graduates stand out in the digital economy, they count towards final results, and are recorded in a digital career passport.

UEL's Docklands campus in the shadow of Canary Wharf was the first new campus in London for 50 years, and its striking waterside buildings have become synonymous with the area's regeneration. Stratford, where the original headquarters are based, is near the Queen Elizabeth Olympic Park, and has been the focus of recent developments. It is the location for a joint venture with Birkbeck, University of London, offering subjects including law, performing arts, dance, music and information technology as daytime or evening courses.

Almost half of UEL's undergraduates are 21 or older on entry – many choosing to start courses in February rather than in the autumn. A guidance unit advises local people considering returning to education. Rio 2016 Paralympian shot-putter Vanessa Wallace (formerly Daobry), took part in the university's New Beginnings courses. Up to 10 weeks long, these show prospective mature students what degree study involves and allow successful participants to move on to a range of degree courses.

The curriculum is being transformed: placement and foundation years were added in about 25 subjects for 2020, plus around 20 new degrees are joining the curriculum in subjects including international law with legal practice, youth work, media and communication, interior design and artificial intelligence. A suite of MBAs is also new.

There are nine degree apprenticeships in the fields of management, civil engineering, nursing, teaching and digital technology and UEL expects more than 200 degree apprentices on its programmes in 2021.

Docklands Campus
University Way
London E16 2RD
020 8223 3333
study@uel.ac.uk
www.uel.ac.uk
www.uelunion.org
Open days: see website

The Times and The Sunday Times Rankings		
Overall Ranking: 129 (last year: 127)		
Teaching quality	78.6%	=80
Student experience	75.5%	=103
Research quality	7.2%	76
Entry standards	111	=111
Graduate prospects	59.7%	=125
Good honours	70.3%	110
Expected completion rate	73.1%	124
Student/staff ratio	19.7	=121
Services and facilities	£1,699	124

UEL is one of only 11 universities in our table awarded bronze in the government's Teaching Excellence Framework (TEF) and was unsuccessful in appealing to be upgraded to silver. Low graduate employment rates were the main stumbling block. They are also one of the factors accounting for its ranking in the bottom 10 of our table, with just 60% of graduates in high-skilled jobs or postgraduate study 15 months after leaving.

Students here are also among the least content with their overall university experience, results from the National Student Survey reveal. In 2020 UEL ranked outside the top 100 for student experience, although it performed better for student satisfaction with teaching quality, ranking joint 80th.

For social inclusion, however, UEL is hugely successful and is placed 12th in our dedicated table. Just under 70% of undergraduates are from ethnic minority populations and more than half are the first in their family to go to university. UEL does better at keeping students on courses, too, and has a projected dropout rate of 12.9%, considerably lower than the 18.5% expected according to the academic and social background of its intake.

UEL's Noon Centre for Equality and Diversity in Business helps black, Asian and minority ethnic (BAME) students to prepare for successful careers. Almost 1,000 businesses take part in mentoring programmes and/or offer accredited placements.

World-class research doubled in the 2014 Research Excellence Framework compared with the 2008 assessments: 62% of the work submitted reached the top two categories. The university was ranked first equal in England for the impact of its research in psychology.

Accommodation is guaranteed for first-years in the university's supply of nearly 1,200 spaces. Campus social life centres around the Docklands student village, though Stratford has the edge as a destination off campus. Hipsters flock to the east of the capital and UEL students are in the thick of the area's fashionable haunts.

UEL has built on the legacy of the 2012 London Olympics. The institution's high-performing sports programme offers £2m in scholarships and bursaries. Jona Efoloko, the World under-20 200m gold medallist, and Shannon Hylton, who won gold in the 4x100m at the 2018 Athletics World Cup, are among the university's 150 sports scholars. The university has also trained two-times Olympian sprinter Adam Gemili and Bianca Williams, who helped England to 4x100m relay gold in the 2018 Commonwealth Games.

Tuition fees

» Fees for UK students	£9,250
» Fees for International students 2020–21	£12,700
» For scholarship and bursary information see www.uel.ac.uk/undergraduate/fees-and-funding	
» Graduate salary	£23,000

Student numbers

Undergraduates	9,013	(736)
Postgraduates	2,330	(1,317)
Applications/places		16,385/2,085
Applications per place		7.9
Overall offer rate		71.4%
International students – EU		3.7%
Non-EU		10.3%

Accommodation

University provided places: 1,169
Self-catered: £148–£193 per week
www.uel.ac.uk/accommodation

Where do the students come from?

State schools (non-grammar)	97.4%	First generation students	54.6%	
Grammar schools	1.1%	Deprived areas	7%	
Independent schools	1.5%	All ethnic minorities	69.4%	

Social inclusion ranking: 12

Black attainment gap	-24%
Disabled	6.9%
Mature (over 21)	49.5%

Edge Hill University

The first trainee doctors at Edge Hill Medical School are enjoying the benefits of the university's new clinical skills and simulation centre. Students on other health and social care courses can also use the facilities, which feature simulations of wards, an operating theatre and consultation rooms, as well as ultrasound resources and the Better at Home suite, where parents and carers can learn to look after people outside hospital.

The medical school welcomed its first students in September 2020 following the introduction of a foundation year in 2019. The scheme aims to widen participation in medical training, targeting pupils from schools in the northwest with below-average performance and accepting applicants with results three grades lower than those required of students entering the first year of the five-year programme.

England's only Unesco Bioethics Unit has been set up at the medical school, tackling ethical issues in healthcare. The school also houses the North West Institute of Radiology, and the university is launching a physician associate MSc in response to demand from the region. An integrated master's degree (MSci) is being pioneered to train nurse paramedics, and new programmes in biomedical sciences and anatomy have joined Edge Hill's portfolio of health courses.

The university's Ormskirk campus in Lancashire has benefited from £300m investment in capital developments over the past decade. When the £27m Catalyst building opened in 2018, study spaces were increased by half. The £13m Tech Hub has industry-standard equipment for biotechnology laboratories, putting Edge Hill at the forefront of genetic technology and supporting research in the prevention of diseases, DNA sequencing, cloning and treatments.

Edge Hill gained university status in 2005 and its ascent of our league table has made it consistently one of the 10 leading post-1992 institutions. However, lukewarm results from the most recent National Student Survey have contributed to a dip in its overall ranking in 2020.

Creative Edge, a £17m complex for the departments of media and computing, allows students to cut their teeth on industry-standard studios for television, animation, sound, photography and radio. There is also a multimedia laboratory. Elsewhere on the 160-acre campus, a performance studio has been created out of a converted 1930s swimming pool.

Edge Hill has been training teachers since the 19th century and is still one of the UK's largest providers of secondary teacher training and courses for classroom assistants. A new education piazza next to the Faculty of Education's Lakeside building has added more space for secondary-level and further education courses.

The university was one of only three in the northwest of England to be awarded gold in

St Helens Road
Ormskirk L39 4QP
01695 650 950
admissions@edgehill.ac.uk
www.edgehill.ac.uk
www.edgehillsu.org.uk
Open days: see website

The Times and The Sunday Times **Rankings**

Overall Ranking: 70 (last year: 55)

Teaching quality	78%	=92
Student experience	76.7%	=86
Research quality	4.9%	=93
Entry standards	130	=56
Graduate prospects	72%	=75
Good honours	71.3%	=97
Expected completion rate	84.2%	=64
Student/staff ratio	14	26
Services and facilities	£2,587	52

the first round of assessment by the Teaching Excellence Framework. The panel noted that "students from diverse backgrounds achieve consistently outstanding outcomes". Almost all the students are state-educated and the projected dropout rate (8.7%) is substantially better than the university's benchmark (12.2%).

Edge Hill's successful outreach work has contributed to a student population where 18% come from areas with the lowest rates of participation in higher education. A seven-week fast-track programme for adults offers an alternative route to entry, outside published UCAS course tariffs. A £1.1m financial package benefits 1,000 students each year, awarding non-means-tested academic scholarships to high-achieving students already studying, as well as new recruits.

Along with medicine, eight further degrees joined Edge Hill's curriculum in 2020, including a suite of nursing degrees, religion, systems automation and biomedical science. Undergraduates joining in 2021 will also have the options of electronic engineering, computer science and artificial intelligence, education and mathematics, and contemporary mental health practice. The new computer science-related programmes are part of the university's longer-term vision to boost its engineering activity and complement work in biotechnology, robotics and automation.

All arts and science undergraduates can take a sandwich year in industry or a year studying abroad. Every student has a personal tutor, as well as access to counsellors and financial advice.

English, sport and media produced the best results in the 2014 Research Excellence Framework. Two new research centres have been introduced in 2020: the International Centre on Racism and the Centre for Child Protection and Safeguarding in Sport.

Student accommodation in the elegant 1930s-designed Main Building has been refurbished and all first-years are guaranteed a residential space on campus. Some of the 2,498 rooms come with a catering allowance.

A free shuttle bus connects the campus with Ormskirk. Edge Hill's £30m sports centre has an eight-court sports hall, 25-metre swimming pool, 80-station fitness suite, aerobics studio and health suite with sauna and steam rooms. Outdoors, there is a trim trail with exercise stations, a running track, rugby, hockey and football pitches, an athletics field and netball and tennis courts. There are two lakes and La Plage is Edge Hill's sandy beach on the Eastern campus.

Tuition fees

» Fees for UK students	£9,250
Foundation courses	£6,165
» Fees for International students 2021–22	£12,500
» For scholarship and bursary information see www.edgehill.ac.uk/studentservices/moneyadvice	
» Graduate salary	£23,000

Student numbers

Undergraduates	9,517	(895)
Postgraduates	1,285	(2,137)
Applications/places		15,210/3,015
Applications per place		5
Overall offer rate		72.2%
International students – EU		0.7%
Non-EU		1.8%

Accommodation

University provided places: 2,489
Catered cost: £112
Self-catered: £60–£140 per week
First years guaranteed accommodation
www.edgehill.ac.uk/study/accommodation

Where do the students come from?

State schools (non-grammar)	96.6%	First generation students	55.3%	Black attainment gap	-13%
Grammar schools	2.2%	Deprived areas	18%	Disabled	6.2%
Independent schools	1.2%	All ethnic minorities	8%	Mature (over 21)	24.9%

Social inclusion ranking: 42

University of Edinburgh

World-leading research at Edinburgh helped to secure a top-20 place again in the latest QS World University rankings, published in summer 2020. In the UK it also makes a welcome appearance in our top 20 for the first time in a decade despite stubbornly low scores for student satisfaction, ranking in the bottom 10 for teaching quality and the wider student experience.

For all health and welfare issues, students have a new £8m Health and Wellbeing Centre, recently opened on Bistro Square, near the students' union buildings and McEwan Hall – the grand venue for graduation ceremonies and flagship lectures. The centre houses a medical practice and pharmacy, counselling and disability services, with 36 one-to-one consultation rooms and a wellbeing lounge for moments of peace or pop-up events promoting better mental health and wellbeing.

The wellbeing centre and other initiatives to boost contentment in the student community – such as personal tutors and peer support – should start to bear fruit in the National Survey of Students in the coming years. A new role, vice-principal students, was created in 2019 to drive a culture recognising that teaching, learning and the student experience are equally as important as research.

An ancient university, opened in 1583,

Edinburgh has much to be proud of – and now counts being at the cutting edge of informatics among its academic strengths. It has the largest computing department in Europe and is to host the £79m national supercomputer, Archer2.

Building on the university's expertise in technology, Edinburgh and the surrounding southeast Scotland region aims to become Europe's data capital. Under the City Region Deal, five data-driven innovation hubs are being established at the university, tasked with tackling society's big issues such as climate change, space exploration and food production using high-speed data analytics.

Edinburgh has more future-facing projects in the pipeline, such as a commitment to becoming carbon-neutral by 2040. The university, which has the third-largest endowment fund of any UK institution, is withdrawing entirely from fossil fuel investments.

Most of the university's buildings border the historic Old Town. The law school has returned to Old College following its refurbishment. Two miles to the south the BioQuarter is a collaboration between the university and public bodies, consolidating Scotland's reputation as a world leader in biomedical science. The Institute for Regeneration and Repair is located here, bringing together Edinburgh researchers from the Centre for Tissue Repair and the Centre for Regenerative Medicine.

Sir Ian Wilmut of Edinburgh's Roslin

33 Buccleuch Place
Edinburgh EH8 9JS
0131 650 4360
https://www.sra.is.ed.ac.uk/
comms/enquiry/
www.ed.ac.uk
www.eusa.ed.ac.uk
Open days: see website

The Times and The Sunday Times Rankings
Overall Ranking: 17 (last year: 25)

Teaching quality	72.8%	=123
Student experience	72.9%	121
Research quality	43.8%	10
Entry standards	187	8
Graduate prospects	81.2%	32
Good honours	89.5%	8
Expected completion rate	93.8%	18
Student/staff ratio	11.9	=7
Services and facilities	£2,379	72

Institute for animal research created Dolly the sheep – the first mammal to be cloned from an adult cell – in 1996. In March 2020 the institute opened the new Large Animal Research Imaging Facility (Larif), where world-leading researchers will seek insights into livestock, genetic modification and human health using CT and MRI scanners.

A new learning in communities degree is planned for 2021, plus a master's in the same subject. Edinburgh's only degree apprenticeship, in data science, expects a larger cohort of 28 in 2021.

The university has worked hard to put widening participation in the spotlight and to lose its exclusive tag. It met government targets for greater diversity three years early, recruiting 11% of 2018's undergraduate intake from the most deprived parts of Scotland. Outreach activities aim to raise aspirations and attainment at partner schools, and targeted applicants may receive a contextual offer that is lower than the standard entry requirements in recognition of the hurdles many will have had to overcome. The university ranks ahead of Glasgow and St Andrews, its two principal academic rivals, in our Scottish social inclusion ranking.

A range of bursaries, some worth up to £8,500 a year, reduce the costs to English, Welsh or Northern Irish undergraduates, who must pay the full tuition fees for all four years of their degree course.

Edinburgh's sports programmes are among the best in the UK, producing past Olympic champions such as the cyclist Sir Chris Hoy and the rower Dame Katherine Grainger. The university has an outdoor centre 80 miles from Edinburgh in a beautiful setting in the southern Highlands. In and around the city there is a network of gyms for student use, where membership packages start at just £15 a year. Students have a choice of 65 sports clubs and can take part in the full range of fixtures from informal games to competitive tournaments.

There are 9,597 residential places, nearly a third of which come with breakfast and evening meals included. All first-years are guaranteed a room.

Edinburgh has international clout as a social and cultural hangout – and students are in the thick of its many attractions. The university has appointed its first director of festival, cultural and city events to strengthen its ties with the venerated Edinburgh Festival and Fringe, both due to return in 2021 after an enforced absence in 2020.

Tuition fees

- » Fees for Scottish students £0–£1,820
- RUK fees £9,250
- » Fees for International students 2020–21 £22,000–£28,950
- Medicine £33,700–£49,900 (clinical years)
- Veterinary medicine £33,500
- » For scholarship and bursary information see www.ed.ac.uk/student-funding
- » Graduate salary £27,000

Student numbers

Undergraduates	21,892	(856)
Postgraduates	8,810	(2,717)
Applications/places		63,160/6,320
Applications per place		10
Overall offer rate		43.8%
International students – EU		11.1%
Non-EU		27.4%

Accommodation

University provided places: 9,597
Catered costs: £204–£273 per week
Self-catered: £101–£1609per week
First years guaranteed accommodation
www.accom.ed.ac.uk/

Where do the students come from?

State schools (non-grammar)	58.4%	First generation students	21.5%		
Grammar schools	7%	Deprived areas	10.8%		
Independent schools	34.5%	All ethnic minorities	11.3%		

Social inclusion ranking (Scotland): 13

Black attainment gap	4%
Disabled	5.3%
Mature (over 21)	6.3%

Edinburgh Napier University

Edinburgh Napier University has three campuses spread across the Scottish capital. Courses are organised under six schools and students tend to study at one site. Creatives, engineering and computing students are based at Merchiston campus in Bruntsfield, one of Edinburgh's hippest enclaves. The site is home to a 16th-century tower where mathematician John Napier – who inspired the university's name – was born.

Merchiston hosts Screen Academy Scotland, run by the university in partnership with Edinburgh College of Art (now part of the University of Edinburgh), reflecting the institution's strong reputation in film education. The creative arts produced the most successful of Edinburgh Napier's entries for the 2014 Research Excellence Framework.

Students taking arts and creative courses benefit from industry links such as internship and project opportunities on the STV Edinburgh channel. Past schemes have included developing Robert Louis Stevenson Day with Edinburgh Unesco City of Literature Trust and taking part in reading projects in prisons with the Scottish Prisons Service.

A partnership with BBC Scotland's new channel is offering three days of industry insight experience for students throughout the year. A relationship with independent television production company Mentorn Media has involved hosting BBC Scotland's Debate Night on campus – which provided on-set work experience for students.

The campus also boasts a 500-seat computer centre, open 24/7, and is home to a Cyber Academy, cyber-attack simulation suite and expanded computer games laboratory which houses a hub for computing and the creative industries, with fully soundproofed music studios and a broadcast journalism newsroom.

The university's degree in cyber-security and forensics has become the first undergraduate course in the UK to be fully certified by the National Cyber Security Centre, whose parent organisation is GCHQ, the Government Communications Headquarters. Computing students can undertake a year-long work placement in their third year. Elsewhere, many of Edinburgh Napier's courses include work placements of varying lengths.

Under the Student Futures banner, there is one-to-one career guidance, work placement support and engagement with local national and international employers. For start-up founders, specialist advice and free office space is on hand at Bright Red Triangle, Edinburgh Napier's entrepreneur adviser.

The university's business school, opened in the late 1980s by Margaret Thatcher, is at Craiglockhart. Facilities include a lecture theatre known affectionately as "the Egg" due to its curvy architecture, and a historic

---

Sighthill Court
Edinburgh EH11 4BN
0333 900 6040
ugadmissions@napier.ac.uk
www.napier.ac.uk
www.napierstudents.com
Open days:
see website

The Times and The Sunday Times Rankings
Overall Ranking: 63 (last year: 101)

Teaching quality	81.6%	=38
Student experience	80.2%	=27
Research quality	4.6%	=95
Entry standards	152	=31
Graduate prospects	74.3%	63
Good honours	78.8%	=45
Expected completion rate	81.1%	94
Student/staff ratio	18.2	=113
Services and facilities	£2,524	59

wing that was used as a military hospital for shellshocked soldiers in the First World War.

Sighthill, the university's newest campus, is a 20-minute tram journey from the city centre. The base for the schools of nursing, midwifery and social care, and life, sport and social sciences, Sighthill – which as its name suggests enjoys excellent views over Edinburgh – has a five-storey learning resource centre, an environmental chamber and biomechanics laboratory, plus a large simulation and clinical skills centre with mock hospital wards and a high-dependency unit simulator suite.

Three new degrees joined the curriculum in 2020, in football coaching, data science and stage and screen acting. The university is looking to grow its portfolio of degree apprenticeships, which currently has 271 students on 11 programmes in the fields of business, computing, construction and engineering.

Edinburgh Napier's work to widen participation includes subject-specific skills workshops, support for adult learners from Midlothian and extra support for access students before and during their course. The university regularly exceeds its benchmark on widening access measures. One third of undergraduates are over 21 when they enter and just under 40% are the first in their family to go to university.

Undergraduates from Scotland qualify for the national scheme for financial help. Around 83% of students from England, Ireland and Wales qualified for a bursary in 2019 – an increase from 70% the year before. There is an unlimited number of £2,000 or £1,000 awards for students from households where income is below a series of thresholds, and access bursaries of £1,000 are paid each year of study for students who enter with BBB at A-level, or equivalent qualifications.

A well-equipped fitness centre and a sports hall are among the sports facilities, as well as the BT Sport Scottish Rugby Academy. Edinburgh Napier is the official partner of four teams in Scottish Rugby's new Super6 rugby league and the university is Cricket Scotland's official training partner. Team Napier encompasses 36 sports clubs and 30 student societies.

There are 1,240 study bedrooms and all first-years from outside Edinburgh are guaranteed a place. Live-in resident assistants are on duty throughout the night at the halls of residence. As well as being able to help anyone who gets locked out, they are trained in first aid, mental health first aid and conflict management – or are available for a chat, even at unsociable hours.

Tuition fees

» Fees for Scottish students   £0–£1,820
  RUK fees   £9,250 (capped at £27,750 for 4-year courses)
» Fees for International students 2020–21   £13,770–£15,960
» For scholarship and bursary information see
  www.napier.ac.uk/study-with-us/undergraduate/
  fees-and-finance
» Graduate salary   £23,000

Student numbers

Undergraduates	9,217	(1,177)
Postgraduates	2,016	(1,183)
Applications/places		19,480/2,635
Applications per place		7.4
Overall offer rate		55.8%
International students – EU		11.7%
Non-EU		9.3%

Accommodation

University provided places: 1,320
Self-catered: £100–£179 per week
First years guaranteed accommodation
www.napier.ac.uk/study-with-us/accommodation

Where do the students come from?

State schools (non-grammar)	93.7%	First generation students	39.2%	
Grammar schools	1.5%	Deprived areas	12.4%	
Independent schools	4.9%	All ethnic minorities	8.8%	

Social inclusion ranking (Scotland): 7

Black attainment gap	-30.8%
Disabled	5.2%
Mature (over 21)	34.5%

University of Essex

Essex is engaged in an ambitious expansion programme, which has seen enrolments grow by almost one third since 2014 and the number of applications increase at almost the same rate. By 2025, it is hoping to expand its student population by a third, to 20,000. Where some experience growing pains when they get bigger so fast, Essex has been busy collecting awards, earning a shortlisting for our University of the Year title in 2017 and winning the *Times Higher Education* magazine's University of the Year gong a year later.

The constant updating of the course portfolio keeps the offer fresh to prospective students. New degrees launched in 2020 featured six with a foundation year option. These included global studies with human rights, sports performance and coaching, sports and exercise science, sociology with data science, global studies with politics and linguistics with data science.

The global studies options are both available without a foundation year and other new degrees include neural engineering with psychology, social change, film and drama, human biology, philosophy with business management, and art history, visual culture and media studies.

Many of the new offerings build on Essex's strength in the social sciences, where it is ranked in the QS global top 30 for politics and the top 50 for sociology. It has set a target of being a UK top-25 university, which it achieved in 2017 in our ranking, although it has fallen back a little since, not helped by a decline in student satisfaction with their wider university experience in 2020.

Several initiatives contribute to two-thirds of graduates being in high-skilled jobs or postgraduate study 15 months after leaving the university. The student development team works with employers of all sizes to help students gain career insights, work experience, commercial awareness and employability skills, and to expand their business networks. An EmployerLink service connects students and graduates to employers looking to recruit them.

Many degrees have accredited work placement years and work-based learning opportunities as part of their programmes, which also provide real-world business challenges and projects for students to work on where appropriate. Language tuition is free and Essex heavily discounts tuition fees for a full year abroad or a placement year.

Essex took gold in the Teaching Excellence Framework. The panel was impressed that student feedback was being used to develop "rigorous and stretching teaching that is tailored to student needs". It said: "Students from all backgrounds achieve outstanding outcomes with regard

Wivenhoe Park
Colchester CO4 3SQ
01206 873 333
admit@essex.ac.uk
www.essex.ac.uk
www.essexstudent.com
Open days: see website

The Times and The Sunday Times **Rankings**
Overall Ranking: 40 (last year: 37)

Teaching quality	78.8%	79
Student experience	78%	=65
Research quality	37.2%	25
Entry standards	107	=120
Graduate prospects	73.6%	65
Good honours	75.4%	=68
Expected completion rate	84.3%	=62
Student/staff ratio	16.7	=84
Services and facilities	£3,691	7

to continuation and progression to highly skilled employment or further study, notably exceeding the university's benchmark."

The university achieved the best results in the 2014 Research Excellence Framework in politics and was in the top 10 for economics and art history. Essex ranks in the top 25 in our research ranking, with almost 80% of its large submission rated world-leading or internationally excellent.

Facilities on this 1960s-generation university are being refurbished, notably the six iconic Brutalist towers at the heart of the 200-acre Colchester parkland campus. The total refit will see windows, floors, doors and lifts replaced with new entrances to all six buildings. In readiness for a return to face-to-face large-group teaching a new teaching centre, close to the North Towers accommodation, has been completed recently, adding 15 teaching rooms, each with a normal capacity of 40 students.

The £12m Sports Arena, with seating for 1,655 spectators, and 634 rooms in a new residential development opened in 2018, along with a zero-carbon business school. The arena is part of a 40-acre sports area that includes an 18-hole golf course, all-weather tennis courts and room for five-a-side futsal.

Essex's student population is unusually diverse for a pre-1992 university. There are high proportions of mature and international students and just under 97% of the UK undergraduates are state-educated. Almost half are the first in their family to go to university. More than 44% of students are drawn from ethnic minorities.

The average number of UCAS tariff points gained by entrants is now among the lowest in the UK, partly as the result of its widening participation initiatives, which inevitably means admitting students who are less well qualified, making it harder to score highly in one of our key league table measures.

Away from Colchester, the university has outposts in Southend-on-Sea and Loughton. The modern seaside campus offers courses in business, health and the arts, and its accommodation complex houses a gym and fitness studio. The Forum at the heart of the Southend campus has a public and academic library, learning facilities, café and gallery – with a floor reserved for student use.

The East 15 Acting School has a theatre in Southend and another campus in Loughton, which has a new double-height studio available to students.

Tuition fees

» Fees for UK students   £9,250
» Fees for International students 2021–22 £16,850–£19,670
» For scholarship and bursary information see
   www1.essex.ac.uk/fees-and-funding/
» Graduate salary   £23,000

Student numbers

Undergraduates	11,471	(579)
Postgraduates	2,359	(1,189)
Applications/places	20,895/3,675	
Applications per place	5.7	
Overall offer rate	71.7%	
International students – EU	12.8%	
Non-EU	17.5%	

Accommodation

University provided places: 4,341
Self-catered: £102–£1916per week
First years guaranteed accommodation
www1.essex.ac.uk/life/accommodation

Where do the students come from?

State schools (non-grammar)	90.8%	First generation students	46.4%	Black attainment gap	-21.3%
Grammar schools	5.7%	Deprived areas	12.3%	Disabled	3.8%
Independent schools	3.5%	All ethnic minorities	44.6%	Mature (over 21)	17.6%

Social inclusion ranking: =72

University of Exeter

When Steve Smith took over as vice-chancellor of Exeter in 2002, the university ranked 29th in *The Sunday Times* Good University Guide with 7,000 full-time undergraduates and laboured under a "preconception that we are all upper middle-class", according to the president of the guild of students.

Sir Steve stepped down in August 2020, leaving a university in 12th place in our rankings with more than 18,000 full-time undergraduates. The university is close to the bottom of our social inclusion table, however, which may go to prove that you can't change everything at once. Only Oxford and the Royal Agricultural universities admit a greater proportion of their students from independent schools.

Exeter's has been one of the more remarkable transformations during Smith's 18-year tenure. It is one of a small number of institutions to rank consistently higher over recent years, while expanding student numbers sharply and keeping entry standards high. A contextual offer scheme, which offers medical school places at grades of ABB at A-level, aims to broaden the socioeconomic background of the intake. Other courses make offers of BBB for courses that would normally require at least ABB. Almost 2,750 students benefit from the Access to Exeter Bursary, awarded to students who come from households with an annual household income of £25,000 or below. The bursary is worth up to £5,200 over the course of a three-year degree.

Project North Park is one of Exeter's largest infrastructure investments in recent times and will deliver a world-class teaching and research facility at the heart of its picturesque Streatham campus. It will house the Global Systems Institute, the Institute of Data Science and Artificial Intelligence, the Humanities Research Institute, Astrophysics, and the Q-Step Centre, which is part of a UK programme to address the national shortage of numerically-skilled social science graduates.

Overall, Exeter's graduates are much in demand, with 81% of them gaining high-skilled jobs or going into postgraduate study within 15 months of graduating. The university is 12th in the rankings of those most targeted by the leading graduate employers in 2019–20.

Exeter was awarded gold in the Teaching Excellence Framework, attracting praise for "optimum" contact hours and class sizes and for involving business, industry and professional experts in its teaching.

A £72m investment in IT infrastructure could not be coming at a better time with the inevitable shift to greater longer-term online learning as a result of the coronavirus pandemic. Laboratories are also being upgraded and about £20m is being put into engineering facilities.

Northcote House
The Queen's Drive
Exeter EX4 4QJ
0300 555 6060 or 01392 723 044
https://www.exeter.ac.uk/
undergraduate/contact
www.exeter.ac.uk
www.exeterguild.org
Open days: see website

The Times and The Sunday Times **Rankings**
Overall Ranking: 12 (last year: 12)

Teaching quality	78.4%	=84
Student experience	79.3%	=44
Research quality	38%	18
Entry standards	163	=20
Graduate prospects	83.3%	19
Good honours	86.7%	=12
Expected completion rate	94.6%	=11
Student/staff ratio	15.2	=58
Services and facilities	£2,805	35

Exeter is aiming to reduce the pressure on accommodation in the city by completing the East Park, Moberly and Spreytonway student residences on campus by September 2021. These developments will add 1,500 student bedrooms to the current accommodation stock of 6,100 rooms.

Exeter recorded much-improved results in the most recent Research Excellence Framework, in 2014. More than 80% of its large submission was rated world-leading or internationally excellent, with the best results in clinical medicine, psychology and education. A £10m donation from *Sunday Times* Rich Listers Sir Dennis and Mireille Gillings will fund a neuroimaging centre at the medical school to accelerate the diagnosis and treatment of dementia.

Working with Falmouth University, Exeter is ramping up its research outputs in Cornwall. The universities operate the Penryn campus, in Falmouth, as a joint venture and are pouring £11.7m into research facilities there. The campus is home to the newly-opened Renewable Energy Engineering Facility (Reef), which provides specialist teaching facilities for the design, building and testing of renewable energy projects.

Three marine science degrees, including options to study abroad or with a professional placement, are among nine new degrees to be introduced in 2021. Others include business and the environment, environmental geoscience, global politics and politics and management.

Unlike many Russell Group universities, Exeter has embraced degree apprenticeships, with 750 students following one of four undergraduate and two postgraduate programmes.

The main Streatham campus, close to the centre of Exeter, has an attractive hillside setting with plenty of green space. The majority of students are based there, served by the £48m Forum building, which features an extended library, student services centre, technology-rich learning areas and auditorium, as well as social spaces and shops.

The nearby St Luke's campus houses the medical school, which also has a health education and research centre at the Royal Devon and Exeter Hospital and a smaller base in Truro, Cornwall. The Graduate School of Education and the sport and health sciences school are also based at St Luke's.

More than £20m has been invested in sports facilities in recent years, providing some of the best in the country. The Sports Park on the main campus includes a 200-station gym, while sport at Penryn is focused around sailing and surfing.

Tuition fees

» Fees for UK students	£9,250
» Fees for International students 2021–22	£18,800–£23,450
Medicine	£37,000
» For scholarship and bursary information see	
www.exeter.ac.uk/undergraduate/fees/	
» Graduate salary	£26,000

Student numbers

Undergraduates	19,069	(318)
Postgraduates	3,878	(1,743)
Applications/places	37,640/5,985	
Applications per place	6.3	
Overall offer rate	88.7%	
International students – EU	5.8%	
Non-EU	19.5%	

Accommodation

University provided places: 6,139
Catered costs: £192–£269 per week
Self-catered: £110–£181 per week
First years guaranteed accommodation
www.exeter.ac.uk/accommodation

Where do the students come from?

State schools (non-grammar)	52.8%	First generation students	26.9%	
Grammar schools	11.9%	Deprived areas	6%	
Independent schools	35.3%	All ethnic minorities	11.3%	

Social inclusion ranking: 111

Black attainment gap	-16.2%
Disabled	7.5%
Mature (over 21)	5.9%

Falmouth University

In the comedian, actress and writer Dawn French, Falmouth has a dedicated and eloquent chancellor. When handing out graduation scrolls to the class of 2019, French, who lives along the Cornish coast in Fowey and likes to be known as the Queen of Falmouth University, said: "The future of our creative and cultural landscape is in your hands. How exciting to be right on the cusp, about to bring your skills and talents into the world."

A specialist art institution that now embraces a broader undergraduate remit, including business entrepreneurship and marketing, journalism, game development and architecture, the university originated in 1902 as the Falmouth School of Art.

There are two campuses: Falmouth and nearby Penryn, where £100m has been invested over the past 16 years. The subtropical gardens and light-filled creative spaces make for an inspiring setting at the Falmouth site, which is near the town centre and a short walk from Gyllyngvase beach, one of the area's finest. Falmouth is proud of its teaching facilities for photography and an in-house photo agency gives students and graduates a leg-up in a fast-changing industry.

Falmouth shares the Penryn campus with the University of Exeter, and the two universities have a unique joint students' union, FXU. Penryn is the base for Falmouth's performing arts courses, which joined the university's portfolio following a merger with Dartington College of Arts, in south Devon, in 2008. The Academy of Music and Theatre Arts at Penryn is used as a performance venue and gives students access to exceptional facilities such as a 129-seat cinema, motion capture studio, video editing suites and specialist animation software, plus fully sprung dancefloors, rehearsal studios and theatre space.

Eight new degree courses were introduced in 2020, mostly sticking to Falmouth's trademark blend of creativity and innovation, including musical theatre, web development and costume design for film and television. Sustainable tourism management, marketing and communications, and web development also joined the curriculum.

The Teaching Excellence Framework (TEF) panel awarded Falmouth gold, and assessors were particularly impressed with students' personalised learning, partly through individual timetabling and a "data-driven approach to monitoring contact and teaching patterns".

Not untypical of largely arts-based institutions, Falmouth did not fare brilliantly in the new Graduate Outcomes data published in the summer of 2020, which showed only 60% of graduates to be in high-skilled jobs or postgraduate study 15 months after completing their degrees.

Falmouth has about 5,000 students, double

Woodlane
Falmouth TR11 4RH
01326 254 350
futurestudies@falmouth.ac.uk
www.falmouth.ac.uk
www.thesu.org.uk
Open days: see website

The Times and The Sunday Times **Rankings**
Overall Ranking: =94 (last year: 72)

Teaching quality	81.7%	37
Student experience	77.2%	=76
Research quality	4.6%	=95
Entry standards	126	69
Graduate prospects	59.7%	=125
Good honours	76.4%	57
Expected completion rate	86.9%	=52
Student/staff ratio	17.3	=95
Services and facilities	£1,704	123

the numbers it had about a decade ago. The university's growth in the early 2000s was driven by the need to boost higher-level skills in Cornwall, and Falmouth retains a staunch commitment to widening access, including to locals. More than nine out of 10 undergraduates arrive from state schools and the university is redoubling its efforts to deliver on ambitious participation targets.

Outreach activities focus on schools in areas of low participation or disadvantage. In partnership with subject heads at more than 20 schools, Falmouth is helping to develop curriculum content to support students' learning and raise their aspirations. It expects to expand the programme among more schools in the coming years, which should help improve Falmouth's present lowly ranking in our social inclusion table.

The university invites all applicants to interview or audition either on campus, online or at regional locations and provides bursaries to help with travel costs if needed. Portfolios are also assessed where relevant. Between 30%-35% of students qualify for some form of direct financial support from the university. The Falmouth bursary of £250 to £500 per year is for students from households with incomes under £25,000.

The For Real award helps with travel and accommodation costs for course-related off-campus trips, and the Falmouth Edge Awards drive creativity by crediting exceptional extracurricular projects with a financial reward.

Falmouth's submission to the Research Excellence Framework in 2014 gained its best results in music, dance, drama and the performing arts, with a third of its work emerging as world-leading or internationally excellent. Almost a quarter of its art and design submission was placed in the top two categories too.

The sports centre on the Penryn campus has a four-court sports hall, fitness studio and gym, as well as multi-use pitches and outdoor gym. Spinning, yoga and Zumba are some of the classes offered. Watersports on Cornwall's coastline are a boon and part-time jobs in the tourist trade help with student living costs.

"One big Cornish party" is how *The Sunday Times* summed up Falmouth when naming it one of 2019's Best Places to Live. It's not all fishermen's pubs and sea shanty singalongs, however, with Falmouth students having venues such as Beerwolf for craft ale and books, and Jam for vinyl and coffee.

There are residential places on both campuses and accommodation is guaranteed to all full-time first-years who apply in time.

Tuition fees

» Fees for UK students		£9,250
		£11,100 for 2-year courses
» Fees for International students 2021–22		£16,000
» For scholarship and bursary information see		
www.falmouth.ac.uk/study/tuition-fees		
» Graduate salary		£20,000

Student numbers

Undergraduates	5,782	(17)
Postgraduates	190	(434)
Applications/places	5,160/1,515	
Applications per place	3.4	
Overall offer rate	64.1%	
International students – EU	6.9%	
Non-EU	3.8%	

Accommodation

University provided places: 1,342
Catered costs: £159–£197
Self-catered: £114–£193 per week
First years guaranteed accommodation
www.falmouth.ac.uk/accommodation

Where do the students come from?

Social inclusion ranking: 97

State schools (non-grammar)	88.3%	First generation students	34.5%	Black attainment gap	n/a
Grammar schools	3.2%	Deprived areas	8.1%	Disabled	10.3%
Independent schools	8.5%	All ethnic minorities	6.1%	Mature (over 21)	16.6%

University of Glasgow

The University of Glasgow's new James McCune Smith Learning Hub is opening to students in the 2020–21 academic year. With technology-enabled space for more than 2,500 students, the £90.5m development boasts a 500-seat lecture theatre, interactive teaching spaces, seminar or group study rooms and a café.

Glasgow is investing £1bn in its estate over 10 years, and is constructing a £113m Research Hub, due to open in 2021, and a new home for the business school by 2022.

One of Scotland's four ancient universities, Glasgow was the first in Britain to have a school of engineering and the first in Scotland to have a computer. A pioneer to this day, it plans a new innovation campus in the former shipyards of Govan, on the banks of the River Clyde. With funding drawn partly from the Glasgow City Region Deal, the plans focus on nanotechnology and precision medicine. The campus will allow academics to work alongside industry partners and its innovation rooms will be open to schoolchildren.

There is plenty to reflect the long history of the university, founded in 1451 – notably its Gothic revival buildings on the Gilmorehill campus in the city's fashionable West End, where the university has been based since 1871. Glasgow's museum, the Hunterian, is at Gilmorehill and includes collections of art, zoology and anatomy.

In the northwest of the city, four miles from Gilmorehill, is the spacious Garscube campus, where the veterinary school and outdoor sports pitches are based. In Dumfries, where liberal arts and teaching courses are delivered, more than £13m has been spent on better sporting and social facilities.

One of only two Russell Group universities in Scotland, Glasgow's research output attracts an annual income of more than £179m. The university is in the top 100 in both the Times Higher Education and QS world rankings. It moved into the top dozen universities in the UK for research after a much-improved performance in the 2014 Research Excellence Framework, ranking in the UK top 10 in 18 subjects. The best results came in architecture, agriculture, veterinary science and chemistry.

Glasgow hosts Scotland's leading centre for music research in the School of Culture and Creative Arts and there are opportunities for student placements within the city's legendary music scene. The university is also to become a 5G-enabled smart campus with technology-enhanced learning and teaching as a founding partner in the Scotland 5G Centre, an industry, research community and government collaboration.

The numbers starting courses at Glasgow in 2019 dropped marginally but were still not

---

University Avenue, Glasgow G12 8QQ
0141 330 2000
ruk-undergraduate-enquiries
@glasgow.ac.uk;
scot-undergraduate-enquiries
@glasgow.co.uk;
student.recruitment
@glasgow.ac.uk
www.gla.ac.uk
www.guu.co.uk
Open days: see website

The Times and The Sunday Times **Rankings**
Overall Ranking: 14 (last year: 16)

Teaching quality	78.4%	=84
Student experience	79.4%	=40
Research quality	39.9%	12
Entry standards	204	3
Graduate prospects	81.3%	=30
Good honours	82.6%	27
Expected completion rate	88%	45
Student/staff ratio	13.4	=17
Services and facilities	£2,747	41

far off the record high of 2017. Applications were up again in the 2020 admissions cycle. More than a quarter of undergraduates are from outside the UK and Glasgow has a branch campus in Singapore, working with the Singapore Institute of Technology, and a joint graduate school with Nankai University in northeastern China.

In the National Student Survey, Glasgow has registered its best results between 2018–20, moving back into the top 50 for satisfaction with the student experience and into the top 100 once more for satisfaction with teaching quality. Both results significantly outdid its principal rival, Edinburgh.

Almost half of the university's applications are for broad arts or sciences degrees, and a flexible system allows students to delay choosing a specialism until the end of their second year. Managed by the internship hub, there are more than 350 paid opportunities each year, including more than 150 on campus. Almost 81% of graduates were in high-skilled jobs or postgraduate study 15 months after completing their degrees, the most recent statistics revealed – a top-30 finish among UK universities.

Four-year courses are the norm in Scotland, and Glasgow sweetens the deal for students from the rest of the UK by waiving their tuition fees for the fourth year on the majority of degrees.

There are access bursaries of £1,000 to £3,000 per year of study for students from England, Wales and Northern Ireland, paid in 10 cash instalments. A wide range of scholarships targets different disciplines and student cohorts – such as science and engineering's Dean's Award of £10,000 per year for international students, James McCune Smith scholarships of £2,000 for UK students of African and African/Caribbean backgrounds and a variety of awards aimed at widening participation.

More than 3,400 residential places means accommodation is guaranteed for new undergraduates. Glasgow's sports union supports more than 50 clubs and activities and there are purpose-built sports facilities on the Gilmorehill and Garscube campuses.

Scotland's biggest metropolis was crowned the world's friendliest and most affordable city by *Time Out* in 2019. It was also the first in the UK to be named a Unesco city of music, where venues such as King Tut's Wah Wah Hut and Sub Club are a big draw.

Tuition fees

» Fees for Scottish students   £0–£1,820
RUK fees £9,250 (capped at £27,750 for 4-year courses. Cap does not apply to Medicine, Dentistry or Veterinary Surgery.)

» Fees for International students 2021–22   £19,350–£23,000
Medicine £49,950 (clinical years); Dentistry £46,950; Veterinary £32,500

» For scholarship and bursary information see
http://www.gla.ac.uk/study/undergraduate/fees/

» Graduate salary   £26,000

Student numbers

Undergraduates	18,359 (2,699)
Postgraduates	8,228 (1,519)
Applications/places	35,035/4,675
Applications per place	7.5
Overall offer rate	57%
International students – EU	10.2%
Non-EU	21.3%

Accommodation

University provided places: 3,470
Catered costs: £166–£184 per week
Self-catered: £127–£243 per week
First years guaranteed accommodation
www.gla.ac.uk/myglasgow/accommodation

Where do the students come from?

State schools (non-grammar)	79.8%	First generation students	26.2%		
Grammar schools	5.4%	Deprived areas	13.3%		
Independent schools	14.8%	All ethnic minorities	10.4%		

Social inclusion ranking (Scotland): 14

Black attainment gap	-33%
Disabled	3.1%
Mature (over 21)	15.4%

Glasgow Caledonian University

Glasgow Caledonian University (GCU) is committed to widening participation, and undergraduates who do not meet standard entry requirements may enter via qualifications that include relevant experience and prior learning, HND college pathways and foundation or modern apprenticeships. International students can complete an academic pathway programme or progress via English courses to GCU, which occupies a single site in the heart of Glasgow. Highers, though, are the standard entry route.

GCU, which aims to be a "university for the common good", is one of the largest providers of graduates to the NHS in Scotland. It trains 90% of the country's eye care specialists and is the only Scottish university offering optometry degrees. Facilities include a virtual hospital and health was one of GCU's strengths in the 2014 Research Excellence Framework, when half its submission attained the top two categories. GCU was in the top 20 in the UK for allied health research and did well in social work and social policy, and the built environment.

GCU was the first Scottish university to open a campus in London, where postgraduate fashion students are based in trendy Spitalfields. Its outpost in SoHo in New York made GCU the first foreign university to be granted a charter to award its own degrees in fashion and business in the city. While the project was a triumph for GCU, it came at a cost, and the university's plan to increase its loan facility to £15m to expand the New York operation attracted criticism.

GCU's fashion courses are its flagship programme and its British School of Fashion has had partnerships with companies including Marks & Spencer, which has a design studio at the London campus and funds scholarships, and fashion brands All Saints and Arcadia. At the Glasgow headquarters, its purpose-built studio, the Fashion Factory, has industry-standard machinery for designing and making clothing.

GCU has helped to set up the African Leadership College in Mauritius, where the first students embarked on GCU degrees in 2017. It also co-founded the Grameen Caledonian College of Nursing in Bangladesh, and has links with institutions in Oman, China, India and South America.

Like other universities north of the border, GCU benefits in our league table from the conversion rate for Scottish secondary qualifications in the UCAS tariff – putting it in the top 25 for entry grades, above the likes of York, Nottingham and Loughborough. Just over half of applicants receive an offer – a proportion that has remained steady over the years.

Cowcaddens Road
Glasgow G4 0BA
0141 331 8630
admissions@gcu.ac.uk
www.gcu.ac.uk
www.gcustudents.co.uk
Open days:
see website

The Times and The Sunday Times Rankings
Overall Ranking: 75 (last year: =96)

Teaching quality	80.8%	=46
Student experience	79%	=48
Research quality	7%	=77
Entry standards	159	=22
Graduate prospects	74.6%	62
Good honours	80.3%	35
Expected completion rate	85%	58
Student/staff ratio	21.4	129
Services and facilities	£1,881	111

The university does well on completion rates, with a predicted dropout rate of around 8% – considerably better than the expected level of 10.3%, based on the social and academic background of its intake. It shows the academic, social and financial support given to those at risk of dropping out is bearing fruit.

Prospects for graduates are strong, too, with nearly three-quarters working in high-skilled jobs or postgraduate study 15 months after graduating – in the top half of UK universities. More than half of the undergraduate programmes are accredited by professional bodies and most include work placements.

The Glasgow School for Business and Society offers highly specialised degrees, and pioneered subjects such as entrepreneurial studies and risk management. It is developing an undergraduate degree in economic policy to be launched in September 2021. The School of Engineering and Built Environment teaches three-quarters of Scotland's part-time construction students.

Nine of the university's MSc programmes were introduced for 2020 in a two-year format with industry placements and four of the master's courses offered in London will come with two-year extended practice routes in options such as entrepreneurial bootcamp and consultancy projects.

GCU sits fourth among Scottish universities in our league table for social inclusion. It has some high-profile names behind it: the singer Annie Lennox became the university's chancellor in 2018 and Sir Alex Ferguson, the Scottish footballing legend who grew up in the city, has pledged £500,000 to a bursary programme. The university offers financial help to students from its own £2 million scholarship fund. Just under half the students are the first in their family to go to university, while almost all GCU students come from non-selective state schools, one of the highest proportions in the UK.

GCU was the first university named as a cycle-friendly campus by Cycle Scotland and is also a platinum-award winning eco campus. The centrepiece of a £32m redevelopment is the Heart of the Campus, which has a striking glass reception area.

Student facilities include the Arc sports centre and 24-hour computer labs. There are only 654 residential places, with priority given to international or disabled students, and those under 19. The historic West End's red brick flats are popular for off-campus student living. Known for its energy and culture, Scotland's largest city has five universities and is well geared for student life.

Tuition fees

» Fees for Scottish students £0–£1,820
  RUK fees £9,250 (capped at £27,750 for 4-year courses)
» Fees for International students 2021–22 £12,250
» For scholarship and bursary information see www.gcu.ac.uk/study/tuitionfees/
» Graduate salary £23,000

Student numbers

Undergraduates	**11,671**	**(2,113)**
Postgraduates	**1,902**	**(1,174)**
Applications/places		**21,085/3,560**
Applications per place		**5.9**
Overall offer rate		**54.5%**
International students – EU		**5.4%**
Non-EU		**7.1%**

Accommodation

University provided places: 654
Self-catered: £100–£118 per week
www.gcu.ac.uk/study/undergraduate/accommodation/

Where do the students come from?

State schools (non-grammar)	96.2%	First generation students	44.5%
Grammar schools	0.4%	Deprived areas	22.6%
Independent schools	3.3%	All ethnic minorities	12.4%

Social inclusion ranking (Scotland): 4

Black attainment gap	-46.8%
Disabled	2.4%
Mature (over 21)	39.7%

University of Gloucestershire

On the edge of the Cotswolds, designated an area of natural beauty, the University of Gloucestershire has long championed green issues. Its sustainability efforts have earned it top spot in the People & Planet league of environmental performance. In a new initiative, Gloucestershire has got rid of paper copies of its 200-page prospectus, instead giving out biodegradable wristbands, embedded with wildflower seeds, which contain QR codes linking to the online version.

The university offers diplomas in environmentalism, as well as sustainability research and development projects that bring together researchers from around the world, undertaking work for agencies such as Unesco. Students on courses with an environmental theme now benefit from new teaching and workshop facilities, as do those studying architecture and construction.

Following a raft of new additions in 2019, 26 more degrees are joining the course offering from 2020 and 2021 ranging from forensic psychology, diagnostic radiotherapy and primary education with qualified teacher status (QTS) to sport coaching science, theatre design and games art. New programmes in biomedical science will be enhanced by the addition of laboratories with decontamination facilities, and space for teaching, technical support and research.

The university is also expanding its portfolio of degree apprenticeships from 12 to 18 programmes, working with more than 60 employers including the NHS, Superdry (founded in Cheltenham) and Virgin Atlantic. In response to skills gaps and the needs of industry, Gloucestershire is introducing programmes in business and management, health and social care, engineering, education, construction and biomedical science, boosting degree apprentice numbers from 300 to 500.

Students rate their teaching highly. Satisfaction with teaching quality in the latest National Student Survey saw Gloucestershire recover most of 2019's lost ground to rank 40=. It scored less well for satisfaction with the wider experience, ranking 82= – a third successive fall that has cost the university just under 50 places in our ranking on this measure since 2017.

Its integrated approach to enhancing employability through volunteering and placements contributed to a silver award in the Teaching Excellence Framework. Relationships with businesses such as Waitrose and financial advisers St James Place oil the wheels for student placements and projects.

However just 65% of graduates were in high-skilled jobs or postgraduate study 15 months after completing their courses, the latest data showed, placing Gloucestershire in the bottom 20 universities in our new measure for graduate prospects. It does better on completion rates: about one in seven students

The Park
Cheltenham GL50 2RH
03330 141 414
admissions@glos.ac.uk
www.glos.ac.uk
www.yourstudentsunion.com
Open days: see website

The Times and The Sunday Times **Rankings**
Overall Ranking: 109 (last year: 95)

Teaching quality	81.1%	=40
Student experience	76.9%	=82
Research quality	3.8%	=108
Entry standards	116	=97
Graduate prospects	64.5%	113
Good honours	71.8%	=92
Expected completion rate	81.4%	=90
Student/staff ratio	17.7	=101
Services and facilities	£1,979	100

are predicted to drop out, which is broadly in line with expectations (12.8%) based on the social and academic background of its intake.

Applications fell by around 9% in 2019, with enrolments falling 7%. About 15% of the intake secured their places through clearing. Students entering via clearing are given guaranteed accommodation and those applying for nursing, education, arts and media courses even get an interview. According to the university, many "trade up" to Gloucestershire through the clearing process.

In the top 40 for social inclusion, almost half of each new cohort of undergraduates tends to qualify for some sort of financial support. More than 200 students were awarded academic merit scholarships in 2020, worth £400 per year if they achieved 128 UCAS tariff points, equivalent to ABB at A-level.

The university has three sites in Cheltenham and another campus in Gloucester, seven miles away. The main Park campus is a mile from the centre of Cheltenham, and houses the business, education and professional studies faculty. Art and design facilities, and the education and public services institute are closer to the town centre at Francis Close Hall. Hardwick is nearby and has photography and fine art studios as well as its own gallery.

The purpose-built Oxstalls campus in the centre of Gloucester caters for sport and exercise sciences, leisure, tourism, hospitality and event management. The site also houses the Countryside and Community Research Institute, the largest rural research centre in the UK, which produced the best results in the 2014 Research Excellence Framework. Only 20% of eligible staff took part and overall, 44% of Gloucestershire's submission was rated as world-leading or internationally excellent.

In 2001, Gloucestershire was the first Church of England-founded institution to achieve university status for more than a century. Originally a teacher training college, its primary and secondary training courses are rated "outstanding" by Ofsted.

Gloucestershire's strong sporting tradition is supported by extensive facilities at Oxstalls Sports Park and in Cheltenham. Students have the run of an indoor and outdoor tennis centre, playing fields, international-standard 3G pitches for rugby and football, fitness suites, a sports hall and cricket pavilion. More than 80 sporting activities are available.

All first-years are guaranteed housing in university halls or managed accommodation. The options include an 800-bed student village in Cheltenham, opened in 2017, and 300 places in the centre of Gloucester.

Tuition fees

» Fees for UK students	£9,250
» Fees for International students 2020–21	£14,680
» For scholarship and bursary information see www.glos.ac.uk/life/finance/pages/fees.aspx	
» Graduate salary	£20,000

Student numbers

Undergraduates	6,455	(328)
Postgraduates	518	(956)
Applications/places		7,380/1,815
Applications per place		4.1
Overall offer rate		81.3%
International students – EU		1.5%
Non-EU		4.7%

Accommodation

University provided places: 1,712
Self-catered: £126–£202 per week
First years guaranteed accommodation
www.glos.ac.uk/life/accommodation/pages/accommodation.aspx

Where do the students come from?

State schools (non-grammar)	92.8%	First generation students	47.6%	Black attainment gap	-27.1%
Grammar schools	4.2%	Deprived areas	15.1%	Disabled	10.3%
Independent schools	3.1%	All ethnic minorities	11.5%	Mature (over 21)	24.3%

Social inclusion ranking: 36

Goldsmiths, University of London

A new Enterprise Hub is opening at Goldsmiths University in 2021. There will be flexible and collaborative work areas for freelancers, small local businesses and social enterprises and its business advice, workshops and networking events will be open for students, alumni and the community to access. The hub will have a particular focus on encouraging female entrepreneurs and those from black, Asian and minority ethnic (BAME) backgrounds.

The university, which ranks among the top 30 for social inclusion, has appointed Dr Nicola Rollock, an academic specialising in racial justice in education and the workplace, to address its BAME attainment gap, an issue experienced across the sector. For example, the latest data in our social inclusion ranking shows 89% of all white graduates achieved a first or 2:1 degree compared with 71% of BAME graduates.

Goldsmiths has pledged to become carbon-neutral by 2025 — another challenge set by Professor Frances Corner, the university's first female warden, who took over in 2019. The university has taken beef off the menu at campus food outlets, and animal rights charity Peta praised Goldsmiths for being one of the UK's most vegan-friendly institutions.

A 10p levy on bottled water discourages single-use plastic sales on campus. Goldsmiths has also stopped its endowment fund from investing in companies generating more than 10% of their revenue from fossil fuel extraction. The university hopes to expand its allotment space and install more solar panels.

Based in New Cross, in southeast London, Goldsmiths was a key partner in Lewisham's successful bid to become the London Borough of Culture — delayed until 2022 due to the coronavirus pandemic. Sadiq Khan, the mayor of London, has awarded Lewisham £1.25m for an arts programme to celebrate diversity and bring Londoners together.

Some of the capital's best facilities help Goldsmiths to cement its position as one of the leading universities for the creative arts. The Goldsmiths Centre for Contemporary Art opened in 2018 in a listed building that once housed the water tanks for the Laurie Grove public baths. The university's £2.9m performance studios and 200-seat theatre are used by the public as well as students.

Goldsmiths also has some big-hitting alumni such as Bernardine Evaristo, whose novel *Girl, Woman, Other* shared the Booker prize in 2019, as well as Steve McQueen, director of the Oscar-winning *12 Years a Slave*, the musician James Blake and nine Turner prize winners including Damien Hirst.

It ranks 14th in the world for art and design and in the top 100 for the performing

New Cross
London SE14 6NW
020 7078 5300
Course-info@gold.ac.uk
www.gold.ac.uk
www.goldsmithssu.org
Open days: see website
Edinburgh
Belfast
Cardiff
LONDON

The Times and The Sunday Times Rankings
Overall Ranking: 97 (last year: 68)

Teaching quality	70%	129
Student experience	63.8%	129
Research quality	33.4%	36
Entry standards	127	=65
Graduate prospects	62.4%	=119
Good honours	79.6%	41
Expected completion rate	78%	113
Student/staff ratio	14.9	=49
Services and facilities	£3,106	18

arts in the QS World University Rankings by subject.

Beyond the creative arts, Goldsmiths' degree portfolio includes management, economics, politics and computing. A degree course in history, heritage and cultural management began in 2020, joined by law with criminal justice and human rights, following the successful introduction of a law honours programme in 2019.

The university managed only bronze in the Teaching Excellence Framework (TEF), dragged down by poor student satisfaction, a common problem in London, and low levels of graduate employment, which is often a challenge for arts-dominated institutions. The TEF panel acknowledged its high-quality resources and said students benefited by connecting with local communities. Goldsmiths is the lowest-ranked UK university for both our measures of student satisfaction in this publication, covering teaching quality and the wider student experience, based on the outcomes of the 2020 National Student Survey.

According to the latest statistics more than 62% of graduates were in high-skilled jobs or postgraduate study 15 months after completing their course, placing the university outside the top 100, while still outperforming many other arts-focused institutions. But Goldsmiths is let down by its dropout rate (21.7%), far higher than the 13.8% expected taking into account the social and academic background of its intake.

Goldsmiths did well in the 2014 Research Excellence Framework: 70% of its submission was judged world-leading or internationally excellent, with the best results in communication and media studies. The entire submission in music had world-leading impact.

Students who enter via schemes to widen access are guaranteed conditional offers, and scholarships for students from low-participation neighbourhoods were introduced for 2020 entry. An estimated 15% of students qualify for financial assistance.

The campus is 10 minutes by train from central London, though the immediate area has more fashionable enclaves. Blur performed their first comeback gig at Goldsmiths' students' union in 2009 and today's students won't go short of entertainment.

More than 1,500 rooms are available in halls of residence — many in New Cross and all within 30 minutes commuting distance. Priority is given to international students and new undergraduates from outside London. The on-campus gym is well-equipped, and outdoor pitches are half an hour away.

Tuition fees

» Fees for UK students	£9,250
» Fees for International students 2020–21	£16,390–£22,950
» For scholarship and bursary information see www.gold.ac.uk/ug/fees-funding/	
» Graduate salary	£24,000

Student numbers

Undergraduates	6,506	(195)
Postgraduates	2,494	(1,215)
Applications/places		12,460/1,635
Applications per place		7.6
Overall offer rate		66.1%
International students – EU		8.6%
Non-EU		18.5%

Accommodation

University provided places: 1,500
Self-catered: £149–£318 per week
www.gold.ac.uk/accommodation/

Where do the students come from?

State schools (non-grammar)	88.9%	First generation students	45.6%	
Grammar schools	4%	Deprived areas	5%	
Independent schools	7.1%	All ethnic minorities	51.1%	

Social inclusion ranking: 27

Black attainment gap	-18%
Disabled	9.3%
Mature (over 21)	21.3%

University of Greenwich

The University of Greenwich's efforts to boost the employability of its graduates are paying dividends, the Graduate Outcomes survey by the Higher Education Statistics Agency revealed in summer 2020. According to the report, 73% of Greenwich graduates were working in high-skilled employment 15 months after finishing their degrees, which places it ahead of all other modern multi-faculty universities in London for graduate job prospects.

Helping to stem the need for stopgap jobs to pay the bills when graduates finish their courses, Greenwich is the only university in the country with an on-campus strategic relationship with a recruitment firm. The service aims to place final-year undergraduates or recent graduates in full-time, graduate-level jobs that suit their skills, and finds them high-quality internships and other opportunities along the way as well.

Under a new scheme recent graduates will also be employed on internships to support the university's teaching staff in delivering virtual sessions, as part of the blended face-to-face and online learning experience developed in response to the Covid-19 pandemic.

For budding company founders, the university launched Powerhouse, its enterprise hub, in 2019. Located on the Greenwich campus, which occupies a World Heritage site overlooking the Thames, the hub hosts entrepreneurs who run social and commercial enterprises plus teaching and learning space for students. The Powerhouse is intended to help the university realise its 2022 target of having 1,000 students a year engaged in enterprise and 20 supported to launch their own businesses.

A £23m refurbishment of the historic Dreadnought building at the Greenwich campus brought all student-facing services together under one roof, including the students' union, a bar, student and academic services, a gym, media suite, radio station and flexible teaching spaces.

The prize-winning Stockwell Street development, also in Greenwich, was designed partly by the university's own specialists in architecture and includes a landscaped roof terrace, large architecture studio, model-making workshop, and television and sound studios.

Redevelopment of the teaching and learning facilities has begun on another of the university's three campuses, Avery Hill, a Victorian mansion on the outskirts of southeast London, which is the base for education, health and the social sciences. There is already a £14m sports and teaching centre, and laboratories for health courses that replicate NHS wards. The campus also contains a student village of 1,300 rooms.

At Chatham, in Kent, the Medway campus houses the schools of pharmacy, science and engineering in the Natural Resources Institute, as well as nursing and some business courses. The campus, which is shared with the

Maritime Greenwich Campus
Old Royal Naval College
Park Row
London SE10 9LS
020 8331 9000
courseinfo@gre.ac.uk
www.gre.ac.uk
www.greenwichsu.co.uk
Open days: see website

The Times and The Sunday Times **Rankings**
Overall Ranking: 98 (last year: 84)

Teaching quality	78%	=92
Student experience	76.3%	=89
Research quality	4.9%	=93
Entry standards	122	=80
Graduate prospects	73%	67
Good honours	77.1%	54
Expected completion rate	81.4%	=90
Student/staff ratio	17.8	=104
Services and facilities	£2,314	78

University of Kent, has a student hub in a listed building featuring study spaces plus a restaurant, bar and nightclub.

Forensic science degrees, with or without criminology, and including industrial placements, launched in 2020. Programmes in urban design and in children, young people and education are launching in 2021. Greenwich plans to expand its portfolio of degree apprenticeships to include paramedic science, teaching, construction site management and social work.

The university gained silver in the Teaching Excellence Framework, attracting accolades for course design and assessment practices that stretch students. Assessors said personalised provision secures good engagement and commitment to learning from most students, and that the university had invested in high-quality physical and digital resources to enhance learning.

The university's Natural Resources Institute was awarded the Queen's Anniversary Prize in 2020 for its work developing smart solutions to tackle pests that cause plague, famine and disease. More than 200 Greenwich academics entered the 2014 Research Excellence Framework – a considerable increase on 2008 – and 42% of their work was placed in the top two categories.

Adding to the research fold is the Institute of Lifecourse Development, which launched in 2019. Its work promotes the lifelong wellbeing of vulnerable and marginalised people, in partnership with healthcare, education, business and public sector organisations.

Greenwich has a heavyweight alumnus in Abiy Ahmed, who became prime minister of Ethiopia aged 42 in 2018, and Africa's youngest leader. His efforts to achieve peace and international co-operation – which have included challenging armed troops who marched on his offices with a press-up competition instead of retaliating with violence – earned him the 2019 Nobel Prize for Peace. The university has a second Nobel laureate in the late Dr Charles Kao, who won the Nobel Prize for Physics in 2009 for his work in fibre optics. Baroness Doreen Lawrence, mother of Stephen Lawrence, is another notable former student.

The university has scored well in our social inclusion tables, ranking 14th in the latest. It takes almost 60% of its undergraduates from ethnic minorities and more than half from homes where parents did not go to university.

Record numbers are engaging with sports clubs and societies, and facilities include two all-weather pitches at the Avery Hill campus. All new entrants who apply in time are guaranteed accommodation.

Tuition fees

»	Fees for UK students	£9,250
	Foundation courses	£6,165
»	Fees for International students 2020–21	£14,000–£15,000
»	For scholarship and bursary information see www.gre.ac.uk/finance	
»	Graduate salary	£25,000

Student numbers

Undergraduates	12,275 (2,157)
Postgraduates	1,908 (2,604)
Applications/places	24,640/3,440
Applications per place	7.2
Overall offer rate	64.7%
International students – EU	7.2%
Non-EU	14.9%

Accommodation

University provided places: 2,488
Self-catered: £118–£287 per week
First years guaranteed accommodation
www.gre.ac.uk/accommodation

Where do the students come from?

State schools (non-grammar)	93%	First generation students	56.4%	Black attainment gap	-17.5%
Grammar schools	5%	Deprived areas	7.7%	Disabled	5.2%
Independent schools	2.1%	All ethnic minorities	59.7%	Mature (over 21)	33.7%

Social inclusion ranking: 14

Harper Adams University

The Harper and Keele Veterinary School opened in 2020, the UK's ninth vet school. The joint venture draws on Harper Adams' expertise in animal health and science and Keele University's strengths in basic science and medicine. Teaching is shared equally between campuses though students have a "home" at one or other university while also having access to support, social activities and facilities at both.

Harper Adams took double honours in the previous edition of the Good University Guide when it was our Modern University of the Year as well as runner-up for our overall University of the Year award. This year it tops our rankings of modern universities for the fifth time in a row and retains a place in our elite top 30 in spite of an 11-place fall. It is the only university created since 1992 to ever break into the top 30.

Strong scores in the National Student Survey, where it is placed in the top 10 for both teaching and the wider student experience, add to its reputation.

Harper Adams is also distinguished by being one of only two institutions to achieve gold in successive years in the Teaching Excellence Framework (TEF). Having earned gold in 2017 it did not need to be reassessed, but vice-chancellor David Llewellyn said the university wanted to test its performance against the latest measures. The TEF panel praised Harper Adams' course design, delivery and assessment practices, which stretched and challenged students to achieve their full potential.

The university has long been renowned as the country's leading specialist agricultural institution and still occupies a single site on the Shropshire country estate where it was founded in 1901. University status came in 2012 and the Princess Royal became Harper Adams' chancellor the following year.

The university takes a global outlook on tackling challenges around food security, sustainable technologies and natural resource management and options reflect the modern landscape, extending well beyond agriculture to include business, veterinary nursing and physiotherapy, land and property management, engineering and food studies.

Veterinary medicine and surgery began at the new dedicated school in 2020, as did a broad range of extended degree programmes that lead to standard or honours degrees, subject to students' performance – the extra year allowing students without the necessary qualifications to prepare for entry to the degree course. An honours course in geospatial sciences took its first students in September 2020 as part of the geospatial mapping and science degree apprenticeship.

A specialist institution for degree apprenticeships, Harper Adams operates three

Edgmond
Newport
Shropshire TF10 8NB
01952 815 000
admissions@harper-adams.ac.uk
www.harper-adams.ac.uk
www.harpersu.com
Open days: see website

The Times and The Sunday Times **Rankings**

Overall Ranking: 28 (last year: 17)

Teaching quality	84.6%	9
Student experience	82.7%	7
Research quality	5.7%	85
Entry standards	124	=74
Graduate prospects	71.2%	82
Good honours	73%	85
Expected completion rate	87.6%	49
Student/staff ratio	14.8	=45
Services and facilities	£4,029	3

main routes, in rural surveying and utilities, food and drink specialists and engineering. There are plans to introduce level 6 programmes in the roles of environmental practitioner, professional forester and professional adviser agriculture/horticulture for 2021 entry.

Placement years and accredited part-time programmes in industry mean that hardly more than half of the 4,500 students are on campus at once. Tuition fees are about a fifth of the full rate during placement years, and students usually earn a wage while also gaining on-the-job experience.

Harper Adams is strong on completion rates and only half of the projected number of students drops out (5.2% against the benchmark level of 10.4%). It scored less well in the new Graduate Outcomes survey, however, which showed 71% of graduates were in high-skilled jobs or postgraduate study 15 months after finishing their courses.

The university launched the Global Institute for Agri-Tech Economics (Giate) in 2019, to push forward the agenda on the application, adaptation and adoption of innovative agricultural technology. Harper Adams is also a partner in Ni-Park, an agri-tech research and innovation hub under construction in nearby Newport, Shropshire, which is creating new full-time skilled jobs and aims to help place the UK at the forefront of advanced sustainable agriculture.

The success of the university's world-first Hands Free Hectare, where a crop was grown and harvested without human hands touching it to demonstrate the automation of agricultural technology, has led to its expansion into a 35-hectare (86-acre) Hands Free Farm on university land. Having started in a neat rectangular plot, the project is now developing the hands-free concept in more realistic conditions. Academics and students from across the university are exploring the impacts of more automated farming on the food production chain.

The students' union, careers service and café are under one roof at the heart of the campus, where open-access computers allow students to work and socialise in the same area. The Bamford library holds one of the largest specialist land-based collections in the UK.

Sports facilities include a shooting ground as well as a gymnasium, heated outdoor swimming pool, rugby, cricket, football and hockey pitches, tennis courts and an all-weather sports pitch. The rural setting does not dent the vigour of the social scene and the campus has its own local, the Welly Inn.

Tuition fees

»	Fees for UK students	£9,250
»	Fees for International students 2021–22	£10,800
»	For scholarship and bursary information see www.harper-adams.ac.uk/apply/finance/	
»	Graduate salary	£24,000

Student numbers

Undergraduates	2,383 (2,358)
Postgraduates	123 (511)
Applications/places	2,745/605
Applications per place	4.5
Overall offer rate	71.8%
International students – EU	2.2%
Non-EU	2.7%

Accommodation

University provided places: 830
Catered costs: £105–£162 per week
First years given priority for accommodation
www.harper-adams.ac.uk/university-life/accommodation

Where do the students come from?

				Social inclusion ranking: 81	
State schools (non-grammar)	79.3%	First generation students	37.5%	Black attainment gap	n/a
Grammar schools	6.8%	Deprived areas	4.7%	Disabled	17.7%
Independent schools	13.9%	All ethnic minorities	3%	Mature (over 21)	13.6%

Hartpury University

Hartpury will make its debut in our academic ranking in the next edition of this book, by which time it will have results for all but one of the measures on which we assess university performance. It is likely to perform strongly if the latest National Student Survey results are anything to go by. Hartpury would have finished joint top for satisfaction with teaching quality had we included it in our latest league table.

Formerly part of the University of the West of England, Hartpury gained taught degree-awarding powers in 2017, which makes it eligible for inclusion in this guide. It was founded in 1949 as an agricultural institute and has retained a strong land-based selection of courses while expanding its portfolio to cover animal, equine, sport and veterinary nursing degrees.

Today there are about 3,500 students following courses in higher and further education at the university and its sister institution, Hartpury College.

The university, based in the Gloucestershire countryside, has at its heart a commercial farm, where the Agri-Tech Centre opened in spring 2020. This development offers students access to smart agricultural technology to improve the productivity, profitability and sustainability of livestock production, and to help meet global food challenges. Research, innovation and best-practice methods will be shared with the local and national farming sector.

Hartpury has five farms in all, spanning about 1,000 acres, which supply Sainsbury's, Muller and Glencore among others. The 180-acre Home Farm is on the main campus. The farms have cows, sheep and arable land and include a dairy bull-beef rearing unit and a 296-cubicle dairy unit.

Hartpury was awarded gold in the Teaching Excellence Framework just prior to gaining university status. The panel praised the institution for course design and assessment practices that provided a high level of stretch and challenge. It also highlighted the "inquiry-based" approach to teaching and learning and its "optimum contact hours, which secure high levels of engagement and commitment to learning and study from students".

There is an extensive bursary scheme from which just under half of the students benefit. Local recruits from specific schools and areas with low progression to higher education can get £1,500 support each year if they come from families with a household income of £21,000 or less. An annual bursary of £1,000 is offered to similar non-local recruits. Among those eligible for a £500 annual progression bursary are students who transfer from a further education programme at Hartpury College to degree-level study at the university.

Hartpury House
Gloucester GL19 3BE
01452 702 244
admissions@hartpury.ac.uk
www.hartpury.ac.uk
https://.hsu.unioncloud.org
Open days: see website

The Times and The Sunday Times **Rankings**
Overall Ranking: No data available

Two degrees introduced for September 2020 — animal training and performance, and canine training and performance — build on Hartpury's development as a centre for excellence in animal welfare, training, performance and rehabilitation and will take advantage of the emerging science, technology and research in this area. The university is exploring training practices that strengthen the human-animal bond while promoting and developing high standards of welfare.

Students began a new course in equine performance and rehabilitation in September 2020, while a degree in equine behaviour and welfare recruits its first intake in September 2021. Hartpury aims to be at the forefront of setting standards in the world of horses and this new BSc is designed to give students a rounded understanding of equitation science and horsemanship.

Sport has a high profile at Hartpury, too. The university calculates that it has developed more than 200 international athletes in various disciplines over the past decade. An £8.8m sports academy opened in 2019, which includes biomechanics and human performance laboratories, an anti-gravity treadmill, an altitude chamber, and high-speed cameras and digital mirrors to map body movement.

Such excellent facilities translate to sporting achievements. Hartpury University RFC plays championship-level rugby and the university's pitches provide the training and playing venue for Gloucester-Hartpury, who compete in the top division of women's rugby.

The quality of facilities for four-legged equine competitors is just as high. There are three international-class arenas for horses — the main indoor Hartpury Arena, the International Outdoor Arena and the small outdoor CoVE Arena — which between them host more than 100 international, national and regional events each year. They will be used to host the 2022 FEI Dressage and Eventing European Championships for young riders and juniors.

Hartpury also has an equine therapy centre to help horses recover from injury or reach peak performance, and the Margaret Giffen rider performance centre, which provides those of all levels and abilities with world-class facilities and expertise. Simulators and a strength and conditioning gym help them to improve their fitness and technique.

Students can even bring their own horse to university thanks to the stabling and livery options available. Campus social life is lively, and Gloucester and Cheltenham are five and 10 miles away for bigger nights out.

Tuition fees

» Fees for UK students	£9,250
» Fees for International students 2021–22	£13,000
» For scholarship and bursary information see www.hartpury.ac.uk/uni-finance	
» Graduate salary	n/a

Student numbers

Undergraduates	1,558	(59)
Postgraduates	40	(159)
Applications/places		2,720/640
Applications per place		4.3
Overall offer rate		n/a
International students – EU		3.6%
Non-EU		4.4%

Accommodation

University provided places: 523
Catered costs: £134–£151 per week
Self-catered: £134–£152
First years given priority for accommodation
www.hartpury.ac.uk/university/facilities/life-at-hartpury/accommodation

Where do the students come from?

State schools (non-grammar)	90%	First generation students	48.8%	Black attainment gap	n/a
Grammar schools	2.5%	Deprived areas	11.7%	Disabled	11%
Independent schools	7.6%	All ethnic minorities	6.4%	Mature (over 21)	21.5%

Social inclusion ranking: 74

Heriot-Watt University

Heriot-Watt has an enviable reputation for producing graduates who are sought after by employers, capable of making an immediate impact in the workplace. The new Graduate Outcomes survey, which tracks graduate employment 15 months after leaving university, found that 81% of Heriot-Watt graduates were in high-skilled jobs or postgraduate study, ranking the university well inside the UK top 40 on this measure.

Many degree programmes include industry placements and projects and carry professional accreditation, and the university teams up with around 200 big companies every year for a variety of projects. Its portfolio of 37 spin-out firms ranks Heriot-Watt fourth in Scotland and 21st in the UK.

The Grid (Global Research, Innovation and Discovery) building opened in 2019, designed with open learning spaces to encourage collaboration. Its enterprise hub supports business innovation and promotes emerging technology and inventions, encouraging staff and students to pursue the commercial potential of their ideas.

Ever responsive to the needs of employers, Heriot-Watt has one of the largest graduate apprenticeship degree programmes of any Scottish university, with 330 currently on campus. The university plans to recruit 220 more across the nine existing programmes including engineering, design and manufacturing; IT management for business; IT software development; civil engineering; built environment (quantity surveying); business management; data science; and instrumentation measurement and control.

As well as offering industry links, Heriot-Watt also broadens its students' horizons with global study opportunities. The university held our inaugural International University of the Year title in 2017 and its Go Global programme allows students to transfer easily between campuses in Scotland, Dubai and Malaysia for a semester, year or longer during their degree.

While the Go Global programme has been inevitably constrained by the pandemic, the university has used the moment to create a new online virtual learning environment and new learning materials. New BSc degrees were introduced in September 2020 in data sciences and computer science (cyber-security).

Only just over a third of the university's 30,000 students are based on the Riccarton campus, Heriot-Watt's leafy headquarters on the outskirts of Edinburgh. Others are studying with "collaborative partners" in 150 countries, as well as on the two international campuses. There are also two smaller bases in Scotland, in Orkney and Galashiels.

Recently completed improvements to the university library have increased capacity to more than 1,000 study spaces, reconfigured the print collections, and provided excellent

Edinburgh EH14 4AS
0131 451 3376
studywithus@hw.ac.uk
www.hw.ac.uk
www.hwunion.com
Open days: see website

EDINBURGH
Belfast
London
Cardiff

The Times and The Sunday Times **Rankings**
Overall Ranking: 35 (last year: 33)

Teaching quality	77.1%	100
Student experience	78%	=65
Research quality	36.7%	28
Entry standards	168	16
Graduate prospects	80.8%	33
Good honours	79.3%	42
Expected completion rate	84.4%	61
Student/staff ratio	17.8	=104
Services and facilities	£3,268	15

digital learning and study facilities for both collaborative and independent learning.

Heriot-Watt began as the world's first mechanics' institute in 1821 and is named after George Heriot and James Watt, two giants of industry and commerce. The university's strategic plan says all academic staff will be required to perform at internationally competitive levels of creativity in research, scholarship and teaching. The panel awarding Heriot-Watt silver in the Teaching Excellence Framework praised its course design "directly informed by research activity".

More than 80% of the work submitted for the 2014 Research Excellence Framework was rated world-leading or internationally excellent, and Heriot-Watt was among the leaders in the UK in mathematics, general engineering and architecture, planning and the built environment, where it made joint submissions with the University of Edinburgh. Heriot-Watt did particularly well in the assessments of the impact of research, and features in the top 30 of our research ranking.

The university recognised its duty to widen participation in higher education long before it became a requirement. A 30-year partnership, Swap-East, provides routes into university for mature students, while Heriot-Watt targets under-represented groups of pupils through partnerships with schools in the Lothians, Borders and Forth Valley, which have low progression rates to university. About 75

Access Bursaries are awarded each year, worth £1,000 annually, and students from low-participation backgrounds are eligible for a free Lothian Buses Ridacard worth £500, for the duration of their studies, removing travel costs from the list of factors that may inhibit progression to university.

The main campus hosts Oriam, Scotland's national centre for performance in many sports, where world-class facilities are available to Heriot-Watt students. The £33m complex features a Hampden Park replica pitch, outdoor synthetic and grass pitches, a nine-court sports hall, a 3G indoor pitch and a fitness suite, plus medical facilities.

The Edinburgh halls of residence are conveniently placed and house more than 2,000 students.

The Orkney campus in Stromness caters exclusively for postgraduates and specialises in renewable energy, while the Scottish Borders campus, 35 miles south of Edinburgh in Galashiels, specialises in textiles, fashion and design. It offers one of the few degrees in the world in menswear.

Tuition fees

» Fees for Scottish students   £0–£1,820
   RUK fees   £9,250 (capped at £27,750 for 4-year courses)
» Fees for International students 2021–22   £15,384–£19,792
» For scholarship and bursary information see
www.hw.ac.uk/study/fees/tuition-fees.htm
» Graduate salary   £25,000

Student numbers

Undergraduates	7,518	(418)
Postgraduates	1,854	(1,143)
Applications/places	9,295/1,545	
Applications per place	6	
Overall offer rate	81.8%	
International students – EU	8.8%	
Non-EU	20.1%	

Accommodation

University provided places: 2,039
Self-catered: £118–£215 per week
First years guaranteed accommodation
www.hw.ac.uk/uk/edinburgh/accommodation.htm

Where do the students come from?

State schools (non-grammar)	80.4%	First generation students	31.6%
Grammar schools	7.1%	Deprived areas	10.9%
Independent schools	12.5%	All ethnic minorities	16.8%

Social inclusion ranking (Scotland): 5

Black attainment gap	-10%
Disabled	5.5%
Mature (over 21)	23.2%

University of Hertfordshire

Hertfordshire's De Havilland campus in Hatfield has a new £12m Enterprise Hub. On the ground floor of the three-storey development are informal and formal social areas for students, staff and the business community. Above is a business incubator for start-ups and graduate entrepreneurs and the top floor has teaching space for students on courses including degree apprenticeships and MBAs.

The resource is fitting for a university which styles itself as a "business-facing" institution. When upgrading Hertfordshire to a gold award in 2018, the Teaching Excellence Framework judging panel commended the strong emphasis on work-based learning, entrepreneurship and enterprise, with employability and transferable skills embedded in the curriculum. There had been high levels of investment in physical and digital resources, the panel noted, and courses benefited from "vocationally informed pedagogy supported by the university's educational research network".

According to the new Graduate Outcomes survey, 71% were in high-skilled jobs or postgraduate study 15 months after finishing their courses – a measure that places Hertfordshire in the middle reaches of UK universities on this measure. Professional accreditations or approvals are often built into courses, and students leave with CV extras such as Microsoft qualifications or City & Guilds awards. Most courses offer work placements.

The opportunity to study at one of 170 universities in 40 countries is promoted to students – for a term, a summer or a whole year. The Go Herts award, which attracted praise from the TEF panel for its links with degree programmes, gives students formal recognition for extracurricular activities.

The university has recruited more than 500 higher and degree apprentices and predicted the number enrolled on programmes to increase by close to 50% in the 2020–21 academic year. There is a broad range of 15 apprenticeship standards, under which 25 programmes are offered. Roles include solicitor, digital and technology solutions professional, aerospace engineer, registered nurse and teacher. Responding to market needs and skills gaps locally and beyond, the university has a number of new degree apprenticeships in the pipeline, in construction, data analytics, environment and transport and logistics. Degrees in creative writing and in graphic design, advertising and branding began in September 2020.

College Lane, Hertfordshire's original campus, is a 20-minute walk from the purpose-built £120m De Havilland base and the two are linked by a free shuttle bus, footpaths and cycle lanes. Hertfordshire has its own teaching observatory for hands-on learning in astronomy and astrophysics six miles from Hatfield. Bayfordbury Observatory, which was

---

College Lane
Hatfield AL10 9AB
01707 284 800
ask@herts.ac.uk
www.herts.ac.uk
www.hertfordshire.su
Open days:
see website

The Times and The Sunday Times **Rankings**
Overall Ranking: 99 (last year: 88)

Teaching quality	79.3%	72
Student experience	78.1%	=61
Research quality	5.6%	=86
Entry standards	107	=120
Graduate prospects	71.3%	81
Good honours	65.7%	123
Expected completion rate	82%	=85
Student/staff ratio	14.8	=45
Services and facilities	£2,859	30

opened by the late Sir Patrick Moore after an upgrade in 2000, features some of the latest technology in the field, such as seven large optical telescopes, four radio telescopes and a high-definition planetarium.

Simulation suites that recreate real-life work environments include a full-scale Crown Court replica and a large clinical simulation centre. The Hutton Hub on the College Lane site houses the students' union, a counselling centre, a pharmacy, banking facilities and a juice bar. The campus contains a £50m science building, an art gallery in the media centre and the £38m Forum, which has three entertainment spaces, a restaurant, café and multiple bars. The Automotive Centre on College Lane delivers up-to-date engineering teaching and many Formula One teams have Hertfordshire graduates on their staff.

In the 2014 Research Excellence Framework, more than half of the work submitted by Hertfordshire was placed in one of the top two categories. The best results were in history: 45% of the submission was assessed as world-leading and all achieved the top grade for external impact.

Few universities have more students drawn from ethnic minorities than the near 60% undertaking courses here – also unusual for a university in a non-urban location in southern England. Half of Hertfordshire's students are the first in their family to go to university.

There are widening participation links with schools across Hertfordshire, including the two which the university helped to establish – Hatfield Community Free School and the Elstree University Technical College. For new students from households of incomes under £25,000 the UH Undergraduate Bursary is worth £1,000 paid in two £500 instalments in the first year of study only.

The £15m Hertfordshire Sports Village was selected as one of 17 training camps for athletes competing in the 2012 London Olympics. It features a 110-station health and fitness centre, 25-metre pool, a physiotherapy and sports injury clinic and a large, multipurpose sports hall.

Prices in the modern student accommodation start below the £100-a-week mark for those willing to share a twin room, which feels like good value considering the university's commuter belt location. Trains to King's Cross take 25 minutes, though there is also plenty to do in the network of local Hertfordshire towns, including St Albans, Watford and Broxbourne as well as Hatfield. There are 4,710 study bedrooms across both campuses, enough to guarantee a place for all first-years.

Tuition fees

»	Fees for UK students	£9,250
	Foundation courses	£6,165
»	Fees for International students 2020–21	£13,450
»	For scholarship and bursary information see www.herts.ac.uk/study/fees-and-funding	
»	Graduate salary	£24,000

Student numbers

Undergraduates	15,562 (2,583)
Postgraduates	2,028 (4,109)
Applications/places	20,480/3,630
Applications per place	5.6
Overall offer rate	71.2%
International students – EU	3.5%
Non-EU	15.2%

Accommodation

University provided places: 4,710
Self-catered: £100–£210 per week
First years guaranteed accommodation
www.herts.ac.uk/life/student-accommodation

Where do the students come from?

State schools (non-grammar)	95.6%	First generation students	49.5%	
Grammar schools	2.2%	Deprived areas	6.2%	
Independent schools	2.2%	All ethnic minorities	58.7%	

Social inclusion ranking: =62

Black attainment gap	-26.4%
Disabled	4.9%
Mature (over 21)	22.3%

University of the Highlands and Islands

Of all the institutions in this guide, the University of the Highlands and Islands (UHI) is perhaps the one best prepared for post-pandemic higher education. Online course delivery has long been the norm in a university federation made up of 13 colleges and research institutions, with 70 local learning centres spread across hundreds of square miles of this beautiful, isolated region of the United Kingdom.

There are no fewer than 113 references to online study in its 2021 prospectus, billing a pre-Covid UHI somewhat presciently as a "university of today for the world of tomorrow". Teaching is often delivered through "blended" learning, combining online and face-to-face tuition with small class sizes and extensive use of video conferencing, although some courses are already available entirely online.

Applications have been running at near-record levels over the past two years (and at eight times the level of 2010), and although they have fallen back by around 5%, this is largely attributable to the uncertainties related to the pandemic.

The same features that are virtues in serving its region and country make comparison with other universities nigh on impossible. UHI was withdrawn from our rankings in 2017 on account of its dissipated nature, and large numbers of part-time staff and further education students within its various colleges.

These stretch from Shetland in the far northeast to Campbeltown in the southwest; from UHI Lews Castle College, set in 600 acres of parkland, on the Isle of Lewis in the northwest to UHI Perth College in the east. There are about 8,500 full- and part-time degree students split between the various sites. They live mostly locally to the colleges, but the university offers just over 600 places in student accommodation, half of them at UHI Inverness College.

The federation operates from some spectacular locations. The university claims that its harbourside Lochmaddy campus in North Uist is "possibly the UK's most attractive location to study art" and the North Highland College has an equestrian centre in Caithness, with international-sized outdoor and indoor arenas.

Some colleges are relatively large and located in the urban centres such as Perth, Elgin and Inverness, while others are smaller institutions. There are a dozen specialist research facilities in all, as well as an enterprise and research centre on the Inverness campus. They helped to produce some extremely good results in the 2014 Research Excellence Framework. Almost 70% of the research submitted for review was classified as world-leading or internationally excellent.

UHI Sabhal Mor Ostaig is the only Gaelic-medium college in the world, set in stunning

---

Executive Office
12b Ness Walk, Inverness IV3 5SQ
01463 279 190
info@uhi.ac.uk
www.uhi.ac.uk
www.uhi.ac.uk/en/students/
get-involved/
students-association/
Open days: see website

The Times and The Sunday Times **Rankings**
Overall Ranking: n/a
No data available

scenery on the Isle of Skye. Across the university, many courses can be studied in the language. UHI was the first in Scotland to produce a Gaelic Language Plan, which includes proposals to enhance the Gaelic curriculum, produce more bilingual resources for students and hold more Gaelic events. Donnie Munro, the former Runrig frontman, is director of development, fundraising and the arts here.

As the university has grown in size and popularity, so its students have increasingly come from outside the Highland region, from Scotland more widely and beyond. More than half of UHI's students are over 21 when they begin their studies.

More new degree programmes – 50 in all – were introduced at UHI in September 2020 than at any other university in the UK, as it seeks to keep its offering in line with the latest requirements from students. The vast majority of new courses feature archaeology, culture, heritage, history, literature, philosophy, politics, Scottish history, sociology, social sciences and theology in combination with other subjects.

Among the new offerings are a BSc in optometry and a BA in literature and creative writing. Already planned for 2021 entry are degrees in sustainable development, sports therapy and rehabilitation, and moral and philosophical studies with religious education. Like all courses, availability varies from campus to campus.

The university is alert to local business and social requirements and tailors provision accordingly. A £9m health, social care and life sciences school was established in 2017 with the aim of further extending UHI's work in these areas. This includes collaboration with Dundee and St Andrews universities on the development of Scotland's first graduate-entry four-year medical programme (ScotGem) to enhance remote and rural training and the supply of GPs. The first 55 ScotGem students started in September 2018.

Elsewhere, UHI works with organisations as diverse as the Crown Estate, the Cairngorm National Park Authority, the Dounreay Partnership and SSE, the Perth-based energy company. A partnership with the software giant IBM has spawned the innovative BSc in applied software development, giving students access to the latest technologies replicating modern software development practices, guest speakers, industry mentors from around the world, and enhanced IBM Cloud access to complement students' learning.

Tuition fees

» Fees for Scottish students £0–£1,820
RUK fees £9,000 (capped at £27,000 for 4-year courses)
» Fees for International students 2020–21 £12,000–£13,200
» For scholarship and bursary information see www.uhi.ac.uk/en/studying-at-uhi/first-steps/how-much-will-it-cost/
» Graduate salary £21,000

Student numbers

Undergraduates	5,505	(2,931)
Postgraduates	364	(727)
Applications/places		4,310/1,065
Applications per place		4
Overall offer rate		58.8%
International students – EU		2.2%
Non-EU		1.3%

Accommodation

University provided places: 612
Self-catered: £111–£159 per week
www.uhi.ac.uk/en/studying-at-uhi/first-steps/accommodation/

Where do the students come from?

State schools (non-grammar)	98.8%	First generation students	44.7%
Grammar schools	0%	Deprived areas	10%
Independent schools	1.2%	All ethnic minorities	3.7%

Social inclusion ranking (Scotland): 9

Black attainment gap	n/a
Disabled	2.7%
Mature (over 21)	54.1%

University of Huddersfield

Teaching quality is centre stage at the University of Huddersfield, where standards have attracted a raft of recognition and awards, although only a lukewarm endorsement from students themselves. The university holds gold in the government's Teaching Excellence Framework (TEF) – the top honour bestowed on only three Yorkshire universities. Huddersfield also has the highest proportion of staff with a postgraduate teaching qualification (94%), remarkable because that is not a prerequisite in the higher education sector. In 2017 Huddersfield won the first Global Teaching Excellence award, beating competitors from five continents.

Huddersfield academics have won 15 National Teaching Fellowships, which recognise individuals who have made an outstanding impact on student outcomes and higher education teaching. The TEF panel commended the university's effective use of learning analytics to target timely interventions that boost students' results. It also praised an institution-wide strategy for assessment and feedback, which ensures that all students are challenged to achieve their full potential.

All of which makes somewhat baffling the university's ranking of 82= in our latest analysis of the teaching quality questions in the 2020 National Student Survey, down almost 40 places on 2019 and a long way short of the UK top-20 ranking the university achieved on this measure in 2017. Huddersfield lies just outside the top 100 for the quality of the wider student experience, also significantly down.

There has been some reshuffling of the curriculum, with computer games design being discontinued for 2021 entry and replaced by a suite of three games-development degrees with specialisms in design, art and production. Eight new engineering-based degrees began in September 2020, including mechatronic engineering and medical engineering technologies.

More new options from 2021 include computer science with artificial intelligence, education with psychology, paramedic science, speech and language therapy. The school of music, humanities and the media is introducing degrees in performance for screen, screenwriting, digital media and communications, television studies and production, and film-making, while three current media and film courses are ending in 2021. Huddersfield has also been expanding its range of degree apprenticeships in the fields of business and of health, which now include podiatry, midwifery studies, business management, nursing and clinical practice.

Huddersfield's single-site campus is two minutes' walk from the town centre. The university has been investing heavily in teaching and research facilities. The £30m Barbara Hepworth Building, named after the sculptor and West Yorkshire native, opened in 2019 for

Queensgate
Huddersfield HD1 3DH
01484 472 625
study@hud.ac.uk
www.hud.ac.uk
www.huddersfield.su
Open days: see website

The Times and The Sunday Times **Rankings**
Overall Ranking: =73 (last year: 61)

Teaching quality	78.5%	82
Student experience	75.6%	=101
Research quality	9.4%	61
Entry standards	128	=60
Graduate prospects	72%	=75
Good honours	75.6%	=63
Expected completion rate	83.5%	=73
Student/staff ratio	15.5	=63
Services and facilities	£2,455	=65

the study of art, design and architecture. Featuring creative studios and technology facilities that combine digital and physical innovation it overlooks the Huddersfield Narrow Canal, which runs through the campus. The £31m Joseph Priestley Building has teaching spaces, workshops and laboratories for science subjects, as well as its own student hub and social area.

Future business founders can cut their teeth with an enterprise placement year, which provides students with the opportunity to set up and run their own commercial operation instead of undertaking a traditional work placement. Every undergraduate does work experience as part of their degree course and a third take extended placements in business or industry.

Significantly fewer students drop out than expected based on the course mix and social background of recruits, and 72% of graduates were in high-skilled jobs or postgraduate study 15 months after finishing their courses, the latest Higher Education Statistics Agency report showed – a result that puts Huddersfield comfortably among the mid-ranking universities on this measure.

Building on Huddersfield's proud record for widening participation in higher education are three specific projects. The year-long Progression Module is a skills boosting programme worth 12 UCAS tariff points to those who complete it successfully, which they can use towards entry requirements at Huddersfield, Leeds Beckett and Leeds Trinity universities. Aspire to Uni is a 10-year outreach programme for pupils from target primary schools, designed to improve their results and progression from SATS up to post-16 courses. Headstart Huddersfield offers applicants who qualify under widening participation criteria an extra eight UCAS points, plus support including guaranteed interviews and help deciding where to apply.

Huddersfield does not have its own halls of residence, but its preferred accommodation provider, Digs, has more than 1,600 rooms – most of them in the Storthes Hall Park student village, where they can be rented either catered or self-catering. There are also 280 spaces at Ashenhurst, just over a mile from the campus.

The Student Central building has a good range of sports facilities, including an 80-station gym, and the town's leisure centre is within 10 minutes' walk of campus. Huddersfield is renowned as a friendly town and with a 20,000-strong student population there is plenty of social life on the doorstep. Nightlife on a different scale opens up in Leeds and Manchester, both accessible by train.

Tuition fees

- » Fees for UK students £9,250
- » Fees for International students 2021–22   £15,000–£18,000
- » For scholarship and bursary information see www.hud.ac.uk/undergraduate/fees-and-finance
- » Graduate salary £22,000

Student numbers

Undergraduates	12,626 (1,052)
Postgraduates	1,811 (1,804)
Applications/places	17,235/3,000
Applications per place	5.7
Overall offer rate	76.2%
International students – EU	3.2%
Non-EU	15.2%

Accommodation

University provided places: 1,666
Catered costs: £114–£142 per week
Self-catered: £83–£115 per week
www.hud.ac.uk/uni-life/accommodation

Where do the students come from?

				Social inclusion ranking: 24	
State schools (non-grammar)	95%	First generation students	56.2%	Black attainment gap	-15%
Grammar schools	3.8%	Deprived areas	16%	Disabled	9.1%
Independent schools	1.2%	All ethnic minorities	42.9%	Mature (over 21)	19.8%

University of Hull

The University of Hull has put environmental sustainability at the top of its agenda. It has committed to becoming carbon neutral by 2027 and has a clutch of eco-friendly initiatives under way. The new £12m Aura Innovation Centre in East Yorkshire, led by the university, is working with businesses to develop renewable energy technologies, and the university-led Strength in Places consortium has been shortlisted for £36m funding to drive economic growth through clean energy in the Humber region.

The university has introduced master's degrees in renewable energy (with Siemens Gamesa) and in flood risk management. Hull is also leading a joint bid with Humberside Fire and Rescue Service for Ark, a £15m Flood Resilience Centre based in the Humber region which will have a full-scale 120-metre-long street and water rapids course for research and training.

The university is in the second year of its unique six-year partnership with Team GB, during which the rescheduled Tokyo 2020 Olympic Games will take place in 2021. It also includes the Paris 2024 Summer Games and the Beijing 2022 Winter Games. Students can volunteer and participate in Team GB events hosted at Hull, and first-year business school students have been tasked with creating a marketing strategy to keep Team GB fans engaged between the Games. The university is helping Team GB athletes prepare for Tokyo through a virtual reality project and students are working on research to inspire athletes.

Hull's course programme is being streamlined and reassessed to prepare students for the future world of work. Recruitment to language degrees, apart from Chinese, was suspended in 2019 and some philosophy courses were cut. A suite of creative industries degrees is due to be introduced, with five specialisms including games design, music production and media production. Physiotherapy and a range of new music degrees took their first students in September 2020 and economics had placement years and study abroad options attached to programmes. In 2021 professional policing will have its first intake, as will three- and four-year courses in applied modern languages – approved for this cycle but suspended since.

Hull holds silver in the Teaching Excellence Framework and was praised by the judging panel for its course design and assessment practices that stretch and challenge students. Assessors were also impressed by Hull's investment in physical and digital infrastructure.

More than 60% of the work entered for the 2014 Research Excellence Framework was rated as world-leading or internationally excellent, although Hull made a relatively small submission for a pre-1992 university.

Cottingham Road
Hull HU6 7RX
01482 466 100
admissions@hull.ac.uk
www.hull.ac.uk
www.hullstudent.com
Open days: see website

The Times and The Sunday Times **Rankings**
Overall Ranking: =60 (last year: 77)

Teaching quality	80.3%	=57
Student experience	78.6%	=55
Research quality	16.7%	54
Entry standards	125	=70
Graduate prospects	75%	=57
Good honours	73.7%	=77
Expected completion rate	82.9%	=76
Student/staff ratio	15.1	=55
Services and facilities	£2,594	50

The best results were in the allied health category, where 87% of the research was awarded three or four stars, while geography and computer science also did well.

The university won a Queen's Anniversary Prize for its research into slavery and played a key role in shaping the UK's Modern Slavery Act. Hull's strength in politics is reflected in a steady flow of graduates into the House of Commons. The Westminster-Hull internship programme offers a year-long placement for British politics and legislative studies students.

Hull announced in 2019 that it would be making redundancies in an attempt to save £25m over two years after a review found that the university's financial position was "unsustainable" and its league table position "untenable". It dropped out of our top 100 for the first time in 2018, recovering 43 places in the past two years – but it remains among the lowest-ranked of the pre-1992 generation of universities.

Professor Susan Lea, Hull's vice-chancellor, said the cost savings would allow it to "continue to make investments in its campus". The university is in the midst of a £300m investment programme to boost the student experience, teaching and research.

The medical school Hull shares with the University of York is expanding after being awarded another 90 places. In the £25m Allam medical building, opened by the Queen and partly paid for by the local philanthropist

Assem Allam, medical students can work alongside nursing, midwifery and allied health undergraduates, as well as PhD students, advanced nurse practitioners and physician associates. It offers a gateway year for students who may not meet the standard entry requirements for the five-year course, and Pathways to Medicine – run with the Sutton Trust – supports talented budding medics by giving them insights into the profession and help with the application and selection processes.

Hull's single-site redbrick campus has industry-standard recording and performance facilities in the redeveloped Middleton Hall and an art gallery in the £28m upgraded Brynmor Jones library. A £4.5m redevelopment of the students' union is underway and a £16m enhancement of the sports facilities is almost complete.

The east coast city of Hull is kind on the student wallet and there is plenty of local nightlife. Leeds is less than an hour away by train.

Tuition fees

»	Fees for UK students	£9,250
	Foundation courses	£7,500
»	Fees for International students 2021–22	£14,800–£17,550
	Medicine	£34,950
»	For scholarship and bursary information see	
	www.hull.ac.uk/choose-hull/study-at-hull/money	
»	Graduate salary	£23,000

Student numbers

Undergraduates	11,817	(1,424)
Postgraduates	1,993	(858)
Applications/places		11,775/2,330
Applications per place		5.1
Overall offer rate		79%
International students – EU		3.8%
Non-EU		10.1%

Accommodation

University provided places: 2,312
Self-catered: £125–£210 per week
First years guaranteed accommodation
www.hull.ac.uk/choose-hull/student-life/accommodation

Where do the students come from?

State schools (non-grammar)	92.1%	First generation students	48%		
Grammar schools	3.3%	Deprived areas	24.1%		
Independent schools	4.6%	All ethnic minorities	10.5%		

Social inclusion ranking: 30

Black attainment gap	-6.5%
Disabled	6.9%
Mature (over 21)	28.8%

Imperial College London

One of the country's elite universities, Imperial College London has set out a new five-year programme to widen participation in higher education among under-represented groups. The only UK university to focus exclusively on science, medicine, engineering and business is piloting new admissions schemes to better take into account the full context of applications and give students from disadvantaged groups a better shot.

Outreach practices vary by department. The Department of Life Sciences and the medical biosciences degree within the School of Medicine will make guaranteed offers to widening-participation applicants based on their predicted grades meeting the minimum entry standard. Interviews, contextual offers and a guarantee to ask for the minimum entry standard are among the range of other considerations made to applicants who qualify under widening-participation criteria.

The university is introducing outreach programmes aimed specifically at black students, whose number has been growing at Imperial. The Access and Participation programme is also exploring the establishment of a maths sixth-form school, which would target under-represented groups, and Imperial is rolling out a free digital platform to support students taking further maths.

The measures should help improve Imperial's record on social inclusion. It has one of the country's largest contingents from independent schools, with a third of the intake arriving from the private sector. Almost a quarter of undergraduates went to selective grammars, and only just over four in 10 students arrive from non-selective state comprehensive schools.

Imperial features in the top 10 of both the QS and Times Higher Education world rankings. It was named by Reuters as the third most innovative university in Europe – and top in the UK. It leads our new graduate prospects measure, with more than 95% of graduates in high-skilled employment or postgraduate study 15 months after leaving Imperial, for which it wins our University of the Year for Graduate Employment award.

Imperial was gold-rated in the government's Teaching Excellence Framework, praised for providing an "exceptionally stimulating and stretching academic, vocational and professional education that successfully challenges students to achieve their full potential".

The university received stellar plaudits in the 2014 Research Excellence Framework, too, when Imperial's research was found to have greater impact on the economy and society than that of any other university. Ninety per cent of its submission was rated as world-

---

South Kensington Campus
Exhibition Road
London SW7 2BU
Engineering.admissions
@Imperial.ac.uk
Medicine.ug.admissions
@Imperial.ac.uk
Ns.admissions@Imperial.ac.uk
www.imperial.ac.uk
www.imperialcollegeunion.org
Open days: see website

Edinburgh
Belfast
Cardiff
LONDON

The Times and The Sunday Times **Rankings**
Overall Ranking: 5 (last year: 4)

Teaching quality	75.5%	117
Student experience	78.5%	57
Research quality	56.2%	2
Entry standards	189	6
Graduate prospects	95.4%	1
Good honours	91.5%	5
Expected completion rate	96.8%	4
Student/staff ratio	11.1	3
Services and facilities	£3,914	4

leading or internationally excellent overall, a performance bettered only by Cambridge.

Undergraduates in most subjects are based at the original South Kensington campus, which is home to the business school and the Dyson School of Engineering, part-funded through a £12m donation from the inventor's foundation. The university's strength in engineering is renowned and it is the only UK university to provide teaching and research in the full range of engineering disciplines.

There are nine Imperial sites in London, with teaching bases attached to a number of hospitals in central and west London. The Faculty of Medicine is one of Europe's largest in terms of its staff and student numbers, while the UK's first Academic Health Science Centre (AHSC), run in partnership with Imperial College Healthcare NHS Trust, aims to translate research advances into patient care.

The landmark new 23-acre White City campus – which is set to cost £3bn in total, making it the most expensive new university building in London this century – is continuing to open new facilities as it develops. Its Translation & Innovation Hub (I-Hub) is a home for research-based businesses, and the £167m Molecular Sciences Research Hub opened in 2019.

Competition for places is stiff, with an offer rate that equates to a little over four in 10 applicants – only students admitted to Cambridge, Oxford, St Andrews, Glasgow and Strathclyde have higher average entry qualifications. New courses for 2021 entry include a five-year degree in aeronautical engineering and a four-year planetary science course, both with a year abroad.

The Imperial Bursary makes financial awards on a sliding scale from £2,000 to £5,000 to UK undergraduates with annual household incomes of up to £60,000 – a far higher threshold than at most universities. In the 2019–20 academic year nearly four in 10 bursary recipients got the maximum amount, and 36% of the UK intake received the bursary overall. There are also scholarships for music, sport and academic excellence.

Imperial remained London's top sporting university in 2018–19, ranked 25th overall in the BUCS (British Universities & Colleges Sport) league. Outdoor facilities are remote, but there is a well-equipped campus sports centre with a swimming pool. New entrants are guaranteed one of the 2,900 residential places, as long as they apply by the deadline. As for social lives, Imperial students have all that London offers on their doorstep.

Tuition fees

- » Fees for UK students £9,250
- » Fees for International students 2021–22 £32,000–£34,500
  Medicine £45,300
- » For scholarship and bursary information see
  www.imperial.ac.uk/study/ug/fees-and-funding/
- » Graduate salary £33,000

Student numbers

Undergraduates	9,979	(4)
Postgraduates	7,505	(1,627)
Applications/places	23,380/2,845	
Applications per place	8.2	
Overall offer rate	43%	
International students – EU	17.3%	
Non-EU	35.4%	

Accommodation

University provided places: 2,900
Self-catered: £112–£302 per week
First years guaranteed accommodation
www.imperial.ac.uk/study/campus-life/accommodation/halls/

Where do the students come from?

					Social inclusion ranking: 112	
State schools (non-grammar)	43.4%	First generation students	22.3%	Black attainment gap	-7%
Grammar schools	23.7%	Deprived areas	4.1%	Disabled	2.7%
Independent schools	32.9%	All ethnic minorities	56.9%	Mature (over 21)	7.3%

Keele University

Keele's new Vet School, a collaboration with Harper Adams University, admitted its first intake of students in September 2020. One of only nine vet schools in the UK, it offers 72 places each year on a five-year bachelor of veterinary medicine and surgery degree, delivered at both campuses. In partnership with local clinical providers and industry, the landmark venture will add new facilities to Keele including a veterinary hospital and a clinical skill centre, due to be built in 2021.

Keele's 600-acre parkland campus is the UK's largest and has ample space for its other new development: the Marriott chain is building one of its Courtyard hotels, with 150 bedrooms, a restaurant and bar, meeting rooms and a fitness suite on site. It will be a handy on-campus bolthole for open-day visitors and delegates to academic conferences, as well as being used by the organisations based at the university's Science and Innovation Park and wedding guests from Keele Hall, the campus's grand 19th-century mansion.

The university is ploughing its largest investment ever into teaching and learning to accommodate its intention to grow by a third over five years, with postgraduates accounting for many of the new places. Sir David Attenborough opened the new life sciences laboratories in 2019 and the Keele Business School building followed in the same year, providing new spaces for undergraduates and graduates, a big-data laboratory and a business incubator. The £34m Central Science Laboratory also opened to students in 2019, bringing together practical teaching across a range of disciplines.

Life at the university, which is located in the heart of England near Stoke-on-Trent, is often referred to affectionately as the "Keele bubble" due to the friendly and safe environment it offers students. The campus has everything a local town would provide – bars, restaurants, shops, a bank, a health centre and a pharmacy – as well as a thriving students' union, all within walking distance of the student accommodation buildings and set amid bucolic greenery.

Keele is a former winner of our University of the Year for Student Experience, although its scores in this area in the latest National Student Survey have fallen back somewhat. The 1949-founded university has students from more than 100 countries, and they tend to like it, with Keele generally being among the leaders on student satisfaction.

The Teaching Excellence Framework (TEF) awarded Keele gold, its highest standard. The judging panel commended an institutional culture that "demonstrably values teaching as highly as research", with outstanding levels of student engagement and excellent teaching and assessment practices resulting in a commitment to learning.

Keele ST5 5BG
01782 734 010
admissions@keele.ac.uk
www.keele.ac.uk
www.keelesu.com
Open days:
see website

The Times and The Sunday Times **Rankings**
Overall Ranking: =51 (last year: 46)

Teaching quality	80.5%	=52
Student experience	79%	=48
Research quality	22.1%	53
Entry standards	123	=76
Graduate prospects	78.2%	43
Good honours	76%	59
Expected completion rate	86.9%	=52
Student/staff ratio	14.3	=30
Services and facilities	£2,266	83

The Keele Curriculum, introduced in 2012, came in for particular praise in the TEF assessment. It covers voluntary and sporting activities, as well as the academic core, contributing to the Keele University Skills Portfolio, which is accredited by the Institute of Leadership and Management.

In the 2014 Research Excellence Framework more than 70% of the work submitted by Keele was placed in the top two categories. Research in primary care and health sciences, pharmacy, chemistry, science and technology, the life sciences and history scored particularly well.

As well as the new veterinary programme, degrees in public health and law with professional legal practice launched in September 2020. Five more open to students in 2021: in data science, cell and tissue engineering, geography (combined honours), geology and physical geography, and business and psychology.

Seventy-eight per cent of Keele graduates were in high-skilled jobs or postgraduate study 15 months after completing their courses, the latest figures show – placing the university comfortably in the top half of UK institutions for this measure. Fewer than one in 10 students drop out, a result that beats the projected benchmark figure based on the social and academic mix of the intake.

Keele succeeds in attracting a more socially diverse intake than many other pre-1992 universities. Almost nine out of 10 undergraduates are state-educated and more than a third are from black, Asian and minority ethnic (BAME) backgrounds. Contextual information relating to applicants' backgrounds and experiences is taken into account for most applications to Keele, and the medical school runs a widening participation scheme to support under-represented groups. Higher Horizons+, the National Collaborative Outreach Programme led by Keele, engages 80 schools and 25 colleges across Staffordshire, Shropshire and Cheshire in free activities – such as residential stays and advice sessions – to boost outreach work.

The students' union organises events on campus every day and night of the week during term time and nearby Newcastle-under-Lyme has options for off-campus nights out. Sports facilities include a full-size 3G football pitch suitable for all-weather play in a variety of sports to supplement the indoor facilities. The university has about 2,800 residential spaces, with prices as low as £90 a week.

Tuition fees

» Fees for UK students £9,250
» Fees for International students 2021–22 £15,500–£23,000
  Foundation courses £14,000; Medicine £37,000
» For scholarship and bursary information see
  www.keele.ac.uk/study/undergraduate/tuitionfeesandfunding/
» Graduate salary £23,000

Student numbers

Undergraduates	7,918	(538)
Postgraduates	645	(1,765)
Applications/places	13,665/1,980	
Applications per place	6.9	
Overall offer rate	82.2%	
International students – EU	2.2%	
Non-EU	6.3%	

Accommodation

University provided places: 2,800
Self-catered: £90–£171 per week
First years guaranteed accommodation
www.keele.ac.uk/discover/accommodation/

Where do the students come from?

State schools (non-grammar)	86.7%	First generation students	43.6%		
Grammar schools	7.1%	Deprived areas	20%		
Independent schools	6.2%	All ethnic minorities	34.8%		

Social inclusion ranking: 56

Black attainment gap	-22.4%
Disabled	7.1%
Mature (over 21)	15.2%

University of Kent

The first intake of trainee doctors started at the new Kent and Medway Medical School (KMMS) in September 2020. The region's first medical school serves a growing population and is a joint venture with Canterbury Christ Church University. Offering a five-year Bachelor of Medicine, Bachelor of Surgery degree jointly awarded by the universities, KMMS is working in partnership with the long-established Brighton and Sussex Medical School.

Kent is constructing the Pears Building at the Canterbury campus for KMMS, which will have a 150-seat lecture theatre, seminar rooms, social spaces and a GP simulation suite among its facilities. The opening of the medical school is in line with its mission to become a leading civic university, delivering social, educational, cultural, public and economic benefits across Kent and Medway by 2025.

The university's digital estate has benefited from a revamp that stands to make the student life cycle easier to manage, and in turn should support its determination to offer a transformative student experience. Thanks to KentVision software, the admissions and student data system has been streamlined into a single administrative journey with the aim of adding clarity, information and seamlessness for applicants and students.

Kent's main 300-acre campus overlooks Canterbury. The original 1960s low-rise buildings blend with modern facilities such as the recently opened £18.8m economics building, which has given students on the popular degree course their own space for the first time. The latest addition is a £4m indoor tennis and events centre, which has four acrylic courts and will offer improved space for exams and conferences.

The university is distinguished by being one of only a handful in the UK with a college system. Every student is attached to a college, the beating heart of social life – especially in the first year – with academic as well as residential facilities. The Canterbury campus has six colleges and there is one at the university's Medway campus on the old Chatham naval base, which is shared with Greenwich and Canterbury Christ Church universities.

The £50m School of Pharmacy and the purpose-built Centre for Music and Audio Technology are at Medway too, along with the refurbished business school. The university also has a base in Tonbridge, mainly for short courses as preparation for degree-level study.

The college system was one of the factors that contributed to Kent securing gold in the Teaching Excellence Framework. The panel saw the system as a vital element underpinning a "flexible and personalised" approach to academic support and praised Kent's "outstanding" Student Success Project,

The Registry
Canterbury CT2 7NZ
01227 768 896
www.kent.ac.uk/contact-us
www.kent.ac.uk
www.kentunion.co.uk
Open days: see website

Edinburgh
Belfast
Cardiff London
CANTERBURY

***The Times and The Sunday Times* Rankings**
Overall Ranking: 48 (last year: 54)

Teaching quality	77.9%	=94
Student experience	76.8%	85
Research quality	35.2%	33
Entry standards	131	=54
Graduate prospects	72.9%	=68
Good honours	78%	53
Expected completion rate	88.8%	43
Student/staff ratio	17	=90
Services and facilities	£1,952	=103

which identifies trends in results and completion rates, and acts to help those likely to fall behind.

Medicine was one of 13 new options for 2020 entrants, many of the others being reworkings of established degrees, such as law with a language (Italian), chemistry with a year abroad and mechanical engineering with a year in industry. Those joining in 2021 will have new degrees in graphic design and in spatial and interior design to choose from. Kent has more than 450 degree apprentices on 14 programmes across roles including professional economist, laboratory scientist and senior leader.

Almost three-quarters of the work submitted for the 2014 Research Excellence Framework was judged world-leading or internationally excellent. Led by successes in social work and social policy, music and drama, and modern languages, Kent achieved its highest ranking on research.

The university is arguably the UK's most active participant in EU programmes. It has postgraduate sites in Brussels, Paris, Athens and Rome, and gives many undergraduates the option of a year abroad. Almost 40% of the academic staff are EU nationals and there are partnerships with more than 100 European universities. Brexit may be felt harder here than elsewhere as a consequence, although the vice-chancellor has insisted the university's European outlook will not change.

Nearly 600 of 2019–20's undergraduate intake received the Kent financial support package, worth £1,500 a year to state-educated students from households where the income is below £42,875, if they meet other criteria, such as living in social housing. The Kent Scholarship – a single £2,000 award – may be paid on top, or by itself, to students with AAA at A-level, or equivalent qualifications, or AAB if one of the subjects is either maths or a foreign language.

With 4,689 residential spaces, Kent is one of the best-provided universities for accommodation. A £3m hub opened in 2018 in the Park Wood student village on the Canterbury campus, which includes a shop, café/bar and dance studios. A fitness suite, strength and conditioning training area and three multipurpose sports halls are among the other sports facilities. The university is also a partner in the £3m Medway Park sports centre, which has squash courts, an athletics track, a gym and swimming facilities.

Canterbury is big on olde-worlde charm, with its cobbled streets, cosy pubs and towering cathedral, but there are more student-centric venues such as The Cuban, which hosts club nights, and a vintage-clothes den, Revivals.

Tuition fees

» Fees for UK students £9,250
» Fees for International students 2021–22 £16,800–£20,500
   Medicine £46,600
» For scholarship and bursary information see
   www.kent.ac.uk/finance-student/fees/index.htm
» Graduate salary £24,000

Student numbers

Undergraduates	14,766	(786)
Postgraduates	2,314	(1,399)
Applications/places	22,450/3,650	
Applications per place	6.2	
Overall offer rate	86.5%	
International students – EU	7.8%	
Non-EU	14%	

Accommodation

University provided places: 4,689
Catered costs: £143–£264 per week
Self-catered: £127–£204 per week
First years guaranteed accommodation
www.kent.ac.uk/accommodation/

Where do the students come from?

State schools (non-grammar)	90.9%	First generation students	46.4%	Black attainment gap	-25.5%
Grammar schools	3.4%	Deprived areas	10.2%	Disabled	6.1%
Independent schools	5.8%	All ethnic minorities	39.1%	Mature (over 21)	8.2%

Social inclusion ranking: 82

King's College London

A new Department of Engineering opened in 2019 at King's College London (KCL), a significant milestone for the university as it builds on strengths in robotics, telecommunications and biomedical engineering.

Headed by Professor Barbara Shollock, who brings links with Nasa and Rolls-Royce to the role, the department has introduced an undergraduate degree in general engineering for 2020, taking a project- and group-based approach to solving practical problems. KCL's Strand campus is adding new laboratories and group learning spaces and the department aims to help KCL train engineers to address global technological and societal challenges in new ways.

The new degree is likely to boost the university's consistent popularity. Applications increased by 9% in March 2020, having risen more than 8% in 2019. Degree programmes in history and political economy, creative, media and cultural industries, and dental therapy and hygiene have been added to the curriculum, as well as a suite of neuroscience and psychology courses with options for a placement year and study abroad.

More than 86% of KCL graduates were in high-skilled jobs or postgraduate study within 15 months of finishing their course, the latest figures show, ranking the university eighth in the UK. Opportunities for students to engage with employers contributed to a silver award in the Teaching Excellence Framework. The panel highlighted the "excellent" extent to which students were stretched academically and the "strong research-led culture" that requires all research staff to teach.

The London universities with high profiles in research tend to struggle with student satisfaction. KCL scores in the bottom five UK institutions for student satisfaction with teaching quality and the wider experience, according to our analysis of the latest National Student Survey. This depresses its rank in our overall league table. Its QS World Universities Ranking – which doesn't take into account student satisfaction – is 33rd, only three places lower than our domestic ranking.

KCL's four campuses near the banks of the Thames occupy such prime territory that students and tourists often converge outside its buildings, all within a square mile of each other. There is a fifth campus in Denmark Hill, south London. KCL is one of the oldest and largest colleges of the University of London, with more than 30,000 students – a third of them from outside the UK.

The Strand site and the Waterloo campus house most of the non-medical departments. KCL's Dickson Poon School of Law has expanded into the east wing of the picturesque Somerset House. Bush House, the former headquarters of the BBC World Service and another London landmark

Strand
London WC2R 2LS
020 7848 5454
Admissions@kcl.ac.uk
www.kcl.ac.uk
www.kclsu.org
Open days: see website

The Times and The Sunday Times **Rankings**
Overall Ranking: 30 (last year: 30)

Teaching quality	72.5%	125
Student experience	70.8%	126
Research quality	44%	9
Entry standards	164	19
Graduate prospects	86.3%	8
Good honours	85.5%	18
Expected completion rate	91.4%	=30
Student/staff ratio	11.9	=7
Services and facilities	£2,810	34

building, is the latest addition to the estate. It houses KCL's business school, the faculty of science and some student services.

Nursing and midwifery and some biomedical subjects are based at Waterloo, while medicine and dentistry are mainly at Guy's Hospital, near London Bridge, and the St Thomas' Hospital campus, across the river from the Houses of Parliament. The Denmark Hill campus, in south London, hosts the Institute of Psychiatry, Psychology and Neuroscience and has facilities for dentistry.

Twelve Nobel prize winners have studied or worked at KCL, which is in our top 10 for research after 85% of the work submitted to the 2014 Research Excellence Framework was judged to be world-leading or internationally excellent. Law, education, clinical medicine and philosophy all ranked in the top three in the country and there were good results in general engineering, history, psychology and communication and media studies. KCL's success in the assessment produced the biggest increase in research funding at any university.

KCL has had a role in some of modern life's big advances, including the discovery of DNA and the development of radar. It continues to collaborate with hundreds of businesses – not least by co-ordinating the Covid-19 Research Registry.

More than half of its undergraduates come from ethnic minority backgrounds, with 65% from comprehensive schools and colleges, ranking KCL second among the highly selective Russell Group universities for social inclusion, behind only Queen Mary, University of London.

About 40% of the intake tends to qualify for a bursary or scholarship and there are some heavy-hitting awards – such as the £50,000 Michael and Saki Ruth Dockrill scholarship for one student taking a war studies degree. The King's Living bursary of £1,200 to £1,600 is paid on a sliding scale to students from households with incomes up to £42,875.

The university sports grounds involve a train ride south of the city centre but have plenty to offer, including facilities for all the main sports, plus rifle ranges, two gyms and a swimming pool.

Accommodation comes catered or self-catered and a space in one of the 4,912 rooms is guaranteed to students who apply by the deadline. Prices start at £155-£169 a week self-catered (nearly 1,000 spaces) but can be up to £410 a week to live in the glare of London's bright lights.

Tuition fees

» Fees for UK students £9,250
» Fees for International students 2021–22 £20,790–£28,050
   Medicine £40,800; Dentistry £45,600
» For scholarship and bursary information see
   www.kcl.ac.uk/study/undergraduate/Index
» Graduate salary £29,000

Student numbers

Undergraduates	17,737 (1,464)
Postgraduates	8,899 (4,793)
Applications/places	52,110/6,020
Applications per place	8.7
Overall offer rate	56.1%
International students – EU	12.9%
Non-EU	24.8%

Accommodation

University provided places: 4,912
Catered costs: £293–£306
Self-catered: £155–£410 per week
First years guaranteed accommodation
www.kcl.ac.uk/study/accommodation

Where do the students come from?

State schools (non-grammar)	65.1%	First generation students	36.4%	Black attainment gap	-11.2%
Grammar schools	12.7%	Deprived areas	3.7%	Disabled	5.9%
Independent schools	22.2%	All ethnic minorities	58.5%	Mature (over 21)	21.8%

Social inclusion ranking:75

Kingston University

Kingston's £50m Town House, which opened in January 2020, has become the new heart of the Penrhyn Road campus. It features a library and archive, an auditorium, dance studios and a studio theatre along with informal learning spaces and two cafés that are open to the public – evidence of Kingston's intention that the building acts as a gateway between the university and the local area. Designed by award-winning architects to exacting standards of environmental sustainability, it has been shortlisted for an industry award.

At the Kingston School of Art's Knights Park campus, facilities have been boosted by a £20m refurbishment. Students have a 3D workshop, a digital hackspace (an electronics and programming workshop that encourages creative collaboration) and professional-level kit for design and architecture among their new resources. The revamp also included retro-fitted studios and roomy workshops that flow into design studios for the university's fashion department.

Since a high point at the start of the decade, applications to Kingston have more than halved and the number of students starting degrees at the university has dropped by about 20% since 2014. The decline has steadied, though, and applications increased by about 5% in 2020, buoyed by rises in nursing, education and business, and by interest from non-EU applicants.

Kingston added one new degree for 2020 in creative and cultural industries: fashion promotion and communications. Its suite of degree apprenticeships is the focus of greater growth. Five programmes in vocational disciplines around construction and health are set to be joined by six new sector subject areas including education and childcare, engineering and manufacturing, strategic leadership and laboratory science – which will more than double the numbers on programmes to around 400 by September 2021.

Just over two-thirds of Kingston graduates were in high-skilled jobs or postgraduate study 15 months after finishing their course, according to the Graduate Outcomes survey, published for the first time in summer 2020. A management programme has begun at the university's business school to help micro firms of up to nine employees use technology to boost their productivity. Kingston has consistently been among the top two universities for its number of graduate start-ups, and the enterprise department gives advice and the possibility of funding to would-be entrepreneurs in any subject.

For teaching quality, Kingston holds the lowest (bronze) rating in the Teaching Excellence Framework. The panel did compliment the university's award-winning

**Holmwood House
Penrhyn Road
Kingston upon Thames
KT1 2EE**
020 3308 9932
admissionsops@kingston.ac.uk
www.kingston.ac.uk
www.kingstonstudents.net
Open days: see website

The Times and The Sunday Times Rankings		
Overall Ranking: =104 (last year: 106)		
Teaching quality	79.1%	=74
Student experience	77.3%	=73
Research quality	5.1%	=91
Entry standards	117	=95
Graduate prospects	70.2%	90
Good honours	71.3%	=97
Expected completion rate	80.9%	95
Student/staff ratio	16.8	=86
Services and facilities	£2,761	40

focus on black, Asian and minority ethnic (BAME) students, and a completion rate which is in line with the national average for Kingston's courses and student profile. It has improved further since the TEF evaluation with about one in eight dropping out, now well below the expected level.

Building on this strength is a new programme to help BAME mental health nurses develop the skills and confidence to access more senior roles. Run jointly by Kingston and St George's, University of London, the bespoke course was shortlisted for a Royal College of Nursing Institute award and offers nurses professional development and one-to-one coaching while exploring how cultural backgrounds influence career trajectories.

With one of the country's most diverse student populations (65% from ethnic minorities), Kingston ranks in the UK top 20 in our social inclusion table. The university will award at least 400 bursaries of £2,000 to new undergraduates enrolling in 2021, provided they meet certain criteria for widening participation including neither of their parents holding a higher-education qualification, and coming from a household where the income is £25,000 or less.

Family bursaries at Kingston offer a 10% reduction in tuition fees to the children of alumni, the spouses of current students or alumni and the siblings of students or graduates.

Kingston's suburban, riverside location and its relative proximity to London's bright lights are a big selling point. Two campuses are close to Kingston town centre; another is two miles away at Kingston Hill, close to Richmond Park. The fourth campus is in Roehampton Vale, where a one-time aerospace factory now contains a technology block. Kingston is the UK's largest provider of undergraduate aerospace education, with its own Learjet and flight simulator.

The health, social care and education faculty is run jointly with St George's and there is a link with the Royal Marsden School of Cancer Nursing and Rehabilitation, enabling some students to spend up to half of their course on clinical placements working in hospital, primary care and community settings.

Good outdoor sports facilities are only three miles from the main campus and there is a gym on the Penrhyn Road site. Kingston has spent more than £20m extending and upgrading its student accommodation and all new entrants are guaranteed one of its 2,141 residential places, although the prices – which go as high as £349 a week – are less appealing.

Tuition fees

» Fees for UK students £9,250

  Foundation courses £7,800 (Early years £6,000)

» Fees for International students 2021–22 £13,500–£15,900

» For scholarship and bursary information see www.kingston.ac.uk/undergraduate/fees-and-funding/

» Graduate salary £24,000

Student numbers

Undergraduates	11,827	(864)
Postgraduates	2,553	(1,577)
Applications/places	20,820/3,355	
Applications per place	6.2	
Overall offer rate	72.5%	
International students – EU	4.7%	
Non-EU	15.1%	

Accommodation

University provided places: 2,141
Self-catered: £132–£349 per week
First years guaranteed accommodation
www.kingston.ac.uk/undergraduate/accommodation/

Where do the students come from?

State schools (non-grammar)	94.5%	First generation students	54.4%	Black attainment gap	-14%
Grammar schools	2.2%	Deprived areas	6.7%	Disabled	7.3%
Independent schools	3.3%	All ethnic minorities	64.7%	Mature (over 21)	27.6%

Social inclusion ranking: 16

Lancaster University

Applications and acceptances at Lancaster reached new highs in 2019, when more than 20,000 applied for places for the first time. The university reported a further 18% rise in applications in 2020 ahead of the coronavirus pandemic.

Lancaster had been the highest-profile proponent of "conditional unconditional" offers – dropping entry conditions for applicants who make a university their firm choice – with around a quarter of all offers to students from England, Wales and Northern Ireland falling into this category in 2019. A similar number was expected to be made for entry in autumn 2020 but the pandemic triggered a ban until 2021 to prevent them skewing the student market as universities scramble to fill places.

The surge in applications has been fuelled by a consistent ranking in our top 10 in recent years, with Lancaster joining Warwick as the most successful of the 1960s generation of universities. It was our University of the Year in 2018 and scooped our International University of the Year title the following year, based on the strength of its overseas activities and their benefits to students.

Lancaster opened a campus in Leipzig, Germany, in January 2020, ready to take its first degree students in September. It provides the chance for German students to gain a UK degree while studying in Europe, and offers UK-based students the option of studying abroad and taking short-term summer programmes. Hundreds of Lancaster students already spend part of their courses in America, Asia, Australia or Europe. Lancaster is the only UK university with a presence in sub-Saharan Africa, having opened a campus in Ghana, and there is a joint institute in China, with Beijing Jiaotong University.

At home, the campus on the outskirts of Lancaster is undergoing significant investment. A three-floor extension of the library, due to open in 2021, will add 400 study spaces and 120 silent study spaces for the university's 10,000-plus undergraduates.

The well-regarded management school is being redeveloped to include a new area for students, staff and partner organisations, while a Health Innovation campus brings together academics, entrepreneurs, business, local government and healthcare providers to help drive forward technological advances and new products.

Appropriately for a university whose chancellor is Alan Milburn, the former chair of the Social Mobility Commission, Lancaster has a good track record for widening participation. It exceeds its targets for state school-educated recruits with nine in 10 students coming through the state system. While still in the bottom 25 in our social inclusion table, it

Bailrigg
Lancaster LA1 4YW
01524 592 028
ugadmissions@lancaster.ac.uk
www.lancaster.ac.uk
www.lancastersu.co.uk
Open days: see website

The Times and The Sunday Times **Rankings**
Overall Ranking: =10 (last year: 8)

Teaching quality	79.4%	=69
Student experience	77.8%	71
Research quality	39.1%	15
Entry standards	150	=37
Graduate prospects	81.9%	=24
Good honours	79.6%	=39
Expected completion rate	93%	24
Student/staff ratio	12.5	10
Services and facilities	£3,588	8

outperforms all bar Loughborough in our academic top 10 in this regard.

Bursary support of £1,000 a year kicks in for students from households with an income of £30,000 or less (a £5,000 higher threshold than at many universities). Around a third of the intake qualifies for some form of financial assistance. There are further provisions for care-leavers or those estranged from their parents.

Academic excellence is recognised too. New UK-domiciled students achieving at least A*A*A at A-level and five or more GCSE grades at A/7 or above are awarded a £2,000 Lancaster Scholarship in their first year, while A-level results of AAA and above coupled with five or more GCSEs at A/7 or above qualify for a £1,000 scholarship paid in each year of study, subject to progression.

Five new degrees are planned for September 2021, including two in zoology (one with study abroad), an MEng in engineering, a BA in politics, religion and values and a new six-year degree in medicine and surgery. The extra year is a "gateway year" that lowers the tariff requirement to ABB at A-level, which should do wonders for increasing access to this most exclusive of subjects.

Awarded gold in the Teaching Excellence Framework (TEF), the university was praised for making students feel valued, supported and challenged academically. The TEF panel said its "culture of research-stimulated learning"

provided the knowledge, skills and understanding that are most highly valued by employers.

The university's research grades improved substantially in the 2014 Research Excellence Framework, when 83% of its work was considered world-leading or internationally excellent. There was a strong performance across the board plus particularly good results in business and management, sociology, English, and maths and statistics.

The 560-acre parkland campus features eco-friendly student residences, which in September 2019 won the best halls award in the National Student Housing Survey for the eighth time since Lancaster first entered in 2010. With more than 10,000 rooms owned, managed or endorsed by the university, all first-years and about 45% of undergraduates overall can be accommodated.

Some of the nation's most unspoilt countryside, including the Lake District, is on the university's doorstep. Sports facilities are good and conveniently placed, with a £20m sports centre on campus, as well as a boathouse on the River Lune.

Tuition fees

- » Fees for UK students £9,250
- » Fees for International students 2021–22 £19,930–£24,070
  Medicine £36,430
- » For scholarship and bursary information see www.lancaster.ac.uk/study/undergraduate/fees-and-funding
- » Graduate salary £24,000

Student numbers

Undergraduates	10,631	(23)
Postgraduates	2,436	(1,375)
Applications/places		20,175/3,405
Applications per place		5.9
Overall offer rate		86.1%
International students – EU		9.6%
Non-EU		22.8%

Accommodation

University provided places: 10,559
Catered costs: £146–£196 per week
Self-catered: £92–£171 per week
First years guaranteed accommodation
www.lancaster.ac.uk/accommodation/

Where do the students come from?

State schools (non-grammar)	78.5%	First generation students	37%	
Grammar schools	11.8%	Deprived areas	7.4%	
Independent schools	9.7%	All ethnic minorities	17.9%	

Social inclusion ranking: 93

Black attainment gap	-19.6%
Disabled	7%
Mature (over 21)	4.2%

University of Leeds

Leeds graduates are among the most sought-after by graduate employers. The university performed well in the new measure of graduate outcomes with 82% of leavers in high-skilled jobs or postgraduate study 15 months after graduating, and ranks seventh in the annual survey of the universities most targeted by leading graduate employers.

This success can be attributed in part to the plentiful partnerships with industry, yielding placement years and summer internships in businesses as diverse as Goldman Sachs and Airbus, Disney and the Leeds and York Partnership NHS Foundation Trust.

The university is working hard to team up with its alumni to provide global opportunities for students – offering jobs and providing employability insights via online and campus sessions. The LeedsforLife service, which provides academic and careers advice plus help finding work placements and volunteering opportunities, is open to students for up to five years after graduation.

Our 2017 University of the Year remains one of the most popular in the country, attracting more than 60,000 applicants last year (second only to Manchester) with applications up a further 4% in 2020 before the pandemic.

The university has invested £520m in its campus in the past five years, improving teaching, research, studying and sporting facilities. The Laidlaw Library – funded in part from the university's largest ever philanthropic donation, from Lord Laidlaw – has been built with the needs of undergraduates in mind, and the Edward Boyle Library has been refurbished.

Leeds students' union building, once famed for having the longest bar in the country, has been given a £17m makeover with improved social spaces and performance venues.

All students in campus accommodation get free off-peak access to the Edge, the award-winning sports centre which boasts the largest fitness suite of any UK university. The facility is complemented by the Brownlee Centre, the UK's first purpose-built triathlon training base, housed at Sports Park Weetwood, three miles from the main city centre campus. The centre is named after the Olympic medal-winning Brownlee brothers, Jonathan and Alistair, who are Leeds alumni.

A major campus-wide investment in IT is coming at a critical time as more teaching is likely to shift online in response to the coronavirus pandemic. Leeds already has one of the largest lecture capture and multimedia management systems in Europe, upgraded in 2019 to improve user experience. Students can access lectures and other teaching facilities through the virtual learning environment, enabling them to study at their own pace.

The Business School and School of Law

Woodhouse Lane
Leeds LS2 9JT
0113 343 2336
study@leeds.ac.uk
www.leeds.ac.uk
www.luu.org.uk
Open days: see website

The Times and The Sunday Times **Rankings**
Overall Ranking: =15 (last year: 13)

Teaching quality	77.7%	97
Student experience	77.2%	=76
Research quality	36.8%	27
Entry standards	163	=20
Graduate prospects	82%	23
Good honours	87.2%	11
Expected completion rate	93.5%	=20
Student/staff ratio	13.7	=20
Services and facilities	£3,096	19

are the latest to be upgraded as part of a £75m transformation project. The Newlyn Building has opened already, offering new teaching space and innovative technologies, with the Esther Simpson Building to follow in 2021. It will offer flexible teaching spaces, behavioural laboratories and other specialist facilities.

A £96m investment in an integrated campus for engineering and physical sciences will bring together engineering, physics and astronomy in the sort of interdisciplinary collaboration that increasingly characterises the best of British higher education. High-quality laboratories and specialised teaching spaces will benefit researchers and undergraduates alike.

Leeds secured gold in the Teaching Excellence Framework, impressing the panel with its emphasis on education inspired by "discovery, global and cultural insight, ethics and responsibility, and employability". The assessors found that students take charge of their experiences with academic and co-curricular opportunities that can enhance their learning while preparing them for the world beyond university.

More than 80% of the research assessed in the 2014 Research Excellence Framework was considered world-leading or internationally excellent, placing Leeds in the top 10 in the UK in 30% of its subject areas. It is also in the top 100 in the QS World University Rankings, one of a minority of UK institutions not to drop down the 2021 rankings.

The university occupies a 98-acre site within walking distance of the city centre, although much of the accommodation is further out. Park Lane and Headingley are particularly popular with students living out. There are about 8,500 places in university-owned, managed or endorsed accommodation. The student population is highly cosmopolitan, with 9,000 international students from 170 countries among a total of more than 38,000.

There are more than 500 undergraduate programmes, with students encouraged to take courses outside their main subject. The Leeds Curriculum scheme requires undergraduates to undertake a research project in their final year, which is intended to be seen as the "pinnacle of their academic achievement" and is weighted accordingly.

The financial support fund at Leeds is one of the largest of any institution, benefiting 31% of UK and EU undergraduates in 2019. An innovative Alternative Entry Scheme takes account of mature students' work and life experiences if they lack the formal qualifications to secure a degree place.

Tuition fees

»	Fees for UK students	£9,250
»	Fees for International students 2021–22	£20,250–£24,500
	Medicine	£35,250
»	For scholarship and bursary information see www.leeds.ac.uk/undergraduatefees	
»	Graduate salary	£25,000

Student numbers

Undergraduates	25,809	(448)
Postgraduates	8,191	(1,804)
Applications/places	60,215/6,595	
Applications per place	9.1	
Overall offer rate	64.9%	
International students – EU	4.3%	
Non-EU	21.2%	

Accommodation

University provided places: 8,500
Catered costs: £91–£210 per week
Self-catered: £91–£154 per week
First years guaranteed accommodation
www.accommodation.leeds.ac.uk/

Where do the students come from?

State schools (non-grammar)	69.1%	First generation students	33.6%	Black attainment gap	-24.2%
Grammar schools	12.2%	Deprived areas	8.1%	Disabled	5.4%
Independent schools	18.7%	All ethnic minorities	21%	Mature (over 21)	7.2%

Social inclusion ranking: =103

Leeds Arts University

In the short time since Leeds College of Art became Leeds Arts University in 2017, the north of England's only specialist arts university has blazed a trail in our league table. Our University of the Year for Student Retention in 2019–20 has kept its dropout rate down again to 3.1% — way below the 8.6% expected, taking into account the academic and social background of its intake.

Ten minutes on foot from the centre of Leeds, the university's Blenheim Walk campus has buildings purpose-built for creative undergraduate and postgraduate degrees. Vernon Street, the original base in the city centre, is where further education courses are taught.

Blenheim Walk gained a raft of modern facilities when its £22m development opened in 2019. It brought on stream studios for film, music and photography as well as a grand 230-seat auditorium, enhanced fashion design studios and a larger specialist arts library. The campus café, Dot the Lions, is an offshoot of Laynes Espresso, an independent Leeds coffeehouse.

There is professional-standard equipment to suit the different disciplines, such as large-format digital printers, 3D scanners and industrial-grade machinery for working with wood, metal and plastics. Acoustically-insulated sound booths, which record the quietest and loudest sounds, can be used to create radio or television advertisements.

Inside the building's open-plan atrium entranceway is the Blenheim Walk Gallery, which exhibited the work of Yoko Ono for its 2019 launch. The artist had previously performed at the Vernon Street building in 1966 when she was hidden in a large black bag on a dais with her then husband, Anthony Cox. They barely moved for an hour, watched by a full house of students and staff.

Leeds Arts has educated many leading creatives since its foundation in 1846 as the Leeds Government School of Art and Design and during its later incarnation as Leeds College of Art. Among them are Henry Moore and Barbara Hepworth, who were contemporaries, and more recently Damien Hirst and the comedian Leigh Francis, better known as Keith Lemon.

The university rates well on student satisfaction. It rises up our rankings to reach the elite top 20 for satisfaction with teaching quality based on our analysis of the 2020 National Student Survey, and the top 40 for the wider student experience.

The institution was awarded silver in the Teaching Excellence Framework when it was still Leeds College of Art. The panel was impressed that a significant number of teaching staff were practising artists or designers, enhancing the students' exposure to

Blenheim Walk
Leeds LS2 9AQ
0113 202 8039
admissions@leeds-art.ac.uk
www.leeds-art.ac.uk
www.leedsartsunion.org.uk
Open days: see website

The Times and The Sunday Times Rankings
Overall Ranking: 55 (last year: =56)

Teaching quality	83.5%	17
Student experience	79.6%	36
Research quality	n/a	
Entry standards	152	=31
Graduate prospects	62.4%	=119
Good honours	76.7%	55
Expected completion rate	93.6%	19
Student/staff ratio	14.1	=27
Services and facilities	£1,334	130

the creative industries, and praised the level of support for mature students and those with disabilities.

The teaching timetable is punctuated by "crits" (critiques), either tutor- or student-led small groups that provide feedback on developing projects. Tutorials may be one-to-one or in small groups (in line with public-health advice), and students prepare work, questions and points for discussion.

Leeds Arts is a small university which in 2019–20 had about 1,600 students taking 15 undergraduate degrees. Further education and postgraduate students add to the population.

A commitment to widening participation is facilitated by activities including Easter and summer schools, a free after-school art club, specialist workshops and taster sessions for learners from primary school age to mature students. The university opens its doors for campus tours, mentoring and presentations. The state education sector accounts for almost all (94%) of the intake, higher than average for its courses and entry standards.

Bursaries add up to £1,100, paid in three instalments over three years to undergraduates whose family income is below £25,000 a year. There is also a £500 scholarship, for the first year only, for those who progress from one of the university's further education courses to a degree.

Students start to build their industry contacts through live briefs, prestigious competitions, work placements and professional events. They show their work at trade fairs, studios and in galleries and all students get free membership to the Association of Independent Professionals and the Self-Employed to help them explore freelance options. Guest speakers at Creative Networks events have included the artist Jake Chapman, historian and broadcaster Andrew Graham Dixon and the fashion designer Jeff Banks.

Formerly bottom of our rankings for graduate prospects, Leeds Arts has performed better than all bar one of the specialist arts institutions in our new measure, with 62% of graduates in high-skilled jobs or postgraduate study 15 months after leaving.

University accommodation is owned and managed privately in Hepworth Lodge (formerly Liberty Park) and, as of 2020, at iQ Leeds in Headingley and Carr Mills, 15 minutes' walk from campus. Most students who want to live in are able to get a place, although accommodation is guaranteed only for international students. Leeds has four universities, and the social scene is bursting with energy.

Tuition fees

- » Fees for UK students £9,250
- » Fees for International students 2020–21 £15,700–£16,700
- » For scholarship and bursary information see www.leeds-art.ac.uk/apply/finance/
- » Graduate salary £20,000

Student numbers

Undergraduates	1,799	(0)
Postgraduates	9	(40)
Applications/places		4,760/835
Applications per place		5.7
Overall offer rate		46.7%
International students – EU		2.4%
Non-EU		6.5%

Accommodation

University provided places: 673
Self-catered: £120–£149 per week
First years given priority
www.leeds-art.ac.uk/life-in-leeds/accommodation

Where do the students come from?

State schools (non-grammar)	94.2%	First generation students	43%	Black attainment gap	n/a
Grammar schools	2.1%	Deprived areas	15.4%	Disabled	12.4%
Independent schools	3.7%	All ethnic minorities	11%	Mature (over 21)	6.4%

Social inclusion ranking: 50

Leeds Beckett University

Students can find out how their body stands up to altitudes of 8,000 metres (more than 26,000ft, not far off the height of Mount Everest) in one of the new environmental chambers at Leeds Beckett's Carnegie School of Sport. The £45m development houses world-class facilities where the chambers can mimic harsh environments from -30C to 50C.

The building also has a teaching kitchen to study nutrition, a rooftop 60m sprint track for performance training and analysis, plus strength and conditioning facilities. It will provide a base for undergraduate and postgraduate courses and research programmes – and the university's elite student athletes.

The university has more development in its sights. In 2021 the Leeds School of Arts will move to an £80m building with a 184-seat theatre and a 220-seat Dolby Atmos cinema providing an immersive sound experience. Professional-standard music studios and post-production equipment will add to the facilities.

The two new buildings are part of a seven-year, £200m plan to create a distinct home for each of the university's 12 schools. Almost £1m has also been invested in 24/7 open-plan libraries with 200,000 e-books as well as journals, databases and a disability resource area.

The City campus in the centre of Leeds features the futuristic Rose Bowl lecture theatre complex and the business school, and will house the arts school when complete. An urban wellbeing garden has been added, where students can work in groups, meditate or socialise while reconnecting with nature.

Sports facilities are at the Headingley campus, three miles away, in 100 acres of park and woodland. The new Carnegie school augments an arena, multi-use sports pitches, indoor and outdoor tennis courts and a running track. The Headingley rugby ground – adjacent to the Test and County cricket ground – has coaching facilities shared by the university and two professional clubs. There are also classrooms for education, informatics, law and business.

Leeds Beckett made significant gains in 2020's National Student Survey. Satisfaction with both teaching quality and the wider experience now rank the university well inside the top 40 on both measures, contributing to Leeds Beckett's 16-place improvement in our overall ranking in this edition.

A silver award from the Teaching Excellence Framework (TEF) came with praise for Leeds Beckett's employability strategies for students, who can learn real-world skills through live project briefs, case studies, practice-related assessments, and placements.

The latest statistics show 70% of Leeds Beckett graduates were in high-skilled jobs or postgraduate study within 15 months of completing their degrees – a UK top-100 result.

City Campus
Leeds LS1 3HE
0113 812 3113
admissionenquiries@
leedsbeckett.ac.uk
www.leedsbeckett.ac.uk
www.leedsbeckettsu.co.uk
Open days: see website

The Times and The Sunday Times **Rankings**
Overall Ranking: 107 (last year: 123)

Teaching quality	81.8%	36
Student experience	80.3%	=25
Research quality	4.1%	=101
Entry standards	107	=120
Graduate prospects	69.7%	94
Good honours	71.3%	=97
Expected completion rate	76.1%	120
Student/staff ratio	19.2	117
Services and facilities	£2,325	77

But the university has yet to achieve its goal of halving its dropout rate. At one in five it is far above the expected level.

Ten new degrees were introduced in 2020, focusing on creative event design, occupational therapy and international tourism with social responsibility, among other specialisms. Another 10 are planned for 2021 including social policy, sports journalism, digital forensics, geography and environmental science and cyber-security.

Two degree apprenticeships in architecture and digital marketing are under consideration for 2021. The university is already a large provider offering 17 programmes. Its broad portfolio of courses ranges from building services engineering to social work, nursing and advanced clinical practice and about 1,000 degree apprentices are expected to be on board by September 2021.

The university almost doubled the number of academics it entered for the Research Excellence Framework in 2014, compared with the previous round in 2008. Just over a third of their work was rated as world-leading or internationally excellent, led by architecture and sports studies. Leeds Beckett has built a reputation mainly for applied research: three interdisciplinary research institutes focus on health, sport and sustainability, and there are 10 centres in more specialist fields.

Six research centres under the Carnegie School of Sport explore rugby, sport coaching, human performance, social justice in sport and society, active lifestyles and applied obesity.

A range of sports scholarships supports elite student athletes, and collectively about 7,000 students take part in some form of sporting activity. The Athletic Union oversees 40 clubs and 85 university teams, many of which do well in national competitions.

Although Leeds Beckett and its predecessor institutions have built a reputation for widening access to higher education, it remains in the lower third of institutions in our social inclusion ranking. The university has set targets with the Office for Students to increase enrolments from students from black, Asian and minority ethnic (BAME) backgrounds and under-represented groups, as well as from mature students and those with disabilities. Leeds nightlife has a well-earned reputation for being lively, wide-ranging and relatively affordable. With more than 3,600 rooms, Leeds Beckett can guarantee accommodation to all students who make the university their firm choice.

Tuition fees

- » Fees for UK students — £9,250
- » Fees for International students 2021–22 — £13,000
  Foundation courses — £11,000
- » For scholarship and bursary information see www.leedsbeckett.ac.uk/undergraduate/financing-your-studies/
- » Graduate salary — £21,000

Student numbers

Undergraduates	15,771	(2,145)
Postgraduates	1,977	(3,383)
Applications/places		26,300/4,825
Applications per place		5.5
Overall offer rate		78.6%
International students – EU		1.8%
Non-EU		4.2%

Accommodation

University provided places: 3,868
Self-catered: £100–£246 per week
First years guaranteed accommodation
www.leeds-beckett.ac.uk/accommodation/

Where do the students come from?

State schools (non-grammar)	91.2%	First generation students	39.1%	Black attainment gap	-15%
Grammar schools	3.9%	Deprived areas	15.6%	Disabled	5.3%
Independent schools	4.8%	All ethnic minorities	22.7%	Mature (over 21)	13.3%

Social inclusion ranking: 84

Leeds Trinity University

Sharp gains in the annual National Student Survey put Leeds Trinity just outside the top 50 for student satisfaction with teaching quality and their wider experience. In 2019 it didn't make the top 100 on either measure – which suggests that an academic restructuring programme begun in 2019 may already be bearing fruit. The university, with its roots in two Catholic teacher training colleges established in the 1960s, has consolidated its operations into two schools – arts and communication, and social and health sciences – plus the Institute of Childhood and Education.

The restructuring exercise aims to make it easier for staff to collaborate and create an experience for students focusing on real-world practice, leading to graduate jobs or further study.

All Leeds Trinity degrees include professional work placements without students needing to take a sandwich year. The university has an extensive network of partnerships and students are placed at local, national and global organisations. However, the placement programme has not translated into competitive graduate prospects, putting the university just outside the bottom 30 on this measure, according to the latest figures which show 68% of Leeds Trinity graduates in high-skilled jobs or postgraduate study within 15 months of finishing their course.

The placement scheme did contribute to a silver award in the Teaching Excellence Framework. The panel highlighted high-quality support mechanisms for employability, including professional placements, as well as excellent use of technology and innovative assessment and feedback.

At its single site in Horsforth, six miles northwest of Leeds city centre, a £40m development programme has produced many new facilities. Two new photography studios are open for product and still-life work and an open-plan dark room has added facilities for analogue photography, with a full-time photography technician available to help students and staff put their ideas into action. The student bar and dining room have been refurbished.

New degree courses – journalism with content creation, and digital marketing, each with the option of a foundation year – welcomed their first intake in September 2020.

The new Centre for Apprenticeships, Work-based Learning and Skills co-ordinates Leeds Trinity's degree apprenticeship programmes and has specialist tutors and support staff. Police constable degree apprentices began training in July 2020, in partnership with West Yorkshire police, taking the number of programmes to seven. Other options lead to qualifications as a

Brownberrie Lane
Horsforth
Leeds LS18 5HD
0113 283 7123
admissions@leedstrinity.ac.uk
www.leedstrinity.ac.uk
www.ltsu.co.uk
Open days: see website

The Times and The Sunday Times Rankings		
Overall Ranking: 110 (last year: 117)		
Teaching quality	80.4%	=55
Student experience	78.7%	=52
Research quality	2%	121
Entry standards	104	126
Graduate prospects	68.3%	100
Good honours	78.7%	=49
Expected completion rate	80.3%	=97
Student/staff ratio	21	127
Services and facilities	£1,952	=103

chartered manager, senior leader, supply-chain leadership professional and business-to-business sales professional. Working with employers to meet demand, the university hopes to add two more programmes and triple the number of degree apprentices to 600 by September 2021.

Teacher training remains Leeds Trinity's strongest suit and true to its Catholic foundation, it "promotes the dialogue and teaching of the Catholic Church" while welcoming students of all faiths or none.

Only 20 academics were entered for the 2014 Research Excellence Framework, but there were good results in communication, cultural and media studies, and library and information management. The flagship research group, the Leeds Centre for Victorian Studies, has a national and international reputation.

Ranked 15th in England and Wales for social inclusion, Leeds Trinity leads the city's four universities on this measure. More than 60% of students are the first in their family to go to university and almost one in five comes from an area with little tradition of sending students to university – one of the highest proportions in the country.

Its social mission to empower individuals to achieve their true potential, regardless of their background or route to higher education, drives the university's extensive outreach activities. Leeds Trinity works with more than 190 target schools and colleges in West Yorkshire to raise aspirations and has formalised partnerships with more than 40. Initiatives to widen participation include contextualised admissions, taster days, careers fairs and parents' evenings.

Undergraduates joining Leeds Trinity can hit the ground running at its new fitness suite at the sports centre on campus, which caters for elite athletes as well as casual users. There is a spin studio and two floors of gym equipment, with specialist strength and conditioning gear. A sports therapy fitness suite and motion-capture analysis lab has been added too, for sport and media students. Other facilities include a 3G pitch and recently upgraded changing facilities.

The university has nearly 800 residential places – enough to guarantee accommodation to first-years who apply by the end of June. A place in catered halls costs £123 per week. Located in Horsforth, a suburb on the edge of Leeds, there are good connections with the city centre by bus and train. With four universities in and around the city, there is no shortage of nightlife.

Tuition fees

»	Fees for UK students	£9,250
	Foundation degrees	£5,000
»	Fees for International students 2021–22	£12,000
»	For scholarship and bursary information see www.leeds-trinity.ac.uk/study/fees-and-finance	
»	Graduate salary	£20,000

Student numbers

Undergraduates	2,664	(45)
Postgraduates	451	(254)
Applications/places		6,470/945
Applications per place		6.8
Overall offer rate		89%
International students – EU		1.1%
Non-EU		0.3%

Accommodation

University provided places: 784
Catered costs: £123 per week
Self-catered: £98–£133 per week
First years guaranteed accommodation
www.leeds-trinity.ac.uk/accommodation

Where do the students come from?

State schools (non-grammar)	96.1%	First generation students	60.6%	Black attainment gap	n/a
Grammar schools	1.2%	Deprived areas	19.2%	Disabled	6.9%
Independent schools	2.7%	All ethnic minorities	35.9%	Mature (over 21)	26.3%

Social inclusion ranking: 15

University of Leicester

The University of Leicester celebrates its centenary in 2021. Its roots are traced to a public fund used for its first endowment to create a living memorial to locals who died in the First World War. Continuing to invest in its estate as part of a £500m capital development plan, Leicester has redeveloped its historic Brookfield site a few minutes from the main campus. Home to the School of Business, it now has new teaching rooms, modern lecture theatres, a trading room and breakout areas.

Building on a longstanding commitment to space research the university's ambitious Space Park Leicester is scheduled to open in spring 2021. The government has contributed nearly £21m of the £100m funding for this unique business park, which is dedicated to companies developing space technology such as satellites or using space-enabled data. It aims to be a world-leading centre for research, enterprise and education in space and earth observation, and students will be part of its collaborative community of academics and industry partners.

A £21m extension to the Percy Gee students' union building has doubled social learning spaces and added a large food court. At Freemen's Common, just opposite, a teaching and learning centre is due to open in autumn 2021 complete with a large lecture theatre, exhibition space and green walls. Student accommodation with 1,200 spaces is also being redeveloped, along with community-friendly facilities such as a cinema and games rooms.

Leicester's main campus and much of the residential accommodation is in a leafy suburb a mile from the city centre. The university's first overseas venture – the Leicester International Institute/Dalian University of Technology – opened in China in 2017. Based in Panjin, it offers degrees taught in English in chemistry, mechanical engineering and mathematics.

Leicester has a silver rating in the Teaching Excellence Framework (TEF), drawing favourable comments for putting in place a system to film lectures (especially useful now in pandemic times), in response to student feedback. The TEF panel also congratulated the university on engaging students with current research on all its courses.

"Your degree, your choice" encapsulates Leicester's flexible approach to the curriculum in which undergraduates can choose single, joint or major/minor programmes. Those taking the major/minor route are able to combine a wide range of subjects, spending three-quarters of their time studying their principal subject and a quarter on the minor element.

Eleven new degrees began in 2020, among them creative writing with English or journalism, policing, and midwifery with leadership. Twenty-four more are being

University Road
Leicester LE1 7RH
0116 252 5281
study@le.ac.uk
www.le.ac.uk
www.leicesterunion.com
Open days: see website

The Times and The Sunday Times Rankings
Overall Ranking: 37 (last year: 41)

Teaching quality	77%	=101
Student experience	77.3%	=73
Research quality	31.8%	=37
Entry standards	132	53
Graduate prospects	76.9%	47
Good honours	78.9%	44
Expected completion rate	94%	17
Student/staff ratio	13.7	=20
Services and facilities	£2,830	32

added in 2021, including a suite of biological sciences degrees with specialisms in genetics, zoology, neuroscience and biochemistry, among others, as well as a foundation-year option. Economics degrees with a range of options are also being introduced, including economics and econometrics, and financial economics and banking. Physical geography and computer science with enterprise will also take their first students in 2021.

Leicester is in the top half of UK universities for graduate prospects, with 77% in high-skilled jobs or postgraduate study within 15 months of finishing their degree.

Nearly half (45%) of Leicester's undergraduates received financial support in 2019–20, a proportion the university expects to continue. The Centenary Scholarship provides 100 one-off awards of £1,000 to students whose 250-word submission explaining how they exemplify the founding spirit of the university cuts the mustard.

Stoneygate Awards of £3,000 per year for up to three years are awarded to students with at least AAB at A-level, or equivalent, and who come from households with incomes under £25,000 in areas of low participation in higher education. Successful applicants also make a written submission describing how they have overcome challenging personal circumstances to start their degree, and how a Stoneygate Award would help them.

Music, sport and choral scholarships add to the provision, along with bursaries for mature students and scholarships for students who make Leicester their firm choice in the main admissions cycle, and meet UCAS tariff point standards.

Leicester may make reduced offers of up to two grades across most undergraduate courses based on contextual data, even without applicants asking for a grade reduction.

There are two sports centres, one on campus and the other at the student village. Both have a gym, swimming pool, spa, sauna and steam room, and studios. Campus also has a sports hall and there are flood-lit tennis courts, all-weather courts and rugby pitches at the Stoughton Road playing fields in Oadby.

Students enjoy the city of Leicester's manageable size, decent nightlife and reasonably priced restaurants. The university's award-winning students' union is the only one in the country with its own O_2 Academy. In 2018 the NatWest Student Living Index ranked Leicester as the third most affordable student city in the UK after Cardiff and Hull, taking account of rents, entertainment prices and other expenses such as taxis.

Tuition fees

» Fees for UK students   £9,250
» Fees for International students 2021–22   £17,450–£21,515
   Medicine   £40,140 (2020–21 clinical years)
» For scholarship and bursary information see
   www.le.ac.uk/study/undergraduate/fees-funding
» Graduate salary   £24,000

Student numbers

Undergraduates	11,920	(277)
Postgraduates	3,126	(1,531)
Applications/places	20,110/2,345	
Applications per place	8.6	
Overall offer rate	75.6%	
International students – EU	3.8%	
Non-EU	19.8%	

Accommodation

University provided places: 3,773
Self-catered: £87–£179 per week
First years guaranteed accommodation
www.le.ac.uk/study/accommodation

Where do the students come from?

					Social inclusion ranking: 77	
State schools (non-grammar)	80.1%	First generation students	39.5%		Black attainment gap	-19.1%
Grammar schools	10.9%	Deprived areas	9.7%		Disabled	5.4%
Independent schools	9%	All ethnic minorities	51.2%		Mature (over 21)	9.4%

University of Lincoln

Our Modern University of the Year, Lincoln welcomed a second round of 80 entrants to its new medical school in September 2020. A first for the county, the medical school is run in partnership with the University of Nottingham, whose BMBS (Bachelor of Medicine, Bachelor of Surgery) degree the students take.

Clinical placements take place at hospitals, GP surgeries and other healthcare units in the region. Once it reaches full capacity the school will train around 400 undergraduates a year.

A six-year degree including a foundation year is also offered to a further 15 students without the necessary qualifications for immediate entry to the five-year course to help widen participation in medicine. Medical students, currently based in Lincoln's modern science and healthcare facilities, are due to move into a new £21m Medical School building in 2021.

Lincoln has also become home to the world's first Centre for Doctoral Training for agri-food robotics. With £6.6m backing from the government's Engineering and Physical Sciences Research Council, the university is leading the new advanced training centre and will create the largest cohort of agri-tech robots for the global farming and food sectors.

There was more good news for Lincoln in the latest National Student Survey, in which it ranked joint 11th in the UK for satisfaction with the wider undergraduate experience, and joint 26th for teaching quality. The scores have contributed to a six-place rise in our overall league table, making Lincoln the top-ranked multi-faculty modern university. The achievement is all the more extraordinary given that its predecessor institution, the University of Lincolnshire and Humberside, finished bottom of our rankings in 1999.

A gold rating in the Teaching Excellence Framework boosts Lincoln's pedigree further. Assessors complimented its strong approach to personalised learning through highly engaged personal tutors, with access to analytics to monitor students' progress proactively. Students were involved in the design of courses, the TEF panel found, enabling them to develop the independence, understanding and skills to reflect their full potential.

Degrees in sport and exercise therapy, international accounting, musical theatre and modern history began in September 2020, as did a four-year integrated master's degree in geography. The curriculum will gain biomedical engineering in 2021. Lincoln's portfolio of degree apprenticeships is also growing and it is looking to add programmes in conservation and in nursing to the current stable of eight courses covering a range of food-related areas, integrated engineering,

Brayford Pool
Lincoln LN6 7TS
01522 886 644
enquiries@lincoln.ac.uk
www.lincoln.ac.uk
www.lincolnsu.com
Open days: see website

Edinburgh
Belfast
LINCOLN
London
Cardiff

The Times and The Sunday Times Rankings
Overall Ranking: 45 (last year: 51)

Teaching quality	82.4%	=26
Student experience	81.3%	=11
Research quality	10.3%	58
Entry standards	120	=87
Graduate prospects	72.9%	68
Good honours	75.9%	60
Expected completion rate	88.7%	44
Student/staff ratio	15.3	61
Services and facilities	£2,295	79

social work and chartered management.

Lincoln runs an expanded graduate internship scheme and a popular summer placement programme. Several degrees can be taken as work-based programmes, with credit awarded for relevant aspects of the job, and the university was the first to win a Charter Mark for exceptional service. There are courses offered with Siemens and pharmacy undergraduates study in industry-standard laboratories at the £22m Science and Innovation Park in Lincoln.

The new measure of graduate prospects shows just under three-quarters of graduates in high-skilled jobs or postgraduate study within 15 months of finishing their degrees.

Lincoln's popularity has been growing, and at 2018's record levels there were almost 1,000 more students starting courses than three years previously, an increase of nearly 28%. Both enrolments and applications dipped by around 4% in 2019, however, against an increasing offer rate: nearly nine in 10 applicants were offered a place.

More than half of a large submission to the 2014 Research Excellence Framework was rated internationally excellent or world-leading. Lincoln was in the top 10 in the health category for the quality of its output. Research in the fields of agriculture, veterinary science and food science got the university's best results.

The university campus is purpose-built on an attractive site next to Brayford Pool near the centre of Lincoln, after moving from Hull between 1996 and 2002. About half of all new undergraduates qualify for some sort of financial support, a proportion the university expects to be the same in 2021–22. Lincoln's extensive provision includes three payments of £500 to UK and EU entrants from households where the income is less than £45,875.

Efforts to widen participation focus on Lincolnshire's higher education "cold spots", as defined by the Office for Students, and aim to raise aspirations and offer opportunities. Outreach initiatives in low-participation neighbourhoods include campus visits, student experience taster days, sports events, a visiting lecture programme, student finance workshops and summer schools.

A sports centre on campus includes a hall and outdoor pitches. There is a £6m performing arts centre, too, with a 450-seat theatre and three large studio spaces. The Engine Shed, also on campus, is a music and entertainment venue operated by Lincoln's students' union. There are 5,261 residential spaces and Lincoln guarantees all first-years a spot.

Tuition fees

- » Fees for UK students £9,250
- » Fees for International students 2021–22   £14,400–£15,900
  Medicine (2020–21)   £43,500 (clinical years)
- » For scholarship and bursary information see
  www.lincoln.ac.uk/home/studywithus/
  undergraduatestudy/feesandfunding/
- » Graduate salary £21,000

Student numbers		
Undergraduates	12,008	(1,552)
Postgraduates	1,142	(1,173)
Applications/places		18,325/3,885
Applications per place		4.7
Overall offer rate		87.2%
International students – EU		1.4%
Non-EU		5.4%

Accommodation
University provided places: 5,261
Self-catered: £93–£201 per week
First years guaranteed accommodation
www.lincoln.ac.uk/home/studentlife/accommodation/

Where do the students come from?				Social inclusion ranking: 61	
State schools (non-grammar)	92.4%	First generation students	52.3%	Black attainment gap	-23.7%
Grammar schools	4.4%	Deprived areas	18.6%	Disabled	6.7%
Independent schools	3.2%	All ethnic minorities	10.7%	Mature (over 21)	10.6%

University of Liverpool

The University of Liverpool is gaining a Digital Innovation Factory (DIF). The centre of excellence in simulation and virtual reality will add more than 1,500 square feet of facilities at the north of the campus. The DIF is intended to promote innovation by linking the university's strength in computer science, robotics and engineering research with businesses. It has been projected to create 400 jobs and boost the city's economy by £44.5m.

Liverpool has been digging deep to invest in its city-centre campus. A new home for the School of Law and Social Justice opened in 2019 – bringing offices, meeting rooms, event space and a boardroom along with seminar rooms, breakout spaces and a café to the redeveloped Cypress building. The department has an agreement with the University of Law (ULaw) to offer its legal practice course so law graduates are now able to remain at the university for their professional training. Those enrolled in other subjects can take ULaw's graduate diploma in law.

When the Tung auditorium opens in 2021 it will add a 400-seat auditorium and accommodate a 70-piece orchestra. Drawing on the city's arts heritage, the space will host concerts, lectures and exhibitions for people of all ages and backgrounds.

Liverpool was upgraded from bronze to silver in the Teaching Excellence Framework. It also fared better for student satisfaction with teaching quality in the 2020 National Student Survey, rising 15 places to joint 62nd. Satisfaction with the wider undergraduate experience revealed an even stronger result, putting Liverpool in the top 30 UK universities.

Enrolments increased by 3% in 2019 and applications nudged up, too. The 2020 admissions cycle showed a further 7% rise in applications by the end of March.

New degrees in avionic systems, computer science and electronic engineering, electrical and electronic engineering and in mechatronics and robotic systems – all with a year in industry – began in September 2020. Games design joins the curriculum from 2021.

The university's Career Studio uses peer-to-peer mentoring and "boot camps" to help new graduates network with employers and develop work-ready skills. AstraZeneca, HSBC, IBM and PWC are among Liverpool's industry partnerships. More than 80% of graduates land high-skilled jobs or go into postgraduate study within 15 months of finishing their courses.

For a research-led Russell Group institution, Liverpool entered a relatively low proportion of its eligible academics for the 2014 Research Excellence Framework. This holds it back in our research ranking even though 70% of the work was judged to be world-leading or internationally excellent. More than half of

Liverpool L69 7ZX
0151 794 5927
ug-recruitment@liverpool.ac.uk
www.liverpool.ac.uk
www.liverpoolguild.org
Open days: see website

The Times and The Sunday Times Rankings

Overall Ranking: 29 (last year: 29)

Teaching quality	80%	=62
Student experience	80.2%	=27
Research quality	31.5%	40
Entry standards	143	=44
Graduate prospects	80.6%	34
Good honours	78.8%	=45
Expected completion rate	92.7%	25
Student/staff ratio	14.4	=33
Services and facilities	£2,899	25

its chemistry research was considered world-leading, with just 1% placed outside the top two categories. Computer science and general engineering also scored particularly well.

Liverpool has a campus in the Chinese city of Suzhou, run in partnership with Xi'an Jiaotong University. It also offers joint courses with the Singapore Institute of Technology and has partnerships with universities in Chile, Mexico and Spain that allow students to complete part of their degree abroad.

Each year about 10% of new students come from neighbourhoods with the lowest participation in higher education – more than at many other Russell Group universities. It fares better than most of them in our social inclusion table too.

Long-term engagement with local disadvantaged schools and colleges underpins the university's widening participation agenda. The two-year Liverpool Scholars programme boosts students' academic skills and builds a sense of belonging. Passing it entitles Scholars to an offer reduced by up to two A-level grades, or equivalent, for entry to an undergraduate course. The FastTrackers mentoring scheme for local Somali and Yemeni students was highlighted by the Office for Students for its good practice.

About a third of UK undergraduates receive Liverpool bursaries, worth £2,000 in cash or fee waivers for each year of study to students whose household incomes are under £25,000, or £750 per year where incomes are up to £35,000. Other scholarships include the elite athlete scheme and bursaries for estranged students, care leavers, mature students and young adult carers.

An £800 housing discount for those who get the Liverpool bursary (both values) or other bursaries is a rare scheme, and means about a quarter of students living in halls of residence receive the saving, at a cost of about £920,000 to the university each year.

The campus sport and fitness centre includes a swimming pool, two sports halls, a squash court, a bouldering wall and spin studios. Off campus at the Wyncote Sports Ground, the university has 10 pitches for football and rugby, one for lacrosse, a floodlit all-weather pitch and 3G rugby facilities.

Accommodation is guaranteed to first-years in Liverpool's supply of 4,400 university-owned rooms, or the 400 it endorses. Student life in Liverpool is hard to beat, combining nights out, affordability and a famously friendly atmosphere.

Tuition fees

- » Fees for UK students — £9,250
  - Foundation courses — £5,140
- » Fees for International students 2021–22 — £18,500–£23,750
  - Dentistry £37,100; Medicine £34,550;
  - Veterinary Science £34,550
- » For scholarship and bursary information see
  - www.liverpool.ac.uk/study/undergraduate/finance
- » Graduate salary — £24,000

Student numbers

Undergraduates	22,199	(535)
Postgraduates	4,055	(2,907)
Applications/places	40,415/4,775	
Applications per place	8.5	
Overall offer rate	77.8%	
International students – EU	3.4%	
Non-EU	26%	

Accommodation

University provided places: 4,800
Catered costs: £219–£220 per week
Self-catered: £143–£219 per week
First years guaranteed accommodation
www.liverpool.ac.uk/accommodation/

Where do the students come from?

State schools (non-grammar)	75.4%	First generation students	41.7%	
Grammar schools	12.2%	Deprived areas	9%	
Independent schools	12.5%	All ethnic minorities	17.2%	

Social inclusion ranking: 98

Black attainment gap	-26.5%
Disabled	5.5%
Mature (over 21)	8.8%

Liverpool Hope University

Liverpool Hope has a new School of Social Sciences building on its main Hope Park campus in Childwall, four miles from the city centre. It features a simulation suite where social work students can tackle common scenarios and assess their performance via video and audio recordings. The school's wider remit encompasses both undergraduate and master's programmes in disciplines including health and wellbeing, social policy, criminology and sociology, childhood and youth, disability studies and special educational needs.

A physiotherapy and sports rehabilitation clinic has also opened at the Hope Park Sports complex, bringing clinical teaching spaces and training facilities and treatment for students, staff and the community. An £8.5m health sciences building is another recent development, housing laboratories for nutrition, genomics, cell biology and psychology, along with a 25-metre biomechanics sprint track.

The university's purpose-built Creative Campus is close to the city centre and has a newly-opened arts centre, food court, study spaces and additional library facilities. There are studios for fine and applied art courses and group study rooms, plus a hub for student support, wellbeing and students' union services, as well as two theatres, a recording studio and dance studios.

The raft of upgrades has contributed to enviable levels of student satisfaction. Liverpool Hope is in the elite top 20 for student satisfaction with teaching quality, and ranks 40= for satisfaction with the wider undergraduate experience. These excellent results, drawn from the most recent National Student Survey, are not a flash in the pan, either: the university was in the top five for both measures of satisfaction three years ago.

Liverpool Hope was the only higher education institution in the city to achieve gold in the Teaching Excellence Framework (TEF). Assessors commented on "outstanding levels of stretch provided through judicious partnerships, good curriculum design and extracurricular activities".

Degrees in applied biomedical health, applied childhood and youth, musical theatre and social care launched in September 2020. The curriculum will gain three more new degrees in 2021 – in film, TV, radio and media production, physical activity, nutrition and health, and interactive and immersive performance. There was a 7% increase in applications in 2020 and enrolments have been steady for some time.

The university has a number of initiatives under way that should enhance its graduates' job prospects. Placement years have been introduced for the majority of degrees and Liverpool Hope's Careers and Employability service, as well as individual academic departments, strive to find placements that fit

Taggart Avenue
Hope Park
Liverpool L16 9JD
0151 291 3899
admission@hope.ac.uk
www.hope.ac.uk
www.hopesu.com
Open days: see website

The Times and The Sunday Times Rankings

Overall Ranking: =80 (last year: 60)

Teaching quality	83.1%	18
Student experience	79.4%	=40
Research quality	9.2%	=62
Entry standards	114	=102
Graduate prospects	62.9%	118
Good honours	71.8%	=92
Expected completion rate	77.3%	=116
Student/staff ratio	15	=51
Services and facilities	£2,147	90

desired career trajectories. Students usually earn between £16,000 and £23,000 during their work experience year, and these may result in graduate job offers afterwards.

With the ambition to "train the next generation of sports industry leaders" Liverpool Hope has launched a partnership with sports coaching and post-16 education firm LLS, an organisation backed by Dr Brian Barwick, the former chief executive of the Football Association and chairman of football's National League. Targeted at international students, the partnership means they can study a range of Liverpool Hope degrees and, away from the lecture theatre, access elite sports training along with professional and academic coaching. The aim is to secure future careers ranging from playing at elite level to roles in physiotherapy, refereeing, nutrition and management.

In a further collaboration, Liverpool Hope has teamed up with the Liverpool Everyman and Playhouse theatres to give creative and performing arts students industry experience and work placements. Senior practitioners from the theatres co-designed a new drama and theatre curriculum, and will also deliver technique masterclasses and set work assessments.

Via the university's new membership of the Council for Christian Colleges & Universities, students have access to professional development conferences, scholarly grants, study programmes in the US and unique research data.

More than half the university's eligible staff were entered for the 2014 Research Excellence Framework – far more than at most post-1992 universities – and there were good results in theology and education. Research-led seminars in the final year of degree courses introduce undergraduates to a research culture, and all students produce a dissertation or advanced research project.

Liverpool Hope was formed by the 1980 merger of two Catholic and one Church of England teacher training colleges and became a university in 2005. Students of all religions and none are accepted, although "taking faith seriously" remains a key value. The university exceeds all the official benchmarks for widening participation in higher education and is up 26 places to sit in the top 30 of our latest league table for social inclusion.

The university's £5.5m Sports Complex includes a sports hall, squash courts, fitness suite, dance studio and artificial pitches. Access to all facilities and classes is just £25 per year. Most residential places are at Aigburth Park, three miles from the Hope Park campus, and accommodation is guaranteed for new entrants who apply before clearing.

Tuition fees

» Fees for UK students	£9,250
» Fees for International students 2020–21	£11,400
» For scholarship and bursary information see	
www.hope.ac.uk/undergraduate/feesandfunding/	
» Graduate salary	£19,819

Student numbers

Undergraduates	3,737	(129)
Postgraduates	806	(430)
Applications/places		9,115/1,125
Applications per place		8.1
Overall offer rate		85.2%
International students – EU		2.2%
Non-EU		1.4%

Accommodation

University provided places: 1,142
Self-catered: £78–£126 per week
First years guaranteed accommodation
www.hope.ac.uk/halls

Where do the students come from?

State schools (non-grammar)	88.4%	First generation students	51.2%		
Grammar schools	9.9%	Deprived areas	24%		
Independent schools	1.7%	All ethnic minorities	14.1%		

Social inclusion ranking: =28

Black attainment gap	n/a
Disabled	9.2%
Mature (over 21)	18.3%

Liverpool John Moores University

Students joining Liverpool John Moores University (LJMU) will soon gain the Copperas Hill development near Lime Street station, where a Student Life Building and Sport Building are being added. Across five storeys the facility will bring together the students' union, advice and wellbeing services, careers guidance, international exchanges, teaching spaces and a study area. The two-floor Sport Building is set to have an eight-court hall, two further multipurpose halls and a modern gym.

The central site with its spaces to relax, study and train will connect the university's City Centre and Mount Pleasant campuses. It will also benefit the local community by regenerating the area. Once Copperas Hill is occupied, the IM Marsh campus four miles from the city centre will close and all of LJMU's activities will be concentrated in one area.

LJMU's focus on ensuring students have high-quality facilities at their fingertips has driven an ambitious programme of developments over the past decade or so. Facilities include the award-winning John Lennon Art and Design Building and the £25.5m Life Sciences Building, with its indoor 70-metre running track and labs for testing cardiovascular function. The £37.6m Redmonds Building houses the Liverpool Screen School, where students use industry-standard television and radio studios. It is also the base for the Liverpool Business School and the School of Law.

Results from the latest National Student Survey showed an improvement in student satisfaction with their experience at LJMU – ranking the university inside the top 40. Responding to feedback from the students' union, the university added spaces for chilling out or to use for social study in six buildings and £1.5m investment paid for features such as indoor lawns, phone-charging docks and IT resources.

The Teaching Excellence Framework awarded silver to LJMU, and assessors complimented its "highly effective institutional strategic drive to improve satisfaction with assessment and feedback", strong recognition of teaching excellence and a consistent commitment to student engagement.

Degrees in climate change (with or without a foundation year), international relations and politics with a foundation year, and musical theatre practice welcomed their first students in September 2020. A part-time professional policing practice degree has also begun.

LJMU was among the pioneers of degree apprenticeships. It currently has 817 apprentices studying for 21 academic degrees in areas including healthcare, civil engineering, construction management, risk and safety management, quantity surveying, professional policing practice, and digital and technology solutions.

Exchange Station
Tithebarn Street
Liverpool L2 2QP
0151 231 5090
courses@ljmu.ac.uk
www.ljmu.ac.uk
www.jmsu.co.uk
Open days: see website

The Times and The Sunday Times **Rankings**
Overall Ranking: 85 (last year: 78)

Teaching quality	79.8%	=64
Student experience	79.5%	=38
Research quality	8.9%	=67
Entry standards	145	43
Graduate prospects	69.8%	93
Good honours	73.7%	=77
Expected completion rate	82.1%	=83
Student/staff ratio	16.8	=86
Services and facilities	£1,829	114

The university's careers service offers one-to-one appointments with advisers and there is a tailored programme of advice to students depending on their level of study, with the aim of ensuring they complete courses with work-ready skills. Second-year students are offered paid summer internships with local organisations such as Sound City, the Liverpool music festival. The most recent statistics show that just under 70% of graduates were in high-skilled jobs or postgraduate study within 15 months of finishing their degrees.

LJMU enjoys a burgeoning research reputation and more than 60% of the work submitted for the 2014 Research Excellence Framework was rated world-leading or internationally excellent. The proportion topped 80% in physics, where the results covered astronomy. Researchers and students use the university's robotic telescope in the Canary Islands. LJMU was ranked second in the UK for sports science and fourth among post-1992 universities for law and education.

The university traces its roots to the Industrial Revolution and upon gaining university status in 1992, took its name from a Liverpool entrepreneur and philanthropist who helped fund its predecessor institutions. Nearly all its students arrive from state schools and LJMU does well at attracting undergraduates whose homes are in areas of deprivation. Forty-three per cent of its intake is from the Liverpool city region, and it recruits more students from Northern Ireland than any university outside Northern Ireland itself. Extensive outreach activities include Law Factor, a programme aimed at widening participation and administered jointly with the legal firm DWF.

Fewer students drop out than the expected level, based on the social and academic background of LJMU's intake. It fields teams in inter-university competitions and the new Sport Building will be a boon for facilities. There are opportunities to get involved at elite or just-for-fun level in activities including men's and women's Gaelic football, tennis, basketball and athletics.

The university endorses 3,800 residential spaces in privately operated halls of residence, enough for all first-years to be guaranteed a room in the heart of the city. Liverpool makes a strong case as a student city with its thriving nightlife, relative affordability and cultural wealth.

Tuition fees

- » Fees for UK students   £9,250
- » Fees for International students 2021–22   £15,600–£16,100
  Foundation years   £11,000
- » For scholarship and bursary information see www.ljmu.ac.uk/discover/fees-and-funding/
- » Graduate salary   £22,000

Student numbers

Undergraduates	17,670	(1,796)
Postgraduates	2,169	(2,396)
Applications/places		31,835/5,400
Applications per place		5.9
Overall offer rate		79.1%
International students – EU		1.9%
Non-EU		5.5%

Accommodation

University provided places: 3,800
Self-catered: £89–£166 per week
First years guaranteed accommodation
www.ljmu.ac.uk/discover/your-student-experience/accommodation

Where do the students come from?

State schools (non-grammar)	89%	First generation students	54.2%	Black attainment gap	-22%
Grammar schools	8.5%	Deprived areas	19.8%	Disabled	4.9%
Independent schools	2.5%	All ethnic minorities	12.8%	Mature (over 21)	16.7%

Social inclusion ranking: =70

London Metropolitan University

Student satisfaction with teaching quality at London Metropolitan improved to reach the top 50 in the latest National Student Survey. The university was 58= for satisfaction with the wider student experience, outdoing many pre-1992 research-led London institutions and representing a big improvement for London Met, which has long held bottom-30 positions for both measures. However, London Met's overall ranking was boosted by only one place.

The university is one of the most diverse in the country and ranks in the top 30 of our social inclusion table. It has the seventh highest proportion of black, Asian and minority ethnic (BAME) students and fifth-highest presence of mature students at any university. There are bursaries for care leavers and social work students, and the university's outreach projects focus on supporting under-represented and disadvantaged students aged nine to 19, plus adult learners.

Social justice is at the forefront of London Met's agenda. It is researching the social challenges disproportionately facing the communities it serves under a new strategy called Giving Back to the City. The university has also established a Centre for Equity and Inclusion to examine and improve its own provision, creating conditions in which every individual can fulfil their potential. A new curriculum strategy, the Education for Social Justice Framework, has been developed by university staff and students to fight racial inequality.

Applications rose 10% early in the 2020 admissions round, placing the university's recruitment ahead of many other modern London institutions. Under the leadership of vice-chancellor Professor Lynn Dobbs, whose research has focused on social exclusion, there are new partnerships with London schools and further education colleges to broaden admissions. Dobbs was named among London's most influential people in the activists: equality section of the *Evening Standard's* Progress 1000 list in 2019. She was the only vice-chancellor to be included.

New degrees to suit the shifting jobs market have proved popular with applicants. Five courses welcomed their first students in September 2020, including business and law, events management and marketing, and public health and health promotion.

London Met was among 61% of British higher education institutions found to be in financial deficit in the latest figures. In 2018–19 it stood just under £14.3m in the red, after a £20.1m deficit the previous year.

Created by the merger of London Guildhall University and the University of North London in 2002, London Met's origins date from the mid-19th century. Most of its

166–220 Holloway Road
London N7 8DB
020 7133 4200
courseenquiries@londonmet.ac.uk
www.londonmet.ac.uk
www.londonmetsu.org.uk
Open days: see website

The Times and The Sunday Times **Rankings**

Overall Ranking: 125 (last year: 126)

Teaching quality	80.8%	=46
Student experience	78.4%	=58
Research quality	3.5%	111
Entry standards	97	131
Graduate prospects	60%	124
Good honours	60.4%	=129
Expected completion rate	64.8%	130
Student/staff ratio	17.8	=104
Services and facilities	£4,053	2

extensive estate is around the Holloway Road campus. The School of Art, Architecture and Design is in Aldgate, close to east London's tech hub, where it provides workshops, boot camps and an incubator programme for budding entrepreneurs. The school recently dropped "Sir John Cass" from its name because of the 18th-century politician and philanthropist's early links to the slave trade.

On Holloway Road the Science Centre's Superlab is among the largest teaching laboratories in Europe, with audiovisual systems able to transmit 12 practical lectures simultaneously for different groups of students – a vital feature in the reshaped university landscape. A social learning hub has high-spec classrooms and a café.

The university's cyber-security research centre is the first of its kind and brings together students and businesses. Languages are another strength: London Met is one of only 22 universities around the world to be a member of the UN Language Careers Network.

London Met received a bronze rating in the government's Teaching Excellence Framework. An unusually negative assessment by the panel said students' achievement was "notably below benchmark across a range of indicators". It acknowledged a range of positive and appropriate strategies to address student satisfaction, but was concerned that comparatively few students continued their studies after graduating.

The university entered just 15% of eligible academics in the 2014 Research Excellence Framework – far fewer than in the previous round in 2008. As a result, it slipped down our research ranking, even though half of its submission was rated world-leading or internationally excellent. English and health subjects scored well.

Nearly three in 10 students drop out, higher than the expected level of just over two in 10, based on the subject mix and social background of London Met's intake. The university also has ground to make up on graduate prospects, where it is in the bottom 10. The figures show only 60% of graduates are in high-skilled jobs or postgraduate study 15 months after graduation.

Students get free membership of the university's modern gym and sports hall. London Met does not own any halls of residence but works with private accommodation providers. Holloway Road is especially lively when Arsenal play at home in the nearby Emirates Stadium and Islington has an enduring appeal for young people, while Aldgate is a hipper neck of the woods.

Tuition fees

» Fees for UK students   £9,250
» Fees for International students 2021–22   £13,200–£14,000
» For scholarship and bursary information see www.londonmet.ac.uk/applying/funding-your-studies/undergraduate-tuition-fees/
» Graduate salary   £22,500

Student numbers

Undergraduates	6,369	(716)
Postgraduates	1,006	(1,107)
Applications/places		11,490/1,100
Applications per place		10.4
Overall offer rate		83.6%
International students – EU		6.5%
Non-EU		4.1%

Accommodation

University provided places: 0
Self-catered: £150–£369 per week (private providers)
www.londonmet.ac.uk/services-and-facilities/accommodation/

Where do the students come from?

State schools (non-grammar)	96.8%	First generation students	50.2%	
Grammar schools	0.7%	Deprived areas	6.2%	
Independent schools	2.5%	All ethnic minorities	70.2%	

Social inclusion ranking: =28

Black attainment gap	-25%
Disabled	0.2%
Mature (over 21)	63%

London School of Economics and Political Science

In a corner of picturesque Lincoln's Inn Fields, the London School of Economics and Political Science (LSE) is preparing to open a modern new facility, the Marshall Building, in September 2021. It will provide a base for the departments of management, finance and accounting as well as the Marshall Institute for Philanthropy and Social Entrepreneurship, funded by a £30m donation from hedge funder Sir Paul Marshall.

The new building will also house a new sports centre, café, arts rehearsal facilities and music practice rooms, plus a teaching and learning hub.

More space for students to study and relax have been created in the LSE's recently opened Centre Buildings at the heart of the campus on Houghton Street, off Aldwych in central London.

The latest development appears already to have had a positive impact on student satisfaction rates, with which the university has struggled in the past. Under our analysis of the 2020 National Student Survey, the school has reached the top 100 for satisfaction with teaching quality. It has also improved its score for student satisfaction with the wider experience, although remaining in the bottom 20 on this measure. In 2018 the LSE came last for both.

Improved student satisfaction has helped to boost the LSE's position within our elite top 10 overall. Now fourth, it has achieved its highest ranking since 2013. Under the leadership of director Dame Minouche Shafik, the university's LSE 2030 strategy has set out its ambition to be the world's leading social science institution with the greatest global impact. It has only Harvard to topple in the QS World University Rankings for social science.

Although LSE was awarded only bronze in the Teaching Excellence Framework (again held back by poor student satisfaction, now rising), students continue to be attracted by the stellar career trajectories of its graduates. The latest figures show 92.5% are in high-skilled jobs or postgraduate study within 15 months of completing their studies. Only Imperial College London does better.

The LSE is top in the UK for graduate earnings in law, based on a study by the Chambers Student guide, while the Institute for Fiscal Studies concluded in 2018 that the prestige of having studied at the school boosted men's wages by 49% and women's by 37%, compared with the average graduate.

Economics and politics may lead the way but the university offers courses in more subjects than its name suggests, including maths, law and environmental policy. A degree in data science joins the curriculum in 2021. More than 30 past or present heads of state

---

Houghton street
London WC2A 2AE
020 7955 6613
www.lse.ac.uk/ask-LSE
www.lse.ac.uk
www.lsesu.com
Open days: see website

The Times and The Sunday Times **Rankings**

Overall Ranking: 4 (last year: 6)

Teaching quality	77.3%	99
Student experience	74.3%	=112
Research quality	52.8%	4
Entry standards	170	14
Graduate prospects	92.5%	2
Good honours	92.2%	3
Expected completion rate	97.2%	3
Student/staff ratio	11.9	=7
Services and facilities	£2,941	22

have studied or taught at the LSE, as have 16 winners of the Nobel Prize in economics, literature and peace. The school has a long history of political involvement, from its foundation by Beatrice and Sidney Webb, pioneers of the left-leaning Fabian movement. Unusually for a UK university, its international profile means that only a small proportion of the LSE's funding comes from government sources.

Competition for places remains fierce and the LSE is among the UK's most selective universities. The offer rate in 2019 was the highest it has been in six years – yet only 35% of applicants succeeded in getting an offer of a place. The LSE is one of the few British universities that do not participate in clearing.

All applicants are considered on individual merit and compete with the admission cycle cohort. As well as academic achievement, the university considers a personal statement, academic reference and contextual social and educational information as part of its efforts to widen participation. However, the LSE has its work cut out to broaden its recruitment. Less than half of LSE students went to a non-selective state school and programmes to attract capable students from under-represented backgrounds have been stepped up. LSE students have been trained as mentors and tutors to work with pupils in schools and there are long-term programmes for pupils in years 11–13.

The LSE had more world-leading research than any other university in the 2014 Research Excellence Framework. It was the clear leader in the social sciences, with particularly good results in social work and social policy, and communication and media studies. A £10m donation from alumnus Firoz Lalji has since created an academic centre focused on Africa.

London life is expensive but the Three Tuns, the LSE's student bar, provides a more affordable option for unwinding after a day at the books. Close to Covent Garden and the River Thames, the university has an enviable location near plenty of downtime distractions.

More than half of the 2,940 residential spaces for full-time undergraduates are in catered halls of residence, the remainder are self-catered. Accommodation is guaranteed for first-years as long as they book online by the end of May.

Tuition fees

»	Fees for UK students	£9,250
»	Fees for International students 2021–22	£22,430
	For scholarship and bursary information see www.lse.ac.uk/study-at-lse/undergraduate/fees-and-funding	
»	Graduate salary	£31,000

Student numbers

Undergraduates	5,009	(47)
Postgraduates	6,446	(349)
Applications/places		21,255/1,695
Applications per place		12.5
Overall offer rate		35.2%
International students – EU		18.4%
Non-EU		49.1%

Accommodation

University provided places: 2,940
Catered costs: £112–£306 per week
Self-catered: £157–£418 per week
First years guaranteed accommodation
www.lse.ac.uk/accommodation

Where do the students come from?

State schools (non-grammar)	49%	First generation students	29.5%	Black attainment gap	-6%
Grammar schools	21.9%	Deprived areas	5.1%	Disabled	3.8%
Independent schools	29.1%	All ethnic minorities	56%	Mature (over 21)	1.8%

Social inclusion ranking: =103

London South Bank University

New arrivals to London South Bank University (LSBU) in 2021 will benefit from the biggest development in the university's Zones project, which LSBU expects to revolutionise the student experience, affecting how they "think, feel and study". The £45m renovation of London Road, LSBU's largest building, will include a 20,000 square metre learning space, with an open-plan library and gym, and improved accessibility to make it as inclusive as possible.

The main campus is close to London's Southbank arts complex, while many health students are based in hospitals in Romford and Leytonstone, in east London, and Havering. Now the university is planning to open a town-centre campus in Croydon in 2021 which will offer degrees including nursing, accounting and business management.

A dozen new degrees were introduced for 2020, half of them in engineering and three in fashion. A BSc in marketing will begin in September 2021. LSBU is also expanding its already extensive portfolio of degree apprenticeships, with the current 1,500 students expected to grow to more than 2,200 in a year's time. Apprenticeships in construction have been added and programmes for operating department practitioners, physiotherapists, rail engineers and occupational therapists are on the way.

The university has enjoyed its second successive increase in applications this year, which at 11% was one of the biggest of the 2020 admissions cycle, due mainly to improved recruitment in health courses after the reintroduction of nursing bursaries.

The health and social care school works with more than 50 NHS partner organisations and has high ratings from the Nursing and Midwifery Council. The university as a whole has a silver award in the government's Teaching Excellence Framework.

LSBU operates its own employment agency to help students find part-time work while they study and also provides strong support for start-up companies. The university's Clarence Centre ranked second in the UK and fourth in Europe for innovative business development in UBI Global's 2018 World Rankings.

However LSBU is one of the universities to have lost out heavily from the change to how graduate prospects are measured in our rankings, now based on the number in high-skilled work 15 (rather than six) months after leaving. There are also different reporting procedures and classifications of the high-skilled jobs which, combined with the proportion who have moved on to postgraduate study, form the basis of our new measure. Three in 10 of the jobs reported by LSBU graduates were classified as medium or low-skilled.

The university believes low response rates

103 Borough Road
London SE1 0AA
0800 923 8888
admissions@lsbu.ac.uk
www.lsbu.ac.uk
www.lsbsu.org
Open days: see website

Edinburgh

Belfast

Cardiff

LONDON

The Times and The Sunday Times Rankings

Overall Ranking: 123 (last year: 86)

Teaching quality	77.9%	=94
Student experience	75.5%	=103
Research quality	9.0%	=64
Entry standards	107	=120
Graduate prospects	70.6%	87
Good honours	70.7%	=104
Expected completion rate	76.4%	118
Student/staff ratio	16.3	=78
Services and facilities	£2,327	=75

may have depressed its graduate prospects score, which is low enough to pull it into the bottom 10 of our overall ranking.

Three-quarters of the students are from London and 70% are drawn from ethnic minorities, helping to place the university in the top 10 for social inclusion once again. Widening participation has always been a priority at LSBU, which makes lower offers to disadvantaged applicants and has partnerships with a number of colleges and academies in south London to encourage progression to higher education.

The projected dropout rate for undergraduates is around the expected level at just under one in six. The university provides grants of between £200 and £1,000 a year from a Student Retention Fund to boost completion rates for those struggling financially. However, there is concern over the attainment gap between black, Asian and minority ethnic (BAME) students and the rest, with a notable 21 percentage-point gap between the proportion of black students getting a first or 2:1 (60%) and their white counterparts (81%). Attainment workshops and race equality action plans are among LSBU's strategies to improve the gap.

LSBU entered more academics for the 2014 Research Excellence Framework than it had for previous assessments and scored well on the external impact of its research, with almost three-quarters of the submission placed in the top two categories. The university boasts the UK's first inner-city green technology research facility, the Centre for Efficient and Renewable Energy in Buildings.

LSBU boasts of being the only UK university to hold four accreditations from the Institute of Customer Service (ICS) for excellent service across its accommodation service, library and learning resources, centre for student life and sports academy. Scores in the National Student Survey declined in 2020, however, after an encouraging rise in student satisfaction with teaching quality and the wider experience in 2019.

The students' union and many support services have been brought together to make them more convenient and accessible. Sports facilities include a multipurpose hall, therapy services and a 40-station fitness suite, dance studio and injury clinic.

All 1,400 halls of residence rooms are under 10 minutes' walk away. First-year full-time students are only guaranteed accommodation if they have accepted an unconditional offer by mid-June, but the university expects to have enough rooms to satisfy the remainder who want one.

Tuition fees

» Fees for UK students	£9,250
» Fees for International students 2020–21	£14,470
» For scholarship and bursary information see www.lsbu.ac.uk/study/undergraduate/fees-and-funding	
» Graduate salary	£25,000

Student numbers

Undergraduates	8,284 (4,316)
Postgraduates	1,754 (2,769)
Applications/places	19,715/2,870
Applications per place	6.9
Overall offer rate	67.4%
International students – EU	3.5%
Non-EU	5.8%

Accommodation

University provided places: 1,400
Self-catered: £135–£147 per week
First years given priority
www.lsbu.ac.uk/student-life/accommodation

Where do the students come from?

State schools (non-grammar)	95.5%	First generation students	52.3%	Black attainment gap	-21%
Grammar schools	2.1%	Deprived areas	5.5%	Disabled	10%
Independent schools	2.4%	All ethnic minorities	70.1%	Mature (over 21)	46.8%

Social inclusion ranking: 10

Loughborough University

Home to the best sports facilities on this side of the Atlantic, Loughborough offers students so much more than just a chance to shine in a tracksuit, as its two University of the Year awards and multiple nominations over two decades attest.

Only Cambridge and Oxford head more subject tables than Loughborough's four with table-topping excellence in diverse areas such as building, criminology, and communication and media studies. Loughborough also enjoys a formidable reputation for engineering excellence – embracing almost 3,000 students. Its partnership with Rolls-Royce, spanning more than 50 years, led to the opening of the National Centre for Combustion and Aerothermal Technology (NCCAT) on campus in 2019.

Its work is focused on developing low-emission, high-efficiency combustion engines for the aerospace industry to reduce the environmental impact of aircraft. The centre will be at the heart of Loughborough's work to train the next generation of aerospace engineers.

Applications jumped nearly 12% in 2019 to a record 33,200. The surge in applications has been achieved without going down the "conditional unconditional" offer route. Professor Robert Allison, the vice-chancellor, has been an implacable opponent of the now outlawed practice. Students have to earn their place at Loughborough, but a contextual offer scheme lowers the asking rate for those whose social and educational background fits the criteria. About one in five students benefits from some form of bursary or scholarship.

The 440-acre campus on the edge of the small Leicestershire market town of Loughborough is the hub around which most student life revolves. Architecturally functional, it has a high density of outstanding facilities, spanning all sports and most subjects. A refurbishment programme of several teaching spaces is nearing completion.

A big-city university experience this isn't, but the camaraderie for which the university is renowned has translated into consistently excellent scores in the annual National Student Survey. After a dip in 2018, NSS scores for teaching quality have recovered to the usual high levels of satisfaction with the student experience.

The addition of 600 new ensuite rooms in the Claudia Parsons Hall, named after the Loughborough alumnus who was one of the country's first female engineers, brings the accommodation stock to around 6,300 rooms, enough to accommodate 44% of all full-time first degree students. The university can usually house all first-years who apply by September 1.

Arts facilities at Loughborough include a 266-seat theatre, a separate auditorium for concerts and film screenings, plus practice

---

Epinal Way
Loughborough LE11 3TU
01509 274 403
admissions@lboro.ac.uk
www.lboro.ac.uk
www.lsu.co.uk
Open days: see website

The Times and The Sunday Times **Rankings**
Overall Ranking: 7 (last year: 5)

Teaching quality	82.4%	=26
Student experience	84.8%	4
Research quality	36.3%	=30
Entry standards	153	=28
Graduate prospects	83.6%	=16
Good honours	84.4%	=22
Expected completion rate	93.3%	22
Student/staff ratio	13.4	=17
Services and facilities	£3,410	11

rooms, exhibition space and a dance studio. The prize-winning students' union is among the most popular in the country with its members. Its community activities received the Queen's Award for voluntary service.

Loughborough has a gold award in the Teaching Excellence Framework (TEF) to add to its attractions. The TEF panel found that students from all backgrounds achieve consistently outstanding outcomes, thanks to a culture of personalised learning and a comprehensive pastoral and academic tutorial programme.

Four new programmes will be introduced in September 2021, including psychology in education; design; and product design and technology with a foundation year or an international foundation year. This follows the introduction of seven new degrees in 2020, which included philosophy, politics and economics; urban planning; architectural engineering; marketing and management; sociology and media; and business analytics.

Most subjects are available either as three-year full-time courses or longer sandwich degrees, which include a year in industry. The university is also a leader in the use of computer-assisted assessment, offering students the chance to gauge their progress online, something that will come into its own in the post-pandemic world.

Only eight universities entered such a high proportion of their eligible staff – 88% – in the Research Excellence Framework in 2014. Almost three-quarters of their research was judged to be world-leading or internationally excellent, with sport and exercise sciences producing the best results in the UK and six other subject areas featuring in the top 10.

The new Graduate Outcomes survey reported that 84% of Loughborough graduates secure high-skilled jobs or go on to further study within 15 months, just outside the UK top 10. The university works hard to support graduate start-ups, incorporating its Studio facility in its Science and Enterprise Park in 2019. The Studio has supported more than 50 graduate businesses since it was established in 2011.

For all its excellence elsewhere, Loughborough remains pre-eminent for sport. Investment of more than £60m in the past 15 years has produced what it claims to be the best facilities concentrated in one square mile in the world. They include national centres for athletics, swimming, cricket, tennis and netball, alongside world-class gym and training facilities. The postponement of the Tokyo Olympics deprived Loughborough of bragging rights as its athletes, alumni and other users of its world-class facilities reliably earn more medals than many whole nations.

Tuition fees

» Fees for UK students	£9,250
» Fees for International students 2021–22	£18,650–£23,100
» For scholarship and bursary information see www.lboro.ac.uk/study/undergraduate/fees-funding/	
» Graduate salary	£27,000

Student numbers

Undergraduates	13,474	(188)
Postgraduates	3,350	(1,013)
Applications/places		33,200/3,775
Applications per place		8.8
Overall offer rate		73.5%
International students – EU		4.9%
Non-EU		18.1%

Accommodation

University provided places: 6,286
Catered costs: £142–£197 per week
Self-catered: £99–£180 per week
First years guaranteed accommodation
www.lboro.ac.uk/services/accommodation/

Where do the students come from?

State schools (non-grammar)	68.3%	First generation students	33.8%	Social inclusion ranking: 90		
				Black attainment gap	-9.8%
Grammar schools	14.5%	Deprived areas	5.7%	Disabled	8.6%
Independent schools	17.2%	All ethnic minorities	26.1%	Mature (over 21)	2.3%

University of Manchester

The largest construction project undertaken by any UK university – the Manchester Engineering Campus Development (MECD) – is due to welcome its first students in September 2021. It will house four engineering schools and two research institutes in a £400m development connecting the university's facilities along Oxford Road.

The project is part of a £1bn programme to create a unified "world-class" campus that Manchester hopes will help it to secure a place among the top 25 research universities in the world. It has only two places to go in the QS World University Rankings, although a little more in other international exercises.

Already by far the biggest university in our table with more than 40,000 students, Manchester saw a big increase in applications in 2019 followed by another 10% rise in the early stages of the 2020 admissions cycle. In recent years, 5,000 students from China have swelled the numbers, providing 14% of tuition fee income.

No fewer than 23 new degrees are scheduled to start in 2021, although more than half are existing courses which are adding an integrated foundation year. Four of the entirely new programmes pair Korean with other languages. Others include ancient history and archaeology, philosophy and religion, business accounting with an industrial or professional placement, and a BA in liberal arts. There is only one degree apprenticeship at present, an MSc in management practice, but others are being explored in health and business.

Manchester has maintained its position in our top 20, having recovered significant lost ground in our rankings in recent years. However, the university is still held back by poor performances in the National Student Survey. Although it has brought in initiatives such as improved digital services that were expected to boost student contentment, it is outside the top 100 for satisfaction both with teaching quality and the wider student experience.

Outstanding teaching is part of the university's strategy, which includes a dedicated initiative to ensure that undergraduates take part in research.

All undergraduates address three "ethical grand challenges", one for each year of their degree – sustainability, social justice and workplace ethics – as part of Manchester's Stellify programme, encouraging students to make a difference in the world. The award recognises extracurricular activities alongside degree studies and is designed to make Manchester students highly employable. It works: the institution was once again the favourite recruiting ground of employers in the latest High Fliers survey of *The Times* top 100

Oxford Road
Manchester M13 9PL
0161 275 2077
study@manchester.ac.uk
www.manchester.ac.uk
www.manchesterstudentsunion.com
Open days: see website

The Times and The Sunday Times Rankings		
Overall Ranking: 18 (last year: 18)		
Teaching quality	76.7%	=107
Student experience	75.5%	=103
Research quality	39.8%	13
Entry standards	165	=17
Graduate prospects	83%	21
Good honours	82.9%	=24
Expected completion rate	93.5%	=20
Student/staff ratio	13.1	12
Services and facilities	£3,349	12

graduate employers, and is just outside the top 20 in our new assessment of graduate prospects.

Recent development projects have included the renovation of the Whitworth art gallery and the refurbishment of the Alliance Manchester Business School and its library, with further teaching and learning spaces added. The school hosts a new institute funded by the Economic and Social Research Council to make the UK economy more productive.

More than 80% of the work entered for the 2014 Research Excellence Framework was considered world-leading or internationally excellent, although the university entered a lower proportion of its academics than several of its Russell Group peers. Manchester has had 25 Nobel laureates, most recently Sir Andre Geim and Sir Konstantin Novoselov, who shared the prize in physics in 2010 for discovering graphene, the strongest material ever measured. The university hosts the National Graphene Institute, set up to explore its industrial potential.

Jodrell Bank, the university's world-famous radio observatory, was made a Unesco World Heritage Site in 2019 and is used as a teaching resource and focus for public engagement with scientific research. The university is also the site of the Henry Royce Institute, a £300m facility run in partnership with nine leading institutions to lead the way on advanced materials research.

Manchester has been trying to broaden its intake, with a focus on increasing recruitment from the city and its surrounding area. The university admits more low-income students than any other in the Russell Group and surpasses its national benchmarks for widening participation. It is the fourth-highest ranked Russell Group university in our social inclusion table for England and Wales, and more than a third of students come from homes where neither parent attended university. A third of UK undergraduates receive financial support and scholarships are available in languages, science and engineering and at the business school.

The city's famed youth culture, plentiful accommodation and huge student population are great attractions for applicants. Manchester owns or endorses 7,800 residential places, enough to guarantee accommodation for all new entrants who apply by the end of August. There are first-rate sports facilities and the university's teams frequently rank near the top of the British Universities and Colleges Sport league.

Tuition fees

»	Fees for UK students	£9,250
»	Fees for International students 2021–22	£19,500–£25,000
	Medicine (clinical years 2020)	£44,000
»	For scholarship and bursary information see www.manchester.ac.uk/study/undergraduate/student-finance/	
»	Graduate salary	£25,000

Student numbers

Undergraduates	26,675	(180)
Postgraduates	9,906	(3,488)
Applications/places		72,300/7,845
Applications per place		9.2
Overall offer rate		61.9%
International students – EU		7.4%
Non-EU		28.5%

Accommodation

University provided places: 7,800
Catered costs: £103–£201 per week
Self-catered: £80–£161 per week
First years guaranteed accommodation
www.accommodation.manchester.ac.uk/ouraccommodation/

Where do the students come from?

State schools (non-grammar)	73.7%	First generation students	33.8%	**Social inclusion ranking: 94**		
				Black attainment gap	-16.6%
Grammar schools	11.7%	Deprived areas	7.3%	Disabled	7.6%
Independent schools	14.6%	All ethnic minorities	32.1%	Mature (over 21)	9.1%

Manchester Metropolitan University

 Manchester Met (MMU) is our University of the Year for Student Retention in recognition of its efforts to support students through their courses. Around one in 10 students drop out compared with the expected level of one in seven – which in an institution of MMU's scale amounts to hundreds of students graduating every year who would not otherwise have done so.

Only four universities recruit more undergraduates than Manchester Met and none can match the size and scope of its degree apprenticeship portfolio. The first degree apprentices arrived in 2015 and by September 2020 there were 1,700 signed up with 300 different employers in the fields of architecture, management and leadership, technology, digital marketing, digital user experience, health and social care, retail and science.

A £400m programme of campus improvements greeted 2020's intake. A new building for the arts and humanities, will house a poetry library and the Manchester Writing School, where former poet laureate Carol Ann Duffy is creative director. There is also a language centre and a 180-seat auditorium for the Manchester School of Theatre. It will be followed in 2021 by the School of Digital Arts (Soda), a £35m investment providing workspaces, networks, teaching and research facilities across all forms of creative content.

The university is also capitalising on its strong reputation in sports studies with the development of a new Institute of Sport, opening in 2022. It will bring together the Department of Sport and Exercise Sciences with researchers from the Faculty of Science and Engineering, sports business experts from the Faculty of Business and Law and a range of specialists in the Faculty of Health, Psychology and Social Care.

MMU has dropped a little in our latest league table, but remains in the top half. Like other big city institutions, it continues to struggle in the National Student Survey, sitting just inside the top 60 for student satisfaction with teaching quality and just outside the top 60 for the wider student experience. The university was awarded silver in the Teaching Excellence Framework.

Students welcome MMU's commitment to green issues. In 2019 it came second in the People & Planet league, comparing universities' all-round environmental performance, having finished in the top three for seven years in a row. Carbon literacy programmes are delivered to students and staff, and the university has been chosen to lead a national project on carbon literacy for public sector employees.

The university has stepped up its emphasis on graduate skills. From September 2020, 1,000 students at the business school will take

All Saints Building
All Saints
Manchester M15 6BH
0161 247 2000
www2.mmu.ac.uk/contact/
course-enquiry/
www2.mmu.ac.uk
www.theunionmmu.org
Open days: see website

The Times and The Sunday Times Rankings
Overall Ranking: 65 (last year: =62)

Teaching quality	80.2%	60
Student experience	78.1%	=61
Research quality	7.5%	75
Entry standards	131	=54
Graduate prospects	66.5%	=109
Good honours	72.8%	86
Expected completion rate	85.1%	57
Student/staff ratio	15	=51
Services and facilities	£2,831	31

part in a new development programme that will help them to discover and develop their natural strengths in preparation for future careers. Under MMU's employability strategy, undergraduates are offered work placements of up to a year, during which students with an annual family income of less than £25,000 receive a full fee waiver.

Almost two-thirds of MMU graduates stay and work in the northwest. The Talent Match service, run in partnership with the Greater Manchester Chamber of Commerce, helps to identify skilled graduates to meet the needs of local employers.

The university has a longstanding commitment to extending access to higher education. More than half the intake comprises students who are the first in their family to go to university and MMU's First Generation scheme provides financial, professional and personal support throughout their studies and into their careers. About 40% of undergraduates qualify for financial support.

MMU closed its campus in Crewe, Cheshire, in 2019 and has concentrated activities at its two Manchester campuses, bordering Hulme and Moss Side. A £75m business school and science and engineering buildings were added at All Saints, while the Brooks campus hosts the education and health faculties.

The Manchester School of Architecture, run in collaboration with the University of Manchester, is rated in the world's top 10 by QS, while the School of Art is in the top 200. Fashion is a successful area for the university, with the multidisciplinary Manchester Fashion Institute covering undergraduate and postgraduate training in design, business, promotion, fashion buying and technology.

MMU was recently awarded a Collaborative Award for Teaching Excellence by Advance Higher Education, the teaching enhancement agency, for its MetMUnch social enterprise, which promotes sustainable and nutritious food. The MetMUnch team runs interactive educational sessions for businesses and schools and set up its own meat-free café in 2019.

All first-years who request accommodation by mid-July are guaranteed a place. The university either owns or endorses more than 3,500 residential places in Manchester.

The university's sports facilities are good and the city's attractions are part of Manchester Met's appeal. The Sugden Sports Centre was redeveloped in 2018, and Manchester Aquatics Centre, with three gyms and a 50-metre pool, is also on the doorstep.

Tuition fees

- » Fees for UK students £9,250
- » Fees for International students 2021–22 £15,500–£17,000
  Architecture £24,500
- » For scholarship and bursary information see www2.mmu.ac.uk/study/undergraduate/money-matters
- » Graduate salary £21,000

Student numbers

Undergraduates	24,501	(1,813)
Postgraduates	3,484	(3,252)
Applications/places	49,040/7,365	
Applications per place	6.7	
Overall offer rate	69.6%	
International students – EU	2.8%	
Non-EU	5.1%	

Accommodation
University provided places: 3,553
Self-catered: £112–£224 per week
First years guaranteed accommodation
www.mmu.ac.uk/study/accommodation/

Where do the students come from?

State schools (non-grammar)	94.1%	First generation students	51.2%	Black attainment gap	-25.2%
Grammar schools	3%	Deprived areas	14.3%	Disabled	4.4%
Independent schools	3%	All ethnic minorities	37.3%	Mature (over 21)	14.3%

Social inclusion ranking: =70

Middlesex University

Middlesex has dropped to just outside of our bottom 10, after falling nearly 50 places in four years. The immediate cause is its performance in the new measure of graduate prospects, which places the university inside the bottom 10 for the proportion of leavers in high-skilled work or postgraduate study 15 months after graduation.

Middlesex is determined to do better, pledging to deliver "learning through doing" with practical courses. The university aims to combine personalised support with active learning to create a distinctive student experience.

A prime example of this approach is the MDX Living Pavilion, a learning and wellbeing space on campus that is used for outdoor classes, student society events, exercise and as a place for quiet contemplation. The pavilion was designed and developed three years ago by architectural technology students, in collaboration with industry professionals.

More conventional examples include the UK's first Cyber Factory training facility, which opened in 2017 to prepare students for the jobs of the future. Midwifery students have new augmented reality equipment to help them to understand real-life scenarios.

Measures to support the diverse student body prepare for the employment market helped to earn the university silver in the Teaching Excellence Framework. The panel was impressed by the way employability is embedded within and alongside programmes of study.

Students are yet to be won over in the numbers that Middlesex might hope, however. The university is in the bottom 20 in both of our measures of student satisfaction. And, while applications were up by 4% when the official deadline passed for courses beginning in September 2020, this followed three years in which both applications and enrolments fell by 25%.

Middlesex has a network of international campuses, where students can take part of their degree if they wish. Although the campus in Malta will close in 2022, those in Dubai and Mauritius are thriving. Almost 1,900 students came from other European Union countries to study at Middlesex in 2018.

For the majority of students based in northwest London, there will be further improvements to the main Hendon campus, which has already benefited from £200m of development. Library services will be brought closer together, two new academic buildings will enhance the business school, and a big expansion of student accommodation is planned.

Eight new degrees are being introduced in 2020 and 2021, most of them in existing subjects with the addition of a foundation year for students without the necessary

The Burroughs
Hendon
London NW4 4BT
020 8411 5555
enquiries@mdx.ac.uk
www.mdx.ac.uk
www.mdxsu.com
Open days: see website

The Times and *The Sunday Times* **Rankings**		
Overall Ranking: 121 (last year: 107)		
Teaching quality	76.1%	=114
Student experience	74.3%	=112
Research quality	9.7%	60
Entry standards	115	=100
Graduate prospects	61.9%	122
Good honours	68.7%	=111
Expected completion rate	78.1%	=110
Student/staff ratio	17	=90
Services and facilities	£2,734	43

qualifications for degree entry. They include business economics, medical science and mathematics with data science.

The flexible course system allows students to start some courses in January and offers the option of an extra five-week session in the summer to try out new subjects or add to their credits with work-based programmes. Two degrees – in computer science and cyber-security and digital forensics – are being relaunched with an updated curriculum in January 2021.

Middlesex is also a significant provider of degree apprenticeships, training police constables, social workers, teachers, nurses, risk and safety management professionals and healthcare science and environmental health practitioners among others. By the end of 2021, the university expects to have more than 1,000 apprentices working with companies such as BT, BAE Systems, Royal Mail and Amazon, as well as public sector organisations. The university has a Centre for Apprenticeships and Skills to bring academics and businesses together and ensure that programmes meet the needs of both employers and apprentices.

More than a third of the eligible staff were entered for the 2014 Research Excellence Framework and 58% of their work reached one of the top two categories. Art and design produced the best results, with three-quarters of the research assessed as world-leading or internationally excellent.

Almost all the British students are state-educated and Middlesex ranks just outside the top 20 in our social inclusion table. More than two-thirds of the students are drawn from ethnic minorities with just under 60% from homes where parents have not attended university. Having previously abandoned bursaries and scholarships in the belief that outreach and retention activities did more for students from low-income households, Middlesex has since reintroduced a variety of awards, as well as hardship funds. In 2020–21, more than £100,000 will be available for them.

There are more than 1,200 residential places on or near the campus, including 630 in a privately-run development near Wembley Stadium. New entrants are guaranteed accommodation if they apply by the end of June.

Sports facilities are extensive and most are conveniently located. They include a bouldering wall and fitness pod and a real tennis court. The West End and London's other attractions are a Tube journey away.

Tuition fees

- » Fees for UK students £9,250
- » Fees for International students 2021–22 £14,000
- » For scholarship and bursary information see www.mdx.ac.uk/study-with-us/fees-and-funding/undergraduate-finance
- » Graduate salary £23,000

Student numbers

Undergraduates	13,632	(1,134)
Postgraduates	2,286	(2,581)
Applications/places	21,270/2,695	
Applications per place	7.9	
Overall offer rate	65.5%	
International students – EU	9.6%	
Non-EU	13.7%	

Accommodation

University provided places: 1,239
Self-catered: £151–£185 per week
First years guaranteed accommodation
www.mdx.ac.uk/student-life/accommodation

Where do the students come from?

						Social inclusion ranking: 22	
State schools (non-grammar)	97.1%	First generation students	57.3%	Black attainment gap	-18%
Grammar schools	1.5%	Deprived areas	5.2%	Disabled	5.7%
Independent schools	1.4%	All ethnic minorities	73.2%	Mature (over 21)	30.5%

Newcastle University

Newcastle University is at the heart of one of the city's biggest regeneration projects. Newcastle Helix – formerly Science Central – is a £350m collaboration with the city council and investment partner Legal & General Capital. The 24-acre site features the newly opened Frederick Douglass Centre with a 750-capacity auditorium and 200-seat lecture theatre ready to come into their own when Covid-19 restrictions are lifted.

The Catalyst building on the former brewery site adjoining the city centre – once the home of Newcastle Brown Ale – hosts National Innovation Centres for Ageing and Data as well as the National Institute for Health Research Innovation Observatory, which specialises in "horizon scanning" for medical technology breakthroughs.

The Newcastle Helix facilities will provide laboratories and offices for businesses, especially in the healthcare and life sciences sector, reflecting the strength of the university's medical school. Its longstanding excellence helped Newcastle, one of the 24 Russell Group universities which share a focus on research and a reputation for academic achievement, to win our University of the Year title in 2000.

Scores for student satisfaction with teaching quality and the wider student experience have been falling for four and five years respectively, dragging the university out of our overall top 30 in our latest rankings. Internationally, the university has performed much better: it is one of just 13 universities out of 150 worldwide to record 5+ stars in the new QS Stars ranking system, graded on factors including teaching, research, employability, academic development and social responsibility. A recent Times Higher Education ranking for impact on society and leadership in sustainable development placed Newcastle 11th in the world.

Newcastle was one of a minority of Russell Group universities awarded gold in the Teaching Excellence Framework in the first round. Assessors were impressed by "exceptional" support for students, including tailored help for disabled students, and how the university consistently engaged undergraduates with developments at the forefront of research.

Almost 80% of the research entered for the 2014 Research Excellence Framework was judged to be world-leading or internationally excellent. Neuroscience, English and computing science were rated as leading departments in the UK. The university's subsequent research initiatives have included the opening of Tyne Pressure Testing, formerly Tyne Subsea, a centre of excellence for hyberbaric testing, and the Emerson Cavitation Tunnel research centre, the UK's only specialist facility testing propellers and turbine blades for the marine industries.

Newcastle upon Tyne
NE1 7RU
0191 208 3333
http://www.ncl.ac.uk/
who-we-are/contact
www.ncl.ac.uk
www.nusu.co.uk
Open days: see website

Edinburgh
Belfast
NEWCASTLE
UPON TYNE
London
Cardiff

The Times and The Sunday Times **Rankings**
Overall Ranking: =31 (last year: 28)

Teaching quality	76.4%	=110
Student experience	77.1%	80
Research quality	37.7%	=21
Entry standards	150	=37
Graduate prospects	81.4%	29
Good honours	82%	30
Expected completion rate	95.1%	7
Student/staff ratio	14.2	29
Services and facilities	£2,483	=63

A £2.5m investment in digital technology to support students' teaching and learning has been accelerated in response to Covid-19 as more student services and teaching move online.

A second successive fall in applications in 2019 – down 6.3% – was more than offset by an 8.2% rise in applications in 2020 up to the outbreak of the pandemic. Newcastle has long been a sought-after choice: four out of five students come from outside the northeast, attracted by the combination of an outstanding university with the city's legendary nightlife. The dropout rate of 3.8% is among the lowest.

Many undergraduates put down roots, with 36% of graduates working in the northeast. The new Graduate Outcomes survey, which records students' occupations 15 months after graduation, showed 81% in high-skilled employment or in postgraduate study.

The university is popular with students from independent schools, who still account for nearly a quarter of admissions, significantly more than the expected level. However, Newcastle meets its benchmark for recruiting students from areas that send the fewest children into higher education. Bursary support of £1,000 a year is provided for students from households with income up to £35,000, rising to £2,000 a year for those from homes with £25,000 a year annual income or less. More than 27% get some form of financial assistance with their studies.

Heavy recent investment in student accommodation saw the opening in 2018 of the £75m Park View student village, next to the main university precinct and medical school. With space for 1,300 students, the university now has more than 3,500 university-owned rooms with a further 600 in managed rooms, enough for all students in their first year who want a place.

The university has invested £30m in its sports facilities, including three artificial-turf pitches and a rowing training centre. The new sports centre, next door to Park View, has teaching and research spaces, an eight-court sports hall, four squash courts and four studio spaces, including one for spinning. A new BSc in sports and exercise science has been introduced.

The main campus, which opens onto the busy Haymarket shopping area near the Civic Centre, hosts an independent theatre, museum and the Hatton Gallery, which has had a £3.8m refurbishment. The students' union has also been upgraded and now counts an outdoor social space among its amenities.

Tuition fees

- » Fees for UK students £9,250
- » Fees for International students 2021–22 £18,600–£23,400
  Dentistry £37,800; Medicine £34,800
- » For scholarship and bursary information see
  www.ncl.ac.uk/undergraduate/finance
- » Graduate salary £25,000

Student numbers

Undergraduates	20,795	(51)
Postgraduates	5,011	(1,356)
Applications/places	31,965/5,345	
Applications per place	6	
Overall offer rate	79.2%	
International students – EU	5.2%	
Non-EU	20%	

Accommodation

University provided places: 5,000+
Catered costs: £137–£197 per week
Self-catered: £97–£173 per week
First years guaranteed accommodation
www.ncl.ac.uk/undergraduate/accommodation

Where do the students come from?

State schools (non-grammar)	64.7%	First generation students	33.7%	**Social inclusion ranking: 107**	
Grammar schools	11.6%	Deprived areas	8.2%	Black attainment gap	-11.7%
Independent schools	23.7%	All ethnic minorities	14%	Disabled	4.4%
				Mature (over 21)	6.5%

Newman University Birmingham

Newman may be outside our top 100 but it ranks eighth for student satisfaction with their wider experience, covering course organisation, the availability of learning resources and the learning community. It is 10th for satisfaction with teaching quality. Its overall ranking in our table is let down by low scores on other measures such as completion, research and graduate prospects.

Applications increased 6% early in the 2020 admissions cycle, reversing two years of decline thanks to better marketing of a revised course portfolio along with Newman's silver award in the Teaching Excellence Framework and a gradual rise up this and other league tables.

This small Catholic former teacher training college is in the top three in England and Wales for diversity in our social inclusion ranking. Nearly half of the undergraduates come from ethnic minorities, more than a third were at least 21 on entry and 10% have disabilities. Three-quarters of all undergraduates come from homes where their parents did not attend university — the highest proportion in the UK.

The campus is in a quiet residential area eight miles southwest of Birmingham city centre, with views over the Bartley reservoir and the Worcestershire countryside. The university has now added Birmingham to its title, underlining its proximity to the city for potential applicants.

Newman has quadrangles of modern buildings around lawns and trees. About £22m has been invested in new halls of residence and upgraded teaching facilities for interactive learning. A mock law court, a new computer science laboratory and a careers and employability hub all opened in 2020 and the drama studio has been refurbished.

A two-year accelerated degree in applied humanities was added for 2020, blending history, literature and philosophy with digital, medical and environmental issues. A BA degree in counselling, mental health and wellbeing will be offered from 2021, following the trend of recent years to reduce the domination of education and traditional humanities degrees in the course portfolio. All full-time degrees include work placements of at least 100 hours, some of which are abroad, and undergraduates can opt to study at a partner university in Europe or further afield.

Newman was one of three Catholic colleges awarded university status in 2012. It takes its name from John Henry Newman, a 19th-century cardinal who wrote *The Idea of the University* and was canonised only in 2019. His vision of a community of scholars still guides the university, which was established in 1968 as a teacher training college but now

Genners Lane
Bartley Green
Birmingham B32 3NT
0121 476 1181
admissions@newman.ac.uk
www.newman.ac.uk
www.newmansu.org
Open days: see website

The Times and The Sunday Times Rankings
Overall Ranking: =112 (last year: 115)

Teaching quality	84.4%	=10
Student experience	82.2%	=8
Research quality	2.8%	115
Entry standards	110	=113
Graduate prospects	63.5%	117
Good honours	66.8%	118
Expected completion rate	78.1%	=110
Student/staff ratio	17.1	92
Services and facilities	£1,778	117

has a wider portfolio of degrees, mainly in the social sciences and humanities.

According to the university, the cardinal's influence lives on in its small class sizes and interactive teaching style. Newman retains its Catholic ethos but recruits students from all faiths and none. Professor Jackie Dunne arrived from the University of Wolverhampton in March 2020 to take over as vice-chancellor.

A higher than average proportion of the academic staff have teaching qualifications and the university received one of eight national awards to improve the use of technology in teaching and learning, following a project designed to boost digital literacy among its students.

Although only 23 academics were entered for the Research Excellence Framework in 2014, the number grew from half that in 2008. Education and history produced the best results, but less than a third of the research submitted was placed in the top two categories. Newman does not employ staff for research alone, in order to ensure that students have regular contact with active researchers.

Nearly a quarter of students entered through clearing in 2019. There will be no bursaries or scholarships for students joining the university in 2021, but student support payments of up to £1,750 can be awarded and the university issues supermarket and travel vouchers to those who can demonstrate hardship.

Newman is part of the Aimhigher Plus consortium, with the five other Birmingham universities and Worcester, which offers a range of activities, information, advice and guidance for young people aged 13–19. The university also has partnerships with six schools and further education colleges, offering intensive support and opportunities to their students, as well as running its own outreach programmes.

With the opening of 100 more ensuite bedrooms, first-year students are now guaranteed a place in university-owned accommodation. The halls of residence are close to the teaching areas and library.

A refurbished fitness suite and performance room give students an incentive to get fit. There is also a 3G sports pitch, sports hall, gymnasium and squash courts. Birmingham city centre, with its cultural attractions and student-oriented nightlife, is within easy reach.

Tuition fees

» Fees for UK students	£9,250
» Fees for International students	n/a
» For scholarship and bursary information see www.newman.ac.uk/knowledge-base/ fees-finance-overview/	
» Graduate salary	£22,765

Student numbers

Undergraduates	1,817	(356)
Postgraduates	347	(280)
Applications/places		2,845/515
Applications per place		5.5
Overall offer rate		88.7%
International students – EU		0.6%
Non-EU		0%

Accommodation

University provided places: 290
Self-catered: £100–£190 per week
www.newman.ac.uk/accommodation

Where do the students come from?

State schools (non-grammar)	97.7%	First generation students	75.5%	Black attainment gap	-19%
Grammar schools	0.5%	Deprived areas	21.3%	Disabled	10.3%
Independent schools	1.9%	All ethnic minorities	48.4%	Mature (over 21)	34.9%

Social inclusion ranking: 3

University of Northampton

Students starting at Northampton still get a laptop to keep, an offer which created a stir when it was unveiled in 2019. But the Northampton Employment Promise may be more valuable in the long run, guaranteeing an internship of at least three months or a postgraduate course to any graduates who have not found full-time work within a year of graduating with a 2:2 degree or Higher National Diploma.

The university was the first in the UK to be named a Changemaker Campus by the Ashoka global network of social entrepreneurs and has since been ranked top in the country for social enterprise. Every student has the opportunity to work in a social enterprise as part of their course, developing entrepreneurial skills to make them more employable.

Northampton's Waterside campus is almost complete now that a new suite of engineering workshops and a printroom for fine art, graphics and textiles students opened in time for the 2020 intake. The £330m campus first opened in 2018 — just before applications and enrolments fell in 2019, although there was increased demand in 2020 in clearing.

The ongoing costs of the campus contributed to a £16m deficit in 2018–19, although the university's board has said it remains confident in Northampton's financial model. Uniquely in UK higher education, the £231m bond that was issued to fund construction of the campus is backed by Treasury guarantee.

The 58-acre campus, a few minutes' walk from the town centre, is focused on a four-storey Learning Hub, where most teaching takes place. Big lecture theatres have been replaced by classrooms for up to 40 people and smaller lecture spaces in accordance with a "flipped learning" model where students prepare in advance for their teaching sessions and interact more with their peers and staff.

Leisure facilities are shared with the local community, while the Senate building includes room for guest lectures and exhibitions. A grade II listed engine shed was restored to house the students' union.

Northampton was awarded gold in the government's Teaching Excellence Framework before the new campus opened. Since the move, student satisfaction with teaching quality has improved, placing the university in the top half of the National Student Survey results. It remains outside the top 100 for student satisfaction with the wider experience, however, despite a small improvement in 2020.

Almost all Northampton undergraduates come from non-selective state schools and the university, which achieves a top-40 finish in

---

Waterside Campus
University Drive
Northampton NN1 5PH
0300 303 2772
study@northampton.ac.uk
www.northampton.ac.uk
www.northamptonunion.com
Open days: see website

The Times and The Sunday Times **Rankings**
Overall Ranking: 111 (last year: 116)

Teaching quality	80.1%	61
Student experience	74.7%	109
Research quality	3.2%	113
Entry standards	102	130
Graduate prospects	69%	97
Good honours	66.9%	=116
Expected completion rate	78.8%	105
Student/staff ratio	16.2	=74
Services and facilities	£2,889	26

our social inclusion table, very nearly meets its benchmark for recruiting students from areas of low participation in higher education.

Northampton runs a wide variety of outreach activities in an attempt to further widen the intake. The Big Bang Northants promotes science, technology, engineering, arts and maths (Steam) subjects through interactive events. A growing portfolio of degree apprenticeships covers training in 12 areas including chartered management, nursing and occupational therapy and provides training for manufacturing engineers, police constables and advanced clinical practitioners.

Northampton co-sponsors a University Technical College at the nearby Silverstone motor-racing circuit. It also works closely with the Northamptonshire Growth Hub, assisting local businesses as well as highlighting opportunities for student placements and part-time jobs.

The university's origins lie in the 13th century when Henry III dissolved the original institution, allegedly because his bishops thought it posed a threat to Oxford. The modern institution, which was awarded university status in 2005, was formed from the town's colleges of education, nursing, technology and art.

In the 2014 Research Excellence Framework only 30% of its research was placed in the top two categories, but the university had entered just a quarter of its eligible staff. Results were outstanding in history, where two-thirds of the work was considered world-leading or internationally excellent. Five research centres focus on subjects from contemporary fiction to exploring psychic and paranormal claims. The China and Emerging Economies Centre studies changes to global business networks.

Northampton is one of few universities in the UK to offer all students free access to sports facilities. The sports dome is used for teaching as well as recreation, and there is a pavilion, outdoor games areas and an artificial pitch.

Some students live on campus and there is more accommodation at the Scholars Green student village, four miles away. New entrants are guaranteed accommodation if they apply by the end of April.

The new campus has freshened the options for socialising and the town centre has a number of popular bars including the Platform, a students' union venue housing a nightclub, bar and café.

Tuition fees

»	Fees for UK students	£9,250
	Foundation years	£6,750
»	Fees for International students 2021–22	£12,900–£15,750
	Foundation years	£12,900
»	For scholarship and bursary information see	
	www.northampton.ac.uk/student-life/fees-and-funding/	
»	Graduate salary	£23,000

Student numbers

Undergraduates	8,558	(1,099)
Postgraduates	939	(1,388)
Applications/places		13,320/2,445
Applications per place		5.4
Overall offer rate		77.2%
International students – EU		3.4%
Non-EU		11.2%

Accommodation

University provided places: 2,500
Self-catered: £77–£170 per week
First years guaranteed accommodation
www.northampton.ac.uk/student-life/accommodation

Where do the students come from?

State schools (non-grammar)	96.3%	First generation students	50.8%	Black attainment gap	-20.6%
Grammar schools	1.5%	Deprived areas	14.1%	Disabled	6.1%
Independent schools	2.2%	All ethnic minorities	43.4%	Mature (over 21)	35.8%

Social inclusion ranking: 35

Northumbria University

The largest university in northeast England prides itself on being a national leader in business and enterprise, through its partnerships with businesses, the public sector, cultural organisations and charities. More than 560 employers and 60 professional bodies sponsor or accredit Northumbria's programmes.

The extensive roll call of international, national and regional business collaborators encompasses Nissan, Nike, IBM, Proctor & Gamble, Santander, the BBC and the NHS. These partnerships foster research projects, work placements, job opportunities and, perhaps most crucially, teaching that is relevant to the outside world.

The university was a big winner in the new measure of graduate employment. The Graduate Outcomes survey takes a longer-term view of employment, looking at what graduates are doing 15 months after leaving university. It found that three-quarters of Northumbria graduates were in high-skilled employment or postgraduate study at this point, enough to rank the university just outside the UK top 50 on this measure.

The institution has enjoyed a good year for rankings: it was the top UK university in the Times Higher Education Young University Rankings 2020, a global league table for all universities that are 50 years old or less (coming 80th in the world), and also improved its place in the latest QS World University Rankings.

In 2019, it topped the annual Higher Education Business and Community Interactive Survey (Hebcis) rankings for the third successive year for generating the highest turnover from graduate start-up businesses — £81.5m — of any UK university.

Such successes vindicate the approach taken by the vice-chancellor, Professor Andrew Wathey, to create a research-intensive modern university, responsive to the needs of business and industry. He had solid ground on which to build. The former Newcastle Polytechnic enjoyed an excellent reputation and in the early years of this guide was consistently the top-performing modern university.

It is returning to those levels domestically now, showing strongly in a number of our key performance measures. The dropout rate of less than 12% is lower than expected given the social and subject mix. That social mix sees just under one in five students recruited from areas with low progression rates to higher education, well above its benchmark level and reflecting strong regional recruitment. The northeast has the lowest higher-education participation rate in England. It is one of very few universities to have a broadly similar position in our tables for academic measures and social inclusion, ranking 57 and 59= respectively.

The university gained a silver rating in the Teaching Excellence Framework, drawing praise for helping students to enjoy their

---

Sutherland Building
Newcastle upon Tyne
NE1 8ST
0191 227 4646
ask4help@nurthumbria.ac.uk
www.northumbria.ac.uk
www.mynsu.co.uk
Open days: see website

The Times and The Sunday Times Rankings		
Overall Ranking: 57 (last year: =65)		
Teaching quality	79.4%	=69
Student experience	77%	81
Research quality	9%	=64
Entry standards	143	=44
Graduate prospects	75.2%	56
Good honours	78.7%	=49
Expected completion rate	83.8%	=70
Student/staff ratio	15.5	=63
Services and facilities	£2,332	74

studies and achieve high attainment through a range of academic and personal support services, plus graduate start-up and careers assistance. High-quality physical and digital resources are used effectively both in teaching and by students, the panel said.

Recent — and diverse — research successes have built on a strong showing in the Research Excellence Framework, in which 60% of the submitted work was judged to be world-leading or internationally excellent. In 2019, Northumbria was named as one of the UK's academic centres of excellence for cyber-security research. It is playing the lead role in a £4m study into how climate change in Antarctica might lead to devastating rises in sea level and it has a £1.2m grant to develop a new technique in forensic research that will help identify previously unidentified bodies.

It is keen for its students to stay on to undertake postgraduate work, offering a 20% discount on postgraduate fees for alumni.

A constantly evolving course programme will see a number of new and revised business courses rolled out in September 2021, covering accounting, finance and investment management, economics and finance, international business management, tourism and events management, marketing, entrepreneurship, business management, and business and marketing.

The extensive degree-apprenticeship programme is expected to see new additions in engineering and health to add to 15 awards currently available. These include a police constable programme launched in 2019. There are more than 800 students enrolled on degree apprenticeships on the Newcastle campus, with a further 250 based at the university's London outpost.

Heavy recent investment in the Newcastle campus has created excellent teaching facilities, alongside new student accommodation (with 3,275 places in university-owned or partner-operated rooms and a 100% guarantee of a place for all first-years) and sports facilities. Sport Central, at the heart of the City campus, is a £30m facility that was refurbished in 2019, containing a pool, sports science laboratories, sports halls and a 3,000-seat arena.

The university has developed sporting partnerships with i2i Sports and the Newcastle United Foundation to support talented footballers through study, training, performance analysis, and strength and conditioning.

The pre-pandemic Newcastle student experience was legendary with a nightlife second to none.

Tuition fees

» Fees for UK students	£9,250
» Fees for International students 2021–22	£16,000
» For scholarship and bursary information see www.northumbria.ac.uk/study-at-northumbria/fees-and-scholarships/	
» Graduate salary	£23,000

Student numbers

Undergraduates	18,252 (2,448)
Postgraduates	3,453 (2,295)
Applications/places	23,525/5,215
Applications per place	4.5
Overall offer rate	85.5%
International students – EU	3.8%
Non-EU	11.7%

Accommodation

University provided places: 3,275
Catered costs: £122–£123 per week
Self-catered: £80–£175 per week
First years guaranteed accommodation
www.northumbria.ac.uk/study-at-northumbria/accommodation/

Where do the students come from?

State schools (non-grammar)	89.6%	First generation students	51.5%		
Grammar schools	4.4%	Deprived areas	18.1%		
Independent schools	6%	All ethnic minorities	11.1%		

Social inclusion ranking: =59

Black attainment gap	-18.5%
Disabled	6.4%
Mature (over 21)	19.7%

Norwich University of the Arts

Every degree at Norwich University of the Arts (NUA) now includes the option of a foundation year to give students the chance to develop the skills to study at that level. All applicants are interviewed, with places awarded on the quality of their portfolio as much as predicted grades. The system has served NUA well as it was able to make all offers unconditional and avoid the chaos surrounding the 2020 A-level results.

Entrants in 2021 will enjoy upgraded facilities and more residential accommodation in the largest building project undertaken by NUA since it became a university in 2012. A seven-storey building adjoining the library and main teaching space will create a large new lecture theatre, teaching rooms, and 100 bedrooms for first-year students.

Other recent developments have provided a new base for the students' union, a café and lounge, as well as laboratories and other teaching facilities for courses including film and moving image production, photography, and fashion communication and promotion. The Sir John Hurt Film Studio, named after the late actor and NUA chancellor, is in a grade II listed building that also houses the School of Architecture and won a design award for its renovation.

The university makes a virtue of focusing entirely on the arts, design and media without branching out into the humanities and social sciences, as other former art schools have done. Degrees in acting, fashion marketing and business, and animation and visual effects were added to the portfolio for 2020.

Applications rose in 2019 and the university was able to admit 30 additional students from about the same number of offers. NUA has dropped 15 places in our league table, however, partly because its dropout rate has increased since 2019, when it was named our University of the Year for Student Retention. It has also dropped out of the top 50 for student satisfaction with teaching quality — another former strength.

It was, however, awarded gold in the Teaching Excellence Framework (TEF). The panel found that course design and assessment practices encouraged experimentation, creative risk-taking and team-working, providing "outstanding levels of stretch for students".

The Ideas Factory, also praised by the TEF assessors, is a start-up incubation space helping graduates to develop new digital businesses. It hosts the university's Digital User Research Lab and its creative agency, which provides opportunities for students to work on commercial projects with local, national and international organisations.

Francis House
3-7 Redwell Street
Norwich NR2 4SN
01603 610 561
admissions@nua.ac.uk
www.nua.ac.uk
www.nuasu.co.uk
Open days: see website

The Times and The Sunday Times **Rankings**

Overall Ranking: 77 (last year: =62)

Teaching quality	80.5%	=52
Student experience	76.9%	=82
Research quality	5.6%	=86
Entry standards	130	=56
Graduate prospects	56.2%	130
Good honours	70.8%	103
Expected completion rate	84.1%	67
Student/staff ratio	15.2	=58
Services and facilities	£3,013	20

Like many specialist arts institutions, NUA struggles in comparisons of graduate employment. It is next to bottom in our new measure of graduate prospects, tracking the percentage of graduates in high-skilled jobs or postgraduate study 15 months after finishing a degree. One of its quirky employability schemes is being introduced across the region, however. Students are placed in non-creative sectors, where they quickly appreciate the value of their creative skillset, and employers see how creative problem-solving can boost business growth.

With most of its facilities in the pedestrianised centre of Norwich, the university's origins can be traced back to 1845, when the Norwich School of Design was established by the followers of the Norwich school of painters, known for their landscapes. Former tutors include the artists Lucian Freud, Lesley Davenport and Michael Andrews.

Almost all of the undergraduates are state-educated and one in six is from an area of low participation in higher education. Both figures exceed the national average for NUA's courses and entry qualifications. Up to half the entrants in 2021 are expected to qualify for financial support, which includes a contribution towards the cost of materials, equipment and other expenses where household income is below £25,000.

NUA has an art materials shop which sells basic and specialist art supplies at discounted prices. Individual studio space is provided for all full-time students in the faculties of art and design. Experienced professionals, artists and NUA graduates give workshops providing specialised resources for processes from digital video editing to laser cutting.

More than half of the work submitted to the 2014 Research Excellence Framework was judged to be world-leading or internationally excellent, with 90% in the top two categories for its impact on the broader cultural and economic landscape.

NUA does not have its own sports facilities but its students have access to the University of East Anglia's Sportspark, which includes an Olympic-sized swimming pool. The city of Norwich is popular with students and is one of the safest and greenest in the UK.

Only international students and those with a disability are guaranteed accommodation, but NUA expects to have enough places for all new entrants in 2021. In addition to its own stock in the city centre, the university keeps a register of more than 1,000 private residential places.

Tuition fees

- » Fees for UK students   £9,250
- » Fees for International students 2021–22   £15,900
- » For scholarship and bursary information see www.nua.ac.uk/study-at-nua/fees-funding/
- » Graduate salary   £20,000

Student numbers		
Undergraduates	2,204	(0)
Postgraduates	48	(54)
Applications/places		2,930/840
Applications per place		3.5
Overall offer rate		68.9%
International students – EU		3.4%
Non-EU		4%

Accommodation
University provided places: 900
Self-catered: £102–£155 per week
www.nua.ac.uk/university-life/accommodation/

Where do the students come from?

				Social inclusion ranking: 43	
State schools (non-grammar)	95.7%	First generation students	46.6%	Black attainment gap	n/a
Grammar schools	2.6%	Deprived areas	18%	Disabled	12.6%
Independent schools	1.7%	All ethnic minorities	10.4%	Mature (over 21)	13.3%

University of Nottingham

A rolling parkland campus is the setting for Nottingham's outstanding reputation for teaching and research. The university's high levels of graduate employability also contribute to its enduring popularity, and applications nudged up again in the 2020 cycle.

It was the sixth most targeted university by the top graduate employers in the latest High Fliers report and ranks just outside the top 10 for the proportion of graduates (85%) in high-skilled employment or postgraduate study 15 months after leaving, according to the new Graduate Outcomes survey.

Nottingham's careers and employability service has outstanding links to employers of all sizes regionally, nationally and globally. About 2,000 of them advertise on its online jobs board, where students are encouraged to seek work experience, internships and industrial placements.

The university has embraced degree apprenticeships, and plans to expand from the current 50 apprentices enrolled on seven programmes in architecture, advanced clinical practice, bioinformatics, social work, data science and laboratory science to 400 by 2021, boosted by new programmes for artificial intelligence, process engineers and pharmacists.

The university continues to do well in our annual awards, although it is yet to land the main prize, due in large part to its poor scores for student satisfaction. In 2020, it achieved the unusual feat of ranking the same for satisfaction with teaching quality as it does for the wider student experience. Unfortunately, that ranking was 101=.

Yet Nottingham was awarded gold in the Teaching Excellence Framework (TEF), outperforming many other Russell Group universities. It drew praise for high levels of contact time, which are prescribed and monitored; a culture of personalised learning that ensures all students are challenged to achieve their full potential; and exceptionally high student engagement with advanced technology-enhanced learning.

Nottingham's 330-acre University Park campus is one of the UK's most attractive, and has won several environmental awards. One of its ambitious developments, the £23m Biodiscovery Institute, brings together experts in serious diseases including cancer, cardiovascular, liver, bone and respiratory conditions to encourage collaboration and drive breakthroughs in treatments and diagnosis.

Much of the university's latest development has been on the Jubilee campus, its second base in the city, where the new Advanced Manufacturing Building, opened in 2019, hosts collaborations with companies such as Rolls-Royce and Siemens. The campus also

---

University Park
Nottingham NG7 2RD
0115 951 5559
www.nottingham.ac.uk/
studywithus/enquiry.aspx
www.nottingham.ac.uk
www.su.nottingham.ac.uk
Open days: see website

The Times and The Sunday Times **Rankings**
Overall Ranking: 26 (last year: 21)

Teaching quality	77%	=101
Student experience	75.6%	=101
Research quality	37.8%	20
Entry standards	150	=37
Graduate prospects	84.9%	12
Good honours	84.4%	=22
Expected completion rate	92.1%	26
Student/staff ratio	14.5	=37
Services and facilities	£2,888	27

houses the Centre for Sustainable Chemistry, part-funded by GSK, featuring the UK's first carbon-neutral laboratories. A £21m, 280-space accommodation development is planned.

A third campus, 12 miles south of the city, at Sutton Bonington, focuses on the biosciences and veterinary medicine. Work is continuing to expand the veterinary school's clinical building and a Centre for Dairy Science Innovation has been completed.

Several new degrees are being introduced, including a part-time postgraduate master's in applied English, delivered by distance learning. The degree has its own microsite and a free taster pod. With pay-as-you-go fees of just under £10,000, students take 18 study pods from a choice of nearly 140 over a recommended three-year timespan. In the post-pandemic world, this style of learning might yet become commonplace.

Conventional degree programmes for undergraduates in computer science with cyber-physical systems, and physical geography and geology are among the new additions to the course portfolio in September 2021.

Nottingham was among the pioneers of overseas campuses, exporting a well-known and trusted educational brand to China and Malaysia, where its campuses are centres of research as well as teaching. There are more than 6,600 students at Ningbo, in China, and almost 5,000 in Malaysia, an hour's drive from Kuala Lumpur, taking Nottingham's total student population to more than 45,000.

With more than 7,000 international students coming to Nottingham, the university justifiably markets itself as a global institution.

More than 80% of Nottingham's work entered for the 2014 Research Excellence Framework was rated as world-leading or internationally excellent. The university was in the top 10 in half of the work submitted in 32 subject areas, led by pharmacy, chemistry and physics.

Nottingham wins our Sports University of the Year award for the second time in three years for being top of the inter-university British Universities and Colleges Sport (BUCS) league at the time of its suspension and ultimate cancellation in March due to the pandemic. Loughborough has never been beaten to the top of the BUCS table — and might well have beaten Nottingham again if the competition had continued. But Nottingham's strong position in March confirms it as an emerging challenger.

That success is built around the new David Ross Sports Village, a £40m complex with an indoor sprint track, hydrotherapy pool and 200-station fitness suite.

Tuition fees

» Fees for UK students	£9,250
» Fees for International students 2021–22	£19,000–£25,000
Medicine (clinical years)	£40,500
Veterinary science (2020–21)	£35,220
» For scholarship and bursary information see www.nottingham.ac.uk/fees/tuition-fees-student-services.aspx	
» Graduate salary	£26,000

Student numbers

Undergraduates	24,576	(494)
Postgraduates	6,523	(1,948)
Applications/places		53,800/7,310
Applications per place		7.4
Overall offer rate		74.2%
International students – EU		4.6%
Non-EU		19.8%

Accommodation

University provided places: 8,932
Catered costs: £171–£216 per week
Self-catered: £107–£183 per week
First years guaranteed accommodation
www.nottingham.ac.uk/accommodation

Where do the students come from?

State schools (non-grammar)	64.8%	First generation students	30.9%	
Grammar schools	15.6%	Deprived areas	6.8%	
Independent schools	19.6%	All ethnic minorities	29.1%	

Social inclusion ranking: 108

Black attainment gap	-20%
Disabled	4.7%
Mature (over 21)	7.4%

Nottingham Trent University

Already among the top two recruiters of undergraduates in our league table, Nottingham Trent (NTU) is now branching out across the East Midlands. NTU in Mansfield has begun offering a wide range of foundation degrees for 2020 in partnership with Vision West Nottinghamshire College and the university has plans to open a £3.5m health campus in Worksop, run with Bassetlaw Hospital and the University of Derby.

Courses in Mansfield include business, computing, education and sport and exercise science, and training for ambulance technicians. There is an option to transfer to the Nottingham campus to upgrade to a bachelor's degree.

The university's first nursing degrees were among 13 to be introduced for 2020 including psychology, politics, agriculture and illustration. They will be followed in 2021 by degrees in electronic and electrical engineering, and mathematics with statistics.

NTU has been enjoying a boom in applications and enrolments, both up by another 10% in 2019. The university puts the growing demand for places down to three University of the Year titles in as many years, including ours for Modern University of the Year in 2018.

Nottingham Trent was awarded gold in the Teaching Excellence Framework but has slipped 13 places in our latest league table and is no longer the leading non-specialist modern university. Its scores have dipped in most of our measures revised this year, although it still performs well in the National Student Survey. NTU has moved up to 11th place for student satisfaction with the wider experience in a year when scores have declined nationwide.

Now just outside our top 50 overall, NTU still has a higher ranking than it did a decade ago. In that time, £420m has been spent on its campuses and more is expected to be invested over the next four years. At the £9m Digital Media Hub, a bespoke facility for creative technology students, the Metronome centre has opened, featuring a venue for 350 people, recording studios, rehearsal rooms and a bar. A new Global Lounge offers international and UK students an environment to meet, host events and promote internationalism.

The main City campus is close to the centre of Nottingham and is the academic base for about half of NTU's students. The Clifton campus, just outside the city, houses the arts and humanities, and science and technology, as well as the Nottingham Institute of Education, while the Brackenhurst campus is a countryside estate 14 miles from Nottingham where Ares (animal, rural and environmental sciences) courses are based. A new teaching and reception building has opened at Brackenhurst followed by a dining area, lecture theatre and exhibition space.

50 Shakespeare Street
Nottingham NG1 4FQ
0115 848 4200
ntu.ac.uk/askntu
www.ntu.ac.uk
www.trentstudents.org
Open days: see website

The Times and The Sunday Times **Rankings**

Overall Ranking: 53 (last year: 40)

Teaching quality	82.3%	30
Student experience	81.3%	=11
Research quality	6.5%	80
Entry standards	125	=70
Graduate prospects	71.7%	79
Good honours	69.7%	=111
Expected completion rate	86.7%	54
Student/staff ratio	14.8	=45
Services and facilities	£2,495	61

The business school has begun integrating the UN Sustainable Development Goals into all its courses, and the School of Art and Design has introduced a new module on all undergraduate courses to encourage students to work and collaborate outside their discipline.

The university has also increased the number and range of degree apprenticeships, with more than 1,000 students enrolled on 23 programmes. It is aiming to double participation by September 2021, expanding the range of subjects and employer partnerships.

NTU is already among the leading universities for the number of students on year-long work placements. Most courses include placements of at least four weeks and a dedicated employment team can help students to find international opportunities to study or work.

The university is also among the top five recruiters of disadvantaged students, and a new system of contextual offers, lowering A-level requirements for eligible applicants, may raise the numbers further. NTU was chosen in 2019 to co-lead the National Social Mobility Research Centre. Almost a third of all undergraduates benefit from an unusually wide range of bursaries and scholarships.

Nottingham Trent has a more developed research function than most of its peer group. More than half of the work submitted to the 2014 Research Excellence Framework was considered world-leading or internationally excellent. The best results were in health subjects and general engineering, where more than 80% of the work was placed in the top two categories.

There is residential accommodation on every campus, and new entrants may book one of the 6,000 rooms that are owned or endorsed by NTU as soon as they have a firm offer of a place. The university has a strong sporting reputation, frequently reaching the top 20 in the BUCS (British Universities and Colleges Sport) league. Social life varies between campuses, but all have access to the city's lively cultural and clubbing scene.

Tuition fees

» Fees for UK students	£9,250
» Fees for International students 2020–21	£14,500
» For scholarship and bursary information see www.ntu.ac.uk/study-and-courses/undergraduate/fees-and-funding	
» Graduate salary	£22,000

Student numbers

Undergraduates	24,921 (1,604)
Postgraduates	3,377 (3,354)
Applications/places	45,155/9,260
Applications per place	4.9
Overall offer rate	88.9%
International students – EU	3%
Non-EU	11.3%

Accommodation

University provided places: 5,994
Self-catered: £103–£184 per week
First years guaranteed accommodation
www.ntu.ac.uk/life-at-ntu/accommodation

Where do the students come from?

State schools (non-grammar)	88.2%	First generation students	43.8%	Black attainment gap	-25.9%
Grammar schools	4.6%	Deprived areas	13.7%	Disabled	6.7%
Independent schools	7.2%	All ethnic minorities	25.5%	Mature (over 21)	10.4%

Social inclusion ranking: 91

The Open University

After a period of turmoil amid course closures, staff cuts and budget deficits, the Open University (OU) is headed for calmer waters under the stewardship of Professor Tim Blackman, appointed vice-chancellor in 2019. His predecessor, Peter Horrocks, a former BBC editor, quit after the OU's governing council rejected his plans to cut the budget.

It was not the ideal backdrop for 2019's 50th birthday celebrations, but the anniversary was one well worth celebrating. The OU championed widening participation in higher education before the term had even been coined, embracing students for whom further study had been beyond reach. It is perhaps the greatest legacy of Harold Wilson's 1960s Labour government.

In more recent times, however, the OU has been hit by a triple whammy: the internet offers free Massive Open Online Courses (Moocs), the conventional university sector has also homed in on its market, and part-time students have faced government funding cuts. Student numbers have dropped from 195,000 in 2011 to just 122,000 in 2019.

The OU is hitting back with a string of new courses, recruiting their first students in 2020 and 2021, offering art history and visual cultures, geography, nursing, biology, chemistry, physics, cyber-security, computing and electronic engineering, and an integrated masters in environmental science. There are high hopes for the new Open Centre for Languages and Cultures, which offers 11 beginners' short courses.

The OU also proved particularly nimble-footed during the coronavirus pandemic, linking up with the Department for Education to provide content for its website, The Skills Toolkit, to help workers who had been furloughed, or those seeking new work. The site borrowed courses from the OU's OpenLearn platform such as maths, learning to code and cyber-security.

It is all far removed from the midnight BBC2 television programming of the 1970s and 1980s, largely fronted by men with beards. Now the OU is championing "microcredentials" — accredited, online courses designed to equip learners with specialised skills relevant to their careers. These are delivered through its part-owned website FutureLearn.com. Launched in June 2020, it places the OU in a vanguard of a move to new-style qualifications, designed to address a need identified by learners and partners.

Its introductory courses include teacher training: embedding mental health in the curriculum; global development in practice: designing an intervention; cyber-security operations (Cisco CCNA); and digital photography: creating a professional portfolio.

The university also offers seven degree

Walton Hall
Milton Keynes
MK7 6AA
0300 303 5303
general-enquiries@open.ac.uk
www.open.ac.uk
www.oustudents.com

The Times and The Sunday Times Rankings
n/a
No data available

apprenticeships (including options for social work, police constables, registered nurses and chartered managers) and one higher apprenticeship in England. In Scotland, there are three graduate apprenticeships and in Wales one degree apprenticeship.

More than two million students in 157 countries have benefited from an OU education since its inception in 1969 and it continues to hone its competitive edge compared with its campus rivals. Annual fees for full-time courses with 120 credits come in at £6,192 a year for English students (against £9,250 for a standard full-time degree elsewhere), or £2,064 for students in Scotland, Wales and Northern Ireland. Access modules of 30 credits cost £753 in England and £258 in the rest of the UK — half the cost of similar courses at campus universities.

There are extensive bursaries on offer, up to a full fee waiver for Access programme first-time students from households with an annual income of less than £25,000 (or individual income of less than £25,000 in Scotland).

Our rankings have never included the OU because the absence of campus-based undergraduates would place it at a disadvantage in comparison with traditional universities. There are no entrance requirements, for example, and no need for physical facilities for students.

On those measures where comparisons are possible, the OU generally performs well.

Just under three-quarters of the OU's submission for the 2014 Research Excellence Framework was considered world-leading or internationally excellent. Music was outstanding, with 94% in the top two categories, and work in art and design and electronic engineering also did well. It is world-ranked by QS in nine subjects.

The OU remains the model for distance learning around the world. Based in Milton Keynes, in Buckinghamshire, the university employs thousands of part-time tutors around the country to guide students through their degrees. Its "supported open learning" system allows students to work where they choose: at home, in the workplace or at a library or study centre. Tutorials, day schools or online forums and social networks provide contact with fellow students (pre-Covid) and work is monitored by continual assessment, examination or assignment.

Although more than a third of new OU students are under 25, three-quarters of its students combine their studies with full- or part-time work.

Tuition fees

» Fees for English students (current)	£6,192
Scotland, Wales and Northern Ireland	£2,064
» Fees for International students	£6,192
» For scholarship and bursary information see	
www.open.ac.uk/courses/fees-and-funding	
» Graduate salary	n/a

Students

Undergraduates	282 (112,764)
Postgraduates	300 (9,013)

Accommodation

Not applicable

Where do the students come from?

Not available

University of Oxford

Oxford is our University of the Year for its response to the Covid-19 pandemic, as well as its commitment — and action — on social diversity. First off the mark to develop a vaccine against the virus, the university was also quick to expand its intake when the chaos surrounding A-level results threatened to narrow the social make-up of its entrants.

The university's academics have also been among the most prominent sources of public information to demystify the coronavirus and scrutinise the government's actions throughout the crisis.

Although still second to Cambridge in our league table, Oxford has narrowed the gap to its smallest since 2017. It leads its ancient rival in two of the three main international rankings — and is No 1 in the world according to Times Higher Education.

Oxford has been addressing criticism of its social mix. Professor Louise Richardson, the vice-chancellor, promised a "sea change" in the numbers admitted from ethnic minorities and disadvantaged areas in 2019, introducing two new access schemes. The additional intake of students in 2020 who missed their required grades under the Ofqual algorithm includes a disproportionate number of candidates from disadvantaged backgrounds.

The university remains in the bottom three in our social inclusion table, however, with the lowest proportion of entrants drawn from non-selective state schools. By 2023 Oxford aims to add 250 state school applicants to the intake, an increase from 15% to 25% of those from under-represented backgrounds.

Oxford is expected to make additional places available again in 2021 to avoid reducing opportunities for candidates due to a higher than usual number of deferrals after colleges reached capacity for the October 2020 term. Competition for places is already fierce with barely one in seven receiving an offer.

One of the university's new access schemes, Opportunity Oxford, is a bridging programme for up to 200 school pupils each year who already have an offer from the university but may need extra preparation to get the most out of their course. Another programme introduces a foundation year for students who have experienced severe disadvantage or educational disruption, enabling them to meet entry standards. The university and its colleges also run a £7m outreach programme in schools.

Oxford offers among the most generous financial support in UK higher education for students from poor backgrounds. Nearly a quarter of all students receive some support, with those from the lowest-income families receiving Crankstart bursaries of £5,000 a year.

University Offices
Wellington Square
Oxford OX1 2JD
01865 288 000
www.ox.ac.uk
www.ox.ac.uk/admissions/undergraduate
www.oxfordsu.org
Open days: see website

The Times and The Sunday Times **Rankings**
Overall Ranking: 2 (last year: 2)

Teaching quality	n/a	
Student experience	n/a	
Research quality	53.1%	3
Entry standards	203	4
Graduate prospects	90.6%	4
Good honours	94%	1
Expected completion rate	98.1%	2
Student/staff ratio	10.3	1
Services and facilities	£3,436	10

There are written admissions tests for certain subjects and applicants may be asked to submit samples of work. Some courses now demand two A* grades and another A at A-level and 99% of successful candidates achieve at least three As at A-level or their equivalent.

Selection is in the hands of the 30 undergraduate colleges. Sound advice on the colleges' academic strengths and social vibe is essential for applicants to give themselves the best chance of winning a place and finding an environment where they can thrive. Most colleges can accommodate undergraduates for two of their three years at Oxford, if not more.

Applicants can make an open application without specifying a college preference, but most do make a choice — and picking one is especially important for arts and social science students, whose tuition is based in-college. Science and technology subjects are mainly taught in central facilities.

The gap in our table between Oxbridge and their nearest challengers cannot be precise while the two universities' undergraduates continue to boycott the National Student Survey. It is an odd stance which sets the university's students apart (not in a good way) and means Oxford's satisfaction levels are based on 2016 responses.

Oxford has a gold award in the Teaching Excellence Framework and had the best results in the UK in nine subject areas in the 2014 Research Excellence Framework, when 87% of its submission was rated as world-leading or internationally excellent. It has a slightly lower overall score than Cambridge in our research ratings because it entered a lower proportion of eligible staff.

The university is in the midst of a £1.5bn programme of improvements. The new Wolfson Centre for the Prevention of Stroke and Dementia provides the only purpose-built research facility of its kind in the UK, while the Beecroft Building has world-leading facilities for theoretical and experimental research in physics. Work continues on the provisionally-named Life and Mind Building for the psychological and life sciences, and new facilities for biochemistry.

Sports facilities are first-class. The Iffley Road sports complex — where Sir Roger Bannister ran the first sub-four-minute mile, in 1954 — has been upgraded with a new gym and sports hall, complementing college facilities.

The deadline for applications to Oxford is October 15, and it is not possible to apply to both Oxford and Cambridge in the same year.

Tuition fees

» Fees for UK students   £9,250
» Fees for International students 2021–22   £26,770–£37,510
    Medicine   £46,730 (clinical years)
» For scholarship and bursary information see www.ox.ac.uk/admissions/undergraduate/fees-and-funding
» Graduate salary   £30,000

Student numbers

Undergraduates	11,688	(3,218)
Postgraduates	7,702	(2,780)
Applications/places	23,480/3,305	
Applications per place	7.1	
Overall offer rate	21.8%	
International students – EU	10.4%	
Non-EU	23.1%	

Accommodation

College websites provide accommodation details
See chapter 14 for individual colleges

Where do the students come from?

State schools (non-grammar)	42.5%	First generation students	14%	Black attainment gap	-5.6%
Grammar schools	18.1%	Deprived areas	3.7%	Disabled	7.6%
Independent schools	39.4%	All ethnic minorities	22%	Mature (over 21)	2.4%

Social inclusion ranking: 114

Oxford Brookes University

Oxford Brookes updated its academic framework for 2020 to streamline the degree system, introducing more interdisciplinary courses favoured by employers. The changes to modules and timetabling, following consultation in 2016, will reduce the number of optional modules but increase the focus on quality.

The move may revive student satisfaction, which fell again in 2020, leaving the university in the bottom 20 for satisfaction with teaching quality despite holding a silver rating in the Teaching Excellence Framework. Overall, Brookes has risen eight places in our rankings, however, taking it back inside the top 60.

Applications have fallen by more than a third in three years, but higher offer rates have ensured that the decline in enrolments has been marginal. The university will have been helped in this regard by almost one entrant in six receiving a controversial (and now outlawed) "conditional unconditional" offer in 2019, requiring the beneficiaries to make Brookes their first choice.

Eight new degrees took their first students in September 2020 — including physical activity and health promotion, business and international relations, law with criminology, and mathematics. Three foundation years have been introduced in law, business and humanities for those without the qualifications for immediate degree-level study. From 2021, a BA in liberal arts and a BSc in information technology for business join the curriculum.

There are degree apprenticeships for nursing associates, advanced clinical practitioners, senior leaders and architects. The university is planning to expand its programmes, but the Covid-19 pandemic forced many health apprentices to take a break in their studies, creating uncertainty over future numbers.

Oxford Brookes has four campuses, although the engineering base at Wheatley, seven miles from Oxford, is to be closed in 2021 and the courses transferred to the main city campus in Headington. Harcourt Hill, three miles from the city centre, houses education, English, communication, philosophy and sport students, and nursing is based in a business park in Swindon.

The university is part of an innovative collaboration sharing education, clinical practice and research in nursing, midwifery and allied health professions with two NHS trusts, Oxford University Hospitals NHS Foundation Trust and Oxford Health NHS Foundation Trust.

New teaching, laboratory, research and study spaces have been created at the Sinclair Building in Headington, where the Faculty of Health and Life Sciences has specialist computing equipment and software. The project was the latest phase in a £220m development programme.

For the third year in succession, Oxford Brookes is the UK's only university to appear in the top-50 QS world rankings for institutions less

Headington Campus
Oxford OX3 0BP

01865 741 111
admissions@brookes.ac.uk
www.brookes.ac.uk
www.brookesunion.org.uk
Open days: see website

The Times and The Sunday Times Rankings
Overall Ranking: 56 (last year: 64)

Teaching quality	76.3%	113
Student experience	76.3%	=89
Research quality	11.4%	57
Entry standards	122	=80
Graduate prospects	78.5%	=41
Good honours	78.8%	=45
Expected completion rate	89.4%	38
Student/staff ratio	14.7	=41
Services and facilities	£2,408	69

than 50 years old. There has been a growing emphasis on its international profile. Through a global partnership with the Association of Chartered Certified Accountants, Brookes has more than 200,000 students taking its qualifications in other countries, far more students than any other UK university.

The university is popular with independent schools, which provide more than 30% of the undergraduates — much the highest proportion among the non-specialist post-1992 universities and three times the national average for the institution's subjects and entry grades. It has been trying to attract more students from the state sector and works with more than 120 schools to encourage progression to higher education, as well as running subject-specific summer schools and taster days.

Support available to students includes subsidised bus passes for those from low-income households. The university offers one of the most valuable bursaries at any UK university: the Tessa Jane Evans bursary for nursing, worth £30,000 over three years to three mature students who have no other forms of funding.

Oxford Brookes excelled in the 2014 Research Excellence Framework, entering more academics than most of its peers and still having almost 60% of its work rated as world-leading or internationally excellent. There were particularly good results in architecture, English and history.

The university's researchers are involved in four projects funded out of the government's £40m investment to fast-track new technology to boost the UK's recovery from the coronavirus pandemic. Two involve mobile fitness apps to help patients get stronger; a third is an artificial intelligence app that monitors people's emotional reactions and helps improve their mental health and wellbeing, while the fourth is a social enterprise venture, using artificial intelligence to devise personalised water-based exercise plans.

New privately-managed halls of residence opened in 2020 in east Oxford, adding 880 rooms for students. Applicants who make Oxford Brookes their firm or insurance choice are guaranteed one of the 5,236 spaces owned or endorsed by the university.

Impressive sports facilities include a 25-metre swimming pool and nine-hole golf course. Oxford Brookes is especially strong in rowing, while the cricketers combine with the University of Oxford to take on county teams.

The students' union runs one of the biggest entertainment venues in Oxford. The city offers plenty to do, although it can be expensive.

Tuition fees

» Fees for UK students		£9,250
	Foundation courses	£7,570
» Fees for International students 2021–22		£14,500–£15,200
	Foundation courses	£9,270
» For scholarship and bursary information see www.brookes.ac.uk/studying-at-brookes/finance/		
» Graduate salary		£24,000

Student numbers

Undergraduates	11,870	(913)
Postgraduates	1,672	(2,211)
Applications/places		18,110/3,775
Applications per place		4.8
Overall offer rate		79.7%
International students – EU		5.4%
Non-EU		11.1%

Accommodation

University provided places: 5,236
Catered costs: £160 per week
Self-catered: £89–£200 per week
First years guaranteed accommodation
www.brookes.ac.uk/studying-at-brookes/accommodation/

Where do the students come from?

State schools (non-grammar)	62.9%	First generation students	39.2%	Black attainment gap	-15.6%
Grammar schools	5.1%	Deprived areas	6.5%	Disabled	9.6%
Independent schools	32%	All ethnic minorities	18.2%	Mature (over 21)	17.8%

Social inclusion ranking: 95

Plymouth University

A rise of 17 places has taken Plymouth into the top half of our league table for the first time in almost a decade – and closer to its traditional position among the leading post-1992 universities. The improvement is largely down to higher spending on student facilities combined with steady student satisfaction at a time when rates have fallen elsewhere.

Plymouth finished just outside the top 20 for student satisfaction with teaching quality in the latest National Student Survey and holds a silver rating in the Teaching Excellence Framework. Less positively, the university has had to cut more than 400 staff since 2017-18 to address "significant financial challenges".

Declining student numbers have brought about Plymouth's plan for a "smaller, higher-quality institution, building on its core strengths including its research excellence, its strong reputation for teaching and its pivotal role in the city and wider region". Applications levelled out in 2019, but only after a 26% decline over the previous four years. The numbers enrolling continued to drop.

While some courses have been cut, expansion continues in other directions. Plymouth's new range of degrees for 2020 included zoology, creative writing, computing, and audio and music technology. The university is planning to add environmental geoscience, and diagnostic radiography with ultrasonography, with an integrated foundation year in 2021.

The university has also expanded physically, opening a school of nursing in Exeter. It is the largest provider of nursing, midwifery and health professional education and training in the southwest of England, with nursing courses in Plymouth and Truro.

More than £200m has been invested on the main campus. A new student hub brings student support services together under one roof at the heart of campus in the main library. The university has also taken over Intercity Place, an 11-storey office block overlooking Plymouth railway station, to convert it into a new health campus. A halo of LED lighting on the roof will make the tower a city landmark at night.

The development will complement a £17m medical, dental and biomedical research laboratory which opened in 2019 at the city's Derriford Hospital. Health will also be the main area of expansion for degree apprenticeships. The university expects to double the number of apprentices to 800 by 2021 to respond to skills shortages in health and construction roles.

At the Plymouth Conservatoire, students develop a creative edge from the only partnership in Britain between a university and theatre to teach the performing arts. Undergraduates divide their time between the university and the Theatre Royal Plymouth.

Drake circus
Plymouth PL4 8AA
01752 585 858
admissions@plymouth.ac.uk
www.plymouth.ac.uk
www.upsu.com
Open days: see website

The Times and The Sunday Times Rankings
Overall Ranking: 59 (last year: 76)

Teaching quality	82.7%	21
Student experience	80%	32
Research quality	15.9%	56
Entry standards	128	=60
Graduate prospects	76.5%	51
Good honours	73.7%	=77
Expected completion rate	83.5%	=73
Student/staff ratio	16.2	=74
Services and facilities	£2,342	73

Only two post-1992 universities produced better results in the 2014 Research Excellence Framework than Plymouth. Its submission involved a far bigger proportion of its academics than most of its peers and still managed to have nearly two-thirds of its research judged world-leading or internationally excellent.

Much of Plymouth's research is focused on business and industry in the region and the university is developing a unique new research facility to explore the cyber-security challenges facing the shipping industry.

Plymouth was the first university to be awarded Regional Growth Fund money to promote economic development and has now received almost £500,000 for its Knowledge Exchange Academy, which will help arts and humanities students develop the skills required by employers.

The university has one of the country's top-10 business incubation facilities, focusing on small and medium-sized enterprises in the southwest. About 12,000 students undertake work-based learning or placements, while the Plymouth Award recognises extracurricular achievements.

There are 13 partner colleges across the southwest and the Channel Islands where students can follow Plymouth degree courses. There are also opportunities to study abroad in Europe, America and Canada. Plymouth is one of the partners in the new South West Institute for Technology, established by the government to train students in technical subjects. The institute will establish new buildings and facilities across the region to help train thousands of students and enhance career opportunities.

Eighty-eight per cent of undergraduates come from state schools and colleges, and 45% are the first in their family to go to university. About four in 10 students receive some form of financial support. There are subject-specific scholarships in mathematics and marine-related subjects, an area of particular strength.

Student facilities include the £3m health and wellbeing centre and 1,754 residential places in Plymouth, with 235 in Truro. Applicants holding Plymouth as their firm choice are guaranteed a place in one of the managed halls or in an accredited private hall if they apply by the end of June.

On campus there is a sports hall, fitness centre, dance studio and squash courts. The university has upgraded its facilities for water sports and sessions are run exclusively for students at the city's international-standard swimming and diving centre. Plymouth city centre has plenty of student-oriented nightlife.

Tuition fees

- » Fees for UK students   £9,250
- » Fees for International students 2021–22   £14,200
  Dentistry & Medicine   £39,900 (clinical years)
- » For scholarship and bursary information see
  www.plymouth.ac.uk/fees
- » Graduate salary   £24,000

Student numbers

Undergraduates	15,004	(1,656)
Postgraduates	1,269	(1,717)
Applications/places		18,020/3,485
Applications per place		5.2
Overall offer rate		76.4%
International students – EU		3.1%
Non-EU		6.3%

Accommodation

University provided places: 1,989
Self-catered: £99–£180 per week
First years guaranteed accommodation
www.plymouth.ac.uk/student-life/services/accommodation

Where do the students come from?

State schools (non-grammar)	88%	First generation students	45.2%		
Grammar schools	6.4%	Deprived areas	15.3%		
Independent schools	5.6%	All ethnic minorities	13%		

Social inclusion ranking: 69

Black attainment gap	-25.6%
Disabled	9.2%
Mature (over 21)	28.3%

Plymouth Marjon University

Plymouth Marjon is homing in on its target of attracting 1,000 students per year. In 2019 the university recorded its third successive rise in the number of students starting degrees, and applications early in the 2020 cycle were up 5% following the introduction of new courses.

A key element of the university's growth plan is a 10-year development of the spacious and attractive campus on the north side of Plymouth, which has views of the sea and Dartmoor National Park. There have already been improvements to enhance the student experience with the addition of social learning spaces, new social areas and versatile new teaching accommodation.

A new student bar and a hub featuring social working space and an information centre opened in 2018. The hub houses all the main student support services, such as learning support, employability and career development, and counselling.

Presciently, the university has also been investing in teaching and learning technology, introducing a Moodle virtual learning environment in 2019 and installing interactive television screens in the main lecture rooms. All lectures are filmed for later viewing by students on mobiles or computers. A new TV and radio broadcasting facility opened a year ago at the BBC studio building in Plymouth.

However, falling student satisfaction levels have prevented Marjon from achieving a place in our top 100. It has gone from a top-10 high in 2019 for its scores in the National Student Survey to featuring in the top 25 for satisfaction with teaching quality and the top 35 for the wider experience this year — still strong results in comparison to other institutions, but they have contributed to a fall of 13 places for Marjon in our overall rankings.

Almost all courses have a form of work placement for students, some in NHS hospitals and local football clubs, as well as media outlets. New degrees starting in September 2020 included journalism with photography, outdoor learning in early years and primary education, physical education and dance, and sport business management.

Six additions planned for 2021 cover history, criminology and law, business and law, accounting and finance, high-performance coaching and football science. So far there is only one degree apprenticeship, in education.

Marjon has a silver rating in the Teaching Excellence Framework. Every student now has a personal development tutor to help with academic skills, careers advice, one-to-one mentoring, confidence-building and resilience.

The university has been awarded £250,000 by the Office for Students and Research England to develop its student-led programmes working with NHS patients into a model for other institutions. Researchers

Derriford Road
Plymouth PL6 8BH
01752 636 890
admissions@marjon.ac.uk
www.marjon.ac.uk
www.marjonsu.com
Open days: see website

The Times and The Sunday Times **Rankings**

Overall Ranking: 115 (last year: =102)

Teaching quality	82.5%	=22
Student experience	79.7%	35
Research quality	0%	127
Entry standards	114	=102
Graduate prospects	70.4%	88
Good honours	73.8%	76
Expected completion rate	79.1%	104
Student/staff ratio	20.5	125
Services and facilities	£1,603	126

and students work in community clinics to help patients understand and manage living with a disease through lifestyle and behavioural changes.

Marjon suffers in our table for a decision not to take part in the 2014 Research Excellence Framework, which leaves it in last place for research quality. One of its key aims for 2025 is to have developed a credible entry to the next research assessment.

Nearly all the undergraduates are state-educated and one in five comes from an area of low participation in higher education. Widening participation is a priority in student recruitment, and about 60% of entrants are the first in their family to go to university. Marjon has long-term progression agreements with 12 local schools or colleges and makes lower offers to pupils who qualify under widening-participation programmes.

Established in London in 1840 as a Church of England teacher training college, Marjon claims to be one of the oldest higher education institutions in England. Its first principal was the son of the poet Samuel Taylor Coleridge. Teacher training remains a strength and Ofsted has rated its courses outstanding for leadership and management.

The College of St Mark and St John moved to Plymouth in 1973. It remains a Church of England institution and its Chaplaincy Centre, at the heart of the campus, welcomes students of all faiths.

Sport is one of the main teaching areas and the university's excellent sports facilities are all available to the public. They include a floodlit 3G pitch for rugby, lacrosse and football, two other floodlit all-weather lacrosse and hockey pitches, a climbing wall, 25-metre indoor swimming pool and gym. There is also a rehabilitation clinic and sports science laboratory.

Sport students have access to a climate chamber and an anti-gravity treadmill. A sports scholarship scheme extends to sports not currently covered by the national Talented Athlete Scholarship Scheme.

There are student bedrooms on campus for 462 students in seven halls of residence and 38 village houses. First-year students are given priority in the allocation of places, and if none is available they are found approved off-campus accommodation. The lively city centre is only a short bus ride from the campus.

Tuition fees

»	Fees for UK students	£9,250
	Foundation courses	£6,000
»	Fees for International students 2021–22	£12,000
»	For scholarship and bursary information see www.marjon.ac.uk/courses/fees-and-funding/	
»	Graduate salary	£21,000

Student numbers

Undergraduates	2,135	(139)
Postgraduates	309	(189)
Applications/places		3,030/750
Applications per place		4
Overall offer rate		85%
International students – EU		1.7%
Non-EU		0.8%

Accommodation

University provided places: 462
Self-catered: £95–£115 per week
First years guaranteed accommodation
www.marjon.ac.uk/student-life/accommodation/

Where do the students come from?

State schools (non-grammar)	96.2%	First generation students	59.9%	Black attainment gap	n/a
Grammar schools	2.1%	Deprived areas	20.6%	Disabled	14.8%
Independent schools	1.7%	All ethnic minorities	5.8%	Mature (over 21)	38.7%

Social inclusion ranking: 6

University of Portsmouth

Portsmouth prides itself on responding to feedback from its students. Improvements introduced in recent years include changes to the academic year, online submission of work, extended opening hours for the library and increased support with IT resources. Students can put forward ideas via an online suggestion box and informal drop-in sessions.

The approach may have helped the university to maintain levels of student satisfaction in the 2020 National Student Survey (NSS), when they were falling across the country. Portsmouth is back in the top 40 for satisfaction with teaching quality and the wider experience based on our analysis of the NSS results.

But that was not enough to stop Portsmouth slipping 16 places overall, taking it out of the top half of our league table. Scores have fallen across most factors — in particular for graduate prospects, now measured in a new way by the Higher Education Statistics Agency, leaving Portsmouth 68=.

Investment has been concentrated on teaching through real-life scenarios, both actual and simulated, to give students the hands-on experience favoured by employers. Students learn to dispense medicines in a pharmacy and to treat NHS patients at a dental clinic. Portsmouth has also opened a forensic innovation centre where students work alongside police officers.

The £12m Future Technology Centre, opened in 2019, also enables students on BEng (Hons) and MEng Innovation Engineering courses to confront real-world health, humanitarian and environmental problems using specialist technology. Additional teaching facilities are available at the heart of the city centre campus through Highbury College's City Learning Centre.

High levels of student engagement and commitment to learning helped Portsmouth to win a gold award in the government's Teaching Excellence Framework. Despite this, however, applications have declined for five years in a row, dropping by more than a quarter in that time, although enrolments have stayed steadier.

Portsmouth made more than 2,000 unconditional offers in 2018 and continued the now-outlawed practice in 2019, adding a £1,000 vice-chancellor's scholarship for those who met or exceeded their predicted grades as an incentive to avoid demotivation.

Nine new degrees for 2020 include three in music technology, journalism with creative writing, and creative computing with a foundation year for those without the necessary qualifications to go straight onto a degree course. Creative media production is being delivered jointly with the Isle of Wight

Academic registry
University House
Winston Churchill Avenue
Portsmouth PO1 2UP
023 9284 5566
admissions@port.ac.uk
www.port.ac.uk
www.upsu.net
Open days: see website

The Times and The Sunday Times **Rankings**
Overall Ranking: 72 (last year: =56)

Teaching quality	81.1%	=40
Student experience	79.4%	=40
Research quality	8.6%	70
Entry standards	113	=106
Graduate prospects	72.9%	=68
Good honours	73.6%	=80
Expected completion rate	83.8%	=70
Student/staff ratio	16.1	=72
Services and facilities	£2,281	82

College, while a new partnership with the Institute for Optimum Nutrition has produced a BSc in nutritional therapy, with a graduate diploma in integrative functional nutrition to follow in 2021.

There are also 18 degree apprenticeship programmes, with more to come in nursing and teaching in 2021. By then, the university expects to have 1,200 students training for roles ranging from surveying to risk management, architecture and healthcare management.

Health subjects produced the best results in the 2014 Research Excellence Framework. About 90% of the work submitted in dentistry, nursing and pharmacy was assessed as world-leading or internationally excellent. Health research links are expected to grow stronger after the local hospital trust was renamed the Portsmouth Hospitals University NHS Trust in summer 2020, marking the next stage in a decade-long partnership.

The university has pioneered new approaches to student wellbeing. Academic staff, including personal tutors, are trained in mental health awareness and how best to support their students. Portsmouth was the first university to use WhatsUp? – a mental health app that promotes better communication between students and pastoral services.

Portsmouth spends almost £1m a year on scholarships to encourage its students to progress to postgraduate courses, where this will help their career plans, including a growing range of MRes programmes to develop research skills. Taking up opportunities for UK and global work placements is encouraged, and new placement years have been introduced for students to set up their own business and develop enterprise skills.

Most of the university's residential accommodation is close to the central Guildhall campus, although many students live in Southsea. The university has 4,000 residential places — enough to guarantee accommodation to all new entrants who apply by the deadline and make Portsmouth their firm choice.

A £6.5m student centre includes alcohol-free areas. The £50m Ravelin Sports Centre is due to open in 2021, with an eight-lane 25m swimming pool, an eight-court sports hall, a 175-station fitness suite, squash courts and a ski simulator. The university's seaside location provides an excellent base for water sports, and outdoor sports facilities include an all-weather 3G pitch suitable for football, rugby, lacrosse and American football.

Tuition fees

» Fees for UK students £9,250
» Fees for International students 2021–22 £15,500–£17,600
» For scholarship and bursary information see www.port.ac.uk/study/undergraduate/undergraduate-fees-and-student-finance
» Graduate salary £24,000

Student numbers

Undergraduates	18,603 (2,488)
Postgraduates	2,389 (2,035)
Applications/places	24,825/5,040
Applications per place	4.9
Overall offer rate	89.9%
International students–EU	4.4%
Non-EU	13.1%

Accommodation

University provided places: 4,062
Catered costs: £134–£173 per week
Self-catered: £99–£163 per week
First years guaranteed accommodation
www.port.ac.uk/student-life/accommodation

Where do the students come from?

State schools (non-grammar)	91%	First generation students	49.2%	Black attainment gap	-22.2%
Grammar schools	5.3%	Deprived areas	15.8%	Disabled	8.4%
Independent schools	3.7%	All ethnic minorities	28.5%	Mature (over 21)	14%

Social inclusion ranking: =62

Queen Margaret University Edinburgh

Queen Margaret (QMU) is aiming to increase the student population over the next five years. Under its new strategic plan looking ahead to 2025, the university also hopes to increase the opportunities for students to take work experience, and to recruit greater numbers from disadvantaged groups.

The strategy also promises to address sustainability in all courses so graduates leave with a "rounded understanding of the sustainability challenges facing the world and the tools to contribute to solutions". QMU aims to reduce the university's own carbon footprint and be one of the greenest institutions in the UK.

Being a sector leader in widening access to university for students from under-represented groups is another QMU goal, and one it is already delivering on: the university is third in our social inclusion ranking for Scotland, with about 40% of entrants the first in their family to go to university.

Overall, the university has fallen seven places in our rankings in this edition, and although student satisfaction scores are close to what they were in 2019 – with a top-60 rank for teaching quality and a top-100 finish for the wider experience – there is some distance to cover before QMU achieves its aim to be Scotland's leader in student satisfaction.

Sir Paul Grice, QMU's new principal, sees challenging times but also opportunities ahead, boosted by the university's location in one of the world's great cities. He was previously clerk and chief executive of the Scottish parliament.

Enrolments have increased a little for the past two years while applications rose another 3% in the 2020 admissions round, due partly to the addition of a popular new degree in paramedic science.

QMU has the broadest range of allied health courses in Scotland and is one of only three universities north of the border to offer paramedic science. Two degrees in acting and performance were added in 2020. Business management is the only graduate apprenticeship, but the university expects to add early learning and childcare by September 2021.

Originally a cookery school for women, the institution was established in 1875 and named after Saint Margaret, the 11th-century wife of King Malcolm III of Scotland. Today three-quarters of the 2,850 undergraduates are women, 85% of them from Scotland. Bursaries of up to £2,000 a year are available for those from low-income households.

The university remains strong in teaching and research on hospitality and food, and has Prue Leith, the restaurateur and Great British Bake Off host, as chancellor. It hosts the Scottish Centre for Food Development and

University Way
Musselburgh
Edinburgh EH21 6UU
0131 474 0000
admissions@qmu.ac.uk
www.qmu.ac.uk
www.qmusu.org.uk
Open days: see website

The Times and The Sunday Times Rankings
Overall Ranking: 89 (last year: 82)

Teaching quality	80.3%	=57
Student experience	76.1%	95
Research quality	6.6%	79
Entry standards	153	=28
Graduate prospects	71.8%	78
Good honours	79.6%	=39
Expected completion rate	79.3%	=102
Student/staff ratio	19.5	=119
Services and facilities	£1,676	125

Innovation and students can gain practical experience during their degree studies in international hospitality management through a partnership with the Edinburgh New Town Cookery School.

QMU moved to its purpose-built campus, designed in consultation with the students, in the seaside town of Musselburgh in 2007, when it gained university status. The campus, which won a string of awards, is one of the most environmentally sustainable in the UK and still exceeds current standards.

The university promises a "student-centred approach" with a culture of personalised support. Nearly a quarter of the QMU's workforce has been trained in mental health first aid — offering a bigger network than any other university in Scotland.

Queen Margaret has a highly successful employer mentoring scheme, matching third- and fourth-year students with professionals who have relevant experience. A business innovation zone supports the creation of student and staff start-up businesses. QMU is the only university in Scotland to host a Business Gateway on campus, offering guidance for new and established local businesses. It is also developing the £80m Edinburgh Innovation Park on land next to the university campus, in partnership with East Lothian council.

With 65% in high-skilled jobs or further study 15 months after completing their degrees the university held on to a top-100 ranking in our graduate employment measure this year.

Only 22% of the eligible staff were entered in the 2014 Research Excellence Framework but almost 60% of their work was considered world-leading or internationally excellent. Its submission in speech and language sciences was the most successful, with 92% of it rated in the top two categories, placing the university second in the UK and first in Scotland in this area.

From the campus, next to Musselburgh train station, Edinburgh's attractions are less than 10 minutes away. There are 800 residential places on campus and a good range of sports facilities. The university does not guarantee accommodation for new entrants, although 96% of those who wanted one were offered a place in 2019. Priority goes to students from outside the Edinburgh area, as well as those who have disabilities or have been in care.

Tuition fees

» Fees for Scottish students £0–£1,820
   RUK fees £9,250 (capped at £27,750 for 4-year courses)
» Fees for International students 2021–22 £13,500–£15,500
» For scholarship and bursary information see www.qmu.ac.uk/current-students/current-students-general-information/fees-and-charges/
» Graduate salary £23,000

Student numbers

Undergraduates	3,033	(473)
Postgraduates	654	(1,066)
Applications/places		6,260/875
Applications per place		7.2
Overall offer rate		57.5%
International students – EU		15.6%
Non-EU		5.7%

Accommodation

University provided places: 800
Self-catered: £119–£144 per week
www.qmu.ac.uk/campus-life/accommodation/

Where do the students come from?

State schools (non-grammar)	95.7%	First generation students	38.7%		
Grammar schools	1.9%	Deprived areas	11.7%		
Independent schools	2.5%	All ethnic minorities	5.8%		

Social inclusion ranking (Scotland): 3

Black attainment gap	n/a
Disabled	9.2%
Mature (over 21)	38%

Queen Mary, University of London

Queen Mary, University of London (QMUL) continues to prove that social inclusion and academic success are not mutually exclusive. In line with its Strategy 2030 vision "to open the doors of opportunity, through world-leading teaching and research, and to become the most inclusive university of our kind" it has risen eight places to rank 41st in our academic ranking and five places to stand 46th in our social inclusion table. This balanced success earns QMUL runner-up spot for our University of the Year title.

Among its fellow research-led Russell Group institutions, high academic rankings tend to be turned on their head in our measure of social inclusion. But at QMUL, 48% of UK students are the first in their family to attend university, seven out of 10 are from black and minority ethnic backgrounds and three in 10 are from households with an income below £35,000.

Many QMUL students grew up near its campuses in the east London borough of Tower Hamlets — one of the most deprived areas in the UK — and rub shoulders with coursemates from around the world. The university believes that through this diversity of ideas and views, truly original work will take place.

QMUL was awarded silver in the Teaching Excellence Framework (TEF), impressing assessors with the quality of its coaching programmes, mentoring schemes and employer engagement programmes, which help students to find good jobs. The latest graduate prospects figures support the TEF's findings, showing that 80% of QMUL graduates were in high-skilled jobs or postgraduate study within 15 months of finishing their degrees — a top-30 result. Significantly fewer students drop out than expected.

Degrees are structured to improve students' networking and communication skills, and provide experience outside their subject. The QMUL Model accounts for 10% of a student's degree, covering activities such as work experience, volunteering in the community, overseas travel, project work with local businesses and other organisations, learning a language, or taking modules from other subjects.

Most of QMUL's 14,300 undergraduates are both taught and housed on a self-contained campus in Mile End, one of east London's more desirable enclaves. Its large medical school, Barts and the London School of Medicine and Dentistry, is based in nearby Whitechapel.

With £100m investment over five years, recent campus improvements have included a new graduate centre, a new dental school and the redevelopment of the engineering and maths buildings. The Neuron Pod is a £1.9m extension of QMUL's award-winning Centre of the Cell science education centre. The art

327 Mile End Road
London E1 4NS
020 7882 5511
admissions@qmul.ac.uk
www.qmul.ac.uk
www.qmsu.org/
Open days: see website

The Times and The Sunday Times **Rankings**
Overall Ranking: 41 (last year: 49)

Teaching quality	72.8%	=123
Student experience	73.9%	=115
Research quality	37.9%	19
Entry standards	152	=31
Graduate prospects	80.3%	35
Good honours	86%	16
Expected completion rate	90.7%	34
Student/staff ratio	13	11
Services and facilities	£2,208	85

deco People's Palace, built to bring culture, entertainment and education to Victorian-era East Enders, has been restored to host events.

Many new degrees to be introduced in 2021 will add a year abroad, placement or foundation years to existing undergraduate courses. Degrees in actuarial science, physics with data science, economics and international relations and business management with Mandarin Chinese are among the new options.

A designated Institute of Technology, QMUL has £28m capital funding to establish a dedicated campus for apprenticeships. It plans to double its current portfolio of four degree apprenticeships by adding programmes in economics, data science, systems engineering, and aerospace engineering — and aims to have 300 participants by September 2021.

Via the Queen Mary Academy, all staff and students can access continuing professional development opportunities online and face-to-face, and in the university's Going for Gold initiative staff and students are co-creating ideas to boost the educational and student experience. Student satisfaction, though, remains an Achilles heel for QMUL in our main league table, as it does with other research-intensive universities in London.

Medicine and other health subjects did well in the 2014 Research Excellence Framework, but the best results came in the humanities. About 95% of the research in linguistics and in music, drama and the performing arts was rated as world-leading or internationally excellent. More than 85% of QMUL's entire submission reached the top two categories.

About half of the university's UK undergraduates receive some form of direct financial support. More than 30% qualify for the Queen Mary University of London Bursary, worth up to £1,700 per year. A range of scholarships helps local students whose household incomes are under £42,875 and subject-specific academic scholarships include awards for law, medicine and dentistry students.

There is also provision for forced migrants and asylum seekers who want to study. QMUL has put together a non-academic support package that covers advice on money, housing, immigration and emotional wellbeing.

QMUL students can use the sports facilities at the nearby Queen Elizabeth Olympic Park, including the Copper Box indoor arena and the Aquatic Centre's swimming pool. The Mile End campus has a refurbished students' union and a subsidised health and fitness centre. Students are on the doorstep of London's most achingly hip social scenes around Brick Lane.

Tuition fees

» Fees for UK students	£9,250
» Fees for International students 2021–22	£19,250–£23,950
Dentistry, Medicine (2020–21)	£38,000
» For scholarship and bursary information see www.qmul.ac.uk/undergraduate/feesandfunding/	
» Graduate salary	£28,000

Student numbers

Undergraduates	14,299	(4)
Postgraduates	4,854	(1,405)
Applications/places		33,930/3,910
Applications per place		8.7
Overall offer rate		64.3%
International students – EU		9.2%
Non-EU		24.6%

Accommodation

University provided places: 2,981
Self-catered: £133–£212 per week
First years guaranteed accommodation
www.qmul.ac.uk/study/accommodation

Where do the students come from?

State schools (non-grammar)	80.4%	First generation students	47.8%	Black attainment gap	-5%
Grammar schools	10.9%	Deprived areas	3.6%	Disabled	6.5%
Independent schools	8.7%	All ethnic minorities	70.5%	Mature (over 21)	9.1%

Social inclusion ranking: 46

Queen's University Belfast

Northern Ireland's leading university has been moving up our league table and is on the verge of the top 30 in this edition after a four-place rise. It has done particularly well under the new system of assessing graduate prospects, taking it close to the top 10 on this measure.

Queen's saw one of the biggest increases in applications at any UK university when the deadline for entry in 2020 passed in June. The volume of applications had dipped slightly for three years in a row, although the numbers starting courses had remained steady. But the development of integrated master's courses and stronger international marketing produced a 12% increase in demand.

Student satisfaction continues to hold Queen's back, however. It has now dropped into the bottom 20 in our analysis of the sections of the National Student Survey focused on satisfaction with teaching quality.

Hillary Clinton has been installed as chancellor as part of the university's internationalisation drive, which is intended to double the number of students coming from overseas. A member of the Russell Group, with a position just outside the top 200 in the QS World University Rankings, the university sees plenty of scope for expansion.

The university is not planning any new honours degrees for September 2021, although it launched an innovative master's programme in professional nursing in 2020 aimed at graduates from other disciplines who want to move into the profession. Expansion is planned for the degree apprenticeship offering however, from a single programme in software engineering and digital technology to include project management and pharmaceutical analysis.

A new teaching centre for the management school is the next project of a £350m 10-year development programme. The £39m School of Biological Sciences opened in 2019, expanding the university's work in the life sciences in areas such as agriculture, food science and the environment.

The university has also opened Queen's Precision Medicine Centre of Excellence, which aims to develop artificial intelligence solutions to enable early, rapid and accurate diagnoses of cancers. A £2.1m grant will pay for a new high-performance computing facility on the campus.

Queen's plays a leading role in initiatives such as the Belfast City Region Deal, a 15-year programme to boost growth. The university has been rated top in the UK for establishment of knowledge transfer partnerships and is co-leader of a national programme to promote the commercialisation of university research.

The university won a record seventh Queen's Anniversary Prize for Higher Education in 2020 for its pioneering work in shared education, which facilitates collaboration between schools serving

---

University Road
Belfast BT7 1NN
028 9097 3838
admissions@qub.ac.uk
www.qub.ac.uk
www.qubsu.org
Open days: see website

The Times and The Sunday Times **Rankings**
Overall Ranking: =31 (last year: 35)

Teaching quality	76.1%	=114
Student experience	76.3%	=89
Research quality	39.7%	14
Entry standards	152	=31
Graduate prospects	84.7%	=13
Good honours	85%	19
Expected completion rate	91.6%	29
Student/staff ratio	14.6	=39
Services and facilities	£2,423	68

different faiths. For more than 100 years the university's own charter has guaranteed non-denominational teaching as well as student representation and equal rights for women.

Most undergraduates come from Northern Ireland, more than 60% of them from grammar schools, which educate a much larger proportion of the population in the province than elsewhere in the UK. The university does not feature in our social inclusion ranking because of this feature of the Northern Irish education system. Our ranking measures recruitment from non-selective state schools, a figure that is unduly depressed at Queen's, Belfast and Ulster.

The university has been increasing efforts to broaden its intake and more than 40% of undergraduates are expected to receive some financial support in 2020/21. A Pathway Opportunity Programme for Northern Irish students living in disadvantaged areas has almost 300 participants, who are guaranteed a conditional offer which may be two grades lower than the norm for their chosen course. The programme has continued online during the pandemic.

Queen's is in our top 20 for research after entering 95% of its academics for the 2014 Research Excellence Framework, a proportion matched only by Cambridge. Of the large submission, 77% of the research was considered world-leading or internationally excellent and 14 subject areas were ranked in the UK's top 20.

The campus, on the south side of the city, has a cinema, an art gallery and theatre, all of which are open to the wider community as well as students. The city centre has plenty of nightlife, but the social scene is mainly concentrated on the students' union and the surrounding area.

Most of the 4,000 residential places are at the Elms student village, close to the university, but a new development of 1,200 rooms with its own services, including pastoral care, security and social activities, has added the option of living in the city centre.

Sports facilities include Mourne Cottage in the mountains, a boathouse on the River Lagan and an arena pitch for football, rugby or Gaelic sport. Facilities have benefitted from a £20m programme of investment, which added a floodlit international standard hockey pitch and a 100-seat spectator stand in 2020.

Friendly, compact and increasingly cosmopolitan Belfast makes a popular student city.

Tuition fees

» Fees for Northern Ireland students	£4,395
Students from England, Scotland and Wales	£9,250
» Fees for International students 2021–22	£17,400–£21,400
Dentistry	£32,800
Medicine	£42,200
» For scholarship and bursary information see	
www.qub.ac.uk/Study/undergraduate/fees-and-scholarships/	
» Graduate salary	£22,000

Student numbers

Undergraduates	15,433 (3,301)
Postgraduates	3,663 (2,300)
Applications/places	27,730/4,130
Applications per place	6.7
Overall offer rate	72.3%
International students – EU	4.2%
Non-EU	11.2%

Accommodation

University provided places: 4,024
Catered costs: £99–£133 per week
Self-catered: £75–£175 per week
First years guaranteed accommodation
www.qub.ac.uk/accommodation

Where do the students come from?

State schools (non-grammar)	34.4%	First generation students	36%		
Grammar schools	63.9%	Deprived areas	6.7%		
Independent schools	1.7%	Ethnic minorities	n/a		

Social inclusion ranking: n/a

Mature (over-21)	19.5%

Ravensbourne University, London

Ravensbourne is off the bottom of our table for the first time, even if only by one place. A sharp rise in the proportion of students awarded good honours, as well as improved staffing levels and graduate prospects, explain the improvement.

The new university, which achieved that status only in 2018, is still hampered by the absence of a score for research quality because it did not enter the Research Excellence Framework in 2014. But it is also in the bottom two in both of our measures of student satisfaction.

Andy Cook, who had served as acting vice-chancellor since June 2019, took the permanent role with a pledge to develop new courses and enhance the student experience. He will oversee the opening of a new Institute for Creativity and Technology and the development of digital-first teaching provision, with courses that meet the needs of industry while widening opportunities to participate in higher education.

Ravensbourne has fewer than 2,500 undergraduates, with male students in a narrow majority — unusual for a specialist arts university. Degrees in creative computing, cloud computing, cyber-security and digital marketing all began in September 2020, and foundation years have been introduced in animation and games design. More than 40% of students taking foundation programmes progress to degree courses. As in other similar institutions, the offer of a place hinges on an applicant's portfolio or showreel as much as on academic grades.

Ravensbourne is planning further degree apprenticeships in 2021 to add to the existing programme in digital and technology solutions. The new programmes for digital UX (user experience) professionals and broadcast and media systems engineers will bring the number of apprentices to about 60.

The university, which brands itself as a specialist design and digital media institution, occupies a striking purpose-built, open-plan building, next to the O2 Arena on the Greenwich Peninsula. The Institute for Creativity and Technology will open in 2021 in the peninsula's new design district, housing Ravensbourne's postgraduate provision and incubation and research activities.

More than 100 creative technology businesses utilise Ravensbourne's technology and media resources, and collaborate with its student body and industry partners. The university has a strong track record for business creation, its incubation unit helping award-winning production companies and digital agencies, as well as internationally recognised fashion labels.

A focus on employability has helped Ravensbourne graduates to the highest starting salaries among the specialist arts universities in recent years. Its extensive collaboration with

---

6 Penrose Way
Greenwich Peninsula
London SE10 0EW
020 3040 3998
admissions@rave.ac.uk
www.ravensbourne.ac.uk
www.ravesu.co.uk
Open days: see website

The Times and The Sunday Times **Rankings**
Overall Ranking: 130 (last year: 131)

Teaching quality	71.7%	=126
Student experience	65.1%	128
Research quality	n/a	
Entry standards	112	=109
Graduate prospects	70.7%	86
Good honours	82.9%	=24
Expected completion rate	72.4%	126
Student/staff ratio	24.2	131
Services and facilities	£1,466	129

industry was one of the factors behind a silver rating in the Teaching Excellence Framework.

Widening participation is another of Ravensbourne's priorities, although it is in the bottom half of our latest social inclusion table. More than 40% of the undergraduates are from ethnic minorities and 93% attended non-selective state schools or colleges. There is a range of bursaries for low-income students, starting with the main Ravensbourne Bursary of £500 a year for those with a household income of less than £25,000. All new students receive a £100 voucher for a laptop or course materials, rising to £500 for those from low-income households.

Established in 1962, Ravensbourne was located on Bromley Common and then Chislehurst, Kent, before moving to its current home nine years ago. Its degrees were validated by the University of Arts London until 2018.

The single-building campus requires the university to manage its student numbers, room use and teaching model carefully, but the strategic plan envisages gradual growth, increased commercial activity and more research in the longer term. Ravensbourne aims to be recognised as a national and international leader in creative industries education and training. A partnership with Berghs School of Communication, in Stockholm, began in 2019, bringing Swedish students to the university.

Ravensbourne's best-known alumni include fashion designers Clare Waight Keller of Givenchy, who designed the dress Meghan Markle wore for her wedding to Prince Harry; Stella McCartney; Bruce Oldfield; Kevin Carrigan, the senior vice-president and creative director at Ralph Lauren; literary scholar Robert Hewison; handbag designer Emma Hill, sculptor Alison Wilding and the co-designer of the Olympic 2012 torch, Jay Osgerby.

The university does not own or manage halls of residence, but it works with a number of private providers to offer accommodation. No guarantees are given, but first-years who request a room are usually found one. The university encourages students to apply as early as possible as most providers fill rooms on a first-come, first-served basis.

Students get discounted membership to use a gym within 200 yards of the university building and there are good transport services on the doorstep for excursions into central London. Ravensbourne students also enjoy discounts at a number of the neighbouring O2 restaurants, bars and shops.

Tuition fees

»	Fees for UK students	£9,250
	Foundation courses	£5,421
»	Fees for International students 2020–21	£14,900
	Foundation courses	£9,500
»	For scholarship and bursary information see www.ravensbourne.ac.uk/study-here/ bursaries-and-scholarships/	
»	Graduate salary	£23,000

Student numbers

Undergraduates	2,446	(5)
Postgraduates	69	(8)
Applications/places	3,175/760	
Applications per place	4.2	
Overall offer rate	58.1%	
International students – EU	5.8%	
Non-EU	7.9%	

Accommodation

University provided places: 100
Self-catered: £216–£299 per week
www.ravensbourne.ac.uk/accommodation/

Where do the students come from?

State schools (non-grammar)	92.9%	First generation students	45.1%		
Grammar schools	2.9%	Deprived areas	6.2%		
Independent schools	4.3%	All ethnic minorities	44.2%		

Social inclusion ranking: 64

Black attainment gap	-18%
Disabled	8.3%
Mature (over 21)	13.9%

University of Reading

Reading is up seven places and close to the top 30 in our latest league table. Its position has been boosted by excellent results in the new Graduate Outcomes survey, which found 78% of graduates were in high-skilled work or further study within 15 months of finishing their degrees.

All first-degree students can take work placements as part of their course, as well as career management skills modules that contribute five credits towards their degree classification. There is also an award-winning career mentoring programme, which connects students with successful alumni, preparing them for graduate recruitment over the summer of their penultimate year and into their final year.

The university, which holds silver in the Teaching Excellence Framework, is aiming to become a "larger, vibrant and more sustainable institution" by the time of its centenary in 2026. Under the 2026: Transform programme, the university is investing more than £200m on improvements to buildings and facilities.

The library on the main Whiteknights campus is newly refurbished and has extra study space. A new £55m health and life sciences building will include one of the largest teaching labs in the UK, as well as the Cole Museum of Zoology, open to the public.

Lecture theatres across the campus have been refurbished, and more than £2m has been spent on the students' union's popular nightclub. A £1m capital fund allows the students' union to select its own projects. So far, they have included free charging points in lecture theatres, more lockers and a relaxation zone in the union.

The latest big project is a new television studio at the university's Thames Valley Science Park, part of a bid to make Reading a global media hub. The university is also extending its Langley Mead nature reserve on one of its two farms, where it offers guided walks to inform the public about plants and wildlife.

The launch of 21 new undergraduate programmes in 2020 may help to reverse four consecutive years of declining applications. Around half of the new degrees involve the addition of foundation years or placements at work or abroad, but wholly new programmes in areas such as archaeology and anthropology, architectural engineering, chemistry with cosmetic science and nutrition have also been added.

Levels of student satisfaction have improved – and contributed to Reading's rise up our academic ranking – although the university remains in the bottom third for teaching quality and only marginally higher for the wider experience.

Whiteknights
PO Box 217
Reading RG6 6AH
0118 378 8372
www.reading.ac.uk/question
www.reading.ac.uk
www.rusu.co.uk
Open days: see website

The Times and The Sunday Times Rankings

Overall Ranking: =31 (last year: =38)

Teaching quality	78.1%	91
Student experience	77.2%	=76
Research quality	36.5%	29
Entry standards	127	=65
Graduate prospects	78.9%	39
Good honours	81.9%	=31
Expected completion rate	91.3%	32
Student/staff ratio	15.8	=69
Services and facilities	£2,880	28

The main campus in 320 acres of parkland on the outskirts of Reading has won a clutch of Green Gown environmental awards. There is a second campus in town. The university's 2,000 acres of farmland are at nearby Sonning and Shinfield, where the nature reserve and the Centre for Dairy Research are located.

Reading's global reputation for courses and research in agriculture and development attracts many of the international students who make up about a fifth of undergraduates. The university wants one student in three to have some experience of studying abroad by 2026, with summer schools at its own branch campus in Malaysia, as well as at longstanding partner institutions in Moscow and Nanjing, China, among the current options.

The university's other main site houses its postgraduate and executive business school, formerly Henley Management College, in an attractive bankside position overlooking the Thames. Business undergraduates are taught at Whiteknights.

An Electronic Management Assessment programme — timely in view of the impact of Covid-19 — was completed in January, allowing students to submit work and receive feedback online, as well as increasing the availability of data and analytics on marks and progress. The programme includes improvements in the privacy, safety and security of assessment and gives access to additional tools to increase the quality of submissions.

A new student welfare team is integrated with an academic tutor system established in 2018 to address personal problems and enhance students' professional development.

Reading entered more academics for assessment in the 2014 Research Excellence Framework than most of its peers and still saw almost 80% of its research rated as world-leading or internationally excellent. Real estate, planning and construction management were among the top-performing areas.

More than 5,000 residential places are either on or a stroll away from the Whiteknights campus, and all new entrants are guaranteed one. The SportsPark, on the edge of the campus, has extensive indoor and outdoor facilities including dance and yoga studios, a soccer park and indoor courts. There are also boathouses on the Thames and a sailing and canoeing club nearby.

Commuter-belt Reading has plenty of nightlife, a popular shopping centre and is within easy reach of London.

Tuition fees

» Fees for UK students £9,250
» Fees for International students 2021–22 £17,320–£20,830
» For scholarship and bursary information see www.reading.ac.uk/ready-to-study/study/fees-and-funding
» Graduate salary £24,000

Student numbers

Undergraduates	12,324	(263)
Postgraduates	2,951	(2,266)
Applications/places		18,095/2,825
Applications per place		6.4
Overall offer rate		83.6%
International students – EU		6%
Non-EU		18.1%

Accommodation

University provided places: 4,982
Catered costs: £129–£200 per week
Self-catered: £131–£266 per week
First years guaranteed accommodation
www.reading.ac.uk/ready-to-study/accommodation.aspx

Where do the students come from?

State schools (non-grammar)	74.8%	First generation students	36.1%	Black attainment gap	-19.7%
Grammar schools	10.3%	Deprived areas	6.4%	Disabled	7.2%
Independent schools	14.9%	All ethnic minorities	32.5%	Mature (over 21)	7.2%

Social inclusion ranking: 92

Robert Gordon University

Robert Gordon University (RGU) achieved its best results ever in the latest National Student Survey, ranking 8= for satisfaction with the wider undergraduate experience and 12th for teaching quality. The modern Aberdeen institution has also risen 17 places in our overall league table – helping earn it our Scottish University of the Year award.

Formerly our leading post-1992 university for graduate prospects, RGU stayed in the top 20 for this measure until 2016 — during some of the peak years of the North Sea oil and gas industry based off Aberdeen. RGU graduates still do well in the careers market and 78.5% were in high-skilled jobs or postgraduate study within 15 months of finishing their degrees — a top-50 result.

Adapting to the changing world of work as digitisation increases, the university has launched a learning and teaching framework to equip future graduates with personal and interpersonal skills. Its eHub app, launched in 2019, has expanded to include careers education modules and subject-specific programmes. The app's jobs facility links students and graduates with vacancies, and international students can access opportunities from companies licensed to sponsor those with a tier two or five visa.

A new tool, CV360, provides instant feedback on compiling curriculum vitae and the university's Startup Accelerator has had more than 180 applications for its mentorship, development and £10,000 seed funding programme — with 62% of those selected having one or more female founder.

When the university gained gold in the Teaching Excellence Framework the judging panel was impressed by the range of opportunities for students to develop knowledge, understanding and skills that are most highly valued by employers, and to engage "consistently and frequently" with developments at the forefront of professional practice. RGU has developed a strategy to be an "innovative, disruptive force in higher education", assessors also found.

Under the RGU Net Zero eco framework the university has set carbon reduction targets and expanded courses that address climate change. It plans to draw on its research expertise in renewables, smart cities, carbon capture and storage, and green buildings to develop innovative solutions and a pipeline of potential spin-out businesses.

There is a new mobile arts school, giving the region's school pupils art and design experience while also providing training and mentoring opportunities for RGU students and graduates. The university's Creative Accelerator programme supports emerging creative industry businesses and offers funding of up to £1,500.

Garthdee House
Garthdee Road
Aberdeen AB10 7AQ
01224 262 728
UGOffice@rgu.ac.uk
www.rgu.ac.uk
www.rguunion.co.uk
Open days: see website

The Times and The Sunday Times Rankings
Overall Ranking: 66 (last year: 83)

Teaching quality	84.3%	12
Student experience	82.2%	=8
Research quality	4%	=104
Entry standards	156	=25
Graduate prospects	78.5%	=41
Good honours	72%	=90
Expected completion rate	84.5%	60
Student/staff ratio	18.7	116
Services and facilities	£1,706	122

All teaching is based at the Garthdee campus overlooking the River Dee on the south side of Aberdeen. RGU, named after an 18th-century philanthropist, has a 250-year-plus pedigree in education and its landmark green glass library tower symbolises its future ambitions following a £135m capital programme.

The Clinical Skills Centre recently completed a £750,000 upgrade, and houses simulations of a ward, home setting, radiography suite, physiotherapy suite and gym, as well as a human performance laboratory and a community pharmacy.

RGU's new drilling simulator is part of the Dart (Dynamic Advanced Response Training) simulation suite. It provides real-time training within a virtual drilling environment using 3D graphics representing a rig floor, oil and gas industry equipment and drilling processes.

The first paramedic practice students started degrees in September 2020. Two art and design entry routes were also introduced, along with dual nursing registration courses (specialising in adult and mental health, adult and children and young people, mental health and children and young people).

One of Scotland's largest providers of graduate apprenticeships, RGU offers seven programmes and expects to have around 475 apprentices by September 2021. A five-year accounting course comprises both degree and professional qualifications. Other options are in construction and the built environment, data science and engineering.

Robert Gordon ranks in the top 10 in our Scottish social inclusion table. A high proportion of students are the first generation in their family to go to university and 95% arrived from non-selective state schools. Merit-based scholarships — some with work experience built in — are funded by industry partners and worth £1,500 to £2,500 a year. Access scholarships of £1,500 to £2,000 a year are available to students from low-income households or deprived regions.

Trained students are available to discuss mental health or wellbeing concerns under a peer support service, and personal tutors have been introduced for all.

Sports facilities are good: three gyms, a swimming pool, badminton courts, a sports hall and climbing facilities are among the on-campus resources. RGU also has a physiotherapy clinic and offers sports scholarships.

Nearly half of the 912 residential places cost less than £100 a week to rent and there is usually space for all who want a room, although there is no formal guarantee.

Tuition fees

» Fees for Scottish students	£0–£1,820
RUK fees	£5,000–£8,500
» Fees for International students 2021–22	£14,000–£24,975
» For scholarship and bursary information see www.rgu.ac.uk/study/courses	
» Graduate salary	£24,000

Student numbers

Undergraduates	7,940	(1,198)
Postgraduates	1,147	(2,052)
Applications/places		9,360/2,070
Applications per place		4.5
Overall offer rate		69.8%
International students – EU		8.4%
Non-EU		8%

Accommodation

University provided places: 912
Self-catered: £98–£160 per week
www.rgu.ac.uk/life-at-rgu/accommodation

Where do the students come from?

State schools (non-grammar)	94.8%	First generation students	34.6%	
Grammar schools	0.5%	Deprived areas	6.7%	
Independent schools	4.7%	All ethnic minorities	11.2%	

Social inclusion ranking (Scotland): 8

Black attainment gap	-16.9%
Disabled	5%
Mature (over 21)	32.6%

University of Roehampton

A new digital media hub, the Sir David Bell Building, opened on Roehampton's campus in 2020. It gives students the opportunity to learn in industry-standard film studios, editing suites and newsrooms, using resources for media, photography and sound production as well as computer facilities and a cinema. Spaces for independent and group study as well as a gallery area to display student work and host creative industry events are also available.

The digital media building is the latest addition to Roehampton's 54-acre campus near Putney and Hammersmith in southwest London. Close to central London but offering a campus community environment, Roehampton gives students a best-of-both-worlds experience. A space in its relatively affordable student accommodation (170 rooms cost less than £100 a week in rent) is guaranteed to all first-years who accept an offer and apply by the deadline.

The university has also boosted resources for students who commute to campus. A free bus runs regularly between Roehampton and nearby Barnes Station, and students can store their bikes securely on campus, take a shower and stow belongings in lockers. Kitchens and lounges with charging points have also been added.

The improvements appear to be going down well with undergraduates, going by Roehampton's fourth successive climb up the ranks of the National Student Survey (NSS). It has done better than many other London universities, which tend to struggle with student satisfaction levels, rising to joint 68th place in terms of the wider experience in our analysis of the 2020 NSS, and joint 76th for teaching quality.

Education courses are a significant area for Roehampton, and account for a quarter of students. The university has additional study locations in Holborn in London, Birmingham and Manchester, where business and computing degrees are taught by staff from QA Higher Education, a private firm.

Roehampton was one of two universities upgraded to silver in the Teaching Excellence Framework in 2019. The panel complimented it on reducing the attainment gap for black, Asian and minority ethnic (BAME) students, and on support to find work experience.

Degrees in English literature and philosophy, and in sports management have been introduced. Top-up bachelor's degrees — completed in one or two years, building on a related foundation qualification — have been added in seven established subjects including accounting, human resource management and international business. January starts for 16 degrees including law, criminology, childhood studies and adult nursing are also now available. An LLM degree in commercial law will accept its first students in 2021.

Grove House
Roehampton Lane
London SW15 5PJ
020 8392 3232
enquiries@roehampton.ac.uk
www.roehampton.ac.uk
www.roehamptonstudent.com
Open days: see website

Edinburgh

Belfast

Cardiff

LONDON

The Times and The Sunday Times **Rankings**

Overall Ranking: 78 (last year: 69)

Teaching quality	79%	=76
Student experience	77.9%	=68
Research quality	24.5%	50
Entry standards	103	=127
Graduate prospects	61.6%	123
Good honours	66.7%	=119
Expected completion rate	75.1%	121
Student/staff ratio	14.8	=45
Services and facilities	£3,321	14

Four 'Women in E-sports' scholarships are now offered. The first of their kind in Europe, they follow the introduction of e-sport scholarships in 2019 and aim to drive up diversity and inclusivity in the multiplayer video game competition industry — reportedly the fastest growing sport in the world. A new e-sports arena with 20 high-specification gaming PCs, professional-standard peripherals and facilities for live streaming has opened to host practice sessions, social events and tournaments.

Two-thirds of Roehampton's eligible academics submitted work in the 2014 Research Excellence Framework and 66% of it was rated world-leading or internationally excellent. The university outperformed all post-1992 universities and had the most highly-rated dance department in the UK, with 94% of research placed in the top two categories. The results in education and English were among the best in London.

The latest completion rate figures showed that nearly a quarter of students dropped out, however — a far higher proportion than the expected level of just over a fifth, based on the academic and economic background of the intake. Roehampton had a bad year for graduate prospects, too, with only 62% in high-skilled jobs or postgraduate study within 15 months of finishing their degrees — ranking in the bottom 10 nationally on this measure.

Roehampton does not offer bursaries to students from low-income backgrounds, but does extend merit-based scholarships in a range of subjects. Mature students account for around a fifth of the intake, and more than half of Roehampton students are the first in their family to go to university.

Anglican Whitelands, one of Roehampton's four foundation colleges, was the first in the country to admit women to higher education. Digby Stuart was established by French Catholic women; Southlands by Methodists; and Froebel follows the humanist teachings of Frederick Froebel. While they retain some of their religious ethos, students of any denomination or none are accepted. The university also has a Jewish resource centre and Muslim prayer rooms.

Four dance studios, which support the renowned dance programmes, add to the provision for sports. Students also have use of the RoeActive gym, a multi-use games area and tennis courts.

Lively local social scenes abound in southwest London. As well as the students' union entertainment, the colleges host balls, events and formal dinners.

Tuition fees

» Fees for UK students	£9,250
» Fees for International students 2021–22	£13,145
» For scholarship and bursary information see	
www.roehampton.ac.uk/undergraduate-courses/tuition-fees/	
» Graduate salary	£24,000

Student numbers

Undergraduates	10,243	(486)
Postgraduates	1,123	(811)
Applications/places		6,680/1,615
Applications per place		4.1
Overall offer rate		93.9%
International students – EU		4%
Non-EU		5.5

Accommodation

University provided places: 1,882
Self-catered: £97–£188 per week
First years guaranteed accommodation
www.roehampton.ac.uk/accommodation

Where do the students come from?

State schools (non-grammar)	95.5%	First generation students	51.4%	**Social inclusion ranking: 31**		
Grammar schools	1.4%	Deprived areas	4.7%	Black attainment gap	-26%
Independent schools	3.1%	All ethnic minorities	64.4%	Disabled	5.3%
				Mature (over 21)	53.3%

Royal Agricultural University

The Royal Agricultural University (RAU) celebrated its 175th anniversary in 2020, having been established as the first agricultural college in the English-speaking world. In the same year the Cirencester-based university opened RAU Swindon, home of the Cultural Heritage Institute, which focuses on archaeology, applied heritage and historic environment management.

The £1.35m development in a converted workshop in Swindon's railway heritage quarter has been designed to encourage collaboration and interdisciplinary studies. An undergraduate archaeology degree is planned to begin in 2021 at RAU Swindon, which also offers taught masters and MBA programmes.

The RAU was awarded silver in the government's Teaching Excellence Framework, winning praise for its specialist facilities. Assessors were impressed by the employer-informed course design, work placements and extracurricular opportunities for students to develop skills and attributes valued by employers.

New degrees in environment, food and society and in rural entrepreneurship and enterprise welcomed their first students in September 2020. Responding to industry needs, the courses are part of a wider £2.5m initiative in partnership with the Countryside and Community Research Institute and University College of Estate Management to create leadership in the agri-food and land management industries, post-Brexit.

Experts from the food supply chain, farming, land management, non-governmental organisations, banks and businesses — such as Barclays and Waitrose — have weighed in on the content of these new courses. Nearly half (£1.1m) of the funding for the work came from a successful Catalyst bid, awarded by the former Higher Education Council for England (Hefce).

Student experience has been a focus for RAU, which shot up the National Student Survey rankings in 2019 to 12th for student satisfaction with the wider experience and into the top 40 for teaching quality. In the 2020 survey, though, it fell back to 73= for the wider undergraduate experience, and 84= for teaching quality. A new Student Hub opened in September 2019, housing all student-facing services in the centre of campus.

Only half the expected number of students (5.5%) drops out, according to the most recent figures. There has been a big improvement in graduate prospects measured by the new Graduate Outcomes survey, with 70% in high-skilled jobs or postgraduate study within 15 months of graduating — placing the university comfortably inside the top 100.

From the 2020–21 academic year, all BSc (Hons) degrees are being offered as sandwich courses, with a year's industry placement.

Stroud Road
Cirencester GL7 6JS
01285 889 912
admissions@rau.ac.uk
www.rau.ac.uk
www.rau.ac.uk/university-life/
social/student-union
Open days: see website

The Times and The Sunday Times **Rankings**

Overall Ranking: =73 (last year: =89)

Teaching quality	78.4%	=84
Student experience	77.3%	=73
Research quality	1.1%	125
Entry standards	120	=87
Graduate prospects	70.3%	89
Good honours	67.6%	115
Expected completion rate	94.4%	=14
Student/staff ratio	19.8	=123
Services and facilities	£3,130	17

Since its foundation in 1845 as the Royal Agricultural College, the institution has been visited by every monarch since Queen Victoria, at least once. Often described as "the Oxbridge of the countryside", RAU has the country's highest proportion of private-school entrants, who study in a splendid Cotswolds setting. Its social life centres on society balls — and the university even has its own beagle pack.

Outreach activities to widen participation target schools and colleges with high proportions of under-represented groups, particularly in rural areas of deprivation in nearby counties. The new Swindon site will be the focus for increasing engagement with the town's schools and community. Foundation years were introduced on all BSc (Hons) programmes from September 2019, and top-up degrees have also been added. Both routes offer flexible entry options. About 16% of new undergraduates received some form of scholarship or bursary in 2019–20, a proportion that is expected to continue.

Practical experience and teaching is based at Coates Manor Farm, next to the campus, and students also have access to a large dairy complex at Kemble Farm, and Leaze Farm. More than 100 agricultural businesses allow staff and students to learn from their up-to-date farming operations off-site.

A £4.2m building opened in 2018 on the main campus, strengthening links with agri-tech companies. One floor is used by the Farm491 project, named after the number of hectares available for research and testing in sustainable food production. The building also houses the Cirencester Growth Hub, helping local businesses of all kinds.

The university achieved one of the lowest scores for research. Only 12 staff were entered for the 2014 Research Excellence Framework — a quarter of those holding research contracts — and just 7% of their work was placed in the top two categories.

Three-quarters of the 334 rooms in eight halls of residence on campus are catered. There is space for about 80% of first-years in university rooms and the university works with local providers to accommodate those who live off campus.

Small student numbers and the bucolic setting make for a collegiate feel and sport plays an important part in student life. Clubs include polo, clay pigeon shooting, beagling and team chasing — a cross-country equestrian sport. Known as the "capital of the Cotswolds", the thriving market town of Cirencester is 15 minutes' walk from campus. Bath and Cheltenham are easily reached.

Tuition fees

» Fees for UK students	£9,250
» Fees for International students 2021–22	£11,000
» For scholarship and bursary information see www.rau.ac.uk/study/undergraduate/ funding-your-time-at-university	
» Graduate salary	£24,000

Student numbers

Undergraduates	1,014	(29)
Postgraduates	90	(16)
Applications/places		1,075/290
Applications per place		3.7
Overall offer rate		n/a
International students – EU		3.9%
Non-EU		8.3%

Accommodation

University provided places: 334
Catered costs: £152 per week
Self-catered: £161–£229 per week
www.rau.ac.uk/university-life/accommodation

Where do the students come from?

State schools (non-grammar)	57.8%	First generation students	36.2%	Black attainment gap	n/a
Grammar schools	2.4%	Deprived areas	3%	Disabled	12.8%
Independent schools	39.8%	All ethnic minorities	2.9%	Mature (over 21)	26.7%

Social inclusion ranking: =100

Royal Holloway, University of London

Royal Holloway has some of the most satisfied students of any University of London institution. Based on a woodland campus in green-belt Egham, in Surrey, it offers a calm student life but with central London's bright lights only 40 minutes away.

Scores in the 2020 National Student Survey put Royal Holloway in the top 50 for satisfaction with the wider student experience and in the top 70 for satisfaction with teaching quality, although they have slipped a little compared with the previous year, when Royal Holloway was shortlisted for our University of the Year award.

There is a majesty to its palatial red-brick Founder's Building, modelled on a French chateau and opened by Queen Victoria. The 135-acre campus near Windsor and Heathrow has plenty of modern facilities too, which are being upgraded as part of a £150m development plan.

SuperFab is a world-class "cleanroom" in the physics department, with advanced electronic nanofabrication equipment for research and development of the technology needed for medical imaging and quantum computers.

The Beatrice Shilling Building, named after the pioneering British aeronautical engineer and amateur motor racing driver, houses the Department of Electronic Engineering, opened in 2017. One of its aims is to attract more female engineering students — fittingly for an institution formed from the merger of two colleges (Royal Holloway and Bedford) which were among the first British institutions to educate women. Bedford's early students included Sarah Parker Remond, the first black woman to carry out a lecture tour around Britain about slavery, the artist Barbara Bodichon and the novelist George Eliot.

The flexibility for undergraduates to take an additional year to complete their degree has been built into all Royal Holloway courses. They can choose to spend their third year working, volunteering or studying abroad — or a combination of all three. The optional placement year is taken in the third year of study (or fourth for those on MSci or MEng degrees), costs 20% of standard tuition fees and is formally recognised on degree certificates.

Royal Holloway was awarded silver in the Teaching Excellence Framework and drew praise for the level of investment in e-learning facilities – which will also have proved useful during the pandemic. Assessors said students were engaged with developments from the forefront of research, scholarship and professional practice.

New degrees in social sciences and modern languages, politics and international relations have been introduced for 2020. The curriculum will grow in 2021 when more than 20 new options will be offered including environment and social change (BSc and BA); genetics; geosciences and sustainable energy; English and

Egham TW20 0EX
01784 414 944
study@royalholloway.ac.uk
www.royalholloway.ac.uk
www.su.rhul.ac.uk
Open days: see website

The Times and The Sunday Times Rankings
Overall Ranking: 22 (last year: 19)

Teaching quality	79.7%	=66
Student experience	79.2%	46
Research quality	36.3%	=30
Entry standards	134	52
Graduate prospects	75%	=57
Good honours	81.5%	34
Expected completion rate	91.2%	33
Student/staff ratio	14.7	=41
Services and facilities	£2,913	24

world literatures, and mathematics and philosophy. A number of law degrees will be introduced with modern languages or philosophy. At MSc level, Royal Holloway will begin running courses in law and economics, finance, economics and econometrics, economics and corporate finance.

The former Speaker of the House of Commons, John Bercow, has been made a professor of politics and will work part-time with undergraduates and postgraduate students at the university.

More than 80% of the work assessed in the 2014 Research Excellence Framework was judged to be world-leading or internationally excellent, placing Royal Holloway in the top 30 institutions on this measure in our table. It would have been higher still if a larger proportion of the academics had been entered.

Geography achieved the best results in England, while earth sciences, psychology, mathematics, music, media arts, and drama and theatre all reached the top 10 in their subject areas. Royal Holloway was named by the government as one of eight acádemic centres of excellence in cyber-security research.

The university ranks 80th in our social inclusion table, and about a quarter of students arrive from independent or grammar schools. Contextual offers, which accept lower A-level grades, take social and economic disadvantages into consideration in an effort to widen participation.

Royal Holloway paid more than £3.6m in scholarships and bursaries in 2019–20. Awards recognise academic, sport and music achievements or help fund those from under-represented groups. Future Leaders awards pay full tuition fees to home or EU students with expected AAA grades and demonstrable leadership skills. The Santander Widening Access Scholarship is a £1,250 cash award for students from qualifying postcodes or schools, and the Barbara Raw English scholarship is a £6,000 award for black students from the UK with expected AAA grades who study in the department of English.

Royal Holloway is one of the University of London's top sporting colleges, with more than 80 teams and good facilities. There is a fitness studio and multi-use sports hall and outdoor facilities such as a 3G pitch. The university also has the use of a boathouse on the Thames.

Nearly a third of the 3,460 residential spaces on campus are catered and with rents no higher than £191 per week, prices are kinder on the student wallet than at many other London universities.

Tuition fees

» Fees for UK students £9,250
» Fees for International students 2021–22 £17,700–£22,600
» For scholarship and bursary information see www.royalholloway.ac.uk/studying-here/fees-and-funding
» Graduate salary £23,857

Student numbers

Undergraduates	7,951	(155)
Postgraduates	2,143	(791)
Applications/places		17,200/2,560
Applications per place		6.7
Overall offer rate		86.5%
International students – EU		7.7%
Non-EU		20.1%

Accommodation

University provided places: 3,460
Catered costs: £120–£182 per week
Self-catered: £168–£191 per week
First years guaranteed accommodation
www.royalholloway.ac.uk/student-life/accommodation/

Where do the students come from?

State schools (non-grammar)	74.8%	First generation students	39.5%	Black attainment gap	-18.3%
Grammar schools	10.4%	Deprived areas	5.3%	Disabled	6.6%
Independent schools	14.8%	All ethnic minorities	43.2%	Mature (over 21)	5.5%

Social inclusion ranking: 80

University of St Andrews

Twice our UK University of the Year, St Andrews has come within a whisker of ousting Oxford from second place in our rankings once again in this edition, while also closing the gap on Cambridge at the top of the table.

It is the highest ranked university in the country for which we can accurately measure student satisfaction with the university experience and the quality of teaching. While Oxbridge students continue to boycott the annual National Student Survey, St Andrews' students tell us they are among the most satisfied in the UK, ranking their institution third for teaching quality and second for student experience.

St Andrews is also pushing ahead by establishing a new degree in Chinese studies that will recruit its first students for September 2021, available in combination with the study of another language, as well as international relations and history. The degree will focus on the linguistic and cultural realities of China and the Chinese-speaking world, exploring mainstream, popular and dissident cultures.

The new focus on China will complement existing strengths that put St Andrews academics at the heart of research into key issues of our time. The university's Centre for Syrian Studies and the Handa Centre for the Study of Terrorism and Political Violence are the first of their kind in Europe and their experts have become familiar faces in the media.

In the past year, the university has enhanced its reputation in marine research by opening the Scottish Oceans Institute. In medicine, the Sir James Mackenzie Institute for Early Diagnosis has opened to target improvements in the detection of cancers, cardiovascular disease, mental health issues and infections.

Not bad for an ancient educational institution that celebrated its 600th anniversary in 2013. A fundraising appeal to mark the milestone met its £100m target five years later, led by the Duke of Cambridge, who graduated from St Andrews with a degree in geography and helped to put the university on the map in terms of global student recruitment, particularly from the United States.

Nearly half of the student population comes from outside Britain, with 16% recruited from Scotland (a number capped by the government) and the remainder from the rest of the UK. Applications are at an all-time high but, unlike many institutions, St Andrews has no plans to expand significantly beyond a 10,000 maximum, a figure it hit inadvertently in September 2020, partly as a result of the Government-inspired mayhem around the calculation of A-level and Higher results.

St Katharine's West
16 The Scores
St Andrews KY16 9AX
01334 462 150
admissions@st-andrews.ac.uk
www.st-andrews.ac.uk
www.yourunion.net
Open days: see website

ST ANDREWS
Edinburgh
Belfast
London
Cardiff

The Times and The Sunday Times **Rankings**
Overall Ranking: 3 (last year: 3)

Teaching quality	86.7%	3
Student experience	86.3%	2
Research quality	40.4%	11
Entry standards	211	2
Graduate prospects	81.9%	=24
Good honours	90.6%	6
Expected completion rate	95%	8
Student/staff ratio	11.2	=4
Services and facilities	£3,725	6

The optimum figure is set not only on academic grounds but in recognition that the town of about 17,000 people, perched on the Fife coast, is already dominated by the university.

First-years are guaranteed a place in halls if they apply by the end of June. Two new halls opened in 2018, allowing about 45% of students to live in. Traditionally, third- or fourth-year students help new arrivals, known as "bejants" and "bejantines", adjust to university life. Students enjoy a lively social life in a tight-knit community.

Six halls of residence encircle University Park, where students can get active at an excellent sports centre, recently extended during a £14m redevelopment to produce some of the best facilities in Scotland. There are 13 grass pitches for football, rugby, lacrosse and ultimate frisbee, as well as the traditional Scottish game shinty, similar to field hockey. Students also have access to two cricket squares, a Fifa-approved 3G pitch, tennis courts and an athletics track.

Unlike many Scottish institutions, St Andrews does not align its fees with English universities. Students from the rest of the UK pay £9,250 per year for courses, so the standard four-year undergraduate course will cost £37,000 rather than £27,750 for the three-year degrees offered in England. However, there is an extensive bursary and scholarship programme (worth £1,000 to £4,000 a year for UK-domiciled students).

Professor Sally Mapstone, principal and vice-chancellor of St Andrews, led the Scotland-wide work on contextual admissions which proposed that applicants from disadvantaged areas should be given offers at no more than the minimum grades needed to complete their chosen course. Now Scottish government policy, the scheme has been embraced by St Andrews, allowing offers up to two A-level grades lower than standard. In 2018, the proportion of students admitted to St Andrews from the most deprived 20% of postcodes in Scotland rose to just over one in 10, although the university remains bottom of our Scottish social inclusion table.

St Andrews has invested heavily in the sciences, which produced some of its best results in the 2014 Research Excellence Framework. More than 90% of work submitted jointly with Edinburgh in chemistry and physics was rated world-leading or internationally excellent. Classics and history of art scored well and more than 70% of the overall submission reached the top two categories.

Tuition fees

»	Fees for Scottish students	£0–£1,820
	RUK fees	£9,250
»	Fees for International students 2021–22	£25,100
	Medicine	£32,910
»	For scholarship and bursary information see	
	www.st-andrews.ac.uk/study/fees-and-funding/	
»	Graduate salary	£26,000

Student numbers

Undergraduates	7,637	(816)
Postgraduates	1,855	(264)
Applications/places	19,050/1,655	
Applications per place	11.5	
Overall offer rate	42.3%	
International students – EU	10.2%	
Non-EU	35.4%	

Accommodation

University provided places: 3,597
Catered costs: £168–£255 per week
Self-catered: £142–£232 per week
First years guaranteed accommodation
www.st-andrews.ac.uk/study/accommodation/

Where do the students come from?

State schools (non-grammar)	60.6%	First generation students	18%	
Grammar schools	4.8%	Deprived areas	10.6%	
Independent schools	34.6%	All ethnic minorities	12.3%	

Social inclusion ranking (Scotland): 15

Black attainment gap	n/a
Disabled	5.4%
Mature (over 21)	8.1%

St George's, University of London

Undergraduate numbers have been rising steadily for three years as St George's pursues a new approach to broadening access to medicine, one of the most socially exclusive subjects in higher education. Its medical school was the first to advertise places in clearing and, taking all subjects into account, now recruits more than a third of its students this way. St George's considers clearing the fairest way to find high-quality candidates and has not seen its entry scores decline unduly as a result.

The Adjusted Criteria Scheme reduces entrance requirements by two A-level grades for anyone applying from a non-selective state school where results are in the bottom 20% nationwide. The scheme applies to medicine, biomedical science, physiotherapy and healthcare science. More than a third of undergraduates qualify for financial assistance, which includes grants of up to £1,700 from the St George's Opportunity Fund for those from the poorest households.

A focus on science and other health subjects, as well as medicine, gives St George's a head start in graduate employment comparisons. It is in the top five in our new measure of graduate prospects, with 90% in high-skilled jobs or postgraduate study 15 months after completing a degree. Scores in the National Student Survey

(NSS) have been more of a problem. There was a substantial increase in overall student satisfaction in 2020, but the school still finished in the bottom 10 for satisfaction with the wider experience and next to bottom for teaching quality under our analysis of the NSS results.

St George's is the only freestanding medical school in the University of London — and the only one in our table — but the full portfolio of courses extends to biomedical science and healthcare science degrees covering respiratory and cardiac physiology and sleep physiology, while paramedic science and radiography degrees are also taught on-site in a partnership with Kingston University. A new MSc in translational medicine launched in 2020.

The original medical school opened in 1868 at St George's Hospital, which had been established in 1733 at Hyde Park Corner, in central London, when it was open countryside. Edward Jenner trained there before inventing the smallpox vaccination and the hide of Blossom the cow, the subject of his early experiments, can still be seen in the library of St George's Hospital in Tooting, south London, the institution's home since the 1970s. The university shares clinical facilities with the hospital.

Sir Patrick Vallance, the government's chief scientific officer (and regular pandemic performer at Downing Street press conferences) is a St George's alumnus, and opened a new 200-seat lecture theatre in February 2020, at the start

Cranmer Terrace
Tooting
London SW17 0RE
020 3897 2032
study@sgul.ac.uk
www.sgul.ac.uk
www.sgsu.org.uk
Open days: see website

The Times and The Sunday Times Rankings
Overall Ranking: 49 (last year: 67)

Teaching quality	71.7%	=126
Student experience	73.1%	=119
Research quality	22.2%	52
Entry standards	156	=25
Graduate prospects	90.3%	5
Good honours	78.1%	52
Expected completion rate	94.4%	=14
Student/staff ratio	13.3	=13
Services and facilities	£5,211	1

of a long-term plan to refresh the university's facilities. A strategic plan to 2022 commits it to immersing students in research and healthcare practice, as well as providing opportunities beyond the curriculum.

However, St George's remains one of only 11 universities in our table awarded bronze (the lowest grade) in the government's Teaching Excellence Framework. Although the panel gave the university credit for an "embedded institutional culture that rewards excellent teaching, and promotes inclusivity among staff and students", low student satisfaction with assessment and feedback held it back, as did comparisons with other largely medically-based institutions with even higher employment rates.

A preparatory centre for international students is based on the campus. St George's also offers a four-year graduate-entry Bachelor of Surgery degree at the University of Nicosia in Cyprus. St George's was the first UK institution to launch the MBBS Graduate Entry Programme, a four-year fast-track medical degree course open to graduates in any discipline, which has become an increasingly popular route into the medical profession.

There are interviews for all undergraduate courses except biomedical science and clinical pharmacology. A shadowing scheme offers sixth-formers from Wandsworth and Merton state schools the opportunity to accompany a doctor or other healthcare professional at St George's or Queen Mary's Hospital.

Historic developments in cardiac pacemakers and IVF are among St George's research achievements. The university was second only to Imperial College, London for the impact of its work in the 2014 Research Excellence Framework. Overall, 70% of its submission reached the top two categories for world-leading and internationally excellent research.

The south London institution has played a highly visible role in tackling the Covid-19 virus: its researchers have collaborated with the associated NHS trust and other universities on 14 different studies on the diagnosis, treatment and prevention of the disease.

There is an active students' union with 120 clubs, societies and community projects. The sports centre is five minutes' walk from campus and competitive teams play in regional and national competitions. Students have use of a rowing club on the River Thames and can also take advantage of University of London facilities for sport.

Tuition fees

- » Fees for UK students £9,250
- » Fees for International students 2021–22 £16,500–£18,500
  Medicine £37,500
- » For scholarship and bursary information see www.sgul.ac.uk/study/undergraduate-study/ fees-and-financial-support/
- » Graduate salary £29,000

Student numbers

Undergraduates	3,094	(643)
Postgraduates	269	(683)
Applications/places		5,940/555
Applications per place		10.7
Overall offer rate		39%
International students – EU		1.5%
Non-EU		6.7%

Accommodation

University provided places: 486
Self-catered: £172–£182 per week
First-years guaranteed accommodation
www.sgul.ac.uk/study/life-at-st-georges/accommodation

Where do the students come from?

State schools (non-grammar)	63.6%	First generation students	35.4%	
Grammar schools	18.2%	Deprived areas	5.3%	
Independent schools	18.2%	All ethnic minorities	64.8%	

Social inclusion ranking: 55

Black attainment gap	-4%
Disabled	6.8%
Mature (over 21)	28.6%

St Mary's University, Twickenham

The horizons of St Mary's, Twickenham are broadening from its leafy southwest London enclave. The university is launching a postgraduate campus north of the border in Edinburgh, in a partnership with the Archdiocese of St Andrews and Edinburgh. St Mary's is occupying a portion of the Gillis Centre, where part-time two-year postgraduate master's programmes in Catholic theology and leadership in Catholic education begin in September 2021.

The courses' flexibility is aimed at attracting mature students, teachers and those with a keen interest in education who can study in the evening and at weekends.

Undergraduate provision, though, is still based solely in Twickenham. With 5,000 students, St Mary's is the largest of three Catholic universities in the UK. It admits students of all faiths and none, but does have the objective to provide "a unique experience for our students and staff by virtue of our values and identity as a Catholic university".

Teacher training accounts for a third of students, harking back to St Mary's foundation in 1850 to meet the need for teachers to educate the growing number of poor Catholic children.

St Mary's was awarded silver in the Teaching Excellence Framework and assessors commended its high-quality resources and good staffing levels which allowed personalised and small-group learning.

There are about 500 undergraduate degree combinations across four schools covering sport, health and applied science; education, theology and leadership; management and social sciences; and the arts and humanities.

Degrees in physiotherapy, sport psychology and sports performance analysis and talent identification were introduced in 2020. A new liberal arts degree may be studied either as an accelerated two-year course or over three years.

Levels of student satisfaction are consistently buoyant, and St Mary's ranks in the top 30 UK universities for how students feel about the wider undergraduate experience. It has done almost as well for teaching quality, ranking 33=.

St Mary's makes the most of its best-of-both-worlds appeal, occupying a picturesque 35-acre campus featuring gardens, parkland and the shimmering white Gothic fantasy Strawberry Hill House near the River Thames — only 30 minutes' from central London. The university also has a community building in the centre of Twickenham, with theatre space, studio rooms and a large conservatory area with a café. The Exchange offers training courses for local residents and firms, as well as providing more teaching space for students.

Waldegrave Road
Strawberry Hill
Twickenham TW1 4SX
020 8240 2314
apply@stmarys.ac.uk
www.stmarys.ac.uk
www.stmaryssu.co.uk
Open days: see website

The Times and The Sunday Times Rankings
Overall Ranking: 86 (last year: 85)

Teaching quality	82%	=33
Student experience	80.1%	=30
Research quality	4%	=104
Entry standards	110	=113
Graduate prospects	70.1%	=91
Good honours	75.1%	71
Expected completion rate	82.8%	=78
Student/staff ratio	18	=108
Services and facilities	£1,922	108

Sport is a big deal at St Mary's — both its study and practice. The university has a superstar alumnus in Sir Mo Farah, who trained at St Mary's from 2001 to 2011 and won a scholarship to its Endurance Performance and Coaching Centre — known as one of the world's best running training setups and established in partnership with the London Marathon.

Sir Mo is one of many elite athletes who have studied at St Mary's. At the Rio Olympics in 2016, 22 St Mary's students and alumni won six medals — including three gold — meaning that had it been a country, the university would have finished 25th in the medals table, ahead of South Africa and Poland.

Across measures of social inclusion St Mary's performs well and ranks within the top 50 in our dedicated table. Just under half of students are the first in their families to go to university and only 7% went to grammar or private schools. More than a third of students come from ethnic minority backgrounds.

The local area surrounding St Mary's has a population well represented in higher education so the university focuses its outreach efforts further afield. Links with several schools in Croydon have included in-school workshop days and online mentoring with year 10 students. Foundation years, with extra pastoral and learning support, are available in most subjects to widen entry to those without the qualifications to study at degree level.

A portfolio of financial awards includes the St Mary's Bursary, worth £2,000 per year to students from households with incomes up to £15,000. The vice-chancellor's Excellence Scholarship of £3,000 annually is given to students entering with at least ABB or equivalent from households with an income of up to £25,000. There are also scholarships in sport and history and for students who have been in care or who are estranged from their parents.

The Sir Mo Farah Athletics Track was named in honour of the runner, and further facilities include a rugby pitch and training pitch, a performance hall, gym, dance studio and indoor tennis centre. The university's Teddington Lock sport campus is a 15-minute walk away and has a range of pitches for football, rugby and cricket.

St Mary's guarantees all first-years one of its 704 spaces in halls of residence if they apply by the deadline. Unusually, nearly all rooms are catered. Accommodation is on campus and in nearby Twickenham.

Tuition fees

»	Fees for UK students	£9,250
	Foundation courses	£5,140–£8,660
»	Fees for International students 2021–22	£12,900
»	For scholarship and bursary information see www.stmarys.ac.uk/student-finance/overview.aspx	
»	Graduate salary	£24,000

Student numbers

Undergraduates	3,307	(229)
Postgraduates	897	(1,058)
Applications/places		5,065/925
Applications per place		5.5
Overall offer rate		88.3%
International students – EU		4.7%
Non-EU		3.5%

Accommodation

University provided places: 704
Catered costs: £195–£248 per week
Self-catered: £177–£187
First years guaranteed accommodation
www.stmarys.ac.uk/accommodation

Where do the students come from?

State schools (non-grammar)	93%	First generation students	48.9%	
Grammar schools	2.3%	Deprived areas	5.7%	
Independent schools	4.7%	All ethnic minorities	34.4%	

Social inclusion ranking: 45

Black attainment gap	-13%
Disabled	10.6%
Mature (over 21)	23.2%

University of Salford

Salford, freshly reorganised following the merger of its science schools, is building a four-storey School of Science, Engineering and Environment with a multidisciplinary approach to prepare students for a world with a growing emphasis on digital technology, automation and energy conservation.

The development on the main Peel Park campus is part of an £800m plan in conjunction with the local authority to create a new 240-acre district linking the centre of Manchester with MediaCityUK, where Salford has another campus.

At Peel Park, the university has invested more than £80m in student facilities and residential places. The £55m New Adelphi teaching centre houses the latest facilities for art, performance, and design and technology students, including a 350-seat theatre, screen acting studios, six recording studios and a range of dedicated art and design workshops.

The £30m MediaCityUK site at Salford Quays is part of the same development as the BBC and ITV, and professional broadcasters lend their expertise as guest editors on Quays News, the university's student-led broadcast channel. Courses in nursing, midwifery, psychology, social sciences, sports and health are based at the Frederick Road campus, 10 minutes' from Peel Park.

A new Centre of Excellence for Robotics is in the pipeline. Here, researchers will be able to collaborate with small and medium-sized businesses to pilot the latest technologies. The Business School holds free workshops to show microbusinesses with up to nine employees how they can scale up their operations.

In the most recent National Student Survey Salford regained some of the ground lost in 2019, edging up to 69= for student satisfaction with teaching quality and 86= for the wider experience. The improved scores have lifted Salford back into our top 100 overall.

The university was awarded bronze in the Teaching Excellence Framework (TEF) and an appeal to upgrade the assessment was rejected in 2018. Despite its good links with employers and a commitment to learning by students, the TEF panel found that progression to employment or further study remained "exceptionally low".

However, Salford ranks in the middle reaches of our graduate prospects measure – derived from the 2020 Graduate Outcomes survey – which showed that 73% of its graduates were in high-skilled jobs or postgraduate study within 15 months of finishing their degrees. Work experience placements and live briefs from industry experts are built into Salford degree courses to boost employability.

A unique degree course for aspiring footballers and those hoping to make a career in the sport welcomed its first students in September 2020. The course, designed in

Maxwell Building
43 The Crescent
Salford
Greater Manchester
M5 4WT
0161 295 4545
enquiries@salford.ac.uk
www.salford.ac.uk
www.salfordstudents.com
Open days: see website

The Times and The Sunday Times Rankings
Overall Ranking: 100 (last year: 111)

Teaching quality	79.4%	=69
Student experience	76.7%	=86
Research quality	8.3%	71
Entry standards	127	=65
Graduate prospects	72.8%	71
Good honours	71.7%	94
Expected completion rate	81.9%	87
Student/staff ratio	16.5	=80
Services and facilities	£2,100	93

partnership with Leeds United football club, is delivered online and aimed at academy players and teaches leadership, digital and business skills along with coaching techniques.

Ten more new degrees were also introduced including production and visual effects, creative writing (multidiscipline), fashion business and promotion, digital construction, and microbiology. Another five will take their first students in 2021: design for sport, health and wellbeing, model making for the creative industries, music management and creative enterprise, intelligence analysis and make-up for media and performance.

The university's substantial portfolio of degree apprenticeships is also growing. New programmes in physiotherapy, podiatry, public health and nursing have been added. The university expects to have about 2,000 student apprentices on 14 programmes by September 2021.

Salford scores well in our social inclusion table, with more than 96% of its students arriving from non-selective state schools, one third from ethnic minorities, and nearly half from homes where their parents did not go to university.

Residential summer schools for year 10–12 pupils are intended to increase recruitment from low-participation neighbourhoods in Salford and Greater Manchester.

Most students qualify for financial help through the Inspire Support Scheme, introduced in 2019, providing £150-£350 for each year of study to help those from low-income backgrounds to buy learning resources from an online shop. Scholarships are also awarded to UK students from low-income homes, especially to those studying engineering, the built environment and arts and media.

Salford entered only a third of its eligible academics for the 2014 Research Excellence Framework, but more than half of their work was assessed as world-leading or internationally excellent. The School of Health Sciences has an international reputation for the treatment of sports injuries.

The Energy House Labs, a commercial and research centre, is building a £16m facility where extreme weather conditions can be replicated to test structures and learn how to improve energy efficiency in housing.

A swimming pool, five fitness suites and a multi-use sports hall are among Salford's sports facilities. Accommodation costs no more than £157.18 per week, and while first-years are not guaranteed a room, they are allocated most of the 2,111 available.

Tuition fees

» Fees for UK students	£9,250
Foundation courses	£8,250
» Fees for International students 2021–22	£14,400–£18.990
» For scholarship and bursary information see www.salford.ac.uk/undergraduate/fees	
» Graduate salary	£23,000

Student numbers

Undergraduates	15,940	(729)
Postgraduates	1,929	(2,215)
Applications/places	25,375/4,830	
Applications per place	5.3	
Overall offer rate	73%	
International students – EU	2.6%	
Non-EU	6%	

Accommodation

University provided places: 2,111
Self-catered: £90–£157 per week
www.salford.ac.uk/accommodation

Where do the students come from?

State schools (non-grammar)	96.4%	First generation students	45.9%	Black attainment gap	-27.2%
Grammar schools	2.2%	Deprived areas	15.7%	Disabled	6.6%
Independent schools	1.5%	All ethnic minorities	32.8%	Mature (over 21)	27%

Social inclusion ranking: =66

University of Sheffield

A curved glass roof undulates over Engineering Heartspace, the recently completed home of Sheffield's Faculty of Engineering. Linking the university's grade II listed Sir Frederick Mappin Building and 1885 Central Wing, the modern space houses world-class laboratories alongside office and social areas. An employability hub has been included, intended to aid collaboration between businesses from the region and beyond with engineering students and to put work placements and graduate opportunities on the doorstep.

Heartspace follows the Diamond, Sheffield's £81m engineering building and its biggest single development, clad in aluminium and with 19 specialist laboratories. The new engineering facilities cater for the growing number of students in one of Sheffield's key areas. The Diamond also features 1,000 study spaces for students from across the university.

In the latest National Student Survey Sheffield ranked joint 66th among UK universities for teaching quality and 22nd for the wider undergraduate experience.

Regularly voted the best in the country, Sheffield's students' union (SU) is central to daily life. As well as housing the Foundry club live music venue, the SU hosts events for the 350-plus student societies and is a focal point for the university's thriving sports scene. The Student Advice Centre, an online resource offering help regarding courses, cash, health and wellbeing, housing and visas, also comes under the SU umbrella, as does a nursery that provides pre-school childcare for the offspring of students, staff and the wider public.

The university has recently switched to a fully renewable power supply for all buildings, a move that will reduce net carbon emissions by up to 17,000 tons of CO_2 per year and help its target of becoming carbon neutral. The main university precinct stretches for a mile, ending near the city centre, and although Sheffield is not a campus university its buildings are fairly near each other and the city itself is a manageable size. The £23m Information Commons operates 24-hours throughout the year.

Rated silver in the Teaching Excellence Framework, the panel commended "high levels of stretch and challenge" which help students to develop skills valued highly by employers.

On our measure of graduate prospects the university is among the top 30, with the latest figures showing that 82% of graduates were in high-skilled jobs or postgraduate study within 15 months of finishing their course. The university is one of Siemens's leading UK suppliers of graduates, who are targeted through unique hackathons, curriculum engagement and internships.

Degree apprenticeships for social workers and nursing associates are among a portfolio of six offered by Sheffield. Programmes in

---

Western Bank
Sheffield S10 0TN
0114 222 8030
study@sheffield.ac.uk
www.sheffield.ac.uk
http://su.sheffield.ac.uk
Open days: see website

The Times and The Sunday Times **Rankings**		
Overall Ranking: =23 (last year: 26)		
Teaching quality	79.7%	=66
Student experience	80.6%	22
Research quality	37.6%	23
Entry standards	152	=31
Graduate prospects	81.8%	26
Good honours	82.7%	26
Expected completion rate	93.2%	23
Student/staff ratio	14.7	=41
Services and facilities	£2,327	=75

manufacturing and engineering at the university's renowned Advanced Manufacturing Research Centre include opportunities for apprentices to work for industry giants such as McLaren, Boeing and Rolls-Royce.

In the 2014 Research Excellence Framework, about 85% of the university's submission was considered world-leading or internationally excellent. Biomedical sciences, control and systems engineering, history and politics were all in the top three in the UK. But Sheffield entered a smaller proportion of its academics than most of its peers, keeping it just outside the top 20 in our research table.

Nearly half of 2020's intake received some form of financial help and the university expects that proportion to be much the same for 2021. Among numerous awards, the Sheffield Bursary is worth between £250 and £1,000 per year to students from households with incomes up to £40,000.

Although it features in the lower reaches of our social inclusion table overall, Sheffield is more diverse than most of its immediate academic peers, ranking third among the English and Welsh Russell Group universities. It has a longstanding commitment to encouraging participation in higher education and engages in outreach initiatives with more than 500 local and regional schools and colleges.

The Discover access programme opens the door to medicine, dentistry, law, Stem (science, technology, engineering and mathematics) subjects, and to studying the arts and humanities and social sciences. Applicants who successfully complete the course may enter with up to two A-level grades lower than the norm.

There are excellent sports facilities near the main university precinct including floodlit synthetic pitches, a large fitness centre, a swimming pool with sauna and steam rooms, a sports hall, four squash courts and a bouldering wall.

Outdoor pitches for rugby, football and cricket are a bus ride away. Sheffield has one of the biggest programmes of internal leagues at any university and scholarships for elite athletes contribute to the university's thriving high-performance sports. Three alumnae brought home either a gold or silver medal from the Rio Olympics in 2016.

There are 5,377 residential spaces, most of them within walking distance of lectures. Known for its green spaces and friendly atmosphere, Sheffield has a big student population (including those from neighbouring Sheffield Hallam University) so its shops and bars cater to a student vibe.

Tuition fees

- » Fees for UK students   £9,250
- » Fees for International students 2021–22   £19,050–£24,450
  Dentistry £38,790; Medicine £36,240 (clinical years)
- » For scholarship and bursary information see
  www.sheffield.ac.uk/undergraduate/fees-funding/
- » Graduate salary   £25,000

Student numbers

Undergraduates	19,025	(586)
Postgraduates	8,160	(2,424)
Applications/places		36,270/3,965
Applications per place		9.1
Overall offer rate		78.7%
International students – EU		5.2%
Non-EU		28.2%

Accommodation

University provided places: 5,377
Self-catered: £102–£166 per week
First years guaranteed accommodation
www.sheffield.ac.uk/accommodation

Where do the students come from?

State schools (non-grammar)	77.4%	First generation students	33.1%	Black attainment gap	-11%
Grammar schools	11.7%	Deprived areas	9.4%	Disabled	8.9%
Independent schools	10.9%	All ethnic minorities	20.9%	Mature (over 21)	11.3%

Social inclusion ranking: 85

Sheffield Hallam University

Under the leadership of vice-chancellor Professor Sir Chris Husbands, Sheffield Hallam has a vision to be the world's leading applied university and a mission to transform students' lives. In line with the first objective, and to help address societal challenges, it has launched two new world-leading research centres putting wellbeing and food engineering under the microscope.

The £14m Advanced Wellbeing Research Centre, opened at the start of 2020, is the centrepiece of Sheffield's Olympic Legacy Park, a joint venture between the university, the city council and Sheffield Teaching Hospitals NHS Foundation Trust. Focusing on innovations that help people move, the AWRC is dedicated to improving the population's health and wellbeing.

At the National Centre of Excellence for Food Engineering, which opened in 2019, a network of businesses, industry groups, academics and engineers are working to solve industry challenges through expertise and the latest facilities.

Hallam has long been on track with its mission to transform students' lives via initiatives that tackle social inequality and widen access to higher education. For a university usually placed in the upper half of our overall league table (and only just outside it in this edition) Hallam has one of the highest proportions — 94% — of students who arrive from non-selective state schools. It rises 12 places in our latest social inclusion table, and more than half of students are recruited from families where the parents did not go to university.

Hallam is now leading a new social mobility programme, South Yorkshire Futures, which aims to improve GCSE attainment and raise aspirations for young people in South Yorkshire, especially those from disadvantaged backgrounds. The university already does well at attracting students locally and almost half of undergraduates come from the Yorkshire and Humber region. An even larger proportion stay and work in the area after graduation. A report in summer 2019 found that Hallam was the UK's biggest recruiter of poor, white students — a group whose educational underperformance is a cause of growing concern to policy-makers.

Sheffield Hallam was University of the Year for Teaching Quality for 2019–20, when it ranked 14th in the UK based on the outcomes of the National Student Survey. Although it did less well in the most recent snapshot of student satisfaction, its top-50 ranking for satisfaction with teaching quality is no mean feat for one of the country's largest universities, with 30,000 students. It ranked 72nd for satisfaction with the wider undergraduate experience.

City Campus
Howard Street
Sheffield S1 1WB
0114 225 5555
admissions@shu.ac.uk
www.shu.ac.uk
www.hallamstudentsunion.com
Open days: see website

The Times and The Sunday Times **Rankings**
Overall Ranking: 67 (last year: =65)

Teaching quality	80.6%	=50
Student experience	77.4%	72
Research quality	5.4%	=89
Entry standards	116	=97
Graduate prospects	77.1%	46
Good honours	75.7%	62
Expected completion rate	85.5%	56
Student/staff ratio	16.8	=86
Services and facilities	£2,702	45

More than three-quarters of graduates were in high-skilled jobs or postgraduate study within 15 months of leaving, the most recent figures showed, putting the university in the top 50. Hallam's employability initiatives helped earn a silver award in the government's Teaching Excellence Framework (TEF), which was chaired by the university's vice-chancellor. He was not involved in the decision, but the TEF panel complimented the institution on an exemplary commitment to the region and support for students to be retained in the area.

The first phase of a 15-year plan to improve teaching and learning facilities at the city centre and at the Collegiate campus will be delivered over the next five years, adding new business school buildings, a refurbished students' union and creating a university green.

Nine new degrees were introduced in 2020 including e-sports, festival and entertainment management, finance, and professional policing. From 2021 the university will offer degrees in film and television production and in international hospitality and tourism management.

Hallam's diverse degree apprenticeship programme is growing. Already one of the country's largest providers, the university expects 1,000 more apprentices to sign up by 2021, bringing the number to more than 2,400. Its National Centre of Excellence for Degree Apprenticeship, launched in 2018, has dedicated learning and teaching spaces. More than 30 programmes are offered in the fields of architecture and chartered planning, construction and chartered surveying, digital and technology, engineering, food and drink, health and social care, healthcare sciences and leadership and management.

Only 16% of eligible academics entered the 2014 Research Excellence Framework. However, 65% of their work was considered world-leading or internationally excellent.

There are fitness suites and sports halls at both campuses. Hallam manages Sheffield's only athletics stadium, two miles from the city site, where the BUCS (British Universities and Colleges Sport) Championships have been hosted. Most outdoor pitches — grass, 3G and sand-dressed — are five miles from the city campus at Bawtry Road, where there is also a cricket hall.

The university makes an unequivocal accommodation guarantee to all first-years seeking one of the 4,457 spaces in the privately-owned halls of residence it endorses. Sheffield's plentiful green spaces, student-friendly venues and affordability make it a popular student city.

Tuition fees

» Fees for UK students	£9,250
» Fees for International students 2021–22	£13,995
» For scholarship and bursary information see www.shu.ac.uk/study-here/fees-and-funding	
» Graduate salary	£23,000

Student numbers

Undergraduates	21,916 (2,402)
Postgraduates	3,105 (3,293)
Applications/places	29,485/5,735
Applications per place	5.1
Overall offer rate	75.1%
International students – EU	1.6%
Non-EU	5.7%

Accommodation

University provided places: 4,457
Self-catered: £85–£160 per week
First years guaranteed accommodation
www.shu.ac.uk/study-here/accommodation

Where do the students come from?

State schools (non-grammar)	94%	First generation students	51.6%		
Grammar schools	3%	Deprived areas	20.7%		
Independent schools	3%	All ethnic minorities	22.1%		

Social inclusion ranking: 44

Black attainment gap	-25.8%
Disabled	7.9%
Mature (over 21)	19%

SOAS, University of London

Soas (the School of Oriental and African Studies) has sold off buildings adjoining its central London headquarters and drawn up plans to cut staff as part of a "turnaround plan" to cope with a £19m deficit and ensure its long-term future as an independent institution. Professor Adam Habib is due to arrive from South Africa in January 2021 to take over as director, as Soas sets about budget cuts of £17m, which threaten parts of its unique course portfolio.

One of the most diverse institutions under the University of London umbrella, Soas draws more than 70% of its UK students from non-selective state schools and more than half from ethnic minorities. But it has struggled to attract enough students overall, despite a global reputation for its focus on Asia, Africa and the Middle East. Although there was a big rise in new entrants in 2019, this followed two years in which the intake fell by 46%, and there was another 10% decline in applications early in the 2020 admissions cycle.

Professor Habib, a radical political geographer, is used to financial constraints, having led the University of the Witwatersrand, in Johannesburg, for seven years during South Africa's ongoing tuition fee crisis. He succeeds Baroness Amos, who was the first black woman to lead a UK university and has gone on to head University College, Oxford.

Under her leadership, Soas pioneered moves to "decolonise" the curriculum. The school has committed itself to challenging Eurocentrism and developed a toolkit for making teaching more inclusive and redressing disadvantage through racism and colonialism. There has been a student working group on the subject since 2016, prompted partly by Soas's own colonial origins.

Soas has also reduced the attainment gap between black students (75% of whom get firsts or 2:1s) and their white counterparts (88%), now 13 percentage points adrift compared with 30 three years before. The figure forms part of our social inclusion ranking, in which Soas places in the top 50 overall.

Soas has introduced a "guided curriculum" where three-quarters of the first-year timetable will be fixed, with more scope to broaden options later in a degree course. Core modules covering Soas values and including study and employment skills are being introduced across the school.

The university plans to replace the traditional three-term system with two semesters, both of which will include exams and assessment. The aim is to make the extent of assessment more equal across all subjects and reduce an overreliance on exams. Soas believes the changes will reduce attainment gaps and dropout rates, and also

---

Thornhaugh Street
Russell Square
London WC1H 0XG
020 7637 2388
study@soas.ac.uk
www.soas.ac.uk
http://soasunion.org
Open days: see website

The Times and The Sunday Times Rankings

Overall Ranking: 50 (last year: 44)

Teaching quality	75%	=120
Student experience	71.3%	125
Research quality	27.9%	46
Entry standards	158	24
Graduate prospects	68.5%	99
Good honours	82.5%	28
Expected completion rate	82%	=85
Student/staff ratio	11.6	6
Services and facilities	£1,469	128

improve employment prospects and student satisfaction.

Low student satisfaction rates have held Soas back in our academic league table, although it returned to the top 50 in 2019, a position it retains in this edition. Satisfaction with the student experience remained in the bottom five in 2020, however.

Soas gained silver in the Teaching Excellence Framework, upgraded from bronze at the third attempt. The panel praised a strong institutional emphasis on personalised learning and small-group teaching, as well as a comprehensive student engagement system and outreach initiatives to widen participation.

The university offers a free week's bridging course to prepare students who are the first in their family to go to university, are over 21, or are from a low-participation neighbourhood. Those with household incomes below £25,000 receive a bursary worth at least £1,500 a year.

Soas covers a much wider variety of subjects than its name suggests. Degrees are available in law, history and the social sciences, but with a specialist emphasis. More than 40% of the 5,800 students are from outside the UK and the school is ranked by QS in the top 50 universities in the world for the arts and humanities. Music, drama and the performing arts produced the best results in the Research Excellence Framework, when two-thirds of the submission was rated world-leading or internationally excellent.

The school celebrated its centenary in 2016 by moving into the north block of Senate House, the Bloomsbury headquarters of the University of London, which adjoins the Soas precinct. The five-floor development brought Soas together on a single site for the first time in many years. It includes a student hub, hosting services such as accommodation, counselling, student finance and careers, and a plaza under a glass canopy.

There is no separate students' union building, although students do have their own bar, social space and catering facilities. The former University of London Union, now a student centre, is close at hand, with a swimming pool, gym and bars.

Almost 1,100 residential places are available within 20 minutes' walk of the school. Soas has few of its own sports facilities and the outdoor pitches are remote. For most students, however, sport is not a priority.

Tuition fees

» Fees for UK students	£9,250
» Fees for International students 2021–22	£18,630
» For scholarship and bursary information see www.soas.ac.uk/registry/funding	
» Graduate salary	£24,000

Student numbers

Undergraduates	2,629	(66)
Postgraduates	1,959	(1,147)
Applications/places		6,175/875
Applications per place		7.1
Overall offer rate		79%
International students – EU		14.8%
Non-EU		28.8%

Accommodation

University provided places: 1,084
Catered costs: £162–£293 per week
Self-catered: £152–£299 per week
www.soas.ac.uk/accommodation

Where do the students come from?

State schools (non-grammar)	70.5%	First generation students	42.8%
Grammar schools	9.5%	Deprived areas	4.5%
Independent schools	20%	All ethnic minorities	69.3%

Social inclusion ranking: =48

Black attainment gap	-13%
Disabled	9%
Mature (over 21)	23.6%

Solent University

Solent's city centre site has at its heart the £33m Spark building, which contains lecture theatres with charging sockets and the technology to upload live lectures to a virtual learning environment. Spark is where the newly-separated schools of law and of business are being housed, too — and features a new moot courtroom to allow students to hone their arguments in a real-life setting.

In another shift, all sports courses now have access to the university's sports complex, a £28m facility opened in 2019 comprising a teaching building, gym, sports halls and fitness studios.

Solent students are among the most satisfied in the country, the latest National Student Survey revealed. The university ranked 22= for student satisfaction with teaching quality and climbed to 33 for satisfaction with the wider undergraduate experience.

Student support facilities have been brought together, making access easier to advice desks specialising in finance, accommodation and assessment. A food garden with growing space for fruit and vegetables has been dug on campus. Students can relax and garden alone or with fellow green-fingered types and raised beds have been included to make access easier for wheelchair users.

Solent was upgraded to silver in the Teaching Excellence Framework. Assessors were impressed by students' high levels of engagement and commitment to learning, and by the substantial investment in learning resources and successful integration of research and professional practice into the curriculum. A low graduate employment rate had been the main factor limiting the university to bronze in 2017. In the latest figures for graduate prospects Solent is in the bottom 20 UK universities, with only 64% in high-skilled jobs or postgraduate study within 15 months of finishing their degree.

A guarantee to put real-world learning into undergraduate courses may help to boost employability. The change to course design followed a rethink of Solent's degree programmes. Students will have placement opportunities and paid assignments, and will be assessed on tasks for employers or community organisations.

The first mental health nursing students started their courses in September 2020, as did those on a new degree in prosthetics and special effects design. The university hopes to launch a degree integrating full commercial pilot training with academic study.

The portfolio of 22 higher and degree apprenticeships is growing however, and the university expects the numbers to increase from 495 to around 995 by September 2021. New programmes awaiting approval include construction project management, cyber-security, software engineering, digital

East Park Terrace
Southampton SO14 0YN
023 8201 5066
admissions@solent.ac.uk
www.solent.ac.uk
www.solentsu.co.uk
Open days: see website

The Times and The Sunday Times **Rankings**

Overall Ranking: 93 (last year: =89)

Teaching quality	82.5%	=22
Student experience	79.9%	33
Research quality	0.5%	126
Entry standards	124	=74
Graduate prospects	64.1%	115
Good honours	70.7%	=104
Expected completion rate	78.5%	=106
Student/staff ratio	15.8	=69
Services and facilities	£2,149	89

and technology solutions and broadcast production. Maritime, social work, healthcare science, and registered nursing (mental health) training courses are also due to be added to the list.

A £43m investment in maritime technology has brought specialist simulation facilities to the main campus, where tuition for Merchant Navy senior officers, yacht certification, maritime safety management, leadership and security courses moved in 2018.

The university has a fleet of 11 manned model ships at its training centre on Timsbury Lake and work has begun at Warsash maritime academy to provide upgraded facilities for maritime safety training, including open water, rescue boat and survival craft, fire school and helicopter underwater escape training, as well as medical facilities.

The world-renowned maritime academy and the superyacht academy serve the training and research needs of the superyacht, shipping and offshore oil industries. More than 50% of the yachts at 2020's Monaco Yacht Show were designed by Solent alumni. Solent is also the premier yachting university in Britain, with a world champion student team and alumni who have gone on to win Olympic and Paralympic gold medals.

More than 96% of students arrive from non-selective state schools and almost half are the first in their families to go to university. Widening participation initiatives include links with 10 local schools and colleges and outreach work with local under-represented groups. From 2021 Solent will also make contextual offers. Bursaries of £500 to £1,500 are available to students from households with incomes under £25,000, the larger sums reserved for those who are also care leavers, estranged from their families, or young carers.

The university's efforts to use big data to identify students at risk of dropping out and support them to increase engagement and achievement has yet to translate into improved completion rates, and more students drop out than the projected rate based on the academic and social backgrounds of the intake.

The new sports complex on the main campus is a boon and at Test Park, a few miles away, there are outdoor pitches for football (both soccer and American) and rugby union.

There is enough space for all new students to be guaranteed one of the 1,249 residential rooms if they apply by June. Along with student-friendly pubs and clubs in the East Park area, Southampton has lashings of sea air and the nearby New Forest to recommend it.

Tuition fees

» Fees for UK students	£9,250
» Fees for International students 2021–22	£13,260
Foundation	£11,660
» For scholarship and bursary information see www.solent.ac.uk/finance	
» Graduate salary	£21,000

Student numbers

Undergraduates	8,562	(699)
Postgraduates	342	(308)
Applications/places		10,165/2,115
Applications per place		4.8
Overall offer rate		85.5%
International students – EU		13.2%
Non-EU		5.1%

Accommodation

University provided places: 1,249
Self-catered: £111–£156 per week
First years guaranteed accommodation
www.solent.ac.uk/studying-at-solent/accommodation

Where do the students come from?

State schools (non-grammar)	96.1%	First generation students	49.1%		
Grammar schools	0.6%	Deprived areas	17.1%		
Independent schools	3.4%	All ethnic minorities	18.9%		

Social inclusion ranking: 54

Black attainment gap	-26.4%
Disabled	5.4%
Mature (over 21)	22.1%

University of South Wales

The University of South Wales (USW) continued its strong record in the latest National Student Survey where it was placed 33= for student satisfaction with teaching quality and 65= for satisfaction with the wider experience. The results have contributed to an impressive 24-place rise up our table overall and a re-entry comfortably inside the top 100.

Formed by a merger between Glamorgan and Newport universities, there is more change afoot for USW. In July 2020 USW and the University of Wales Trinity Saint David agreed to a strategic alliance in which they will work together more closely on academic and administrative issues, while stopping short of a merger. The health pandemic and its economic fallout were catalysts to the move to better secure the universities' futures.

USW's vice-chancellor Julie Lydon sees the move as positive, saying: "The opportunity of crafting a new direction of travel which addresses the planning and delivery of education and skills development across further, higher and employment-based education through Wales will have a significant impact and will deliver key outcomes which will support economic and civic regeneration."

USW has a record of weathering storms. When it closed and sold the attractive Caerleon campus outside Newport (later used as a filming location for the Netflix series Sex Education), student satisfaction scores soared despite the controversy. Its largest campus is now in Pontypridd, 10 miles outside Cardiff, where two sites cater mainly for science, engineering and health subjects. Recent developments there have included a new Law School and upgraded laboratories, as well as a £6m Learning Resource Centre.

At USW's Cardiff campus for the creative industries, the recently opened Atrium building has professional advertising, television and film set design and fashion space. It also has room for dance studios, rehearsal spaces and photographic studios. USW's simulated learning facilities include a trading room, hospital wards and a scene-of-crime house. The Startup Stiwdio incubation space is also at the Cardiff campus, and provides programmes to help develop and grow new business ideas.

The £35m Newport City Campus opened in 2011, and is the site of USW's Security Operations Training Centre, part of its National Cyber Security Academy, which offers students first-hand experience in responding to cyber-threats by simulating real-world incidents and how to handle them. The National Cyber Awards organisation named UWS as the UK's best university for cyber-education in 2019.

Degrees in building surveying, applied biosciences, artificial intelligence with computer science, and international event management are among those to have been

---

1 Lantwit Road
Pontypridd
CF37 1DL
03455 76 77 78
admissions@southwales.ac.uk
www.southwales.ac.uk
www.uswsu.com
Open days: see website

The Times and The Sunday Times Rankings		
Overall Ranking: =90 (last year: 114)		
Teaching quality	82%	=33
Student experience	78%	=65
Research quality	4%	=104
Entry standards	121	=84
Graduate prospects	68%	=101
Good honours	70.4%	109
Expected completion rate	81.7%	89
Student/staff ratio	15.1	=55
Services and facilities	£1,955	102

added to the course portfolio in 2020. Sports therapy, music producing and visual journalism will be ready in 2021.

The university is adding programmes in cyber-security and data science to its stable of degree apprenticeships, which also covers mechanical, manufacturing, electrical and electronic engineering, compound semi-conductors, policing, and digital technology solutions. The number on courses is likely to grow to about 200 by September 2021. USW also recruits for police constable degree apprenticeships in the southwest of England and expects 350 on the programme.

Like many universities in Wales, USW has not entered the Teaching Excellence Framework. Of its relatively small submission in the 2014 Research Excellence Framework, half of the work was considered world-leading or internationally excellent. The best results came in a joint submission with Cardiff Metropolitan and Trinity St David universities in art and design. Results were also good for sport and exercise science, and social work and social policy.

The university ranks outside the top 100 for graduate prospects, with the latest figures showing 68% were in high-skilled jobs or postgraduate study within 15 months of finishing their degree.

Three-quarters of USW's students are from Wales and more than one in five comes from an area of low participation in higher education. Bursaries include £500 awards for college students with USW-accredited foundation or HND qualifications, who progress to USW to top them up to honours degrees. Those from Birmingham Metropolitan College who progress to a full degree at USW qualify for £1,000. There are Welsh medium scholarships of between £250 and £1,000 depending on how many degree credits are studied in the Welsh language.

Sports facilities were boosted by the opening of a new 3G pitch and 270-seat stand at USW Sport Park at the end of 2019. It doubles as the home pitch for Pontypridd FC. The Sport Park includes specialist equipment for sports degree studies and a centre for strength and conditioning with 12 lifting platforms and a full-size 3G indoor football pitch, the only one in Wales and one of five in the UK.

The university has 1,656 residential spaces, some in each of its locations. First-years get priority but there is no guarantee of accommodation. City, seaside and countryside life is on the doorstep.

Tuition fees

» Fees for UK students	£9,000
» Fees for International students 2020–21	£13,200–£13,500
Foundation courses	£10,000
» For scholarship and bursary information see www.southwales.ac.uk/study/fees-and-funding/	
» Graduate salary	£21,000

Student numbers

Undergraduates	14,088	(3,441)
Postgraduates	1,878	(2,921)
Applications/places		11,490/2,585
Applications per place		4.4
Overall offer rate		73.3%
International students – EU		5.5%
Non-EU		6.3%

Accommodation

University provided places: 1,656
Self-catered: £96–£170 per week
www.southwales.ac.uk/student-life/accommodation

Where do the students come from?

State schools (non-grammar)	95.6%	First generation students	43.3%		
Grammar schools	1.4%	Deprived areas	21.8%		
Independent schools	3%	All ethnic minorities	10.9%		

Social inclusion ranking: 33

Black attainment gap	-19.5%
Disabled	7.2%
Mature (over 21)	33.2%

University of Southampton

There has been teaching at Southampton's Highfield campus for more than 100 years, a milestone marked in the naming of the new Centenary Building, where teaching and learning facilities focus on improving the student experience. Independent study spaces come with views across the campus and the city, seminar rooms are bookable and private study pods are plentiful. Opened in 2019, the building has an 80-seat Harvard lecture theatre and large teaching spaces.

Higher levels of student satisfaction have contributed to a five-place climb up our league table for Southampton, the largest improvement among our elite top-20 universities in this edition.

A founding member of the research-led Russell Group of universities, Southampton was upgraded to silver in the Teaching Excellence Framework. The panel of assessors complimented the institution on a strategic commitment to enhancing the quality of teaching and a learning environment in which students participate actively in research. Southampton is in the top 100 in the QS global rankings and is No 1 in the UK for consultancy income earned.

Students are encouraged to spend time studying abroad and most subject areas offer a year in employment. Southampton does well on our measure of graduate prospects, with 82% in high-skilled jobs or postgraduate study within 15 months of finishing their degrees — only 27 UK universities did better. And it was among the 20 UK universities most targeted by leading graduate employers, according to the 2020 High Fliers graduate market report.

The main Highfield campus enjoys a green setting two miles from Southampton city centre. The Avenue campus nearby houses most of the humanities departments, while clinical medicine is based at Southampton General Hospital. Winchester School of Art has been part of the university since 1996 and other sites include the National Oceanography Centre Southampton, based in the revitalised dock area. Further afield, the university has a campus in Malaysia dedicated to engineering, which it plans to expand in both curriculum and estate.

The final phase of the 10-year £140m Boldrewood Innovation Campus redevelopment completed in 2019 with the opening of the National Infrastructure Laboratory, housing the latest teaching and research facilities for geomechanics, heavy structures, solid mechanics and infrastructure engineering. The campus is dedicated to marine engineering and engineering sciences and was developed jointly with Lloyd's Register.

Southampton was quick off the blocks in the race to find a vaccine for Covid-19. It commenced clinical tests in March 2020 with drug-development company Synairgen and

---

University Road
Highfield
Southampton SO17 1BJ
023 8059 9699
enquiry@southampton.ac.uk
www.southampton.ac.uk
www.susu.org
Open days: see website

The Times and The Sunday Times **Rankings**
Overall Ranking: =15 (last year: 20)

Teaching quality	79%	=76
Student experience	78.8%	51
Research quality	44.9%	7
Entry standards	153	=28
Graduate prospects	81.6%	28
Good honours	85.8%	17
Expected completion rate	92%	27
Student/staff ratio	13.3	=13
Services and facilities	£2,700	46

announced positive results for an inhaled medicine in those most at risk. In July 2020, results showed the odds of developing severe disease (requiring ventilation or resulting in death) during the treatment period were reduced by 79% for patients receiving the drug compared with those given a placebo.

The university was also central in testing for Covid-19 among the city's households and helped to build and fly a light drone to take medical supplies across the Solent to the Isle of Wight.

Southampton performed well in the 2014 Research Excellence Framework. It ranks seventh for research quality in our survey after entering nine out of 10 eligible academics for assessment. More than 80% of their work was rated world-leading or internationally excellent.

The best results came in health subjects, environmental science, psychology, physics, chemistry, electronic engineering and music, drama and performing arts. Computer science is another of Southampton's flagship departments: Dame Wendy Hall is a Regius professor in the subject and Sir Tim Berners-Lee, inventor of the worldwide web, is an honorary professor.

Although it has a more diverse intake than most of its Russell Group peers, Southampton is only just inside the top 100 in our social inclusion ranking. More than a third of students are the first in their families to go to university, and a quarter of undergraduates come from ethnic minority backgrounds.

About a quarter of admissions will receive some form of financial assistance in 2021, as was the case in 2020. Bursaries of £1,500 or £2,000 are awarded to students where household incomes are up to £30,000 or £16,000 respectively. There are also 150 A2S access bursaries of £1,000 awarded to undergraduates who enrol having successfully completed the university's widening participation access programme, which includes summer school (when Covid-safe), student mentoring and skills workshops.

An indoor sports complex next to the students' union and a 25-metre pool add to Southampton's excellent facilities. There are numerous gyms at halls of residence, while the outdoor sports complex has multiple grass and synthetic pitches. Flying Formula is the university's Sigma 38 yacht, available for taster sessions or bareboat charter.

Southampton has more than 7,000 residential places, enough for all new entrants who apply by the deadline — and most others. Southampton nightlife has a lively reputation, and students can roam to nearby beaches and the New Forest.

Tuition fees

»	Fees for UK students	£9,250
»	Fees for International students 2021–22	£18,520–£22,760
	Medicine	£23,738–£46,992
»	For scholarship and bursary information see www.southampton.ac.uk/courses/fees/undergraduate.page	
»	Graduate salary	£25,000

Student numbers

Undergraduates	15,731	(59)
Postgraduates	5,588	(1,336)
Applications/places	35,795/3,485	
Applications per place	10.3	
Overall offer rate	68%	
International students – EU	7.7%	
Non-EU	21.7%	

Accommodation

University provided places: 7,000
Catered costs: £150–£201 per week
Self-catered: £116–£331 per week
First years guaranteed accommodation
www.southampton.ac.uk/uni-life/accommodation.page

Where do the students come from?

State schools (non-grammar)	72.5%	First generation students	35.5%	Black attainment gap	-20.9%
Grammar schools	14.7%	Deprived areas	7.9%	Disabled	5.7%
Independent schools	12.8%	All ethnic minorities	25%	Mature (over 21)	9.3%

Social inclusion ranking: 99

Staffordshire University

Students at Staffordshire are among the country's most satisfied with teaching quality. Their warm feedback in the latest National Student Survey ranks the institution 15 on this measure, and 40= for satisfaction with the wider undergraduate experience. This level of performance helped earn Staffordshire a shortlisting for our University of the Year award for 2019–20.

The latest results reconfirm the university's strong long-term record for student satisfaction. It also holds the highest rating — gold — in the government's Teaching Excellence Framework (TEF), following an upgrade in 2019. The TEF panel said students from all backgrounds achieve outstanding outcomes and complimented the university on high rates of progression to high-skilled employment or further study as well as its strong commitment to supporting students' personal and professional development.

However, this picture was not confirmed by the new measurement of graduate prospects, which put Staffordshire among the biggest losers, with a ranking just outside the top 100 for the proportion of graduates in high-skilled jobs or postgraduate study 15 months after leaving university. The decline has contributed to its 23-place fall in our overall rankings, though this follows three consecutive years in which Staffordshire climbed to its highest position.

The university's efforts to engage and support students have translated to better completion rates, and the most recent figures showed fewer students dropped out than the projected level based on the social and academic backgrounds of the intake. The TEF panel noted the effectiveness of initiatives that help students into university and support them during their studies, such as the Student Journey scheme — which was co-created by students and staff to address any areas of disadvantage. The Quiet Induction offers a calm, personalised registration and welcome experience for students on the autistic spectrum.

The university's main campus is in Stoke, where Staffordshire is at the heart of the University Quarter, linking the train station with the city. Its Smart Zone has two storeys of dedicated workshop space, the latest digital technology and high-end computing facilities, allowing students on courses including fashion and engineering computing to invent, innovate and create.

In 2019 the university extended its reach beyond the Potteries and opened a Digital Institute campus at Queen Elizabeth Olympic Park in east London. Building on Staffordshire's strengths in computing and computer games, the campus is dedicated to new and emerging technologies and offers some of the university's most popular degrees, in e-sports, computer games design and games

College Road
University Quarter
Stok-on-Trent ST4 2DE
01782 294 400
enquiries@staffs.ac.uk
www.staffs.ac.uk
www.staffsunion.com
Open days: see website

The Times and The Sunday Times **Rankings**
Overall Ranking: 76 (last year: 53)

Teaching quality	83.7%	15
Student experience	79.4%	=40
Research quality	16.5%	55
Entry standards	120	=87
Graduate prospects	66.7%	108
Good honours	73.4%	84
Expected completion rate	79.7%	=100
Student/staff ratio	17.5	=98
Services and facilities	£2,289	81

PR and community management. A cyber-security degree began in 2020.

Primary teacher training programmes are based at Lichfield, where there is an integrated further and higher education centre, developed in partnership with South Staffordshire College. Nursing and midwifery students are based in the Royal Shrewsbury Hospital and there are also 15,000 students taking Staffordshire courses outside the UK, almost half of them located around the Pacific Rim.

Degrees in digital content creation, big data analytics, acting for stage and screen and international relations: history and global politics were among the diverse range of new options making their debut for 2020. The university has also set up new optional pathways for its degrees in games art, computer science, music, sound design and production and film and media production. For 2021 entry, undergraduates will have three more degrees to choose from: architecture, security and intelligence sciences and e-law.

Staffordshire has a portfolio of 10 degree apprenticeship programmes across the fields of business and administration, health and science, manufacturing and engineering and law and policing. New options are being developed for 2020–21 in accountancy/taxation and advanced forensic practice. Staffordshire also offers seven higher apprenticeships.

Provision for apprenticeships is to benefit from a £40m Catalyst Building on the Stoke campus, due to open in September 2021. Designed to be a hub for apprentices and digital skills, the building was part-funded by the Office for Students and will be an innovative study base for 6,500 new apprentices by 2030. The venue will also house Staffordshire's new library along with food outlets and event space.

The university's goal to promote social mobility is borne out by its diverse intake. It has risen 20 places in our latest social inclusion ranking to sit 13th. Almost all students arrive from non-selective state schools, nearly six in 10 are the first in their family to go to university and more than a quarter come from areas of deprivation.

Sports facilities on the Leek Road site of the Stoke campus are close to university accommodation and include a gym, grass and synthetic pitches, a sports hall and a strength and conditioning suite. There are 1,000 residential places and those who make Staffordshire their firm choice are guaranteed one.

The students' union has a range of venues for drinks, club nights and food. Off campus, the Hanley area is known for clubbing and nearby Newcastle-Under-Lyme for its pubs.

Tuition fees

- » Fees for UK students   £9,250
- » Fees for International students 2021–22   £14,000-£18,000
- » For scholarship and bursary information see www.staffs.ac.uk/courses/undergraduate/fees-and-funding
- » Graduate salary   £21,000

Student numbers

Undergraduates	8,407	(4,226)
Postgraduates	715	(1,505)
Applications/places	11,460/2,730	
Applications per place	4.2	
Overall offer rate	81.1%	
International students – EU	0.9%	
Non-EU	2.3%	

Accommodation

University provided places: 1,075
Self-catered: £95–£125 per week
www.staffs.ac.uk/student-life/accommodation

Where do the students come from?

State schools (non-grammar)	97%	First generation students	57.8%	Black attainment gap	-30.4%
Grammar schools	1.6%	Deprived areas	28.4%	Disabled	11.1%
Independent schools	1.4%	All ethnic minorities	19.6%	Mature (over 21)	35.3%

Social inclusion ranking: 13

University of Stirling

Already one of the most distinctive — and beautiful — campuses in Britain, Stirling is investing heavily in sports facilities and its new Campus Central development to provide a learning environment for the 21st century.

Founded in the late 1960s, today's campus retains original features such as the Pathfoot Building, an architectural masterpiece designed by John Richards, unmissable near the entrance. Now listed, it mixes lecture theatres with a permanent art collection and temporary exhibitions in its 17 courtyards, where students can grab a moment of contemplation.

Stirling makes a competitive offer to students, lying in eighth place among Scottish universities for the average UCAS tariff points attained by their recruits. A contextual offer scheme benefiting applicants from the 20% of Scottish postcodes classified as the most deprived helps keep the average lower than it might be for an institution of Stirling's calibre.

The clear commitment to widening access to higher education is echoed in joint degrees with Forth Valley College, where students split their time between the two institutions. Stirling also offers a growing number of articulation agreements providing direct entry into the second or third year of its degree courses. A mentoring scheme pairs new recruits from under-represented groups with more experienced students to help keep the dropout rate in check.

To find the university at the cutting edge in widening access is no surprise. Breaking the mould has been part of Stirling's DNA from its inception. It was the UK pioneer of the semester system, now popular throughout higher education. The academic year is divided into two 15-week blocks with short mid-semester breaks. Students have the option of starting courses in January, rather than September, and can choose subjects from across all five faculties.

Undergraduates can switch the direction of their studies as their interests develop, after academic advice. Part-time students can speed up their progress by taking a summer academic programme, which jams a full semester's teaching into July and August.

Teaching for two new degrees — paramedic science and data science — began in 2020, with funding also secured for 25 graduate apprenticeships in data science.

Campus Central should be complete in time for the new intake of students in September 2021. The three-storey building at the heart of the campus will provide new study and social spaces for students, staff and visitors. Taking its cue from the Pathfoot Building, the £21.7m development will maximise the impact of the university's

---

Stirling
FK9 4LA
01786 467 044
admissions@stir.ac.uk
www.stir.ac.uk
www.stirlingstudentsunion.com
Open days: see website

The Times and The Sunday Times Rankings
Overall Ranking: 38 (last year: 47)

Teaching quality	82.2%	31
Student experience	78.6%	=55
Research quality	30.5%	42
Entry standards	165	=17
Graduate prospects	77.4%	45
Good honours	76.3%	58
Expected completion rate	81.3%	93
Student/staff ratio	16.2	=74
Services and facilities	£2,011	97

stunning surroundings at the foot of the Ochil Hills on the shores of a loch.

Already the Atrium has been refurbished to provide improved catering and retail facilities for students, just over one-third of whom live on campus in nearly 2,900 student bedrooms. About two-thirds of students come from Scotland.

A spin-off project as part of the Campus Central development has created a new facility where students can borrow a laptop for four hours free of charge — which could come in handy in any move towards more online lectures following the Covid-19 crisis. All lectures are already filmed and accessible online.

New sports facilities are adding purpose-built fitness studios, a gym, a three-court sports hall, an indoor cycling studio and strength and conditioning areas. Stirling stood 11th in the inter-university sports league run by BUCS (British University and Colleges Sport) when competition was suspended last year, easily the best performance for a university of its size in the UK.

Even before the addition of the new £20m sports centre, facilities were top-notch and mostly open to the local community. Stirling won our Sports University of the Year title for 2019–20 and has been Scotland's designated University for Sporting Excellence since 2008. The campus hosts national centres for swimming, triathlon and tennis (which helped to foster the careers of Andy and Jamie Murray), and

has a nine-hole golf course with wide fairways and smoother greens to help encourage students to take up the sport.

Almost three-quarters of the work submitted to the 2014 Research Excellence Framework was judged to be world-leading or internationally excellent. The best results were in agriculture, veterinary science and food science, where Stirling was ranked fourth in the UK. The university was top in Scotland for health sciences and third for psychology.

The Institute of Aquaculture, based on campus, is a research and business hub providing consultancy, scientific collaboration and expertise to develop new technology and work practices in a key area of the Scottish economy.

The award-winning students' union oversees a lively social scene. The Macrobert Arts Centre runs cultural activities, while the surrounding countryside holds its own attractions for walkers and climbers. The campus has been described by Police Scotland as one of the safest in Britain and there is a safe-taxi scheme.

Tuition fees

» Fees for Scottish students   £0–£1,820
    RUK fees   £9,250 (capped at £27,750 for 4-year courses)
» Fees for International students 2021–22   £15,100–£17,900
» For scholarship and bursary information see
    www.stir.ac.uk/study/fees-funding/
» Graduate salary   £23,000

Student numbers

Undergraduates	8,006	(558)
Postgraduates	2,475	(1,460)
Applications/places	16,320/2,120	
Applications per place	7.7	
Overall offer rate	63.2%	
International students – EU	8.8%	
Non-EU	13.8%	

Accommodation

University provided places: 2,894
Self-catered: £84–£179 per week
First years guaranteed accommodation
www.stir.ac.uk/student-life/accommodation

Where do the students come from?

State schools (non-grammar)	87.7%	First generation students	37.6%		
Grammar schools	6.3%	Deprived areas	14.4%		
Independent schools	6%	All ethnic minorities	6%		

Social inclusion ranking (Scotland): 11

Black attainment gap	-51.9%
Disabled	6.4%
Mature (over 21)	24.9%

University of Strathclyde

Shortlisted for our UK University of the Year award, Strathclyde has entered our top 25 after a rise of 13 places — the biggest leap among the top 30 universities. Student satisfaction with the wider experience has risen for the second consecutive year and brought Strathclyde — which won our Scottish University of the Year title for 2019–20 — into the top 40 for that measure. Satisfaction with teaching quality has also improved again.

The quality of "StrathLife", as insiders refer to the student experience here, has evidently been undisturbed by a busy programme of campus developments. The university is investing £1bn over 10 years in its estate and work is under way on a £60m learning and teaching building at the heart of the Glasgow city centre John Anderson campus, where all courses are taught. The building will add study spaces and house Strathclyde students' union plus other student-facing services under the same roof.

The Wolfson Building is undergoing an £18m refurbishment to better provide for the Department of Biomedical Engineering. Strathclyde's engineering faculty is the largest in Scotland, and home to one of Europe's biggest university electrical power engineering and energy research groupings.

The university has retained its hard-to-get-into distinction, with an offer rate that equates to less than half of applications. Even taking into account the high conversion rate for Scottish secondary qualifications in the UCAS tariff system (which also benefits other Scottish institutions), Strathclyde's entry standards are stiff.

Established in 1796 to be a "place of useful learning" — words the university continues to live by — Strathclyde is the third-largest university in Scotland and is aiming to be one of the world's leading technological universities. With more than 83% of graduates in high-skilled jobs or postgraduate study within 15 months of finishing their degrees, the university features in the top 20 for graduate prospects. It delivers both Scotland's graduate apprenticeships and degree apprenticeships validated in England.

The Hunter Centre for Entrepreneurship, a unit endowed by the Scottish businessman and philanthropist Sir Tom Hunter, is one of Europe's leading centres for the study of entrepreneurship, innovation and strategy and offers degrees in business enterprise.

Widening access to higher education is also central to Strathclyde's purpose and it is on course to exceed government targets, a decade ahead of schedule. Its award-winning Breaking Barriers initiative is run in partnership with the charity Enable Scotland and ScottishPower and offers young people with learning disabilities the chance to gain a Certificate in Applied Business

McCance Building
16 Richmond Street
Glasgow G1 1XQ
0141 548 4400
study-here@strath.ac.uk
www.strath.ac.uk
www.strathunion.com
Open days: see website

The Times and The Sunday Times Rankings
Overall Ranking: =23 (last year: 36)

Teaching quality	78.5%	=82
Student experience	79.5%	=38
Research quality	37.7%	=21
Entry standards	200	5
Graduate prospects	83.4%	18
Good honours	84.9%	20
Expected completion rate	87.8%	=46
Student/staff ratio	19.5	=119
Services and facilities	£2,090	95

Skills and an eight-week work placement.

Given its high entry standards and the calibre of courses, Strathclyde does well to recruit nine out of 10 students from state schools, and far exceeds the UK average. More than a third of students have parents who did not go to university and Strathclyde ranks 10th once again in Scotland in our social inclusion index.

Like most Scottish universities, Strathclyde did not enter the Teaching Excellence Framework, but it excelled in the 2014 Research Excellence Framework. Almost 80% of an exceptionally large submission was rated world-leading or internationally excellent. The university was top in the UK for physics and top in Scotland for business, among a clutch of impressive performances.

In 2019 Strathclyde was awarded the Queen's Anniversary Prize for excellence in energy innovation. The award recognises institutions that show "quality and innovation" and deliver "real benefit to the wider world and public through education and training". In the same year Strathclyde also announced it had won its largest single research contract, the £20m One Ocean Hub project, bringing together 50 international partners to transform the world's response to plastic pollution, rising sea levels and overfishing.

Strathclyde's Advanced Forming Research Centre, a partnership with international engineering firms, is a centre of excellence in innovative manufacturing technologies. It is the European partner for South Korea's global research and commercialisation programme.

Financial help underpins Strathclyde's commitment to inclusivity, and as well as merit-based scholarships and bursaries that support students from low-income backgrounds, it extends to assistance with childcare costs for UK students. There are also awards for international undergraduates. The Strathclyde Accommodation Bursary helps full fee-paying new entrants from England, Wales and Northern Ireland with £1,000 towards their halls of residence rent.

The recently opened £31m sport centre has a six-lane, 25-metre swimming pool, two sports halls, squash courts, a café and specialist health facilities. Outdoor pitches are at the Stepps facility, 15-minutes from the Cathedral Street headquarters.

New entrants are guaranteed accommodation in one of the university's 1,500 rooms as long as their application is received before August 21. Glasgow is one of the UK's leading university cities.

Tuition fees

» Fees for Scottish students £0–£1,820
  RUK fees £9,250 (capped at £27,750 for 4-year courses)
» Fees for International students 2021–22 £16,000–£22,500
» For scholarship and bursary information see
  www.strath.ac.uk/studywithus/feesfunding/
» Graduate salary £26,000

Student numbers

Undergraduates	13,332 (1,721)
Postgraduates	4,949 (2,640)
Applications/places	27,045/4,040
Applications per place	6.7
Overall offer rate	48.9%
International students – EU	6.2%
Non-EU	12.1%

Accommodation

University provided places: 1,500
Self-catered: £104–£141 per week
www.strath.ac.uk/studywithus/accommodation/

Where do the students come from?

State schools (non-grammar)	90.1%	First generation students	36.9%	Black attainment gap	-35.9%
Grammar schools	2.1%	Deprived areas	17.4%	Disabled	3.1%
Independent schools	7.9%	All ethnic minorities	11%	Mature (over 21)	13.8%

Social inclusion ranking (Scotland): 10

University of Suffolk

Student numbers at Suffolk are swelling with each admissions round. The Ipswich-based university exceeded its target of having between 6,000 and 7,000 students by 2020 and at last count had a 7,700-strong student community. In 2019 alone enrolments increased by 20%. The university makes good use of the clearing process, which accounted for 30% of 2019's intake.

Facilities are expanding to accommodate the burgeoning population. In the library and students' union building a new social space has opened, featuring an 80-seat social learning area complete with power units, a small kitchen, table tennis and pool tables, and a shop.

A Digitech Centre is being developed in collaboration with BT, to become home to the university's ICT and digital creative courses and provide training for careers in the information and communications technology sector. The centre is to offer research and training programmes in emerging technologies, such as artificial intelligence, data software defined systems, cloud computing and smart metrology.

The library has had a £2.5m renovation and a revamp to one of the main teaching buildings has added specialist facilities for psychology, computer games design and network and software engineering. The Atrium also houses the Ipswich Waterfront Innovation Centre for business and innovation activities, where students have access to a range of 3D printers.

The Hold, near Ipswich waterfront, will be opened officially in 2021. A £20m building that has teaching spaces and new facilities for students, it is also a heritage research centre housing the region's historic treasures dating back to 1119, the date of the Royal Charter of King Henry I.

The university, founded in 2007, is also participating in the AWS Academy, an Amazon Web Service programme that teaches cloud computing skills, which will benefit students on computing degrees. Degrees in crime, justice and society and in art, culture and society have welcomed their first students and one in exercise prescription and public health will launch in 2021.

Suffolk offers seven degree apprenticeships, in chartered management, network engineering, software engineering, business management, civil engineering, health and wellbeing and social work. There are more than 600 learners taking the courses which are delivered to apprenticeship levy-paying employers. The portfolio of programmes is set to grow, focusing on health, social science, humanities and digital technology.

The university was given a bronze rating in the Teaching Excellence Framework (TEF) because it was "substantially" below its benchmarks for student satisfaction and graduate employment. The panel did

Waterfront Building
Neptune Quay
Ipswich IP4 1QJ
01473 338 348
admissions@uos.ac.uk
www.uos.ac.uk
www.uosunion.org
Open days: see website

The Times and The Sunday Times Rankings
Overall Ranking: 122 (last year: 129)

Teaching quality	78.3%	=89
Student experience	74.2%	114
Research quality	n/a	
Entry standards	105	125
Graduate prospects	75.7%	54
Good honours	71%	=100
Expected completion rate	72.5%	125
Student/staff ratio	16.7	=84
Services and facilities	£2,591	51

acknowledge the contribution of employers to course design and found a "developing approach to the creation of research and practice-based communities of staff, enabling students to benefit by exposure to scholarship, research and professional practice".

But Suffolk's efforts to boost the employability of its graduates are paying off. There were 76% in high-skilled jobs or postgraduate study within 15 months of finishing their degrees according to the new Graduate Outcomes survey — which places Suffolk just outside of the top 50 in the UK.

Student satisfaction remains an issue, and while the university is within the top 100 for satisfaction with teaching quality, it falls well outside it in terms of the wider undergraduate experience. Completion rates are also a stumbling block, with more than one in five students dropping out — higher than the projected level based on the academic and social backgrounds of the intake.

Suffolk classes itself as a widening participation institution and has filled a higher education gap in the region. It works actively with schools and colleges to encourage progression and does well in our social inclusion ranking. About one in five undergraduates come from areas of low participation in higher education – among the highest proportions in the country. Almost 60% of students are from homes where parents did not go to university and three-

quarters are aged over 21 when they start their courses. Almost all Suffolk students went to non-selective state secondary schools.

Bursaries of £500 are awarded for three years to those from households with incomes up to £25,000, and to entrants who have been in care. For 2020 entry, students holding unconditional offers prior to receiving their results qualified for a vice-chancellor's scholarship of £250 if they met course entry requirements, or £300 if they also achieved or exceeded their predicted grades.

There are plenty of sports facilities near the campus, though Suffolk does not have its own. The students' union co-ordinates activities for fun and competition. Lots of students live at home but the privately-operated Athena Hall residence near the campus has space for 590 students, with rooms allocated on a first-come, first-served basis.

The modern Waterfront development around Ipswich's marina is a popular hub of bars and restaurants, and the surrounding countryside boasts some of the UK's most desirable holiday spots, such as Aldeburgh and Southwold.

Tuition fees

» Fees for UK students	£9,250
Foundation courses	£8,220
» Fees for International students 2020–21	£11,790–£13,330
» For scholarship and bursary information see www.uos.ac.uk/feeesandscholarships	
» Graduate salary	£24,000

Student numbers

Undergraduates	6,460	(621)
Postgraduates	143	(469)
Applications/places		4,165/1,115
Applications per place		3.7
Overall offer rate		73.8%
International students – EU		6.7%
Non-EU		1.5%

Accommodation
Available places: 590
Self-catered: £130–£177 per week
www.uos.ac.uk/accommodation

Where do the students come from?

State schools (non-grammar)	96.7%	First generation students	58.9%	Black attainment gap	-29%
Grammar schools	1%	Deprived areas	18.9%	Disabled	6.4%
Independent schools	2.3%	All ethnic minorities	12.2%	Mature (over 21)	74.7%

Social inclusion ranking: 25

University of Sunderland

Sunderland is all about giving opportunities in higher education to those that might not be given them elsewhere. Very few universities can match its record in widening participation: it is one of a handful of universities where more than 60% of the intake are the first in their family to go to university and more than 98% are educated in non-selective state schools. Sunderland is once again in the top 20 of our social inclusion ranking, and wins our University of the Year for Social Inclusion title.

The second intake of 100 students at the new Sunderland School of Medicine for September 2020 was double the number admitted in 2019. The cohort was even more socially diverse than in 2019, with one in five meeting the criteria for widening participation. In a subject that demands high grades, Sunderland is attempting to break the mould for the "typical" medical student. Schools in areas that are among the lowest 40% for progression to higher education have been targeted and the university has introduced a medical summer school for year 12 schoolchildren who qualify under widening participation measures.

An anatomy laboratory within the new medical school opened in September 2020 and cadaveric dissection facilities will be available from 2021 as the university steps up its medical offer. Working in partnership with Keele University School of Medicine, the course has a significant general practice focus.

Across all subjects, the university works with more than 40 schools in the northeast — which has England's lowest overall participation rate in higher education — targeting middle-achieving children who have the capability but not the motivation to consider higher education. The First Choice Progression Scheme offers sessions on access to university, balancing finances, writing a CV, study skills and subject tasters. Successful completion is worth 16 UCAS tariff points to those who then apply to an eligible course at Sunderland.

More than 80% of British undergraduates come from within the region and the university works hard to ensure they complete their courses. The dropout rate is 15.9%, better than expected allowing for the subject and social mix. There is an extensive bursary and scholarship scheme targeted at students from homes with an annual income lower than £42,875. It also offers broader support and medical students are eligible for generous contributions towards accommodation costs. Many students qualify for free public transport.

Although it remains outside the top 100, Sunderland has risen six places in our latest academic ranking overall after a recovery in student satisfaction scores. The university is in the top half of tables for both student satisfaction

---

Edinburgh Building
City Campus
Chester Road
Sunderland SR1 3SD
0191 515 3000
student.helpline@sunderland.ac.uk
www.sunderland.ac.uk
www.sunderlandsu.co.uk
Open days: see website

The Times and The Sunday Times **Rankings**
Overall Ranking: 103 (last year: 109)

Teaching quality	80.4%	=55
Student experience	78.1%	=61
Research quality	5.8%	=83
Entry standards	113	=106
Graduate prospects	66.2%	111
Good honours	61.3%	128
Expected completion rate	78.4%	108
Student/staff ratio	15.5	=63
Services and facilities	£2,946	21

with teaching quality and their wider student experience.

Students have the option of spending part of their degree at the university's east London campus, in Canary Wharf. There is another campus in Hong Kong, opened in 2017 and currently delivering all courses online with students barred from the campus because of the coronavirus risk. It offers bachelor's and top-up degrees in business and management, marketing or human resources, accounting and financial management, and international tourism and hospitality management.

Closer to home — and in tune with Sunderland's access agenda — a string of degrees with integrated foundation years took their first students. These include biomedical science, nutrition, exercise and health, physiological sciences, biochemistry, cosmetic science, medicinal chemistry and biopharmaceutical science.

An already extensive programme of 15 degree apprenticeships has 550 students enrolled and is expected to expand. The list of degree apprenticeships includes courses in engineering, nursing, teaching, social work and digital skills.

The university holds silver in the Teaching Excellence Framework. The panel said students' academic experiences were tailored to the individual, with personalised support available. It also praised the exposure of students to professional practice through engagement with industrial and community partners, and employers' involvement in course development. Among an extensive list of business partners regionally and nationally are Caterpillar, Sage, Accenture, Northumbria police, Santander, the BBC and South Tyneside and Sunderland NHS Foundation Trust.

There are two campuses in Sunderland, one in the city centre and the other, the Sir Tom Cowie campus on the banks of the River Wear, was built around a 7th-century abbey described as one of Britain's first universities and incorporating the National Glass Centre. All arts and creative industry courses will be based at the latter within the next three years. The London campus focuses on business, tourism and nursing degrees.

The city of Sunderland is fiercely proud of its identity and has the advantage of a riverside and coastal location. Leisure facilities are good: the city has the northeast's only 50-metre swimming pool and dry ski slope, as well as Europe's biggest climbing wall and a theatre that shows West End productions. A short Metro or bus journey brings the culture and legendary nightlife of Newcastle within reach.

Tuition fees

»	Fees for UK students	£9,250
	Foundation courses	£8,200
»	Fees for International students 2021–22	£12,500
»	For scholarship and bursary information see www.sunderland.ac.uk/about/your-finances/	
»	Graduate salary	£21,000

Student numbers

Undergraduates	10,420	(1,503)
Postgraduates	1,956	(827)
Applications/places	8,290/1,615	
Applications per place	5.1	
Overall offer rate	72.3%	
International students – EU	7%	
Non-EU	11.9%	

Accommodation

University provided places: 911
Self-catered: £78–£154 per week
www.sunderland.ac.uk/about/accommodation/

Where do the students come from?

State schools (non-grammar)	98.2%	First generation students	60.1%	Black attainment gap	-18.8%
Grammar schools	0.2%	Deprived areas	26.9%	Disabled	5.8%
Independent schools	1.5%	All ethnic minorities	31%	Mature (over 21)	65.6%

Social inclusion ranking: 11

University of Surrey

Surrey's School of Health Sciences has a new £14m home, the Kate Granger Building. Opened by the Countess of Wessex at the start of 2020 it has a simulation suite that recreates clinical scenarios, and replica wards where student nurses and midwives can practise in hospital situations. Named after an NHS doctor whose *#hellomynameis* campaign encouraged healthcare staff to establish personal connections with patients, Surrey wants the building to be at the forefront of educating the UK's next generation of nurses, midwives, physicians' associates and paramedics.

A new £5m psychology facility has also been completed recently, adding virtual and augmented reality suites, soundproof neuropsychology laboratories, a to-scale dummy MRI scanner and a neurostimulation lab. There are also 20 student research labs, observation suites, a 96-person computer-enhanced learning lab and an electroencephalography (EEG) recording room.

These are the latest fruits of £400m of development in the past two decades. Surrey's two campuses, Stag Hill and Manor Park, are 10 minutes' walk from the centre of Guildford. The separate Surrey Research Park is one of the largest in the UK still to be owned, funded and managed by its host university.

Other developments include a £1.7m

upgrade to the Innovation for Health building's computer science laboratory, a new flexible teaching space for mechanical engineering science, advanced teaching facilities for geotechnics and Fair-Space, a cross-disciplinary £800m hub for artificial intelligence research called Future AI for Robotics in Space.

The university was awarded gold in the Teaching Excellence Framework. A glowing reference from the panel described "innovative and personalised provision", "high levels of teaching excellence" and "an effective approach to the development of professional skills and employability".

The new way of measuring graduate prospects, which looks at the proportion of graduates in high-skilled jobs within 15 months of completing their degrees, has given the university a considerable shot in the arm. It now ranks in the top 10 nationally for graduate prospects.

Employability-boosting professional training placements of up to 12 months are offered on most degrees. Taken in between the second and third years in the UK or overseas, the placements mean that most Surrey students are at university for four years. New entrants apply for them via UCAS as sandwich courses when making their main application to Surrey. The university has partnerships with more than 2,300 businesses including the Bank of England, Nintendo, Walt Disney, Tesla and AstraZeneca.

Foundation years in mathematics and in social sciences were introduced in 2020. A

Senate House
Guildford GU2 7XH
01483 682 222
admissions@surrey.ac.uk
www.surrey.ac.uk
www.ussu.co.uk
Open days: see website

Edinburgh
Belfast
Cardiff London
GUILDFORD

The Times and The Sunday Times Rankings
Overall Ranking: 39 (last year: 32)

Teaching quality	75%	=120
Student experience	76.9%	=82
Research quality	29.7%	44
Entry standards	146	42
Graduate prospects	85.5%	10
Good honours	79.9%	=37
Expected completion rate	88.9%	=41
Student/staff ratio	15.8	=69
Services and facilities	£2,800	36

new degree in applied and contemporary theatre will welcome its first students in 2021. Surrey, which ranks eighth in the world for hospitality and leisure management in the QS World Rankings, is planning a degree apprenticeship in international hospitality, tourism and events management practice, as well as one in management practice.

Surrey has slipped down our overall league table for the second year running however, due largely to a fourth successive drop in student satisfaction. Scores taken from the National Student Survey have sent the university toppling to 120= for teaching quality and 82= for the broader student experience. Completion rates remain healthy in spite of student satisfaction being at a low ebb, and fewer drop out than projected by the intake's academic and social mix.

Almost 80% of the work submitted by Surrey academics to the 2014 Research Excellence Framework was assessed as world-leading or internationally excellent. The best results were in nursing and other health subjects. Surrey's research is organised around "grand challenges" such as global wellbeing, sustainable cities and communities, and connecting societies and cultures.

About three in 10 students are from outside the UK and of the British contingent, independent and selective grammar schools account for just over one fifth of the intake. More than four in 10 students come from ethnic minority backgrounds. Less than 8% of students come from areas categorised as deprived, but the university is working to widen participation. There are links with local non-selective schools, and In2Surrey is a scheme that identifies and supports students from under-represented groups by offering entry-grade reductions, a financial award upon enrolment and access to an e-mentor to students who complete an academic assignment.

The £36m Surrey Sports Park is on the Manor Park campus, next to the School of Veterinary Medicine and on the same site as 2,934 of Surrey's 6,013 residential rooms. Under the Team Surrey banner are more than 40 sports clubs for all abilities. Facilities — both indoors and outdoors — are extensive and up to standard for elite athletes and teams including Harlequins rugby union, Surrey Storm netball and Guildford City swimming club.

Guildford is known as being an affluent and safe town surrounded by bucolic English countryside. It has plenty of pubs and is a good spot for shopping. For clubbing, Casino or the students' union tend to be the student haunts.

Tuition fees

» Fees for UK students	£9,250
» Fees for International students 2021–22	£17,300–£22,400
Veterinary Medicine	£34,400
» For scholarship and bursary information see www.surrey.ac.uk/fees-and-funding	
» Graduate salary	£26,000

Student numbers

Undergraduates	12,666	(765)
Postgraduates	2,420	(963)
Applications/places		32,600/3,275
Applications per place		10
Overall offer rate		66.5%
International students – EU		10.7%
Non-EU		18.4%

Accommodation

University provided places: 6,143
Self-catered: £75–£231 per week
First years guaranteed accommodation
www.surrey.ac.uk/accommodation

Where do the students come from?

State schools (non-grammar)	77.9%	First generation students	42.3%	
Grammar schools	12.5%	Deprived areas	7.4%	
Independent schools	9.6%	All ethnic minorities	40.7%	

Social inclusion ranking: =88

Black attainment gap	-24.4%
Disabled	5.1%
Mature (over 21)	10.9%

University of Sussex

Sussex launched its new School of Media, Arts and Humanities in 2020. Echoing the university's 1960s interdisciplinary roots, it brings together a broad range of existing schools to create a hub for teaching, learning and collaborative research. The school is home to subjects including English, art history, drama and theatre, philosophy, media, film, music, American studies and languages.

A focus on graduate employability is being brought to life with an industry-facing curriculum and work placements at cultural institutions such as the BBC and theatres and galleries worldwide. Academically the school combines theory, practice and activism with critical and creative work.

This fresh take on established educational forms is par for the course for Sussex, which has built a tradition of being disruptive and experimental, and a place where radicalism and dissent are espoused. With its 2025 vision — "a better university for a better world" — Sussex plans to reimagine its pioneering spirit within the context of a new generation.

In 2019 the university became one of the global organisations that declared a climate emergency. Sussex has invested £3m over recent years in establishing a global research programme to help speed up the delivery of the United Nations' 17 sustainable development goals.

The university's 2025 vision also involves investing in infrastructure and £19m was invested in capital developments in 2018 alone. With the architectural integrity of Sir Basil Spence's original modernist designs kept intact, regeneration is under way at Sussex's campus on the edge of the South Downs in Falmer, just outside Brighton. New residences at East Slope are being built in phases. More than 1,000 students are already living in the 800 bedrooms that opened in 2018, another 500 opened last year and the remaining 570 should be ready in early 2021.

Made up of townhouses and flats, the student village has a new student centre. Due for completion in spring 2021 it has been designed to become the main source of student-facing information, advice and guidance on campus. East Slope will have shops, an unlicensed café and a launderette.

Sussex gained silver in the Teaching Excellence Framework, winning praise for its "outstanding" employment strategy, designed to help students develop transferable employment skills. Undergraduates are encouraged to take work placements, study abroad and learn a language to broaden their experiences. There are also opportunities to study a core area for 75% of the time and an additional area for 25% of the time with a major/minor course.

A liberal arts degree will welcome its first students in September 2021, bringing together the arts, humanities and social sciences. A new

Sussex House
Falmer
Brighton BN1 9RH
01273 876 787
ug.enquiries@sussex.ac.uk
www.sussex.ac.uk
www.sussexstudent.com
Open days: see website

The Times and The Sunday Times **Rankings**

Overall Ranking: 44 (last year: =38)

Teaching quality	76.1%	=114
Student experience	73.6%	117
Research quality	31.8%	=37
Entry standards	142	46
Graduate prospects	76.2%	=52
Good honours	75.3%	70
Expected completion rate	89.9%	=36
Student/staff ratio	17.4	97
Services and facilities	£2,563	56

degree in digital media and culture also launches in 2021. Combining a practical element of digital media creation with critical analysis of the digital world, it joins Sussex's long-established stable of media-related courses.

A successful joint medical school is shared with the neighbouring University of Brighton, and split between the Royal Sussex County Hospital and the two universities' Falmer campuses.

Sussex, which was in our top 20 four years ago, has fallen outside the top 40 in this edition. Poor rates of student satisfaction are largely to blame, with the university now ranking in the bottom 20 nationally both for satisfaction with teaching quality and the wider student experience.

Three-quarters of the work submitted for the 2014 Research Excellence Framework was assessed as world-leading or internationally excellent and Sussex was among the leaders in history, English, psychology and geography. The university has launched a new centre for Jewish studies, with backing from the German government, to address the rise in antisemitism.

The university has topped the QS world ranking for development studies for four years in a row and has a sustainability research programme headed by the former chief scientist at the UN environment programme, Professor Joseph Alcamo.

Though Sussex is in the bottom 30 of our social inclusion ranking it outdoes many of its academic peers, and around four-fifths of students went to non-selective state secondary schools. Widening participation activities include summer schools for sixth-formers and contextual offers up to two grades lower than the norm for applicants from low participation areas.

About 25%-30% of admissions qualified for the Sussex bursary in September 2020, worth £1,000 in the first year and £500 per subsequent study year to those whose family income is under £25,000, and care leavers. Merit-based scholarships include the £2,000 Sussex and EU Excellence Scholarships, awarded to high academic achievers.

On-campus sports facilities can be used via memberships or on a pay-and-play basis. Two sports halls, glass-backed squash courts, a well-equipped gym, a dance and martial arts studio and outdoor pitches are among the facilities.

Most students move into Brighton from their second year and commute easily to campus by train or bus. Its diversity, seaside location and non-stop nightlife makes the city enduringly popular with students.

Tuition fees

- » Fees for UK students £9,250
- » Fees for International students 2020–21 £18,500–£22,500
  Medicine £35,517 (clinical years)
- » For scholarship and bursary information see www.sussex.ac.uk/study/fees-funding
- » Graduate salary £24,000

Student numbers

Undergraduates	14,024	(3)
Postgraduates	4,147	(979)
Applications/places	22,095/3,470	
Applications per place	6.4	
Overall offer rate	88%	
International students – EU	7.9%	
Non-EU	24.2	

Accommodation

University provided places: 5,300
Self-catered: £123–£168 per week
First years guaranteed accommodation
www.sussex.ac.uk/study/accommodation

Where do the students come from?

State schools (non-grammar)	78.7%	First generation students	41.4%	Black attainment gap	-19.9%
Grammar schools	10%	Deprived areas	7.3%	Disabled	9.4%
Independent schools	11.3%	All ethnic minorities	25%	Mature (over 21)	9.7%

Social inclusion ranking: 87

Swansea University

Swansea University's foundation stone was laid by King George V on July 19, 1920 on the site its Singleton Park campus occupies today. His great-grandson, the Prince of Wales, broadcast a birthday message for the university charting its history from an initial cohort of 89 students to today's dual campus institution of around 20,500.

The global health pandemic got in the way of the planned centenary celebrations. Funding earmarked for cancelled centenary events is instead being funnelled into research projects related to Covid-19 and supporting student wellbeing, explained Prince Charles, whose Foundation for Building Community helped develop Swansea's Bay campus.

The £450m, 65-acre beachside site doubled the size of the university when it launched in 2015 and helped cement Swansea's standing as one of the UK's leading universities. It is the base for the College of Engineering and a new £35m research centre, the Institute for Innovative Materials, Processing and Numerical Technologies (known as Impact), which opened in 2019, where industry and academics are collaborating in advanced engineering and materials. The campus has direct access to the beach, a stone's throw from university buildings, and there are halls of residence for about 1,000 students.

At the other end of this stretch of Swansea Bay's waterfront, the original Singleton campus has seen significant investment as well. The Hillary Rodham Clinton School of Law, named after the former US presidential candidate who received an honorary degree from Swansea in 2017, has new facilities including teaching and study spaces, a courtroom and a law clinic. Clinton is supporting a postgraduate scholarship programme intended to produce the next generation of leaders committed to addressing urgent global challenges.

The university has secured an EU grant to establish Legal Innovation Lab Wales, a £5.6m initiative to encourage research and innovation in legal tech, access to justice and countering cyber-threats.

Swansea is down five places in our rankings in this edition, falling below Cardiff, which becomes the top ranked university in Wales. Student satisfaction has always been a strength and Swansea is 19= for students' assessment of the wider undergraduate experience. It placed lower for teaching quality, but still well within the upper half of UK universities.

The university rolled out a new virtual learning environment during 2020, Canvas, which offers opportunities to review academic content and introduce new approaches to learning to benefit students and improve the study experience.

Swansea holds gold in the Teaching Excellence Framework thanks to its clear employability strategy and strong staff-student

Singleton Park
Swansea SA2 8PP
01792 205 678
admissions@swansea.ac.uk
www.swansea.ac.uk
www.swansea-union.co.uk
Open days: see website

The Times and The Sunday Times Rankings
Overall Ranking: 36 (last year: 31)

Teaching quality	80.6%	=50
Student experience	80.7%	=19
Research quality	33.7%	35
Entry standards	129	59
Graduate prospects	82.6%	22
Good honours	79.1%	43
Expected completion rate	89.2%	39
Student/staff ratio	15	=51
Services and facilities	£2,293	80

partnerships. With close on 83% of graduates in high-skilled jobs or postgraduate study within 15 months of finishing their degrees, the university ranks just outside the UK top 20 on our graduate prospects measure. The Swansea Employability Academy provides paid internships and co-ordinates programmes for career development.

Undergraduates are encouraged to take modules outside their specialist area in their first year. Many degrees include opportunities to work abroad or study at one of more than 100 partner institutions.

Swansea's medical school is introducing a new pharmacy course in September 2021. Reflecting the collaboration between pharmacists, doctors and nurses in clinical settings, the degree will adopt an interdisciplinary approach.

The university delivers a degree apprenticeship in applied software engineering in Swansea and two more, in aeronautical and manufacturing engineering and in advanced manufacturing engineering via a further education college in north Wales.

Four-fifths of the work submitted for the 2014 Research Excellence Framework was assessed as world-leading or internationally excellent, with health subjects, English and general engineering getting Swansea's best results.

The £20m Sports Village beside the Singleton campus has an athletics track, grass and all-weather pitches, squash and tennis courts, plus an indoor athletics training centre and 80-station gym. There are 50-metre and 25-metre pools at the Wales National Pool next door.

The university is the higher-education partner for Swansea City FC and the team's front-of-shirt sponsor for the 2020–21 season. Its grass and 3G pitches at Fairfield, five miles away, were built in partnership with the club. For rugby fans, Swansea students get concession rate tickets to Ospreys games. The Bay campus has a sports hall, gym and two outdoor multi-use areas.

There are plenty of good beaches in Swansea and the nearby Gower Peninsula has some of the UK's finest, Rhossili and Three Cliffs among them. Student surfers take their own boards, though these can also be rented. Students' union venue Rebound promises cheap drinks and classic tunes, while Wind Street is the local stretch of bars and restaurants. The social scene at Mumbles seaside resort has outgrown the infamous Mumbles Mile pub crawl but the area remains popular for nights out.

The university has 4,598 residential spaces, 660 of them costing only £95 a week. A small proportion of rooms are catered.

Tuition fees

» Fees for UK students   £9,000
» Fees for International students 2021–22   £15,400–£20,3500
   Medicine   £36,750 (clinical years)
» For scholarship and bursary information see
   www.swansea.ac.uk/undergraduate/fees-and-funding
» Graduate salary   £24,000

Student numbers

Undergraduates	**15,432** (1,244)
Postgraduates	**2,804** (1,141)
Applications/places	**17,355/3,275**
Applications per place	**5.3**
Overall offer rate	**81.1%**
International students – EU	**4.8%**
Non-EU	**12.4%**

Accommodation

University provided places: 4,598
Catered costs: £143–£148 per week
Self-catered: £95–£158 per week
First years guaranteed accommodation
www.swansea.ac.uk/accommodation

Where do the students come from?

				Social inclusion ranking: =88	
State schools (non-grammar)	90.5%	First generation students	37.2%	Black attainment gap	-17.1%
Grammar schools	1%	Deprived areas	10.7%	Disabled	4.6%
Independent schools	8.5%	All ethnic minorities	18.2%	Mature (over 21)	18.1%

University of Teesside

Bold plans to transform the centre of Middlesbrough include a cluster of university buildings, reinventing Teesside's central campus and putting the institution at the heart of the town's regeneration.

By 2026, about £300m is due to have been invested in the campus, where the main thoroughfare has been pedestrianised, bringing a new air of space and modernity. The most recent addition is the Student Life building, which amalgamates student support services in one place and has social spaces and a digital learning hub.

The £21m Cornell Quarter for student residences will be completed during the 2020–21 academic year, housing 300 students and increasing the university's accommodation stock by nearly a third — an important step towards broadening Teesside's appeal beyond the local region it serves so well. Refurbishment of the students' union building is in the pipeline, along with the construction and conversion of more buildings to form a student village.

A second campus in nearby Darlington has not been overlooked in the development spree. The £22m National Horizons Centre (NHC) opened there in 2019 as a research, teaching and business hub for the biosciences. Its laboratory equipment was used to help the NHS Covid-19 testing operation, while researchers worked alongside NHS staff to map the clinical course of cases and help identify risk factors to guide future treatment strategies.

Collaboration with outside agencies and between disciplines is at the core of Teesside's academic operation. Allied to the NHC, a new school of health and life sciences brings together scientific disciplines alongside health courses with the aim of delivering world-class research and transforming healthcare in the northeast.

Another newly configured division — the school of computing, engineering and digital technologies — will work across conventional academic boundaries to equip graduates with the right skills according to industrial priorities and growth sectors. An excellent record in digital technologies is exemplified by Teesside's DigitalCity initiative, which has helped to create nearly 300 businesses and 700 jobs since 2004. The university will introduce a new BSc in computer games development in September 2021.

Data from the new Graduate Outcomes survey shows 78% of Teesside graduates are in high-skilled employment or postgraduate study 15 months after leaving, an excellent result good enough to rank the university in the top 50 on this measure.

Teesside embodies the spirit of levelling up, sitting in the top 10 in our social inclusion ranking once again. Almost 99% of the students enrol from state schools and just under 30% come from areas with the worst record

Middlesbrough
TS1 3BX
01642 218 121
enquiries@tees.ac.uk
www.tees.ac.uk
www.tees-su.org.uk
Open days: see website

Edinburgh
Belfast
MIDDLESBROUGH
London
Cardiff

The Times and The Sunday Times Rankings

Overall Ranking: 92 (last year: 87)

Teaching quality	82.1%	32
Student experience	78.7%	=52
Research quality	3.6%	110
Entry standards	120	=87
Graduate prospects	78.1%	44
Good honours	71.6%	95
Expected completion rate	77.9%	114
Student/staff ratio	18.2	=113
Services and facilities	£2,634	47

of sending children into higher education, double the expected level for institutions with Teesside's course and student profile.

Figures for 2018-19 show that 80% of students were drawn from disadvantaged backgrounds, 46% from within a 15-mile radius of Middlesbrough, and 73% from the wider northeast, the region of England with the lowest rate of progression to higher education.

When they arrive on campus, all new full-time undergraduate students, including those doing a foundation year, are given an iPad and keyboard and up to £300 to spend on course texts as part of the Teesside University Advance scholarship programme.

The university has aspirations to climb much higher in our academic rankings and has made modest gains in recent years, assisted by a strong performance in the National Student Survey (NSS), measuring satisfaction with teaching quality and the wider student experience. However, a small decline in NSS performance and a lower degree completion rate has triggered a small fall in Teesside's overall ranking.

A diverse range of new courses was offered from September 2020, including degrees in artificial intelligence, mathematics with data analytics, innovative home design and construction, business and cyber-security, professional policing and clinical optometry.

The university has embraced degree apprenticeships with 850 students on campus following 18 different programmes. Ten further apprenticeship programmes are planned, to nearly double the numbers by September 2021 to 1,500. All courses moved to virtual delivery when the campus closed due to Covid-19.

A strong culture of partnership with students was cited by assessors for the Teaching Excellence Framework (TEF), who awarded Teesside silver. The TEF panel was also impressed by innovative and well-resourced support for developing employability. Support for graduates continues for a minimum of two years after they leave university through more than 200 paid internship and training opportunities. Second-year students undertake summer work placements.

Sports facilities are available on and off campus. The Olympia sports complex on campus incorporates a sports hall with capacity for 500 spectators, a climbing wall and gym. The Saltersgill Pavilion, two miles away, has seven rugby union pitches, while the university is a stakeholder in the River Tees Water Sports Centre offering waterskiing, rowing, kayaking, white water rafting and canoeing around the Tees barrage, four miles from campus.

Tuition fees

» Fees for UK students	£9,250
Foundation courses	£6,150
» Fees for International students 2021–22	£13,000
» For scholarship and bursary information see www.tees.ac.uk/sections/fulltime/fees.cfm	
» Graduate salary	£23,000

Student numbers

Undergraduates	10,155 (5,324)
Postgraduates	1,721 (1,467)
Applications/places	11,560/2,905
Applications per place	4
Overall offer rate	72.4%
International students – EU	1.6%
Non-EU	6.8%

Accommodation

University provided places: 1,001
Self-catered: £58–£115 per week
www.tees.ac.uk/sections/accommodation

Where do the students come from?

				Social inclusion ranking: 8	
State schools (non-grammar)	98.9%	First generation students	56.8%	Black attainment gap	-14.3%
Grammar schools	0.4%	Deprived areas	29.9%	Disabled	10.5%
Independent schools	0.6%	All ethnic minorities	13.2%	Mature (over 21)	44.1%

University of Wales, Trinity St David

For the third successive year, the University of Wales Trinity St David (UWTSD) holds a top-10 spot for student satisfaction with teaching quality — partly as a result of investment in teaching facilities. It has inched back towards the top 100 in our overall league table at the same time as moving up a place in our rankings for teaching quality.

The Advanced Manufacturing Academy (AMA), based in the department of engineering at the university's SA1 waterfront campus in Swansea, is equipped with the latest CNC (computer numerical control) machine tools, robotics and advanced manufacturing technologies, allowing students to graduate with the skills needed to operate at the cutting edge in engineering and manufacturing.

Equipping students with the emerging skills required by the manufacturing and engineering sector extends through UWTSD's course provision in these areas at both degree and degree-apprenticeship level. Degree apprentices in advanced manufacturing operations, mechanical and manufacturing engineering and manufacturing systems engineering are among 580 following earn-while-you-learn programmes on campus. There are plans to add another 120 degree apprenticeship places.

UWTSD's Construction Wales Innovation Centre, also based in Swansea, is home to construction course undergraduates, giving them access to laser measurement and surveying equipment. Like the AMA, it offers students the use of pioneering technologies, including virtual reality construction applications and the drones used in building environments. These facilities have also delivered bespoke training programmes to more than 600 construction companies in the past three years.

Automotive engineering students work as part of a race team involved in UK motorsport events, using an on-campus simulator for big data analysis that feeds back into the design of the vehicle for further on-track testing. The university has good links with Aston Martin, Jaguar Land Rover and McLaren Automotive.

These up-to-the-minute technologies all come packaged within one of the UK's oldest higher education institutions, created in its present form in 2010 when the University of Wales Lampeter and Trinity University College Carmarthen came together to form UWTSD. Swansea Metropolitan University joined UWTSD in 2013. Lampeter's original royal charter, as St David's College, dates from 1822, making it the third-oldest university in England and Wales after Cambridge and Oxford.

UWTSD remains split across three main sites — Swansea, Lampeter and Carmarthen. The university experience varies at each site, perhaps playing into a satisfaction score for the wider student experience ranking 44=,

Carmarthen Campus
College Road
Carmarthen SA31 3EP
0300 500 5054
admissions@uwtsd.ac.uk
www.uwtsd.ac.uk
www.tsdsu.co.uk
Open days: see website

The Times and The Sunday Times Rankings
Overall Ranking: =101 (last year: =102)

Teaching quality	84.9%	7
Student experience	79.3%	=44
Research quality	2.6%	116
Entry standards	135	=50
Graduate prospects	57.3%	=128
Good honours	73.5%	=82
Expected completion rate	77%	117
Student/staff ratio	16.3	=78
Services and facilities	£1,873	112

still excellent but below the stellar level of its teaching quality outcomes. Swansea offers the big-city university experience; Lampeter and Carmarthen something more intimate and niche.

Five new degrees focus on advocacy, cloud software development, mental health, professional policing and work with young people.

UWTSD was one of six Welsh universities to enter the Teaching Excellence Framework (TEF) in 2017. An initial bronze rating that year was upgraded to silver in 2019, with the panel praising "optimal" contact time, leading to outstanding personalised provision.

The TEF panel also drew attention to UWTSD's lower-than-expected performance on graduate prospects, below its benchmark. The latest Graduate Outcomes data suggests this remains an issue: just over 57% of graduates were in high-skilled employment or postgraduate study 15 months after the end of their course — in the bottom 10 in the country.

The £350m SA1 campus, shared by businesses, may provide a conducive environment for the university to turn around those statistics, encouraging close working relationships between students and industry. A number of courses have been co-created and delivered with industrial partners since the first phase of the campus opened in 2018.

There are about 10,000 students overall and the university performs strongly in our social inclusion ranking, beaten in Wales only by Wrexham Glyndŵr. There are a range of bursaries worth up to £1,000 a year, and students can access a hardship fund.

The Lampeter campus, in particular, makes a virtue of its small size by emphasising its friendly atmosphere and intimate teaching style. Based on an ancient castle and modelled on an Oxbridge college, it offers subjects including anthropology, archaeology, Chinese, classics and philosophy.

The Carmarthen site, established in 1848 to train teachers, offers programmes in the creative and performing arts, as well as a growing portfolio within the school of sport, health and outdoor education.

The original Swansea campus began as a college of art, but its automotive engineering courses — especially those focused on motorsport — are now its best known.

First-year undergraduates are guaranteed accommodation. Sports facilities are available at the Carmarthen, Lampeter and Swansea campuses, offering plenty of indoor and outdoor facilities. A 40ft climbing wall at Carmarthen is a good place to start before students consider venturing up the crags of Pembrokeshire.

Tuition fees

» Fees for UK students	£9,000
» Fees for International students 2020–21	£11,850
Foundation courses	£10,250
» For scholarship and bursary information see www.uwtsd.ac.uk/student-finance/	
» Graduate salary	£19,500

Student numbers

Undergraduates	7,784	(1,473)
Postgraduates	928	(950)
Applications/places		3,295/935
Applications per place		3.5
Overall offer rate		80.8%
International students – EU		2.1%
Non-EU		3.5%

Accommodation

University provided places: 794
Catered costs: £121 per week
Self-catered: £75–£140 per week
First years guaranteed accommodation
www.uwtsd.ac.uk/accommodation

Where do the students come from?

State schools (non-grammar)	97.8%	First generation students	40.5%	Black attainment gap	-34.4%
Grammar schools	0.3%	Deprived areas	15.4%	Disabled	17.2%
Independent schools	1.9%	All ethnic minorities	8.4%	Mature (over 21)	61%

Social inclusion ranking: =17

Ulster University

Ulster is knocking on the door of our top 50 after a third successive rise in our rankings, at the same time as its city centre campus in Belfast continues to develop apace. The £263m project is one of the largest single capital developments in higher education in Europe. It will see many courses transfer from Jordanstown, presently the largest of Ulster University's four campuses, seven miles north of Belfast, and is considered central to the city's long-term regeneration.

The new campus in Belfast's Cathedral Quarter, where art and design, architecture, hospitality, event management, photography and digital animation courses are already based, will have room for students taking courses in business and management, the built environment, computing and engineering, health and sport sciences, and social sciences, who will relocate from Jordanstown.

The university is working hard to improve the student experience across all campuses after successive falls in student satisfaction, measured across the past two National Student Surveys, which have sent Ulster's ranking for satisfaction with teaching quality and the wider student experience plummeting from 30= and 21= respectively to 68 and 50.

Experiential as well as structural improvements have been a focus. Central to this, has been the appointment of ResLife co-ordinators to help students in halls of residence by offering a range of activities and events to help build communities and support wellbeing, as well as to assist with the moving-in process. The university was shortlisted for the best application experience and best moving-in experience in the 2020 National Student Housing Survey.

On the Magee campus, in Derry, the library has been refurbished with new social and collaborative learning spaces, group study pods and digital information hubs, dovetailing with the recently-opened teaching block.

A Spatial Computing and Neurotechnology Innovation (Scani) hub opened on the Magee campus in January to enable research and education in the next generation of human/computer and human/machine interaction for able-bodied and physically impaired people. The centre uses cutting-edge technology to determine the brain and body's response to stress, fatigue, achievement, awareness, error and threats in simulated virtual environments.

Northern Ireland's emergence as a leading film and television centre has inspired many students, who gain insight into the industry at a £6.5m media centre opened three years ago at Coleraine. It has a BBC television studio at its heart, with a multimedia newsroom and editing suites. The Centre for Molecular Biosciences, at Coleraine, produced the university's most highly-rated work in the 2014 Research Excellence Framework. More than 70% of Ulster's

Cromore Road
Coleraine BT52 18A
028 9036 6565
study@ulster.ac.uk
www.ulster.ac.uk
http://uusu.org
Open days: see website

The Times and The Sunday Times Rankings
Overall Ranking: =51 (last year: =58)

Teaching quality	79.6%	68
Student experience	78.9%	50
Research quality	31.8%	=37
Entry standards	128	=60
Graduate prospects	76.6%	50
Good honours	78.6%	51
Expected completion rate	80.3%	=97
Student/staff ratio	18.1	=111
Services and facilities	£2,574	55

submission was considered world-leading or internationally excellent.

At Magee, the focus is on the creative and performing arts, nursing and social work, computing, business and management, and social sciences. Its expansion will be mainly in computer science, engineering and creative technologies.

In the long term, only the High Performance Sports Centre, which houses the Sports Institute of Northern Ireland, will remain in Jordanstown.

Four new BSc degrees in marine science, financial technology, planning, regeneration and development, and paramedic science are planned for 2021, as are new degree apprenticeships within the existing areas of provision. There are currently 200 students following nine programmes within accountancy and finance, built environment, business studies, civil engineering, computing, health science and management with plans to expand the number of degree apprentices by between 100 and 300.

Just under 77% of graduates were in high-skilled jobs or postgraduate study 15 months after leaving the university, placing it comfortably in the top half of the table on this measure.

This success is built on solid foundations. Ulster's degree programmes often feature work-based learning. More than 2,000 students annually undertake a professional practice placement or a placement year, and employers are actively engaged in the design and delivery of many courses. PwC sponsors a university Employability Award (Ulster Edge) which provides 1,000 students a year with recognition and accreditation for the extra- and co-curricular activities they undertake.

Almost all the undergraduates are from state schools, but the university does not feature in our social inclusion ranking because the education system in Northern Ireland is radically different from the rest of the UK, with selective grammar schools making up a significant proportion of state secondary schools. Our ranking measures recruitment from non-selective state schools, a figure that is unduly depressed at Ulster and Queen's, Belfast.

Ulster has an extensive outreach programme that encompasses summer schools, lectures, laboratory experiments, workshops and school visits. The university's Tutoring in Schools initiative places hundreds of student volunteers annually in primary, post-primary and special needs schools in disadvantaged areas.

A place in one of the university's 2,200 rooms is guaranteed for all first-year students who apply by the July deadline.

Tuition fees

»	Fees for Northern Irish students	£4,395
	RUK fees	£9,250
»	Fees for International students 2021–22	£14,910
»	For scholarship and bursary information see www.ulster.ac.uk/finance/student	
»	Graduate salary	£22,000

Student numbers

Undergraduates	14,817 (3,507)
Postgraduates	2,014 (4,191)
Applications/places	28,165/4,985
Applications per place	5.6
Overall offer rate	80.5%
International students – EU	6.5%
Non-EU	3.1

Accommodation

University provided places: 2,203
Self-catered: £83–£201 per week
First years guaranteed accommodation
www.ulster.ac.uk/accommodation

Where do the students come from?

State schools (non-grammar)	58.6%	Working-class homes	n/a	Black attainment gap	n/a
Grammar schools	41.3%	Deprived areas	10.7	Disabled	n/a
Independent schools	0.2%	All ethnic minorities	n/a	Mature (over 21)	23.4%

Social inclusion ranking: n/a

University College London

UCL may be a better bet than usual for UK students seeking a place at a top university in 2021 if, as expected, students from the European Union are put off by having to pay full international fees in a post-Brexit world. UCL has by far the largest number of European students in the UK — more than 5,000 in 2018–19 — as well as a much larger international contingent. Since it makes offers to little more than half of the UK students who apply, filling its places should not be a problem.

Winning a place is never easy, however. Applications have been running at record levels, increasing by more than 4,000 in the three years up to 2019. UCL students' entry scores are frequently in the top 10, despite considerable expansion since recruitment restrictions were lifted. Students are also expected to have a foreign language at grade C/5 at GCSE or the equivalent, which they can achieve during their degree if they have not taken a language at school. British sign language also meets this requirement.

The recent growth has prompted a huge building plan, spreading the college eastwards from its central London base. Under the Transforming UCL programme, £1.2bn will be spent over 10 years to improve its sites. In Dagenham, construction has begun on UCL's new Person-Environment Activity Research Laboratory, which will test how different designs for public spaces affect behavioural responses. Two new research facilities have been added at the Zayed Centre for Research into Rare Disease in Children and the Eastman Dental Institute, with a third on the way for neuroscience.

A new campus is also being built at the Queen Elizabeth Olympic Park in Stratford. The development, which will be part of the East Bank cultural and educational quarter, will involve all eight faculties in interdisciplinary teaching and research, with the first phase opening in 2022. Two new buildings will cater for 4,000 students and house laboratories and research space for robotics, smart cities, culture and conservation. There will also be accommodation and workspace for projects with schools, charities and local groups.

At the Bloomsbury headquarters, a new student centre opened in 2019, with 1,000 extra study seats and group collaboration areas. UCL's Institute of Education has also been refurbished. The university topped the QS world rankings for education and remains in the top 10 in the global list overall, although it has slipped two places this year.

Poor ratings in the National Student Survey have held the college back in our league table. Although there was marginal improvement in student satisfaction with teaching quality and the wider experience in

---

Gower Street
London WC1E 6BT
020 3370 1214
study@ucl.ac.uk
www.ucl.ac.uk
http://studentsunionucl.org
Open days: see website

The Times and *The Sunday Times* **Rankings**
Overall Ranking: 8 (last year: 9)

Teaching quality	75.4%	118
Student experience	75.7%	=99
Research quality	51%	5
Entry standards	175	11
Graduate prospects	86.1%	9
Good honours	88.9%	10
Expected completion rate	94.6%	=11
Student/staff ratio	10.4	2
Services and facilities	£2,823	33

both 2020 and 2019, UCL remains towards the bottom of the rankings on both measures. A strong top-10 performance in the latest survey of graduate prospects, however, has helped UCL to move up to eighth place overall in our academic ranking.

Every student at the university gets the opportunity to engage in research as part of the connected curriculum framework. With almost 30 Nobel prize-winners among its staff, researchers and graduates, UCL's strength in research is towering. Only Oxford received a higher research grant following the 2014 Research Excellence Framework assessment, when 90% of UCL's eligible academics made submissions and at least 80% of their work was rated world-leading or internationally excellent.

UCL had the most world-leading research in medicine and the biological sciences, the largest volume of research in science, technology, engineering and maths, and the biggest share of top grades in the social sciences. The medical school, with several associated teaching hospitals, is among the largest in Europe. UCL was a founding partner in the Francis Crick Institute, which undertakes leading research in health and disease.

Four new degrees were introduced in 2020 in architecture, pharmacy, professional policing and sociology. Two more, in global humanitarian studies and media, will take their first students in 2021.

UCL is comfortably the biggest of the University of London's colleges. It runs summer schools, outreach activities and campus-based programmes to try to make the intake more diverse, but the share of places won by independent school students remains among the highest in the UK, at more than a third.

A contextual offer scheme was launched in 2019. Applicants may be asked for two A-level grades lower than the standard UCL offer if they come from areas of low progression to higher education, less advantaged backgrounds or low-performing schools.

Close to the West End and with its own theatre and recreational facilities, UCL offers plenty of leisure options. More than 7,000 residential places are owned or endorsed by the college, enough to guarantee accommodation for new entrants who apply by the end of May. Indoor sports and fitness facilities are close at hand, but the main outdoor pitches are a (free) coach ride away in Hertfordshire.

Tuition fees

- » Fees for UK students   £9,250
- » Fees for International students 2021–22   £23,300–£34,100
      Medicine   £36,900
- » For scholarship and bursary information see
      www.ucl.ac.uk/students/fees-and-funding
- » Graduate salary   £30,000

Student numbers

Undergraduates	18,674	(1,329)
Postgraduates	15,329	(5,847)
Applications/places		54,890/5,950
Applications per place		9.2
Overall offer rate		52.3%
International students – EU		12.3%
Non-EU		35.4

Accommodation

University provided places: 7,149
Catered costs: £152–£252 per week
Self-catered: £99–£315 per week
First years guaranteed accommodation
www.ucl.ac.uk/accommodation

Where do the students come from?

State schools (non-grammar)	49.4%	First generation students	26.3%	Black attainment gap	-8.9%
Grammar schools	16.5%	Deprived areas	3.7%	Disabled	3.8%
Independent schools	34.1%	All ethnic minorities	50.9%	Mature (over 21)	6.8%

Social inclusion ranking: 110

University of Warwick

The University of Warwick has never been out of our top 10. Research-led since its foundation in 1965, the university's strength and reputation places it 62nd in the QS World University Rankings.

A £250m investment programme is under way at the leafy 750-acre campus. The latest development is an expansion and upgrade of the Warwick Arts Centre, which is due to be completed to coincide with Coventry's year as City of Culture 2021. (Despite its name, the university sits on the edge of Coventry.)

Warwick's renown for successful collaborations with business is well-deserved. The £150m National Automotive Innovation Centre (NAIC), which opened in 2020, is a shining example. Featuring 33,000 square metres of cutting-edge workshops, laboratories, virtual engineering suites and advanced powertrain facilities, it is a partnership between the Warwick Manufacturing Group (part of the university), the government and local manufacturers Jaguar Land Rover and Tata Motors. One of Europe's largest automotive research and development facilities, the NAIC's 1,000-plus designers, engineers and researchers are working on future-facing projects such as carbon emissions reduction and driverless technology.

More than 85% of Warwick's graduates were in high-skilled jobs or postgraduate study within 15 months of completing their degrees, the latest figures showed, earning it a ranking just outside the UK top 10 for our graduate prospects measure. It is also among the top three recruiting grounds for the leading graduate employers in the most recent *Times* Top 100 Graduate Employers survey.

In the government's 2017 Teaching Excellence Framework (TEF), though, Warwick was restricted to silver, in spite of consistent high achievement by its students and staff, excellent completion and employment rates and exceptional employer feedback — criteria suitable for a gold award.

The TEF panel was impressed by the culture of research-stimulated learning that challenged students, but said Warwick had missed its benchmarks for satisfaction and continuation rates among some groups of students. It is in our top 10 for completion rates, however, with just 4.4% of students dropping out and in line with the low proportion projected.

Warwick is continuing to grow its portfolio of degree apprenticeships, which currently spans five academic departments and includes civil engineering, healthcare science practitioner and social work. New programmes are being introduced in the roles of career consultant, electro-mechanical engineer, advanced clinical practitioner (with and without clinical care), electrical/electronic technical support engineer and control/technical support engineer.

Almost 90% of the work submitted for

Admissions Office
University House
Coventry CV4 8UW
024 7652 3723
ugadmissions@warwick.ac.uk
www.warwick.ac.uk
www.warwicksu.com
Open days: see website

The Times and The Sunday Times **Rankings**

Overall Ranking: =10 (last year: 10)

Teaching quality	78.6%	=80
Student experience	77.9%	=68
Research quality	44.6%	8
Entry standards	171	13
Graduate prospects	85.2%	11
Good honours	86.7%	=12
Expected completion rate	94.9%	10
Student/staff ratio	13.8	24
Services and facilities	£2,580	54

the 2014 Research Excellence Framework was rated as world-leading or internationally excellent, confirming Warwick's place among the top eight universities for research. English and computer science produced the best results, and Warwick ranked in the UK's top 10 in 14 different subject areas.

Many miles from its single site campus, Warwick also has a library and teaching rooms in Venice, used by third-year history students who spend the autumn term there. The university's large business school has a London base in the Shard, which delivers part-time programmes. Undergraduates taking global sustainable development courses can spend part of their second year at Monash University — either in Melbourne, in Australia, or Kuala Lumpur, in Malaysia.

The Warwick Scholars programme for widening participation engages with post-16 students from the region and supports them to apply successfully to Warwick and do well once there. Extensive bursary and scholarship provision includes the Warwick Bursary of up to £3,000 for students from households with incomes below £35,000. Royal Television Society scholarships are for undergraduates from lower income backgrounds who intend to pursue television careers.

The Warwick Business School Undergraduate Scholarship Programme helps students from under-represented groups with £2,000 per academic year plus guidance

from tutors and a tailored programme of networking events. Nearly four in 10 students come from ethnic minority backgrounds and almost a third have parents who did not go to university. Independent and grammar school admissions account for around 40% of the intake and Warwick ranks 102nd in our social inclusion index.

A £49m sports and wellness hub opened in April 2019, bringing a 230-station gym, a 25m swimming pool, fitness studios, bouldering and climbing walls, a sports hall, squash courts and 4G outdoor pitches.

The first 383 bedrooms at the new Cryfield Village of townhouses and flats on campus have opened to students. They are part of a £62m investment in student accommodation that will see 830 spaces added. Students usually live on campus in their first year and Warwick has well over 7,000 residential places, enough to guarantee one to all who apply by the deadline. The towns of Leamington Spa, Kenilworth and the Earlsdon area of Coventry are the Warwick student hubs, post-halls.

Tuition fees

- » Fees for UK students £9,250
  Foundation courses £6,750
- » Fees for International students 2021–22 £21,220–£27,060
  Medicine £43,170 (clinical years)
- » For scholarship and bursary information see
  www.warwick.ac.uk/study/undergraduate/studentfunding/
- » Graduate salary £29,000

Student numbers

Undergraduates	**15,909**	**(1,149)**
Postgraduates	**6,301**	**(2,719)**
Applications/places		**41,555/5,035**
Applications per place		**8.3**
Overall offer rate		**70.9%**
International students – EU		**10.3%**
Non-EU		**26.4**

Accommodation

University provided places: 8,959
Self-catered: £77–£198 per week
First years guaranteed accommodation
www.warwick.ac.uk/services/accommodation/

Where do the students come from?

State schools (non-grammar)	59.6%	First generation students	31.5%	Black attainment gap	-14.1%
Grammar schools	18.4%	Deprived areas	4.9%	Disabled	5.4%
Independent schools	22%	All ethnic minorities	38.3%	Mature (over 21)	9.9%

Social inclusion ranking: 102

University of West London

 Students' assessment of their time at the University of West London (UWL) translated into stellar scores in the latest National Student Survey. Not only does UWL have the most satisfied students of any London university, it ranks in the top five of all UK institutions for both the wider undergraduate experience and teaching quality. It is a deserving winner of our University of the Year for Student Experience award.

Anyone entering the Ealing campus cannot miss the student support services building, a sign of how seriously UWL takes supporting its students and a convenient centre for them to use. The Street is its dedicated area for accessing advice from trained professionals in services that include academic support, careers, counselling, health and wellbeing, funding and accommodation.

UWL has a student engagement team that tracks attendance and troubleshoots any issues that may be causing students to struggle. The team provides mentoring and extra study help, too. Staff have been trained in mental-health first aid and thanks to UWL's mental health strategy, which was developed with the students' union, workshops on topics such as "how to look after your mate" are at the heart of its wellbeing strategy.

More than £150m has been invested in student facilities over the past few years. The modern library has around 250 computers, comfy seating and spacious study areas, and the students' union has been revamped.

A number of work-based simulations include a "simbulance" for trainee paramedics, a mock courtroom, replica hospital wards and a radio station. UWL's Boeing 737 flight simulator is said to be as close to flying the real deal as possible, and was recently upgraded with commercial airline software and a flight management system.

An on-campus sports centre with two gyms, two large fitness studios and plenty of changing-room space was opened in February 2020 by the Paralympian Ade Adepitan. Rami Ranger House, named after its businessman benefactor, is the focal point for international and postgraduate students.

At UWL's Brentford campus, the landmark Paragon Building is the headquarters of one of the largest healthcare faculties in Britain, with top ratings for nursing and midwifery. There is also an outpost in Reading, which houses the Berkshire Institute of Health, and has nursing and midwifery students.

UWL achieved silver in the government's Teaching Excellence Framework (TEF). The panel complimented the university on its investment in high-quality physical and digital resources, with students fully involved in the design of the new facilities. It also

St Mary's Road
Ealing
London W5 5RF
0208 231 2220
undergraduate.admissions@uwl.ac.uk
www.uwl.ac.uk
www.uwlsu.com
Open days: see website

The Times and The Sunday Times Rankings
Overall Ranking: =60 (last year: 52)

Teaching quality	86.3%	5
Student experience	85.2%	3
Research quality	1.6%	122
Entry standards	123	=76
Graduate prospects	68%	=101
Good honours	75.4%	=68
Expected completion rate	77.8%	115
Student/staff ratio	15.2	=58
Services and facilities	£2,483	=63

commented favourably on peer mentoring and targeted financial support programmes to improve the engagement of those most at risk of dropping out.

The university is building a reputation for using industry connections to boost graduate prospects, and makes the most of being close to the capital's businesses. Students can undertake work experience on every course.

The number of undergraduates starting courses was up by 16% in 2019 and applications for 2020 were up by 7%. Numbers have swelled with the new School of Biomedical Science's first intake of students on degrees in biomedical science, human nutrition and pharmacology. UWL has also expanded its capacity on nursing and midwifery courses. In partnership with an airline training academy UWL is delivering its new aviation with commercial pilot licence degree at Gloucestershire airport.

UWL's work in widening access to higher education for under-represented groups was recognised by the Queen when Professor Peter John, the vice-chancellor, was awarded a CBE for services to higher education. This recognised the transformative change that has made UWL a flagship university for the benefits of widening participation, social inclusion and meritocracy.

Almost two-thirds of UWL students, 62%, are from households where the income is less than £25,000, and 53% are the first in their family to study at higher education level. Bursaries and part-time fee waivers help financially.

UWL's business school has reduced its ethnic minority attainment gap to a historic low of 0.8% through its Fulfilment Through Challenge programme, which aims to break down barriers to social mobility by raising student confidence and aspirations, and making the transition from university to work seamless for those from less privileged backgrounds. The number of UWL associate professors and professors from black, Asian and minority ethnic (BAME) backgrounds has increased.

Research centres have been established in subject areas aligned to courses that focus on societal issues. The National Centre for Gang Research is a UK first and the Geller Institute of Ageing and Memory is looking into new technologies, effective psychosocial care and multisensory approaches to help those with dementia.

UK and international first-years are guaranteed a place within the 959 residential spaces that UWL manages. Students at Ealing and Brentford are Tube rides away from all that London has to offer.

Tuition fees

» Fees for UK students	£9,250
» Fees for International students 2020–21	£12,500
» For scholarship and bursary information see www.uwl.ac.uk/courses/undergraduate/fees-and-funding	
» Graduate salary	£24,000

Student numbers

Undergraduates	7,957	(1,100)
Postgraduates	911	(1,089)
Applications/places		12,625/1,765
Applications per place		7.2
Overall offer rate		61.6%
International students – EU		11.2%
Non-EU		6.4%

Accommodation

University provided places: 959
Catered costs: £196–£276
Self-catered: £179–£259 per week
www.uwl.ac.uk/student-life/accommodation

Where do the students come from?

				Social inclusion ranking: 22	
State schools (non-grammar)	95.3%	First generation students	52.5%	Black attainment gap	-20%
Grammar schools	2.3%	Deprived areas	10.1%	Disabled	7.4%
Independent schools	2.4%	All ethnic minorities	68.1%	Mature (over 21)	58.2%

University of the West of England Bristol

Students at UWE Bristol are among the most satisfied with their university life. Our analysis of the most recent National Student Survey places the university sixth for satisfaction with the wider undergraduate experience and 13th for students' assessment of teaching quality.

Plenty of investment in facilities is under way to support their learning, teaching and living, as part of a £300m spend on capital developments in recent years. A new engineering building on the Frenchay campus has been built for hands-on learning. It has engine test cells, wind tunnels and collaborative learning spaces.

The Foundry Technology Affinity Space was developed with the Institute of Coding. Formerly a disused students' union bar at Frenchay, it launched in 2019 as a technology and innovation hub with co-working zones and a boardroom among its resources. A venue for outreach digital events across cyber-security, computer science and creative technologies, it has been designed to widen participation in coding and digital skills. It also allows employers to set live briefs for UWE students. Elsewhere on campus, the Lab Zone of new and upgraded science laboratories benefited from a £7m redevelopment.

At the City campus in Bower Ashton, new design studios have been added as part of a £37m investment in facilities for creative industries. Featuring flexible workshops and collaborative learning areas, they also house the Fabrication Centre and the Centre for Fine Print Research.

The £5m optometry and clinical skills centre on the Glenside campus is housed in a grade II listed former NHS laundry. It is now the base for trainee paramedics, occupational therapy students, nurses and undergraduates on the optometry programme.

The university received a gold rating in the government's Teaching Excellence Framework (TEF). The panel noted the above-benchmark levels of student satisfaction with academic support and rates of progression to high-skilled employment. TEF assessors also commended UWE Bristol's outstanding learning resources at institutional and subject-specific levels, the systematic embedding of enterprise and entrepreneurship throughout curricula, and successful approaches to personalised learning.

UWE has one of the largest internship programmes, and its graduates can apply to the Centre for Graduate Enterprise for help to set up a business in an incubator hub on the Frenchay campus. There are 500 employability bursaries of £1,000 set aside for students who take part in a sandwich placement or year abroad, a summer internship with an employer or as a researcher, or short

Frenchay Campus
Coldharbour Lane
Bristol BS16 1QY
0117 328 3333
admissions@uwe.ac.uk
www.uwe.ac.uk
www.thestudentsunion.co.uk
Open days: see website

The Times and The Sunday Times Rankings
Overall Ranking: 58 (last year: =58)

Teaching quality	83.9%	13
Student experience	83%	6
Research quality	8.8%	69
Entry standards	121	=84
Graduate prospects	76.8%	48
Good honours	74.5%	73
Expected completion rate	82.5%	=80
Student/staff ratio	15.4	62
Services and facilities	£1,897	110

international projects. More than 150 of UWE's degrees come with professional accreditation from industry bodies and 76% of graduates were in high-skilled jobs or postgraduate study within 15 months of finishing their degrees, a top-50 result.

New degrees in media communications and media production launched in September 2020. The university also introduced more top-up courses for students with lower-level qualifications to build up to full degrees in business and human resource management, business and events management, marketing and international business communication.

One of the university's ambitions is to drive forward growth in apprenticeship provision and it works with local councils to close regional skills gaps. It says that by September 2021 the numbers on apprenticeship courses could double from the 1,000 currently on 16 programmes, thanks to the addition of courses for paramedics and in construction site management, environmental health practice and occupational therapy.

After 12 student suicides in eight years from 2010 to 2018, a mental health strategy provides a framework for UWE's wellbeing initiatives. At the Frenchay campus a student centre is open 24/7 offering an alcohol-free hangout with sofas and bean bags where students can host film nights, have society meetings or just chill out. All students have academic tutors and emotional resilience training is embedded into courses. A wellbeing service offers broad support and there is a round-the-clock crisis text helpline and out-of-hours online counselling platform.

A UWE bursary of £500 a year goes to students from households with incomes up to £25,000. There are many more bursary schemes and around a third of new students qualify for some form of financial assistance.

The Frenchay campus has fitness suites next to student residences as well as a sports hall, indoor climbing wall, squash courts and an all-weather pitch. Sports teams including soccer, American football and rugby are based at the recently-opened £4.5m Hillside Gardens facility a few miles away, which has artificial and grass pitches and undercover spectator seating.

All first-years who apply by June 8 are guaranteed one of UWE Bristol's 5,580 residential spaces. Characterful Bristol has something for everyone in its different neighbourhoods, from the indie pubs and shops of Gloucester Road to the modern waterside developments and the kerb appeal of Clifton. Lots of graduates end up never leaving the city.

Tuition fees

» Fees for UK students	£9,250
» Fees for International students 2020–21	£13,250–£15,750
» For scholarship and bursary information see www1.uwe.ac.uk/courses/fees	
» Graduate salary	£24,000

Student numbers

Undergraduates	19,786 (2,144)
Postgraduates	2,272 (5,355)
Applications/places	31,330/6,075
Applications per place	5.2
Overall offer rate	72.8%
International students – EU	3.5%
Non-EU	9.8

Accommodation

University provided places: 5,580
Self-catered: £94–£214 per week
First years guaranteed accommodation
www.uwe.ac.uk/life/accommodation

Where do the students come from?

State schools (non-grammar)	90.4%	First generation students	43.1%	
Grammar schools	3.7%	Deprived areas	14.9%	
Independent schools	6%	All ethnic minorities	19.3%	

Social inclusion ranking: 68

Black attainment gap	-26.6%
Disabled	9.3%
Mature (over 21)	24%

University of the West of Scotland

The reach of the University of the West of Scotland (UWS) extends much further than the border with England. Its newly expanded London campus opened in 2020 next to the Docklands area in the east of the city, bringing students a light-filled atrium and technology-rich study and breakout spaces.

Of the university's four Scottish campuses, the £110m Lanarkshire site is the most eye-catching modern addition. Located in the highly-successful Hamilton International Technology Park, the award-winning campus has brought the latest in learning and teaching facilities and is powered by 100% renewable energy sources.

Courses in health, computing and some business and social science subjects are based at the Lanarkshire campus, which has space for 4,000 students and features simulations of hospital wards and of community and primary care settings.

Paisley, which remains UWS headquarters, has benefited from a £30m spend on student facilities and more accommodation. At the Ayr site, £81m has gone into modern facilities for 2,300 students. The campus has a prize-winning library shared with Scotland's Rural College.

The smallest campus, Dumfries, has 550 UWS students who join others from the University of Glasgow and Dumfries and Galloway College on the 85-acre parkland site on the Crichton estate, half an hour from the town centre.

Between them the campuses form one of the largest modern universities in Scotland with more than 16,000 students. UWS was founded in 2007 from the merger of Paisley University and Bell College, in Hamilton — serving two areas of low participation in higher education. The university has stayed true to its roots and succeeds at widening participation in higher education where others fail.

After coming top in 2019, UWS now ranks second among the most socially inclusive universities in Scotland. More than a quarter of students, the highest proportion at any Scottish university, are from areas deemed the poorest by the Scottish Index of Multiple Deprivation. Around half its students are 21 or older when they enrol and a similar number have parents who did not go to university.

The rates of student satisfaction with the wider undergraduate experience have gone up more than 10 places in our analysis of the 2020 National Student Survey, bringing UWS inside the top 60. For students' assessment of the teaching quality, the university now ranks in the UK top 40, after a three-place rise.

These results are not enough to prevent UWS's decline of eight places in our overall league table. Scores were hampered by its

Paisley Campus
Paisley PA1 2BE
0800 027 1000; +44 141 849 4101 (international)
ask@uws.ac.uk
www.uws.ac.uk
www.sauws.org.uk
Open days: see website

The Times and The Sunday Times **Rankings**
Overall Ranking: 116 (last year: 108)

Teaching quality	81.6%	=38
Student experience	78.4%	=58
Research quality	4.3%	=98
Entry standards	130	=56
Graduate prospects	72%	=75
Good honours	70.9%	102
Expected completion rate	78.5%	=106
Student/staff ratio	22.6	130
Services and facilities	£2,389	71

completion rates — the fifth of students dropping out is far higher than the benchmark level of 12.8% based on the intake's academic and social backgrounds. The new measure of graduate prospects, published for the first time this summer, also did UWS no favours, ranking the institution in the middle reaches of the table when it had previously been much closer to the top.

Employability is a key focus of UWS, however. If their degree does not already have work placements built in — which many, such as nursing, teaching and social work, do — students can make use of the university placement scheme to make one happen. The EU Erasmus+ programme enables students to study or work with partners in 32 countries across Europe, at the same time as completing their UWS courses.

A new degree in paramedic science joined the curriculum in September, and one in criminal justice and forensic science will welcome its first students at the start of the 2021–22 academic year. There are 172 learners on the five graduate apprenticeship programmes offered by UWS in IT software development, engineering design and manufacture, civil engineering, business management and early learning and childcare.

The School of Health, Nursing and Midwifery, the largest in Scotland, produced the university's best results in the 2014 Research Excellence Framework.

In a collaboration with the International Space School Education Trust to encourage young people into Stem (science, technology, engineering and maths) subjects, UWS invited local school pupils to design an experiment that could be carried out in space, with the help of Nasa astronauts on the International Space Station. Academics from UWS have also been testing their research in space.

The university has just 696 residential places, which are allocated based on distance from campus on a first-come, first-served basis. The high proportion of students who live at home means that although there is no accommodation guarantee, it has been possible to allocate a space to all first-years who want to live in.

There are students' union social venues across the three main campuses and also free gym memberships for all students to use UWS-operated sports facilities across the Ayr, Lanarkshire and Paisley sites. The university fields 15 teams in sports including swimming, hockey, judo and football.

Tuition fees

- » Fees for Scottish students £0–£1,820
  RUK fees £9,250 (capped at £27,750 for 4-year courses)
- » Fees for International students 2020–21 £13,000–£18,500
- » For scholarship and bursary information see www.uws.ac.uk/money-fees-funding/
- » Graduate salary £24,000

Student numbers

Undergraduates	12,376 (1,841)
Postgraduates	1,667 (1,141)
Applications/places	19,630/3,900
Applications per place	5
Overall offer rate	57%
International students – EU	3.7%
Non-EU	8%

Accommodation

University provided places: 696
Self-catered: £95–£160 per week
www.uws.ac.uk/university-life/accommodation

Where do the students come from?

State schools (non-grammar)	98.7%	First generation students	47.1%	Black attainment gap	-46.2%
Grammar schools	0.2%	Deprived areas	28.2%	Disabled	1.5%
Independent schools	1.1%	All ethnic minorities	8.3%	Mature (over 21)	48.5%

Social inclusion ranking (Scotland): 2

University of Westminster

The University of Westminster's Harrow campus in northwest London houses the media, arts and design faculty — its best-known feature, where the Emerging Media Space provides open access for students to experiment with cutting-edge technology such as 3D scanning and printing, robotics, virtual reality and drone imaging. The equipment can be used on audio synthesis projects, sound and video processing, making 3D models and installations using sensors.

There are more digital advances at the Marylebone campus near Regent's Park. Here the fabrication lab has added a 3D print farm, new facilities for virtual, augmented and mixed reality, and projection mapping.

Regent Street is where Westminster was founded as the UK's first polytechnic in 1838 and it is still the university's headquarters. At the separate Cavendish campus nearby, a stone's throw from Oxford Circus, courses include biological and biomedical sciences, engineering and psychology.

Options to study abroad are built into a broad range of degrees and taken at partner institutions across Europe, Asia, the Americas and Australasia. There is an international air to the campuses in London, too. Westminster had nearly 2,300 EU students in 2017-18, close to 20% of the undergraduate population, and an even higher proportion from outside the EU.

Westminster's longstanding commitment to widening participation has translated to a top-25 rank in our social inclusion table, in contrast to its academic ranking – where it has slipped into the bottom 10. Two-thirds of undergraduates come from ethnic minorities and more than half are the first in their family to go to university.

The university has increased and diversified its outreach activities, and prospective students from areas with a poor record in higher education are now invited to on-campus taster sessions led by Westminster academics. The outreach team also helps students with their personal statements.

Preference is given to students from under-represented groups in the allocation of 50 Great Start scholarships worth £1,500 a year to those from households with incomes below £35,000. Ten access scholarships of £3,000 a year are awarded to students with a documented disability, financial need and who show academic excellence. A Living Expenses Support Scheme helps with costs such as rent, travel and childcare.

Westminster was given a bronze rating in the Teaching Excellence Framework. The awarding panel praised the consistent support for students at risk of dropping out and acknowledged a strategic approach and commitment to improving employment and entrepreneurship.

According to the latest figures, only 64% of graduates were in high-skilled jobs or postgraduate study within 15 months of finishing their degrees, which places

309 Regent Street
London W1B 2HW
020 7911 5000
UGAdmissions@westminster.ac.uk
www.westminster.ac.uk
www.uwsu.com
Open days: see website

The Times and The Sunday Times **Rankings**

Overall Ranking: 126 (last year: 119)

Teaching quality	76.8%	=104
Student experience	76%	96
Research quality	9.8%	59
Entry standards	119	=92
Graduate prospects	63.9%	116
Good honours	66.2%	121
Expected completion rate	82.4%	82
Student/staff ratio	20.9	126
Services and facilities	£1,764	118

Westminster in the lower reaches of our graduate prospects measure.

As the world of work changes, so too do Westminster's careers programmes. The Creative Enterprise Centre supports students and recent graduates whose aspirations include becoming entrepreneurs, freelancers and designers. It has engaged with more than 3,000 students in two years via workshops, mentoring, one-to-one business advice, paid freelance work, live briefs and business competitions.

Employing Humanities, a new programme of work-based and professional learning integrated across humanities courses, focuses on careers in the field. Criminology and sociology students can gain practical and academic skills in prison education via the prison-university partnerships at Westminster, which were recently awarded funding from the Quintin Hogg Trust.

September 2020 brought new degrees in English language and global communications, fashion business management, psychology and criminology, medical sciences, business management, data science and analytics and smart computer systems. Foundation years have been added to several property and construction courses.

The curriculum for the computer science degree has been revamped, bringing in new study areas such as artificial intelligence, machine learning, robotics, and the Internet of Things. An update to the history degree from 2021 will shift the focus to contemporary histories and social change.

Westminster plans to expand its degree apprenticeship offering from the two current programmes in healthcare science practice and chartered surveying. The number on courses is expected to grow from 150 to more than 500 by September 2021.

The university held its position among the leading institutions for communication and media studies in the 2014 Research Excellence Framework, when almost two-thirds of the work submitted was judged to be world-leading or excellent. There were even better results in art and design, and a good performance in English. Although less than 30% of the eligible staff entered the exercise, the university is in our top 60 for research, comfortably its best position among the nine measures in our league table.

There are 1,514 residential places in Wembley, Harrow, Hoxton and Marylebone but only students with disabilities are guaranteed accommodation. Sports facilities include gyms at the Regent Street and Harrow campuses. Best of all is the 45-acre sports ground overlooking the River Thames in Chiswick, also home to the university's boathouse.

Tuition fees

» Fees for UK students	£9,250
» Fees for International students 2021–22	£14,400
» For scholarship and bursary information see www.westminster.ac.uk/study/fees-and-funding/	
» Graduate salary	£23,000

Student numbers

Undergraduates	12,631 (2,146)
Postgraduates	2,290 (1,816)
Applications/places	26,670/3,910
Applications per place	6.8
Overall offer rate	79.6%
International students – EU	11.7%
Non-EU	22.4

Accommodation

University provided places: 1,514
Self-catered: £181–£279 per week
www.westminster.ac.uk/study/accommodation

Where do the students come from?

				Social inclusion ranking: 23	
State schools (non-grammar)	93.5%	First generation students	55.3%	Black attainment gap	-25%
Grammar schools	2%	Deprived areas	4.1%	Disabled	5.2%
Independent schools	4.5%	All ethnic minorities	69.8%	Mature (over 21)	21.2%

University of Winchester

A drum-shaped auditorium stands out at Winchester's new West Downs development. With seating for 250, it is part of a £50m home for Winchester's Digital Futures computer and digital-related degrees when it opens in early 2021. It will also host the university's business and management programmes and its new facilities will include a library, social learning and teaching spaces, an art gallery, café, food hall and a zero-waste shop.

Green finance rubberstamps the development's eco credentials, via funding from Europe's leading sustainable bank, Triodos. The building, with its rainwater harvesting and green roof, will form a gateway into the city and will encourage wellbeing via a contemplation space, healthy food options, a courtyard garden and landscaped areas.

The university campus is split into four quarters. Most of student life centres on the main King Alfred quarter on a wooded hillside overlooking the cathedral city, a 10-minute walk away. It houses faculty buildings where lectures and seminars take place, along with the performing arts studios and multimedia centre. There is also the Medecroft quarter and Bar End, where the sports facilities are found.

The investment in teaching and learning resources with emphasis on student wellbeing, should help lift student satisfaction scores.

Having historically been a strength for the university, rates of satisfaction with the wider undergraduate experience and with teaching quality saw a downturn for the second year running in the latest National Student Survey.

In its new 10-year Strategic Vision 2030, Winchester has outlined its intention to be a beacon for academic excellence, sustainability and social justice, in alignment with the UN's Sustainable Development Goals (SDGs). Helping to deliver on its ambitions, Winchester recently joined the UN Sustainable Development Solutions Network (SDSN), which tackles global challenges including climate change.

Professor Joy Carter, the vice-chancellor, has been appointed to the council of the Climate Commission for UK Higher and Further Education Leaders, which is galvanising the sector into action. A university-wide pledge to eliminate all unnecessary single-use plastics had a deadline of December 2020.

Winchester has a silver rating in the Teaching Excellence Framework. The panel was impressed by its "appropriate" contact hours, tutorials and buddy schemes that produce personalised learning and high levels of commitment from students. Most are stretched sufficiently to make progress, and acquire the knowledge, skills and understanding valued by employers, assessors added. However, Winchester is in the bottom 25 on our graduate prospects measure, with only 66.5% in high-

---

Sparkford Road
Winchester SO22 4NR
01962 827 234
admissions@winchester.ac.uk
www.winchester.ac.uk
www.winchesterstudents.co.uk
Open days: see website

Edinburgh
Belfast
Cardiff London
WINCHESTER

The Times and The Sunday Times **Rankings**
Overall Ranking: 96 (last year: =98)

Teaching quality	79.8%	=64
Student experience	75.9%	97
Research quality	5.8%	=83
Entry standards	110	=113
Graduate prospects	66.5%	=109
Good honours	74.3%	75
Expected completion rate	84.2%	=64
Student/staff ratio	16.5	=80
Services and facilities	£1,810	115

skilled jobs or postgraduate study within 15 months of finishing their degree.

First established as a Church of England foundation for teacher training, Winchester was known as King Alfred College until 2004. The university has been broadening its curriculum, with 50 new programmes added in two years. New degrees in commercial music, forensic science and nutrition and dietetics will welcome their first students in 2021. They follow the launch of 17 degrees in September 2020, including acting, music journalism, nursing (child) and software engineering.

Winchester is also expanding its range of degree apprenticeships and adding programmes in disability registered nursing and in data science in 2020–21. These join a range of digital and technology solutions specialisms, business management, senior leadership and social care.

The university ranks 59= in our social inclusion ranking, with almost half the students from homes where parents did not go to university. Winchester's work to widen participation is extensive.

About 40% of 2020's admissions received some sort of financial assistance, a proportion the university expects will be higher in 2021 due to the economic effects of Covid-19. A broad range of scholarships and bursaries includes the Helena Kennedy Foundation bursary, worth £1,500, which supports students from further education and sixth-form colleges and adult education centres who have overcome significant obstacles — either personal or financial — to get to university.

Winchester held its own in the 2014 Research Excellence Framework. Almost 45% of its work was considered world-leading or internationally excellent and its best results were recorded for communications and history.

The two-floor university gym is at the heart of the £12m Burma Road student village and offers daily classes at no extra charge to members. On campus there is also a fitness studio, a sports hall and a multi-use games area. The Winchester Sports Stadium nearby is open to the public as well as students and has an athletics track and a floodlit all-weather pitch.

With 1,973 residential spaces, the university guarantees accommodation to all first-years. The city of Winchester won 2016's Best Place to Live award in *The Sunday Times*, thanks in part to its low crime rates and local attractions. For student nights out, think charming pubs rather than all-night clubbing. Festivals of food and culture pepper the city's calendar and London is an hour away by train.

Tuition fees

» Fees for UK students   £9,250
» Fees for International students 2021–22   £13,800
» For scholarship and bursary information see www.winchester.ac.uk/accommodation-and-winchester-life/students-and-money/
» Graduate salary   £22,000

Student numbers

Undergraduates	**6,104**	**(352)**
Postgraduates	**566**	**(746)**
Applications/places		**10,080/2,380**
Applications per place		**4.2**
Overall offer rate		**87.1%**
International students – EU		**1.6%**
Non-EU		**4.1%**

Accommodation

University provided places: 1,973
Catered costs: £167–£170 per week
Self-catered: £88–£154 per week
First years guaranteed accommodation
www.winchester.ac.uk/accommodation-and-winchester-life/accommodation

Where do the students come from?

State schools (non-grammar)	92.2%	First generation students	49.8%	Black attainment gap	-31.9%
Grammar schools	3.9%	Deprived areas	14.4%	Disabled	13.1%
Independent schools	3.8%	All ethnic minorities	12.9%	Mature (over 21)	13.1%

Social inclusion ranking: =59

University of Wolverhampton

The University of Wolverhampton's ambitious plans to create the £100m architecture and built environment Springfield super-campus are bearing fruit. Work has completed on the £28m School of Architecture and Built Environment at the campus, which has space for nearly 1,100 existing students and room to grow to 1,600. Courses in architecture, civil engineering and quantity surveying, as well as facilities management, housing and commercial will be taught at the new school.

Developed on the site of a former brewery, there are design studios and multi-disciplinary workshops along with a lecture theatre, specialist teaching and social learning spaces, offices and a café. The campus is also home to the West Midlands University Technical College and the Elite Centre for Manufacturing Skills.

In another skills-boosting development for the Midlands, a new £9m Centre for Cyber Security is under construction in the cathedral city of Hereford, 45 miles south of Wolverhampton. A trailblazing project shared between the university and Hereford city council, the new centre aims to tap into the booming cyber-security sector. It is being built at Skylon Park in Hereford Enterprise Zone.

The original city centre site in Wolverhampton is one of the university's three main campuses. A second in Walsall is the base for sport, performing arts, health and education. The third is a purpose-built campus in Telford, Shropshire, which focuses on business and engineering.

Wolverhampton was awarded silver in the Teaching Excellence Framework in 2018, upgraded from bronze. The university still missed its benchmarks for student satisfaction and progression to high-skilled employment, but the panel praised the commitment to enhancing students' learning experience, as well as the involvement of employers in the development and review of courses. It was also impressed by Wolverhampton's mental health provision and support systems.

The university is in the top half of UK institutions for student satisfaction with teaching quality according to our analysis of the 2020 National Student Survey, however, and not far outside the top half for satisfaction with the wider undergraduate experience.

Less impressive is Wolverhampton's record on graduate prospects, which is in our bottom 20. The latest figures showed 66% of graduates were in high-skilled jobs or postgraduate study within 15 months of finishing their course. Meanwhile, more than one in five students (21%) are projected to drop out of their courses, somewhat above the benchmark level of 18%, based on the academic and social background of the intake. These results have helped drag

Wulfruna Street
Wolverhampton WV1 1LY
01902 323 505
admissions@wlv.ac.uk
www.wlv.ac.uk
www.wolvesunion.org/
Open days: see website

WOLVERHAMPTON

Belfast
Edinburgh
Cardiff
London

***The Times* and *The Sunday Times* Rankings**
Overall Ranking: 128 (last year: 124)

Teaching quality	80.5%	=52
Student experience	77.2%	=76
Research quality	5.9%	82
Entry standards	109	=117
Graduate prospects	65.9%	112
Good honours	65.6%	=124
Expected completion rate	70.4%	128
Student/staff ratio	17.2	=93
Services and facilities	£2,098	94

Wolverhampton down our overall academic rankings and into the bottom four.

New degrees in biology with secondary education and in architecture welcomed their first students in September 2020. Wolverhampton also offers 15 degree apprenticeships in subjects including nursing, social work, building control, healthcare science practice and digital technology solutions. The university is hoping to enrol 1,000 degree apprentices on programmes by 2021, up from the current 800, with the possible introduction of architectural assistant and environmental health practitioner programmes.

Wolverhampton has maintained a top-10 position in our social inclusion table, with almost two-thirds of undergraduates the first in their family to go to university, nearly half aged 21 or above when they start their degrees, and more than half from black, Asian and minority ethnic (BAME) backgrounds.

Via the Aspire 2 Uni outreach programme, Wolverhampton students offer continuous mentoring to young people in care. The university is leading Aspire to HE, the Black Country and Telford and Wrekin Uni Connect partnership introduced in 2020, allocating funds to local schools to support targeted students' progress to university.

Wolverhampton's research mainly serves the needs of business and industry, as well as underpinning teaching. By far the best results in the Research Excellence Framework were in information science, where almost 90% of the work submitted was considered world-leading or internationally excellent.

The high-quality sports facilities at the Walsall campus are up to scratch for the university's research centre for sport, exercise and performance. They include grass and 3G pitches, outdoor courts for tennis and netball, a gym and strength facility and a 200m running track. Gymnast Kristian Thomas, who was on the British team which won a historic bronze at the 2012 Summer Olympics, graduated with a first-class degree in strength and conditioning from Wolverhampton.

First-years are guaranteed a residential space as long as they are flexible about which room type they are allocated. The relatively low cost of living is one of Wolverhampton's advantages: prices go no higher than £108 per week. Wolves Civic Hall and the Slade Rooms — named after the city's most famous glam rock export — host live acts and transport links include the 20-minute train ride to Birmingham's bright lights.

Tuition fees

» Fees for UK students	£9,250
Foundation courses	£8,400
» Fees for International students 2020–21	£12,250
» For scholarship and bursary information see www.wlv.ac.uk/apply/funding-costs-fees-and-support/	
» Graduate salary	£23,000

Student numbers

Undergraduates	12,260 (3,152)
Postgraduates	1,384 (2,251)
Applications/places	16,135/2,940
Applications per place	5.5
Overall offer rate	83.7%
International students – EU	1.2%
Non-EU	3.3%

Accommodation

University provided places: 1,251
Self-catered: £90–£108 per week
www.wlv.ac.uk/university-life/accommodation

Where do the students come from?

State schools (non-grammar)	97.2%	First generation students	63.4%		
Grammar schools	1.2%	Deprived areas	20.5%		
Independent schools	1.6%	All ethnic minorities	56.9%		

Social inclusion ranking: 7

Black attainment gap	-21.6%
Disabled	7.9%
Mature (over 21)	49.3%

University of Worcester

The University of Worcester's pitch to create a Three Counties medical school to serve Gloucestershire, Herefordshire and Worcestershire is gathering steam. With the backing of the region's NHS trusts and clinicians from across the counties, Worcester has submitted its proposal to the General Medical Council (GMC). An anticipated start date for its Bachelor of Medicine and Bachelor of Surgery programme is September 2022, depending on GMC approval.

A Three Counties medical school would build on Worcester's strong record in educating nurses, midwives and physician associates as well as paramedics, occupational therapists and physiotherapists. First founded in 1946 as an emergency teacher training college, Worcester's subject range and student numbers have multiplied and developed into today's multi-disciplinary institution of nearly 11,000 students.

Another stand-out strength is Worcester's commitment to disability sport. A 2,000-seat indoor sporting arena on the Riverside campus is designed specifically for wheelchair athletes as well as the able-bodied. At the Lakeside campus, a 10-acre lake has been adapted for inclusive watersports.

An inclusive cricket centre is planned next, and the architects who designed facilities at Lord's and the English Cricket Board headquarters have been appointed. Once open, the estimated £8m investment should result in a facility that becomes the base for all national disability cricket squads — including the blind, deaf, learning disability and physical disability teams.

Worcester was given a silver rating in the Teaching Excellence Framework. Assessors said teaching at the university encourages high levels of student engagement and commitment, with "excellent" levels of contact time. The panel also praised its schemes involving students in the enhancement of their learning experience.

Located in the historic cathedral city of Worcester, on the banks of the River Severn, the university achieved some of the best scores in the country in the 2020 National Student Survey. It ranked 10th for student satisfaction with the wider undergraduate experience and 16th for satisfaction with teaching quality. The results are not a flash in the pan: Worcester was in the top 10 for both measures in 2019.

The glowing reviews from students are at odds with the university's performance in some of our other measures, however, and it has fallen nine places in our overall rankings to a position just outside the top 100.

The university's three teaching campuses are less than a mile from each other and all close to the city centre. The attractive City

Henwick Grove
Worcester WR2 6AJ
01905 855 111
admissions@worc.ac.uk
www.worcester.ac.uk
www.worcsu.com
Open days: see website

The Times and The Sunday Times **Rankings**

Overall Ranking: =101 (last year: =92)

Teaching quality	83.6%	16
Student experience	81.7%	10
Research quality	4.3%	=98
Entry standards	117	=95
Graduate prospects	72.4%	73
Good honours	66%	122
Expected completion rate	82.1%	=83
Student/staff ratio	17.8	=104
Services and facilities	£1,715	121

campus incorporates the former Worcester Royal Infirmary and the striking and contemporary Hive library. The business school, health and wellbeing centre and Jenny Lind law building are also at the City site.

Just opposite is the Art House, opened in 2019, which has modern facilities for art and illustration courses in a grade II listed art deco building, complete with clock tower. St John's campus, the headquarters, is 15 minutes from the city centre and houses science facilities, the National Pollen and Aerobiology Research Unit and the digital arts centre and drama studio.

Eight new degrees launched in 2020, including music theatre and performance, health psychology, and law with policing. There are more to come in 2021, ranging from two integrated masters degrees, one in cricket coaching and management, the other in applied psychology. BSc degrees in medical science, and computing with a foundation year are also planned, as well as a BA honours in creative writing.

The portfolio of degree apprenticeships is gaining a sixth programme in advanced clinical practice. Paramedicine and health and social care practice are also under consideration.

Worcester does well on some of our measures of social inclusion, drawing more than half of its intake from families where neither parent went to university. A third are over 21 when they start their degrees and most (95%) went to non-selective state schools.

Worcester was one of the most improved universities in the 2014 Research Excellence Framework compared with previous assessments: it went up 20 places in our research ranking, partly because it entered five times as many academics as it had in 2008. A third of the work submitted was considered world-leading or internationally excellent, with history and art and design achieving the best scores.

Accommodation is guaranteed to first-years among 1,200 spaces on the St John's and City campuses. There are sports facilities throughout the sites including a rubber crumb pitch at St John's and a sport therapy suite at City. The Lakeside campus has 50 acres of open grass and woodland for bushcraft. For American football there is a full-size grass pitch and grass training grids at the Moors playing field.

Clubs and societies are a big part of the social scene and the university has an active students' union. Worcester has plenty of atmospheric pubs and the surrounding Malvern Hills countryside is some of England's finest.

Tuition fees

»	Fees for UK students	£9,250
»	Fees for International students 2021–22	£13,100
»	For scholarship and bursary information see www.worcester.ac.uk/study/fees-and-finance/l	
»	Graduate salary	£23,000

Student numbers		
Undergraduates	7,588	(821)
Postgraduates	746	(921)
Applications/places	10,485/2,430	
Applications per place	4.3	
Overall offer rate	84.2%	
International students – EU	4.3%	
Non-EU	2.1	

Accommodation
University provided places: 1,200
Self-catered: £105–£169 per week
First years guaranteed accommodation
www.worcester.ac.uk/life/accommodation

Where do the students come from?

State schools (non-grammar)	95.1%	First generation students	51.1%	Social inclusion ranking: 79	
				Black attainment gap	-35.9%
Grammar schools	2.1%	Deprived areas	15.6%	Disabled	10.5%
Independent schools	2.8%	All ethnic minorities	13.7%	Mature (over 21)	36.4%

Wrexham Glyndŵr University

For the third successive year, Wrexham Glyndŵr is the most socially inclusive university in England and Wales. It has done well to gain six places in our main league table, too, helped by top-20 student satisfaction with teaching quality. For satisfaction with the wider undergraduate experience, it ranks a respectable 60th.

Supportive lecturers who know their students by name, a sense of personalised learning and a friendly community atmosphere are points of pride for the university, which was named after the 15th-century Welsh prince Owain Glyndŵr, who championed the establishment of universities throughout Wales. It became a university in 2008 and now has 6,000 students, more than half of them part-timers.

The university gained a new chancellor in 2019 in Colin Jackson, the Cardiff-born athlete and former 110m hurdles world record holder, now a BBC sports pundit. "The university excels in a lot of things that I believe in, such as social inclusion, and I look forward to being hands-on in this new role", he said when accepting the appointment.

Wrexham Glyndŵr has the highest proportion of disabled students and second-highest proportion of mature students, who begin their studies aged at least 21. Nearly a quarter of students come from an area of deprivation and only six universities have more students who went to non-selective state schools. The majority of Wrexham Glyndŵr undergraduates are the first in their family to go to university.

The university gained silver in the Teaching Excellence Framework (TEF), scoring well for its part-time courses. Part-timers who live in Wales are eligible for a scholarship waiving 40% of the tuition fee. The TEF panel was impressed by the high levels of interaction with industry, business and the public sector and commented favourably on the quality of work-based learning that matches the region's priorities.

Of the university's three campuses, the main site is Plas Coch on Mold Road on the outskirts of Wrexham, where most courses are taught. The art school is in the town centre. As well as hosting teaching and learning facilities, the campus is the hub for student services and the union and has a nursery for those who need childcare in order to study.

The Wrexham campus also hosts the Centre for the Creative Industries, which has high-quality studios used by students on television production degree courses, and is the regional home of BBC Cymru Wales. Other specialist facilities reflect the university's diverse subject areas and include a complementary medicine clinic, laboratories for computer game development and for

Mold Road
Wrexham LL11 2AW
01978 293 439
enquiries@glyndwr.ac.uk
www.wgu.ac.uk
www.wrexhamglyndwrsu.org.uk
Open days: see website

Edinburgh
Belfast
WREXHAM
Cardiff
London

The Times and The Sunday Times Rankings
Overall Ranking: 124 (last year: 130)

Teaching quality	83%	=19
Student experience	78.2%	60
Research quality	2.3%	119
Entry standards	110	=113
Graduate prospects	67.1%	105
Good honours	71%	=100
Expected completion rate	74.2%	123
Student/staff ratio	19.4	118
Services and facilities	£1,784	116

the study of crime scenes, as well as a flight simulator and supersonic wind tunnel.

The rural Northop campus in Flintshire specialises in animal studies and biodiversity courses, and has a small animal unit and an equine centre. The St Asaph campus in Denbighshire is a research centre for the opto-electronics industry, focusing on the technology to make high-resolution telescopes. The campus incubator offers a programme for space industry start-ups.

In partnership with Airbus, which has a large plant nearby, Wrexham Glyndŵr's Advanced Composite Training and Development Centre in Broughton carries out research to help improve the efficiency of aircraft, and feeds into the university's engineering courses.

Sixty-seven per cent of graduates were in high-skilled jobs or postgraduate study within 15 months of finishing their degrees, a proportion that places Wrexham Glyndŵr among the bottom 30 UK universities. The university's first degree apprenticeships may help improve graduate outcomes. Five programmes have been introduced in cyber-security, computing, production engineering and industrial engineering — both mechanical and electrical.

Wrexham Glyndŵr also offers two-year fast-track degrees and four-year master's degrees in art and design, and computing. Foundation years can be added to a range of the university's courses and provide a gateway to an honours-degree course for those without the qualifications for direct entry.

The university entered only 34 academics for the 2014 Research Excellence Framework, but a third of their work was judged to be internationally excellent, with some world-leading, notably in media subjects.

Lots of students are local and live at home, which eases the pressure on the student accommodation at Plas Coch and Northop. The supply of spaces does not meet demand, though, and rooms are allocated to those who need them most, with first-years among the priority tenants.

The university owns the Racecourse stadium, the world's oldest international football ground currently in use, which hosted the first Welsh home international match in 1877. The students' union runs the popular Cent bar there. The campus also has a modern sports centre with two floodlit artificial pitches, a human performance laboratory and indoor facilities.

Wrexham has its own bars and clubs, and its location in the northeast of Wales offers easy access to the lively cities of northwest England.

Tuition fees

» Fees for UK students	£9,000
» Fees for International students 2021–22	£11,750
» For scholarship and bursary information see www.glyndwr.ac.uk/en/feesandstudentfinance/	
» Graduate salary	£21,000

Student numbers

Undergraduates	2,647	(2,545)
Postgraduates	190	(511)
Applications/places		1,650/415
Applications per place		4
Overall offer rate		71.6%
International students – EU		13.7%
Non-EU		1.1%

Where do the students come from?

State schools (non-grammar)	97.4%	First generation students	59.2%	Black attainment gap	-25.5%
Grammar schools	0.9%	Deprived areas	22.7%	Disabled	21.5%
Independent schools	1.7%	All ethnic minorities	5.1%	Mature (over 21)	70.8%

Accommodation

University provided places: 341
Self-catered: £90–£168 per week
www.glyndwr.ac.uk/en/Accommodation

Social inclusion ranking: 1

University of York

Back in our top 20, York's academic clout comes with a parkland campus and modern collegiate system — all within walking distance of the historic cathedral city. It is a combination that has long been popular with students.

York is focusing on driving forward its employability initiatives. The York Futures programme, for instance, engages students in mapping out bespoke paths that identify their strengths and help them to take charge of their careers. With prompts about when summer internships open for applications, and when is the best time to publish an inaugural LinkedIn profile, students can start to fill their CVs long before graduating, with a view to hitting the careers market running.

On the digital front, York has its own careers and placements podcast and hosts a mentors' platform where current students can connect with alumni. Online tools for honing skills from interview techniques and CV reviewing to job hunting are also at students' fingertips. A support package for graduates has been created in partnership with recruiters and careers coaches and the university has teamed up strategically with Transform Society, the network for the five fast-track public sector graduate recruitment schemes, including the highly-rated Teach First and Unlocked programmes.

York's work to develop employability skills and careers support contributed to its upgrade to gold in 2018's Teaching Excellence Framework. The panel found excellent academic support and a research-strong environment that engages students and provides outstanding levels of stretch.

A two-place rise in our main league table comes in spite of a decline in student satisfaction. Although York remains in the top 50 for satisfaction with teaching quality — ranked above all of its Russell Group peers, which find this a tough nut to crack— its ranking has fallen from the top 25 in 2019. For satisfaction with the wider student experience, it has slipped just outside the top 50.

The university's investment in research, teaching and campus facilities is ongoing. In the past 20 years, 20 new buildings have been added on the original Heslington West campus and a £750m expansion has delivered modern resources at the linked Heslington East campus.

The Hull York medical school has recently finished a complete redesign and gained clinical skills spaces nearby — a welcome upgrade in light of the government's expansion of undergraduate medical education and Hull York's extra 90 medical students per year. A new building for the management school opens in early 2021, fitted with bespoke teaching and learning areas.

In line with the university's continuing investment in mental health, staffing levels

---

Heslington
York YO10 5DD
01904 324 000
ug-admissions@york.ac.uk
www.york.ac.uk
www.yusu.org
Open days: see website

The Times and The Sunday Times **Rankings**		
Overall Ranking: 20 (last year: 22)		
Teaching quality	80.7%	=48
Student experience	78.7%	=52
Research quality	38.3%	17
Entry standards	151	36
Graduate prospects	81.7%	27
Good honours	82.4%	29
Expected completion rate	94.3%	16
Student/staff ratio	14.4	=33
Services and facilities	£1,982	99

are being boosted among its dedicated support teams. For 2021 there will be 10 wellbeing officers based across the campus and in academic departments. The Open Door team, which provides professional support to students experiencing mental health or psychological difficulties, is gaining another three practitioners. The benefits of sleep, effective studying methods and managing perfectionism and procrastination are the subjects of wellbeing events and workshops.

York is one of a few UK universities with a college system, and all students join one of nine. The student communities cross year groups and academic disciplines, and are the bases for accommodation, social activities, inter-college sports and support networks. Every student has a supervisor responsible for their academic and personal welfare and York's completion rates are excellent.

Like most other Russell Group universities, York is outside the top 100 of our social inclusion ranking. Bursary and scholarship provision is good, however. Students from households with incomes up to £35,000 qualify for bursaries of £2,000 towards accommodation costs in the first year and cash instalments of up to £1,100 in subsequent years. Forty York Opportunity awards per year worth £3,300 each go to students who have overcome significant barriers to reach their educational goals.

York lost ground on some competitors in the 2014 Research Excellence Framework, when it submitted a lower proportion of its academics for assessment than most leading universities. Nevertheless, more than 80% of the research was considered world-leading or internationally excellent, and York was in the top 10 for the impact of its research. Eight departments were ranked in the top five for their subject and the university remains in the top 20 for research quality overall.

Sports facilities are good, and include four sports halls and a dance studio. The £12m York Sports Village features a 25-metre pool, trainer pool, 120-station gym, 3G pitch and five-a-side pitches. The university has the only velodrome in Yorkshire, a 1km cycling track and an athletics track, as well as its own boathouse on the River Ouse.

Accommodation is guaranteed for all first-years who apply by the deadline, and there is usually enough space for those who want to stay on campus for their second and third years to do so.

Tuition fees

» Fees for UK students £9,250
» Fees for International students 2021–22 £18,350–£22,650
  Medicine £34,950 (Hull-York Medical School)
» For scholarship and bursary information see
  www.york.ac.uk/study/undergraduate/fees-funding/
» Graduate salary £24,000

Student numbers

Undergraduates	13,555	(477)
Postgraduates	4,049	(1,388)
Applications/places	25,045/3,710	
Applications per place	6.8	
Overall offer rate	81.6%	
International students – EU	4.3%	
Non-EU	17.2%	

Accommodation

University provided places: 6,054
Catered costs: £136–£196 per week
Self-catered: £99–£174 per week
First years guaranteed accommodation
www.york.ac.uk/study/accommodation/

Where do the students come from?

State schools (non-grammar)	69.9%	First generation students	30.3%	Black attainment gap	-7.7%
Grammar schools	12.3%	Deprived areas	7.5%	Disabled	5.7%
Independent schools	17.8%	All ethnic minorities	13.5%	Mature (over 21)	7.2%

Social inclusion ranking: 109

York St John University

Students at York St John (YSJ) are among the country's most content with their university lives. For the second year running YSJ has achieved a top-10 ranking for student satisfaction with teaching quality. Our analysis of the latest National Student Survey places the university in the top 20 for satisfaction with the wider undergraduate experience, too.

These results have contributed significantly to YSJ's position in our latest league table overall, where it has largely held on to the substantial gains of the past two years. A dropout rate of just 6.6%, considerably below the expected level, is no surprise given the high rates of satisfaction.

Founded in 1841, YSJ was a teacher training college for most of its history and had a Ripon campus that closed in 2001. It now offers a full suite of degrees under nine academic schools and gained university status in 2006. The main 11-acre Lord Mayor's Walk campus is near York city centre and faces York Minster — where YSJ graduation ceremonies take place in some style. A postgraduate London campus in the Barbican opened in 2018, within easy reach of King's Cross station and the train to York.

More than £100m has been invested lately, and a new Creative Centre is being built at the main York campus. Sustainably designed, it will bring a 210-seat auditorium, editing suites, games laboratories and flexible working space as well as a critical listening room and lecture theatre. With inspiring views over York Minster, the atrium will host exhibitions, lectures and performances and will be open for use by the community.

The separate Haxby Road sports campus, a mile away, has new sports science laboratories and teaching rooms, along with 57 acres of outdoor space and indoor sports facilities.

A degree in international relations is new for 2020, as is applied biosciences — specialising in either medical biochemistry or cancer biology. A degree in musical theatre will begin in September 2021, along with one in applied biosciences — bioinformatics.

The university's stable of degree apprenticeships is growing, too. New programmes are being offered in healthcare science, senior leadership — real estate sector, project management and professional policing.

Low rates of graduate employment in high-skilled jobs contributed to a bronze rating in the Teaching Excellence Framework but the panel was impressed by a scheme that involves undergraduates in research and by the innovative measures to support vulnerable students, including those experiencing mental health difficulties. Progression to high-skilled jobs has also hampered York St John in

Lord Mayor's Walk
York YO31 7EX
01904 876 598
admissions@yorksj.ac.uk
www.yorksj.ac.uk
http://ysjsu.com
Open days: see website

Belfast
Edinburgh
YORK
London
Cardiff

The Times and The Sunday Times Rankings
Overall Ranking: =83 (last year: 81)

Teaching quality	84.4%	=10
Student experience	80.7%	=19
Research quality	4.1%	=101
Entry standards	103	=127
Graduate prospects	66.9%	=106
Good honours	73.6%	=80
Expected completion rate	86.4%	55
Student/staff ratio	18	=108
Services and facilities	£2,204	86

our league table — with just 67% in high-skilled work or postgraduate study within 15 months of graduation in the latest survey, the university is in the bottom 30 on our graduate prospects measure.

Psychology produced the best results in the 2014 research ratings, when the 30% of research regarded as world-leading or internationally excellent represented a big improvement on the 2008 assessments. The strategy promotes interdisciplinary research, building on current areas of expertise and targeting further improvement in the 2021 exercise.

YSJ continues to charge some of the lowest fees in England — £4,200 in the coming 2021–22 academic year for its foundation degrees in education and theology for a limited range of mature students without traditional qualifications. Fees for all honours degrees are at the standard UK rate of £9,250.

A small number of vice-chancellor's scholarships of £1,000 per study year are awarded to students according to a range of widening participation criteria. There is also financial help for children bereaved by the death in service of parents in the armed forces. YSJ's sanctuary scholarships award full tuition fee waivers plus £1,000 per study year and one-to-one support to students who have sought refuge in the UK. The Aspire scheme gives all UK undergraduates £100 a year towards course materials. Those whose household income is below £25,000 receive an extra £400.

YSJ does well to recruit more than one in six students from areas of low participation in higher education — well above average for its courses and entry qualifications. It sits in the top half of our latest social inclusion ranking for England and Wales.

The Lord Mayor's Walk campus has a sports hall, climbing wall, facilities for basketball, netball and indoor football and cricket nets. The sports park 15-minutes' walk away offers 3G and grass pitches, outdoor courts for tennis and netball and a sprint track. The indoor centre includes a sports hall and a strength and conditioning suite.

First-years are guaranteed one of 1,598 residential places if they apply by the deadline. The university's central location makes meeting at the students' union a good way to start an evening out on the town. Historic York is a student-friendly city that offers hip cocktail bars as well as plenty of pubs which cater to a young crowd.

Tuition fees

»	Fees for UK students	£9,250
	Foundation degrees	from £4,200
»	Fees for International students 2021–22	£12,750
»	For scholarship and bursary information see www.yorksj.ac.uk/students/your-finances/	
»	Graduate salary	£22,000

Student numbers

Undergraduates	5,676	(154)
Postgraduates	489	(299)
Applications/places		8,755/1,550
Applications per place		5.6
Overall offer rate		89.4%
International students – EU		n/a
Non-EU		n/a

Accommodation

University provided places: 1,598
Self-catered: £102–£160 per week
First years guaranteed accommodation
www.yorksj.ac.uk/study/accommodation

Where do the students come from?

State schools (non-grammar)	94.2%	First generation students	46.7%	Black attainment gap	n/a
Grammar schools	2.9%	Deprived areas	18.6%	Disabled	7.6%
Independent schools	3%	All ethnic minorities	7%	Mature (over 21)	12.2%

Social inclusion ranking: 53

Specialist and Private Institutions

1 Specialist colleges of the University of London

This listing gives contact details for specialist degree-awarding colleges within the University of London not listed elsewhere within the book. Those marked * are members of GuildHE (**www.guildhe.ac.uk**). Fees are given for UK undergraduates for a single year of study.

Courtauld Institute of Art
Somerset House Strand
London WC2R 0RN
020 3947 7777
www.courtauld.ac.uk
Fees 2020–21: £9,250

London Business School
Regent's Park
London NW1 4SA
020 7000 7000
www.london.edu
Postgraduate only

London School of Hygiene and Tropical Medicine
Keppel Street
London WC1E 7HT
020 7636 8636
www.lshtm.ac.uk
Postgraduate medical courses

Royal Academy of Music
Marylebone Road
London NW1 5HT
020 7873 7373
www.ram.ac.uk
Fees 2020–21: £9,250

Royal Central School of Speech and Drama*
Eton Avenue
London NW3 3HY
020 7722 8183
www.cssd.ac.uk
Fees 2020–21: £9,250

Royal Veterinary College
Royal College Street
London NW1 0TU
020 7468 5147
www. rvc.ac.uk
Fees 2020–21: £9,250

University of London Institute in Paris
9–11 rue de Constantine
75340 Paris Cedex 07, France
(+33) 1 44 11 73 83
https://ulip.london.ac.uk
Degrees offered in conjunction with
Queen Mary and Royal Holloway colleges
Fees 2020–21: £9,250

2 Specialist colleges and private institutions

This listing gives contact details for other degree-awarding higher education institutions not mentioned elsewhere within the book. All the institutions listed below offer degree courses, some providing a wide range of courses while others are specialist colleges with a small intake. Those marked * are members of GuildHE (www.guildhe.ac.uk). Fees are given for UK undergraduates for a single year of study.

Arden University
Business, finance, health and others
Arden House,
Middlemarch Park,
Coventry CV3 4FJ
  Campuses in London, Birmingham,
  Manchester & Berlin
0808 274 1535
www.arden.ac.uk
Fees 2020–21: £7,750-£8,250 (blended learning)

BPP University
Mainly law, business & health
Aldine Place, 142–144 Uxbridge Road,
London W12 8AW
  Campuses in Abingdon, Birmingham,
  Bristol, Cambridge, Doncaster, Leeds,
  Liverpool, London, Manchester,
  Maidstone, Milton Keynes, Newcastle,
  Nottingham, Reading, Southampton
03300 603 100
www.bpp.com
Fees 2020–21: £13,500 (two-year course);
£6,000–£9,000 (three-year course)

Conservatoire for Dance and Drama
Comprised of:
  Bristol Old Vic Theatre School, Central
  School of Ballet, London Academy of
  Music and Dramatic Art (LAMDA),
  London Contemporary Dance School,
  National Centre for Circus Arts,
  Northern School of Contemporary
  Dance, Rambert School of Ballet and
  Contemporary Dance, Royal Academy of
  Dramatic Art (RADA)*
The Energy Centre, Units 1–3,

Bowling Green Walk, London N1 6AL
020 7387 5101
www.cdd.ac.uk
Fees 2020–21: £9,250

Dyson Institute of Engineering and Technology
Tetbury Hill Malmesbury
Wiltshire SN16 0RP
01285 705228
dysoninstitute@dyson.com
www.dysoninstitute.com
Paid degree courses – no fees

Glasgow School of Art
167 Renfrew Street, Glasgow G3 6RQ
0141 353 4500
www.gsa.ac.uk
Fees 2020–21: Scotland, no fee,
RUK £9,250

Guildhall School of Music and Drama
Silk Street, Barbican,
London EC2Y 8DT
020 7628 2571
www.gsmd.ac.uk
Fees 2021–22: £9,250

The University of Law*
Birmingham, Bristol, Chester, Exeter,
Guildford, Leeds, London (Bloomsbury and
Moorgate), Manchester, Nottingham
01483 216 000
www.law.ac.uk
Fees 2020–21: £11,100 (two-year course)
£9,250 (three-year course)

Liverpool Institute for Performing Arts*
Mount Street,
Liverpool L1 9HF
0151 330 3084
www.lipa.ac.uk
Fees 2020–21: £9,250

The London Institute of Banking and Finance*
4–9 Burgate Lane
Canterbury, Kent CT1 2XJ
01227 818609
   Student campus:
   25 Lovat Lane, London EC3R 8EB
   020 7337 6293
www.libf.ac.uk
ftp@libf.ac.uk
Fees 2020–21: £9,250

New College of the Humanities*
19 Bedford Square,
London WC1B 3HH
020 7637 4550
www.nchlondon.ac.uk
Fees 2021–22: £9,250

Pearson College*
Business, law & video games
190 High Holborn,
London WC1V 7BH
020 3503 8343
www.pearsoncollegelondon.ac.uk
Fees 2021–22: £9,250

Plymouth College of Art*
Tavistock Place,
Plymouth PL4 8AT
01752 203402
www.plymouthart.ac.uk
Fees 2020–21: £9,250

Regent's University London*
Business, design, media & psychology
Inner Circle,
Regent's Park, London NW1 4NS
020 7487 7505
www.regents.ac.uk
Fees 2021–22: £18,500–£21,500

Rose Bruford College of Theatre and Performance*
Lamorbey Park,
Burnt Oak Lane,
Sidcup, Kent DA15 9DF
020 8308 2600
www.bruford.ac.uk
Fees 2020-21: £9,250

Royal College of Music
Prince Consort Road,
London SW7 2BS
020 7591 4300
www.rcm.ac.uk
Fees 2021–22: £9,250

Royal Conservatoire of Scotland
100 Renfrew Street,
Glasgow G2 3DB
0141 332 4101
www.rcs.ac.uk
Fees 2021–22: Scotland, no fee; RUK £9,250

Royal Northern College of Music
124 Oxford Road,
Manchester M13 9RD
0161 907 5200
www.rncm.ac.uk
Fees 2021–22: £9,250

Royal Welsh College of Music and Drama
Castle Grounds, Cathays Park,
Cardiff CF10 3ER
029 2034 2854
www.rwcmd.ac.uk
Fees 2021–22: £9,000

St Mary's University College*
Teaching & liberal arts
191 Falls Road, Belfast BT12 6FE
028 9032 7678
www.stmarys-belfast.ac.uk
Fees 2020–21: £4,395; RUK £9,250

Scotland's Rural College
Agriculture, environment & land
management
Peter Wilson Building,
The King's Buildings,
West Mains Road,
Edinburgh EH9 3JG
   Campuses at Aberdeen, Ayr, Cupar,
   Dumfries, Oatridge, West Lothian and
   Edinburgh
0131 535 4000
www.sruc.ac.uk
Fees 2020–21: Scotland, no fee; RUK £6,950

Stranmillis University College
Teaching courses
Stranmillis Road, Belfast BT9 5DY
028 9038 1271
www.stran.ac.uk
Fees 2020–21: £4,395; RUK £9,250

Trinity Laban Conservatoire of Music and Dance
Music Faculty: King Charles Court
Old Royal Naval College,
Greenwich, London SE10 9JF
020 8305 4444
Dance Faculty: Laban Building, Creekside
London SE8 3DZ
020 8305 9400
www.trinitylaban.ac.uk
Fees 2021–22: £9,250

University Academy 92
Business, media & sport
UA92 Campus,
Talbot Road, Trafford,
Manchester M16 0PU
0161 507 1992
www.ua92.ac.uk
Fees 2020-21: £9,000

University College, Birmingham (UCB)
Further and Higher Education courses.
Mainly hospitality, tourism, business, sport
and education
Summer Row,
Birmingham B3 1JB
0121 604 1000
www.ucb.ac.uk
Fees 2020-21: £9,250

UCFB (University Campus of Football Business)*
Burnley FC Turf Moor, Burnley
Lancashire BB10 4BX (BTec courses)
Wembley Stadium
London HA9 0WS
   Etihad Campus, Manchester M11 3FF
   0333 060 2196
www.ucfb.com
Fees 2021–22: £9,250

Writtle University College*
Land management
Lordship Road,
Chelmsford, Essex CM1 3RR
01245 424200
www.writtle.ac.uk
Fees 2021–22: £9,250

Index